Evangelistic Lectures: A Reproduction Of Sermons Delivered In 1946 In The Free Evangelistic Style

John Lewis Shuler

EVANGELISTIC LECTURES

By

JOHN LEWIS SHULER

National Bible Lecturer for the American Bible Institute

and

Professor of Evangelism at Takoma Park Seminary

Washington, D. C.

A Foreword

These sermons were delivered in an evangelistic campaign conducted in Des Moines, Iowa, during September, October, November and December of 1946. The first sermon was given on Sunday night, September 8.

The sermons were mechanically recorded at the meetings, and are reproduced in this volume exactly as spoken to the audience with scarcely any editing. No attempt has been made to place them in precise literary form. One of the objectives of this book was to reproduce the full length sermon in the free evangelistic style with its directness and appeal.

The typewritten material for the printer has of necessity been hastily prepared, and it is inevitable that some errors in construction would creep in. The doctrines presented, however, stand as being in strict accordance with the Scriptures of Truth. In some instances, certain texts, as quoted from memory by the speaker, may not be exactly word for word as recorded in the Bible, or with the same punctuation, but there is no deviation from the declaration or apparent meaning of the Scriptures.

A brief word on the plan followed in these evangelistic meetings will be in order. During the first two weeks, sermons were delivered on Sunday, Tuesday, Thursday and Friday nights. Beginning with the third week a central Bible class was conducted at the meeting place with the interested people each Thursday night. From the third week to the tenth week inclusive, sermons were presented on Sunday, Tuesday and Friday nights, and on Saturday afternoons at three o'clock beginning with the fifth Saturday. From the eleventh week to the fifteenth week inclusive, the Bible class was conducted on Tuesday nights, and sermons were presented on Sunday and Friday nights and Saturday afternoons.

Above each sermon title we have indicated the number of each sermon in the series. Beneath the sermon title is a notation designating at what point in the series it was presented. This will enable any worker to discover the plan followed in the order of subjects.

Special Bible lessons were mimeographed on punched note sheets. These were given to all who attended the weekly Bible class. They were made with blank lines after certain statements of Bible doctrine, on which the people recorded the respective Scripture references as the Bible lessons were presented. The first Bible lesson was mechanically recorded as it was given to the class, and is reproduced in this volume. It will convey to workers, some concrete idea as to how the Bible class was conducted.

In connection with these sermons, twenty-two appropriate after meeting talks were presented. These were recorded mechanically and may be published in a separate volume, and made available, if there is sufficient demand for them. A postal card has been inserted in each sermon volume, which the purchaser may use to register his desire for the additional material.

We send these forth with the earnest prayer that God will use these sermons, to establish many interested souls in the present truth, and, that many of the heralds of the third angel's message will find herein help, inspiration and guidance in presenting God's message for these closing days.

Yours in Him,

J. L. SHULER.

Peace or Pieces?

As we watch the swift moving events of our day, certain great questions arise in our minds. What does this new Atomic Age hold in store for man? Will the atomic bomb blast civilization into oblivion? What about the riddle of Russia? Will Russia absorb and rule all Europe? Can Stalin succeed where Hitler failed? World Peace! World security! How will it ever be achieved? What lies ahead for our world? What kind of a world tomorrow?

I don't know what is coming. You don't know what is coming. But there is a God in heaven Who does know. He knows the end from the very beginning, and from ancient times the things which are not yet done. And it has pleased that great God of heaven Who knows the future, to reveal in this Bible some of the events of the future, which we need to know. It is to some of these items that we direct your attention tonight.

In 2 Peter 1:19 the apostle Peter says, "We have a more sure word of prophecy whereunto ye do well that ye take heed as unto a light that shineth in a dark place." I have placed this text on a piece of muslin, that you may see for yourself what the Word of God says. Notice how it reads: "We have a more sure word of prophecy whereunto ye do well that ye take heed as unto a light that shineth in a dark place." Just as the headlights of your automobile show the road ahead, the prophecies of the Bible show what is coming before it happens.

The course of this world's history for the past 2,500 years has been exactly in accordance with a prophetic outline found in the second chapter of the book of Daniel. In Dan. 2 28 I read, "There is a God in heaven that revealeth secrets, and maketh known to the King Nebuchadnezzar what shall be in the latter days." By means of a wonderful dream God revealed to Nebuchadnezzar, king of Babylon, what would happen in the latter days.

Now I have something very remarkable to bring to you. I want you to notice the striking device that God used to portray the future history of nations. (At this juncture a large wooden figure of a man was unveiled on the stage beside the speaker's desk.) I want you to notice that what you see here on the stage is just what I am going to read from God's holy Word. I am turning now to Dan. 2:31-35.

"Thou, O King, sawest, and behold a great image. This great image, whose brightness was excellent, stood before thee; and the form thereof was terrible. This image's head was of fine gold, his breast and his arms of silver, his belly and his thighs of brass, his legs of iron, his feet part of iron and part of clay. Thou sawest till a stone was cut out without hands, which smote the image upon his feet that were of iron and clay, and brake them to pieces. Then was the iron, the clay, the brass, the silver, and the gold, broken to pieces together, and became like the chaff of the summer threshing-floors; and the wind carried them away, that no place was found for them: and the stone that smote the image became a great mountain, and filled the whole earth."

A gigantic statue of a man made of different metal segments was shown to Nebuchadnezzar in his dream. This man's head was of fine gold, his breast ard arms of silver, his thighs of brass, his legs of iron, his feet part of iron and part of clay. Beginning with the most precious metal, gold, there was a uniform depreciation to finally terminate with the most base of all, clay. There you have, if you please, evolution in the reverse. A stone cut from the moun-

3

tain without hands, smote this man upon his feet and dashed him to pieces. The wind from that concussion blew the fragments into oblivion. Then the stone expanded and expanded and expanded until it filled the entire world.

What a mysterious 'dream'! What can it mean? As soon as Daniel told the king his dream, he proceeded to explain the meaning of the gold, the silver, the brass, the iron, the clay and the stone. Now follow me and you will see.

I am turning now to Dan. 2:38, reading the last sentence in the verse. "Thou art this head of gold." The pronoun "thou" refers to Nebuchadnezzar that mighty king of ancient Babylon. To Nebuchadnezzar, king of Babylon, the prophet says, "Thou art this head of gold." O how plain that is! It shows us that this head of gold represented or symbolized the empire of Babylon over which Nebuchadnezzar was then ruling.

Now notice, he goes on to explain the meaning of the breast and arms of silver. I am reading now from Dan. 2 39, the first part of the verse. "And after thee shall arise another kingdom inferior to thee." Daniel makes it plain that this breast and arms of silver represented a second world empire that would follow Babylon upon the stage of world dominion. History tells us that this second world empire was Medo-Persia. So the breast and arms of silver symbolized Persia.

Next he explains the third part of the man. I am reading now Dan. 2:39, the last part of the verse. "Another third kingdom of brass shall bear rule over all the earth." How plain! He tells us in so many words that this third part of the man is a third world empire that will succeed or follow the second one. History shows that the third world empire that followed Persia was the empire of Grecia.

Then notice how he explains the meaning of the legs of iron. I am reading Dan. 2.40. "The fourth kingdom shall be strong as iron." How plain! It shows that these legs of iron symbolized the fourth world empire that would follow the third. History shows that the fourth world empire that followed Grecia was the great empire of Rome.

Mark this. Every school boy in Des Moines can testify to the accuracy of this prophecy in the Bible. Every school boy in Des Moines can tell you that Persia followed Babylon, that Grecia followed Persia, and that Rome followed Grecia. There it is, as plain as two and two make four. The head of gold, Babylon. The breast and arms of silver, Persia. The sides of brass, Grecia. The legs of iron, Rome. The four metals: the gold, the silver, the brass, and the iron symbolized four world empires that were to arise one after another along the pathway of history, as the scroll of the future would be unrolled in the days to come from Daniel's time.

What about the feet and toes? What about this mixture of iron and clay in the feet and the toes? The Word of God tells. I read Dan. 2:41. "Whereas thou sawest the feet and toes, part of potters' clay and part of iron, the kingdom shall be divided." Daniel tells us in so many words that the mixture of iron and clay represented the breaking up of the fourth world empire into smaller kingdoms.

Other prophecies of the Bible even foretold the exact number of those divisions. Dan. 7:24 indicates that this fourth empire was to be divided into ten parts. Did this come true? It certainly did. During the fourth and fifth centuries of the Christian era, ten distinct independent nations established themselves within the boundaries of Western Rome.

I have a chart here which gives a list of these ten kingdoms of Western Rome. These ten kingdoms were as follows: the Anglo-Saxons, the Burgundians, the Franks, the Alemanni, the Visigoths, the Suevi, the Lombards, the Heruli, the Ostrogoths, and the Vandals. Seven of those nations are found on the map of Europe today. The Anglo-Saxons are what we now call the English; the Franks are the French people of France; the Alemanni constitute Germany; the Burgundians are that little nation of Switzerland; the Visigoths constitute Spain; the Suevi are that little country of Portugal and the Lombards are of Italy. These seven nations of England, France, Germany, Spain, Switzerland, Portugal and Italy find their place in this prophecy of Daniel 2 as the toes of this composite metal man

Now follow me closely. Here's where the prophecy touches our day. Here is where it touches 1946, if you please When we deal with England, Germany, France, Spain, Portugal, Italy and Switzerland, we are dealing with Western Europe of 1946. Here is the verse that defeated Hitler Did you know that there was a verse in the Bible that actually defeated Hitler? I am going to read that verse in just a moment.

Many people are worried about Russia. They think Russia is going to absorb and rule all Europe Here is a verse that forever precludes Russia from gaining permanent domination over all Europe. I can tell you on the basis of this Holy Word, that if Russia grows to be ten times as strong as she is now, she'll never be able to absorb and permanently hold all Europe under her sway. Here it is I hope you have your notebook to record all these Scriptural references.

I read Dan. 2 43. "Whereas thou sawest the iron mixed with miry clay, they shall mingle themselves with the seed of men; but they shall not cleave" (referring to these divided nations of Western Europe) "they shall not cleave one to another, even as iron is not mixed with clay." The prophecy shows that these divided nations of England, France, Germany, Spain, Switzerland, Portugal, and Italy will never be welded together into a world empire, as they once were under the Caesars of Rome. You know, I know, everybody knows that you cannot weld iron and clay together. Iron will not cohere with clay. These nations of western Europe cannot be welded into one world empire as they were back in the days of the Caesars when Rome ruled the world.

Notice those seven famous words of prophecy. Here they are: "They shall not cleave one to another." There are the seven words that defeated Napoleon Bonaparte. In the 19th century Napoleon swept over nation after nation of Europe It looked as though Napoleon would rule all of Europe It looked as though no nation or combination of nations could stand against his onslaught. In 1811 Napoleon said, "In five years I shall be the master of the world." But God had said that what Napoleon was trying to do, to make Europe into a world empire, could not be done, even as iron will not cohere with clay. "They shall not cleave one to another"

So his dreams of world empire vanished in smoke on the field of Waterloo with Napoleon fleeing for his life He bowed his head in defeat and said, "God Almighty is too much for me" Yes, God Almighty was too much for Napoleon. More than twenty-three hundred years before Napoleon was ever born, this prophecy declared that those nations of western Europe could not be welded into a world empire to be ruled by one man "They shall not cleave one to another.

Those are the seven words that deprived Germany of victory in World War I and again, in World War II. In 1914 William the II of Germany, Kaiser of Germany, started out to make himself the ruler of all Europe. It seemed for a time that no power could stand against the German army. But the Word of God was on record in Dan. 2:43 that those nations of Western Europe could not be welded into a world empire to be ruled by one man Consequently, the Kaiser's dream of a world empire turned into a nightmare with him fleeing into Holland and spending the rest of his days in exile sawing wood at Doorn, Holland.

In 1939 Mr. Hitler started out to make himself the ruler of all Europe. When Hitler struck at Poland in 1938 he knew England was not prepared for war. He didn't think she would come to the defence of Poland. But Mr. Hitler forgot a number of things. He forgot that the "English Bulldog" will fight whether he is ready or not. He forgot that America lies over the Atlantic Ocean, and that millions of brave Americans would rise as one man to defend the fairest flag ever flown in the breeze—the Stars and Stripes forever. He forgot God. The Word of God had declared that these nations of Western Europe could not be welded permanently into a world empire by any man.

My friends, as Hitler advanced, occupying vast portions of Europe, the Word of God was at stake. The Bible was on record that those divided nations could not be fused into a world empire to be ruled by one man no matter what his name, Hitler or anybody else. Thus it was that Mr. Hitler's dream of world empire turned into a nightmare of suicide amid ashes and ruins of his own capital city, Berlin.

Notice this carefully, don't miss it. The outcome of World War I and the outcome of World War II confirm this Book as the Word of God. This prophecy of Daniel 2 43, "They shall not cleave one to another," stands true amid all the overturnings and upheavals among the nations of Western Europe for the past fourteen centuries. Time and again the mightiest men who ever trod the soil of Western Europe have tried to weld those nations into one great world empire as it was in the days of the Caesars. But everyone has failed. All the armies they could muster have not been able to break the force of these seven words of God's Holy Writ: "They shall not cleave one to another."

Listen to me. One verse of God's Bible is stronger than all the armies in the world. Jesus Christ says, "The Scripture cannot be broken." "Heaven and earth," says He, "shall pass away, but my Word shall not pass away."

I wonder if there is an infidel in this audience tonight. Please be especially free to invite all infidels and skeptics to these American Bible Institute meetings. Many will find faith in God in these lectures. If there is an infidel here tonight, I have a question for you, brother. Here it is. Think it through. How could any man of himself in the days of ancient Babylon look ahead for 2,500 years in advance as Daniel did, and accurately foretell that beginning with Babylon there would be only four world empires, and that the fourth would be divided into segments, and remain divided in spite of all man's attempts to reunite them. Come on, infidel, what do you say?

I'll tell you what you'll have to say. You will say, "Mr. Shuler, the fact is, that there isn't any man of himself who could look ahead 2,500 years." That is right. Man cannot look ahead even through tomorrow. This good Book says, "Boast not thyself against tomorrow, for thou knowest not what a day may bring forth." You'll have to say, Mr. Infidel, that no man of himself could look ahead and prophesy accurately for 2,500 years in advance. Doesn't the fact, then, that Daniel did accurately foretell the future 2,500 years in advance, prove that this prophecy is inspired by that great God Who alone knows the future? This Book foretells things. You can't do that. I can't do that. The fact that his Book foretells things before they happen proves that this book was inspired by that great God Who alone knows the future. Infidelity is silenced; the Bible is vindicated by the unerring fulfillment of its predictions.

The most thrilling and breath-taking part of the dream of the future was when this stone smote the image on his feet and dashed it to pieces and the wind blew the fragments into oblivion. This represents what will happen in the great battle of Armageddon. This is the most interesting item in all the prophecy. It is the most important item for you to understand. In fact it is one of the biggest prophetic subjects in all the Bible. It is such a big subject that I am devoting my entire lecture next Sunday night here at the KRNT

Radio theatre to "The Impending, World-ending Battle of Armageddon as Prophesied in the Bible." I will show from the Bible next Sunday night, when it will come, where it will be fought, who will win, and who is the one man who will rule the entire world after that battle. You must plan to be present to hear that subject.

Tonight I promised to tell you what lies ahead for our world. What kind of a world tomorrow? What will be the final outcome of these unsettled conditions that we see today? Well, here it is in Dan. 2:44. "In the days of these kings shall the God of heaven set up a kingdom, which shall never be destroyed: and the kingdom shall not be left to other people, but it shall break in pieces and consume all these kingdoms, and it shall stand forever."

On the authority of this blessed Word I can tell you that the final outcome of this world situation will be the return of the Lord Jesus Christ to this earth to reconstruct this world into a new, perfect world where there will be no more sorrow, no more sickness, no more trouble, no more wars and no more death. In Rev. 21:1 the prophet says, "I saw a new heaven and a new earth, for the first heaven and the first earth were passed away." In Rev. 21:4 he declares that God shall wipe away all tears from their eyes; and there shall be no more death, neither sorrow, nor crying, neither shall there be any more pain.

This is the answer to the question, "How and when will lasting peace be established?" It will be in the kingdom of God. Here's the answer to the question. Will the atomic bomb blow the world to pieces? The answer is, "No." This world will not be blown to pieces by atomic bombs. This world in due time is to be transformed under the creative hand of the Lord Jesus Christ into a new earth.

Wouldn't you like to know how this sin-sick, tear-smitten, war-dazed world will be made into a sinless, happy paradise? Yes. Don't fail then to be at the Hoyt Sherman Place on Tuesday night and you will hear. Ever since Jesus Christ lived among men 1900 years ago, millions of people have been praying, "Our Father which art in heaven, hallowed be Thy name. Thy kingdom come. Thy will be done in earth, as it is in heaven." This prayer has never been answered yet. The will of God is not being done in this earth today as it is done by the angels in heaven. But that prayer will be answered. Wouldn't you like to know how and when the will of God will be done on this earth, as it is in heaven? Be at the Hoyt Sherman Place Tuesday night when I speak on "Heaven" and you will get the answer from the Word of God. You will see also the mystery of this stone that demolished the image and then expanded and expanded and expanded until it filled the entire world.

I can deal with only a few highlights of the prophecy in this lecture. This is why you want to be sure to mark that stub in the program folder so that we may mail you a free printed copy of this lecture that gives everything I say and much more that I cannot say for lack of time.

Do you know that everything in this prophecy has been fulfilled except the last item, the smiting of the man to pieces? Yes, that is exactly the way it is. I want you to notice where we are in the stream of time.

I have a long chart here that contains an outline of this prophecy of Daniel 2. The head of gold was Babylon, ruling the world from B. C. 606 to B. C. 538. In 538 B. C. Cyrus overthrew Babylon. Then Persia began to rule the world. The breast and arms of silver was Persia ruling the world from B. C. 538 to 331 B. C. In 331 B. C. Alexander overthrew the Persian empire in the battle of Arbela. Then Grecia ruled the world. These sides of brass represented Grecia ruling the world from 331 B. C. to 168 B. C. In B. C. 168 Rome took over Grecia. Then Rome ruled the world from 168 years before the birth of Christ until 476 years after Christ when the Roman empire in the west fell.

Rome ruled the world when Jesus was born. If you have ever heard the
Christmas story you have heard this verse, "It came to pass in those days, that
there went out a decree from Caesar Augustus that all the world should be
taxed." Caesar Augustus, a Roman Emperor, ruled the world when Jesus
was born. Notice that the course of history was in the legs of iron when Jesus
was born, nineteen centuries ago. Then between A. D. 351 and A. D. 483 the
Roman Empire in the west was divided into ten kingdoms, as indicated by the
feet and the toes being part of clay and part of iron. England, France, Germany, Spain, Portugal, Italy and Switzerland are the remnants of these divisions in our day.

Now, what next? Where are we today? Let us look at God's time-table.
We are not in the head of gold. Babylon passed away as a world empire in
B. C. 538. We are not in the breast and arms of silver. Persia passed away
as a world empire in 331 B. C. Where are we today? Not in the days of
Grecia. Grecia as a world empire passed away in B. C. 168 when Rome took
over Grecia. Where are we today? Not in the days when Rome ruled the
world. The Roman empire fell in the West in 476 A. D. Where are we today?
We are in the very last division of the composite metal man. The course of
history is almost run. We are on the last lap of the journey. The next act, according to the prophecy, is the return of Jesus as "King of Kings and Lord of
Lords."

> "Down in the feet of iron and of clay,
>   Weak and divided soon to pass away,
> What will the next great glorious drama be?
>   Christ and His coming, and eternity."

Friends, I wonder if I have really made this prophecy plain. I've tried
my best to make it clear. I believe everyone here is ready to signify by the
uplifted hand that I have made the prophecy plain and that according to my
explanation we must be on the verge of the last mighty act. How many believe that I have made this prophecy plain and according to my explanation
we must be on the verge of that last mighty act? Will you please signify it
by lifting your hand just now? Thank you. It looks as though I see every
hand. I'm glad that you recognize the truthfulness and the import of this
prophecy.

Friends, this brings everyone, hearers and preacher, face to face with the
most vital issue of all our lives. Are we ready to enter Christ's everlasting
kingdom? Are we prepared to meet Jesus Christ the coming King? There
isn't anything in our lives more important than for us to make sure of an eternal happy home in Christ's kingdom.

A home in His kingdom is actually worth more than all the gold, the silver, the diamonds, the stocks, the bonds, the farms, and the houses in the
world. "What will it profit a man if he gain the whole world and lose his own
soul?" If you should fail to prepare for a home in Christ's kingdom, it would
be better for you to have never been born. However, every soul may have an
eternal happy home in Christ's kingdom if he wants it. "God so loved the
world that He gave His only begotten Son, that whosoever believeth on Him
should not perish, but have everlasting life." "Believe on the Lord Jesus
Christ and thou shalt be saved." All you need to do is to surrender your
heart and life to the blessed Jesus and let Him live in you a life of obedience
day by day.

I think tonight of one of those thieves who was crucified when Jesus was
nailed to the cross for our sins. This man lived all his life in sin. He was now
face to face with death. He knew he wasn't ready to die. In his dying hour
he turned to Jesus and said, "Lord, remember me when Thou comest in Thy

kingdom." O, how graciously Jesus responded to his request for salvation, and gave him the immediate assurance that he would be with Him in paradise.

Friend of mine, Jesus is ready to do the same thing for you if you will but look to Him. "Look unto Me and be ye saved, all ye ends of the earth." Don't you want Jesus to remember you when He comes in His kingdom? I'm sure you do. I've never met anybody in all my travels who didn't want Jesus to remember him with an eternal happy home in His kingdom. I believe everyone here tonight desires to raise his hand as a silent prayer to Jesus Christ "Lord, remember me when Thou comest in Thy kingdom" How many of you with me, want to send up a silent prayer tonight to Jesus, "Lord remember me when Thou comest in Thy kingdom?" Would you lift the hand just now as a silent prayer to Jesus? Thank you. Let us look to Him now.

(Praying) O Lord Jesus, we thank Thee that Thou art our Saviour. O we thank Thee for Thy great love in giving Thyself upon the cross for our sins. And now, Jesus, we have raised our hands to Thee as a silent prayer. Jesus, Thou hast heard the prayer. Thou hast seen every hand that has been uplifted here tonight. And O, blessed Christ, precious Saviour, undertake for every man and woman, boy and girl in this great audience, O, Lord, we thank Thee that Thou hast heard our prayer and that Thou wilt remember us with an eternal happy home when Thou comest in Thy kingdom, and we will give Thee all the praise in the name of Jesus, Amen.

What and Where Is Heaven?

(Preached on the First Tuesday Night of the Campaign)

(An outline setting forth the leading items, which are brought forth from the Scriptures in this lecture, was placed in the hands of each hearer, before the lecture began. Some of these propositions on the outline had blank lines after them, on which the hearers were requested to fill in certain Bible references. These propositions from the outline and the Bible references involved, appear in the transcript of this lecture.)

A mail carrier was making his way from house to house. Suddenly a voice called out, "Got anything for me today?" Looking up he saw it was the man who lived in the second house ahead. He replied, "Yes, I have. I have a letter for you that is postmarked Honolulu." "Fine," said the man, "that must be from my wealthy brother who lives in Honolulu." And sure enough when he opened the letter it was from his wealthy brother, inviting him to come and spend the rest of his life on his lovely estate near Honolulu.

In this letter he told about the lovely mansion that he had built for him next to his own palatial home. He told of the lovely flower gardens laid out all around the home. He described the wonderful fruit trees laden with the most luscious fruits. Then he added, "My plan is, that if you are willing to accept my offer, I'll come with my plane to bring you and your family to this lovely home, and I will share all of my fortune with you."

Do you think he was interested in such an offer? He certainly was. He accepted it, double quick. O, how he looked for that day when that plane would arrive to take him and his family to that lovely mansion. I can hear some of you say, "O! I wish I could be that lucky." Listen, this blessed Bible, the Word of God, puts into the hands of everyone in this auditorium an offer that is far better than this. Here it is, John 14:1-3. And listen, this is an offer from **your** brother. You have a wealthy brother in heaven. His name is Jesus. He is your elder Brother. He is the friend that sticketh closer than a brother.

Shortly before He left this world He told His disciples that He would come again to receive His people unto Himself and to take them to glorious mansions in heaven. Notice, as I read, John 14:1-3.

"Let not your heart be troubled: ye believe in God, believe also in Me. In My Father's house are many mansions: if it were not so, I would have told you. I go to prepare a place for you. And if I go and prepare a place for you I will come again, and receive you unto Myself; that where I am, there ye may be also."

Notice, Jesus says, "I go to prepare a place for you." Have you ever wondered what that place is that Jesus has prepared for His own? Wouldn't you like to know what that place is like and where it is located? And how you may be sure of having a home in that fair and happy land? Your Bible tells.

Heb. 11:16 shows that this place that Jesus Christ has prepared is the New Jeresalem, the city of God, in the heaven of heavens. Jesus said in John 14:3, "I go to prepare a place." Then Hebrews 11:16 tells us, He has prepared a city for His people. In the context, in verse 10, that city is identified as the New Jerusalem, a city whose builder and maker is God. This indicates that this place which Jesus has prepared for our future is the New Jerusalem.

We have placed an outline in your hands that you might have a record of the striking facts about this home in the land of the "sweet by and by." Be sure to bring your notebook Thursday night. Look at No. 1 on the outline that you have in your hand. "Mansions in heaven are available through the Lord Jesus Christ," and on the blank line, record John 14:1-3.

Look at No. 2. "There are three different heavens," and on the blank line, record 2 Corinthians 12.2. Here Paul is the speaker. "I knew a man in Christ above fourteen years ago, (whether in the body, I cannot tell; or whether out of the body, I cannot tell: God knoweth;) such an one caught up to the third heaven."

Paul declares that he was caught up to the third heaven. Since there is a third heaven, there must be a first and second heaven. If you tell me that your brother lives in the third house from the corner, I know I must pass two houses before I can contact your brother in the third house. When Paul says he was caught up to the third heaven, he must have passed through the first and second heavens before reaching the third.

The question naturally comes, what are the three different heavens? Are they three degrees of happiness in the life to come? Will people progress from one to the other?

Look at No. 3 on the outline, "The first heaven is the aerial heaven." Fill in the word "aerial" on the blank line before the word "heaven." Then after the words "aerial heaven" fill in the reference Rev. 19:17. This verse speaks about the birds flying in the midst of heaven. Everybody knows that the birds fly in the air above the ground. The Bible designates the air or atmosphere above the surface of the earth as the first heaven. This first heaven or atmospheric heaven is the heaven from which the rain and the snow come down. This is where the clouds float around. In the Bible in its own picturesque way of describing things, it calls the clouds, "the bottle of heaven." Isn't that colorful and expressive?

Look at No. 4, "The second heaven is the stellar heaven." Fill in the word "Stellar," and then record the reference, Psalms 19:1-6. This second heaven is far above the atmospheric heaven. It is the heaven where the sun, moon, and stars move in their orbits. This is the heaven that is mentioned in Psalms 19:1-6.

One beautiful night David went out and looking up on high at those millions of twinkling orbs he broke out in a most rapturous song, "The heavens declare the glory of God; and the firmament sheweth His handywork . . . In them hath He set a tabernacle for the sun, which is as a bridegroom coming out of his chamber, and rejoiceth as a strong man to run a race. His going forth is from the end of the heaven, and his circuit unto the ends of it."

Next look at No. 5, "The third heaven is Paradise." Fill in the word "Paradise," and after the word, record the reference 2 Corinthians 12:2, 4. In the second verse, which I read just a moment ago, Paul says he was caught up to the third heaven. In the fourth verse, in speaking of the same experience, he says he was caught up into Paradise. Now you can see how plain that makes it, that the third heaven is Paradise.

Look at No. 6, "This identifies the third heaven with the New Jerusalem." On the blank line record Rev. 2:7 and Rev. 22:1, 2. You see, the way to understand the Bible is to compare scripture with scripture and not scripture with man's idea. Compare scripture with scripture and the Bible explains itself, and you have the right explanation.

Rev. 2:7 declares that the tree of life is in the middle or midst of the paradise of God. Rev. 22:1, 2 declares, that the tree of life is located on the banks of the river of life in the New Jerusalem. So that identifies the

New Jerusalem with the third heaven and Paradise. This third heaven is the place where Jesus has prepared those lovely mansions for His people.

We have a chart here that will help you to understand this. You will notice that here is the line of the earth's surface, or what we call the ground Here is where the buildings are resting The air, or the atmosphere above the earth's surface is the atmospheric or aerial heaven. It is called "aerial heaven," because aerial is a Latin word for air. This is the heaven where the clouds float around, where the aeroplanes travel. This is the heaven where birds fly, and from which the rain and the snow come down.

Then far above the atmosphere is the "stellar heaven." It is called the stellar heaven, because the word "stella" is the Latin word for star. In the stellar heaven is the moon some 240,000 miles away. And the sun, 95,000,-000 miles away. The nearest fixed star, Alpha Centauri, is some 19 billion miles away, or nineteen-thousand-million miles distant.

Then far above the starry sky is the third heaven, Paradise, the New Jerusalem. This is where the throne of God is located. This is where the angels dwell, and where the righteous will go, to live forever with the Lord.

I promised to tell you about the two men who passed through the first and second heaven into the third heaven, and then came back to this earth to talk to men. You will find this in Matt. 17:1-5. Put this reference down. It isn't on the outline. On the Mount of Transfiguration, Moses and Elijah came from God's dwelling place in the third heaven. As they appeared upon the holy mount, they talked with Jesus and the chosen three of His disciples.

The transfiguration of Christ was a miniature representation of His second coming. Elijah, who was taken to heaven without tasting death, represented the righteous living, who will be changed in the twinkling of an eye and caught up to meet the Lord at His coming. Moses, who was resurrected from the dead, represented the righteous dead, who will be raised from the grave with immortal bodies when Jesus comes.

Everybody in this world craves happiness. But O, there are so many things in this world that mar our happiness, such as, sickness, pain, trouble, disappointment, and death. Friends, in this home that Jesus has prepared for you that craving for happiness will find full and lasting satisfaction. In Rev. 21:4 I read some of the most blessed words that have ever been penned. "God shall wipe away all tears from their eyes; and there shall be no more death, neither sorrow nor crying, neither shall there be any more pain: for the former things are passed away."

In this heavenly home there will be no more sickness, no pain, no trouble, no poverty, no war, no sorrow, no death. We will have perfect immortal bodies that will never have an ache or a pain; that will never get old; that will never die.

"There's no disappointment in heaven,
    No weariness, sorrow or pain;
No hearts that are bleeding and broken,
    No song with a minor refrain;
We'll never pay rent for our mansion,
    The taxes will never come due;
Our garments will never grow threadbare,
    But always be fadeless and new;
There'll never be crepe on the door-knob,
    No funeral train in the sky;
No graves on the hill-sides of glory,
    For there we shall never-more die;
The old will be young there forever,

Transformed in a moment of time;
Immortal we'll stand in His likeness,
The stars and the sun to outshine.
I'm bound for that beautiful city
My Lord has prepared for his own;
Where all the redeemed of all ages
Sing "glory" around the white throng;
Sometimes I grow homesick for heaven,
And the glories I there shall behold:
What a joy that will be when my Saviour I see,
In that beautiful city of gold!"

My friends, when you think of all the suffering, trouble, sorrow, sickness, and disappointment in this world, aren't you glad that your loving Saviour has prepared such a wonderful home for you, where there will be no trouble, sorrow, sickness, pain, or death. Wouldn't you like to thank Jesus just now, for providing such a happy future for you? How many, with me, would like to express your thanks to Jesus tonight for providing such a happy future? Will you lift your hands? Yes, it seems that all hands are raised.

Friends, if there were a country in this world where people could go and never be sick, and never have any trouble and be perfectly happy, and never get old, and never die, wouldn't there be a rush for such a country? Yes! Everybody in the world would want to go to that country. In heaven God has prepared just such a place, for you and me. Why shouldn't we seek with all our hearts to have an eternal happy home in heaven?

A home in that heavenly land is worth more than all the wealth of this world. "What shall it profit a man if he gain the whole world, and lose his own soul?" Just ask yourself, what would it profit me if I could gain the whole world, and then lose an eternal happy home in heaven? This ought to put into your hearts, and into my heart a determination to follow Jesus all the way, no matter what it costs, even if it costs us our life.

Look at No. 7 on the outline, "The New Jerusalem is a place of perfect and everlasting happiness," and on the blank line record Rev 21:4. Remember that the last two chapters in the Bible, Rev. 21, 22, describe the infinite glories and beauties of this heavenly country. When you get home tonight, please take the Bible and turn to the last two chapters before you put your head on the pillow. If you want to have something sweet on your mind as you fall asleep tonight, just take the Bible and read the last two chapters of Revelation.

In those two chapters you will find that the New Jerusalem, the City of God, is laid out in a perfect square. It measures 375 miles on each side It contains 140,625 square miles. It has twelve foundations composed of 12 precious stones. These are so arranged that it will look like a gigantic rainbow. This city has twelve gates, three on each of its four sides. Each gate is composed of one massive pearl. The streets possess the power of perfect transparency, so that when you walk on those streets it will be like walking on air. The throne of God and the throne of His Son, Jesus, is located in the center of this New Jerusalem. Proceeding from the throne of God is the river of life, clear as crystal. On the banks of the river of life with the branches beautifully arched over the river is the tree of life. The fruit on that tree possesses such magic power that when you eat of it you will never be sick again. You will never die. This is the tree of life.

This New Jerusalem is a sinless city. In Rev. 21 27 we are told that "There shall in no wise enter into it anything that defileth." Sin is what defiles. This New Jerusalem will be free forever from every trace of sin. It will be the only city that I have ever heard about in which there will never be any liquor. There will be no tobacco in the New Jerusalem. There will be no dance halls, no gambling dens, no swearing, no hatred, no immorality, no stealing, no Sabbath breaking, no sin of any kind. You see, we get rid of every sin before we can go there. "There shall in no wise enter into it anything that defileth."

The big question is, how can we get rid of every sin? There is only one way. "The blood of Jesus Christ His Son cleanseth us from all sin." Not just nine-tenths, but from "all sin."

Modern chemistry is performing great miracles, but listen, all the chemistry in the world has never been able to find anything that will wash sin out of the soul of man. What can wash away my sins? Nothing, but the blood of Jesus. Our only hope of a home in heaven is the precious blood of the Lamb. If you really want to know how to get ready for a home in heaven be sure to hear the lecture on Thursday night.

You have heard much in recent months about the atomic bomb, atomic power, the atomic age. Listen, do you know that there is coming a super-atomic explosion that will be as much greater than any of these atomic explosions that man has produced, as the ocean is to a tin cup full of water. Beyond that great super atomic explosion there will come a new world in which the righteous will live forever. Here it is in 2 Peter, listen as I read. This is really a marvelous thing in view of what has happened since the advent of the atomic age in 1945.

In II Peter 3:10 I read, "The day of the Lord will come as a thief in the night; in the which the heavens shall pass away with a great noise." This heaven which will pass away refers to the first heaven, the atmospheric heaven. The Bible says in Rev. 21:1, "I saw a new heaven and a new earth: for the first heaven," (not the second heaven, not the third heaven, but) "the first heaven was passed away." The heavens shall pass away with a great noise. This will be a super-explosion of the gases in the air. Then will come the conflagration of the world. The elements shall melt with fervent heat, the earth also and the works that are therein shall be burned up."

This is a very significant point. The Bible is just as up to date as Big Ben. It says, "the elements shall melt with fervent heat." What are the elements? The elements are the fundamental forms of units of matter. This material world is composed of some 90 elements. Some of these are: iron, lead, copper, silver, gold, radium, uranium, oxygen, hydrogen, etc. It says the elements shall melt. The Greek word that is used here in connection with the elements means to loose, or untie. It is the same Greek word that is used where John the Baptist said he wasn't worthy to untie the shoe laces of the Messiah.

Here is the principle of the atomic bomb. In the atom are tiny particles held together by enormous cohesive forces. The atomic bomb is a loosening of the particles that make up the atom. That's why they talk about splitting the atom. God knew all about that before the first man ever walked on the earth. In the day of the Lord, God will use the forces of atomic action. The heavens shall pass away with a great super-atomic explosion. Then will come the conflagration of the world.

But this world will never be wiped out of existence as a planet. When the Bible talks about the end of the world that doesn't mean that this physical world or globe will be wiped out of existence. How do I know this? Friends, if we read the Bible we don't have to worry about this world being wiped out of existence. The earth abideth forever. It will never be wiped out of existence The atmospheric heaven will pass away. There will be a conflagration that will burn sin out of the world. Then beyond this, there will arise a new earth.

I turn to verse 13. "Nevertheless we according to His promise, look for a new heaven and a new earth wherein dwelleth righteousness." This physical sphere on which we are living will never be wiped out of existence. It will be reconstructed, recreated, remade, renewed into a perfect new world, just as it was in the beginning. There the righteous only shall live. There is only one way you can survive this impending destruction "He that doeth the will of God shall abide forever."

Look at No. 8, "At the final day Jesus Christ will reconstruct our present world into a perfect, happy, and sinless new earth in which only the righteous will dwell." On the blank, record 2 Peter 3:10, 13.

Look at No. 9. "This new Jerusalem will descend from the third heaven to become the capital of the new earth." Put down Rev. 21:1-3 on the blank line.

Under 10 and 11 you have some striking items about this coming new earth, with the Bible references already recorded. Notice these. Christ, will rule over this new earth from the New Jerusalem, on the throne of David. (Luke 1:31-33; Isa. 9:6, 7.)

The will of God will then be done on this new earth as it is now done in heaven, in accordance with the Lord's prayer. (Matt. 6:10.) This new earth with the New Jerusalem as its glorious capital will constitute the heavenly home of the righteous for eternity. (Matt. 5:5; 2 Peter 3:13.) This new earth will be the earth which the meek will inherit according to Matt. 5:5. It will be the place where the saints will reign on earth according to Rev. 5:10.

A party of Americans were touring Great Britain one summer. They decided when they came to Liverpool they would stay at the Northwestern Hotel. When the train arrived at Liverpool they called a taxi that took them to the Northwestern Hotel. Stepping up to the desk to register the clerk said, "Sorry, there isn't a room available. See that sign, 'No rooms available unless reservation confirmed'."

They called another taxi, picked up their luggage and started to find some other place. As they were leaving the hotel, they noticed one of the ladies in their party remaining at the desk. They said to her, "Come on. There isn't a room here." "I'm going to stay here. They have a nice room for me."

They returned to her and said, "How is this? We all came here at the same time. He told us there wasn't a chance to get a room." "O," she said, "I wired the hotel five days ago from London to reserve a room. It's all ready for me now."

Friend of mine, if you want a place in God's heavenly home at the end of the way, you must make a reservation now, during this life To those who make a reservation, Jesus will saay, "Come ye blessed of My Father inherit the kingdom prepared for you from the foundation of the world. "To those who fail to make a reservation, Jesus will have to say, "Depart from me into everlasting fire prepared for the devil and his angels."

Do you know how to make a reservation for a mansion in the new Jerusalem? Here it is. "Believe on the Lord Jesus Christ and thou shall be saved." "God so loved the world that He gave His only begotten Son that whosoever believeth in Him should not perish, but have everlasting life." Jesus says, "I am the door, if any man enter in by me he shall be saved."

Wouldn't you like to send on your reservation tonight? I know I do. I believe everybody in this auditorium is ready to say by the uplifted hand, "Lord help me to so believe on You that You can reserve a place in that wonderful home for me." How many want the Lord's help to so follow

Him that He can give you an eternal happy home in the city of God?
Would you lift your hand just now? Thank you.

(Praying) Our Dear Heavenly Father, O, we do thank Thee that Thou
hast provided such a happy future. Lord, in this world of disappointment,
sorrow, sickness, pain and death, O, how we do thank Thee that Thou hast
provided such a happy future. Father, Thou hast even given Thine own
dear Son that we might have an eternal happy home in Thy kingdom and
in Thy glorious city. Father, Thou hast seen every hand that has been
raised and we pray that Jesus will undertake for everyone.

We do want that Thou shouldst help us to so believe on Jesus, to so follow Him that we might have that wonderful everlasting life, that eternal
happy home in the land of the Sweet by and by where dreams will come
true. Father, do grant that everyone of us will so make a reservaton now,
that at the end of the way, Jesus can welcome us into this wonderful home
that He has prepared. We ask it in His precious name. Amen.

(This is a copy of the outline which was placed in the hands of the
hearers, preceding the presentation of the Bible lecture on heaven.)

SOME STRIKING SCRIPTURAL FACTS ABOUT HEAVEN

1. Mansions in heaven are available through the Lord Jesus Christ..........
2. There are three different heavens .... _ ....
3. The first heaven is the..... . ... heaven ....
4. The second heaven is the . ... .heaven . . . . -
5. The third heaven is....... .. ..: .. ... .
6. This identifies the third heaven with the New Jerusalem....................... ..

    In order to learn something of the glories and the beauties of the New
    Jerusalem, you are advised to read Revelation 21 and 22 when you re-
    turn to your home.
7. The New Jerusalem is a place of perfect and everlasting happiness.............
8. At the final day Jesus Christ will reconstruct our present world into a
    perfect, happy, and sinless new earth, in which only the righteous will
    dwell..................... ....
9. This new Jerusalem will descend from the third heaven, to become the
    capital of the new earth . ..._............
10. Christ will rule over this new earth from the new Jerusalem, on the throne
    of David. (Luke 1:31-33; Isa. 9:6, 7.)
11. The will of God will then be done on this earth as it is now done in
    heaven, in accordance with the Lord's prayer. (Matt. 6:10.)

    This new earth with the new Jerusalem as its glorious capital will con-
    stitute the heavenly home of the righteous for eternity. (Matt. 5:5; 2
    Pet. 3:13.)

    This new earth will be the earth which the meek will inherit according
    to Matt. 5:5:

    This new earth will be the place where the saints will reign on earth
    according to Rev. 5:10.

    Those who accept the Lord Jesus Christ as their personal Saviour and
    obey His teachings will have an eternal happy home in heaven. (John
    3:16; Rev. 22:14.)

The Man Who Wrote His Own Autobiography Before He Was Born

(Preached on the First Thursday Night of the Campaign)

The most stupendous claim that ever has been advanced by any person, was that put forth by a young carpenter from an obscure village in the hills of Galilee some 1900 years ago. His family was poor and unknown. His foster father was the village carpenter. This young man worked unnoticed by the world in the carpenter shop of his foster father, in the little village of Nazareth until he was thirty years of age.

When he reached his thirtieth birthday he stepped out from the family circle; out from that carpenter shop; out from the quiet hills of Nazareth and boldly proclaimed to the world that he was the Saviour of mankind, the long expected Messiah, the Son of God. He told the people, "If men do not believe on Me as the Saviour, they will die in their sins and perish, but if a man believes on Me as His Saviour he will live forever." The all-important question before you and me is to ascertain the correctness of this claim.

Questions have come to me in this Bible Institute something like this, "Mr. Shuler, how can a person like me who has never seen Jesus really come to the place where he can be absolutely sure that Christ is the only Saviour? How can I know for a certainty that Christ can forgive my sins and give me eternal life beyond the grave? Well, here's the answer in the Word of God. Put it down, Acts 18:28. Speaking of Apollos, the record says, "For he mightily convinced the Jews, and that publicly, showing by the scriptures that Jesus was Christ." Apollos showed by the Scriptures, the Old Testament scriptures, that Jesus was the Christ, the Saviour of the world. He took up the Messianic prophecies of the Old Testament and showed how all those prophecies were fulfilled to the letter in the life of Jesus of Nazareth.

Do you know that Jesus wrote His own autobiography hundreds of years before He was born? Whoever heard of a man's life story from birth to death being recorded in a book hundreds of years before that man was born, and then, every item coming true in his life? That would be an outstanding wonder, wouldn't it?

Tonight, I'm going a step further than this. Strange as it may seem, or as Robert Ripley says, "believe it or not," tonight we are going to show you how that carpenter of Nazareth directed the writing of His own life's story even hundreds of years before He was ever born as a baby. This is the wonder of wonders!

I direct you to 1 Peter 1:10-12. Here we learn that it was the Spirit of Christ Who directed the Old Testament prophets to predict the coming of the Saviour beforehand. Everyone who has ever heard the story of Christmas knows that Jesus was born in Bethlehem. Even little children can tell you that. But do you know that it was recorded 700 years before Jesus was born, that His birth would take place in that little village of Bethlehem?

Here is is, Micah 5:2: "Thou, Bethlehem Ephratah, though thou be little among the thousands of Judah, yet out of thee shall He come forth unto Me that is to be ruler in Israel; Whose goings forth have been from of old, from everlasting."

This was recorded on the scroll of the prophets B. C. 710, over 700 years before the birth of Jesus Christ. Notice that Micah points out the very town

17

where the Messiah was to be born. Out of a million places in the world where He could be born, the prophet puts his finger on a little hamlet five miles from Jerusalem, and says, "Out of Bethlehem will this Messiah come forth." You will notice that while he prophesied that the Messiah would be born in Bethlehem, he very clearly shows us that this would not be the beginning of Christ. He declares that while He would be born in Bethlehem, His goings forth have been from the days of eternity. Yes, Christ is the eternal Son of God. He was with the Father before the world was.

Everybody in the world that has ever heard the story of Christmas must testify that Micah 5:2 has been fulfilled. I dare say that I could take the children here tonight and ask them where Christ was born, and six out of eight would say in Bethlehem, just as prophesied by Micah.

If we examine the facts in the case, we shall see the Master hand of God in the fulfillment of Micah 5:2. Mary, the mother of Jesus, lived in Nazareth. Nazareth is 92 miles north of Bethlehem. Ninety-two miles was about a four or five days journey in those days on donkey back. At present it requires a full day's run by bus. If you had been living back there three weeks before Jesus was born, knowing that Mary was living in Nazareth, you would have said her child will be born in Nazareth. That was the natural thing to expect, for Nazareth was her home.

But what happened? "God moves in a mysterious way His wonders to perform." At the right time there came from Rome a decree that everybody in the world must be taxed. This decree of the Roman Emperor Augustus, brought Mary and Joseph to Bethlehem at just the right time for the birth of the Christ to take place in this village, as was prophesied 700 years before. Isn't it wonderful that Micah could look ahead 700 years by the Spirit of God and see how even though Mary would be living in Nazareth, a decree would come from Rome from a ruler who knew not God, which would cause her to journey 92 miles to Bethlehem at just the right time for the birth of that wonderful Son in that place? This is one of the numerous remarkable fulfillments of prophecy, which forever establishes the Messiahship of Jesus Christ.

A biography usually tells something about a person's parents. Isaiah foretold 700 years beforehand that Jesus the Christ would be born of a virgin. Put down Isaiah 7:14: "Behold, a virgin shall conceive, and bear a son, and shall call His name Immanuel."

There are some people who say it is very difficult to believe in the virgin birth of Christ. They say it is contrary to nature. You need have no difficulty with this, if you will just remember that prophecy never fails. What God says is to be, always happens. God said 700 years beforehand that Jesus would be born of a virgin. It is very easy to believe that what God said was exactly fulfilled.

The prophecy of Zechariah pointed out some amazing details hundreds of years beforehand. I want you to notice with me three items outlined in Zechariah 11:12, 13. You talk about television! Here is super-television! I'm going to read how the scripture pointed out the exact price that Christ would be sold for over 500 years beforehand. It specified where the one who took that money would throw it down. It specified what disposition would be made of that money. It is really remarkable.

I read from Zech. 11:12, 13. "I said unto them, If ye think good, give me my price; and if not, forbear. So they weighed for my price thirty pieces of silver. And the Lord said unto me, Cast it unto the potter: a goodly price that I was priced at of them. And I took the thirty pieces of silver and cast them to the potter in the house of the Lord."

Think of it! Five hundred years beforehand it was foretold that this

Christ would be sold for thirty pieces of silver and it specified that the money would be thrown down in the temple and it would be used to purchase a field as a burial ground for strangers. How did it come out? All these three details were fulfilled to the very letter in the life of Jesus of Nazareth.

When Judas asked them, "How much will you give me if I betray Him into your hands?" He struck the bargain for thirty pieces of silver. It says "They weighed for my price thirty pieces of silver." After he had betrayed the Saviour his conscience smote him. He came back to the priests with whom he had made the bargain to betray Christ and cried, "I have sinned in that I have betrayed innocent blood." Then he threw down the money on the temple floor. This was exactly where God had foretold 500 years beforehand he would cast it down.

They said to one another, "What shall we do with this money?" One man evidently made the suggestion that it might be put into the treasury box of the temple. Listen to me. Do you know that if they had put that money into the treasury box of the temple, this wouldn't be a true book tonight? When that suggestion was made someone said, "No! you can't put that money in the treasury box. It is the price of blood. It is not lawful to put that money in the treasury box. We will take that money and buy a potter's field." And this is what they did. Notice that they did with this money just what the scripture foretold 500 years before.

Tell me, how could any man of himself look ahead 500 years and predict such minute details, the exact price, what the man would do with the money, and what they would use the money for. Nobody knows such things ahead of time except God. The prognostication of such minute details forever stamps the Bible as the Word of God and Jesus Christ as the only true Saviour.

One thousand years before Jesus was due to appear on this earth, Scripture even foretold where they would drive the nails into His body. Think of it! Put down Psalm 22:16. It says: "They pierced my hands and my feet." And that's exactly what happened to Jesus when He was hung on the old rugged cross. They nailed Him to the cross. They pierced His hands and His feet.

Now this is remarkable. This was written by David one thousand years before the birth of Christ, and in the time of David, death by crucifixion was not even known. It was the Romans who invented death by crucifixion at a later date. Just think of it! Even when death by crucifixion was unknown a thousand years ahead the Bible foretold exactly where they would pierce the body of the Messiah.

The Bible record indicates that four soldiers were on guard around the cross where Jesus hung. They stripped Him of His clothing. Jesus evidently had five different pieces of clothing. They took four pieces and divided them amongst themselves. This was one apiece. One apiece, but one left over Then one of the soldiers said, "What shall we do with this remaining piece? I tell you, we will tear it into four pieces and then every man will have exactly the same." Do you know if that suggestion had been followed, this wouldn't' be a true book tonight?

Here it is. Put down Psalm 22:18. It is uncanny how these minute details were specified and came to pass so clearly. It says here in Psalm 22:18, "They part my garments among them and cast lots upon my vesture."

Prophecy did not say that they would tear it into pieces and everyone take a piece. It said they would divide his garments among them and cast lots for what was left. When this one soldier suggested that they tear it into four pieces the others said, "No! We will not tear it into four pieces.

We will cast lots and see who gets it." They did exactly as God had said they would do a thousand years ahead.

More wonderful than all this, the Bible foretold a thousand years ahead that Christ would be resurrected before His body would begin to decay. Put down Psalm 16:10: "Thou wilt not leave my soul in hell; neither wilt thou suffer thine Holy One to see corruption." It was foretold that He would be raised from the dead even before His body began to decay.

Nor is that all, listen to me. It was foretold 700 years ahead that His resurrection would take place on the third day. Here it is in Hosea 6:2. "After two days will He revive us: in the third day He will raise us up, and we shall live in His sight." Actually it said on the third day, the Father would raise His Son, and He did.

Again, the Bible foretold that He would ascend to the Father. In the Old Testament it told how He would take His place on the Father's right hand as a Priest and Mediator to plead the cases of all who accept Him. You will find this in Zech. 6:13.

I have a chart here tonight that is really remarkable. By the way, I'm going to give you a copy of it. My! how you will treasure it. This card contains what you see on these three charts. It tells the complete life-story of Jesus from the Old Testament.

PROPHECIES OF JESUS

"We have found Him of whom Moses . . . and the prophets, did write, Jesus of Nazareth." John 1:45.

Micah 5.2	Birthplace	Matt. 2:1
Isa. 7:14	Mother	Matt. 1:18-23
Gen. 49:10	Tribe	Heb. 7:14
Isa. 11:1	Family	Rev. 22:16
Hosea 11:1	In Egypt	Matt. 2:13-15
Daniel 9:25	The Time	Mark 1:14, 15

CAREER OUTLINED

Isa. 61:1-3	His Work	Luke 4:16-21
Deut. 18:15	A Prophet	Acts 7:37
Isaiah 9.1, 2	Light Bearer	Matt 4:12-16
Isa. 53.4	A Healer	Matt. 8 16, 17; 12:12-21
Ps. 78:2	Teach in Parables	Matt 13:34, 35
Isa. 40:11	Shepherd	John 10:14
Ps. 69:8; Isa. 53:3	Rejection	John 1:10, 11
Isa. 49:4-6	Known as Saviour	Rev. 7:9
Zech. 9:9	Triumphant Entry	Matt. 21:1-11
Ps. 41:9; 55:12, 13	Betrayer	John 13:18, 19, 26
Zech. 11:12	Price Sold For	Matt. 26:14-16
Zech. 11:13	How Money Used	Matt. 27:3-8
Isa. 50:6	Spit Upon	Matt. 26:67
Micah 5:1	Smitten With Rod	Matt. 27:30
Isa. 53:7	Silent Before Persecutors	Matt. 27:12-14
Zech. 13:7	Disciples Forsake	Matt. 26:31

CLOSING SCENES

Zech. 12:10	Manner of Death	John 19:18
Ps. 22:10	Location of Wounds	John 20:25

HIS DEATH

Dan. 9:26; Ex. 12 6	Year, Day, Hour	Matt. 27:45-50

Isa. 53:13	With Criminals	Mark 15:27, 28
Ps. 22:7, 8	Taunting Words	Matt. 27:39, 41-44
Ps. 22:1	Agonizing Cry	Matt. 27:46
Isa. 53:12	Pray for Persecutors	Luke 23.34
Ps. 69:21	Drink Offered	John 19:28-30
Ps. 22:18	His Garments	John 19:23, 24
Ps. 34-20; Ex. 12.46	No Bones Broken	John 19 36
Isa. 53:9	His Burial	Matt. 27·57-60
Ps. 16:10	His Resurrection	Acts 2.30, 31
Hosea 6:2	The Third Day	Mark 8 31
Ps. 24:7-10	His Ascension	1 Peter 3:22
Zech. 6:13	To the Throne as Priest	Heb. 8:1, 2

Here on the left-hand side are the Old Testament prophecies about the Christ Who was to comse, what He would do and all that. Then over here on the right are the New Testament references where these prophecies were fulfilled to the very letter. Not one word failed. Beginning with His birthplace on this chart there are thirty-seven advance items concerning the Messiah. They are traced out here one by one.

I have touched only a few of these in my lecture, but you will have all the references on the card. In the prophecy it foretold His birthplace He was to be born in that little hamlet of Bethlehem. It foretold who His mother would be. She would be a virgin. It foretold the tribe from which He would come, the family from which He would come. It foretold how He would be called into Egypt. It foretold the very year when He would begin his ministry.

It told what kind of work He would do. He would be a prophet, a light bearer, a healer. He would preach in parables. All of this, mind you, was in the Old Testament centuries before Jesus was ever born. It foretold that He would be rejected by His own people, the Jews. It told of his triumphant entry into Jerusalem It told how He would be betrayed by one of His own disciples. It told the exact price He would be sold for and how they would use the money. Then it told how they would spit upon Him; how they would smite Him with a rod, how He would be silent before His accusers; and how His disciples would forsake Him.

As for the closing scene, it told how He would die, even foretold just where they would drive the nails. It told the year, the day, and the hour that His death would take place. It told how He would be crucified with criminals; numbered with transgressors It told about the taunting words that hundreds of years afterwards they used when they taunted Him as He hung upon the cross It even foretold the agonizing cry, "My God, My God, why hast Thou forsaken Me?"

All this was prophesied hundreds of years ahead. It told how He would pray for His persecutors. It even told the very liquid they gave Him to drink as He hung upon the cross. It marked out what they would do with His garments It told that not one bone of His body would be broken. It told how He would make His grave with the rich; how He would be resurrected before His body began to decay; how it would take place on the third day. Then how He would ascend to the Father and would sit upon the Father's throne as our great high priest.

Now the very fact that the life of Jesus in the New Testament corresponds to every prophetic detail about the Messiah is unimpeachable evidence that Jesus of Nazareth is the only true Saviour and the only true Redeemer. Mark this well. There is no chance for a mistake on this point. There is absolutely no room for doubt. Why not? Because **no other man ever lived, nor ever can** live to whom these prophecies can apply except Jesus Christ. So we know Jesus is the right one; the only one; the true Messiah; the true Saviour. This is how people who have never seen Jesus can be absolutely sure that He is the only true Saviour and put all their trust in Him. This is how to cure your doubts and increase your faith.

Dr. Arthur Pearson has wisely said: "There would be no honest infidel in the world were these Messianic prophecies studied, and there would be no doubting disciple if this body of predictions were understood."

When we find that the life of Jesus corresponds in every detail to the prophetic blueprint, we can say we have found Him of whom Moses and the prophets did write, the Messiah, the only true Saviur.

> "Yes, there's One, only One,
>   The blessed, blessed Jesus,
>   He's the One;
> When afflictions press the soul,
>   When waves of trouble roll,
> And you need a friend to help you,
>   He's the One."
>   * * * * *
> "Wonderful, wonderful Jesus!
>   Who can compare with Thee!
> Wonderful, wonderful Jesus!
>   Fairer than all art Thou to me!
> Wonderful, wonderful Jesus!
>   Oh, how my soul loves Thee!
> Fairer than all the fairest,
>   Jesus art Thou to me!"

(Musical rendering of this was then sung by the choir.)

Yes, friends, it just takes one thing now to make this complete. And that is for every soul here to make sure that he receives Jesus into his heart as his personal Saviour. If you accept Him, you will live forever. If you reject Him, you will die in your sins and perish. The supreme issue before every man and woman, every boy and girl, is, "What shall I do with Jesus which is called the Christ?" The only wise course, the only safe way, the only right decision is to receive Jesus into your heart as your personal Saviour.

Lord Kelvin, that great English scientist was once asked, "What has been your most valuable discovery?" Lord Kelvin had made many great scientific discoveries. The Kelvinator refrigerator is named after Lord Kelvin. He discovered the principle of mechanical refrigeraton. People thought when they asked him this question, he would go on to explain his different discoveries. Looking them in the eye he said, "Gentlemen, the most valuable discovery I ever made is when I discovered that Jesus Christ was my personal Saviour."

Have you made this discovery for yourself? O, I hope you have. This good Book says, "To as many as receive Him He gave the power to become the Sons of God and they were born, not of flesh nor of the will of men but of God."

O, friends, I believe everyone of us wants the Lord to help us to follow this wonderful Jesus, whom we have been talking about, and singing about. How many of you tonight want the Lord to help you to truly follow this wonderful Jesus? Will you lift your hand just now? Yes, it seems that every hand is raised.

(Praying) Blessed Jesus, precious Saviour, Son of God, O, how we do thank Thee for what we have learned tonight from the word of God. We are so thankful that in Thee we have a solid rock. Lord, how plain this is! How sure it is! O, Lord, we cannot thank Thee enough for these prophecies that give us such a sure foundation for our faith. We know no one ever lived to whom these could apply except Thee.

Our faith, Lord, seems stronger. We go from this auditorium tonight with more faith in Thee than we've ever had before. We have raised our hand as a silent prayer to Thee asking for Thy help. Lord, we need it. We live in an evil world. We need help and strength to follow Thee all the way. Lord, we know Thou will hear our prayer and grant us strength and help to follow Thee all the way, that finally we may be with Thee forever in Thy wonderful kingdom. We ask it in Thy precious name. Amen.

Why Doesn't God Kill the Devil?

(Preached on the First Friday of the Campaign)

(An outline setting forth the leading propositions, which are established from the Scriptures in this lecture, was placed in the hands of each hearer, before the lecture began. These propositions had blank lines after them, on which the hearers were requested to fill in certain Bible references. These propositions from the outline and the Bible references involved appear in the transcript of this lecture.)

Some time ago I stood on the street corner of a certain city and saw an empty automobile without anybody at the wheel make a tour of the business section of that city. When the driverless car came to a red light it stopped. When the light changed to the green, the car would proceed. When the car came to another car in the middle of the road, it would turn and go around it just as you would do if you were at the wheel. But remember, nobody was in the car; and nobody was at the wheel. Thousands of people lined the streets of that city watching the movements of that automobile.

Do you think the people who watched that car thought that it was doing this of itself? Certainly not! They understood, that, behind the scenes, someone was directing the movements of that machine. So we know that all of the crime, wickedness, sin, and evil in this world does not come of itself. Back of all this crime, evil, and wickedness there is some superior intelligence engineering the great fight against God and against the right. The Bible explains that this intelligence is the devil or Satan.

I turn to 1 Peter 5:8. As I read this text I would like you to notice that the scripture makes it plain that the devil is a real personage just as much as a lion is a real animal. "Be sober, be vigilant; because your adversary the devil, as a roaring lion," (he is just as real a personage as a lion is a real animal) "your adversary the devil, as a roaring lion, walketh about, seeking whom he may devour."

The New Testament mentions the devil in 34 places; it mentions Satan in 37 places. When you take the 34 places in the New Testament that mention the devil and add to that the 37 places that mention Satan you have 71 direct proofs in the New Testament for the existence of the devil and Satan. A man who doesn't believe in the devil is the worst fooled man in Des Moines.

There was a noted robber and his gang who lived in a cave on a high mountain range. He was the terror of all the country round about. When he wanted to make a raid on a certain valley, he would hire men to go from house to house in that valley telling the people that this great robber whom they had so long feared was now dead. This was to put them off their guard so they would leave their property exposed. Then suddenly, the robber and his gang would sweep down on that valley unawares and plunder their goods without resistance.

The devil is using the same kind of tactics to capture the people of this world. He has invented the lie that there is no devil. This is to throw people off their guard so that he might capture them the more readily in his snares. O, how we need to heed the counsel of the scripture! "Be sober, be vigilant; because your adversary the devil, as a roaring lion, walketh about, seeking whom he may devour."

Some people will tell me, "Mr. Shuler, you are wrong. I know there is no

24

devil because I've never met him." Do you know why? It's because you and the devil are going the same way. If you will step out and accept the Lord Jesus Christ, you will not go one day without knowing that there is a real devil fighting against people who endeavor to walk in the ways of Jesus.

Look at the first statement on the outline. "There is a real devil, who is fighting against all who follow Christ." On the blank line record 1 Peter 5 8.

The question comes, Who is the devil? Does the word "devil" in the Bible denote merely an abstract principle of evil? Or is he a personality? I turn to John 8 44. Jesus Christ declares that the devil is a liar and the father of lies. Tell me, can a mere influence tell a lie? I hear you say no! Can a mere influence be considered the father of lies? No! Since Jesus Christ declared that the devil is a liar and the father of lies, it is plain that the devil and Satan is a personality. Jesus Christ, who is supreme authority on all questions of religion, taught that the devil is a personal being.

I turn next to James 2·19 This verse declares that the devils believe there is only one God Tell me, can a mere abstract principle believe in God? NO! A horse and a cow are real creatures, but a horse or a cow cannot believe in God. Nothing short of an intelligent personality can believe in God. The very fact that the devils believe there is only one God is proof that the devil is a personality. Just as surely as there is a personal God, and a personal Christ in heaven, there is a personal devil in this world fighting against those who serve God and follow Christ.

Look at No. 2 on the outline. "The devil, or Satan, is a personal being." On the blank lines please record John 8.44 and James 2:19.

The question arises, Who made the devil? Where did the devil come from? It may surprise you to learn that the one we call the devil was once a happy, perfect, sinless angel, next to the very throne of God in the heaven of heavens. The devil came from heaven Here is the text. Don't forget to bring your notebook to every lecture. You will want these valuable Scripture references.

I turn to Luke 10·18 This text contains a direct statement from the Lord Jesus Christ. He says· "I beheld Satan as lightning fall from heaven " The devil came from heaven Jesus Christ so declares, "I beheld Satan fall as lightning from heaven."

In harmony with this, the third proposition on the outline sheet says, the devil is a fallen angel from heaven, and on the blank line record Luke 10:18.

The Bible even tells his original name when he lived in heaven. His name has not always been the devil or Satan. The Bible tells his original name when he lived in heaven. Here it is. Put down Isaiah 14:12-14. "How art thou fallen from heaven, O Lucifer, son of the morning!" Before he sinned against God, before he was cast out of heaven, his name was Lucifer. When he rebelled against God his name was changed from Lucifer, which means Day Star, to Satan, which means "adversary" and to devil, which means "false accuser" or "deceiver." In harmony with this the fourth proposition on the outline is, his name was Lucifer, and on the blank line after this statement, please record Isaiah 14:12-14.

We now go a step further. This Bible even tells the position he held in heaven before he sinned. Put it down, Ezekiel 28 13, 14. The 28th chapter of Ezekiel speaks of Satan under the personification of the King of Tyre. Notice as I read from verse 13 and verse 14: "Thou hast been in Eden the garden of God," "Thou art the anointed cherub that covereth; and I have set thee so." Lucifer was one of those covering cerubim to the throne of God. He was one of those mighty angels whom God had chosen to stand next to His throne.

Does the Bible explain what is meant by "covering cherub?" Yes, it does. I have it pictured here upon a chart of the ark of the covenant. In the holy of holies of the earthly sanctuary there stood what was called the ark of the covenant. This ark was a chest made of wood, overlaid with gold. The cover of this chest was beaten out of one piece of gold and was so fashioned as to make not only the cover, but to form the figures of two beautiful golden angels one on either end of the cover of the chest with their wings stretched so as to meet exactly in the center. These golden angels were called "covering cherubim." Cherubim is the plural of cherub. They were called "covering cherubim" bcause they covered the mercy seat which was the top of this sacred chest. Between these angels was the Holy Shekinah or the visible manifestation of the presence of God.

In the heaven of heavens, Jehovah, the Monarch of the Universe, the King of Kings, sits between the cherubim, not between golden cherubim as you see pictured on this chart, but between the living cherubim. I read in Psalm 80:1: "Give ear, O Shepherd of Israel, Thou that leadest Joseph like a flock; Thou that dwellest between the cherubim, shine forth."

Before Lucifer sinned, he was one of these Cherubim that covered the throne of the great God in the heaven of heavens. "Thou art the anointed cherub that covereth, and I have set thee so." In accordance with this the fifth proposition on the outline declares, his position was that of a covering cherub to the throne of God, and on the blank line record Ezekiel 28:13, 14.

When he rebelled against God he was cast out of heaven to this earth. We find this in the book of Revelation. In Revelation 12:7-9 I read: "There was war in heaven." Isn't that a startling declaration? If I had read there was war in China or war in Persia, you wouldn't be surprised. This says, "there was war in heaven."

When you think of heaven, you think of a place of perfect peace, perfect security, perfect rest. So it is now and ever will be. But there was a time when there was war in heaven. Does the Bible tell between whom that war was fought? Yes. Listen to this scripture. "There was war in heaven: Michael and his angels fought against the dragon; and the dragon fought and his angels." This war was between Michael and His angels and the dragon and his angels. Michael is one of the many names that the scriptures give to Christ, the Son of God. The dragon, as mentioned here, is one of the many names that scripture gives to the devil.

On one side stood Christ and the loyal angels who took God's side in the controversy; on the other side stood Lucifer and certain angels who followed him in his disobedience to the law of God. What was the outcome of the war? Look at Revelation 12:9. "The great dragon was cast out, that old serpent, called the Devil, and Satan, which deceiveth the whole world: he was cast out into the earth, and his angels were cast out with him."

This war which began up in heaven between Christ and Satan has been raging in this world ever since man sinned in the beginning. The last battle of this war will be the battle of Armageddon, on which I will preach next Sunday night at the Shrine Auditorium. "The Impending World Ending Battle of Armageddon." Don't miss hearing it.

In accordance with what we found in Rev. 12:7-9, the sixth proposition on the outline declares that he was cast from heaven to this earth because of rebellion. On the blank line you may record Revelation 12:7-9.

The seventh proposition says, he goes to and fro in the earth. On the blank line record Job 1:7. There was a day when the sons of God met and Satan came also. The Lord said to Satan, "Whence comest thou?" Where do you come from? Satan's answer was "From going to and fro in the earth, and from walking up and down in it."

I promised to tell you what the devil looks like. If I were to ask an artist to draw me a picture of the devil, he would likely draw a most hideous looking creature with two great horns coming out of his head, a long dark pointed tail, his mouth breathing forth fire and brimstone, and a great pitchfork in his hand. There is no such devil as this. That is a relic of the superstition of the Dark Ages. Lucifer, or the devil, is actually noted for his beauty. Here it is in Ezekiel 28:12: "Thou sealest up the sum, full of wisdom, and perfect in beauty." Lucifer was one of the most beautiful angels God ever made. He was so bright, he was so glorious, that he was given the name Lucifer which means "Son of the Morning."

Some may say, "If God made the devil, isn't he directly responsible for all the evil that Satan has done through the ages? Why did a Good God make a bad devil?" A simple little illustration will clear up these questions.

Here is a man by the name of John Doe. His mother of course is Mrs. Doe. His mother did everything possible to bring up John Doe in the right way, but John Doe turns out to be a drunkard. One day you are walking down the street and there you see John Doe wallowing in the gutter—drunk. His eyes are bleary, his nose is red, his hair is matted and dirty. He is a most revolting sight. Would you say what a terrible specimen of humanity Mrs. Doe brought into the world? No, you wouldn't think of blaming that mother for bringing a drunkard into the world. She brought a pure, sweet, innocent boy into the world. He corrupted his own way and made himself a drunkard.

So I am bold to say, **God never made a devil.** He made Lucifer pure, holy, perfect, sinless. He of his own accord corrupted his way; disobeyed the law of God; rebelled against God; and made himself a devil. This is exactly what the Bible says. Put down Ezekiel 28:15. It actually declares that he was perfect **until** he sinned. "Thou was perfect in all thy ways from the day that thou wast created, till iniquity was found in thee."

We come now to that question that has puzzled millions. If God is all-powerful and the devil is the originator and the instigator of all evil, why hasn't God killed him long ago, and put an end to his evil work? Why doesn't God kill the Devil?

God is love. The only service God can accept from His creatures is one that is prompted by love. If God had slain Lucifer the moment he took the first wrong step, the other angels would have begun to serve God from fear and not from love. The rebellion of Lucifer would not have been settled or cured. There would have been a question as to the truth or falsity of the charges he had made against God. It took Christ's death on the cross to settle the devil's doom.

Look at the eighth proposition: Christ's death on the cross gives Him the right to destroy Satan. On the blank line record Hebrews 2:14. In speaking about Christ having been made flesh and blood it declares, "that through death He might destroy him that had the power of death, that is, the devil.

Christ's death on the cross rang Satan's death knell. The cross of Calvary, not only made salvation sure for you and me, if we accept Jesus, but it settled the fact that Satan will finally be destroyed.

The appointed time for his destruction is not yet come. Some Sunday night soon I am going to speak on the 20th chapter of Revelation. This is one of the biggest chapters in all the Bible so far as depicting things to come, is concerned. When I lecture on this 20th chapter of Revelation you will see how and when his destruction will take place.

Look at the ninth proposition. Satan's destruction will take place at an appointed time, and on the blank line record Romans 16.20. "The God of Peace shall bruise Satan under your feet shortly."

Why hasn't God killed the devil? The time hasn't yet come. Paul says, "The God of peace shall bruise Satan under your feet shortly." God is making Satan's rebellion **an everlasting lesson to the universe.** He permits Satan to

run his course so that in the future no one will ever have the least reason to
ever rebell against God again. When God makes final settlement with Satan,
He will also settle with the people who take Satan's side. That is why we
should not be on his side now.

God doesn't want to punish you and me when He punishes Satan. God
wants to give us an eternal, happy home in His kingdom. "God so loved the
world, that He gave His only begotten Son, that whosoever believeth in Him
should not perish, but have everlasting life." God is giving you and me an opportunity to accept His way of escape so that whenever He does finally deal
with the devil and those who follow the devil that we may escape.

Notice the tenth proposition. There is victory over sin for everyone who
will surrender his will to Christ. On the blank line record 1 Corinthians 15:57.
"Thanks be to God, which giveth us the victory through our Lord Jesus Christ."

The devil has led every person who ever lived in this world into sin excepting one, the Lord Jesus Christ. He was tempted in all points like as we
are yet without sin. Jesus met the devil in hand to hand conflict and conquered
him. This is good news! He says in John 16:33, "be of good cheer; I have
overcome the world."

As Christ overcame the devil and sin, we through Christ can overcome the
devil and sin. There is victory over sin for everyone if he will only look to
Jesus Christ. "Look unto me," he says, "and be ye saved all the ends of the
earth."

> "In a look there's life for thee;
> In a look at Calvary.
> Blessed thought! Salvation's free,
> By a look at Calvary."

Don't you want victory in your life? Of course you do. You can have it.
"Thanks be unto God Who giveth us the victory through our Lord Jesus Christ."
Why not ask Christ just now to give you the victory? How many with me
want to look to Jesus Christ just now to give us the victory in our lives? Will
you lift your hand, please? Thank you. It appears that every hand is raised.

One day a minister was walking on the Boston common. He met a boy
who had a hand-made cage full of different birds which lived in that vicinity.
He said, "Boy, where did you get those birds?"

"I trapped them."

"What are you going to do with them?"

"I'm going to play with them."

"Well, after you get tired playing with them, what are you going to do?"

"I'm going to give them to the cat to eat."

"O!" the minister said, "I'd like to buy those birds."

"Mr., you don't want those birds. They're not canaries. They won't sing.
They're no good."

Those little birds were sitting there in the cage all drooped, not moving
a feather, just waiting for their doom.

"But," the minister continued, "I want to buy them. How much will you
take?"

"O! they're no good to you, you don't want them."

"Yes, but how much will you take?"

He finally got the boy to say, "I'll take $2.00 for the cage, birds and all."

The minister gave the boy the $2.00 and walked away. The boy watched
the preacher. He turned into an alley. He opened the door in the cage. Not
one of the birds moved. They didn't realize they were free. He gently patted
the side of the cage and one after another hopped out the door and flew into
God's free air. The minister said, "It made me happy every time one of those

little birds took to the air. It seemed as if their wings said, 'Redeemed! redeemed from death'."

Friends, the devil has trapped you and me in sin. He once had the entire world in his cage of sin. Nineteen hundred years ago Jesus Christ left heaven and came down here to throw open the devil's cage of sin. He came to open the prison to them that are bound. O, sinner, the cage door is open tonight! Why not soar out to liberty in Christ? Why stay in the cage of sin when Jesus has opened the door?

We, like those birds, can go to freedom. How many who feel bound in the chain of sin want Jesus to set you free? How many would like to say, "Preacher, pray for me in this closing prayer that Jesus will set me free." Just lift the hand. Thank you I see many hands. God is speaking to your hearts by His Holy Spirit.

(Prayer.) Blessed Jesus, precious Saviour, we thank Thee that Thou art the victor over Satan. We thank Thee that Thou hast overcome and that we, through Thee, can overcome. We pray, Lord, for every soul here tonight, but we especially pray for those who have just lifted their hands. O, Jesus, undertake for them, Thou canst set them free no matter what chain of sin may bind them in their life. O, blessed Christ, we pray to set everyone free from every sin and help us that we may so serve Thee that we may have an eternal happy home with Thee in Thy kingdom forever. We ask it in Thy precious name. Amen.

(This is a copy of the outline which was placed in the hands of the hearers, preceding the presentation of the Bible lecture on "Why Doesn't God Kill the Devil?")

SCRIPTURAL NOTES ON WHY DOESN'T GOD KILL THE DEVIL?

1. There is a real devil, who is fighting against all who follow Christ...... .

2. The devil or Satan is a personal being . ..   .

3. The devil is a fallen angel from heaven .. ..

4. His name was Lucifer. ..   . .   ' .   ...

5. His position was that of a covering cherub to the throne of God. .   .... .

6. He was cast from heaven to this earth because of rebellion .   _ .

7. He goes to and fro in the earth ..   ..

8. Christ's death on the cross gives Him the right to destroy Satan.   .   .

9. Satan's destruction will take place at an appointed time . .   ..

10. There is victory over sin for everyone who will surrender his will to Christz   .   ..   .   _ . ..   . =

Armageddon and the Atomic Bomb

(Preached on the Second Sunday Night of the Campaign)

The Bible tells of a final battle in which so many people will be slaughtered, that it is spoken of figuratively as a river of blood two hundred miles long. You will find this in your Bible in Rev. 14:19, 20. There you will read: "And the angel thrust in his sickle into the earth, and gathered the vine of the earth, and cast it into the great winepress of the wrath of God. And the winepress was trodden without the city, and blood came out of the winepress, even unto the horse bridles, by the space of a thousand and six hundred furlongs."

This Scripture declares that the blood ran to the horse bridles for the space of sixteen hundred furlongs. Sixteen hundred furlongs amount to two hundred miles. A furlong is one-eighth of a mile. When you divide sixteen hundred by eight, the result is two hundred. So when the Scripture says that the blood came out to the horse bridles for sixteen hundred furlongs, that is equivalent to saying that there was a river of blood to the horse bridles two hundred miles long.

This is a figurative description of the wholesale slaughter that will take place in the final battle of Armageddon. There will be so many millions of people slain that it is compared to a river of blood two hundred miles long. In fact all the people in the world will be slain in this final conflict except those whose names are written in the Book of Life. Thus it is written in Dan. 12:1 that "there shall be a time of trouble, such as never was since there was a nation even to that same time: and at that time thy people shall be delivered, every one that shall be found written in the book."

The battle of Armageddon will decide the fate of every person on this earth. You and I, and every other living soul at that day, will either be slain in this final conflict and be lost forever, or we will be delivered by the Lord Jesus Christ to live forever in His kingdom. The most vital question is, will you be among those who will be spared in this final conflict, and live forever with Jesus Christ in His kingdom? You can be, and you will be, if you obey His commandments and make the preparation that He asks you to make.

Jesus Christ declares that as it was in the days of Noah, so it will be in this final day. The deluge swept all the people in the world to destruction except this man of God and his family. Noah was delivered out of that universal destruction because he made the preparation that God asked him to make. So it will be in reference to this wholesale slaughter in the battle of Armageddon at the last day. Every soul who makes the preparation that God has specified in His Holy Word will be delivered. All who fail to make this preparation will be slain in this final struggle.

The question naturally arises, What is this battle of Armageddon? You will find the answer to this question in Revelation 16:14, 16. These verses read as follows: "For they are the spirits of devils, working miracles, which go forth unto the kings of the earth and of the whole world, to gather them to the battle of that great day of God Almighty . . . and he gathered them together into a place called in the Hebrew tongue Armageddon."

Please notice that the 14th verse declares that the kings of the entire world will be gathered to the battle of the great day of God. The 16th verse in speaking of this same gathering of the nations, declares that they will be gathered to Armageddon. Thus when we place these two verses of Scripture to-

30

gether, it is as plain as can be, that the battle of Armageddon is the battle of the great day of God Almighty.

The great day of God refers to that final day which will usher in the return of the Lord Jesus Christ to this world. This final struggle is called the battle of the great day of God Almighty because this is the conflict in which God Himself will fight according to Zechariah 14:3. "Then shall the Lord go forth and fight against those nations, as when He fought in the day of battle."

It will be interesting to note some of the things God will do in connection with this final war of Armageddon. In Rev. 16:16-21 we have a record of some of the most startling events in the entire history of our world that will take place in the final struggle. Verse sixteen declares that the nations will be gathered to a place called Armageddon. What will God do when the nations gather at Armageddon? The next verse, the seventeenth verse, tells: "And the seventh angel poured out his vial into the air, and there came a great voice out of the temple of heaven, from the throne, saying, "It is done."

When the nations gather for the battle of Armageddon, the voice of Almighty God will proclaim, "It is done." This is the last. The end has come. Man's day is ended. Mark well this point. **Armageddon is the world-ending battle.** It will mark the end of the present order of things. It will ring down the curtain on the history of the human race. The battle of Armageddon is the most momentous and most decisive struggle that ever has taken place or ever will take place. You and I certainly need to know what the Bible says about it.

A man in Chicago pulled out his watch before a crowd and said. "If there is a God in Heaven, I give Him five minutes to strike me dead." People went into hysterics. Women fainted. When the five minutes was up, the man announced, "You can see now, there is no God." This didn't prove anything except that he was a fool, because the Scripture says "The fool hath said in his heart, there is no God."

Some day God is going to talk, and every human being will know about it When the nations gather for Armageddon the voice of God will be heard from one end of the earth to the other, saying, "It is done." These three words of God, "It is done," will turn this world upside down. Verse eighteen tells about this: "And there were voices, and thunders, and lightnings; and there was a great earthquake, such as was not since men were upon the earth, so mighty an earthquake, and so great."

This will be the greatest earthquake that ever has been, or ever will be. In fact the verse says, "there was a great earthquake, such as was not since men were upon the earth." This earthquake will cause the entire world to reel to and fro like a drunken man. Isaiah 24:20 declares that "the earth shall reel to and fro like a drunkard, and shall be removed like a cottage."

This final earthquake will reduce every city in the world to a heap of rubble, as though super-atomic bombs had struck every city at the same time. Notice how the prophet describes this in the next two verses of this 16th chapter of Revelation. "And the great city was divided into three parts, and the cities of the nations fell: and great Babylon came in remembrance before God, to give unto her the cup of the wine of the fierceness of His wrath And every island fled away, and the mountains were not found."

When this universal destruction comes where will you go for safety? There will be only one safe place in that tremendous day, and that will be, to be hid in the Lord Jesus Christ. "Rock of Ages, cleft for me, let me hide myself in Thee." If you are obedient to the Lord Jesus Christ you will be able to say with the psalmist, "God is our refuge and our strength, a very present help in trouble. Therefore will not we fear, though the earth be removed and though the mountains be carried into the midst of the sea."

Friend of mine, will you be found safe in the Lord Jesus Christ in this final conflict? There is only one way to be sure about this and that is to be true to the Lord Jesus Christ every day that you live. If you have never given your heart to Him, I hope you will do it now.

When will the battle of Armageddon come? Rev.16:12-20 shows that the kings of the earth will be gathered for this final battle under the sixth plague, shortly before the appearing of the Lord Jesus Christ from heaven at His second advent. Armageddon takes place in connection with the return of Jesus Christ to this earth. In connection with Armageddon there will come the greatest aerial bombardment that has ever been known. God will hurl down ice bombs from heaven weighing over fifty pounds each. Some will say, "Is this really in the Bible?" It certainly is. You will find it in Revelation 16:21. This verse says: "And there fell upon men a great hail out of heaven, every stone about the weight of a talent: and men blasphemed God because of the plague of hail; for the plague thereof was exceeding great."

A talent is an ancient Hebrew standard of weight that equals fifty-seven pounds. When it says that every stone was about the weight of a talent, that means there will be a barrage of ice bombs from heaven about the size of half bushel baskets. Some will say, "I don't believe anything like this could ever happen." It is just as easy for God to rain hailstones weighing fifty pounds each, as it is for Him to rain little drops of water from heaven. The casting of these great hailstones from heaven is a part of God's plan. He talked to Job about this. God asked Job, "Hast thou seen the treasures of the hail, which I have reserved against the time of trouble, against the day of battle and war? Job 38:22, 23.

What can man do against this bombardment of ice bombs from heaven? Fighter planes will be helpless. Anti-aircraft guns will be useless. God has promised that everyone who obeys His word will be protected from these great hailstones. In Isaiah 32:18, 19 we find that when these great hailstones fall and every city is laid low, God's people shall dwell in a peaceful habitation and in quiet resting places.

On that memorable September day in 1945, when the Japanese surrender document was signed on board the battleship Missouri in Tokyo harbor, General Douglas MacArthur made a significant reference to Armageddon in a speech, which was heard around the world. He said, "Military alliance, balances of power, League of Nations—all in turn failed . . . We have had our last chance. If we do not now devise some greater and more equitable system, Armageddon will be at our door."

You have heard much about the atomic bomb and atomic energy. But here is one special point you should mark well. What about the deep significance of the discovery of the atomic bomb in the light of these Bible prophecies which show that Armageddon will wipe out civilization, level the cities to the ground, and destroy man from the face of the earth? Before the advent of the atomic age in 1945, skeptics declared that such prophecies were simply absurd. But no infidel needs to doubt them now. Scientists openly declare that when schemes are devised for converting to energy even as much as a few per cent of the matter of some common material, civilization will have the means to commit suicide at will. The scientists are preaching the end of the world.

Dr. M. L. E. Olphant, of the University of Birmingham recently declared that "the atomic scientist is now able to produce an atomic poison gas which, if used in and with an atomic bomb, would kill every living thing within a radius of 1,000 miles. Three such bombs, if dropped at the proper spots, would wipe out the entire population of the United States.

The Federal Council of the Churches of Christ in America in its official organ, the **Federal Council Bulletin for Nov. 1945**, declared that **this atomic** "discovery of a method of transmuting physical elements produced the most stupendous change in man's relation to the natural order since man was created. Everyone knows that it is fraught with incalculable good or incalculable harm. As one of the responsible scientists has said: 'It has been demonstrated that the universe is inflammable.' He went on to add that he trembled to think of what would happen if some fool set a match to it."

Everybody knows that with the new super-destructive weapons that men are now forging, in the realm of electronics, atomic energy, cosmic rays, transoceanic rockets, and germ sprays, that the wiping out of civilization and the destruction of the human race is at hand, unless men and nations see to it that there is never again a major war.

When the first atomic bomb was tested in the New Mexican desert, as a prelude to Hiroshima and Nagasaki, Dr. George B. Kistiakowsky, one of the nuclear scientists, who was on the scene said to his colleagues, "I am sure that at the end of the world—in the last milli-second of the earth's existence—the last man will see what we saw." He like many other scientists, recognized that man in taking hold of atomic power, had at last taken hold of a force that was capable of annihilating all life on our planet.

Men are alarmed because some genius, with the madness of war upon him, might, with some new fissionable material set off an atmospheric chain of reaction, which would transform our earth into a bright new star, or ball of fire, consuming all life within it. Bible prophecy however makes it clear that God will intervene before man can do this. Christ will appear, and according to Rev. 11:18 will destroy them that destroy the earth. Isn't this a most significant, up-to-the-minute statement in view of the possibilities that atomic scientists are pointing out today?

Bible prophecy shows that in due time God will transform this world into a new perfect earth in which the righteous only shall live. The apostle Peter tells about this in 2 Pet. 3.10-13. In this prophecy Peter declares that in the world conflagration soon to come the "elements" will be "dissolved." He does not say that all the elements will be dissolved. He does say that the conflagration will be brought about by a dissolution of elements.

The Greek word here translated "dissolve" is the simple word "luo," meaning to loose, surely a perfect word to describe the setting free, the releasing, of neutrons and protons from the power which for ages has locked them in and bound them so tightly together in the atoms of which our universe is built. It is clear that the principle of nuclear fission, of atomic energy, is the same as that which God will use in the global conflagration which will result from a dissolution of the elements of our earth. God knows how to split atoms, too, because He created them with His Word, and they will obey His Word.

Every battle that has ever been fought has been a matter of men arrayed on two opposing sides. But the battle of Armageddon will be different from every other battle. There will be more than men arranged on two opposing sides. It will be a contest between the armies of earth and the armies of heaven, between the Lord Jesus Christ and the devil, between the Son of God and Satan.

The devil himself will lead the charge on the field of Armageddon. You will find this set forth in Revelation 16:14. There we are told that the spirits of devils go forth to gather the kings of the entire world to the battle of the great day of God Almighty. Armageddon is the last battle in the age-long struggle between Jesus Christ and Satan, between the Son of God and Lucifer. Armageddon is Satan's last effort to install himself as the sole ruler of mankind.

What nations will be involved in the battle of Armageddon? In Rev. 16:14 we find that the kings of the entire world will be gathered to this final battle.

Every nation in the world will take part in this last mighty conflict. You and I will act a part, and we will be found either on the side of the Lord Jesus Christ, or on the side of Satan.

Where will this battle of Armageddon be fought? Since Armageddon is a universal conflict, the battlefield will embrace the entire world. The Bible shows however that this last conflict will especially center in Palestine, commonly called the Holy Land. In Joel 3:2, 12 God says: "I will also gather all nations, and will bring them down into the valley of Jehoshaphat . . . Let the heathen be wakened, and come up to the valley of Jehoshaphat: for there will I sit to judge all the heathen round about."

The valley of Jehoshaphat is between the Mount of Olives and Jerusalem. This prophecy of Joel indicates that the territory around Jerusalem will be a pivotal spot in the final struggle of the nations.

Revelation 16:14, 16 shows that the kings of the whole world will be gathered to a place called Armageddon. Armageddon means literally the mountain or hill of Megiddo. This word is compounded from two Hebrew words, "Har," meaning mountain or city; "Mageddon" which refers to Mount Megiddo, which overlooks the plain of Esdraelon in Northern Palestine. These plains are marked the plain of Armageddon on some maps.

It is a vast, triangular plain in the northern part of Palestine, about sixty miles north of Jerusalem. It is bounded on the west by the range of mountains terminating in Mount Carmel; on the northeast by Mount Tabor; and on the southeast by Mount Gilboa. The area enclosed by these mountain ranges has probably seen as much fighting as, or perhaps more than, any other similar area on the surface of the earth. It is one of the most historic battlefields of antiquity. More blood, likely, has been shed on this spot than any other spot on earth of equal size.

These prophecies suggest that the Near East will be the great storm center in Armageddon. While the conflict will likely especially center in Palestine, its implications will reach out to every part of the habitable globe and affect every soul on the face of the earth.

The question comes, who will win in the battle of Armageddon? The East? The West? Russia? England? United States? The battle of Armageddon will not bring triumph to any nation or worldly power. Jesus Christ, the King of kings and Lord of lords, will be the victor on the field of Armageddon. I refer you to Psalm 2 2-9.

The second verse tells how the kings of the earth will set themselves against the Lord. "The kings of the earth set themselves and the rulers take counsel together, against the Lord, and against His anointed" Then in the sixth and seventh verses, the Lord God tells how He will crown His Son Christ, King of the world. "Yet have I set My King upon My holy hill of Zion. I will declare the decree; The Lord has said unto Me, Thou art My Son; this day have I begotten Thee."

Then in verses 8 and 9 the prophecy tells what will happen when Jesus Christ appears in connection with the battle of Armageddon. "Ask of Me, and I will give Thee the heathen for Thine inheritance, and the uttermost parts of the earth for Thy possession. Thou shalt break them with a rod of iron; Thou shalt dash them in pieces like a potter's vessel."

The battle of Armageddon brings the last act in that prophetic dream recorded in the second chapter of Daniel, on which I talked last Sunday night in the first Bible lecture of this Bible Institute. God showed Nebuchadnezzar the figure of a man, whose head was composed of fine gold, his breast and his arms of silver, his sides of brass, his legs of iron, his feet part of iron and part of clay. The last act in the dream was a stone that smote the man on his feet and dashed the entire man to pieces. Then the stone became a great mountain, and filled the entire world. This stone, smiting the man to pieces. represents what Jesus Christ will do to the nations in the battle of Armageddon. The prophecy of this second Psalm declares that He will break them with a rod of iron and dash them in pieces like a potter's vessel.

I promised to tell what man will rule the entire world after the battle of Armageddon. This prophecy of the second Psalm shows that the Son of God will rule the entire world after this final conflict. In Rev. 11:15 we find that the kingdoms of this world will become the kingdoms of the Lord Jesus Christ. The man Christ Jesus, the man of Calvary, will rule supreme over the entire world after this final battle.

Some night soon during this Bible Institute I will give a lecture on the wonderful prophecy of Rev. 20. There we shall find that after the final phase of Armageddon, Jesus Christ will reconstruct the earth into a perfect paradise where none but the righteous will ever dwell. Then the will of God will be done in this earth as it is now done in heaven. Then the meek will inherit the earth, as Jesus said.

The battle of Armageddon will come to a more sudden stop perhaps than any other battle that has ever taken place. Why? Because the Bible shows there will be, as it were, a blast of atomic power or a new kind of death ray that will slay millions of people in a second of time. The heavens will be split wide open and Jesus Christ will appear in person, surrounded by an army of millions and millions of angels. This will bring this great battle of Armageddon to a sudden termination.

Wouldn't you like to know more about these momentous coming developments in our world? Certainly you would. Then don't fail to be on hand Tuesday night when I will take up these significant items and trace them out from the Bible. Time will not permit me to read the striking texts on these matters in this lecture, but by the help of the Lord we will do it in the next lecture You owe it to yourself to hear from the Bible these essential facts about this impending, world-ending battle of Armageddon. I hope you will not let anything keep you from being on hand Tuesday night to hear about the momentous outcome of this final battle.

I hope no one will think to himself, "I will wait until I see those armies gather in Palestine, then I will get ready to meet Jesus Christ." If you delay your preparation until you see this, you will never be able to prepare. Why not? Because Revelation 16:12-21 shows that Armageddon comes under the sixth and seventh of the seven last plagues. The scriptures show that man's opportunity for salvation and forgiveness closes before the first plague begins. It will be too late for any person to prepare to meet Jesus Christ when the armies gather in Palestine for the last mighty struggle. The door of mercy will have been closed forever at that time.

God says, "Now is the accepted time, now is the day of salvation." He says, "Come now and let us reason together, though your sins be red like crimson, I will make them white as snow." The Lord is ready to save you now. Jesus Christ is able to save to the uttermost, all who come unto God by Him seeing He ever liveth to make intercession for them. If you will do the coming, Jesus Christ will do the saving. I appeal to you to put your case in the hands of Jesus Christ while you have the opportunity.

A wealthy lady was notified one day that she must appear before the court within seven days, in regard to a certain case. Her husband said, "You better see Mr. Foster and get him to represent you." "Oh," she said, "I am having a party and a dance today. I have no time today to see Mr. Foster. I will go and see him tomorrow." The next day she went to the office of this noted lawyer. After she had told him her story that she must appear before the court within seven days to answer to a certain charge, he said, "Lady, I cannot take your case." She pleaded with him, "Please take my case. Name any fee you wish and I will give it to you." "Lady," he said, "If you offered me one million dollars, I couldn't take your case. If you had come yesterday I would have gladly taken your case. This morning just before you arrived I received word that I have been appointed judge of the court. I could have been your lawyer yesterday, now I must be your judge."

Jesus Christ wants to be your lawyer at the court of God. In I John 2:1 we read, "If any man sin, we have an advocate with the Father, Jesus Christ the righteous." Jesus Christ guarantees a verdict of acquittal for you before the Supreme Court of the universe. He will forgive every sin and cover it with His blessed righteousness. Some day soon He will cease to be the Advocate for sinners, and will come to judge the quick and the dead. O, I beg you not to put off the matter of placing your case in the hands of Jesus Christ. He is coming soon as judge. Take Him as your lawyer while you have the opportunity.

Don't you want Jesus Christ to forgive all your sins and make you ready to meet Him? God can do everything for the person who earnestly desires His help. I am sure everyone in this auditorium is ready to say by the uplifted hand that you want God to help you, to trust in Jesus Christ for full salvation. How many want to be remembered in prayer that the Lord will help you to trust in Jesus Christ for full salvation. Will you lift a hand please? Yes, it seems that every hand is raised.

(Praying.)

"Our dear heavenly Father we thank Thee for Thy great love in giving Jesus, Thy dear Son, to be our Saviour. We thank Thee for His infinite sacrifice upon the cross. O Lord we want to put our cases fully in the hands of Jesus. Lord, Thou hast seen all these uplifted hands, I pray that Thou wilt undertake for every soul in this audience. Bestow full salvation on each one and make him ready to meet Jesus Christ at His coming. We ask this in the precious name of Jesus and for His sake. Amen."

Heaven Split Wide Open

(Preached on the Second Tuesday of the Campaign)

Men have been watching and studying the heavens for centuries. Their nightly vigil has been rewarded, for they have seen some wonderful sights in the sky. I suppose we would all like to look through that new 200 inch telescope on Mt. Palomar in California and view the wonders of God's creation.

The day is coming however when men will see a dazzling sight in the sky, the like of which men never have seen. Heaven will be split wide open and they will see Jesus Christ, Son of man and Son of God, who trod this earth 1900 years ago, descend through the portals of the sky, surrounded by millions of countless angels. As King of Kings and Lord of Lords, Jesus Christ will appear in the midst of that final, world-ending battle of Armageddon, **and the battle will stop immediately.** You will find that in your Bible in Revelation 19.11-21. I hope you have your notebook to put down the valuable scripture references.

I read the 11th verse. "I saw heaven opened." Yes, heaven will be opened. Heaven will be split wide open. "I saw heaven opened, and behold a white horse; and He that sat upon him was called Faithful and True, and in righteousness He doth judge and make war. His eyes were as a flame of fire, and on His head were many crowns; and He had a name written, that no man knew, but He Himself. And He was clothed with a vesture dipped in blood: and His name is called The Word of God."

You will notice he saw heaven opened, and through the opening in the sky Christ was riding forth as the mighty, all-conquering Lord. Some people will say, "O, I don't believe that will ever be. It is impossible that the heavens will open and that Jesus Christ will ride forth from the sky." Listen, fifty years ago people said it was impossible for men to fly across the sky like the birds. Nobody talks that way now. Men are flying five times, yes, ten times faster and higher than any bird ever flew.

The wonders of science confirm the truths of the Bible. Things in the Bible that once seemed almost beyond the realm of reality are now seen to be easily possible. Radio helps us to believe in the reality of prayer. Radar and television help us to understand the all-seeing eye of God.

I read in the 14th verse, "The armies which were in heaven followed Him upon white horses, clothed in fine linen, white and clean." You will notice, "the armies in heaven," or the angels will come with the Lord Jesus when He rides forth from the sky. Jesus Himself said it would be just this way.

Put down Matt. 25.31: "The Son of man shall come in His glory, and **all** the holy angels with Him." We have a chart here on which the artist has endeavored to give us some concept of this great day of days, when the Lord Jesus will appear surrounded by countless millions of bright shining angels.

(At this juncture a chart was lowered depicting Jesus coming upon a cloud, surrounded by the angels.)

Notice verse 15: "Out of His mouth goeth a sharp sword, that with it He should **smite**," (notice that word and think of Daniel 2) "that with it He should **smite** the nations: and He should rule them with a rod of iron; and He treadeth the winepress of the fierceness and wrath of Almighty God."

You will notice that Jesus will "smite the nations" just like that stone smote the man whose head was of gold, breast and arms of silver, thighs of brass, legs of iron, feet part of iron and part of clay. Jesus will appear in the midst of the battle of Armageddon. It is just as plain as can be. You can't help but see it. Take down the text, Revelation 19:19. After he describes how heaven will be opened and Christ will appear, he says: "I saw the beast, and the kings of the earth, and their armies, gathered together to make war against Him that sat on the horse, and against His army."

Mark this point. When the kings of the earth and their armies are gathered for the last battle, that great world-ending battle of Armageddon, Jesus appears from the open heaven and the battle stops instantly.

I want you to notice with me how Jesus Christ will come down from the sky at His second advent and what He will do. I turn to Acts 1:9-11. I want you to notice that what the artist has placed upon this piece of canvas is exactly what we read in the Bible in Acts 1 9-11.

(At this juncture a chart showing the ascension of Jesus was lowered in the sight of the audience.)

Notice what the Scripture says, "When He had spoken these things, while they beheld, He was taken up; and a cloud received Him out of their sight. And while they looked steadfastly toward heaven as He went up behold, two men stood by them in white apparel; Which also said, "Ye men of Galilee, why stand ye gazing up into heaven? this same Jesus, which is taken up from you into heaven, shall so come in like manner as ye have seen Him go into heaven."

Forty days after our Lord's resurrection He led His disciples out of the city, down across the brook Kidron, then up over the brow of the Mount of Olives. Many times they had walked by His side over the hills and valleys of old Judea. But this was to be the last time that He would ever walk visibly by their side. As He walked along He explained to them matters pertaining to the kingdom of God. When He reached a certain spot across the summit, in the vicinity of Bethany, He raised His hands in blessing. Then His feet began to leave the ground. He began to go up, and they watched Him as He went higher and higher and higher. Then He entered a cloud and disappeared from view. They watched the cloud as it appeared smaller, and smaller, and smaller, until it became a mere speck. Then it faded from their view. . Still they stood there, looking up into heaven, hoping to get one more glimpse of the dear Lord whom they loved. Then they heard voices. Looking around, they saw two angels, who said to them: "Ye men of Galilee, why stand ye gazing up into heaven? this same Jesus, which is taken up from you into heaven, shall so come in like manner as ye have seen Him go into heaven."

Please notice that the angels told the disciples exactly how Jesus Christ will come from heaven at His second advent. I have this text printed in large letters on muslin, so you may see for yourself just what scripture says. (A large piece of muslin was lowered in the sight of the audience on which the last part of Acts 1:11 was printed in large letters, with the words—"in like manner as ye have seen Him go into heaven"—heavily underscored.)

Tonight I want you to help me preach. When I come to these words that are underlined, I would like everyone here, who can see the words, to read them aloud with me, in a good strong tone. The angels will tell us how Christ will come down from the sky at His second advent. They said, "This same Jesus which was taken up from you into heaven, shall so come **in like manner as ye have seen Him go into heaven.**" This is very clear. He is coming back, just like He went away. His return will correspond to His departure.

If you want to understand how Jesus Christ will come from heaven at His second advent, all you need to do is to notice how He was taken up to heaven at His ascension, because the angels declared, "This same Jesus shall so come in like manner." He is coming back, exactly as He went away.

Did He go up with a real body? Certainly, He did. His body was resurrected on the third day, and when Christ ascended, He went up with a tangible resurrected body of flesh and bones. When He returns He will descend from heaven with a real body. **The second coming of Jesus Christ is a literal, bodily coming; and not some figurative or spiritual coming.**

Did Christ go away visibly or did He go away invisibly? Well, the answer is, that while they were looking at Him, while they beheld, He was taken up. The angels said, "ye have seen Him go" Just as they saw Him go up into the sky, the people of earth will see Him come down from the sky. He is coming in like manner. As His disciples saw Him go up, the people of earth will see Him come down.

The angels of God know more than the wisest man on the face of the earth. These angels said He is coming in "like manner as ye have seen Him go." Christ went up to heaven literally, bodily, visibly and personally. So at His second advent, He will come down from heaven bodily, literally, visibly and personally.

Would you like to know the first thing the Lord Jesus will do when He appears in the sky? Here it is Put down 1 Thessalonians 4 16. "The Lord Himself shall descend from heaven with a shout" Notice this He will descend from heaven with a shout. This shout will be heard from one end of the earth to the other. Thirty years ago people said it was impossible for a person's voice to be heard from one end of earth to the other Nobody doubts this today. The radio has revealed a law by which your voice, my voice, or any person's voice can be heard from one end of the earth to the other.

Do you know what effect this shout will have on the city of Des Moines? I will tell you what it will do. It will tear up every cemetery in Des Moines. Not only that, it will tear up every cemetery in the world. This is what we find in this 16th verse. "The Lord Himself shall descend from heaven with a shout, with the voice of the archangel, and with the trump of God· and **the dead in Christ shall rise first.**"

Graves will be torn wide open. Tombs will fall apart. And the millions of Christ's people, who have died, will rise with glorious, immortal bodies. We have a representation of this here on a chart.

(A chart was lowered at this juncture showing the graves being opened, and the angels gathering the saints from the earth, to meet the Lord in the air).

Think what a grand reunion the second coming of Jesus Christ will bring! It will be the home-coming of the ages. Death has severed the dearest ties this world knows. If I were to ask everyone here who has lost a loved one to raise his hand, I think that every hand would be raised. There is hardly a person but can think of some mound of earth somewhere that holds the form of one who was very near and dear to him

When Jesus comes, the righteous meet their loved ones, never to part again. Friends will be reunited never to be separated. Yes,

> "The golden morning is fast approaching
> Jesus soon will come
> To take His faithful and happy children
> To their promised home.
> The loved of earth who have long been parted
> Meet in that glad day
> The tears of those who are brokenhearted shall be wiped away "

There was a time when Jesus walked up to the tomb of a man who had been buried three days and said just three words, "Lazarus, come forth." This man who had been dead three days walked out of that tomb. So when He comes the second time He will say, "Awake, awake ye that sleep in the dust of the earth." All over the world millions of graves will be opened and the righteous dead will rise with immortal, glorious, incorruptible bodies.

Some of you are thinkng of what will happen to the living people when the Lord descends from the sky? The Bible tells. Put down 1 Cor. 15:51, 52, and Phil. 3.20, 21. Paul tells us that the true Christian people, who will be living on the earth when the Lord descends from the sky, will be changed in the twinkling of an eye from mortality to immortality and be caught up to meet the Lord to be with the Lord forever. They will go to heaven without tasting death just like Enoch and Elijah were taken to heaven without ever seeing death.

In Phil. 3:20, 21 Paul declares that the Christian people who are living on the earth at the time when the Lord comes will have their bodies made like His glorious body. O, friends, think of the unspeakable joy that will come to you, if you are found true to Jesus Christ when He comes. In a second of time this mortal body will be changed to an immortal, incorruptible body. Then you will have a body that will never have an ache or a pain; a body that will never get old; a body that will never die. You will never have any trouble of any kind. Perfect happiness without end.

Think of all the items that people long for or desire. Think of all the benefits with which man could be favored. Can you think of anything better than to have your body changed in a moment of time, in the twinkling of an eye from mortality to immortality and never have any more pain; never get old and never die and be caught up to be with Jesus forever. This is absolutely the **best benefit, the greatest boon, the grandest prize** that can ever come to a human being. I bring you the good news tonight that this prize of prizes is yours in Christ Jesus. It is for you if you give your heart to Jesus Christ and be true to His word.

As for me there isn't anything in all this world that I desire as much as that immortal body. I'm determined by the grace of God to do what Jesus Christ asks me to do in order to secure it. I feel sure that you in your heart share that same great purpose.

How many of you with me desire to have this immortal body more than any thing else and are determined by the grace of God to do what Jesus wants you to do that you may have it, will you lift your hand? Thank you! It looks as though every person has put up his hand on this.

We need to desire this more than anything else In Jeremiah 29:13 God says, "Ye shall seek Me, and find Me when ye shall search for Me with all your heart." Don't forget that the lecture Thursday night is going to help you on this point. It will deal with God's great message which will help people get ready to meet Jesus.

When Jesus Christ descends from heaven the righteous dead will rise from the grave with immortal bodies The righteous living will be changed in the twinkling of an eye from mortality to immortality. Then what? Where does Jesus take them? Read right on in 1 Thes. 4 16, 17. "The Lord Himself shall descend from heaven with a shout, with the voice of the archangel, and with the trump of God· and the dead in Christ shall rise first: then we which are alive and remain shall be caught up together with them in the clouds, to meet the Lord in the air: and so shall we ever be with the Lord."

They will be caught up from the earth to meet Jesus in the air at His second coming. He will take them to those glorious mansions in heaven which He has prepared for His own. This is according to Christ's own promise in John 14:1-3. He says: "I go to prepare a place for you. And if I go and prepare a place for you, I will come again, and receive you unto myself; that where I am, there ye may be also."

O think what a happy day that will be. The second coming of Jesus

Christ means that we will say good-bye forever to all our troubles, our sorrows, our diseases, our heartaches, our disappointments, and our trials. It means that we will go to those mansions that Jesus has prepared, where there will be no more sickness. No more trouble. No more trials. No more suffering. No more sorrow. No more pain. No more death. In view of all this, friends, how can we do otherwise than love His appearing as Paul says in 2 Timothy 4·6-8. I love that chorus·

> "Some golden daybreak, Jesus will come,
> Some golden daybreak battles all won;
> We'll rise to glory, through heaven's blue,
> Jesus is coming for me, for you"

I want you folks to learn this chorus. You will like it. You will be humming it the next day at your work. It will make you happy all the day long. It is really a beautiful little chorus and it is strictly Biblical.

Yes, when Jesus descends the righteous dead rise. The living are changed and all these righteous ones are caught up from the earth to meet Jesus and go to the heavenly mansions. Now the question comes· What will happen to the millions of disobedient people when Jesus descends from the sky? Put down Jeremiah 25 33: "The slain of the Lord shall be at that day from one end of the earth even unto the other end of the earth: they shall not be lamented, neither gathered, nor buried: they shall be dung upon the ground."

Wherever the disobedient are, they will be struck dead by the presence of the Lord. Notice it says that, **"the slain of the Lord will be from one end of the earth even unto the other end of the earth."** Men have tried to invent a death ray that would slay thousands in a second. Here is a death ray that will actually slay every person in the world that isn't ready to meet Jesus. "The slain of the Lord shall be from one end of the earth even unto the other end of the earth." Here is a death ray that will slay millions in a moment. The divine glory of Christ, when He appears from heaven will strike every sinner dead just as if a bolt of lightning smote him, or as if a live wire fell on him. This is what will stop the battle of Armageddon instantly.

In Psalm 50:3-5 we learn that when the Lord appears from heaven a fire shall devour before Him. In Isaiah 66·15-17 we are told that the Lord will come with fire and the disobedient will be slain by this blast of fire. There will be a blast of atomic energy that will destroy millions in a second. The world witnessed a blast of this atomic power in the destruction of Sodom. In Genesis 19.24 it says: "The Lord rained upon Sodom and upon Gomorrah brimstone and fire from the Lord out of heaven;" It is very significant that not a blade of grass nor a tree has ever grown in that vicinity since. Jesus cites this as an illustration of what will happen to the wicked people when He comes the second time.

Some of you may say, "Mr. Shuler, is the slaying of these disobedient people at the second coming of Jesus Christ the final end of these sinners?" No! All who have done evil must come forth in the resurrection of damnation to receive their punishment. Revelation 20 shows that when they are resurrected the battle of Armageddon will actually be resumed again. This 20th chapter of Revelation is perhaps the greatest prophetic chapter in all the Bible. Some night soon I shall speak on this 20th chapter of Revelation and it will be one of the greatest outlines of future events you have ever listened to. Be sure and hear it.

The second coming of Jesus Christ will not only be the grandest reunion but it will be the saddest separation that has ever taken place. Ungodly husbands will have their godly wives separated from them for eternity. Ungodly children will have their godly mothers and fathers separated from them forever. Jesus Christ says, "two shall be in the field; the one shall be taken and the other left." The Christian wife will be taken to meet Jesus and be with Him forever. The sinner husband will be left behind dead. O, how we need to be ready to meet Jesus when He comes.

A man lay on a hospital bed dying. People knew he could not last but a few days. His friend came and said, "Isn't there something I can do to help you?"

"No, there is nothing you can do."

"May I bring you some ice cream or fruit?"

"No."

"Well, tell me isn't there something I can do for you?"

"No, there is nothing."

"Could I read to you?"

"No, there is nothing you can do."

His friend came back the next day and said, "Isn't there some little thing I can do for you?"

"No." Then he said with great earnestness, "O, if there were only some one who could undo."

Thank God, there is some one who can undo the sin question. Jesus came into this world to save sinners. He says, "Come and let us reason together, saith the Lord though your sins be as scarlet, they shall be as white as snow." Jesus can undo the sin question. He can blot out sin so it will never be seen. He can make the profligate pure, the drunkard sober, the thief honest, and the infidel into a believer.

Every person in the world is lost without Jesus. This good Book says, "All have sinned and come short of the glory of God." All we like sheep have gone astray. We have turned every one aside to his own way but God's invitation is, "Look unto me," the Saviour on the cross with outstretched hands says, "Look unto Me and be ye saved all ye ends of the earth."

Jesus used the brazen serpent that Moses made to illustrate how people are saved. You will find that in John 3 14, 15, "As Moses lifted up the serpent so must the Son of man be lifted up: that whosoever believeth in Him should not perish, but have everlasting life."

How long did it take a bitten Isralite to be cured? One moment he was dying; the next minute by simply looking at the brazen serpent he was completely healed. So the very moment you give yourself to Jesus and take Him as the One who bled and suffered for you, you are pardoned and saved

"There is life in a look at the Crucified One,
There is life at this moment for thee,
Then look, sinner, look unto Him and be saved—
Unto Him who was nailed to the tree."

I believe everyone in this auditorium wants to look at Jesus Christ to-night for full salvation. How many want to be remembered just now in prayer that the Lord may help you to receive Jesus Christ for full salvation? May we see your hands? (Hands were raised.)

(Prayer) O, blessed Jesus, precious Saviour, we do thank Thee for Thy sacrifice upon the cross and for the invitation! 'Look unto me and be ye saved all ye ends of the earth.' We thank thee, O Lord, that in a look there is life for us. In a look at Calvary. Tonight, O God, we've raised our hands to Thee, and we pray that Jesus will minister to us His own grace, His own saving power. He is able to save to the uttermost all who come to Him. Lord we do come to Thee knowing that Thou wilt save us. So we pray tonight to undertake for every man, woman, boy and girl here. Grant that we may so receive Jesus that we shall have full salvation because we ask it in His dear name. Amen.

The Way of Jesus Christ in 194—

(Preached on the Second Thursday of the Campaign)

If you were walking in the country and looked up into the sky and saw an angel flying over your head and heard him speaking certain words to you, wouldn't you be interested to know the meaning of what he said? Certainly. The Bible tells of a certain man who looked up into the sky and saw three angels flying along one behind the other He heard them broadcasting a certain mysterious message to every nation, kindred, tongue, and people You will find this in your Bible in Revelation 14 6-14

You will recall that on Tuesday night I asked you to read Revelation 14 between Tuesday night and this Thursday night I wonder how many have done this. Will all of you who have read Revelation 14 in the last two or three days raise your hands please? (Many hands were raised.) Well, that is fine. I appreciate this, and you will get more from this sermon for having read that chapter. During this Bible Institute I will be preaching oftentimes upon a certain chapter in the Bible, and if you read that chapter beforehand, you'll get much more from the sermon.

Your Heavenly Father has certain secrets that He wants you to understand, and you can know those secrets by studying the prophecies of the Bible. I turn to Amos 3 7. "Surely the Lord God will do nothing but He revealeth His secret unto His servants the prophets." God has revealed His secrets to His prophets. That means that if you will heed what the prophets wrote, you will know the secrets of truth that the Lord has provided for man.

The Bible shows that at different periods in the history of man God has sent special messages to meet man's needs. In the days of Noah just before the flood man became so sinful, so depraved, so wicked that God determined to wipe man off the face of the earth by a great flood of water. God revealed to Noah that the flood was coming and He told Noah what to do. "He revealeth His secrets unto His servants the prophets."

God commissioned Noah to warn the world of its impending doom. Noah began to tell the people, "A flood is coming. God is going to wipe man off the face of the earth with a great flood of waters. Repent of your sins. Turn to God with all your heart. Obey His commandments and get ready to enter this ark that I am preparing." Mark this point well. Everyone who obeyed this message was saved. Everyone who failed to heed this message perished.

The Bible shows that when Jesus Christ was about to appear as the Messiah at His first advent, God sent a special message to prepare people to meet the coming Christ. I read about that message in Matt. 3:1-3. "In those days came John the Baptist preaching in the wilderness of Judea. And saying, Repent ye: for the kingdom of heaven is at hand. For this is He that was spoken of by the prophet Esaias, saying, The voice of one crying in the wilderness, Prepare ye the way of the Lord, make His paths straight."

John the Baptist declared, "The Lord is coming. Get ready. Prepare ye the way of the Lord. Repent of your sins. Turn to God with all your hearts. Be baptized for the remission of sins."

Do you know that God actually revealed that secret 700 years beforehand to the prophet Isaiah? Put down Isaiah 40 3: "The voice of Him that crieth in the wilderness, Prepare ye the way of the Lord, make straight in the desert a highway for our God." This was written 700 years before Christ was born. Over 700 years beforehand God revealed that there would be a forerunner that would go before the Messiah to prepare the way of the Lord. This predicted forerunner was John the Baptist.

Notice this. John the Baptist preached the very message that God had appointed for that hour. When the people asked John the Baptst what denomination he belonged to, he referred them to this prophecy of God's message for that time. Put down John 1.19-23. You will find that a deputation of preachers was sent down from Jerusalem to interrogate John regarding his denominational affiliations. They said to John, "Who art thou? that we may give an answer to them that sent us? What sayest thou of thyself?" His answer was, "I am the voice of one crying in the wilderness, make straight the way of the Lord." He referred them to the message that God had appointed to be preached at that hour.

I want to raise a question that ought to be very interesting to you and me. It is a big question too; when you think of the crisis that this world is in tonight; when you think of this world situation that we are facing and what we have gone through since 1939. The question is this: "Does God have a special message for our day as He had for the people of Noah's time before the flood, and as He had for the Jews in the time of John the Baptist?"

I will let the Bible answer this question. The Bible shows that our day sustains the same relative position to the second coming of Christ as the time of John the Baptist did to our Lord's first advent, also, as the days of Noah did to the impending flood We are living in the time when the second coming of Jesus Christ is about to take place. Remember "the Lord God will do nothing but He revealeth His secrets unto His servants the prophets."

God has placed in the prophecy of Revelation 14:6-14 a special message that is to be preached to all the world when Christ is about to return. I turn to Revelation 14, reading verses 14 and 15, and will you notice please that here on the chart you see depicted just what I will read from Revelation 14·14, 15.

(At this juncture a chart depicting the scene of Christ's coming as described in Rev. 14:14, 15 was lowered in view of the audience.)

"I looked, and behold a white cloud, and upon the cloud one sat like unto the Son of Man, having on His head a golden crown, and in His hand a sharp sickle. And another angel came out of the temple, crying with a loud voice to Him that sat on the cloud, "Thrust in thy sickle, and reap; for the time is come for them to reap: for the harvest of the earth is ripe "

There's no mistaking what this means. Everybody in the auditorium knows that that is a representation of the second coming of Jesus Christ. He saw Christ coming on the cloud with a sickle in His hand to reap the harvest. In Matt. 13 39 Jesus Himself says, "the harvest is the end of the world." This is a representation of Christ coming at the end of the world or at the end of the age.

Notice how three angels are used to picture God's message for our day. I turn to Revelation 14·6, 7. (At this juncture a chart was lowered in the sight of the audience which depicted the scene of the angel flying in midair as described in Rev. 14 6, 7.)

"I saw another angel fly in the midst of heaven, having the everlasting gospel to preach unto them that dwell on the earth, and to every nation, and kindred, and tongue, and people. Saying with a loud voice, Fear God, and give glory to Him; for the hour of His judgment is come: and worship Him that made heaven and earth."

He saw an angel flying through mid-air over every country in the world preaching the gospel in the setting of the judgment hour. What does this mean? Does this mean that a visible angel will fly over every country preaching to the people, "Fear God for the hour of His judgment has come?" No! It doesn't mean that. The preaching of the gospel to all the world

has not been committed to angels. It has been committed to men. Put down
Mark 16·15: To His chosen disciples and their successors to the end of time
Jesus said: "Go ye into all the world, and preach the gospel to every creature."

You can see, friends, that when John saw this angel flying in mid-air
preaching this great gospel message to every nation, it must represent a body
of people whom God will call in the last days, to preach this special message
to all the world. You will notice that there are two special truths set forth in
this first angel's' message.

First, "Fear God for the hour of His judgment is come." This message will
show people when the judgment began, and it will show people what to do to
be ready for the judgment. Again, this message will call upon men to worship Him that made heaven and earth. This message will reveal God as the
personal and direct Creator of man and the world. "Worship Him that made
heaven and earth." Nearly all the world, sad though it is, even the Christian
world, has been led astray by the error of evolution. Man has attempted to
rule God out as the Creator. This message contains God's answer to evolution.

Notice the special truths set forth in the second part of God's message.
Turn to Revelation 14·8. (A chart depicting the second angel's message was
lowered in sight of the audience.) What I read from Rev. 14·8 is what you see
depicted upon this chart. "There followed another angel, saying, Babylon is
fallen, is fallen, that great city, because she made all nations drink of the wine
of the wrath of her fornication."

You will notice that the second part of this message will tell people that
Babylon is fallen. In Revelation 18:2, 4 this message is amplified a bit. There
we read: "He cried mightily with a strong voice, saying, Babylon the great is
fallen, is fallen." Then in verse 4 notice what God will do: "I heard another
voice from heaven, saying, Come out of her," (that "her" refers to Babylon,)
"Come out of her, my people, that ye be not partakers of her sins, and that ye
receive not of her plagues." This second message calls God's people out of
Babylon.

Notice the special truth set forth in the third part of this message. (A
chart depicting the third angel's message was lowered in the sight of the audience.) What I am going to read in Revelation 14.9-11 is what you see depicted upon this chart.

"The third angel followed them," (that is, followed the first and the second angels,) "saying with a loud voice, If any man worship the beast and his
image, and receive his mark in his forehead, or in his hand, The same shall
drink of the wine of the wrath of God, which is poured out without mixture
into the cup of his indignation: and he shall be tormented with fire and brimstone in the presence of the holy angels, and in the presence of the Lamb: and
the smoke of their torment ascendeth up for ever and ever: and they have no
rest day nor night, who worship the beast and his image, and whosoever receiveth the mark of his name."

This third part of the message will show the people what the beast is;
what the image of the beast is; what the mark of the beast is; and it will show
people how to refrain from worshipping the beast and his image. It will show
people what to do to avoid receiving the mark of the beast in their forehead
or in their hand.

What could be the purpose of this message? Let us read Revelation 14:12.
"Here is the patience of the saints: here are they that keep the commandments
of God, and the faith of Jesus." Notice how plain this is. The purpose of this
message is to call out a separate people in every land, in every country to keep
the commandments of God and the faith of Jesus.

The 14th verse shows that when this three-fold message has been preached
to every nation, then Christ will come on the cloud. There we read, "I looked,

and behold a white cloud, and upon the cloud one sat like unto the Son of man, having on His head a golden crown, and in His hand a sharp sickle."

Notice how plainly God has marked out the true way of Jesus Christ for 1946. This 14th verse shows that the second coming of Christ will take place when this three-fold message has been preached to every nation, kindred, tongue and people. This shows plainly that this three-fold message is God's message for the people who live in the last days just before Jesus comes on the cloud.

I wonder if I have made this plain. I want to be sure that you understand it. How many can see that Revelation 14:6-14 indicates that this three-fold message must be God's message for the people who will live in the very last days? Will you raise your hands? (Nearly all raised their hands.) Yes, I am glad you see it.

Someone handed me this question: "Mr. Shuler, I understand that there are 212 different denominations in America. Each one claims to be right, yet many teach just the opposite on certain points. I have no time to search into 212 different religions. How can an ordinary man like me ever be sure which is the true faith of Jesus Christ in these days?"

This man can be just as sure which is the true faith of Jesus Christ in 1946 as 2 and 2 make 4. This three-fold message is the true way of Christ for these last days. The people who accept this three-fold message are said to have the faith of Jesus. Be sure to put down this text, Rev. 14:12, "Here is the patience of the saints: here are they that keep the commandmens of God, and the faith of Jesus." This three-fold message is the faith of Jesus, or the way of Jesus for the people who live just prior to His second advent.

All that this man, or any man, needs to do to find the true way of Christ for 1946 is to learn and heed these truths of this three-fold message. Notice that there are six of these special truths: The hour of God's judgment is come; the worship of God as the Creator; the calling of God's people out of Babylon; the warning against the beast, his image, and the mark of the beast; the keeping of the commandments of God and the faith of Jesus; and the coming of Christ on the cloud. Listen to me. These are the truths that Almighty God has appointed to be preached, to be believed and to be obeyed in these days.

In Revelation 14 6 this three-fold message is called the everlasting gospel or the gospel of the ages. This three-fold message is the gospel of Jesus Christ in the correct setting for the last days. Mark this point well. The purpose of these Bible Institute meetings is to explain these special truths. Can you tell me then what kind of a message these meetings represent? You can see that since this message is to be preached to every people, it must be an inter-denominational, universal message. These truths are for the people of every denomination. This is why I feel so badly that a few people in Des Moines want to brand these meetings along narrow denominational lines, in an attempt to keep people from attending these meetings.

My friends, I refuse to be so narrow as to put a denominational tag on this Holy Book. Jesus Christ and the Bible are bigger than any denomination or all of them put together. These truths are for the people of every denomination, and those who do not belong to any church. These meetings, as we have advertised, are dedicated to the exposition of this great inter-denominational message

We have the authority of the Bible for this kind of an evangelistic approach to the people. When they asked John the Baptist who he was. or what denomination or party he represented, he didn't say, I'm some kind of an "ite" or "ist." He put his finger on Isaiah 40 3 that foretold the very message that God had appointed for that very time. So when people ask, who we are, and why we are here, we point them to this great prophecy of Revelation 14 that sets forth God's inter-denominational message for our day. This is why these meetings are different than any ordinary revival you have ever attended. This is why it is so important not to miss a single subject.

The study of these truths of God's message takes precedence above denominationalism. We cannot explain these truths in just three or four talks. You can't take my word; and you shouldn't take my word or any other man's word as to when the hour of God's judgment came; or how you should worship God as the Creator; or what Babylon is; or what the beast is; or what the image of the beast is; or what the mark of the beast is; and how that mark is received on the forehead or the hand. We must let the Bible speak on these matters. The psalmist says in Psalm 119 105, "Thy Word is a lamp unto my feet, and a light unto my path." Jesus says in John 8 31, 32, "If ye continue in My word . . . ye shall know the truth, and the truth shall make you free."

So dear friends, we shall take up these subjects, one by one, in these meetings and trace out their meaning from the word of God. In the Bible lecture tomorrow night, Friday night, we will show the seven great facts that constitute the everlasting gospel of Jesus Christ. These are the seven most important facts worth knowing. You want to be sure to hear that subject tomorrow night.

Then on Sunday night we will show the meaning of these tremendous times in which we live in the light of Bible prophecy. The following Friday night, just one week from tomorrow night, we will show who is this beast power against whom God has uttered this most solemn warning.

The following Sunday night we will show you from Bible prophecy when the hour of God's judgment began; the very year that this three-fold message was to arise upon the earth. Other lectures will follow and show what it means to worship God as the Creator; what is the beast; what is the image of the beast; what is the mark of the beast; and how the mark is received in the forehead or in the hand; and what is Babylon.

Those who learn the meaning of these truths and obey them will be ready to meet Jesus when He appears on the cloud. The purpose of this message is to make ready a people for the second advent of our Lord, just as John the Baptist's message made ready a people for our Lord's first advent.

> "I want to be ready when Jesus comes,
> I want to be ready when Jesus comes,
> Earth's pleasures grow dim,
> While I'm waiting for Him
> Lord keep me till Jesus comes."

You will be ready if you obey Christ's special message for these last days as set forth in Revelation 14 6-12. Mark this point well. In the days of Noah, every person in the world settled his own fate by what he did with God's message. When the flood came the only people who were saved were those who accepted God's message.

Christ said in Matt. 24:37: "As the days of Noah were, so shall also the coming of the Son of man be " What does this mean to you and me? It means that it is more important for you and me to study our Bibles and learn the meaning of these truths than anything else. It means that we ought to make up our minds not to let anything keep us from attending these meetings where we may learn the meaning of God's message for our day. It is just as important for you and me to know the meaning of these truths and heed them as it was for the people of Noah's time to know about the coming of that flood; and for the people in the days of John the Baptist to know about the coming of Jesus Christ at His first advent.

If God has a special message for you, don't you want to know about it? How many would like to bear a solemn testimony to our dear Saviour tonight, saying by the uplifted hand, "Lord help me to learn and follow the great truths that Thou hast for me in these last days?" Will you please raise your hands? (Nearly every hand was raised.)

Let us pray. O blessed Lord, precious Saviour, we thank Thee for this great revelation of Jesus Christ. We thank Thee, Lord, especially for this 14th chapter which we have been studying tonight. O Lord, we have pictured Thy coming upon the cloud, and just before Thy coming this great three-fold message is preached to every people. Lord, how plain it is that this three-fold message is Thy message to the people who live in these last days. Lord, we want to know the meaning of this message. We love Thee and we want to know Thy will. O God, we pray that as we open up these prophecies in these meetings that Thou wilt give us divine enlightenment to see the truth, then give us divine grace to follow the truth as it is in Christ Jesus. May we each one follow in the way of Thy message that when Jesus shall come upon the cloud, every soul here may be ready to meet Him. We ask this in His precious name. Amen.

The Bridge from Trouble to Eternal Happiness

(Preached on the Second Friday of the Campaign)

Have you ever heard about the man who made a bridge out of his own body in order to save three people from death? In one of our large eastern cities a four-story frame apartment house in one of the poorer sections of the city was afire. Trapped in the top story was a father with his three little boys, ages 7, 5 and 3. It looked as if they were doomed to a most horrible death, to be burnt alive. The father noticed that the window in the adjoining apartment building was opened on the same level where they were. There was a space of about three feet between the two buildings. He saw that by making a supreme effort he could reach out and grasp the window sill of the adjoining building and make a bridge out of his own body on which his three little boys could crawl to safety.

He called them to his side and explained the plan. He reached out and grasped the window sill and the seven year old boy, crawling along on his father's body, went through the open window into the adjoining building to safety. Then came the five year old boy. Then the baby boy came crawling along. He crept along on his father until he was helped through the open window by his brothers to safety. But at last the father's strength failed. He fell to the ground and was picked up dead. He gave his life to save three. He made a bridge out of his own body on which three went from death to life.

Tonight I turn to the Bible and bring you the thrilling story of how the Son of God has made a bridge out of His own body on which we can go from death to life. Sin had doomed every person in this world to perish in everlasting fire, but "God so loved the world, that He gave His only begotten Son, that whosoever believeth in Him should not perish, but have everlasting life." The blessed Son of God so loved you and me that He came from heaven to make a bridge of salvation on which we may go from death to eternal life.

(At this juncture the speaker directed attention to a large chart on which was depicted a bridge supported by seven piers. Strips of paper were pinned over each of these piers, so that the name of each successive pier could be disclosed to the audience as the seven great facts of the gospel were unfolded.)

This bridge of salvation is outlined before you upon this chart. This is the gospel bridge from death to life. Notice it spans the awful gulf of sin. It illustrates the way by which men lost in sin may be saved forever with eternal life in the kingdom of God.

You will notice that this bridge is sustained by seven piers. So we shall find from the Bible that the gospel of salvation rests upon seven mighty facts about the Lord Jesus Christ. The purpose of this study is to discover what those seven facts are.

We uncover the first one and you notice that upon it is inscribed, "I-N-C-A-R-N-A-T-I-O-N." By "Incarnation" we mean the entrance of the Son of God into human flesh to save mankind. In order to save us Christ, the Son of God, had to leave His place in heaven at the Father's side, come to our earth, take our flesh and be born as a baby. So the Scriptures declare that the virgin Mary conceived a son by the power of the Holy Ghost.

The best news that men have ever heard is the news of the first Christmas recorded in Luke 2:10, 11 where the angel said, "Behold I bring you good tidings of great joy, which shall be to all people. For unto you is born this day in the city of David, a Saviour, which is Christ the Lord."

By being born into this world, Christ commenced the construction of a bridge that would save men, that would take men from death to life. So the first pier of the bridge of salvation is labeled "Incarnation." But after He was born He must live a sinless life. So we uncover the second pier and there you read, "Sinless Life."

If Jesus Christ had committed one little sin, every person in the world would be without hope tonight. Why? 1 John 3·4 says, "Sin is the transgression of the law." If Christ had broken the ten commandments, even one time, He would have become a sinner; and if He had been a sinner, He couldn't be your Saviour. If He had transgressed any of the ten commandments, it matters not which one, He would have come under the penalty of the law; then He wouldn't be able to save you from the penalty of your sins. But thank God, Jesus stood true under every test. Hebrews 4 15 says, Jesus "was in all points tempted like as we are, yet without sin." Aren't you glad He stood every test for you? How could you refuse to serve such a loving Saviour?

By living a sinless life Jesus extended this bridge of salvation a little further. But in order to save you and me Jesus not only must be born into the world, not only must He live a sinless life after He is born; but He must die for our sins. So we uncover the third pier and you read that great word, "Crucifixion." To save us He must die for our sins.

The ten commandments condemn every person in the world to death because everyone has sinned. The law of God says, "I condemn you as a sinner. I sentence you to death." But here comes the good news "God so loved the world that He gave His only begotten Son, that whosoever believeth in Him should not perish, but have everlasting life." Jesus says, "I love you   I don't want to see you perish. I died in your place. I went to the cross for your sins. By accepting Me as your Saviour, you are free from condemnation and death." So by His vicarious death on Calvary Jesus built another section of this bridge so that men may pass from death to life, or from being lost in sin to have eternal life in the kingdom of God.

However, after He died He must rise again. This brings us to the fourth pier   There you read that great word, "Resurrection." If Christ had not risen from the dead, man would have been eternally lost. 1 Corinthians 15:17 says, "If Christ be not risen, your faith is vain; ye are yet in your sins."

A dead Saviour couldn't save anybody. Even though He died upon the cross, if He hadn't come out of that tomb, we would still be lost. A dead saviour couldn't save anybody. Thank God He arose.

"Not in the tomb where once He lay,
    A risen Christ, a living Saviour;"
"Up from the grave He arose!
    With a mighty triumph o'er His foes."

By His resurrection Jesus built another section of the bridge over the river of death and destruction. But He must not only rise from the dead, He must ascend to heaven to represent us at the Father's throne, and to mediate cases of those who accept Him. This brings us to the fifth pier. There you see the word, "Ascension." He must ascend to the Father. He went to the Father to undertake a work of intercession for you and me. This brings us to the sixth pier that is inscribed, "Mediation," His priestly mediation.

Notice how all these great facts of Christ fit together so beautifully. In order to save us He must first be born into the world—"Incarnation." After He was born He lived a "Sinless Life." Then He died for our sins—"Crucifixion." After He died he rose again—"Resurrection." Then He ascended to the Father—"Ascension." Then He became our great High Priest to intercede for us with the Father.

Paul tells us in Hebrews 7:25 that, "He is able also to save to the uttermost them that come unto God by Him, seeing He ever liveth to make intercession for them." Listen to me. If you will do the coming, He will do the saving. If you will step out and accept Jesus Christ, He will meet you with peace, pardon, and salvation. If you will give yourself to Him tonight for a closer walk with Him, He will meet you with more power so you can live a true Christian life. If you will confess your sins to this wonderful Jesus, He will raise those nail pierced hands as He stands before the Father and cry, "My blood! MY Blood! I shed My blood, Father, for that poor soul who is trusting Me, and for my sake, Father, forgive him and give him eternal life." O, I hope everyone will put his case fully in the hands of this wonderful Saviour.

By His intercession, by His mediation, Christ extends this bridge of salvation a little bit further. But notice that it takes one more section to complete this wonderful bridge across the gulf of sin. What is that completing link or section? Turn with me to John 14:1-3.

"Let not your heart be troubled: ye believe in God, believe also in me. In my Father's house are many mansions: if it were not so, I would have told you. I go to prepare a place for you. And if I go and prepare a place for you, I will come again and receive you unto myself; that where I am there ye may be also."

In addition to His priestly mediation Christ must come again from heaven to this earth to receive His people unto Himself and to take them to those wonderful mansions that He has prepared. This brings us to the seventh pier, "His Second Advent." The second coming of Christ is just as necessary in the complete gospel as His resurrection or His crucifixion. So we read in Hebrews 9:28. "So Christ was once offered to bear the sins of many; and unto them that look for Him shall He appear the second time without sin unto salvation." Paul strikes the two great focal points of the plan of redemption. He shows us that it is just as necessary for Christ to come the second time as it was for Christ to die upon the cross.

These seven great facts about Jesus Christ constitute the bridge of salvation that will take man from being lost in sin to have eternal life in the kingdom of God. These seven great facts are as follows: His incarnation, His sinless life, His crucifixion, His resurrection, His ascension, His priestly mediation, and His second Advent. **These are the seven most important facts worth knowing.**

Christ was born. He lived. He died. He arose. He ascended. He pleads for us. He is coming again. Listen to me. The gospel of Jesus Christ is not speculation. It is not merely a theory. It isn't a philosophy. It isn't merely theology. **The gospel of Jesus Christ is based on actual facts about an actual person.** Thank God, "On Christ the solid rock I stand, All other ground is sinking sand."

It takes all these seven facts to make the true gospel. If you remove any of those seven piers, this bridge breaks down and that leaves an uncrossable gap, so that men could not go from being lost in sin to be saved forever in the kingdom of God. If a man denies the incarnation, (and many do) if a man denies that Jesus Christ was virgin born, his bridge is broken down before he ever starts across the river. He has nothing on which to start because in order to save us the Son of God must become incarnate in human flesh.

If a man denies the crucifixion, the bridge breaks down in the middle. There are those who deny the atoning blood of Jesus Christ. They say that the blood of Christ has no more power to save people from sin than the blood that flows in your veins. Such teaching leaves an uncrossable gap in their bridge so that they cannot get across the river.

There are those who deny the second advent. Many churches have forgotten about the second advent. How many sermons have you ever heard in Des Moines on Christ's second advent? It is largely lost sight of, yet it is just as necessary in the gospel as the crucifixion or the resurrection.

Anyone who denies or sets aside any one of these seven great facts simply doesn't have the one complete true gospel. Mark this well. These seven essential facts apply to only one person who ever lived and that is Jesus Christ. It is exactly true what Paul wrote in 1 Cor. 3:11. "Other foundation can no man lay than that is laid, which is Jesus Christ." This is why Christianity is the only true religion in the world.

> "Wonderful, wonderful Jesus,
>   Who can compare with Thee?
> Wonderful, wonderful Jesus,
>   Fairer than all art thou to me.

> "Wonderful, wonderful Jesus,
>   O, how my soul loves Thee;
> Fairer than all the fairest,
>   Jesus, art Thou to me."

Friends, what does Jesus mean to you? A person may believe a great deal about Jesus and still not be saved. Just ask yourself quietly, "What do I believe about Jesus? Many will say, "I believe Jesus died upon the cross." But merely believing this will not save you. You may say, "I believe Jesus died on Calvary for sinners." Believing that will not do you any good. You must say, "He loved me and gave Himself for me. I believe Jesus bled and died on account of my sins." We must make a personal application of these great facts of Jesus to our own soul.

An ungodly sea captain was stricken with a fatal disease in mid-ocean. He called the ship's doctor. The doctor said, "Captain, you cannot live more than twenty-four hours." He was terrified. He wasn't prepared to die. So he sent quickly for the first mate, a man named Williams.

He said, "Williams, the doctor declares I can't last more than twenty-four hours. I want you to get a Bible and read something to me. I must have help. I'm going to die. I want you to get a Bible and read to me and pray with me."

Mr. Williams said, "Captain, you've never given me an order in all these years but what I've carried it out to the letter, but you have given me an order now that I cannot carry out. I don't have a Bible and I don't know how to pray."

Then he said, "You may go. Send in the second mate." His name was Thomas. They brought him in. He said, "Thomas, my rope is about run out. I want you to get a Bible and read to me and pray with me. I'm dying."

Thomas said, "Captain, I've always carried out your orders, but this is an order I can't carry out. I don't have any Bible and I don't know how to pray. I've forgotten. My mother taught me when I was a little boy at her knee. She taught me how to pray, but I've forgotten. However, I've seen a Bible in the hands of a little boy on this ship, the cook's boy named Willie Platt."

The captain said, "Bring him in quickly." He went down to the kitchen. There he was working. He was the cook's boy, the cook's assistant. "Willie, get your Bible and go up to the captain's cabin." Willie took his Bible and went to the captain's cabin. The captain said, "I want you to read something about God having mercy on a sinner like me"

The poor boy didn't know what to read at first. Then he thought of that chapter that his mother had had him read so often. The 53rd chapter of Isaiah which so wonderfully pictures the love of Jesus Christ for sinners. So he turned to the 53rd chapter of Isaiah. He came to the 5th verse where it says, speaking of Jesus: "He was wounded for our transgressions, He was bruised for our iniquities: the chastisement of our peace was upon Him; and with His stripes we are healed."

The captain said, "That sounds like what I need. Won't you read that over again?" So the boy read the words over again. Encouraged by the captain's response he said, "Captain, wouldn't you like to have me read this verse like my mother taught me to read it?" The captain said, "By all means, you read the verse just as your mother taught you to read it."

Then he took the verse and in place of that word "o-u-r" he put his own name into the text. Slowly and reverently he read, "He was wounded for Willie Platt's transgressions, He was bruised for Willie Platt's iniquities: the chastisement of Wille Platt's peace was upon Him; and with His stripes Willie Platt is healed."

By this time the captain was half way over the edge of the bed. He says, "Son, read it again and put your captain's name in there." Then the boy again reverently read, "He was wounded for John Clout's transgressions. He was bruised for John Clout's iniquities: the chastisement of John Clout's peace was upon Him and with His stripes John Clout is healed"

The captain fell back upon his pillow and repeated over and over again this beautiful text, putting his own name into it every time. Finally light from heaven broke in upon his darkened soul. He received Him who saves to the uttermost. "If any man be in Christ he is a new creature; old things have passed away and all things are become new."

Friends, I want to put my name into this text, don't you? I want the Lord to save me from all my sins. Every soul in this auditorium tonight needs help from God to give this blessed Christ a larger place in his life.

Friends, we have had a number of good meetings here The Lord has met with us. His Spirit has spoken to our hearts. You have been raising your hands for prayer here in every meeting, and I appreciate it. It is right that you should. But tonight wouldn't you like to draw still closer to Jesus? Wouldn't you like to form a prayer circle here in front of the pulpit? I invite every soul in this auditorium who wants to give Christ a larger place in his life to form a prayer circle here in front of the pulpit. This call has nothing to do with joining any church. It is a call to prayer. It is a call to give Christ a larger place in your life.

I invite forward everyone who wants to live a better life. I invite forward those who have unconverted loved ones whom you want to see saved and for whom you want us to pray in this closing prayer. I invite forward every soul who wants to go across on this great gospel bridge and have eternal life in the kingdom of God. The choir is going to sing one stanza. We will stand as the choir sings, "I've Wandered far away from God, now I'm coming home."

While the choir continues the song I want to invite quietly everyone who would like to give Christ a larger place in his life; you who have unconverted loved ones for whom you want us to pray; everyone who wants to lead a better life, just come and fill in here at the front while the choir sings.

(As the choir sang, hundreds came forward)

The night I was converted in Billie Sunday's meetings I said to myself, "Every time I have a chance to take a step forward for Christ I'll do it." And I've been doing it all the time. Every time a call like this is given I love to press in because I get a blessing.

Thank God, so many are coming. This is really wonderful. I don't want to see anybody left out of this closing prayer. I am glad it is full down here at the front, yet there are many others who want the Lord's help. God can do everything for the person who wants His help. But God can't do anything for a person who doesn't desire His help. How many of you, who haven't been able to come forward because there wasn't room, want to say, "Preacher, just count me in as one down there who wants a part in this prayer for the help of God?" Yes, it seems that every hand in the back part of the audience is raised.

Many of us are conscious of a lack of reality in our Christian experience. We would like to have Jesus be more real in our every-day life. How many would like to have Christ be more real in your every-day life, would you just lift the hand? (It seemed that nearly every person at the front and those further back raised their hands.) Yes, I would like to put up both of my hands on this. I do want Jesus to be more real in my life.

Here is something that will help you. This prayer that I offer now closes the regular meeting It is still early. It is only about eighteen minutes to nine. I have closed the sermon early so we could do this. Immediately after this closing prayer I will give a twelve minute Bible lesson, right here at the front on four ways that Christ can be more real in your life, just like you want Him to be. This lesson will tell you of four simple things that you can do that will make Christ more real in your life. I hope everyone will stay and get the blessing of this after-meeting study. Shall we bow our heads as we look to the Lord in this prayer?

(Prayer.)

Our dear heavenly Father, we thank Thee that Thy Holy Spirit has spoken to our hearts. We thank Thee for this great number who have come forward to have a closer walk with Jesus They want to give Christ a larger place in their life.

We pray also, Lord, for those in the rear who couldn't come forward, but who so quickly raised their hands for help. Lord, we want to remember these unconverted loved ones. We know that many of these dear hearts are thinking of their own loved ones who are out of the fold of safety. O, Lord, we pray that Thy Holy Spirit will speak to them. Wherever they are, Lord, even if they are in a show somewhere, or at a dance, not even thinking of Jesus, may the Spirit speak to them. Lord, make them dissatisfied with the things of the world and may they see the lovely Jesus as He is.

Bless us Lord as we participate in this Bible Study. We know it will be a blessing to our hearts to find these four ways whereby Jesus will be real in our lives. So we pray to bless us each one and may we so appropriate these great facts of Jesus to our souls, that we shall have full salvation because we ask it in His precious name. Amen.

(At this juncture the many scores who were standing at the front took seats at the front. Almost every one remained for the after meeting study.)

THE AFTER MEETING LESSON
Four Ways Whereby Jesus Will Be More Real To You

I don't know what your special needs are but there is one thing I do know—Jesus knows. He knows the individual needs of every soul This isn't all. Jesus not only knows your individual needs, but He is able to supply your individual needs. This isn't all. 'He not only is able to supply your needs, but He will supply your needs if you will contact Him by faith.

We read in Philippians 4.19. "My God shall supply all your need according to His riches in glory by Christ Jesus" It just takes one thing on your part. This is very important. Just one little sentence here in Mark 6 56. You read this in Mark 6:56 when you go home because there is something here I want you to get. "As many as touched Him were made whole." Did you get that? As many as touched Jesus were made whole. How can you be made whole? Simply by touching Jesus Christ. Everything depends on making contact, actual contact with Jesus

In the Gospels we have a wonderful story about a woman who had an issue of blood for twelve years She had spent everything she had on doctors, but none could help her. She said, "O, if I could but see Jesus, the great Doctor, and ask Him to cure me, then 1 would be healed." One day she heard that Jesus was in her neighborhood. But when she went out to find Jesus there was such a crowd around Him that she couldn't get anywhere near Him. She couldn't go up and talk to Him. All she could do was to edge her way in between other people. Finally she succeeded reaching in between other people and just touched the hem of His garment as He was walking along." Instantly power was released. There flowed into her being the healing and the help that she needed. "As many as touched Him were made whole."

Power flows from Jesus Christ just like electricity from a dynamo. All you need to do is to make contact with Him I want you to notice this. There were a lot of people in that crowd who were closer to Jesus physically than this woman. She couldn't get near to even talk to Him. She had to reach between other people to touch a part of His clothing as He walked along. These other people were closer to Jesus, yet they received nothing. The big crowd got nothing but this one woman got something. What made the difference? The difference was the touch of faith. "As many as touched Him were made whole."

Faith makes the contact that releases power. You don't have to touch Jesus physically to get that power. You can make that contact by faith. In Mark 9.23 He says, "all things are possible to him that believeth."

There are four ways by which every person may have constant contact with the Lord Jesus Christ, and have his spiritual needs supplied. I can definitely promise you on the authority of this precious Word that if you will follow these four simple ways, Christ will be more real in your life in the future than He has ever been in the past And your spiritual needs will be supplied.

First of all, let me tell you that there is a way to read the Bible that makes Jesus Christ real to you. You must take God's promises as the voice of God speaking to you personally. Just like my story tonight about Willie Platt. You must put your own name into the text, see?

Here is an example. Hebrews 13 5, a very precious text. It's a promise. "I will never leave thee, nor forsake thee" Listen, when you read that in the Bible, who is the "thee?" Why it is you. Yes, that's exactly it. You must take it to yourself Put your own name into it. That will make Christ more real to you. Put your own name into the promise. When He says "I'll never leave thee" that "thee" is you, and believe it. Then the blessing comes because you know Christ is with you and is never going to leave you. Just like the poet says:

> "If our lives were but more simple,
>   We would take Him at His word,
>   And our lives would be all sunshine
>   In the sweetness of our Lord."

So here is the first way to make Christ more real in your life, take God's promises in the Bible to yourself, individually and personally.

There is a way to pray that will make Christ more real to you. Real prayer is the opening of the heart to Chirst as to a friend. So here is the second way to make Christ more real. When you pray talk to Jesus just as you talk to your dearest friend. Talk to Jesus simply and naturally. Don't think you have to use formal words or set phrases. Just talk to Jesus in your language. He understands. So the second way is to talk to Jesus in prayer as you would to your dearest friend.

There is a way to begin a day that makes Christ more real to us. Jesus has promised that He will dwell in our hearts every day by the Holy Spirit. Put down Rev. 3:20. He says, "Behold, I stand at the door, and knock: if any man hear my voice, and open the door, I will come in to Him and will sup with him, and he with me." He will come into our hearts and live in our being.

We need to give ourselves anew to Jesus every morning. The first thought in the morning should be of Jesus. Turn to Jesus the first thing in the morning. Even before you get out of bed say, "Lord, I give myself to Thee for another day. I thank Thee, Jesus, that Thou art in my heart." This is the third way to make Jesus more real in your heart. Just open up your heart and pray that Jesus will come in and abide with you every day.

There is a way to go through a day that makes Jesus more real to us. Talk to God intimately as you go about your work. Put down Isaiah 26:3. "Thou wilt keep him in perfect peace, whose mind is stayed on thee." Wouldn't you like that perfect peace? O, yes! we have some peace, but it isn't perfect you know. So many things mar our peace. God wants us to have perfect peace. "Thou wilt keep him in perfect peace," (on one condition,) "Thou wilt keep him in perfect peace, whose mind is stayed on thee." So the fourth way to make Christ more real is to keep your mind stayed on Him as you go about your work.

There is a lovely book, it is called the Ministry of Healing. If you ever get a chance to buy that book, do so. In Ministry of Healing, page 182, we have this lovely sentence, "By prayer, by the study of His word, by faith in His abiding presence, the weakest of human beings may live in contact with the living Christ, and He will hold them with a hand that will never let them go."

Now as we look to Jesus in the closing prayer, I hope you will reach out with that living touch of faith and touch Him and then you'll get the help and the power that you need. After I pray, just keep your heads still bowed and we will sing a lovely prayer song which will be your prayer after my prayer.

> "My faith looks up to Thee,
>   Thou Lamb of Calvary,
>   Saviour divine;
>   Now hear me while I pray
>   Take all my guilt away,
>   O let me from this day
>   Be wholly Thine."

After we sing that, I want us all to repeat Isaiah 53:5. This is the text I used in my sermon which says, "He was wounded for our transgressions, He was bruised for our iniquities, the chastisement of our peace was upon Him; and with His stripes we are healed."

I want you to put in the word "my." "He was wounded for my transgressions, He was bruised for my iniquities: the chastisement of my peace was upon Him; and with His stripes I am healed."

All right now we are going to have prayer, then the prayer song, and the verse of Scripture.

(Prayer.)

Blessed Jesus, precious Saviour, we thank Thee for the blessing that Thou hast given to us tonight. Lord, we have had our hearts warmed. Thy Holy Spirit is here. We have drawn a little nearer to Him tonight than ever before and we've felt His presence. Lord, we thank Thee for these four simple ways by which Thou wilt be more real in our life. May it be just now, that every soul here may just reach out with that living touch of faith and touch Jesus.

O, blessed Christ, all powerful Saviour, just reach down Thy mighty arm into every life here and do for each one what he needs to have done. Our faith, Lord, does claim the promise, and we thank Thee that Thou wilt do this for each one because we ask it in Jesus' name. Amen.

Now then the song. Every head bowed. (All joined in singing My Faith Looks Up to Thee.)

Heads still bowed, let us quote the text "He was wounded for my transgressions, He was bruised for my iniquities: the chastisement of my peace was upon Him; and with His stripes I am healed."

I feel sure you have been blessed in this after meeting. I think you feel like John Wesley, the man who founded the great Methodist church. He went to a little meeting one night in Aldersgate Street in London. He heard some one read from Luther's writing how Jesus Christ changes our heart when we have faith in Him and as he listened he said, "I felt my heart strangely warmed." How many of you really got a blessing out of this after meeting and felt your heart warmed tonight? Will you raise your hands? (Many hands were raised.)

(Then the topic for the next after meeting was announced and those present were urged to come forward promptly when the invitation to the after meeting would be extended on Sunday night.)

Last Day Signs

When the Son of God came to this earth at His first advent a sign was given of His arrival into our world. A beautiful star appeared that led the wise men step by step to the very spot where the wonderful Christ child was born at Bethlehem. So the Scriptures tell of certain signs which will appear when this same Son of God is about to make His second advent to our world.

Let us read the words of Jesus as recorded in Matt. 24 32, 33. "Now learn a parable of the fig tree, when his branch is yet tender, and putteth forth leaves, ye know that summer is nigh: so likewise ye, when ye shall see all these things, know that He is near, even at the doors."

At the close of the winter season when the bare trees begin to leaf out, of what is this a sign? Everybody knows what this means It is a sign that summer is near This Scripture declares that when the branch puts forth its new leaves you know that summer is nigh Jesus Christ declares that just as the swelling of the buds is a sign that summer is near, so the fulfillment of certain signs He has given will show that His coming is near.

Mark this point well. Jesus actually commands us to know that His coming is near when these appointed signs are fulfilled. He says "When ye see all these things, know that it is near, even at the doors."

Some have tried to set a date for the end of the world. Jesus Christ declares that it is impossible for any man to figure out the exact date on which He will return. You will find this in Matt. 24.36 where He says, "But of that day and hour knoweth no man, no not the angels of heaven, but my Father only." While it is impossible for any man to know the exact day when Jesus will return, it is the duty of every believer to know that the coming of Christ is near, when the appointed signs are seen in the world

Jesus reproved the Pharisees for their inability to read the signs of the times. We read about this in Matt. 16 1-3. "The Pharisees also with the Sadducees came, and tempting desired Him that He would shew them a sign from heaven. He answered and said unto them, when it is evening, ye say, it will be fair weather for the sky is red. And in the morning, it will be foul weather today: For the sky is red and lowering. O ye hypocrites, ye can discern the face of the sky; but can ye not discern the signs of the times?"

If the Jewish people in the days of Christ had understood the prophecies which pertained to the first advent of the Messiah, they would have recognized Jesus of Nazareth as the promised Messiah, and the Saviour of the world. But they rejected Him, because they did not understand the prophecies that pertained to His first advent This is a warning to professed Christians today. Unless professed Christians heed the prophecies that pertain to Christ's second advent they will be in the dark and caught unprepared at His second coming, as the Jews were at His first advent.

Jesus has a question for every soul "Can ye not discern the signs of the times?" May God help me to take His Holy Word and make the signs of Christ's coming stand out so plainly, that you will be able to discern the signs of the times.

If you want to know what time it is, what do you do? You note the relative positions of the hour and minute hands on the dial of your watch. So if we want to know where we are going today, if we want to know what is coming, and where we are on the stream of time, we must look at the hands on

God's prophetic clock. The last day predictions of the Bible, these prophecies which tell what is to be in the last days, constitute the hour hand on God's clock. The fulfillment of these last-day predictions in modern history and in current conditions is the minute hand on the face of God's clock. I invite you to take note where the hands are on God's clock. I shall take the Bible and read what God prophesied would be in the last days, and then I shall leave it with you to say if this is what you now see in our world.

Everybody knows that there has been a greater increase of knowledge in the last seventy-five years than in all the rest of the history of mankind put together. What does this mean? You will find this explained in Daniel 12:4. "But thou, O Daniel, shut up the words, and seal the book, even to the time of the end. many shall run to and fro, and knowledge shall be increased."

What did the prophecy say would happen in the last days? In the time of the end knowledge shall be increased. The last days of earth's history would be characterized by an increase of knowledge.

Is this true of our day? Look at the endless list of inventions and wonderful discoveries that are being brought out with every passing year. Life has been completely revolutionized during the last fifty or seventy-five years. The old tallow candle has become the electric light. The horse and buggy has become the automobile the aeroplane and the streamliner. The needle has become the electric sewing machine. The old fashioned broom has become the electric sweeper. The old oaken bucket has become the water faucet with running water. The old goose quill has become the typewriter. The messenger on horseback who carried messages has become the telegraph, the telephone and the radio. The horse drawn plow has become the tractor. The scythe and the old-time binder have become the modern reaper. And so we might go on with many other items.

There seems to be no end to this increase of knowledge in our day. New wonders are discovered and developed with almost every passing day. The other day the Associated Press reported the development of a radio facsimile machine that prints a four column newspaper at the rate of five hundred words a minute. News, photographs, maps, charts and cartoons were reproduced during the demonstration by means of signals from a frequency modulated type of broadcasting station. The machine itself is only a little larger than a portable typewriter. It can be used as an attachment in combination with a frequency modulation home receiver. The device turns out printed papers measuring $9\frac{1}{2}$ x 12 inches at the rate of twenty-eight square inches per minute. This is truly a great wonder. But before the ink is hardly dry which recites the story of this newest wonder there will likely be another wonder developed that will eclipse this latest one.

Little school children today have far greater knowledge along some lines than their grandparents had when they were seventy years old. It is safe to say that any person who is sixty years old has seen in his brief lifetime a greater increase of knowledge than all the people of all past generations put together. What does this mean? It means that we are in the time of the end. Daniel 12:4 says, "In the time of the end knowledge shall be increased." Just as surely as you know that there has been this great increase of knowledge in recent decades, just so surely you may know that the end is near.

Up until about a century ago men were not able to travel faster than men before them had traveled for all past generations. Then all of a sudden a change came. Men began to find ways of traveling faster. And during the last ten years they have been traveling decidedly faster and ever faster. How did it come that there was no change in the speed at which men could travel until about the last one hundred twenty years?

Bible prophecy shows that there would be an increased speed of travel in the closing period of earth's history. Dan. 12:4 indicates that in the last days men would travel very swiftly. In the time of the end the prophecy says, many shall run, not walk, but run. Every aeroplane, automobile, train and steamer is a traveling sign of the end of time. Every plane that roars overhead every automobile dashing along the street or highway, every train rushing along the shiny rails, every steamer cutting across the ocean deep, is saying, "it is the day of God's preparation and you should be ready to meet the King."

Let us notice two striking signs in the business and industrial world of our day. In James 5:3 we read: "Ye have heaped treasure together for the last days." The Revised Version says, "Ye have heaped treasure together in the last days." Bible prophecy indicated that in the last days men would pile up fortunes very quickly. Do we see this today? Since 1900 there has been a piling up of colossal fortunes on a scale and at a rate that exceeds all the past history of mankind.

Here is a typical case. In 1900 Henry Ford did not have enough money to buy a turkey for Thanksgiving day. Forty years later he was a billionaire. Think of it! There are hundreds of people in our day who have made, or are making, a million or more dollars in one year. Do you know how much a million dollars amounts to? If you saved five hundred dollars per year, and that would be a tidy sum for most of us to save, how long would it take you to get a million? You would have to save five hundred dollars a year for two thousand years to have a million dollars. If you had been here on the night that Jesus was born in Bethlehem, and had lived on every year since, and had saved five hundred dollars every year, you wouldn't have a million dollars yet. Hundreds of men have made this much or more in one year in our day. What does this mean? It means exactly what Bible prophecy says in James 5:3. They have heaped up treasure in the last days.

In James 5:4 it is made plain that during this same period when men will be piling up these colossal fortunes, there will be a most bitter struggle of the working man against his employer. Do we see this? Since 1910 there have been the most extensive and intensive labor troubles of all past history. What does all this mean? We find the answer in James 5:8. "Be ye also patient; establish your hearts: for the coming of the Lord draweth nigh."

This rapid accumulation of wealth and these great labor troubles in our day are a double sign of the nearness of the second coming of the Lord Jesus Christ. During our day we have seen the greatest accumulation of wealth and the greatest labor troubles in the history of mankind. As surely as we have seen these things, we may know from Bible prophecy that the coming of the Lord draweth nigh.

Jesus prophesied that fear and distress would dominate the thinking and conditions of the people of the world, just before He would appear on the cloud at His second advent. We find this recorded in Luke 21:25-27: "And there shall be signs in the sun, and in the moon, and in the stars; and upon the earth distress of nations, with perplexity; the sea and the waves roaring; Men's hearts failing them for fear, and for looking after those things which are coming on the earth."

Is this what you see now? There never has been a time when so many people have lived in distress and fear as since 1940. There has been distress among all classes among all nations. Mankind today is afraid.

In an article entitled "Must We Be Scared To Death?" appearing in The Christian Century (Jan. 9, 1946) Winthrop S. Hudson says that "now there is fear—real fear, stark naked fear, a fear that is not a figment of the imagination—and we do not know how to live with it, nor how to handle it."

This is true. Humanity is in the grip of terrifying fear, and doesn't know how to free itself from it. This is a time of distress, fear and insecurity that surpasses any other time of which we have ever heard, or seen or read.

What does this mean? Look at the very next verse in this prophecy of Jesus. In verse 27, after speaking in verse 26 how men's hearts would fail them for fear, how fear would dominate the thinking of people in the last days, Jesus declares, "And **then shall they see the Son of Man coming in a cloud with power and great glory."**

Bible prophecy indicated that in the last days there would be the worst disasters and calamities in the history of the world. We read about this in Luke 21:11: "And great earthquakes shall be in divers places, and famines, and pestilences; and fearful sights and great signs shall there be from heaven."

Look at the earthquakes, the floods, the tidal waves, the cyclones, the hurricanes, and the famines of our day. Authentic records show that from the 12th to the 17th centuries there was on the average only one destructive earthquake in the period of each one hundred years. During the eighteenth century there were six destructive earthquakes. In the nineteenth century there were twelve destructive earthquakes. Since 1900 there has been an average of one destructive earthquake every year. During the last fifty years there have been more destructive earthquakes than occurred during the preceding eight hundred years.

When an old man draws near the grave he staggers as he walks. This world today is staggering to its end. These calamities and disasters are fore-runners of the approaching end of the world.

Bible prophecy declared that n the last days there would be the greatest preparation for war and the greatest plans for peace in the history of the world. You will find these predictions recorded in Joel 3 9, 10 and Isaiah 2 2-4. Do we see this in our day? Since 1900 we have witnessed the greatest war preparation and the greatest peace plans in the history of mankind. What does all this mean? It means that we have come to the final movements of this world's history.

Bible prophecy indicated that in the last days men would develop unparalleled powers of destruction. We read about this in the prophecy of Jeremiah 4:19, 20. "My bowels, my bowels! I am pained at my very heart; my heart maketh a noise in me; I cannot hold my peace, because thou hast heard O my soul, the sound of the trumpet, the alarm of war. **Destruction upon destruction is cried; for the whole land is spoiled:** Suddenly are my tents spoiled, and my curtains in a moment."

Do we see anything like this today? Look at the fearful destruction that was wrought by the bombing raids in world war II. Think of the atomic bomb and its fearful implications for destruction. Look at the projected trans-oceanic rockets, the germ sprays, cosmic rays, etc. These show us that the time is fast approaching when God will intervene, and as we read in Rev. 11:18, He will destroy them that destroy the earth.

Have you been impressed how fast things are moving in our world today? I am sure that you have. I don't see how anybody could live in these strenuous days without being conscious of the rapid march of events from day to day. More history is made in one year now than formerly in a century. Ever since 1910 there has been a most marked speeding up of history.

Scripture shows that in the last days there would come just such a speeding up in living. You know of course, that the faster you keep moving, the quicker you reach your destination. This very speeding up of affairs shows that we are swiftly approaching the end of time.

Jesus declared that the last days would be like the days of Noah before the flood, and the days of Lot just before Sodom was destroyed. How was it in the times of Noah and Lot? The Scriptures reveal that these were times of intemperance, immorality, lawlessness, easy divorce, a craze for pleasure and a marked indifference to the requirements of the law of God Isn't this exactly what we see today?   Everybody knows that our day is a day of marked intemperance, immorality, crime, lawlessness, easy divorce, a craze for pleasure and a disregard for the law of God.

In a little town in one of our mid-western states two girls went for a ride with some boys in a car. There was an accident. The girls were killed. They took them to the morgue. Nobody knew just who they were, so the city clerk announced over the radio that mothers whose girls had gone out and not returned that night should come to the morgue to assist in the identification of the girls. The next morning seventy mothers in that little town appeared at the morgue to identify the girls. If this is the way in a small town, how about conditions in a larger city?

Crime has become so bad that day after day, night after night, some person is murdered on the average of every forty minutes. One out of every four hundred people is doomed to be shot, stabbed, poisoned, choked or black-jacked. What will the outcome be? Jesus says in Matt. 24:37: "but as the days of Noah were, so shall also the coming of the Son of man be." In the time of Noah man became so corrupt, so sinful, that the only thing God could do was to take the few good people out of the world into the ark and blot out the rest with the flood. So, Jesus Christ is coming to take the righteous to heaven, and destroy the wicked.

The most positive sign that He is coming soon is the fact that the message of His coming has already been carried to almost every nation on the globe. Christ's disciples asked Him, "What shall be the sign of Thy coming and of the end of the world?"   In His answer Jesus indicated, that the most direct sign of the approach of His coming would be the proclamation of a special message to the people of every nation, to inform them of the nearness of His return. We find this in Matt. 24:14: "And this gospel of the kingdom shall be preached in all the world for a witness unto all nations; and then shall the end come."

This message of the soon coming of Christ is being preached now to almost every nation in the world. Hence the end must be very near. Jesus declares, that when this gospel of the kingdom, the good news of his soon coming kingdom, has been preached to the people of every nation, then—at that very time—the end shall come.

Some people ridicule the idea that Christ is coming soon. They say that there is nothing to indicate that the end is now near, any more than there ever has been. Do you know that people who talk this way are themselves a sign that the end is near?

A minister preached on the prophecies one night to show that the coming of Christ is near. A man stopped him on the street the next day and said, "I understand Sir, that you preached last night that Christ is coming soon I tell you there is nothing to it. Things will go on forever just as they always have. Show me one sign that the end is really near."

The minister pulled out a little Bible which he always carried with him. He turned to II Peter 3.3-4 and read to the man. "Knowing this first that there shall come in the last day scoffers, walking after their own lusts, and saying, Where is the promise of his coming? for since the fathers fell asleep, all things continue as they were from the beginning of the creation."

After reading the text and emphasizing the appropriate portions of it, the minister said quietly to the man, "Brother, according to this prophecy, you are the last sign I have seen."

Do you know that there are in particular eleven characteristics that mark our day as different from any other generation of mankind who have ever lived on this earth? According to Bible prophecy each of these is an infallible sign and incontrovertible evidence that the second coming of Christ is at the door. What are these eleven great signs of Christ's coming? Here they are.

The greatest increase of knowledge of all past ages.

The introduction and development of rapid transit

The unprecedented speeding up of events.

The greatest and most rapid accumulation of wealth.

The most extensive and intensive labor troubles.

The two greatest and worst wars that the world has ever seen.

The most marked unrest, insecurity and distress

The most extensive and destructive war preparations.

The greatest peace plans that have ever been proposed.

The most appalling moral degeneracy according to the light and knowledge that God has given to men.

The greatest missionary movement ever known to carry God's special last day message to every nation.

What do these eleven great signs mean? Here is the answer in Matt. 24:33, "So likewise ye, when ye shall see all these things, know that He is near, even at the doors." It means that the coming of Jesus Christ is at the door.

I have here a chart that gives a list of twenty-four different items from Bible prophecy regarding conditions in the last days.

The last days are to be characterized by a great
1. Accumulation of Wealth—Jas. 5:3.
2. Labor Troubles—Jas. 5.4-8
3. War Preparations—Joel 3:14, 9, 10.
4. Disarmament Talk—Isa. 2·2-4.
5. Awakening of the East—Joel 3:12.
6. Increase of Knowledge—Dan. 12:4.
7. Unrest and Upheaval—Luke 21:25-27.
8. Craze for Pleasure—2 Tim. 3 1-4.
9. Religious Skepticism—Luke 18.8.
10. Intemperance and Physical Degeneracy—Luke 17:29, 30; Ezek. 16:49, 50.
11. Falling Away from Bible Truth—2 Tim. 4:1-4; Isa. 30:8-10.
12. Moral Degeneracy and Decline of Spirituality—2 Tim. 3:1-5.

The last days are to be a time of
13. Rapid Transit—Nahum. 2 3-5.
14. Unparalleled Travel—Dan. 12 4.
15. Destructive Earthquakes, Cyclones, etc.—Luke 21·11.
16. Destructive Insects, Pests, etc.—Joel 1:1-4, 2.1.
17. Abounding Lawlessness—Matt. 24:12.
18. Bloody Crimes—Eze. 7:23.
19. Breaking of Marriage Ties—Matt. 24:37-39
20. Scoffing at Lord's Coming—2 Peter 3 3-5.
21. Turning to Spiritism—1 Tim. 4·1, 2.
22. Deceptive Miracles—Rev. 16·14.
23. Rise of Many False Religions—2 Peter 1:2.
24. Giving of special message of Rev. 14·6-14, to all the world to prepare way for the coming of Christ

This makes a list of 24 different items that Bible prophecy declared would be seen in the last days of this world's history. Every person knows that every one of these twenty-four items is now taking place before our very eyes. This day are these Scriptures fulfilled in your ears. What does all this mean? It means exactly what Jesus said in Matt. 24:33, "When you see all these things know that it is near, even at the door."

This is the last generation that will ever live on this earth in its present condition. We find that in Matt. 24.34, after Jesus told how the time would come when all these signs would be fulfilled. He declares that the generation of people, who see all these signs fulfilled, will not pass off the stage of action until all is consummated.

This is the last hour. Time is shorter than you think. I wonder if I have made this subject plain to you. How many believe that according to the prophecies of the Bible, the return of Jesus Christ must be very near? Will you signify by the uplifted hand, please? Yes, I am glad to see that you believe the prophecies of God's word.

Friends, this brings you and me face to face with the most vital issue of all our lives. Are we ready to meet Jesus Christ? Prepare to meet thy God. Get ready to meet the coming King.

Your only hope for the future is to be ready when Jesus comes. Every soul who is not ready will be lost forever. Jesus says, "Be ye also ready. for in such an hour as you think not, the Son of man cometh."

Years ago in Ohio a young man committed a terrible crime. He was sentenced to death. His parents begged the governor to go and see the young .man and talk with him and try to help him. The governor agreed to go if no announcement was made beforehand about his coming. When the young man saw the governor approaching his cell he said to himself, "Here comes some preacher to bother me, I won't see him."

The governor stepped up to the bars and said, "Good morning, James." But he turned his back and refused to answer. The governor said, "Your friends have been talking to me about you. I have come to see you." "I don't care to talk today." The governor said, "If you knew the importance of my mission, I am sure you would give me an audience." "I don't care to talk, you will do me a favor to go away."

Sometime afterward the guard came by and said, "Well Jim, how did you and the governor come out?" "The governor! You don't mean to tell me that little man who looked like a preacher was the governor of this state?" "Yes, He came to see if he could help you."

A few days later when this young man was led to the gallows, and they put the black cap over his face, he cried out, "Oh what a fool I was. He wanted to help me and I wouldn't let him."

Friend of mine, Jesus wants to help you. He came and died on the cross that you might have eternal life. He is able to save to the uttermost, all who come unto God by Him. He wants to save you. Oh, I hope you will let Him help you tonight. How many are ready to say, "Preacher, I feel my need of being ready to meet Jesus, I want you to pray to Christ to help me to be ready." Will you lift your hands, please? Yes, it seems every hand is raised to God for help.

Let us pray. "Heavenly Father, we thank thee for thy great love in giving Jesus, Thine own dear Son to save us. Help us to accept the wonderful salvation that Thou hast provided. We thank Thee that thou hast shown us so plainly too that Jesus Christ is coming soon. Lord, we want to be ready. The saddest thing that could ever happen to any of us would be if we were found unprepared. We thank Thee, Lord, that thou wilt help us to be ready if we will only look to Thee and receive Jesus into our hearts. Lord, Thou hast seen all these hands that have been raised to Thee for help. O Lord, I do pray that Thou wilt reach down Thy mighty saving arm from heaven into every life here and by Thy saving power make each of us ready to meet Jesus. We ask it in His precious name and for His sake. Amen."

The Destiny of the Four Great Powers

(Preached on the Third Tuesday of the Campaign)

Daniel spake and said, "I saw in my vision by night, and behold the four winds of the heaven strove upon the great sea. And four great beasts came up from the sea. diverse one from another" This is the reading of Daniel 7 2, 3.

Daniel was standing by the sea shore. He saw the four winds lashing the sea in all their fury. Up from the surging waters came four great monsters one after another. The question naturally arises, What does all this mean? What does the great sea signify? What do those four winds represent? What are those four beasts?

If I should give you my opinion as to what this great sea signifies, what those four winds represent, and who those four beasts are, that would not settle the matter for a certainty. There is only one way to be sure what these items really mean and that is to compare scripture with scripture, and let the Bible declare what these things mean.

We inquire first, what are the four great beasts? I turn to Daniel 7:17: "These great beasts, which are four, are four kings, which shall arise out of the earth." Isn't that plain? A child of six or seven years old may understand that.

These four beasts are four kings or four kingdoms that are to arise one after another upon the earth. Notice Daniel 7.23, the words of the angel Gabriel speaking to Daniel: "Thus he said, **The fourth beast shall be the fourth kingdom upon the earth.**" Think of this for a moment. The fourth beast is the fourth kingdom. You can see, anybody couldn't help but see, that since the fourth beast is the fourth kingdom, the third beast is the third kingdom, and the second beast must be the second kingdom, and the first beast must be the first kingdom. These four beasts represent the first, second, third and fourth world empires of prophecy.

I want you to mark this point well. This is not my opinion or my interpretation. This is God's own interpretation of God's own word. This is why I refuse to have people place a denominational tag on these Bible lectures. The interpretation that these four beasts are four world kingdoms is not a Methodist interpretation; it is not a Baptist interpretation; it is not the Presbyterian interpretation. It is God's own interpretation of His own word.

It is very interesting to note that men use this same principle that God used so long ago. God used certain animals to represent certain powers or nations. Men today are following this principle. They use certain animals to represent certain powers. For example, in the field of international politics, what does the lion represent today? Tell me right quick. Yes, England. What does the bear represent? Russia. What does the eagle represent? The United States. In the field of national politics in the United States you know what the donkey represents, don't you? You know what the elephant stands for? Listen, if you don't know what the donkey and the elephant stand for, you had better stay away from the polls.

A glance at a cartoon which gives pictures of certain powers under symbols, may more effectively teach a given idea than the reading of many columns of newsprint. I hold in my hand the **Des Moines Register** of Monday morning of this week, September 23, 1946. I want you to notice a cartoon which appeared just a little over twenty-four hours ago. Everybody knows that Uncle Sam is having a lot of trouble just now in getting along with Russia. We don't know how to do business with Russia. Our statesmen and diplomats are puzzled. The cartoonist depicts this difficulty by Uncle Sam holding a bear by the tail. He doesn't know what to do with the bear. He doesn't dare let go of the tail, for fear it will bite him.

Looking at this cartoon gives you a better idea of the strained relations between the United States and Russia than by reading many columns of newsprint. It puts the idea over. As the Chinese say, one picture is worth ten thousand words. God knew this long before men ever knew it. Here in Daniel 7 God has used cartoons to depict the history of nations. A glance at these cartoons may give us a better idea than to read volumes of history.

I have a clipping from the **Washington Evening Star.** An article appeared with the headline, "Lion and Bear Renew Their Ancient Feud." Do you think people understood what this meant? Everybody knew that the lion and bear meant that England and Russia were still in trouble about their rights in the Near East. I come now to the second figure. Remember these four great beasts came up from the great sea. What does this great sea signify? Put down Revelation 17 15 and see how plain this is: "The waters which thou sawest . . . are peoples, and multitudes, and nations." The Lord couldn't make it any plainer. He says in so many words that the waters represent the peoples of the earth. We still use the same figure. If we see a great audience of ten thousand or fifty thousand, we say, "A great sea of faces." This great sea from which these four beasts came up represents the peoples of the earth.

Now take the third figure. What about those four winds? What does scripture say? In Isaiah 21:1, 2, the wars that the Medes waged against Babylon are compared to winds from the south. In Zechariah 7.14 the wars by which the Jews were scattered all over the earth are compared to a whirlwind. So the four winds represent wars, uprisings, revolutions among the nations.

Thus we have God's own interpretaton of these three similitudes. The "four beasts" are four world powers that will arise one after another. The great "sea" is the peoples of the earth. The "four winds" are wars and uprisings among the people.

Notice how strikingly the Master Artist pictures the truth. Daniel was standing by the sea shore. The four winds were lashing the sea in their fury. Up from those surging waters came four great beasts one after another. This is God's way of picturing, that, as a result of wars and upheavals among the people of the earth, four great powers will arise one after another and rule the world.

Let us look at the first cartoon set forth in this seventh chapter of Daniel. I read from Daniel 7 4. "The first was like a lion, and had eagle's wings:" (As the speaker read these words from the Bible, a chart depicting this lion was lowered in view of the audience.) What world power does this represent? Put down Jeremiah 50.43, 44, reading: "The king of Babylon hath heard the report of them . . . Behold, he shall come up like a lion from the swelling of Jordan unto the habitation of the strong:" The king of Babylon is compared to a lion.

These four beasts cover the same four kingdoms, the same four world powers, as the four divisions of that composite, metal man of Daniel 2, on which I spoke at the first meeting of this Bible Institute at the Shrine auditorium on Sunday night, September 8. (At this juncture a chart depicting this metal man was lowered.) In Daniel 2 we found that the gold, the silver, the brass, and the iron represented the four world powers of Babylon, Persia, Grecia, and Rome The prophecy of Daniel 2 shows that the fourth kingdom would be followed in due time by the establishment of the everlasting kingdom of God. In Daniel 7:17, 18 the angel explained to Daniel that these four beasts are four kingdoms and that the fourth kingdom would be followed in due time by the establishment of God's everlasting kingdom. On the basis of the mathematical axiom that "things equal to each other are the same thing," it is proven that the four beasts of Daniel 7 represented the same four world empires as the gold, the silver, the brass, and the iron of the composite, metal man of Daniel 2.

Hence this first beast represented the kingdom of Babylon. The lion, as the first beast, corresponds exactly to the first division of the composite metal man, the head of gold.

In the British museum there is a stone lion with two wings that was actually dug up from Nebuchadnezzar's palace in Babylon. Babylon thus acknowledged that their empire was the one that God pictured as a lion with two wings

What is the meaning of those eagle wings on the back of the lion? You can see that this is a cartoon. There never was a real lion that had two wings on its back like an eagle. What do those eagle's wings signify? Here it is. Put down Deut. 28:49. Every point is explained in the Bible. This text used the figure, "As swift as the eagle flieth" In Bible symbolism eagles' wings denote swiftness or celerity of movement This meant that Babylon would come to a position of world dominion in a very short time. This is exactly what happened. Babylon attained a position of world supremacy during the forty-three years of Nebuchadnezzar's reign. In B. C. 690 Babylon was subject to Assyria and was a part of the Assyrian empire. Ninety years later she was mistress of the world She flew to the supremacy of power as if on eagle's wings The prophecy of Habakkuk 1.6-8 in describing the conquest of the Babylonians or the Chaldeans says, "They shall fly as the eagle that hasteth to eat"

Daniel saw a change come over this lion I read from Daniel 7.4, "The first was like a lion and had eagle's wings· I beheld till the wings thereof were ·plucked, and it was lifted up from the earth, and made stand upon the feet as a man, and a man's heart was given to it" This pictures the decline of Babylon after the time of Nebuchadnezzar The glory of ancient Babylon passed away with Nebuchadnezzar. His successors were not brave and aggressive like that great king. The empire made no more conquests. The eagle's wings had been plucked. No longer did he fly as the eagle that hasteth to eat. You will recall that when the mysterious handwriting appeared on ·the wall on the night that Babylon fell, Belshazzar, instead of being lion-hearted, was so weakhearted that his knees smote one against the other. The courage and the boldness of the lion were gone and a man's heart, weak, timorous, and faint had been given to the Babylonian lion.

Notice how graphically, how impressively God pictured the rise and decline of ancient Babylon in a few bold strokes. The wings showed how quickly it would come to world dominion. Then the wings were plucked. There would be no more conquests. The empire would decline. This may give you a better idea of the history of ancient Babylon than if you went to the library and spent weeks pouring over volume after volume of old Babylonian history.

Now we come to the second beast I read Daniel 7·5: "And behold another beast, a second, like to a bear, and it raised itself on one side," (and notice) "it had three ribs in the mouth of it between the teeth of it: and they said thus unto it, Arise, devour much flesh." (As the speaker read this verse, a chart showing this scene was disclosed to the audience.)

This second beast represented the world power that followed Babylon which was Persia. Notice that the second beast, the bear, corresponds exactly to the second division of the composite metal man, the breast and arms of silver. Those three ribs in the mouth of that bear represent the three provinces of Babylon, Lydia, and Egypt. They are said to be between the teeth of the bear because those countries were ground down and oppressed by Persia. They are called ribs because those provinces as they were added to the Persian empire greatly strengthened the empire.

Next we come to the third beast. I read from the 6th verse. "After this I beheld, and lo another, like a leopard, which had upon the back of it four wings," (just twice the number the lion had) "had upon the back of it four wings of a fowl; the beast had also four heads; and dominion was given to it" (As this verse was read a chart depicting this scene was lowered in view of the audience)

This third beast, the leopard, represented the third world power that followed Persia, which was Grecia. Notice again, the third beast, the leopard, corresponds exactly to the third division of the composite metal man the sides of brass.

What about those four wings? You can see through this. Since the two wings on the back of the lion meant that Babylon would come to supremacy speedily, the four wings on the back of this swift-footed animal meant that this third power would come to world supremacy in an exceedingly short space of time. This is exactly what happened. The conquest of the world by the Grecians under Alexander is without parallel in ancient history in the swiftness of its accomplishment. Alexander conquered the known world in a military campaign of twelve years

This leopard had four heads. What does this mean? Within fifteen years after Alexander died his great world empire was divided into four parts, just as you see the four heads upon that Leopard. It was divided among his four leading generals who were known as Cassander, Lysimachus, Ptolemy and Seleucus.

Alexander had dozens of generals. Why didn't his great world empire break up into ten parts, among ten of the generals? Why wasn't it divided into five parts among five generals? Or why not into three parts among three generals? Over two hundred years before this, Bible prophecy had indicated that the leopard with four heads meant that this third kingdom would be divided into four parts. And that is what happened. This shows how the Bible accurately forecasts the future centuries in advance. This is one of the unimpeachable evidences of the authenticity and divine inspiration of the Holy Scriptures. Thousands of infidels have been converted by the witness of Bible prophecy. As they see how the Bible foretold things centuries ahead, and everything has been fulfilled to the very letter, they are forced to conclude that the Bible comes from a higher source than human, and what could that source be except from the great God of heaven, Who alone knows the future.

Men know that nobody can read the future except God. The fact that the Bible foretells events proves that it is inspired by Him who alone can read the future. Thus it is that we read in 2 Peter 1:21: "The prophecy came not in old time by the will of man: but holy men of God spake as they were moved by the Holy Ghost." What else can the honest skeptic do in the face of these prophetic witnesses but admit that the Bible is a true book, the inspired Word of God?

Now we come to the fourth beast. I read from Daniel 7:7. "After this I saw in the night visions, and behold a fourth beast, dreadful and terrible, and strong exceedingly; and it had great iron teeth: it devoured and brake in pieces, and stamped the residue with the feet of it: and it was diverse from all the beasts that were before it; and it had ten horns." (As the speaker read this verse, a chart depicting this beast was lowered in view of the audience.)

Daniel was especially excited about this fourth beast. Notice verse 19: "Then I would know the truth of the fourth beast, which was diverse from all others, exceeding dreadful, whose teeth were of iron, and his nails of brass; which devoured, brake in pieces, and stamped the residue with his feet." In verse 23 the angel said that this fourth beast would be the fourth kingdom. This terrible beast represents the fourth world power that followed Grecia, which was Rome. The fourth beast corresponds exactly to the fourth division of the composite metal man, the legs of iron.

This beast has ten horns. What do they mean? Here it is in verse 24: "The ten horns out of this kingdom are ten kings that shall arise:" You see God tells us in so many words that those ten horns represented ten kingdoms into which this fourth world power would be divided. History tells us that between A. D. 351 and 483 the Roman empire in the West was divided into ten parts. Those ten kingdoms are the Anglo-Saxons, the Franks, the Visigoths, the Suevi, the Alemani, the Burgundians, the Lombards, the Heruli, the Ostrogoths, and the Vandals. Seven of these are on the map of Europe today under the names of England, France, Spain, Portugal, Germany, Switzerland, and Italy.

Daniel noticed a strange movement among these ten horns. An eleventh horn thrust itself up among the ten. This eleventh horn plucked up three of the ten horns by the roots. I read in Daniel 7.8 "I considered the horns, and, behold, there came up among them another little horn before whom there were three of the first horns plucked up by the roots." (As this was read a little horn appeared among the ten on the chart of this fourth beast.)

Some peope have asked why, even though this metal man had ten toes, we still have only seven of those kingdoms left on the map of Europe. It is because this eleventh horn came up and uprooted three of the ten. This is why only seven are on the map of Europe tonight.

Daniel inspects this little horn. He says: "Behold, in this horn were eyes," (not the uncultured eyes of a brute, but the keen, shrewd, intelligent eyes of a man, and more wonderful it had a mouth with which it put forth proud sayings, arrogant claims, and preposterous sayings) Here is the most remarkable symbol of the entire chapter of Daniel 7. This little horn is the Anti-Christ, who is destined to be a world dictator in the very near future. This is the most important part of the prophecy for you to understand. What power is this? Who is this little horn with eyes like the eyes of a man and a mouth speaking great things? Come back Friday night and we will begin just where we have stopped, and the Bible will tell you.

(Closing Prayer)

Our heavenly Father, we thank Thee for this prophecy. We thank Thee that the Word of God is true We know that no man could ever give a book like this that could tell the future beforehand. Help us to believe this Word. At last take us to be with Thee forever. We ask it in His precious name Amen.

The Key to Your Bible

(Bible Lesson Presented on the Third Thursday of the Campaign)

THE INAUGURATION OF THE WEEKLY BIBLE CLASS

(On the third Thursday night of the campaign the weekly Bible class was inaugurated. With this lecture is a copy of the lesson outline, which was mimeographed on punched note sheets and given to each person in attendance at this eleventh meeting. At the bottom of the outline are the Scripture references which the people were asked to fill in on the blank lines, as the lesson was presented. These are numbered according to the respective propositions on which they were used.)

(These Bible lesson outlines, as used for this weekly Bible class, from the third week to the fifteenth week inclusive, are reproduced in this volume on the above basis and in the respective order in which they were presented, in relation to the subjects presented in the sermons. The first two Bible studies are reproduced in full as they were given; the remainder are presented in outline form, with the Scripture references attached and numbered in relation to the propositions in the lessons.)

Since this is Bible class night we want everyone to bring his Bible. If you failed to bring your Bible tonight, be sure and bring it next Thursday night. We will have a count made on Bibles. We hope there will soon be a Bible for every person present. We have 58 Bibles tonight. Let us make it 100 next week, what do you say?

Our first lesson is quite significant, "The Key to Your Bible." This lesson is designed to help you see the great plan that lies back of the 66 books which we call the Bible, the Holy Scriptures, the Word of God. Notice the first proposition on the lesson outline. "An understanding of the general plan which lies back of the entire Bible becomes a key to admit us into the great truths of the Bible."

If you were making an automobile trip to a certain city you might secure a map on which you would trace your route before you start. This helps you to find the way. In the same manner, by knowing the great central plan of the Bible it helps us to find our way into the truths of the Bible.

Look at the first item under the second proposition. "The first two chapters in the Bible present our world as a new perfect earth." On the blank line fill in Gen. 1.1, 31.

I will ask Mr. Jayne to read these two verses. "In the beginning God created the heaven and the earth." Verse 31: "And God saw everything that He had made, and, behold, it was very good. And the evening and the morning were the sixth day."

Tell me, in what condition was the earth when God made it? He said that it was "very good." After God had prepared his world as a habitation for man, He surveyed what He had done, and He pronounced it "very good." Not simply good, but very good. It was perfect. It could not be improved upon.

Look at the second item under the second proposition. "The first two chapters in the Bible present—"Man pure and holy, talking with God face to face." On the blank line fill in Gen. 1:26. I will ask Mr. Reynolds to read this text.

"God said, Let us make man in our image, after our likeness: and let them have dominion over the fish of the sea, and over the fowl of the air, and over the cattle, and over all the earth, and over every creeping thing that creepeth upon the earth."

According to this verse God made man in His own image, after His own likeness. God made man pure and holy. Man was able to talk to God face to face.

Notice the third item under the second proposition. "The first two chapters in the Bible present—God's purpose to have a perfect world filled with a perfect number of perfect people with perfect bodies, for their enjoyment of perfect happiness forever." On the blank line write in Gen. 1.27, 28. We will ask Mr Felt to read this.

"So God created man in His own image, in the image of God created He him; male and female created He them. And God blessed them, and God said unto them, Be fruitful, and multiply, and replenish the earth, and subdue it: and have dominion over the fish of the sea, and over the fowl of the air, and over every living thing that moveth upon the earth."

There are three words in verse 28 that give us a key which unlocks God's plan for this world—"multiply, replenish, subdue." Those are the three words which enable us to see what plan God had in mind for this world.

Adam and Eve were perfect and holy. To this holy and perfect pair God said, "multiply." This shows it was God's plan to have this earth inhabited by holy beings just like the first pair. Then God said, "replenish the earth." The original Hebrew word signifies to fill to the full. It was God's plan to have the right number of people in this earth that would properly fill the world.

Please don't ask me what that number was that God had in mind. I do not know. It doubtless corresponds to the total number of people who will be saved from this world. God's plans are perfect. He never does too little. He never does too much. When He made this earth, He made it the right size according to the number of people He had in mind by whom it was to be inhabited.

Here is an illustration. I hold in my hand a half-pint tin cup. It holds exactly a half pint. If I say, fill this cup to the full with milk, that means to pour into this cup a half pint of milk. If you pour only a quarter of a pint, the cup will not be filled to the full. If you try to pour three-fourths of a pint of milk into this cup, it will run over.

So God's plan was to fill the earth to the full with righteous people. That meant that God had in His mind a certain definite number, a perfect number, just the right number of people to properly fill the earth

Now notice the last of these three key words. God said, "Subdue." God placed the first pair in this beautiful garden of Eden as their home. Other pairs in due time were to make themselves homes like the one that God gave to Adam and Eve In other words God's plan was for the entire world to be a perfect paradise in due time, filled up with the perfect number of perfect people. Each one was to have a perfect body and was to enjoy perfect happiness forever. A beautiful plan, wasn't it? A wonderful plan. If God's plan had been carried out. there never would have been any sickness, trouble, war, poverty, sorrow or death in this world. Why wasn't God's plan carried out from the beginning?

Look at the first item under the third proposition. "The third chapter in the Bible (Genesis 3) reveals how Satan led men to disobey God, hoping thereby to wreck God's beautiful plan for our world and man." On the blank line fill in Gen. 3.17, 19, 23. Mr. White will you read please

"Unto Adam He said, Because thou hast hearkened unto the voice of thy wife, and hast eaten of the tree, of which I commanded thee, saying, Thou shalt not eat of it: cursed is the ground for thy sake; in sorrow shalt thou eat of it all the days of thy life." "In the sweat of thy face shalt thou eat bread, till thou return unto the ground: for out of it wast thou taken: for dust thou art, and unto dust shalt thou return." "Therefore the Lord God sent him forth from the garden of Eden, to till the ground from whence he was taken."

You will notice in the 17th verse that because of man's sin the curse was pronounced. Then came the death sentence, "Dust thou art, and unto dust shalt thou return." Then He drove Adam and Eve out of the garden. They lost their beautiful Eden home, because of sin.

Look at the second item under the third proposition. "The third chapter reveals—how through Christ, the Son of God, the divine plan for our world will be accomplished in spite of sin." On the blank line record Gen. 3:15. The devil tried to wreck God's plan, but that plan will be accomplished through Jesus. Mr. Amundson please read the verse.

"I will put enmity between thee and the woman, and between thy seed and her Seed; it shall bruise thy head, and thou shalt bruise His heel." This promised Seed Who was to redeem man from the power of Satan was the Lord Jesus Christ, the Father's only begotten Son.

Notice the first item under the fourth proposition. "The last two chapters in the Bible present—our world as a new perfect world." On the blank line write Rev. 21:1; 22:3   Mr. Jayne we are back to you again.

"I saw a new heaven and a new earth. for the first heaven and the first earth were passed away; and there was no more sea."

You will notice that the next to the last chapter in the Bible tells how God is going to reconstruct, remake, regenerate this world into a new earth. Let us see what will be the condition of that new earth. Now read Revelation 22:3 "There shall be no more curse: but the throne of God and of the lamb shall be in it; and His servants shall serve Him:"

It says, "there shall be no more curse." If God removes the curse of sin, when He makes this earth new, then what kind of an earth will that new earth be? You tell me. It will be perfect. It will be just as it was in the beginning before sin entered. It will be restored to its Edenic beauty.

Notice the second item under the fourth proposition. "The last two chapters in the Bible present—man pure and holy, talking with God face to face." On the blank line record Rev. 22:4. Mr. Reynolds, we will hear from you on this verse. "They shall see His face; and His name shall be in their foreheads."

In talking about this New Jerusalem and this new earth where the righteous will live scripture says, "They shall see His face." Yes, redeemed man will be pure and holy, just like Adam and Eve before they sinned. They will talk with God face to face as Adam and Eve talked with God before they sinned.

Look at the third item under the fourth proposition. "The last two chapters in the Bible present—a perfect world filled with a perfect number of perfect people with perfect bodies, who will enjoy perfect happiness forever and ever." On the blank line fill in Rev. 21:3, 4. Mr. Felt, we will hear from you on this Scripture.

"I heard a great voice out of heaven saying, Behold, the tabernacle of God is with men, and He will dwell with them, and they shall be His people, and God Himself shall be with them, and be their God. And God shall wipe away all tears from their eyes; and there shall be no more death, neither sorrow, nor crying, neither shall there be any more pain: for the former things are passed away."

In this new earth the people will be perfect. There will be no crying, no sickness, no disease, no sorrow, no death. They will have perfect immortal bodies in which they will enjoy perfect happiness. Think of the first two chapters of the Bible, and then the last two chapters and note how God's plan is to be accomplished.

Look at the fifth proposition. "The Bible then is the unfolding of God's plan through Christ for the gathering out of this world an obedient people, to live forever in a perfect world." (John 3:16.)

Notice the sixth proposition. "The Bible has been given as man's Guidebook to this heavenly home." (Ps. 119:105.) This Scripture says, "Thy word is a lamp unto my feet, and a light unto my path."

Look at the seventh statement. "The third chapter from the beginning of the Bible, or Gen. 3, marks the entrance of sin, sorrow, and death, the pronouncing of the curse, the first glimpse of Satan, and man driven from Eden.

Now notice the eighth statement. "The third chapter from the close of the Bible, or Rev. 20, marks the exit of sin, sorrow and death, the removal of the curse, and the last glimpse of Satan, and man led back into Eden."

(At this juncture three slides were thrown on the screen to show how wonderfully the Bible traces out the plan of God for our world.)

Genesis 1 and 2, the first two chapters in the Bible, open the story with a new earth, everything perfect, man pure and holy, talking with God face to face. Then Revelation 21 and 22, the last two chapters of God's Book, close the story with a new earth again, everything perfect, and those who accept Jesus Christ, pure, holy, talking to God face to face.

Genesis 3, the third chapter from the beginning, marks the entrance of sin, sorrow, death, the curse pronounced, the first glimpse of Satan, man driven from Eden. The third chapter from the end of the Bible, Revelation 20, marks the exit of sin, sorrow, death, the curse removed, the last glimpse of Satan, and man led back into Eden.

(A large chart was then lowered into view on which God's plan for our world was traced out in harmony with the description which follows.)

Genesis 1 and 2 tells how the kingdom of God was inaugurated in the garden of Eden. Then comes the fall of man. The entrance of sin is recorded in the third chapter of Genesis. Notice when man disobeyed God the kingdom was lost through sin. Then the Bible picks up the story, beginning with Genesis 3, and from Genesis 3 to Revelation 20, it tells how the kingdom is to be restored. Then in Revelation 21 and 22 we have the kingdom restored in the New Jerusalem and in the new earth.

This chart reveals that if man had never sinned, he would have always walked in the way of holiness. He would have always enjoyed the kingdom of God. But when man sinned, he took the downward path, the way of disobedience. This way of disobedience ends in hell. If people keep on the path of disobedience, they will end in the lake of fire or in hell, as traced out upon this chart.

Here is something that is very important. After the fall men began to walk the way of disobedience. But in due time Jesus came. Do you see the cross set up along the way? Jesus came to take men off the way of disobedience and put them on the way of holiness that leads into the New Jerusalem. You will notice how graphically this is illustrated here. The way of holiness leads from the cross into the New Jerusalem and the new earth where the kingdom will be restored.

Here is a very special point. Do you see this little door at the foot of the cross? Jesus said in John 10:9, "I am the door: by Me if any man enter in, he shall be saved." It is only through Jesus that you can get off the way to hell and get on the path to heaven. He is the way. John 14:6 He says, "I am the way" There is no other. Acts 4:12 says, "There is none other name under heaven given among men, whereby we must be saved."

Friends, the big question is, Have you accepted Him? There are only two ways for travelers in the journey of life from the cradle to the grave. There is the way of disobedience that ends in hell, and the way of holiness that leads to the New Jerusalem Friend of mine, which of these ways are you traveling? You are bound to be on one way or the other tonight. There is no third route Words can never express how thankful I am that I made my decision to accept Jesus Christ and take the cross and follow the blessed Saviour all the way I thank Jesus that He took me off the way of disobedience and put me in the way of holiness.

You may talk against Billy Sunday all you want to, but it was in one of Billy Sunday's meetings that Mr. Shuler stepped off the way of disobedience into the way of holiness

How many with me want to bear a silent testimony of thanks to Jesus Christ for leading you to accept Him and putting you on the way of holiness? Would you raise your hands just now? Yes, I'm glad to see every hand raised I want to thank Jesus for doing that for me I wonder if there is one here tonight who has never received Jesus as his personal Saviour? Would you like to have us pray for you that you would receive Him? Do I see a hand? Is there one here who has never accepted Jesus and wants us to pray for you that you will receive Him? I am glad that we all have accepted Him

Look at the ninth proposition "In this new world the redeemed will have real bodies, life will be as real as it was with Adam at creation" On the blank line record Isa 65·17, 21-25 Mr White it is your turn to read

"For, behold. I create new heavens and a new earth and the former shall not be remembered, nor come into mind And they shall build houses, and inhabit them, and they shall plant vineyards. and eat the fruit of them They shall not build, and another inhabit, they shall not plant, and another eat· for as the days of a tree are the days of my people, and mine elect shall long enjoy the work of their hands They shall not labour in vain, nor bring forth for trouble; for they are the seed of the blessed of the Lord, and their offspring with them And it shall come to pass, that before they call, I will answer, and while they are yet speaking, I will hear The wolf and the lamb shall feed together, and the lion shall eat straw like the bullock and dust shall be the serpent's meat. They shall not hurt nor destroy in all my holy mountain, saith the Lord"

Notice how real life will be in heaven In the kingdom of God we will have real bodies; we will live in real houses; and we will eat real food I thank God it is real. It is not visionary, it is not fanciful; it's real.

Notice the tenth proposition (a) "This new earth will see the time when the will of God will be done in earth as it is in heaven. (Matt 6 10)

(b) When the meek will inherit the earth (Matt. 5·5)

(c) When the knowledge of God will cover all the earth. as the waters cover the sea (Heb. 2 14.)

(d) When Christ will reign forever on David's throne (Luke 1.31-33, Isa. 9.6, 7)

(e) When the promised inheritance will be bestowed upon Abraham and his seed. (Rom 4 13; Gal. 3 39) These are references you can look up when you go home. They will help you

Notice the eleventh proposition. "God invites every soul to have eternal happiness in His eternal plan, by choosing to obey His Son Christ Jesus." (John 3:16; Rev. 22:17.)

"The Spirit and the bride say, Come. And let him that heareth say, Come. And let him that is athirst come. And whosoever will, let him take the water of life freely."

Look at the twelfth statement. "Each person decides his own fate for eternity by whether or not he decides to obey the Lord." (Isa. 1·19, 20.) This is why it is so important to make your decision to obey God. Your fate depends on whether or not you decide to obey God. Isa. 1:19, 20 says, "If ye be willing and obedient, ye shall eat the good of the land; But if ye refuse and rebel, ye shall be devoured with the sword: for the mouth of the Lord hath spoken it."

Here is God's proposition. He says, if you will be willing and obedient to Me, I will give you a home in this glorious new world where you will eat the good of the land forever. But if you refuse to obey My commandments and rebel against My word. then you will be devoured with the sword. It is up to us. Which way will we take? I don't see how anyone could help but choose the first one. Surely none of us wants the Lord to destroy him. Why shouldn't we decide to be willing and obedient to God?

How many by the help of God do want to choose the first proposition, you want to be willing and obedient to God that you may live forever in His wonderful kingdom? May I see your hands? Yes, it seems that every hand is raised.

(Prayer)

Our heavenly Father, we thank Thee for this beautiful lesson from Thy word. Tonight we have received a new glimpse of Thy great plan. We thank Thee for this great group of people who love the Bible. and who are here tonight to earnestly search in its pages. Dear Lord, we pray that the Word of Gid will indeed be that light that will lead us along step by step until we come to the great city of light and live with Thee forever. We ask in Jesus' name. Amen.

LESSON I — THE KEY TO YOUR BIBLE

1. An understanding of the general plan which lies back of the entire Bible becomes a sort of key to admit us into the great truths of the Bible.
2. The first two chapters in the Bible present—
   (a) Our world as a new perfect earth
   (b) Man pure and holy and talking with God face to face
   (c) God's purpose to have a perfect world filled with a perfect number of perfect people with perfect bodies, for their enjoyment of perfect happiness forever .....
3. The third chapter reveals—
   (a) How Satan led man to disobey God, hoping thereby to wreck God's beautiful plan for our world and man ..
   (b) How through Christ, the Son of God, the divine plan for our world will be accomplished in spite of sin .
4. The last two chapters in the Bible present—
   (a) Our world as a new perfect world
   (b) Man pure and holy, and talking with God face to face
   (c) A perfect world filled with a perfect number of perfect people with perfect bodies, who will enjoy perfect happiness forever and ever...
5. The Bible then is the unfolding of God's plan through Christ for the gathering out from this world an obedient people, to live forever in a perfect world (Jno. 3:16.)
6. The Bible has been given as man's guidebook to this heavenly home (Ps. 119:105.)
7. The third chapter from the beginning of the Bible, or Gen. 3 marks the entrance of sin, sorrow, and death, the pronouncing of the curse, the first glimpse of Satan, and man driven from Eden.
8. The third chapter from the close of the Bible, or Rev. 20, marks the exit

of sin, sorrow and death, the removal of the curse, and the last glimpse of Satan, and man led back into Eden.

9. In this new world the redeemed will have real bodies, life will be as real, as it was with Adam at creation.. ..   . .

10. This new earth will bring the time—

(a) When the will of God will be done in earth as it is in heaven   (Matt. 6.10.)

(b) When the meek will inherit the earth.` (Matt 5:5)

(c) When the knowledge of God will cover all the earth, as the waters cover the sea. (Hab. 2·14.)

(d) When Christ will reign forever on David's throne.   (Luke 1·31-33; Isa. 9:6, 7.)

(e) When the promised inheritance will be bestowed upon Abraham and his seed.   (Rom. 4:13; Gal. 3:29.)

11. God invites every soul to have eternal happiness in His eternal plan, by choosing to obey His Son Christ Jesus.   (Jno. 3:16; Rev. 22 17.)

12. Each of us decides our own fate for eternity by whether or not we decide to obey the Lord. (Isa. 1:19, 20.)

(2a) Gen. 1 1, 31; (2b) Gen 1:26; (2c) Gen. 1.27, 28; (3a) Gen. 3:17, 19, 23; (3b) Gen, 3 15; (4a) Rev. 21:1; 22:3; (4b) Rev. 22:4; (4c) Rev. 21:3, 4: (9) Isa. 65:17, 21-25.

Who Is the Anti-christ?

The day is fast approaching when every person will have to decide whether he will obey Jesus Christ or Anti-christ. The Bible plainly shows that every soul will finally be brought to the place where he will either choose to obey Jesus Christ and be saved forever, or he will obey Anti-christ and be lost forever. The purpose of this Bible lecture is to let the Bible speak and show who is the Anti-christ and how we can take our stand for Jesus Christ.

Many people have a wrong understanding of this word Anti-christ. This word Anti-christ is composed of two Greek words, "Anti" and "christos." Some people think that the word "anti" in this case of the Anti-christ means against Christ, just as Anti-Cigarette League means a league against the use of cigarettes. It is true that the word "anti" in some cases means against, but in the case of Anti-christ the word "anti" means in the place of, or in the room of. This Greek preposition "anti" is used as a separate word twenty times in the New Testament and in every case except five it means in place of, or in the room of. For instance the Bible talks about an eye for an eye.

Anti-christ will appear as a Christian power acting for Jesus Christ. Anti-christ will have Christian names, Christian forms. In fact this power will claim to be the only true church of Jesus Christ. But it will be Satan's masterful counterfeit. Here it is set forth in 2 Thess. 2 3, 4.

"Let no man deceive you by any means: for that day shall not come, except there come a falling away first, and that man of sin be revealed, the son of perdition; who opposeth and exalteth himself above all that is called God, or that is worshipped; so that he as God sitteth in the temple of God, shewing himself that he is God."

Notice Anti-christ will claim to be God on earth, and he will sit in the temple of God. He will sit in the church and set himself forth as God. Anti-christ will claim to do the work of Christ. He will claim to hold the place of Christ on earth. He will claim to speak for Christ, but in reality he is Satan's counterfeit for Christ.

Tell me, how does a counterfeiter work? If some criminal wants to make counterfeit ten-dollar bills and pass them off on people, what does he do? Does he print those ten-dollar bills on pieces of brown paper? O, no! There isn't anybody in the United States that would be fooled by a piece of brown paper as being a ten-dollar bill. What does he do?

He makes those counterfeit ten-dollar bills just as nearly as he can like the genuine ones that are issued in the Bureau of Engraving in Washington, D. C. The more nearly he can make his counterfeits look like the genuine ten-dollar bills, the more people he can fool. **Never forget, the devil is the master counterfeiter.** That is the way he works in religion.

Put down 2 Cor. 11:14, 15. "No marvel; for Satan himself is transformed into an angel of light. Therefore it is no great thing if his ministers also be transformed as the ministers of righteousness." The more the devil can make his doctrines look like God's doctrine the more people he can fool with his counterfeit system.

You can know now that Anti-christ is the greatest counterfeit of Christianity that the world has ever known. In fact it is such a master counterfe that all the people in the world will be deceived by that system excepting a f people who really follow God. Here it is in the Bible. This is really shocki

But listen, it is time to tell the truth. It is time to get the facts. Put down Revelation 13:8. It is speaking here about that beast power against which the third-angel's message warns people. Speaking here of that beast power, it says, "And all," (not just a few) "And all that dwell upon the earth shall worship him, whose names are not written in the book of life of the Lamb slain from the foundation of the world." This shows us that the entire world will be deceived by this Anti-christ except a few people who really follow God. That is why it is so important that we understand this subject for ourselves.

Every person who doesn't know the real truth for himself will be deceived. Put down Matt. 24:24, 25. Jesus said, "There shall arise false Christs, and false prophets, and shall shew great signs and wonders; insomuch that if it were possible, they shall deceive the very elect." Notice that those deceptions will be so strong that they will almost deceive the elect. Why will not the elect be deceived? The 25th verse of this 24th chapter of Matthew tells. Jesus says, "Behold, I have told you before." To be forewarned is to be forearmed. In the Bible Christ has forewarned us of these coming deceptions. That is why it is so important to know for yourself what the Bible teaches. The Bible unmasks these great deceptions that will take the world captive. Plan not to miss a single lecture at this Bible Institute.

There is so much in the prophecies of Daniel and Revelation about the Anti-christ, that I can explain only a small part of it in this lecture. In Revelation 13 God tells us that the number of the Anti-christ is three 6's, 666. Listen. Some night, I will have that man's name hanging up here on a chart in 5 inch letters. When you count it, it will be exactly what God said it would be— 666. This Anti-christ has a mark which the Scripture calls the Mark of the Beast. He will attempt to impose that mark on every person.

Some night in the very near future behind closed doors I will let the Bible tell you what the Mark of the Beast is. Tickets will be free. There will be no charge to get in, but you can't get in without a ticket. The tickets will be offered free a week beforehand. This coming Sunday night I will show from Bible prophecy when the time came for God's special message for the last days to go forth, which will restore all these truths that Anti-christ has taken away.

I want to let the Word of God tear off the mask of the Anti-christ and show who he is. The mask must be torn off from the Anti-christ, or you will not know who he is because he is so cleverly masked in Christian forms. But remember that I do this with the utmost love to all.

The Bible shows there are three aspects of the Anti-christ. There is the Anti-christ of the past, the Anti-christ of the present, and the Anti-christ of the future. Anti-christ is set forth in Daniel 7 under the symbol of a little horn with the eyes like the eyes of a man and a mouth speaking great things. You will recall that on Tuesday night at this Bible Institute I gave a lecture on Daniel's vision of the four great beasts from the raging sea. We found that the first beast, the Lion, symbolized the empire of ancient Babylon. The bear with three ribs in his mouth was a symbol of the dual monarchy of Medo-Persia. The leopard with four heads and four wings was a figure of the Grecian empire. The terrible nondescript beast with ten horns was a symbol of the empire of Rome.

We found in Daniel 7:24 that those ten horns represented the ten kingdoms that were to arise out of the empire of Rome. We further discovered that these ten kingdoms came into existence on the map of Western Europe between 351 A. D. and 483 A. D.

Now I turn to Daniel 7:8 and read about this little horn: "I considered the horns, and behold there came up among them another little horn, before whom there were three of the first horns plucked up by the roots: and, behold, in this horn were eyes like the eyes of man, and a mouth speaking great things."

He tells us that this little horn came up among the ten and plucked up three of the original ten by the roots. Now the question to which you want the answer is, who is this power with eyes like the eyes of man, and a mouth speaking great things? All you need to do is to read closely Daniel 7. Note the specifications given regarding this power, and then find the power that fulfills the specifications.

Daniel 7 shows that this little horn or Anti-christ will operate in the realm of religion. This 7th chapter of Daniel also shows that this power will arise out of the ruins of the ancient Roman empire. Notice again as I direct your attention back to this 8th verse which I just read. Daniel 7:8, "I considered the horns and behold there came up among them," (among the ten,) "another little horn." This little horn arose among the ten. Those ten horns represented the ten kingdoms of Western Europe. Since this little horn arose among the ten, this shows that it represents some power that will come up in Western Europe. Hence the territory of Western Europe is where we must look for the little horn power or Anti-christ development.

Now look at Daniel 7 24. "The ten horns out of this kingdom are ten kings that shall arise and another," (referring to this little horn) "and another shall rise after them;" This little horn came up after the ten were already in existence. These ten horns as covered by the ten kingdoms of Western Rome came into existence from 351 A. D. to 483 A. D. Since this little horn came up after the ten, this shows it is some power that will come to its supremacy after 483 A. D.

Put the specifications together and what do you have? You have this. This little horn, the Anti-christ, is some religious system which arose in Western Europe after 483 A. D. and gained the supremacy over the nations. What power was this? There was only one power, not two, there's only one power that has ever been known in history that answers to these three specifications of Daniel 7, and that power is the **Papal power.**

This little horn plucked up three of those ten horns by the roots. So we find that in connection with the rise of the Papacy three of the orginal ten kingdoms of Western Rome were destroyed. Those three were· The Heruli in 493 A. D.; the Vandals in 534 A. D.; and the Ostrogoths in 538 A. D.

This prophecy of Daniel 7 foretold how long this little-horn power or Anti-christ would continue in power after he began to rule. You will notice Daniel 7·25: "He shall speak great words against the most High and shall wear out the saints of the most High, and think to change times and laws· and they shall be given into his hand until a time and times and the dividing of time."

This little-horn power is to continue in power for a time, times, and the dividing of time. You say, "That sounds pretty mysterious, Mr. Shuler." Yes, it does if you have not compared the Scriptures on this point. If you will read Revelation 12·6, 14 you will find that the Bible actually tells us that this time, times, and dividing of time is a period of 1260 days.

The Bible also shows us that in prophecy a day represents a year. Just as a beast represents a power or nation, a day in prophecy represents a year. You will find this in Ezekiel 4 6. God revealed two prophetic periods to Ezekiel. After He revealed these periods to him, He told him that He was to count each day as a year. This Papal power was to continue in power for 1260 days or 1260 years.

The time of this Papal supremacy began in 538. So if you will add 126(to 538 when the Papal supremacy began, what do you have? You have 179 Do you know what happened then? In 1798 on the 10th day of February French army entered the city of Rome and took the Pope prisoner and carr him back to France where he died in captivity. He continued in power for a time, times, and a dividing of time just as the Bible had prophesied. The Bible foretells that this Papal power is to be restored to power again in the last days, and in the closing scenes of earth's history will dominate the world once more.

Notice three items which this Anti-christ was to do. God gives the specifications here. I read from Daniel 7 25: "He shall speak great words against the most High, and shall wear out the saints of the most High, and think to change times and laws." This power is to speak great words against God. Has the Papal power done this? I want to read to you some of the Catholic teachings regarding the power of the Pope. I read from the Catholic National of July, 1895.

"The Pope is not only the representative of Jesus Christ, but he is Jesus Christ Himself, hidden under the veil of the flesh."

I want you to think of this. They claim that the Pope is Jesus Christ Himself in human flesh.

I haven't anything against the Pope as a man. I have no personal animosity against any Catholic. Every Catholic has as much right to his religion as I have to mine. There are just as good people in the Catholic church as there are in any other church. Nothing that I say here tonight is aimed at any Catholic or even against the Pope as a man personally. I am merely preaching what the Bible says and showing wherein the Papal system has fulfilled the prophecy of the Holy Scriptures.

Scripture declares that this power would speak great words against God. I have read their own claim, where they say that the Pope is Jesus Christ Himself in human flesh. No matter how wise the Pope is; no matter how good he is, he can't take the place of Jesus Christ for me. As a Protestant, as a believer in the Bible, as a lover of the Lord Jesus Christ, I protest with all my heart against any teaching that puts a mere man in the place of Jesus Christ. (Large number of amens heard.)

I read from Ferrari's Ecclesiastical Dictionary, a standard Catholic work which deals at length with the power of the Pope.

"The pope is so great in dignity and so exalted that he is not mere man, but as it were God, and the vicar of God."

Think of this! They claim that the pope is not mere man, but he is God n earth. As a protestant, as one who loves God, I cannot help but protest ·ainst any teaching that would take a mere man and make him God on earth. The pope claims to be the Vicar of Christ. Do you know that in claiming the vicar of Christ he actually admits that he is Anti-christ? Anti-christ Greek word. Vicar is an English word. Anti-christ translated into Eng- s vice-Christ or vicar of Christ. And vicar of Christ put into Greek is christos or Anti-christ. Just think of it! By claiming to be the vicar of t he actually pleads at the bar of the world that he is the Anti-christ.

Notice this next clause in Daniel 7.25, "He shall speak great words against ost High, and shall wear out the saints of the most High." Has the Pa- lone this? During the Dark Ages millions of saints were put to death ish persecutors. I read from Dr. William Edward Lecky from his book alism in Europe, Vol. 2, Part 2, Chap. 4, pp. 40, 41, revised edition. the church of Rome has shed more innocent blood than any other insti- that has ever existed among mankind, will be questioned by no Prostest- o has a complete knowledge of history." Yes, they have worn out the f the most High.

This was the time of which Isaac Watts sang,

"Must I be carried to the skies on flowery beds of ease;
While others fought to win the prize and sailed through bloody seas?"

Yes, millions sealed their testimony with their blood in the Dark Ages when this power ruled supreme.

Notice the third item in Daniel 7:25 It says, "He shall think to change times and law." Has the Papacy done this? I have two charts here that I think will make this so plain that nobody will miss seeing it. I have a chart giving the Ten Commandments as they were spoken by the Lord Himself in Exodus 20 3-17. Then here is another chart which lists the ten commandments as they are given in the Catholic catechism, as they are taught by the Catholic church. Now please compare the two and see for yourself.

God said, he will think to change the law of God. Let us read the 1st commandment of God: "Thou shalt have no other gods before Me" The first commandment according to the Catholic catechism is, "I am the Lord thy God. Thou shalt have no strange God's before me." This is essentially the same as it was given by the Lord.

Notice the second commandment as God gave it: "Thou shalt not make unto thee any graven image, or any likeness of anything that is in heaven above, or that is in the earth beneath, or that is in the water under the earth: thou shalt not bow down thyself to them, nor serve them:" Look now at the second commandment according to the Catholic catechism as taught by the Catholic church: "Thou shalt not take the name of the Lord thy God in vain." Tell me, does this second commandment in the Catholic catechism correspond in any way with the second commandment as given by God? No, it does not.

The second commandment, as given in the Catholic catechism agrees with the third commandment as God gave the commandments. The third commandment according to the ten as given by God is: "Thou shalt not take the name of the Lord thy God in vain" This corresponds to the second commandment as given in the Catholic catechism. Tell me what have they done with the second commandment about not bowing down to graven images? They have wiped the second commandment out completely from the list of God's precepts. Yes he has thought to change times and the law.

We read now the fourth commandment as given by the Lord in the Bible: "Remember the Sabbath day to keep it holy. Six days shalt thou labour, and do all thy work: But the seventh day is the Sabbath of the Lord thy God: in it thou shalt not do any work." Then He tells us that the reason is because "in six days the Lord made the heaven and earth, the sea, and all that in them is, and rested the seventh day: wherefore the Lord blessed the Sabbath day, and hallowed it."

Notice the third commandment according to papal authority "Remember that thou keep holy the Sabbath day." Don't you see how they have changed the Sabbath commandment? God is particular to tell us which day is the Sabbath. He tells us that the seventh day of the week on which He rested is the Sabbath for man. He says that He has hallowed or set apart the seventh day for man because on that day He rested after He had made the world in six days.

In the ten commandments as taught by the Catholic church it simply says, "Remember that thou keep holy the Sabbath day." They have left out all the part that refers to the seventh day. In fact there is no certain day specified. They changed that Sabbath commandment to make it apply to any day they wish to select. And believe it or not, millions have followed this Catholic power in this change without being aware of it. God's message for the last days will bring light on this question so men will know how to be true to God.

Next we read the fifth commandment of the Lord: "Honour thy father and thy mother:" The fourth in the papal list agrees with that exactly: "Honour thy father and thy mother."

God's sixth commandment is, "Thou shalt not kill." The fifth in the papal list is in accord with this

God's seventh precept says, "Thou shalt not commit adultery." The sixth in the list as given in the Catholic catechism is identical with this.

The eighth commandment says, "Thou shalt not steal." The seventh in the Catholic catechism agrees with this.

The ninth commandment—"Thou shalt not bear false witness against thy neighbor"—is identical in both lists.

But watch! The tenth commandment of God says, "Thou shalt not covet thy neighbour's house, thou shalt not covet thy neighbour's wife, nor his manservant, nor his maidservant, nor anything that is thy neighbour's." The ninth in the Catholic list reads, "Thou shalt not covet thy neighbour's wife Then the tenth in the Catholic list says, "Thou shalt not covet thy neighbour's goods."

Do you see where they got into trouble? Having done away with the second one, they only had nine left. They couldn't call it ten commandments and only have nine, so they cut the tenth one in two, to make up for the one they left out. Yes, "He shall think to change the times and the law of God."

Now I have a plain question for you. I think I know your answer in advance. Do you think they had any right to change God's Ten Commandments? What do you say? (Many No's heard) God has positively forbidden man to change one word of these Ten Commandments.

Here it is. Put down Deut. 4 2 and Matt. 5:17, 18.

In Deut. 4:2 He says, "Ye shall not add unto the word which I command you, neither shall ye diminish ought from it, that ye may keep the commandments of the Lord" Then Jesus said in Matt. 5:17, 18: "Think not that I am come to destroy the law, or the prophets; I am not come to destroy, but to fulfill. Verily I say unto you, till heaven and earth pass, one jot or one title shall in no wise pass from the law, till all be fulfilled."

Here is another question that we need to think through. What shall we do about this? Shall we keep God's commandments as they have been changed by the Catholic power? or shall we keep the commandments as God has given them and as they are recorded in the holy Scriptures?

> "Keep me true, Lord, true to You,
>   Keep me true, Lord, true to You;
>   May all I say or strive to do,
>   Prove dear Lord that I am true to You."

Friends, I want God to help me to be true to Him. There is only one way we can be true to the Lord and that is to receive the righteousness of Jesus Christ. There is only one person who has ever been born into this world who has never committed a single sin and that is the Lord Jesus Christ He was tempted in all points like as we are, yet without sin

He offered Himself as a lamb without spot. By His sinless life and atoning death He has provided a perfect righteousness for all who will receive Him. In 2 Cor. 5.21 we read: "He hath made Him to be sin for us, who knew no sin; that we might be made the righteousness of God in Him" Just think of it! Jesus actually offers to take all your sins on Himself and give you back His perfect righteousness in exchange for your sins. This is the best deal that you can ever make.

Suppose there was a man who had no other clothes but a soiled, thread-bare, ragged suit. A kind friend offers him a new, nice-fitting suit of the best material in exchange for his worthless suit. Would it take him long to decide what to do? No! He would make that exchange in a second. Why don't we just as quickly decide to give up all our sins to Jesus Christ and receive from Him righteousness and have all our sins covered by His spotless life? How many want to be remembered in prayer tonight that all your sins may be covered with the righteousness of Jesus? Will you lift the hand just now? Yes, it seems that every hand is raised.

(Prayer)

Blessed Lord Jesus, we do thank Thee that Thou didst give Thyself without spot for us We thank Thee that Thou didst stand every test We thank Thee that we can have Thy righteousness by faith. Our righteousness is like filthy rags. Tonight, O Lord, we want to give up every sin to Jesus and just take from Him His own righteousness. Grant that every soul here may be complete in Christ by taking His righteousness, and know the power of that blessed righteousness for righteous living day by day until He comes, then we may be ready to meet Him and go to be with Him forever. We ask in His precious name. Amen.

Infidelity Challenged, Refuted and Silenced

There isn't anybody in the world with a sound mind who doubts that 2 and 2 equal 4. In fact if a man did doubt it, he could very quickly prove it to himself. I hold two books in my right hand and I have two books in my left hand If I put these two books together, you can see it makes four books; 2 and 2 do equal 4.

Listen to me. There is a prophecy in Daniel which shows that just as surely as 2 and 2 make 4, just so surely the Bible is the true inspired Word of God and Jesus Christ is the true and only Saviour. Put down Daniel 9:24: "Seventy weeks are determined upon thy people and upon thy holy city, to finish the transgression, and to make an end of sins, and to make reconciliation for iniquity and to bring in everlasting righteousness, and to seal up the vision and prophecy, and to anoint the most Holy."

These are the words of the angel Gabriel to the prophet Daniel. He told him that seventy weeks were allotted to Daniel's people or the Jews as their special day of opportunity. "Seventy-weeks are determined upon thy people."

The question naturally arises, "When does this period of seventy weeks begin? The very next verse gives us the starting point of the seventy weeks. Put down Daniel 9.25. "Know therefore and understand, that from the going forth of the commandment to restore and to build Jerusalem unto the Messiah the Prince shall be seven weeks, and threescore and two weeks."

Gabriel declares that seven weeks, three score and two weeks, from the going forth of a certain commandment or decree for the restoration of Jerusalem will reach to the time when the Messiah will appear among men at His first advent. Does the Bible tell us when this decree went forth for the restoration of Jerusalem? Yes, it does

There are two certain books in the Old Testament, the books of Ezra and Nehemiah, that are devoted to the story of the restoration of Jerusalem after it was destroyed by Nebuchadnezzar in B. C. 606. Put down Ezra 6.14. It reads, "The elders of the Jews builded," (that is they rebuilt Jerusalem,) "and they prospered through the prophesying of Haggai the prophet and Zechariah the son of Iddo. And they builded, and finished it, according to the commandment of the God of Israel, and according to the commandment," (listen now,) "the commandment of Cyrus, and Darius, and Artaxerxes, king of Persia."

Three Persian kings acted a part in issuing the decree for the rebuilding and restoration of Jerusalem. In B. C. 538 Cyrus, king of Persia, issued a decree providing for the rebuilding of the Jewish temple at Jerusalem. Darius, king of Persia, reaffirmed this decree in B. C. 519. Then in B. C. 457 Artaxerxes Longimanus issued a decree providing for the restoration of the Jewish state at Jerusalem.

In Ezra 7.7-9 we learn that Artaxerxes issued this decree in the seventh year of his reign. History very clearly shows that the seventh year of Artaxerxes was B. C 457. By a close study of the seventh chapter of Ezra we learn that this decree of Artaxerxes went forth in the autumn of B. C. 457. We are ready now to drive down the first stake. This banner says, "Autumn of B. C 457, the beginning of the seventy-weeks "

84

(At this juncture a banner was lowered before the audience on which these words appeared in four inch letters. Seven other banners with inscriptions marking the various steps in the computation of the seventy weeks of Dan. 9:24 and the 2,300 days of Dan. 8:14 were lowered, as the speaker came to these respective points in his lecture.)

Gabriel declares that seven weeks, and three score and two weeks will reach from the going forth of this commandment to restore Jerusalem unto the time when the Messiah appears among men. Tell me quickly, How much is seven weeks, three score and two weeks? A score is 20. Three score is 60, 7 and 60 and 2 equals 69. How many days are there in 69 weeks? How many days in one week? Seven. If you want to know how many days there are in 69 weeks, you must multiply 69x7 and the result is 483.

We must remember that we are dealing with prophetic days and prophetic weeks In the Bible God has plainly shown to us that in prophecy we must count a day as a year. You will find this in your Bible in Ezekiel 4:6. God revealed certain prophetic periods to Ezekiel and then He told him that when he computed those periods he was to reckon each day as a year. "I have appointed thee," He says, "each day for a year."

This means that 69 weeks or 483 days in prophecy must be reckoned as 483 literal years. Now we will look at our measuring line. Unto the Messiah shall be 7 weeks (or 49 years,) three score and two weeks (or 434 years,) or unto the Messiah shall be 69 weeks (or 483 years) from the time the decree went forth in the autumn of B. C. 457 for the restoration of Jerusalem. Four hundred eighty-three years from the autumn of B. C 457, when that decree went forth for the restoration of Jerusalem, reached to the autumn of A. D. 27, the time when the Messiah was to appear according to Daniel 9:25.

Here's the way you can prove this. Four hundred fifty-six full years from the autumn of B. C. 457 reaches to the autumn of A. D. 1. If you subtract 456 from 483, the answer is 27. This would be A D. 27.

Did the Messiah appear in the autumn of A. D. 27? It was prophecied over 500 years beforehand that 483 years from the going forth of that decree of Artaxerxes in 457 B. C. would reach to the time when the Messiah would appear to men. Did this come true? I will give you some references. In John 1:41 we learn that the word Messiah signifies "the Anointed One." In Acts 10:38 we are told that God anointed Jesus of Nazareth with the Holy Ghost. Jesus is God's anointed one. He is the Messiah, and God anointed Him with the Holy Ghost. You know without my even telling you that God anointed Jesus with the Holy Ghost at His baptism· Put down Luke 3.21, 22. He was anointed with the Holy Ghost when He was baptized by John the Baptist in the river Jordan.

Did the baptism of Jesus Christ take place in A. D. 27, sixty-nine weeks from the going forth of that decree to restore Jerusalem in the autumn of B. C. 457? Put down Luke 3.1, 21, 22. There you find that the Bible shows us that Christ was baptized in the fifteenth year of Tiberius Caesar, a Roman Emperor. Tiberius Caesar began to reign jointly with his step-father, Augustus Caesar in A. D. 12. Thus the fifteenth year of Tiberius Caesar was A. D 27. Jesus Christ appeared as the Messiah exactly at the end of 69 weeks from the going forth of the commandment to restore and rebuild Jerusalem, as Daniel had prophecied over five hundred years beforehand. Now we drive down our second stake. "Autumn of A. D. 27, Messiah begins His work."

If you had been standing on the bank of the river Jordan in the autumn of A. D. 27, you would have seen a crowd on the bank of the river. There is a man in the river baptizing people. Now we see a man of outstanding, pure, and noble countenance press His way through the crowd. He walks into the river where John the Baptist is baptizing people He says, "I should like you to baptize Me." John the Baptist recognizes that he is in the presence of a superior being, a superior person. John the Baptist replies, "No, I ought not to baptize You; You baptize me." Then the man says, "Suffer it to be so now for thus it becometh us to fulfill all righteousness."

Isn't this a wonderful lesson to you and me? The perfect Son of God didn't leave anything off that God wants man to do. John took this Man and laid Him back in the water, and as He raised Him up from the water the heavens opened, and the Holy Ghost came down and rested upon Him as the Father's voice proclaimed, "This is My beloved Son in Whom I am well pleased." John turned to the people and said, "Behold the Lamb of God that taketh away the sins of the world "

Have you ever noticed the significance of the first words used by Jesus in His preaching? You will find these in Mark 1·14, 15. He said, "The time is fulfilled. Repent ye and believe the gospel." Jesus knew the prophecies. He had inspired the prophets to write them The time was fulfilled. The 69th week had expired It was the set time for the Messiah to appear. When God's great clock struck the end of the 69th week, the Messiah appeared.

Here's a question for the infidel. If the Bible is only the product of men's minds, as infidels claim, how could any man, of himself, foretell 565 years beforehand the exact year when Jesus Christ would be baptized and appear as the Messiah? Man cannot accurately foretell the future even one day ahead. The wisest of men observed this. He says in Proverbs 27:1, "Boast not thyself of tomorrow, for thou knowest not what a day may bring forth."

Yet here is a book that actually foretold 565 years ahead in Daniel 9.25, the year when the Messiah would appear. Doesn't this show that this must be the inspired word of that great God Who alone knows the future? Yes! As Peter says in 2 Peter 1:21, "The prophecy came not in old time by the will of man: but holy men of God spake as they were moved by the Holy Ghost."

Every Bible reader knows that the very moment Christ died on the cross, the moment He said, "It is finished," the veil in the temple was rent from the top to the bottom. This showed that the entire ceremonial system that God gave the Jews was brought to an end by the sacrifice of Jesus on the cross.

Daniel 9:26 tells what was to happen in the middle of this seventieth week I read: "He shall confirm the covenant with many for one week: and in the midst," (note that word,) "in the midst," or the middle of the week. That is in the middle of this seventieth week, "He shall cause the sacrifice and the oblation to cease." If you cut a week into two equal parts(tell me how much will you have in each half? You will have three and one-half days. There are seven days in the week and if you cut a week exactly in the middle, you will have three and one-half days in each of the equal parts.

Now we come to another one of our measuring rods. One-half of the seventieth week on the basis of the year-day principle would be 3½ years. The sixty-ninth week ended, as you have seen, in A. D. 27. If you add 3½ years to the autumn of A. D 27, it brings you to the spring of A D. 31. Now we drive down our third stake. "In the spring of A. D. 31 the Messiah puts an end to the sacrificial system by offering Himself as the Lamb of God." At this very time Jesus was crucified and caused the sacrificial system to end, by becoming the great sacrifice for sin.

There are four texts in the Bible which when put together actually show that it was foreshadowed 568 years beforehand how the Messiah would die, the very year, the month, the day, and the exact hour, if you please, that He would be cut off.

In Ps. 22:16 it was foretold that He would die by crucifixion. "They pierced My hands and My feet."

In Daniel 9 26, 27 it was foretold that He would be cut off in the middle of the seventieth week. This figures out to be the spring of A D 31.

In 1 Cor. 5:7 Paul declares that "Christ our passover is slain for us." He is the true pascal lamb

In Exodus 12.6 we find that the passover lamb was slain on the 14th day of the 1st Jewish month at 3 o'clock in the afternoon

Now just put them together. It means the Messiah was to be crucified and die in the spring of A. D. 31 on the 14th day of the first Jewish month at 3 o'clock in the afternoon. And that is exactly what happened   He was nailed to the cross on the 14th day of the first Jewish month, and at 3 o'clock in the afternoon He gave up the ghost as He said, "It is finished " Think of it! Five hundred sixty-eight years beforehand the Bible foretold how He would die, the year, the month, the day, and the exact hour

Now comes the challenge to the infidel   Where is the infidel that can tell 568 years beforehand the year, the month, and the exact hour that something is going to happen?   This is a challenge that no infidel ever has answered or ever can answer   The fact that the Bible did foretell this shows it to be the inspired word of the God of heaven Who knows the future   Infidelity is challenged, refuted, and silenced by the prophecy of Daniel 9.

You can be just as sure that Jesus Christ is the true Saviour, as that 2 and 2 make 4   Listen to me   Just as you take 2 and 2 and add them together and find it equals 4, you can take your pencil and by the same law of mathematical computation, according to Daniel, find for an absolute certainty that Jesus Christ is the One Who appeared as the Messiah at the end of the sixty-nine weeks from the going forth of the commandment to restore and rebuild Jerusalem. O, think what a sure basis we have for our faith in Jesus Christ!

"How firm a foundation, ye saints of the Lord,
  Is laid for your faith in His excellent word!"

What does all this mean to you and me? It means just what you read in Acts 4 12 and John 8 24. It means that there is no other name whereby you can be saved except the name of Jesus   It means, as Jesus said, "Except ye believe that I am He, ye shall die in your sins and perish " It means, friends, that the only wise course, the only safe way, the only right thing for you and me is to make sure that we receive Him as our personal Saviour

Did you notice how the love of God for your soul is revealed in the prophecy of Daniel 9? Put down Daniel 9 26. I read "After threescore and two weeks shall Messiah be cut off, but not for Himself." O, how the love of God is revealed in those three words, "not for Himself!" Jesus Christ never did anything for which He deserved to die   Pilate, the judge who tried Him and sentenced Him to death, said three times over, "Behold I have found no fault in this man " He died, but not for Himself. He was cut off, but not for Himself   He died for you; He died for me   All we like sheep have gone astray. We have turned everyone aside to his own way, but the Lord laid on this wonderful Lamb of God the iniquity of us all

As we read in 2 Cor. 5 21, "He hath made Him to be sin for us, who knew no sin; that we might be made the righteousness of God in Him " O, friends, think of this wonderful gospel! God actually takes your sins and charges them up against Jesus Christ's account   Then He takes the perfect life of Jesus Christ and credits you with that   O, such a wonderful gospel! The wonderful love of God.

Go back with me a little over nineteen hundred years ago to a little hill just outside of Jerusalem. There are three crosses raised on Golgotha's brow. Tell me if you will, Who is this One on the middle cross? You say, it is just a man named Jesus. No, the Man on that middle cross is the very Son of God Himself. The fact that it was the Son of God who died on the middle cross proves there is no other way to be saved except by the death of Jesus Christ. Jesus Christ is God's one and only and all-sufficient remedy for sin.

The next question is most vital. What have you done about the death of this Son of God on the cross? I hope you will bow before that cross tonight, and say, "Lord, I'll take the cross and follow all the way"

Mr. Gladstone, the great English statesman, was once asked, "What is the greatest question before the people of England today?" His friends thought he would discuss the relative importance of various political issues. Mr. Gladstone quietly said, "The supreme question before every person in England today is the relation of his heart to the Lord Jesus Christ." I believe Mr. Gladstone was exactly right. The supreme question before every soul is, What shall I do with this Jesus who is called the Christ? If you accept Him, you gain everything. If you reject them, you lose everything.

Suppose you fell into a deep lake and couldn't swim. You are sinking for the last time. A man plunges in and rescues you. Wouldn't you have some feeling in your heart toward that man? Wouldn't you want to show your appreciation? Jesus Christ has done far more than save you from drowning in any lake. He died to save you from everlasting destruction in hell. Don't you love Jesus for what He has done for you? O, I am sure that you want God to help you to follow this wonderful Jesus.

"Wonderful, wonderful Jesus,
    Who can compare with thee;
Wonderful, wonderful Jesus,
    Fairer than all art Thou to me.

Wonderful, wonderful Jesus,
    O how my soul loves thee;
Fairer than all the fairest
    Jesus art Thou to me."

We turn now to the remaining half of this seventieth week. Remember we have another half of this 70 weeks left In this half there are 3½ days in prophetic time or 3½ years. When we go forward 3½ years from the spring of A. D. 31, it brings us to the autumn of A. D. 34, as the end of the 70 weeks or 490 years allotted to the Jews. What happened in A. D. 34? I will tell you. The special day of opportunity given to the Jews came to an end and the apostles began to teach the gospel to the Gentiles.

Some Bible teachers apply this seventieth week to a future seven-year period that they say will come in between Rapture and the Revelation. Think how unreasonable to detach this seventieth week from the 69 weeks by an interval of over 1900 years and apply it to something yet in the future! Doesn't the seventieth week of a child's life begin directly following his sixty-ninth week? That is the way my mother counted my age.

The 70 weeks of Daniel 9 are bound to be the next seven years from the end of the sixty-ninth week Just as the sixty-ninth week began when the sixty-eighth week ended, so the seventieth week began when the sixty-ninth week ended. It could not cover any other seven-year period except from 27 A. D. to 34 A. D. It is a great mistake for any Bible teacher to apply this seventieth week to some seven-year period connected with the second advent of Christ.

Gabriel said, "Seventy weeks are **determined** upon thy people." This word "determined" means "cut off." The seventy weeks were "cut off" for the sake of the Jews. Cut off from what? Here is the answer in Daniel 8:14. I read:

"He said unto me, Unto two thousand and three hundred days; then shall the sanctuary be cleansed." The seventy weeks are cut off from the 2300 days. Seventy weeks are 490 days. Subtract 490 from 2300 and you have 1810 left. We have the 70 weeks or 490 days reaching from B. C. 457 to the autumn of A. D. 34. Then we have 1810 day-years left of this 2300 day-year period. Follow this closely, we are coming to something that is tremendously interesting.

If you take 34 and add 1810, what do you get? 1844! Now we drive down our last stake. It is inscribed, "Autumn of 1844, end of 2300 days." What was to happen then? Daniel 8·14 says, "Unto two thousand and three hundred days; then," (then what?) "then shall the sanctuary be cleansed." What is meant by the cleansing of the sanctuary set for 1844? Friends, do you know that more depends upon that 1844 date than upon any other date since the crucifixion and resurrection of Jesus Christ? According to Bible prophecy 1844 was to mark the greatest event in God's program since the crucifixion and resurrection of Jesus Christ.

It was to mark the opening of a special work in heaven that affects the destiny of every soul. It marked the rise of a movement in our world that is giving the last message to the world. The only way we can understand the real truth for our day is to understand the real significance of this cleansing of the sanctuary that has been going on ever since 1844. What is meant by this deeply significant phrase, "the cleansing of the sanctuary," that was set for 1844? Come back Tuesday night and we will open up the Bible on that subject. Shall we bow our heads in prayer?

(Prayer)

Our heavenly Father, we thank Thee for this wonderful prophecy. O, we thank Thee for the sure foundation we have in the Bible, the sure Rock, Christ Jesus. Tonight, Lord, our faith is stronger. We go out from here loving Jesus more. We have been drawn closer to Him. Help us to understand this great event in Thy program—the cleansing of the sanctuary. O, Lord, bring us all back Tuesday night to hear the rest of this vital prophecy. We pray in Jesus' name. Amen.

The Greatest Religious Discovery of the Twentieth Century

(Preached on the Fourth Tuesday of the Campaign)

"He said unto me, Unto two thousand and three hundred days; then shall the sanctuary be cleansed." This is the reading of Daniel 8:14.

In the lecture on Sunday night we found that the two thousand three-hundred days began in B C. 457 and ended in 1844. Here on this chart we have traced out how the 2300 days of Daniel 8 began in the autumn of B. C. 457, when that decree went forth for the restoration of Jerusalem, and reached down through the ages, past the cross of Christ, to that memorable date of 1844

What does the prophecy say will happen in 1844? Here it is in Daniel 8:14: "Unto two thousand and three hundred days; then shall the sanctuary be cleansed." Before we can understand what is meant by the cleansing of the sanctuary, we must first find out what constitutes the sanctuary What is the sanctuary? We find a direct answer to this question in Hebrews 9 1. "Then verily the first covenant had also ordinances of divine service, and a worldly sanctuary."

This verse declares that the old covenant had a worldly sanctuary. During that 1500-year period of the old covenant from the time of Moses to the cross of Christ, there was a building on the earth, that the Bible called "the worldly sanctuary." What was this worldly sanctuary? Scripture tells us in the next four verses, or Hebrews 9 2-5. I want you to notice how this description refers to the Mosaic tabernacle as portrayed on this chart. (A chart of the sanctuary was lowered into view)

We read in Heb. 9:2-5: "There was a tabernacle made: the first, wherein was the candlestick, and the table, and the shewbread; which is called the sanctuary. And after the second veil, the tabernacle which is called the Holiest of all; which had the golden censer, and the ark of the covenant overlaid round about with gold, wherein was the golden pot that had manna, and Aaron's rod that budded, and over it the cherubim of glory shadowing the mercy seat; of which we cannot now speak particularly."

There is no mistaking what object this Scripture refers to. This is a description of the tabernacle that Moses built in the wilderness at the Lord's direction. This tabernacle was later on merged into that wonderful Jewish temple at Jerusalem.

This worldly sanctuary, as you see pictured on the chart, had two apartments. The first apartment was called the holy place. The second apartment was called the most holy place, or the holy of holies. The priests entered this first apartment every day to perform certain ceremonial functions. Into the holy of holies, only one man could ever go, and he only one time in a year, and that was on the day of atonement when the worldly sanctuary was cleansed.

You will notice that in this first apartment there are three articles of furniture, the golden candlestick, the table of shewbread, and the golden altar of incense. In the second apartment, or the holy of holies, there was just one article of furniture, the ark of the covenant. This ark of the covenant was a box made out of a certain kind of oriental wood overlaid with gold. The cover of that box was beaten out of one piece of gold, and so beaten as to form the cover and at the same time form the figures of two golden angels with their wings outstretched, meeting exactly in the middle. These golden angels were called, "covering cherubim."

In this ark or chest was the most sacred document that the Lord ever gave to man. Do you know what that was? It was the ten commandments. This decalogue is the only document we have in this world today that came direct from God. The Bible is the inspired Word of God, but the ten commandments are above inspiration. They were spoken directly by the Lord and written by Him upon two tables of stone.

The cover of this ark was called the Mercy Seat, because there mercy was granted to the penitent sinner when the blood of the sacrificial victim was sprinkled either before the mercy seat, or upon it

This earthly sanctuary fulfilled a place in God's plan only until the crucifixion of Christ. At the very moment Jesus died upon the cross, when He said, "It is finished," the veil in this temple was rent from the top to the bottom. This showed that the service of God in the earthly sanctuary had come to an end.

The book of Hebrews shows that the worldly sanctuary was superseded by the heavenly sanctuary after the crucifixion of Jesus Christ. The earthly sanctuary in which the Levitical priests performed their ministry was a **type**, or **figure**, or **shadow** of the true tabernacle in heaven, where Jesus our High Priest now ministers the merits of His shed blood for us Put down Hebrews 8.1, 2. These are very interesting verses in which the writer sums up the first seven chapters of Hebrews.

In these verses he says, "Now of the things which we have spoken this is the sum "We have such an high priest, who is set on the right hand of the throne of his Majesty in the heavens; a minister of the sanctuary, and of the true tabernacle, which the Lord pitched, and not man."

He tells us that Jesus Christ, our High Priest, is ministering for us in the heavenly sanctuary. He is the minister of the sanctuary, the true tabernacle in heaven, which the Lord pitched and not man You will notice the contrast between the two sanctuaries The earthly tabernacle was where the Levitical priests performed their ministry. The heavenly temple is where the Lord Jesus Christ, our High Priest, performs His ministry The earthly tabernacle was built by Moses, built by man. The heavenly temple is the one that the Lord pitched, and not man.

By the ministry of the priests and the offering of the sacrifices, the record of the peoples' sins was transferred to the worldly sanctuary. Then once each year on the day of atonement, the earthly sanctuary was cleansed At that time a final disposition was made of the sins of the people. Do you know that one entire chapter in the Bible, Leviticus 16, is devoted to a description of the cleansing of the sanctuary on the day of atonement? This earthly sanctuary was cleansed on the day of atonement, which came upon the tenth day of the seventh Jewish month

On this day two goats were brought to the door of the tabernacle These goats were brought before the high priest. They had to be just alike in color, size, age, and appearance The high priest put his hands into a golden urn, and took out two lots. One of these lots was inscribed "La Jehovah " That is for the Lord. The other lot was inscribed "La Azazel," which means for the scapegoat. Then he placed these lots on the heads of these goats, and thus one goat was set aside for the Lord and the other was set aside for the scapegoat. Then he took a knife and thrust it into the heart of the Lord's goat. He caught the blood in a basin, and then, notice, for the only time in the year he passed right through the inner veil into the holy of holies and sprinkled the blood on the mercy seat.

After he had done this, he came out of the door of the tabernacle and placed his hands on the head of the scapegoat and, in type, cast the responsibility and burden of all sin upon this goat. Then the scapegoat was taken into the wilderness to perish.

Now follow me closely. The book of Hebrews in the New Testament shows that all that was a type, a figure, a shadow of Christ's redemptive work in the heavenly sanctuary. Put down Hebrews 8:5. There we learn that these priests in the worldly sanctuary served unto a "shadow" or "example" of heavenly things.

On the cross Jesus Christ offered Himself as the Lamb of God for our sins. Then forty days after His resurrection He ascended to heaven and began His work as our High Priest in the first apartment of the true tabernacle in heaven, which the Lord built and not man.

What was to happen in 1844? Daniel 8:14 says, "Unto two thousand and three hundred days; then shall the sanctuary be cleansed." This means in 1844 Jesus Christ moved his seat of His priestly ministration from the first apartment to the second apartment. In 1844 He entered upon the closing phase of His mediatorial work. What does this mean? It means that in 1844 the final period of this world's history began, and whatever we intend to do to be ready to meet Jesus, we must do quickly.

This day of atonement when the sanctuary was cleansed was a day of judgment of the professed people of God. The record of all their sins of the past year was blotted out when the sanctuary was cleansed. This means that the cleansing of the heavenly sanctuary between 1844 and the end of time will be a time of judgment of God's professed people, when their records will pass in review on the antitypical day of judgment.

A message in code is easily deciphered if you have a key to the code. You know every government has a code with which they can send messages. For instance our government can send messages to our ambassadors or our military men anywhere in the world, but they are in code. Nobody understands them, but the man who has the key to the code.

Daniel 8:14 is a message in code. "Unto two thousand and three hundred days then shall the sanctuary be cleansed." This contains two coded expressions, "Unto 2,300 days" and the "cleansing of the sanctuary." The Bible furnishes the key to these two coded expressions. When we compare the Scriptures, as we did here Sunday night, we find that "unto two thousand three hundred days," figures out to be 1844. Tonight as we compare the Scriptures, we find that the cleansing of the sanctuary means a work of divine judgment. According to the Bible this text in Daniel 8.14, "Unto two thousand and three hundred days then shall the sanctuary be cleansed," simply means this—Unto 1844, then shall the judgment begin.

In this judgment between 1844 and the end of time, decisions are being made, or will be made, as to who among the dead will rise with immortal bodies when the Lord Jesus descends from heaven at His second advent, and as to who among the living will be changed in a moment in the twinkling of an eye at His coming. Listen. Ever since 1844 the cases of men, beginning with the first man who died, Abel, have been passing in review before God. The judgment is making up the list of those who will live forever in God's glorious kingdom. Wouldn't you like to know how that list is made up for the heavenly kingdom? Then be sure and be here Thursday night. The Bible lesson Thursday night will show how that list is being made up for the heavenly kingdom. Don't miss hearing about it from the Bible.

You will notice how Daniel 8:14 is a key that opens up a most important religious discovery. It shows that the judgment began in heaven in 1844. The Bible shows that when the judgment begins in heaven, God's special last day message of Rev 14 6-12 will begin to go forth among men When the judgment sits in heaven, the great God will send a special message to tell the people that the judgment has begun and to show them how to prepare for the judgment. Here it is just as plain as can be. It is really wonderful what we are bringing out tonight. We are going into the very heart of the truth for our day. Put down Revelation 14.6, 7, 14.

"I saw another angel fly in the midst of heaven, having the everlasting gospel to preach unto them that dwell on the earth, and to every nation, and kindred, and tongue, and people, saying with a loud voice, Fear God, and give glory to him;" (get this next phrase,) "for the hour of His judgment is come: and worship Him that made heaven, and earth, and the sea, and the fountains of water." Then reading the 14th verse, "I looked, and behold a white cloud, and upon the cloud, One sat like unto the Son of man, having on His head a golden crown, and in His hand a sharp sickle."

I wish you would notice how this message is worded. Did you get the wording of God's message about the judgment? It didn't say that the hour of God's judgment has come, as though it pertained to some time in the past. It didn't say that the hour of God's judgment will come as though it pertains to some future time. What does the message say? "Fear God, for the hour of His judgment is come:" The judgment has begun. The time has arrived for the judgment to begin its session. "The hour of His judgment is come."

This special message for the last days, as pictured by the three angels preaching in mid-air, was to arise in the earth when the time came for the judgment to begin in heaven in 1844. We have this pictured here upon a chart. (At this juncture a chart depicting the three angels of Revelation 14.6-12 was lowered into view.)

He saw three angels flying one behind the other. Each was preaching a certain part of a great three-fold message. In verse 6 it says that the message of these three angels was to be preached to every nation, every kindred, every tongue, and every people.

Then in the fourteenth verse, it shows that when this three-fold message has been preached to every nation in the earth, Christ will come on the cloud. You will remember that I just finished reading this. "I looked, and behold a white cloud, and upon the cloud One sat like unto the Son of man, having on His head a golden crown, and in His hand a sharp sickle."

Notice how plainly this enables you to find what is the one true way of Jesus Christ for these days in which we live. You who have been attending these meetings will recall that on the second Thursday night of this Bible Institute, I spoke on the prophecy of these three angels of Revelation 14. I am interested to know how many are here tonight who heard that lecture. How many heard that lecture? (Many hands went up.) Yes, this shows that the same folks keep coming to these meetings, and they will get the most from these Bible lectures.

We found that this three-fold message is the true way of Jesus Christ for our day. Follow me closely. The fact that the hour of God's judgment came in 1844, shows that this three-fold message about the arrival of the judgment hour belongs to the period between 1844 and the end of time. This special three-fold message couldn't be preached before 1844.

Martin Luther could not have preached it. John Wesley could not have preached it. No. This three-fold message could not be preached before 1844, because the hour of God's judgment didn't come until the end of the twenty-three hundred day-years of Daniel 8.3, or in 1844. When this three-fold message has been preached to every nation, Christ will come the second time. How plain it is, that this three-fold message belongs to that period between 1844 and the end of time.

Mark this point well. This means that in our day there is some God-ordained movement that arose in 1844 by which this three-fold message is being carried to all the world. When you find that movement, connect yourself with it, you can know for an absolute certainty that you have found the true way of Jesus Christ for our time   All this will be made extra plain in subsequent meetings.

Let me say again that the purpose of these meetings, in harmony with our repeated announcements, is to unfold this special three-fold message for the last days. The movement which gives this message to the world is not merely another denomination. I want to repeat this. The movement that gives this three-fold message to the world will not be merely another denomination. This is why I refuse to have a denominational tag placed on these Bible lectures dealing with this three-fold message. The movement that gives this three-fold message to the world will not be merely another denomination added to a long list that is already in existence, **but it will be God's movement for the consummation of the gospel of Jesus Christ.**

We face the solemn facts that the final period of man's day began in 1844, and that Jesus Christ, our High Priest, is soon to close His work for sinners Soon the last case will be decided in the judgment. Then Jesus Christ will pronounce that solemn decree recorded in Revelation 22:11, 12 "He that is unjust, let him be unjust still: and he which is filthy let him be filthy still and he that is righteous, let him be righteous still: and he that is holy, let him be holy still. And, behold, I come quickly; and My reward is with me, to give every man according as his work shall be."

Friend, are you ready for that hour? As that decree finds you, so you will have to be. You can't make any change after that. He that is unjust, let him be. Whatever you intend to do to get ready to meet Jesus Christ, you have to do it before that decree is pronounced.

Under the Mosaic law in order for a sinner to receive pardon, he had to actually put his hand on the head of the lamb that he brought, and with his hands on the lamb's head confess the sins of which he was guilty. It was believed that by doing this, his sin was transferred from the man to the lamb, which represented Jesus This is why the lamb was killed and its blood taken to satisfy the claims of the ten commandments which this man had broken.

Now get this lesson. Christ is the true Lamb of God. We must actually lay our sins on Jesus Christ by repentance, by confession, by faith in Him as our personal Saviour. Unless you choose to put your sins on Jesus Christ, then your sins are still with you. The man who fails to obey Jesus Christ will be punished for his sins just the same as if Christ had never died at all.

A man employed in the Russian government under Czar Alexander I, found himself hopelessly bankrupt. He drew up a list of all his debts, and at the bottom of the list he wrote, "Who is going to pay all these debts?" He had lost much sleep over this. This day he fell asleep at his desk with the list on his desk. It so happened that Alexander I, the great Czar of all Russians of that day, was making a tour of this very department of the government. He saw the man asleep at his desk, and tiptoed close to him. Looking down over the sleeping head of the man, he saw the long list of debts, and there was that tremendous question, "Who is to pay all these debts?" Being seized with a good impulse, he pulled out his golden pen, and put two words after the question: "I, Alexander." When the man awoke, he was the happiest man in Russia. His great master, the Czar of all the Russians, had said that he would be responsible for these debts.

My friends, nobody here would like to see a list of all his sins on the screen. I guarantee if there were a list of your sins placed on this screen, you would go away, just as they went away that day when Jesus began to write in the sand.

Who is going to pay for all those sins? In the Bible sin is compared to a debt. In the Lord's Prayer it says, "Forgive us our debts, as we forgive our debtors." Sin is compared to a debt. Who is going to pay all these debts? O, thank God, Jesus is ready. He says in Isaiah 43 25, "I, even I, am He that blotteth out thy transgressions for mine own sake."

The big question is, "Have you put your case fully in the hands of Jesus Christ as your heavenly Advocate?" He says He is able to save to the uttermost all who come unto God by Him, seeing He ever liveth to make intercession for them. If you will do the coming, He will do the saving. Thank God, many people have found this to be so true here in these Bible Institute meetings. They have come to Jesus, they have surrendered their all to Him, and the Lord has wrought a work in their hearts. Jesus never fails. If we come to Him, He will save us to the uttermost.

No one ever came to Jesus and found that He didn't do the saving as He promised. How many of you want to put your case tonight fully in the hands of Jesus Christ? Just lift your hands. Yes, I am sure everyone here wants to do this.

(Prayer)

O, blessed Lord Jesus, we thank Thee that we know where Thou art tonight. Thou art at the right hand of the Father as our Great Mediator, our Intercessor, our High Priest, our Advocate. We are so thankful to know that if any man sins we have an Advocate with the Father, Jesus Christ, the righteous One, and that He is able to save to the uttermost all who come to Him because He ever lives to make intercession. Tonight, dear Lord, we want to put our cases fully in Thy hands. We are so glad we can do this We pray that every woman and man, and boy and girl in this audience may make sure that they put their case fully in the hands of such a wonderful Saviour. May it be that every one may so put his case in Thy hands, that when the judgment comes to our name, our name may be retained in the book of life for an everlasting happy home with Thee in Thy kingdom. We ask it in Thy precious name Amen.

The Key to Present Truth

Our Bible lesson tonight is entitled THE KEY TO PRESENT TRUTH. Notice the first proposition: "There is nothing more important for us than to know and obey the truth." Write on the blank line Isaiah 26.2. Mr. Hagen, we shall hear from you as to what the Bible says in Isaiah 26 2.

"Open ye the gates, that the righteous nation which keepeth the truth may enter in."

This text tells how many people in this auditorium, yes, how many people in the world, will actually go to heaven. How many people will go through the gates of heaven? To whom will the gates be opened? Listen now to what God says: "Open ye the gates, that the righteous nation which keepeth," (what?) "which keepeth the truth may enter in."

This word, "keepeth," is used in the sense of obey or follow. You cannot obey the truth until you first know what is the truth. We first need to learn the truth. This is why we have this Bible class. How lovely to see so many come here with their Bibles to learn the truth! We first need to learn the truth; then obey the truth; then adhere to the truth to the end. The three most important items in the world so far as you and I are concerned are first, learn the truth; second, obey the truth; third, stick to the truth to the end.

In view of the fact that those who keep the truth will pass through the gates to have an eternal, happy home in the city of God, isn't it plain that there is nothing more important for us than to know and follow the truth? The Bible speaks of "the present truth." Take your pencil and write in after Isaiah 26 2 the text, 2 Peter 1:12. The apostle Peter exhorts us to "be established in the present truth."

Present truth is truth which is especially adapted to a certain time or certain period. For instance, the message of Noah about the coming flood was a **present truth** to the generation of people who lived just prior to the deluge. The message of John the Baptist about getting ready to receive the Messiah was present truth to the Jews who lived in the days of John the Baptist. Listen! Here is a most vital item. Just as God had a message of present truth for the people who lived before the flood, for the people who lived before Christ appeared as the Messiah, He has a message of present truth for us who are living just before the second coming of Jesus Christ.

Notice the second proposition on the lesson sheet. "The real truth for our day and the true way of Christ for this generation is set forth in the threefold message of Rev. 14:6-14."

You will recall that on the second Thursday night of this Bible Institute I gave a sermon on the fourteenth chapter of Revelation verses 6-14. Here is a picture of what we find in Revelation 14.6-14. (At this juncture a chart was lowered depicting the three angels of Rev. 14.6-14.) He saw three angels flying along one behind the other. As he listened, he heard the first angel preach a certain message about the hour of God's judgment being come. He called upon men to "fear God; for the hour of His judgment is come: and to worship Him that made heaven and earth."

Then he listened again, and he heard the second angel add the solemn warning that Babylon the great is fallen, and that God's people are to come out of her. Next, he heard the third angel issue a solemn warning against worshiping the beast and his image, and against receiving the mark of the beast in the forehead or in the hand. Then what? The very next item after he heard this great three-fold message preached to the world was the coming of Jesus on the cloud to reap the harvest.

This makes it plain that this three-fold message is the present truth for the people who live in this closing period of earth's history. Hence this second proposition is firmly established. "The real truth for our day and the true way of Christ for our generation is set forth in the threefold message of Rev. 14 6-14."

Look at the third proposition. "The purpose of this message is to call out a people in every nation to keep the commandments of God and the faith of Jesus." On the blank line write Revelation 14 12.

Mr. Howard, we shall hear from you as to what God says in Revelation 14·12. "Here is the patience of the saints: here are they that keep the commandments of God and the faith of Jesus."

This makes it clear that the purpose of this message is to call out a people in every land to keep the commandments of God and the faith of Jesus.

Look at the fourth proposition. "This message was to arise in the earth when the hour came for God's judgment to begin in heaven." On the blank line record Revelation 14 6, 7.

Mr. Esquilla, let us hear from you. "I saw another angel fly in the midst of heaven, having the everlasting gospel to preach unto them that dwell on the earth, and to every nation, and kindred, and tongue, and people, saying with a loud voice, Fear God, and give glory to Him; for the hour of His judgment is come: and worship Him that made heaven, and earth, and the sea, and the fountains of waters."

Did you notice how this is worded? He says, "Fear God, and give glory to Him; for the hour of His judgment is come." He doesn't say that the hour of God's judgment will come as though it pertained to some time in the future But the burden of his message in that "the hour of His judgment is come." It has begun. The judgment is in session. This shows that this message will be preached in the earth when the time comes for the judgment to begin in heaven

Look at the fifth proposition. "The prophecy of the 2,300 days furnishes a key as to when the hour of God's judgment would come." This is based on Daniel 8:14 which says: "Unto two thousand and three hundred days; then shall the sanctuary be cleansed.

Look at the sixth proposition. "The 2,300 days began in B. C. 457 and ended in A. D. 1844."

On Sunday night of this week we figured this upon the blackboard. We had the banners here on the stage, which revealed the successive steps in the computation of this 2,300 day-year period.

We found that the 2,300 days began in B. C. 457 and reached to the autumn of A. D. 1844.

Notice the seventh proposition. "The cleansing of the sanctuary is identical with the hour of God's judgment in Rev. 14:6, 7. (Lev. 23.29, 30.)"

The day of atonement, when the earthly sanctuary was cleansed, was a day of judgment on the Jewish people. There isn't any day in the year that the Jews celebrate so carefully as this day of atonement. Did you read the Evening Tribune for today? It tells how the Jews in Des Moines are celebrating Friday sunset to Saturday sunset of this week as the great day of atonement. They regard it as the annual day of judgment.

According to Lev. 23:29, 30 whatsoever soul did not find pardon on this day was cut off. It was a day of judgment of the house of Israel. This shows that the cleansing of the heavenly sanctuary will be the hour of God's judgment of the church, or of the people of God.

Notice the eighth proposition. "Daniel 8:14 means unto 1844, then shall the judgment begin." In Daniel 8:14 we have two expressions in code. "Unto two thousand three hundred days." That is a code expression. The "cleansing of the sanctuary," is another expression in code. The only way to understand the Bible is to compare scripture with scripture. When we compare scripture with scripture we find that the two thousand three hundred days, when figured out, bring us to 1844. When we compare the scriptures we find that the "cleansing of the sanctuary" is a work of judgment.

Now we can understand Daniel 8:14. "Unto two thousand three hundred days," means 1844. "The cleansing of the sanctuary," is a work of judgment. Unto 1844 then shall the judgment begin.

Notice the ninth proposition. "Since God's special message for the last days was to arise when the hour of his judgment came (Rev. 14:6, 7,) it must have arisen in 1844." You will remember that the first angel's message is, "Fear God, for the hour of His judgment is come." This shows that this message will arise in the world when the hour of God's judgment is ushered in at the end of this 2,300 day-years in 1844. This means that there is some God-ordained movement in this earth that arose in 1844, by which this three-fold message is to be preached to every nation, kindred, tongue and people before the end of time. When you find that movement and connect yourself with it, as you will want to do, you can know for an absolute certainty that you have found the true way of Jesus Christ for our day.

It will not be difficult to find that movement. God describes this people in Rev. 14:12. "Here are they that keep" (what) "the commandments of God and the Faith of Jesus." This is how God tells the way to find the right people. You must find the people who keep the commandments of God and the faith of Jesus.

Those who give this message for the last days will show the people that the judgment has begun. If the ministers in that God-ordained movement didn't know when the judgment began, how could they tell the people "the hour of His judgment is come?" They will know from the Bible when the judgment began. The people of this message will not be merely another denomination. It will be God's movement for the consummation of the gospel of Jesus Christ.

Look at the tenth proposition. "In order to be sure of finding the true way of Christ for our day, we must identify ourselves wih the God-ordained movement, which arose in 1844, by which this threefold message is being given to every nation. "This is why it is so importaant for you to understand this three-fold message.

Look at the eleventh proposition. "The prophecy of Daniel appointed 1844 as the time when the truth which had been lost sight of would be restored again. On the blank line write Daniel 8:12-14.

Mr. Caviness, please read Daniel 8:12-14: Pause at the end of the twelfth verse, because I want every person to notice a special point in this text. "An host was given him against the daily sacrifice by reason of transgression, and it cast down the truth to the ground; and it practised and prospered." This is speaking of the little horn power that symbolized Rome. Notice it says, "it cast down," (what to the ground?) "It cast down the truth to the ground." This means that under the rule of that power the truth was buried and hidden from view.

Now read the 13th verse. Notice that the angels are tremendously interested in how long these truths will be hid from the people. "Then I heard one saint speaking, and another saint said unto that certain saint which spake, How long shall be the vision concerning the daily sacrifice, and the trangression of desolation, to give both the sanctuary and the host to be trodden under foot?" The angel wanted to know how long these truths would be hidden from view. Now read the fourteenth verse and you will find the answer. "And he said unto me, Unto two thousand and three hundred days; then shall the sanctuary be cleansed."

The 2,300 days ended in 1844. This means that the prophecy appointed 1844 as the time when the truth that had been lost sight of in former generations would be restored in this great three-fold message for the last days.

Look at the twelfth proposition. "Bible prophecy marked 1844 as the time for five of the greatest events since the crucifixion and resurrection of Christ: (1) The beginning of the judgment. (2) The inauguration of the final period of human history. (3) The rise of God's last gospel message. (Rev. 14·6-14.) (4) The inauguration of the final phase of Christ's mediatorial work. (5) The rise of the true gospel movement for these last days"

Look at the thirteenth proposition. "The judgment will be in session in heaven prior to the second coming of Christ" Many people think that the judgment is a great final day of twenty-four hours when all the human race will file before God one by one to receive their sentence. However the Bible shows that one phase of the judgment will begin in heaven some time before Christ comes at the last day. On the blank line write Daniel 7:9-11.

Mr. Funk, we shall hear from you as to what this says. "I beheld till the thrones were cast down, and the Ancient of days did sit, whose garment was white as snow, and the hair of His head like the pure wool: His throne was like the fiery flame, and His wheels as burning fire. A fiery stream issued and came forth from before Him: thousand thousands ministered unto Him, and ten thousand times ten thousand stood before Him: the judgment was set, and the books were opened."

Just pause here a moment. It says, "the judgment was set, **and the books were opened.**" The judgment will be conducted according to certain books. In the next verse we find that after the prophet saw the judgment begin in heaven, he heard some remarkable words of blasphemy spoken by this little-horn power upon the earth. Read verse 11, please.

"I beheld **then** because of the voice of the great words which the horn spake: I beheld even till the beast was slain, and his body destroyed, and given to the burning flame."

Underline that little word "then." He saw the judgment begin. The books were opened Then shortly after the judgment began, his attention was attracted by this little-horn power upon the earth. He heard this little horn issuing certain great claims. This shows that the judgment will be in session in heaven during the closing period of earth's history.

The judgment will be conducted according to certain books. "The judgment was set and the books were opened." What books will be used in the judgment?

Look at the fourteenth proposition. "Three sets of books are used in the judgment. On the blank line record Revelation 20 12.

Mr. Hagen, will you please read this? "I saw the dead, small and great, stand before God; and the books were opened: and another book was opened, which is the book of life: and the dead were judged out of those things which were written in the books, according to their works."

He says the books were opened. The least that "books" could mean would be two, wouldn't it? Then he says "another book" was opened. He names that third book. What was it? The book of life.

The Bible shows there will be three sets of books used in the judgment. The book of life contains the names of all who choose to serve God. The Bible talks about the book of remembrance, which contains the record of the good deeds, the good words, and the tears of penitence. There is a book of recorded sins that contains a record of every sin. In the judgment each one will be judged according to his record in the books. If the record shows that a person was faithful to God to the end, his name will be retained in the book of life, as one who will be given an eternal happy home in heaven. If he was not obedient to the end, then his name will be blotted out of the book of life.

We find in Revelation 3:5 that the one who overcomes will have his name retained in the book of life. The important thing is to be obedient to the end, and have our name retained in the book for a home in God's kingdom forever.

Look at the fifteenth proposition. "The ten commandments are the standard by which men will be judged." On the blank line write James 2:8-12.

Mr. Howard, will you please read this text? Please pause after the eighth verse, so I may ask a few questions.

"If ye fulfill the royal law according to the scriptures, thou shalt love thy neighbour as thyself, ye do well."

What kind of law is he talking about? He says, "If ye fulfill the royal law." You know very well that royal is something that pertains to a king. He is talking about the law of the great King of heaven and earth. "If ye fulfill the royal law." What law is the law of the great King? Just read on and we will see.

"But if ye have respect to persons, ye commit sin, and are convinced of the law as transgressors. For whomsoever shall keep the whole law, and yet offend in one point, he is guilty of all. For he that said, Do not commit adultery, said also, Do not kill. Now if thou commit no adultery, yet if thou kill, thou are become a transgressor of the law."

Tell me what law says, "Do not commit adultery," and "Do not kill." What law is this? We call that law the ten commandments. We know that he is talking about the law of the ten commandments, because he quotes two of them. He is talking about the law that says, "Thou shalt not kill, "and the law that says, "Thou shalt not commit adultery." These are the sixth and seventh precepts of the ten commandments.

Notice what he calls the ten commandments, as they are in Christ. Please read the twelfth verse. "So speak ye, and so do, as they that shall be judged by the law of liberty."

When you are redeemed from sin and have Jesus living in your heart, the ten commandments become the great law of liberty. It is that law of liberty which will judge us. This shows how important it is that we have Christ in our hearts, that we may be in harmony with all of His commandments. Since we shall be judged by these commandments we should make careful study of them, that by the grace of God we may live in harmony with them.

Some people tell us that the ten commandments are not for today. They say that they are out of date. They claim that they were abolished at the cross when the old covenant came to an end. If you want to know the real truth about this, make a careful study of this text, James 2:8, 12. Remember that the apostle James wrote this epistle in A. D. 60, twenty-nine years after the crucifixion, twenty-nine years after the old covenant had ended. He wrote this epistle to all Christians. The epistle of James is what we call a general epistle. It is addressed to all Christians everywhere. Jesus shows that everyone of the ten commandments is binding as a rule of life and conduct. Notice that he says, "Whosoever shall keep the whole law, yet offend in one point, he is guilty of all.

If any one of these ten commandments were not binding, if you offend in one point, you are guilty of sin. However, he declares, if you offend in one point, you are guilty of sin. This shows that every one of the ten is binding.

The ceremonial laws of Moses about the offering of lambs and circumcision and certain annual sabbath days were abolished at the cross. But the ten commandments continued binding after the cross.

Some of you will have a question about verse 10. "Whosoever shall keep

the whole law and offend in one point, he is guilty of all." Does that mean
that a person who breaks one commandment is as bad as the man that
breaks all? No, it does not mean this. The Bible recognizes degrees of sin
and degrees of guilt.

I think I can illustrate the meaning of this   Suppose there is a lamp sus-
pended by a chain of ten links. How many links must I cut for the lamp to
fall? Five? Three? Two? What? Yes, one. If I cut one link the lamp
will fall just as hard as if I cut all ten links. So, if a man transgresses any
one of the ten commandments, knowingly and persistently, he will miss heaven
just as much as if he trangressed all ten. The man who breaks all of the ten
will be punished far more than the man who breaks only one. But, the man
who breaks one, knowingly and persistently, will miss heaven just as much
as the man who broke all ten.

Our only safety is to permit Jesus Christ to live in us a life of obedience
to every one of God's commandments. If in these meetings the Holy Spirit
shows you where you are not living accordingly to God's commandments, then
the only safe thing, the only wise thing, the only right thing, is to pray God
to give you grace and strength to come into harmony with His law. Our attitude should be, "I delight to do Thy will, O my God; yea, Thy law is within
my heart."

Now we have ten minutes for your questions.

(Then those present sent a number of written questions to the desk by
the hands of the ushers, which the speaker aanswered from the Bible.)

(Copy of the Bible Lesson outline, which was distributed to the people preceding the fifteenth lecture.)

LESSON II — THE KEY TO PRESENT TRUTH

1. There is nothing more important for us than to know and obey the truth . . . .

2. The real truth for our day and the true way of Christ for this generation is set forth in the threefold message of Rev. 14:6-14.

3. The purpose of this message is to call out a people in every nation to keep the commandments of God and the faith of Jesus... . .. .

4. This message was to arise in the earth when the hour came for God's judgment to begin in heaven   ....

5. The prophecy of the 2,300 days furnishes a key as to when the hour of God's judgment would come. (Dan. 8:14.)

6 The 2,300 days began in B. C. 457 and ended in A. D. 1844.

7 The cleansing of the sanctuary is identical with the hour of God's judgment in Rev. 14 6, 7. (Lev. 23 29, 30)

8. Dan. 8:14 means unto 1844, then shall the judgment begin.

9. Since God's special message for the last days was to arise when the hour of His judgment came (Rev. 14 6, 7,) it must have arisen in 1844.

10. In order to be sure of finding the true way of Christ for our day, we must identify ourselves with the God-ordained movement, which arose in 1844, by which this three-fold message is being given to every nation.

11. The prophecy of Daniel appointed 1844 as the time when the truth which had been lost sight of would be restored.. ....

12. Bible prophecy marked 1844 as the time for five of the greatest events since the crucifixion and resurrection of Christ.
    (a) The beginning of the judgment.
    (b) The inauguration of the final period of human history.
    (c) The rise of God's last gospel message. (Rev. 14:6-14.)
    (d) The inauguration of the final phase of Christ's mediatorial work.
    (e) The rise of the true gospel movement for these last days.

13. The judgment will be in session in heaven prior to the second coming of Christ.... .. ..

14. Three sets of books are used in the judgment...... . ...
    (a) The book of life. (Phil 4 6; Rev. 13 8.)
    (b) The book of remembrance. (Mal. 3:16.)
    (c) The book of recorded sins. (Jer. 2:22.)

15. The ten commandments are the standard by which men will be judged......

References which were filled in as the study was presented: (1) Isa. 26:2; (3) Rev. 14:12; (4) Rev. 14 6, 7; (11) Dan. 8.12-14; (13) Dan. 7:9-11; (14) Rev. 20:12; (15) Jas. 2:8-12.

Three Steps from Your House to the City of Eternal Happiness

(Preached on the Fourth Friday of the Campaign)

If there were a highway to the moon, it would take twenty months of constant driving at the rate of 400 miles per day to reach the land of the moon. If there were a railroad to the sun, a streamliner making ninety miles per hour would have to run without stopping day after day, year after year, for **116 years** to reach sunnyland. An airplane travelling at 300 miles per hour would have to fly without a stop year after year, century after century, millennium after millennium, for **seven million years** to reach the nearest fixed star.

Far beyond the starry sky lie the pearly gates of God's heavenly home. Nobody knows how far it is to the heavenly Jerusalem, the place that Christ has prepared for His own. But this I know, no matter how far it is to the heavenly Jerusalem, every soul in this auditorium can get there in just three steps—if he wants to.

We have this illustration upon a chart. (At this juncture a chart was lowered depicting three steps from a cottage upon the earth to the city of God in heaven. The inscriptions on the three steps were covered with pieces of paper, which were removed as the speaker successively developed these three steps from the Scriptures.) This house in the lower lefthand corner represents your house. This is where you reside Above your house is God's great home, the heavenly Jerusalem, the city of God. You will notice as we unfold the Scriptures tonight that there are three steps which will take you from your house to God's house.

What are those three steps which a person must take in order to go from his house to the city of eternal happiness? Here are three Bible texts that will tell you. Put down Revelation 21:27, "There shall in no wise enter into it anything that defileth, neither whatsoever worketh abomination, or worketh a lie: but they which are written in the Lamb's book of life."

This is speaking of those who will enter heaven. "There shall in no wise enter into it anything that defileth." Sin is what defiles. Even one sin will defile a person. In order to go to heaven, we must get rid of every sin. "There shall in no wise enter into it **anything** that defileth." Every sin must be forgiven and covered by the righteousness of Jesus Christ.

When John saw the saved stand before the throne of God in heaven as described in Revelation 7:9-14, he said that they were clothed with white robes. One of the elders asked John, "Who are these arrayed in white robes?" The answer was given, "These are they who have washed their robes and made them white in the blood of the Lamb " Yes, if we want to go to heaven, we must be washed in the blood of the Lamb. The blood of Jesus Christ His Son cleanseth us from all sin.

So the first step is inscribed—Sins Forgiven. This is the first step from your house to God's house. All your sins must be forgiven.

The second step is presented in John 3 3. These are a part of the words of the Lord Jesus Christ in that interview that He had with that great Jewish ruler, Nicodemus. "Jesus answered and said unto him, Verily, verily, I say unto thee, Except a man be born again, he cannot see the kingdom of God."

Jesus Christ is the supreme authority on what it takes on our part to go to heaven. Notice that Jesus doesn't say, "Except a man be born again he **may**

103

not get to heaven." No! He doesn't say, "Except a man be born again he might not get inside the pearly gates." No! But, "Except a man be born again he cannot see the kingdom of God."

Jesus Christ stands across the pathway of every man, every woman, every young person, and with uplifted hands he says, "Except you are born again you cannot go to heaven" So this second step is inscribed BORN AGAIN. Along with accepting the Lord Jesus Christ for pardon for all our sins we must experience conversion and be born again.

The third step is presented in Hebrews 5 9. This text will tell you how many people are going to heaven. It will tell you how many people in this auditorium are going to heaven. Speaking of Jesus it says, "Being made perfect, He became the author of eternal salvation unto all them that obey Him." In order to go to heaven we must obey Jesus Christ just as far as we have knowledge of His will. So the third step is inscribed OBEY Christ.

It is only three steps from your house to the city of eternal happiness. SINS FORGIVEN; BORN AGAIN; and OBEY Christ. Don't you want to take those three steps from your house to God's heavenly house to enjoy eternal happiness? Certainly you do. There isn't anybody who wants to go to hell. I have never met anyone in all my travels who wanted to be lost. Thank God, you don't have to be lost. God doesn't want you to be lost. "God so loved the world that He gave His only begotten Son that whosoever believeth in Him should not perish, but have everlasting life."

In 2 Peter 3:9 we find that God doesn't want any man to perish but He wants all to come to repentance. In 1 Thess 5:9 He says that, "We are not appointed unto wrath, but to obtain salvation through our Lord Jesus Christ." Friend of mine, why not make up your mind to take these three steps this very night, if you haven't already taken them.

How can a person take this first step? How can we have all our sins forgiven? God forgives all our sins on three conditions: repentance, confession, and faith in the Lord Jesus Christ as our personal Saviour.

Repentance means being sorry for the wrong things which we have done, and turning from the wrong to do what is right. God has made a wonderful promise to us in 1 John 1:9: "If we confess our sins, He is faithful and just to forgive us our sins, and to cleanse us from all unrighteousness." If you will confess your sins, God forgives and cleanses you. If you will do the confessing, God will do the forgiving; and God does the forgiving the moment we do the confessing.

Confession includes restitution Some people have forgotten about this. It is not popular to preach this kind of doctrine today. The popular doctrine is just to give assent in the brain to the fact that Jesus is the Son of God, and people say that this is all it takes This is a part of it, but it isn't all.

Confession includes restitution. I want to tell you that I believe in the old-time religion, what do you say? (Amens from audience.) Confession includes making things right with our fellow men If a man has taken something that doesn't belong to him, he must restore it. I can tell you, that if the people in Des Moines, who belong to even twelve churches in this city, would go tomorrow and give back what they have stolen, we would have a revival in Des Moines before tomorrow night. If they have lied about anyone then they ought to make that right.

Think of Zacchaeus who had to climb a tree in order to be sure of seeing Jesus in the crowd. He said to Jesus, "If I have taken anything from any man, I restore him fourfold." That is to say, if I have taken $1.00, I will give him $4.00 The first thing Jesus said to him was, "This day is salvation come to this house."

You see, getting right with God includes restitution. You can take this first step from your house to the city of eternal happiness by coming to Jesus just as you are in repentance and confession.

> "Just as I am, without one plea,
>   But that Thy blood was shed for me,
>   And that Thou bid'st me come to Thee,
>   O Lamb of God, I come, I come."

You don't have to wait for a certain kind of feeling Go to Jesus in prayer and in confession Thank Him that you are forgiven, and you will get whatever feeling God wants you to have.

Now we come to the question, How can a man take this second step? How can a person be born again? You will find the answer in John 1·12, 13. "As many as received Him, to them gave He power to become the sons of God, even to them that believe on His name: Which were born, not of blood, nor of the will of the flesh, nor of the will of man, but of God "

Receive Jesus Christ and you are born of God Everyone who truly receives Jesus Christ into his heart is born of God. If you have received Him, you are born again

People say to me, "I don't see much difference between Christianity and the religion of Confucius and Buddha or Mohammed." Let me tell you something. A man may call long and loud on Confucius, Buddha, and Mohammed, but nothing happens in response to his prayers. But when a man kneels before the old rugged cross and earnestly calls on Jesus Christ for salvation, something happens in that man. An unseen power lifts the burden of sin and creates in him a new heart. He is born again. He becomes a new creature in Christ Jesus.

You will notice the scripture doesn't say, "As many as join the church are born again." It doesn't say, "As many as were baptized are born again " Now I believe in baptism. It is Biblical. I believe in joining the church. This is also Biblical It doesn't say, "As many as profess Jesus Christ are born again." No' It says, "As many as received Him, are born of God."

"Received Him " What does Him stand for? I think I can show you here on the blackboard:

> H is for He
> I is for Is
> M is for Mine

"Him" means He is mine. "As many as received Him," He is mine. This is receiving Jesus.

In 1939, when the King and Queen of England visited the White House in Washington, D C., an Indian chief named White Feather sang for them the hymn, "I'd Rather Have Jesus Than Silver or Gold." After he sang this hymn he asked Queen Elizabeth, "Your majesty, I would like to ask you if you know Jesus as your personal Saviour?" The Queen looked at him and said, "Some people know about God and some know about Christ, but the Lord Jesus Christ is the possessor of my heart." The King, a deeply religious man, smiled and said. "I would rather have Jesus too."

When Jesus is the possessor of our hearts, we can sing just like the Indian,

> "Nor gold nor silver hath obtained my redemption,
>   Nor riches of earth could have saved my soul;
>   The blood of the cross is my only foundation.
>   The death of my Saviour now maketh me whole."

I would rather have Jesus too, wouldn't you ? Oh, friends, how thankful you ought to be to the Lord for saving your soul. I wonder if we really appreciate what Jesus has done for us. I wonder if we thank Him as much as we should.

(Choir sang:)

"Thank you Lord for saving my soul.
Thank you Lord for making me whole;
Thank you Lord for giving to me,
Thy great salvation so rich and free."

Some will ask, "How can I know that I have been born again?" Here is the answer in 2 Cor. 5.17, "If any man be in Christ, he is a new creature: old things are passed away; behold, all things are become new." What is the real evidence that a man is born again? If the old habits have passed and he is living in newness of life to God, he has been born again.

Friend of mine, all you need to do is ask yourself Has the love of the world gone out of my heart? Has the love of God come in? If that is so, you are born again. Can you say, "The things of the world, like drinking, gambling, theatre-going, card playing—I may have loved them once but I don't care for them now?" Can you say of the things of God like reading the Bible, prayer, and attending preaching like this—"I once didn't care for it but now I love it?" "If any man be in Christ, he is a new creature: old things are passed away, and behold all things are become new."

Now we come to the question, How can we take this third step? It is a very important step. In fact, it is the step that puts a man inside God's house. It is the last step. How can we take the third step? How can we obey Christ? Put down Gal. 2 20. This is perhaps the clearest statement that has ever been written on what it means to be a Christian. Paul says, "I am crucified with Christ: nevertheless I live; yet not I, but Christ liveth in me: and the life which I now live in the flesh I live by the faith of the Son of God, who loved me. and gave Himself for me." There is only one way that we can ever obey the Lord, and that is for Jesus Christ to live in our hearts a life of obedience day by day.

It means that we are to so yield to Christ and to so receive Christ that He lives in us a life of obedience to God's commandments. This is why the faith of Jesus and the keeping of the commandments of God must go together, and never be separated. Revelation 14:12, in describing the true people of God, under God's last message that was to arise in 1844, says "Here are they that keep the commandments of God and the faith of Jesus."

Some people unfortunately and unwisely, try to separate the keeping of the commandments from the faith of Jesus. There will be plenty said about this within two weeks. I am not a prophet. However, I can tell you that within two weeks people will likely tell you that since salvation is entirely by grace, you don't need to keep the ten commandments any longer. They will tell you that keeping the ten commandments is contrary to grace, and that Christians are under grace and don't have to keep the ten commandments. Is this true? What does God say? In Revelation 14 12 God Himself links grace and obedience together. "Here are they that keep the commandments of God." (that is obedience) "and the faith of Jesus," (that is grace.) God links grace and obedience together. "What God has joined together, let no man put asunder."

The ten commandments and grace are perfectly united in the person of Jesus Christ. Jesus is full of grace. At the same time He is the ten commandments in living form. The ten commandments are pure, holy, righteous, perfect, and good. Jesus Christ is pure, holy, righteous, perfect and good. What the law is, He is. He is the law in living form.

No man has ever been saved by keeping the ten commandments. No man ever can save himself by keeping the ten commandments. Jesus Christ and His grace and His blood alone can save men. However, when Jesus Christ saves a man from sin by grace, that man will obey Jesus Christ as far as he knows the will of Jesus. If he doesn't, he hasn't been saved by grace. He just didn't go all the way.

If a man loves Jesus Christ, he will obey Jesus Christ. In John 14·15 it says, "If ye love Me, keep My commandments." If we love Jesus, we will want to do what He says. If we love Him, our love will be spelled out in obedience. He says in 1 John 5:3, "This is the love of God, that we keep His commandments, and His commandments are not grievious."

The Bible tells us that "love is the fulfilling of the law." If a person loves God with all his heart, he will keep the first four of the ten commandments If he loves his neighbor as himself, he will certainly keep the last six of the ten commandments. Listen! It is all of grace on the Lord's part in saving us.; and it must be all of love on our part in serving Him. As salvation is all of grace from God, it must be all of love on our part in receiving salvation.

Instead of grace doing away with or superseding obedience to the ten commandments, the very purpose of grace is to bring the believer into harmony with the ten commandments. This is made plain in Rom. 3:31. Paul raises a vital question, "Do we then make void the law through faith?" Some people would immediately answer in the affirmative. They would say, "Yes, when you have faith in Christ, the ten commandments are done away with." Paul taught no such doctrine. He asks, "Do we then make void the law through faith?" Then he summoned the strongest negative he knew, "God forbid: yea, we establish the law."

Did you get that? Instead of faith in Christ doing away with the ten commandments, it establishes obedience to the ten commandments in the Christian's heart. Instead of grace doing away with or superseding the ten commandments, the very purpose of grace is to make the believer obedient to God.

Some people say, "Those ten commandments belong to the Old Testament. We don't follow the Old Testament now. We take the New Testament. Those old laws were abolished at the cross. We Christians are living under a new law in Christ Jesus." What does the Bible really teach? The Bible plainly shows that those Jewish laws about the offering of lambs for sins, the rite of circumcision, and certain annual feast days, and yearly sabbaths were abolished at the cross. But the ten commandments are separate and distinct from the ceremonial law, and continued in force after the cross.

The apostles of Jesus Christ recognized the ten commandments as a binding code under the new covenant. Here are four texts to prove this. In Ephesians 6:2 Paul wrote the following, and remember this was some twenty-nine years after the crucifixion of Christ: "Honour thy father and mother; which is the first commandment with promise." He didn't say, "Honour thy father and mother; which was or used to be the first commandment. But he recognized the fifth commandment as being binding twenty-nine years after the cross of Christ. He quotes from the ten commandments as a binding code on Christians twenty-nine years after the old covenant had passed away at the cross.

In Romans 7.7 Paul says, "I had not known lust, except the law had said, Thou shalt not covet." There he quotes the tenth commandment as a binding commandment, and this was years after the old covenant had passed away at the cross.

In James 2:10 we read, "Whosoever shall keep the whole law," (speaking directly of the ten commaandments) "and yet offend in one point, he is guilty of all."

Then the beloved apostle makes, I think, the strongest statement of all in

1 John 3:4: "Whosoever commiteth sin transgresseth also the law: for sin is the transgression of the law " And the law of which sin is the transgression is the ten commandments.

These are great facts, and let us accept facts as they are. The apostles of Jesus Christ, long after the cross, quote from the ten commaandments as a binding code on Christians. Hebrews 8:10 shows that the same ten commandments that the Jews had written upon stone under the old covenant are written by the Holy Spirit on the believer's heart under the new covenant

Friends, I want to take all three of these steps and go from my house to the city of eternal happiness, don't you? You can take the first two steps in an instant. It doesn't take a long time to take these first two steps. Just the moment you receive Jesus Christ and confess and repent of your sins, they are forgiven. The moment you receive Him, you are born again You can take those two steps in just an instant, if you surrender to Jesus Christ.

The third step covers a life time You can take it tonight, but you can't take it tonight for tomorrow You take it each day, yielding yourself to be obedient to Him. After a man is born again he is to obey Jesus Christ for the rest of His life. If he keeps on obeying Christ, he will go through the gates into God's house. Here it is in Revelation 22·14 "Blessed are they that do His commandments, that they may have right to the tree of life, and may enter in through the gates into the city."

O thank God, if a man gives his heart to Jesus Christ his sins are forgiven, he is born again, and if he obeys Jesus Christ every day, he will go through the gates into the city of God That is where I want to go, don't you ?

Everybody in this auditorium tonight needs help from God to take these three steps from his house to the city of eternal happiness. Some people here need help regarding this first step. Their sins have never been forgiven. They haven't repented of their sins and confessed them and personally received Jesus. Some people here have never been born again. They need help on this. Many people need help to obey Christ This is one step that you need help on as long as you live

Dear friends, shouldn't we look to God and get this help that we need? How many would like to raise their hands as a silent prayer and say, Lord Jesus, I want help to take these three steps and go from my house to that lovely house that Thou has prepared for me ? How many want to put up their hands on this ? Yes, every hand is raised

(Prayer)

We thank Thee, Lord, that it is just three steps from our house to Thy house. Lord, many of us here have taken all three of these steps. We are on the way tonight, but, Jesus, we need help to obey Thee better. We pray that Thou wilt come into our hearts in a fuller way that we may have Christ live in us, His life of obedience. Some here have never taken the first step toward Thy house. We pray that they may come to Jesus just as they are in repentance and confession and have all their sins forgiven. Some here have never been born again. Oh, may this be the night when they will receive Him, and in receiving Him be born again We pray that each of us may take these three steps just now, and then keep on walking in the way of obedience until we pass through the gates into Thy heavenly house We ask it in Jesus' name Amen.

The Twelve Greatest Coming Developments

(Preached on the Fifth Sunday Night of the Campaign)

Would you like to know the twelve greatest coming developments destined to take place in our world? A close study of the one thousand year period mentioned in Revelation 20 will furnish you with this information. In this chapter, God draws aside the curtain and reveals the future for a thousand years ahead. I wonder how many of our friends have read the twentieth chapter of Revelation since last Sunday night. May we see your hands? I appreciate this. (Many hands went up.) You will get more from this lecture for having read the chapter. For the benefit of those who did not read this chapter I shall read Revelation 20·1-9 in part.

"I saw an angel come, down from heaven, having the key of the bottomless pit and a great chain in his hand And he laid hold on the dragon, that old serpent, which is the Devil, and Satan, and bound him a thousand years, and cast him into the bottomless pit, and shut him up, and set a seal upon him, that he should deceive the nations no more, till the thousand years should be fulfilled: and after that he must be loosed a little season. And I saw thrones, and they sat upon them· ... and they lived and reigned with Christ a thousand years.

But the rest of the dead lived not again until the thousand years were finished. This is the first resurrection. Blessed and holy is he that hath part in the first resurrection: on such the second death hath no power, but they shall be priests of God and of Christ, and shall reign with Him a thousand years And when the thousand years are expired, Satan shall be loosed out of his prison, and shall go out to deceive the nations which are in the four quarters of the earth, Gog and Magog, to gather them together to battle. the number of whom is as the sand of the sea.

"And they went up on the breadth of the earth, and compassed the camp of the saints about, and the beloved city and fire came down from God out of heaven, and devoured them "

Will you join me in a word of prayer?

(Prayer.) Our heavenly Father we thank Thee for this great prophecy We pray that by the Holy Spirit Thou wilt make plain to us what these things mean. Help every man, and woman, and young person in this audience to sustain the right relation to these great events which are shortly to come to pass. Help us, O Lord, to take our stand on the side of Jesus Christ that we may do our part in this great drama of things to come. We ask it in Jesus' name. Amen.

(In this lecture the speaker used a large diagram on which some fifteen events were listed in relation to the one thousand years of Revelation 20. The wording of these events and developments was covered with various pieces of paper. These were successively removed, so as to disclose the wording to the audience as the speaker came to each respective point in his discourse.)

We reproduce below a copy of the diagram which was used.

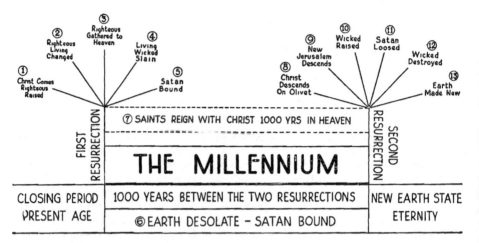

This twentieth chapter of Revelation shows that there will be two general resurrections; the first of which will take place at the beginning of the one thousand years commonly called the millenium; while the other will take place at the end of the one-thousand-year period. One of the first items that we must discover is, What class of people will be raised from the dead in the first resurrection? Put down Revelation 20.6.

"Blessed and holy is he that hath part in the first resurrection." Isn't that plain? No one need misunderstand it. It declares in so many words that it is the holy people, the righteous people, the good people, who will have part in the first resurrection.

Now the question naturally comes, "When will this first resurrection in which the righteous will be raised from the dead take place?" Put down Revelation 20:4, 5. There you will find that the righteous will be brought to life and will reign with Christ one thousand years. I have placed this text on a piece of muslin according to the rendering in the Modern Speech New Testament. I should like everyone who can see these words to read them with me.

(The audience read with the speaker as follows:)

"They (the righteous) came to life and were kings with Christ, for a thousand years. This is the first resurrection." How plain that is! These righteous people are raised in the first resurrection, in order that they may reign with Christ during the one thousand years. It is as plain as 2 and 2 make 4 that the first resurrection in which the righteous are raised will take place at the beginning of the one thousand years.

We shall remove the first paper. You are looking at the words, "First resurrection." You will notice that the first resurrection marks the beginning of the millennium. The next question is, "When will the unjust people, the wicked people be resurrected?" Put down Revelation 20.5. Here we read, "The rest of the dead lived not again until the thousand years were finished." Verse four tells how the righteous will be raised in the first resurrection at the beginning of the one thousand years, then Revelation 20:5 declares that the rest of the dead, the unjust, lived not again until the thousand years were finished.

Now we shall remove the second paper. When the second paper is removed you will notice, the "Second Resurrection, marking the end of the one thousand years." Notice the diagram shows that the millennium reaches from the first resurrection to the second resurrection. What, then, is the millennium?

We take off the next paper and we see—"The Millennium is One Thousand

Years between the Two Resurrections" The word millennium means one thousand years. It comes from two Latin words, "Mille" meaning **one thousand,** "annum" meaning **years.**

I wonder if I have really made this plain. How many see that the millennium, or this one thousand years of Revelation 20, is a period of time in between the two resurrections? Will you just lift your hands? Thank you. I am glad you see this, because it is vital to the right understanding of the subject.

The scripture shows that the resurrection of the righteous which marks the beginning of the millennial period will take place at the second coming of Jesus Christ. You will find this in 1 Thess. 4:16. Paul says, "The Lord Himself shall descend from heaven with a shout, with the voice of the archangel, and with the trump of God. and the dead in Christ shall rise first." The righteous dead will rise when the Lord Jesus Christ descends from heaven at His second coming.

Five of the greatest events that have ever taken place in the history of the world will happen at the beginning of this one-thousand-year period. Follow me closely as we proceed with these events.

As we remove the next paper we find that the first of those five greatest events, which will happen at the beginning of the one-thousand-years is, "Christ will come, and the righteous dead will be raised."

Now we remove the next paper. When this paper is removed we see that the second one of those five greatest events which will mark the beginning of the millennium is, that at the coming of Jesus the righteous living will be changed in the twinkling of an eye from mortality to immortality. You will find this in 1 Cor. 15:52.

We shall remove the next paper. When we remove this paper, we notice that the third of these five greatest events which mark the beginning of the millennium is, that when Jesus comes all the righteous, the resurrected saints, the changed living saints, are caught up to meet the Lord in the air to be with Him forever. You will find this in 1 Thess. 4:16, 17. The resurrected saints and the living saints are caught up from the earth to meet the Lord in the air at His coming.

Where will the Lord take all these righteous people? John 14 3 tells. Jesus said, "I go to prepare a place for you. And if I go and prepare a place for you, I will come again, and receive you unto myself; that where I am, there ye may be also." At the second coming of Christ all the righteous, the resurrected saints, and the changed living saints will be caught up to meet Jesus and go with Him to those glorious mansions in heaven that He has prepared for His own.

"Some golden daybreak, Jesus will come;
Some golden daybreak, battles all won,
We'll rise to glory, through heaven's blue;
Jesus is coming for me, for you."

The next question is, What will happen to the millions of wicked people who will be living on the earth at that last day when Jesus comes the second time? Now we shall remove the next paper. When this paper is removed, you find that the fourth of these greatest events to happen at the beginning of the one thousand years is that, when Jesus comes the living wicked will be slain. Here are the references: 2 Thess. 2 8, and Jeremiah 25 33.

In 2 Thess. 2 8 it says, "The wicked will be destroyed by the brightness of His coming." Jeremiah 25·33 says, "The slain of the Lord shall be at that day from one end of the earth even unto the other end of the earth: They shall not be lamented, neither gathered, nor buried; they shall be dung upon the ground."

This describes the death of the wicked in connection with the first phase of the battle of Armageddon. The wicked all over the earth will be struck dead by the glory of Christ as He descends from heaven. Wherever the wicked are, when Christ appears, they will be struck dead by His glory, as though a bolt of lightning or live wire fell upon them. They will lie here on top of the earth unburied. This verse in Jeremiah 25 33 says, "They shall not be lamented, neither gathered nor buried." Why will they not be buried? As Jesus appears, all the righteous people are caught up to meet the Lord in the air. There is no one left on the earth to bury the wicked.

Notice that when the one thousand years or millennium begins, **there will not be a single living human being left upon the earth.** It says here in Jeremiah 25:33 that these slain wicked shall not be lamented. This will be the first time in the history of the world that people will die and nobody will ever shed a tear for them. Why not? There is no one left on the earth to cry over them —except the devil, and he doesn't care. He has them on his side.

There can be only one of two things happen to every soul on this earth when Jesus Christ appears. Either He will pray for the rocks to fall upon him and be struck dead, at the presence of Jesus, or he will look up as he sees the Lord coming to sing and shout for joy as he is caught up from the earth to meet the Lord in the air. "One shall be taken and another left." Friend of mine, which one will you be? Why not surrender your heart to the Lord Jesus Christ and follow Him each day so that you will be ready when He comes?

Some people think that many of those who have never accepted the gospel during their lifetime will be raised in little groups during this one thousand years and that the righteous people will preach to them and that many of them will accept the Lord during this one thousand years. This is not true. Here is the proof. Put down Revelation 20:5. I have also placed this on a piece of muslin that you would not miss seeing what the scripture says. This too is rendered according to the Modern Speech New Testament. It says, "No one else who was dead rose to life until the thousand years were at an end."

Notice that in the place of the wicked being alive and having some one preach to them during the one thousand years, they are all dead . None of them come to life until the one thousand years are at an end. It is just as impossible for any person to hear the gospel and be saved during the millennium as it is for a corpse to rise up in the coffin and be converted during the funeral service.

I hope no person in this audience will put off accepting Jesus Christ, thinking you will have another chance after death. You will not. The Bible shows that death seals a man's fate for eternity. Here it is in Isaiah 38:18. "They that go down into the pit cannot hope for Thy truth." God says to you and me, "Now is the accepted time: now is the day of salvation." "Today, if you will hear My voice and harden not your heart. You are having your chance now, make the most of it " The best thing anybody can do is to accept Jesus Christ now. One of the worst things any one can do is to put off accepting Jesus Christ.

At the beginning of this one thousand years, as we have already noticed from the Scriptures, all the righteous are taken from the earth to the mansions Jesus has prepared for them The wicked who are alive at His coming will be struck dead and lie unburied. This will make the earth temporarily empty. This is exactly what the Bible says. Put it down. Isaiah 24:1. "Behold, the Lord maketh the earth empty . . . and scattereth abroad the inhabitants thereof."

That is what will bind the devil for one thousand years as described in Revelation 20:1-3. There are two ways to bind a person. You can take a rope or a chain and bind a man literally so he can't do anything; or you can put a man in a position where he can't do what he would like to do. I have heard people say, "I would like to help you, but my hands are tied." Was there a rope around their hands? No! They were under a chain of circumstances where they couldn't help, even if they had a desire to help

Notice the situation of the devil during this one thousand years All during this one-thousand-year period the devil cannot tempt any of the righteous. Thank God, they will be in heaven beyond his reach. He cannot deceive the wicked and work through them, because they are all dead—He is out of a job. He takes an enforced vacation for one thousand years.

Notice as we remove the next paper. The fifth great event to happen at the beginning of this one thousand years is that Satan is bound. During the one thousand years the earth will be desolate. Removing the next paper we notice that during the one thousand years, Satan is bound and the earth is desolate.

This is what the Bible means by the bottomless pit. This may have perplexed you, but it will not perplex you if you will think a little bit. The Greek word for bottomless pit is "abussos." It means an abyss, or a desolate place. During the one thousand years the earth is desolate It is a veritable bottomless pit or abyss in which Satan is forced to stay. He is bound.

You say, "Mr. Shuler, aren't the saints going to reign on earth with Christ during the millennium?" The Scriptures show that the saints will reign over the earth when it is made new. During the one thousand years the saints will reign with Christ in the New Jerusalem

We remove the next paper and find that during this one thousand years the saints reign with Christ in heaven. The millennial reign of Christ with the saints cannot be on this earth because there will not be a single righteous person left on this earth during the millenium. All the righteous are taken to heaven at the beginning of the one thousand years.

At the close of the one thousand years there will be five or more of the greatest developments that will ever take place in the history of this world. We remove the next paper and we find that the first one of these is that at the end of the one thousand years Jesus Christ will descend upon Mount Olivet. Put down Zechariah 14·4, 5. This says, "His feet shall stand in that day upon the mount of Olives . . . and there shall be a very great valley; and half of the mountain shall remove toward the north, and half of it toward the south . . . And the Lord my God shall come, and all the saints with Him."

Some people have thought there would be seven years between the coming of Jesus Christ for His saints, and the coming of Jesus Christ with His saints. The Scriptures show that Christ comes for His saints at the beginning of the one thousand years, and He comes with His saints at the end of the one thousand years. In connection with the descent of Christ to Mount Olivet with the saints, the New Jerusalem will come down to this earth.

We remove the next paper and find that the second one of these five great events that will happen at the end of the one thousand years is that the New Jerusalem descends from heaven to this earth. Put down Revelation 21:2. "I John saw the holy city, the New Jerusalem, coming down." He saw it coming down to the earth.

We remove the next paper and we see that the third one of these five greatest events at the end of the one thousand years is that the wicked dead are resurrected. In Revelation 20:5 we found that the wicked dead would not live again until the thousand years were ended. This shows that at the end of the one thousand years the wicked will be resurrected.

In Revelation 20 3 we read that after the one thousand years is finished, Satan will be loosed for a little season. Follow me closely. It is the resurrection of the wicked at the end of the one thousand years that looses the devil for a little season. It furnishes him with subjects with whom he can resume his work of deception. Put down Rev. 20 7, 8. "When the thousand years are expired, Satan shall be loosed out of his prison, and shall go out to deceive" (see, he is loosed, because he has power to deceive the resurrected wicked people.) Notice what he does with the millions of wicked people. I read verses 8 and 9, "And shall go out to deceive the nations which are in the four quarters of the earth, Gog and magog, to gather them together to battle· the number of whom is as the sand of the sea. And they went up on the breadth of the earth, and compassed the camp of the saints about, and the beloved city;" (notice that the New Jerusalem will then be on the earth.)

Satan will organize these millions of people into the greatest army that ever trod this earth. The millions who marched in World War II will be as nothing compared to this mighty host which Satan will-marshal against the city of God. We have some idea of its vastness. It says, "The number of whom is as the sand of the sea." It tells you very plainly where the vast majority of the people will be' found at the last day.

Satan gathers these people together. He leads the millions of wicked people in a great drive to capture the New Jerusalem, which will then be resting upon the earth. This is the final phase of the battle of Armageddon on which I preached on the second Sunday night of this Bible Institute. This will be a fight to the finish . This will be the war that will end wars.

This army will completely surround the New Jerusalem. It tells you in the first part of the 9th verse, "They went up on the breadth of the earth, and compassed the camp of the saints about, and the beloved city." It looks as if the city will be captured. But what happens? "Fire came down from God out of heaven, and devoured them." Those coals of fire will burn the flesh off of their bones as they stand on their feet. You will find this in Zechariah 14.12.

This fire from God will purify the earth and in due time God will recreate, remake, reconstruct, and regenerate this earth into a new earth that will be just as perfect as it was before sin entered. John says in Revelation 21:1, "I saw a new heaven and a new earth: for the first heaven and the first earth were passed away."

We now remove the last two papers. The two great events which will come at the close of the one thousand years will be that Satan will be loosed a little season and the wicked destroyed, and the earth will be made new. This new earth, with the New Jerusalem as its capital, will be the eternal happy home of the saved In this new earth Jesus Christ will rule on the throne of David forever In the new earth—that will be when the saints will reign on earth.

Friend of mine, where will you stand in the great day of judgment? Listen to me. All the people who have ever lived on this earth will stand before God at the same time—at the end of this one thousand years. This is the judgment of the great white throne described in Revelation 20. Everyone who has ever given his heart to Jesus Christ will be **inside** the glorious New Jerusalem, saved forever. Everyone who refused to give himself to Jesus Christ will be **outside** the New Jerusalem in the army of the devil lost forever. The most vital question that you ever have faced, or ever can face, is on which side will you stand? There will be no **third** side on which you can stand. Every man, every woman, every young person is bound to be, at that day, either **inside** the New Jerusalem, saved forever, or **outside**, lost forever. Which will it be? Every person in this auditorium is deciding for himself whether he will be saved forever, or lost forever, in the way he responds to the call of Jesus Christ each day that he lives.

To the people who are outside the New Jerusalem, Jesus will say: "Depart from Me, ye cursed, into everlasting fire prepared, for the devil and his angels." O, what weeping, wailing and gnashing of teeth there will be when they realize that they are lost forever!

Those who are inside the New Jerusalem will hear the sweetest words ever spoken, "Come, ye blessed of My Father, inherit the kingdom prepared for you from the foundation of the world." O, what never-ending, ever-deepening joys will be theirs!

Dear friends, think it through. Which will it be with you? Which will it be with me? We can't help being there on one side or the other. If you don't believe a word that I have said tonight, you will be there just the same. If you don't believe in God, if you don't believe in the Bible, you will be there just the same. "We must all appear before the judgment seat of Christ that everyone may receive the things done in his body, according to that he has done, whether it be good or bad."

You and I cannot help being there. The fact that you are alive proves that you will be there. There is one thing you can do. There is one thing you can care for. You can decide upon which side you want to stand. You can give yourself to Jesus Christ and be on His side. God has given you the power of choice. O, I hope you will use that wonderful power of choice to put yourself on the side of Jesus Christ and be on the inside of the city of God at that great day! I appeal to you tonight to choose for heaven, and not for hell.

It takes only two steps, and everyone here may take those two steps before he leaves this meeting if he wants to. The first is, accept the Lord Jesus Christ as your personal Saviour. The second is, permit Jesus Christ to live in you by the Holy Spirit a life of obedience to all His commandments. He says in Revelation 22:14, "Blessed are they that do His commandments, that they may have right to the tree of life, and may enter in through the gates into the city." Are you ready to take these two steps tonight? Jesus cannot save you unless you come to Him.

About 115 years ago a man in Pennsylvania was convicted of murder. He was sentenced to be hung. Andrew Jackson, who was then President of the United States, granted this man, George Wilson, a pardon. Mr. Wilson refused to accept it. Strange as it may seem, he refused to accept the presidential pardon. He argued that it wasn't a pardon unless he accepted it. They appealed to the State's Attorney. The State's Attorney said that the law was silent upon this point. They took the case to the Supreme Court. John Marshall, Chief Justice of the United States, ruled that a pardon is only a piece of paper unless it is accepted by the person who is implicated. If he refuses a pardon, then it is not a pardon. George Wilson must hang. And he was hanged.

Even the United States Government couldn't force a prisoner to take a pardon, if he did not want it. God Himself does not force men to take a pardon or salvation. Jesus is ready to forgive you, but you must be ready to accept it. Some of you will say, "Well, Mr. Wilson was about the most foolish man I ever heard of, to reject a pardon and thus lose his life." Pray tell me, what about the people who refuse the pardon of Jesus Christ and lose eternal life?

Sinners are saved through simple faith in the finished work of Jesus Christ upon the cross. We need to pray. Yes, we should ask God to forgive all our sins. But you don't need to pray to make God willing to save you. He is at this very moment beseeching you to take salvation. Salvation is a gift from the pierced hand of the Lord Jesus Christ. Romans 6:23 says, "The wages of sin is death; but the gift of God is eternal life through Jesus Christ our Lord." "Whosoever will," let him come, "and take the water of life freely." The gift of God is for you, will you take it?

How many are ready to say, "Preacher, pray for me, that I may truly fol-

low the Lord Jesus Christ and be saved"?   Will you lift your hand just now?
Yes, it seems to me that every hand is lifted.

(Prayer)

Our blessed Lord, we thank Thee for this great prophecy.   Lord, help us
each tonight to realize that these are real events which will soon transpire in
this world.   Help us to act our part well.   We thank Thee that salvation is a
free gift through Jesus Christ.   Help us to accept this gift.   Help us, that we
may permit Jesus to live in us every day a life of obedience to His precious
word   We ask it in Jesus' name   Amen.

Which Day Shall Christians Keep?

The sermon tonight will be an introduction to the Sabbath question. The limitations of time will not permit me to cover all the aspects of the Sabbath question in one sermon. So please remember that if some of the items I present are not clear to you, they will be cleared up as I cover the other aspects of the Sabbath question in succeeding sermons.

If some man says things, which are just the opposite from the way you or I have been brought up, that doesn't necessarily mean that he is wrong. The only safe thing for any person to do, is to prove all things, and hold fast to that which is good. I don't ask you to take my word on any point, but I do ask you to take your Bible and check up on my statements and find the real truth for yourself.

I was brought up to believe that Sunday and Sabbath meant the same thing. When I became a Christian, I kept Sunday strictly because I sincerely believed that it was the day that Jesus Christ had appointed for Christians to observe in honor of His resurrection on the first day of the week. In fact I felt so sure that Sunday was the right day for Christians to keep, that when a certain man attempted to show me that Christians should keep the seventh day, or Saturday, I told my friends that the man was crazy. I said they ought not even to allow him to walk the streets. They ought to put him in an asylum. But that man stirred me to search my Bible to find the facts. Tonight I want to tell you what I found. I want to take you on a delightful tour of investigation of God's Word for a discovery of the real truth about the Sabbath.

Jesus tells us in John 8 31, 32 that if we continue in His word, we shall know the truth, and the truth shall make us free. Please bear in mind that this matter of which day we should observe is not a question of denominationalism. It cannot be settled by what I say or what any other minister says. It cannot be settled by what any certain church teaches; or by what any denomination does; or by what the law of the land says, or by what the encyclopedia or the dictionary may say. If you want the real truth, you must let the Bible speak and tell you which day Jesus Christ wants you to keep.

> "What says the Bible, the blessed Bible?
> This should my only question be.
> Teachings of men so often mislead us,
> What says the Book of God to me?"

The first fact that I discovered was that Sunday is not the day God commands men to keep. Write Exodus 20:10 in your notebooks. I have placed this text on a piece of muslin that you might see for yourself just what God says in Exodus 20 10. (At this juncture a banner containing the words of Exodus 20.10 was lowered in view of the audience.)

Exodus 20 10, a part of the fourth commandment, is one of the ten. The fourth commandment constitutes Exodus 20 8-11 in your Bible.

I would like to have all of us read this. "The seventh day is the Sabbath of the Lord Thy God. In it thou shalt not do any work." Exodus 20:10.

God says, keep the seventh day. Which day is the seventh day? If you look at your calendar, you see at once that the seventh day is the day we call Saturday. Then Saturday is the Sabbath according to the ten commandments.

I discovered further that Sunday cannot be the right day to keep, because Sunday is the first day of the week, while God commands us to keep the seventh day or the last day of the week. So I learned that Sunday and Sabbath do not mean the same thing. Many of you have used those terms synonymously. I once thought that Sunday and Sabbath meant the same thing, but that is not according to the Bible. Sunday and Sabbath do not refer to the same day any more than Thursday and Friday refer to the same day.

Sunday is a name that men gave to the first day of the week, because on that day from time immemorial the heathen people worshipped the s-u-n. Hence they called it the sun's day, or Sunday. The Sabbath is a name that God gave to the seventh day of the week.

Like many other people I formerly thought that the keeping of the seventh day was intended only for the Jews. I would like to have you notice what Jesus says in Mark 2:27. "The sabbath was made for—"whom? The Jews? No, Jesus says, "the Sabbath was made for 'm-a-n'." Does that spell Jew? No! "The Sabbath was made for m-a-n," and that means the race of mankind. I discovered that the keeping of the seventh day was no more intended for just the Jews than the commands, "Thou shalt not kill," and "Thou shalt not steal," and "Thou shalt not commit adultery," were only for the Hebrew people. The ten commandments are ten great principles of righteousness applicable to all people.

Then I thought to myself, the seventh day is the Sabbath of the Old Testament, but Sunday, the first day of the week, is the Sabbath of the New Testament. You know there are a lot of people who think that if you go by what they call the old Bible, the seventh day is the right day, but if you go by what they call the new Bible, then the first day or Sunday is the day we should observe.

I thought that too once. So I searched the New Testament. I came to the second book in the New Testament, which is the book of Mark. I want you to notice Mark 16:1, 2 and see what I found there. "When the sabbath was past, Mary Magdalene, and Mary the mother of James, and Salome, had bought sweet spices, that they might come and anoint Him. And very early in the morning the first day of the week," (notice that after the sabbath was past,) "very early in the morning the first day of the week, they came unto the sepulchre at the rising of the sun."

The Sabbath was passed and gone when they came to the tomb at sunrise. I think you can see that the first day of the week could not be the Sabbath in the New Testament, because the Sabbath was past before the first day of the week dawned. The fact that the first day of the week was the next day after the Sabbath in the New Testament, showed me that the Sabbath, the day Jesus Christ wants me to keep, must be the day that comes just before the first day of the week, which everybody knows is Saturday.

As I read the New Testament I found that the word "Sabbath" in the New Testament refers to the same seventh day of the week that is called the "Sabbath" in the Old Testament. When it comes to the weekly day of observance, the word "Sabbath" in the entire Bible, the New Testament and the Old Testament, is applied to no other day except the seventh day as appointed by the Lord in the ten commandments. The Bible no more speaks of two different weekly Sabbaths, than it talks about two different true Gods or two different true Christs. One true God; one true Christ; one true Sabbath. And there need be no doubt as to which day is the one true Sabbath, because it is the seventh day that God specifies in the ten commandments.

Like many of you, I formerly thought that the resurrection of our Lord on the first day of the week made Sunday the right day for Christians to keep. But when I searched the New Testament, I found that there is no scripture, not a single text, that says that Christians should keep the first day of the week in honor of our Lord's resurrection. The resurrection of Jesus Christ on Sunday did not make Sunday the Sabbath or the Lord's day any more than our Lord's crucifixion on Friday made Friday the Lord's day or the Sabbath.

Here is something I did find. Put this down. In the very beginning of the Bible in Genesis 2.3 I found this. "God blessed the seventh day, and sanctified it because that in it He had rested from all His work which God created and made." You will notice it says, "God sanctified the seventh day." The word "sanctified" means set apart for a holy use. This is the only day for weekly observance that the Lord ever sanctified for man according to the record given in the Bible. This shows that the seventh day is the only day of the week that the Lord ever set apart for man. It is the only weekly day He ever made holy for man or commanded man to keep.

After I learned this the question came to me, just as it is coming to some of you right now, "Does it really make any difference which day a person keeps just so he keeps one day?" Many people think that if only a person keeps one day in seven that that is all that the Lord requires. They think any day that people want to select is satisfactory to the Lord.

We need to look at God's answer to this question. Put down Exodus 20·10, 11. Again we shall read a part of the fourth commandment. We have placed it here on muslin so that you might see what God says. (At this juncture the words of this text on a piece of muslin were disclosed to the view of the audience.)

God says, "The seventh day is," (not used to be, but is **right now**) "the Sabbath." Notice He doesn't say that a seventh day is the Sabbath. He doesn't say **your** seventh day. He doesn't say **any** seventh day is the Sabbath, but He says, "**the** seventh day is the Sabbath." Then He tells us why. He says, "**For,**" (which means because) "in six days the Lord made heaven and earth . . . and rested on the seventh day: wherefore the Lord blessed the Sabbath day, and hallowed it."

Here is something we need to follow very closely. God actually designates the seventh day, which He asks us to keep, to be the same day of the week upon which He rested. In fact God says, You keep the seventh day, because on that day I rested. God defines the seventh day that He wants us to keep as being the last day of the week, the day on which He rested.

God specifies two reasons why man should keep the seventh day of the week. First, because the Lord rested on the seventh day after He made the world in six days. Second, because the Lord set the seventh day apart as a holy day.

Do you know friends that if you put any other day in that fourth commandment except the seventh day, you make the Bible contradict itself? We shall put in the first day of the week and read it to see how it comes out. "The first day is the sabbath of the Lord thy God . . . for in six days the Lord made heaven and earth, and rested the first day." Hold on there! Right there you have a contradiction. You have God resting and working on the same day. You say, He made the world in six days. Well, the first day of the week was one of those six days. Then you say that He rested on the first day. You see it makes the commandment contradict itself. It destroys the commandment.

That isn't all! God has fixed the Sabbath so that man cannot tamper with it. You can take any other day of the week aside from the seventh—the first day, second day, third day, fourth day, or sixth day and place it in the fourth commandment as the Sabbath and it makes the commandment contradict itself. There isn't any day that will fiit in this commandment except the one that God placed in it—the seventh day. This is a very significant point. There is only one way to obey this commandment and that is to keep the last day of the week, the day on which the Lord rested. The Sabbath cannot be any other day except the particular day of the week on which He rested and the day which He set apart or sanctified for man. Since the seventh day is the only day on which the Lord rested after He made the world, the only day He ever sanctified, **then it must be the only right day to keep.**

After I learned this, the thought came to me, as some of you are thinking now, "Yes, the seventh day is the right day to keep, but hasn't the calendar been changed, so that we cannot be sure that the seventh that God specifies in the ten commandments is the identical day that we call Saturday?" If you will study this, you will find that the change in the calendar did not alter the order of the days in the week. The order of the days of the week that we have in our calendar today is the same order of the days of the week that they had when Jesus Christ was here.

We have three charts here which will show that the seventh day which God specifies in the fourth commandment is identical with the day we now call Saturday. (Three charts were displayed depicting the sixth day as the day of the Lord's crucifixion, the following day as the Sabbath according to the commandment, and the next day—the first day of the week, as the day of the Lord's resurrection.)

On this first chart we see the three crosses and Christ on the middle cross. Jesus Christ was crucified on the sixth day of the week. The Bible plainly teaches this. The Bible shows that He was crucified on the day before the Sabbath. Here it is in Mark 15:42. Speaking of the day of the crucifixion it says "It was the preparation, that is, the day before the Sabbath." Jesus was crucified on the day before the Sabbath.

Notice the next day in this cycle of three days as illustrated on the next chart. The next day after He was crucified was the seventh day. He was crucified the day before the Sabbath, so the next day was the Sabbath day. Notice in Luke 23:56 what Christ's own followers did on the day after the crucifixion. After they had seen Christ taken down from the cross and put in Joseph's new tomb, they returned to their homes. Then what did they do? It says, "They rested the Sabbath day according to the commandment" He was crucified the day before the Sabbath and the next day His followers kept the Sabbath according to the commandment of God.

Then what happened on the next day? The next day was the first day of the week. On this third chart you see the women at the tomb and the angel telling them that the Lord is risen. We find in Luke 24:1, that after they had kept the Sabbath, "Upon the first day of the week, very early in the morning, they came unto the sepulchre, bringing the spices which they had prepared."

You have three great days standing side by side. The sixth day of the week, when He was crucified; the next day, which His followers kept as the Sabbath; and the first day of the week upon which He arose. How plain! The day that God asks you and me to keep is the day that came in between the crucifixion on Friday and the resurrection on Sunday. It is a historical fact and no one can rightfully deny that Jesus was crucified on the day we call Friday; and rose on the day we call Sunday. If you know what day comes in between Friday and Sunday, then you know what you ought to do. If there is anybody in this auditorium who doesn't know what day comes between Friday and Sunday, will you please see me privately?

Mark well this point The calendar that was in use in the time of Christ was the Julian Calendar named after Julius Caesar. This calendar was arranged by him forty-six years before Christ was born. That calendar without any modification so far as **the weeks** are concerned is the calendar that hangs on your wall tonight. This is positive evidence that the day we call Saturday is the seventh day of the fourth commandment.

I hold in my hand photostats of certain pages from Dio Cassius' **History of Rome,** which you all recognize as a standard work on the history of Rome. In these citations we find that the seventh day of the week, which we now call Saturday in English, was the day which the heathen anciently dedicated to Saturn. Roman history shows that this day of Saturn or Saturday was the same day of the week which is called the Sabbath in the ten commandments, and was so observed by the Israelites. These two photostats of citations from Dio Cassius' **History of Rome** identify the day of Saturn, now called Saturday, as being the same day of the week which the Israelites kept as the Sabbath according to the fourth commandment of the decalogue.

In his history he tells how Pompey captured Jerusalem by attacking it on the day of Saturn which was the same day as the Sabbath observed by the Jews. On that day the Jews would not fight so the city was taken.

In Dio Cassius' **History of Rome b. 37, ch. 16, Loeb Classical Library, vol. 33, pp. 125, 127** we read "Most of the city, to be sure, he took without any trouble, as he was received by the party of Hyrcanus, but the temple itself which the other party had occupied, he captured only with difficulty. For it was on high ground and was fortified by a wall of its own, and if they had continued defending it on all days alike, he could not have gotten possession of it. As it was, **they made an exception of what are called the days of Saturn, and by doing no work at all on those days** afforded the Romans an opportunity in this interval to batter down the wall." This was sixty-three years before Christ.

Then we have the identity of Saturday with the Sabbath made certain from that time to the present, because the orthodox Jews still consider the seventh day to be holy, and it still coincides with the day called Saturday in the calendar.

Some people told me that the New Testament calls the first day of the week the Lord's day in honour of Christ's resurrection. What are the facts? I found this. The Lord's day is mentioned only one time, not two times, but only one time in the New Testament. This is in the last book in the New Testament in Revelation 1.10. John says, "I was in the Spirit on the Lord's day, and heard behind me a great voice, as of a trumpet."

You will notice that he does not specify which day of the week is the Lord's day. We have no right to read into the Bible something that isn't there. He simply says, "I was in the Spirit on the Lord's day." Of course, the Lord's day means Christ's day. There is no question about that, but he doesn't specify which day of the week it was. There is only one way we can find out for a certainty which day of the week is the Lord's day, and that is to compare scripture with scripture and let the Bible decide.

The Lord's day must be the day of which Jesus Christ is the Lord. What day is Jesus Christ Lord of? In Matthew 12:8 we read, "The Son of man is Lord even of the Sabbath day." Since the Lord's day is the day of which Jesus Christ is Lord, and He is Lord of the Sabbath day, then the Sabbath day is the Lord's day. Since the seventh day is the Sabbath of the Lord, then the seventh day or Saturday is the true Lord's day.

If Jesus Christ is in the Sabbath, and He is, then you want Jesus Christ and the Sabbath. It seems to me, friends, that we should all be willing to follow the example of Jesus. In 1 Peter 2 21 the apostle says that Jesus left us an example, that we should walk in His steps.

When we take the New Testament and trace out Who is the Lord mentioned in this fourth commandment it becomes very clear that the seventh day is Christ's day, because He is the Lord that made the day holy for man to keep. The New Testament shows in seven different places that Christ, the Son of God, is the creator of this world. I shall give you those texts. John

1:1-3; John 1:10; Eph. 3:9; Col. 1:13-17; 1 Cor. 8:6; Hebrews 1:1-3, and Hebrews 1:8-10.

Who is this Lord that made the seventh day to be the Sabbath by resting upon the seventh day, after He made the world in six days, and by sanctifying or setting apart that day? The New Testament tells us it was the Lord Jesus Christ. Isn't it plain that since Christ is the Lord Who made the seventh day the Sabbath by resting on that day after He made the world in six days, and by sanctifying that day that the seventh day is bound to be Christ's day, the **Lord's** day, the **Sabbath of Christ** for all Christians to keep? The keeping of the Sabbath day is a part of following Jesus as our Saviour. It is Christ's day. I love that day, because I know it is Christ's day. The seventh day is the only weekly day that the Lord Jesus Christ ever set apart or ever made holy for man to keep. When He lived here, He kept the seventh day holy. He says to you and me, as Christians, "Follow me."

Some people told me that the keeping of the seventh day was binding only until Jesus died upon the cross. When I searched my Bible, I found that this was not true. I found that the keeping of the seventh day was binding after the crucifixion and resurrection of our Lord. The apostles kept the right day. You can depend on that. They followed the real truth which they had received direct from Christ. If you want to be sure which is the right day to keep, all you need to do is to find what day the apostles called Sabbath and keep it. Put down Acts 13:14, 15.

This thirteenth chapter of Acts gives an account of a striking sermon Paul preached in the Jewish synagogue in Antioch about A. D. 45, or about fourteen years after the crucifixion and resurrection of our Lord. Notice what it says: "When they departed from Perga, they came to Antioch in Pisidia and went into the synagogue on the Sabbath day, and sat down."

They went into the Jewish synagogue on the Sabbath day, when the Jews were assembled for their weekly worship. Tell me upon what day of the week did the Jews in the time of Paul meet for their weekly worship? There can be only one answer to that question. The Jews in the time of Paul met for their weekly worship on the seventh day or Saturday. Notice that the Holy Spirit speaking through Luke calls this seventh day or Saturday when the Jews met for their weekly worship, "the Sabbath day."

This reveals two very important facts. The seventh-day Sabbath was not abolished at the cross for here we have the Acts of the Apostles calling it "the Sabbath day," some fourteen years after the crucifixion and resurrection of Christ. The apostles recognized Saturday as the Sabbath in their religion by calling this day upon which the Jews met for their weekly worship, "the Sabbath day." You will find this fact set forth eight times in the book of Acts. As a matter of fact the seventh day or Saturday on which the Jews met for their weekly worship is called the Sabbath eight times in the book of Acts.

It is true that the ceremonial laws of Moses were nailed to the cross and have been abolished. However, the ten commandments, as the eternal law of righteousness, were binding after the cross just as before. Hebrews 8:10 shows that the same ten commandments which God wrote on stone under the old covenant are written upon the Christian's heart by the Holy Spirit under the new covenant.

In Numbers 28.9 we learn that the Israelites were required by the Mosaic Law to offer two lambs as a burnt offering every Sabbath day or every Saturday. Christians today don't need to offer lambs as sacrifices. Jesus Christ, the Lamb of God, offered Himself on Calvary's cross nineteen hundred years ago once for all. In fact if we should offer lambs for our sins, we would be denying Jesus Christ as the Lamb of God. That Mosaic law about offering two lambs every Sabbath was nailed to the cross. This is why Christians should not keep the Sabbath according to the Mosaic Law, but should keep the Lord's day according to the example of Jesus Christ.

If I should ask how many believe that these ten commandments such as Thou shalt not kill; Thou shalt not steal; Honor thy father and thy mother; and Thou shalt not take the name of the Lord thy God in vain, are binding today, everyone here would raise his hand. Mark this. The keeping of the seventh day, or Saturday, is a part of those ten commandments. It is the fourth one of the ten. This means just as surely as the ten commandments are binding, the keeping of the seventh day is binding. The ten commandments constitute the only document in this world which ever came to man direct from God. God spoke the ten with His own voice and wrote them on everlasting stone. The great God of all, has forever settled this Sabbath question by saying, "The seventh day is the Sabbath of the Lord thy God: in it thou shalt not do any work "

Some of you will say, "Mr. Shuler, I thought you weren't going to preach denominationalism in this Bible Institute." Listen, the keeping of the seventh day is not denominationalism   It is one of God's ten commandments for everybody in the world. Jesus Christ and the ten commandments are not confined to any one denomination. They are for all Christians. The keeping of the seventh day is for all Christians. The keeping of the seventh day is not denominationalism any more than the keeping of the commandment, "Thou shalt not take the name of the Lord thy God in vain." You can't make one of those ten commandments belong to one denomination and give the remaining nine to the rest. You don't want to do that, do you? They belong to all, and that is why I am preaching this. I am not referring to any denomination at all. I am simply telling you what the Bible says.

Did you know that this fourth commandment for the keeping of the seventh day is a commandment of the Lord Jesus Christ? Here are two references. Put them down. 1 Cor. 10 4 and Nehemiah 9:12-15. 1 Cor. 10:4 shows that the Lord God, Who led Israel through the wilderness by that pillar of cloud by day, and pillar of fire by night, was Christ. Paul says, "They drank of that spiritual Rock that followed them: and that Rock was Christ."

Nehemiah 9:12-15 shows that the same Lord God Who led them through the wilderness was the One Who spoke the ten commandments at Sinai. That shows that Christ is the Lord God who spoke the ten commandments. Consequently the fourth commandment for the keeping of the seventh day is a command of Jesus Christ.

The words of the ten commandments about the seventh day being the Sabbath of the Lord are equivalent, according to the New Testament, to saying, the seventh day is the Sabbath of the Lord Jesus Christ because He spoke the ten commandments. If you read this New Testament through one hundred times, you will not find where Jesus Christ ever told anybody to keep the first day of the week for any reason whatsoever. Christ did speak the ten commandments and told men what day they should keep. The seventh day is the only day that the Lord Jesus has ever asked anybody to keep. My friends, if we obey the Lord Jesus Christ, what else can we do but keep the seventh day as He tells us?

What does all this mean to you? What does it mean to me? It means that if we are not already keeping the seventh-day Sabbath, we had better make up our minds to begin keeping it as one of God's commandments just the same as the commandments Thou shalt not steal; and Thou shalt not bear false witness, etc.

There are two facts which forever settle this whole question. **The seventh day is the only day of weekly observance that Jesus Christ ever told man to** keep. The seventh day is the only day of weekly observance that Christ ever blessed or sanctified or hallowed or set apart for man.

Now I am going to put the capstone on all this evidence by reading a text that shows that this seventh-day Sabbath will be kept throughout eternity by the redeemed in the earth made new. You may put down Isaiah 66:22, 23. The prophet is talking about the new earth. He says, "As the new heavens and the new earth, which I will make, shall remain before me, saith the Lord, so shall your seed and your name remain. And it shall come to pass, that from one new moon to another, and from one Sabbath to another, shall all flesh come to worship before me, saith the Lord."

This shows that the seventh-day Sabbath will be kept throughout eternity. It was here before sin entered. It will be here when sin is gone. It is like a great rainbow arch reaching from Eden lost to Eden restored; from paradise forfeited through disobedience to paradise regained by obedience to Jesus

The most important matter of all is for us to make sure of an eternal happy home in God's wonderful new earth. We need Jesus to help us to be there. It would be better for us never to have been born than to miss a home in His wonderful kingdom "What will it profit a man, if he gain the whole world and lose his-own soul?"

Friends, I want to be there and I want Christ to help me to be there. How many of you with me want to raise your hand as a silent prayer, "Lord help me to so follow Thy Word that I may live forever in Thy wonderful kingdom?" Yes, it seems that every hand is raised.

(Prayer)

Blessed Lord Jesus, we thank Thee for Thy great sacrifice upon the cross We thank Thee that through that sacrifice we have the hope of eternal life We thank Thee for this glorious new earth that Thou wilt prepare, this New Jerusalem that Thou hast already prepared for Thine own. Dear Lord, we want to be there. It is all we have to live for, and tonight .we have raised our hands for Thee to help us. Oh, Lord, do help us to follow Thee that we may have an eternal happy home in the place Thou hast prepared for us. We ask it in Jesus' name. Amen.

ADDITIONAL NOTES ON THE IDENTITY OF THE SEVENTH DAY

Some people think that the calendar has been changed therefore we cannot be sure that the seventh day commanded in the ten commandments is the day now called Saturday Since the days of Christ only one change has been made in the calendar, and that was the change from the Julian calendar to the Gregorian This did not in any way affect the days of the week. By 1582 A. D., due to Julius Caesar having inserted a leap year too often, the calendar had drifted away from the seasons The spring equinox, instead of coming on March 21st came on March 11th. To correct the calendar ten days were dropped. Friday, October 5th was called Friday, October 15th. It was still Friday, and Saturday followed as usual Neither Saturday nor Sunday was affected. Some countries who delayed adoption of the reform calendar till 1752 found it necessary to call September 3rd of that year September 14th, thus dropping eleven days. It was a Thursday, and Friday followed as usual. In other words, the changes in the calendar did not affect in any way the order of the days of the week. Hence the seventh day of the week continues as the true seventh day of the week, the day we call Saturday

The Key of Knowledge

(Presented at the Bible Class on the Fifth Thursday Night)

Look at the first item on the lesson outline: "A right understanding of God's law is a key which unlocks the truth of God" On the blank line record Luke 11.52.

Mr. Reynolds, will you please read this text for us? "Woe unto you, lawyers! for ye have taken away the key of knowledge: ye entered not in yourselves, and them that were entering in ye hindered"

You will notice that Jesus Christ addressed those words to the lawyers. The lawyers of Christ's day were men who interpreted the meaning of the laws of God. Jesus shows that by misinterpreting the law of God, they had taken away the key of knowledge. This indicates that a right understanding of God's law is the key of knowledge which unlocks the truth of God.

It is easy to open a lock if you have the right key. So you may readily gain an understanding of the real truth, if you have the key of knowledge, which is a true understanding of the Law of God

Look at the second proposition "A failure to recognize the difference in the nature, application and duration of the Ten Commandment law in contrast to the Ceremonial Law of Moses has caused millions to miss the real truth in regard to the true Lord's day for Christians."

One of the main arguments which people use against the keeping of the seventh day is that all the laws given in the Old Testament, including the Ten Commandments, passed away at the cross. Notice the third statement on the lesson outline: "The Bible presents two distinct systems of law." On the blank line record Deut. 33:2-4.

Mr. Heglund, we shall hear from you on this reference. "The Lord came from Sinai, and rose up from Seir unto them; he shined forth from Mount Paran, and He came with ten thousands of saints: from His right hand went a fiery law for them. Yea, He loved the people; all His saints are in Thy hand: and they sat down at Thy feet; every one shall receive of Thy words. Moses commanded us a law, even the inheritance of the congregation of Jacob."

How many different laws are mentioned in this Scripture? Two different laws are mentioned. First, a fiery law which came direct from God's right hand; then second, another law, which was commanded by Moses. One law which came direct from God's own hand; another law that was commanded to the people by Moses at the Lord's direction.

God Himself made a clear distinction between the laws of the Old Testament. The Ten Commandments were spoken by God's own voice, and written by the Lord Himself on stone, and placed inside the ark of the covenant. The Ceremonial Laws of Moses were promulgated by the voice of Moses—were written by him with a pen in a book, and placed in a pocket outside the ark.

Look at the fourth proposition. "The New Testament shows that the principles of the Ten Commandments, with the seventh-day Sabbath in their very heart, are binding upon Christians today as a rule of life and conduct." You will notice that we list three references on this: Eph. 6.2; James 2:8-12; Acts 13:14.

In Eph. 6:2 Paul quotes from the Ten Commandments as being a code, binding on Christians some twenty-nine years after the old covenant had passed away he said, "Honour thy father and mother; which is the first commandment with promise." In writing to them he quotes from the Ten Commandments as a binding code on Christians.

In James 2.8-12 it speaks directly of the Ten Commandments and says, "Whosoever shall keep the whole law, and yet offend in one point, he is guilty of all." This shows that every one of the Ten Commandments is binding on Christians.

Acts 13:14 shows that the same seventh-day which was the Sabbath before the crucifixion continued to be the Sabbath after the crucifixion and resurrection of Christ.

Notice the second item under the fourth proposition. "The New Testament also shows that the offering of animal sacrifices, meat offerings and drink offerings, and the observance of the feast days, new moons and yearly sabbaths of the Mosaic law were abolished at the cross." On the blank line write in Col. 2·14-17.

Here is something which is especially important for you to understand. Col. 2:14-17 is the reference which many people use to prove that the seventh-day Sabbath was done away with at the cross. I am not a prophet, but I know that in the next two or three weeks many of you will have this reference thrust at you. Preachers will use this text and say, "Just look at this! This proves that the Sabbath was done away with in Christ." Jesus said, "How readest thou?" It is very necessary that we have the true understanding of this text.

All right, Mr. Jayne we shall hear from you as to how this Scripture reads. "Blotting out the handwriting of ordinances that was against us, which was contrary to us, and took it out of the way, nailing it to His cross; And having spoiled principalities and powers, he made a show of them openly, triumphing over them in it. Let no man therefore judge you in meat, or in drink, or in respect of an holy day, or of the new moon, or of the sabbath days: Which are a shadow of things to come; but the body is of Christ."

Notice that the sabbath days which Paul refers to were a part of the handwriting of ordinances, because in Col 2:14-17 he definitely is speaking of the handwriting of ordinances that was nailed to the cross. Just ask yourself the question, "Does the handwriting of ordinances that was nailed to the cross and abolished, mean the ten commandments, or does that refer to the ceremonial law?" The very word "ordinances" shows that it refers to the Ceremonial Law. What is an ordinance? The dictionary says, "An ordinance is a religious rite or ceremony." There are no ordinances in the Ten Commandments. The ordinances are found in the Ceremonial Law. An ordinance is a ceremony and Paul is talking about the Ceremonial Laws.

Look at the fifth item on the lesson outline: "The twenty-third chapter of Leviticus (remember, Leviticus is the ceremonial law) reveals that in addition to the weekly seventh-day Sabbath, which originated at creation, the Jews were given seven yearly sabbaths when they came out of Egypt. These were the fifteenth and twenty-first day of the first month, the day of Penecost, the first, tenth, fifteenth and twenty-second days of the seventh month.

Look at the sixth proposition: "Paul expressly shows that the sabbath days which were done away with in Christ, were these yearly sabbath days connected with the new moons and the feast days of the Jews, which pointed forward to Christ's death on the cross.

Paul is very careful to define which sabbath days he is talking about. He says in the 16th and 17th verses, "The sabbath days which are a shadow of things to come." It was the ceremonial sabbaths that pointed forward to the cross; those ceremonial sabbaths, with which certain offerings were connected, which pointed forward to the Saviour's death.

We have a chart here which reveals the differences between the weekly seventh-day Sabbath, and the yearly sabbaths of the ceremonial law. Notice that the seventh-day Sabbath of the ten commandments was made at creation, when God rested on the seventh day, and then sanctified or set apart for man to keep holy.

These yearly sabbaths of the ceremonial law in Lev 23 were made twenty-five hundred years after creation, when the Jews came out of Egypt. Jesus said it was made for man The yearly sabbaths were for the Jews only. The seventh-day Sabbath was for all ages and times The yearly sabbaths were only for the Mosaic dispensation, and passed away at the cross The seventh-day Sabbath came once a week. The sabbaths of the Ceremonial Law came once a year. The seventh-day Sabbath points back to creation, the yearly sabbaths pointed forward to the cross.

(At this juncture a chart showing the shadow of the cross was lowered in view of the audience.)

This chart illustrates the shadow of the cross Notice in this scene how the cross is the great center around which God's plan revolves. The shadow of the cross reaches back to the garden of Eden, when they offered the first lamb. Every lamb they offered pointed to the great Lamb of God, Who was to die for the sins of the world. Notice that since the cross we have ordinances that point back to Calvary. The cross is the great center. The people of Old Testament times looked forward to the cross. In our days we have ordinances that point us back to the cross We have the Lord's Supper and Baptism, which point back to the crucifixion and resurrection of Christ.

Notice this line at the top which runs all the way across the chart. This shows that the Ten Commandments, as the great law of God, are eternally binding. Notice that the law of Moses came in when Israel left Egypt, and continued only to the cross. The law of Moses was nailed to the cross and abolished, but the Ten Commandments were separate from the laws of Moses, and continued binding after the cross.

Notice the seventh propositon· "The New Testament clearly teaches that the keeping of the seventh-day Sabbath remains after the cross" The first reference is Acts 13.14, where the term Sabbath is identified with the Saturday-meeting day of the Jews in the days of the apostles

On the blank line fill in Hebrews 4 9, 4, 10

Mr L. R Holley, will you please read Heb 4 9 for us? "There remaineth therefore a rest to the people of God"

In the margin it says, "the keeping of a Sabbath." The Greek word is "Sabbatismos," which means, "sabbath keeping" In other words the writer of Hebrews says, Sabbath keeping remains The sacrifices of the old covenant are abolished. The worldly sanctuary has ended But Sabbath keeping remains. "There remaineth the keeping of a Sabbath to the people of God."

What Sabbath is it that remains for the people of God? Listen to verse 4: "For he spake in a certain place of the seventh day on this wise, And God did rest the seventh day from all His works." Notice that in the context, he specifically mentions the seventh day as the day of God's rest. This shows us that the Sabbath keeping which remains is the keeping of that seventh day on which God rested.

Suppose I had a 2x4 piece of lumber 10 feet long. I cut off 2 feet, 8 feet remains What will this 8 feet be like? Will it be 2x6? No! Will it be a 2x8? No! Will it be a 1x4? No! It will be 8 feet of 2x4. It is simply a continuation of the same size piece of wood from which I cut 2 feet. Therefore, the Sabbath that remains must be a continuation of the same weekly Sabbath they had before the cross, which was none other than the seventh-day Sabbath.

Now, Mr. Holley, please read verse 10: "He that is entered into his rest, he also hath ceased from his own works, as God did from His."

The import of this text is that a Christian is to rest as God rested. Tell me, dear friends, if a Christian rests as God rested, on what day will he rest? Yes, the seventh day. This is very plain. If a Christian rests as God rested, he will rest on the seventh day.

God set the seventh day apart for man to keep because He rested upon that day. In Genesis 2.3 we read, "God blessed the seventh day and sanctified it: because that in it He had rested from all His work which he had made." God actually set the seventh day apart for man, because on that day He had rested. Resting as God rested must include resting on the day that God rests, which is none other than the last day of the week, or the seventh day.

Look at proposition No. 8: "While the cross of Christ testified of the abolition of the ceremonial law, it witnesses to the immutability and perpetuity of the Ten Commandments " Two references are listed: 1 Cor. 15·3 and 1 John 3:4.

I want to show you how **law and grace meet at the cross.** Take the word "law." The middle letter of law is what? "a." Now what is the middle letter of "grace?" The middle letter of "Grace" is "a" also. L-a-w, "a" is the middle letter of law. G-r-a-c-e, "a" is the middle letter of "grace." When you place "law" and grace together, so the "a" in each coincides, it forms a cross. The cross of Christ didn't do away with the law. The cross of Christ only testifies to the immutability and perpetuity of the great law of God, the Ten Commandments.

Now look at proposition No. 9: "When the Jewish Christians who still kept these yearly holy days of the Mosaic Law condemned the Gentile Christians for not observing them, Paul urged that the matter be left to each person's choice."

This text has been greatly misunderstood. People quote this reference to justify themselves in the idea that it makes no difference what day we keep, just so we keep a day. Paul does not mean this at all.

I read Romans 14 5, 6: "One man esteemeth one day above another: another esteemeth every day alike. Let every man be fully persuaded in his own mind. He that regardeth the day, regardeth it unto the Lord, and he that regardth not the day, to the Lord he doth not regard it. He that eateth, eateth to the Lord, for he giveth God thanks; and he that eateth not, to the Lord he eateth not, and giveth God thanks."

Paul is talking about days of esteem, days that men esteem. He is not thinking about the day that God commands man to keep. There were two classes of people in the early Christian church. There were the Jewish Christians, who went on keeping these yearly Sabbaths. They had been brought up that way. They kept the day of atonement; they kept the day of Pentecost; they kept the Passover. They went on keeping these yearly sabbaths according to their custom even when they had been done away with at the cross.

The Gentile Christians who had never been under the ceremonial law paid no attention to those yearly sabbaths. The result was that one class began condemning the other about it. Paul exhorted them not to condemn one another about this matter, but to let each do as he thought best. This had reference not to the keeping of the seventh day, but to the Jewish feast days, which had already passed away, and were not binding. He urged that this be left to each person's own choice. It is a misinterpretation of this scripture to use it to support the idea that it makes no difference which day we keep, just so we keep a day.

Now look at Proposition No. 10: "Not being under the law, but under grace, does not release Christians from the obligation to keep all the Ten Cmmandments." On the blank line record Romans 6:14, 15.

Mr. Reynolds will you read this reference? "Sin shall not have dominion over you: for ye are not under the law, but under grace. What then? Shall we sin, because we are not under the law, but under grace? God forbid."

Notice how this reads. He says, "Sin shall not have dominion over you, for ye are not under the law, but under grace." A lot of people stop right there. They say this proves that a Christian is not under the Ten Commandments at all. He doesn't have to keep the Ten Commandments. He is under grace. If they would just read on, they wouldn't draw such a conclusion. Paul evidently knew that people would get the wrong idea. He says, "What then? shall we sin?" What is sin? I John 3:4 says, "Sin is the transgression of the law." All right, "Shall we transgress the law because we are not under the law, but under grace?" What is the answer? "God forbid!" Evidently Paul had no idea of conveying the impression that being under grace gave a Christian the right to live contrary to the Ten Commandments.

Does being under grace, and not under the law, give a man the right to break the eighth commandment, which says, "Thou shalt not steal?" You say, "No." Even so, being under grace and not under the law doesn't give a Christian the right to break the fourth commandment. Why would a Christian want to be free from a law that forbids stealing, lying, murder, swearing, and such? A true Christian wouldn't want to be free from such a law as this.

Notice proposition No. 11. "Instead of the keeping of the Sabbath being contrary to grace, it is one of God's own appointed signs of the work of grace in the believer's life." Put down on the blank line Eze. 20·12.

Mr. Heglund will you please read Eze. 20.12? "Moreover also I gave them My sabbaths, to be a sign between Me and them, that they might know that I am the Lord that sanctify them"

Notice that God says, "I gave them My sabbaths, to be a sign between Me and them, that they might know that I am the Lord that sanctify them." The Sabbath is a sign of sanctification. The keeping of the Sabbath is a sign that God is sanctifying you. It is a sign of the work of grace in your heart and life. The keeping of the Sabbath shows that we are looking to Jesus alone to save us and that we could no more save ourselves, than we could create a world. The same seventh-day that is a sign of creation is also a sign of redemption.

Look at proposition No. 12: "The doctrine of keeping the seventh day stands God's tests for being a part of His truth." The reference is Isa. 8:20. It says, "To the law and to the testimony. If they speak not according to this word, it is because there is no light in them."

This is God's test for true doctrine. The true doctrine will be according to the law of God and the Word of God You know that the keeping of the seventh day is according to the law of God and according to the word of God. Then there must be light in that doctrine for you. The doctrine of keeping the first day of the week doesn't stand the test of the law of God. He says, "To the Law and to the testimony: if they speak not according to this word, it is because there is no light in them."

Look at proposition No. 13. "God is particular that we obey His law exactly as He worded it. In Deut. 4 2 He tells us, that we are not to add unto the commandments nor take anything away from the Commandments, but keep them as He gave them: If we do not keep the seventh day, we are actually taking something away from the law. If we kept the first day in place of the seventh day, we would be adding something to His law. God says, we are not to do this, but to keep it as He gave it.

Look at proposition No. 14: "God requires implicit obedience even in what may seem to us like small matters." In Luke 17:32 you have the shortest sermon Jesus ever preached. It is these three words, "Remember Lot's wife." What about Lot's wife? The angel said to her, "Do not look behind you." This seemed like a little thing. In fact it is rather difficult to keep from looking around when something interesting is going on behind you. In this case the whole town was being burned up. The angel said, "Do not look back." She disobeyed and lost her life and lost her soul. Jesus says, "Remember Lot's wife."

It shows us that when God gives a command, even though it seems like a little thing, God expects us to obey. In John 13:8 we have the statement that Jesus made to Peter. Jesus was washing His disciple's feet. Peter said, "Lord are you going to wash my feet?" Jesus answered him, "What I do thou knowest not now; but thou shalt know hereafter."

Then Peter said, "Thou shalt never wash my feet." Jesus said, "If I wash thee not, thou shalt have no part with me."

Peter said, "Lord, not my feet only, but also my hands and my head." His "never" lasted just about two minutes

Even a little matter like having his feet washed meant everything, because it was a matter of obedience to the Lord Jesus Christ. Hence, the right understanding of the importance of God's law is in your hand a key of knowledge. Let obedience open the door to new vistas beyond.

Now we are ready for the ushers to bring your questions to the desk, to be answered.

(Copy of the Bible lesson outline, which was distributed to the people preceding the nineteenth lecture.)

LESSON III—THE KEY OF KNOWLEDGE

1. A right understanding of God's law is a key, which unlocks the truth of God ....
2. A failure to recognize the difference in the nature, application and duration of the ten commandment law in contrast to the ceremonial law of Moses has caused millions to miss the real truth in regard to the true Lord's day for Christians.
3. The Bible presents two distinct systems of law........ . ...
4A. The New Testament shows that the principles of the ten commandments, with the seventh-day Sabbath in their very heart are binding on Christians today as a rule of life and conduct. (Eph. 6:2; Jas. 2:8-12; Acts 13:14.)
4B. It also shows that the offering of animal sacrifices, meat offerings and drink offerings, and the observance of the feast days, new moons and yearly sabbaths of the Mosaic law were abolished at the cross ....
5. The twenty-third chapter of Leviticus reveals that in addition to the weekly seventh-day Sabbath, which originated at creation, the Jews were given seven yearly sabbaths when they came out of Egypt. These were the fifteenth and twenty-first day of the first month, the day of Pentecost, the first, tenth, fifteenth and twenty-second days of the seventh month.
6. Paul expressly shows that the sabbath days which were done away with in Christ, were these yearly sabbath days connected with the new moons and the feast days of the Jews, and which pointed forward to Christ's death on the cross.
7. The New Testament clearly teaches that the keeping of the seventh-day Sabbath remains after the cross. (Acts 13:14.).... ....
8. While the cross of Christ testifies of the abolition of the ceremonial law, it witnesses to the immutability and perpetuity of the ten commandments. (I Cor. 15:3) (I Jno. 3:4.)
9. When the Jewish Christians, who still kept these yearly holy days of the

Mosaic law, condemned the Gentile Christians for not observing them, Paul urged that the matter be left to each person's own choice. (Rom. 14:5, 6.)

10. Not being under the law, but under grace, does not release Christians from the obligation to keep all the ten commandments... ....

11. Instead of the keeping of the Sabbath being contrary to grace, it is one of God's own appointed signs of the work of grace in the believer's life......

12. The doctrine of keeping the seventh-day stands God's test for being a part of His truth. (Isa. 8:20.)

13. God is particular that we obey His law exactly as He worded it. (Deut. 4:2.)

14. God requires implicit obedience even in what may seem to us like small matters. (Luke 17:32; Gen. 19:17; Jno. 13:8.)

References which were filled in as the study was presented: (1) Luke 11: 52; (3) Deut. 33 2-4; (4B) Col. 2:14-17; (7) Heb. 4:9, 4, 10; (10) Rom. 6:14, 15; (11) Eze. 20:12.

"$5,000 for One Text"

(Preached on the Fifth Friday Night of the Campaign)

I hold in my hand a letter from A. N. Dugger, a leading minister in a denomination known as the Church of God. He is also editor of their official CHURCH OF GOD ADVOCATE. Mr. Dugger writes me as follows:

> Elder J. L .Shuler
> Dear Sir:
> In regard to the matter of what day we ought to keep holy, I will say that I hereby offer you or anyone else $5,000 if they will produce one text from the New Testament which says that we ought to keep the first day of the week or Sunday as a holy day. The law setting apart the first day of the week or Sunday as a rest day or holy day was made by the Catholic church long after the Bible was written; hence, said law cannot be found in the Bible.
> Yours sincerely,
> (Signed) A. N. DUGGER, Editor
> CHURCH OF GOD ADVOCATE.

He offers to give me, or anyone, $5,000 if we will produce one text of scripture which says that Christians are to keep the first day of the week. I could use this 5,000 dollars. It would come in very handy. Hence if it is possible to produce such a text, I want to find it. I plan to examine every text in the New Testament that mentions the first day of the week and see if this $5,000 can be won.

The first day of the week, the day we now call Sunday, is mentioned eight times in the New Testament. I have placed these eight references on the blackboard, so that everyone here may see for himself the eight instances where the New Testament mentions the first day of the week. These are: Mark 16 9, 1, 2, Matt. 28:1; Luke 24:1; John 20 1, 19; 1 Cor. 16:2; Acts 20·7.

It is evident that if there be any proof for the keeping of the first day of the week, or Sunday, it will be found in connection with the eight places in the New Testament which mentions the first day of the week. This $5,000 offer is open to everyone in this audience. You notice he said, "I hereby offer you or anyone else." If you know of any text which says we ought to keep the first day of the week, and I fail to read it, then I want you to place that text on a slip of paper and have an usher bring it to me, and you will receive the $5,000. At a certain time in my lecture I will pause for the ushers to pass up and down the aisles and collect any such texts.

I turn to Mark 16.9. "Now when Jesus was risen early the first day of the week, he appeared first to Mary Magdalene, out of whom He had cast seven devils." This text merely states the fact that when Jesus arose, early on the first day of the week, He appeared first to Mary Magdalene. I cannot claim the $5,000 with this text, because there is not a word in the text to the effect that Christians should keep the first day of the week in honor of the Lord's resurrection.

Next, I turn to Mark 16·1, 2: "When the Sabbath was past, Mary Magdalene, and Mary the mother of James, and Salome, had brought sweet spices, that they might come and anoint him. And very early in the morning, the first day of the week, they came unto the sepulchre at the rising of the sun."

You will notice that this text declares that when the Sabbath was **past**, certain women came to the tomb early on the first day of the week.

Nobody could get the $5,000 on this text, because there isn't a word there to the effect that Chrisians should keep the first day of the week. In fact, it shows that Sunday, the first day of the week, cannot be the Sabbath. The text declares that the Sabbath was past when these women came to the tomb at daybreak on the first day of the week. The first day of the week cannot be the Sabbath, because the Sabbath was **past** when they came to the tomb at the rising of the sun.

The first day of the week cannot be the Sabbath any more than 1945 could be 1946, because 1945 was passed when 1946 began. Since the Sabbath was passed before the first day of the week dawned, that Sabbath must be the day that comes before the first day of the week, which you know is the seventh day, the day we call Saturday. Hence, Mark 16 1, 2 shows that the seventh day or Saturday is the Sabbath of the New Testament.

It is really impossible to keep the Sabbath on Sunday. Why? Because the Sabbath is passed before Sunday dawns. No matter how early you get up on Sunday morning, you couldn't keep the Sabbath, because the Sabbath is already passed before you rise from your bed on Sunday mrning. Mark 16.1, 2 says that the Sabbath was passed when they came to that tomb at sunrise.

I turn now to Matthew 28:1. "In the end of the Sabbath, as it began to dawn toward the first day of the week, came Mary Magdalene and the other Mary to see the sepulchre." This simply states the fact that these women came to the tomb early in the morning on the first day of the week.

Next, I turn to Luke 24 1. "Now upon the first day of the week, very early in the morning, they came unto the sepulchre, bringing the spices which they had prepared, and certain others with them." I cannot qualify for the $5,000 award with this text, because there is not a word there to the effect that Christians are to keep the first day of the week in honour of the resurrection.

Now I turn to John 20 1. "The first day of the week cometh Mary Magdalene early, when it was yet dark, unto the sepulchre, and seeth the stone taken away from the sepulchre." This simply states that on the first day of the week when Christ arose, Mary Magdalene came to the tomb while it was yet dark, and she found the stone had been rolled away from the door of the tomb.

I have now read five of the eight texts which mention the first day of the week in the New Testament. So far I have found nothing with which I could claim the $5,000. I still have three more chances.

I turn next to John 20 19. This is a text that some people believe contains proof that Sunday is the right day for Christians to keep. They tell us that this text shows that Christ's disciples held a special meeting on the very Sunday of Christ's resurrection, to inaugurate the keeping of Sunday as the Christian Sabbath, or the Lord's day. If the text says this, I will be $5,000 better off. I want you to listen carefully as I read the text and see what it says.

"Then the same day at evening, being the first day of the week, when the doors were shut where the disciples were assembled for fear of the Jews came Jesus and stood in the midst, and saith ûnto them, Peace be unto you."

Does this text say that the disciples had gathered on the Sunday evening of the day on which Christ arose, to honour His resurrection? No! People have read something into this text that doesn't belong there In fact, the Scriptures show that these disciples had not met to worship in honour of Christ's resurrection. How do I know this? I know it for two reasons from the Bible. Put down Mark 16.9-13.

In this reference you will find that when Jesus arose early on the first day of the week, He appeared first to Mary Magdalene. She ran and told the disciples. She said, "The Lord is risen. I've seen Him." They refused to believe it. A little later in the day Jesus appeared unto two of the disciples as they walked out into the country. They ran back and told the others. They said, "The Lord is risen! Jesus is alive." They said, "Not so." They refused to believe it. So you can see that those men could not possibly have gathered in honour of Christ's resurrection when they didn't believe He was risen.

The second point to put down is Mark 16:14. Mark refers to this very same meeting that John describes in John 20:19. He says, "He appeared unto the eleven as they sat at meat." In other words, they had gathered in their common abode to eat their evening meal. They had not met to worship in honour of Christ's resurrection. They had simply gathered in their common abode to eat their evening meal.

When Jesus appeared in their midst, they were terrified. He said, "Have you any food?" They had been eating their supper, so they handed Jesus a piece of broiled fish and a piece of honey comb and He ate them. The fact that they had gathered on this Sunday evening to eat their supper proves nothing in favor of Sunday observance.

I should like to have the $5,000, but I cannot ask for it on the basis of what I find in John 20:19. The text says nothing to the effect that Christians were keeping the first day of the week or ever were to keep the first day of the week. You will notice that this makes six texts that mention the first day of the week in direct connection with the very Sunday on which the Lord Jesus arose, and yet they do not say one word to the effect that Christians are to keep the first day of the week in honour of our Lord's resurrection on that day.

I still have two more chances. The next reference is I Corinthians 16:2. Let us read: "Upon the first day of the week let everyone of you lay by him in store, as God hath prospered him, that there be no gatherings when I come."

Some people claim that here is proof that Sunday is the right day for people to keep. They say, "Doesn't Paul give an order for the church to take a collection upon the first day of the week? How could they take up a collection unless they had a meeting?" So the claim is made that Sunday was the regular day for Christians to keep in the days of the apostles.

What does the scripture say? If you read the text carefully, you will see that it has no reference to a collection being taken at church. Does it say, "Upon the first day of the week let everyone drop an offering in the collection basket?" No! "Upon the first day of the week let everyone of you lay by him."

The money was to be laid aside at home. In fact, the Portuguese version of the Scriptures, the Italian version, the Spanish version, and many other versions of the Scriptures render this text, "Lay by at home." It was a private laying by at home.

Paul was gathering relief funds for the poor saints at Jerusalem. He planned to stop at Corinth on his way to Jerusalem. So he wrote on ahead, and as it were, saying, "Now I am coming through on my way to Jerusalem. I want you to lay aside something on the first day of every week at home so you will have something to turn over to me, that I can take with me to the poor saints at Jerusalem."

I still have one more chance, and that is Acts 20:7. Here we read, "Upon the first day of the week, when the disciples came together to break bread, Paul preached unto them, ready to depart on the morrow; and continued his speech until midnight."

Some people say that here is proof that the first day of the week was the regular meeting day for the Christian people in the days of the apostles. If the text said that, I would have the $5,000. Notice that the text does not say anything about the Christians meeting every week upon the first day of the week.

Read the context and you will see that this was only an incidental meeting held upon what we call Saturday night. It tells you in the context that Paul was leaving the next morning. They never expected to see him again in this world, and that is why he talked all night long. Of course you know that no church ordinarily holds a meeting all night long. This was simply an extraordinary occasion, a farewell occasion, and that is why Paul preached all night long.

In the Bible, the day of twenty-four hours is measured from sunset to sunset. This all night meeting must have begun on Saturday evening and continued unto day break on Sunday morning. If you will read this twentieth chapter of Acts, you will find that Paul took a nineteen or twenty-mile journey on foot Sunday morning following this all night meeting. In other words, the context gives evidence that Paul didn't keep the first day of the week as a holy day of rest. He regarded Sunday as an ordinary working day, just like Monday, Thursday or Tuesday.

Now I must be frank and tell you that cannot find any text that says that Christians should keep the first day or Sunday. I cannot win this $5,000. If you know of any text which I did not read which says that Christians should keep the first day of the week, please write it quickly and hand it to an usher, so he can bring it to the front. Attention all ushers. Please arise and pass through the aisles and bring to the front any text that people hand to you on a slip of paper.

According to the Bible, it is no more necessary to keep Sunday to honour Christ's resurrection than to keep Friday every week to celebrate our Saviour's death that took place on Friday. Why do I say this? Here are two references. I Cor. 11:26 and Colossians 2:12. Jesus Christ instituted the Lord's Supper, the Communion of bread and wine, to celebrate His crucifixion. Paul says, "As oft as ye eat this bread and drink this cup, ye shew the Lord's death till He come."

Even so Jesus Christ instituted Christian baptism to celebrate His resurrection. Paul says in Col. 2:12, "Buried with Him in baptism, wherein also ye are risen with Him through the faith of the operation of God, who hath raised Him from the dead."

Follow me closely. There is a real kernel of truth here. There is no need to keep Friday to celebrate the Lord's crucifixion, because He has ordained the Lord's supper to commemorate His death upon the cross. So there is no need to keep Sunday to honor Christ's resurrection, because He has ordained Christian baptism as the means of celebrating His resurrection, and to show our faith in His resurrection. So there is no more authority for keeping Sunday than there is for keeping Friday.

Ushers, do you have any texts? Nobody seems to want this $5,000. If a millionaire offered a million dollars for one Bible text that says Christians should keep the first day of the week and gave people fifty years to find it, no one would be able to produce the text.

If you read the Bible through one hundred times, with reference to the Sabbath question, what will you find? You will find ten notable facts.

1. The word "Sunday" never occurs in the Bible.

2. Jesus Christ and His apostles never changed the Sabbath from the seventh day to the first day of the week, or Sunday.

3. Jesus Christ and the apostles never observed the first day of the week for the Sabbath.

4. There is no divine command in the New Testament for keeping the first day of the week, or Sunday.

5. There is nothing to indicate that the first day is to be kept for any reason.

6. There isn't anything to indicate that the keeping of the

first day of the week, or Sunday, took the place of the seventh day of the week during Bible times.

7. The fourth commandment of the ten commandments which required the keeping of the seventh day, is still binding upon all men just like the command, "Thou shalt not steal."

8. Neither God, Christ, Angels, nor inspired men have ever said one word in favor of Sunday as a holy day.

9. The seventh, or Saturday, is the only day of the week that Jesus Christ ever sanctified, or set apart for man to keep holy.

10. The seventh day is the only day of weekly observance that the Bible ever directs man to keep.

Have you ever noticed what Christ's followers did upon the day before Sunday? Put down Luke 24:1 and Luke 23.56. Luke 24:1, which I have read, tells how they came to Christ's tomb at sunrise on Sunday morning. The preceding verse or Luke 28:56, tells what they did upon the day before the first day of the week. Listen as I read Luke 23.56, "They returned, and prepared spices and ointments; and rested the Sabbath day according to the commandment."

Isn't that plain? Christ's followers kept the day before Sunday as the Sabbath according to God's commandment. You know and I know, and everybody else knows, that the day before Sunday is Saturday, or the seventh day of the week. Christ's followers had to keep the day before Sunday in order to obey Christ's commandments.

Friends, think this through. If you and I obey God, what day will we keep? We will keep the seventh day according to the commandment. The fifth book in the New Testament which is the Acts of the Apostles, gives the history of Christ's church for about twenty-eight years after the crucifixion and resurrection of Jesus Christ.

This Book of Acts mentions the Sabbath eight times. Here are the references: Acts 13:14; Acts 13:27; Acts 13 42; Acts 13:44; Acts 15:21; Acts 16:13; Acts 17:1-3; Acts 18:4. You will find that every time, eight times over, the Acts of the Apostles speaks about the Sabbath, it identifies the Sabbath with the Saturday meeting day of the Jews in the days of the Apostles.

Let me ask you a plain question. Do you think anybody who lived after the apostles had the right to change the Sabbath from the seventh-day to the first? What do you say? No! No! Then it is evident that since Saturday was the Sabbath in the days of the apostles, it is bound to be the Sabbath for Christians today. All Christians today should follow the book of Acts and keep the seventh-day or Saturday, which the book of Acts calls the Sabbath in eight different places.

Now the question comes, what does all this mean to you and to me? What shall I do about it? What of it? It means that since there is no Bible authority for keeping Sunday, the only wise course is to turn and henceforth keep the seventh day, or Saturday, which Jesus Christ sanctified and set apart for man and commands us to keep in the ten commandments.

Did you ever find yourself on a wrong road in your travels? Yes, I have many times. I have found myself going in the wrong direction, when I honestly thought I was on the right road. What did I do? I turned around and took the right road. That is the only wise thing to do.

Some mischievous boys will turn a roadsign around, so that it points in the opposite direction from the way it should. It misleads people. If a man is misled by such a sign all he can do is turn around and get on the right road. Somebody has turned the Sabbath signpost around, so it is leading Christian travelers in the wrong direction regarding the Sabbath. Millions are keeping Sunday, honestly believing it is God's holy day according to the Bible, when it is directly contrary to the Bible. At the same time they are unknowingly working on the very day God says we should keep holy.

Sunday night you will find out from the Bible who is the guilty party. This jury trial scheduled for Sunday night will discover who changed the Sabbath from Saturday to Sunday, how it was changed, and when it was changed.

Some time ago a man at Detroit bought a railroad ticket for Grand Rapids, Michigan. Unknowingly he boarded a limited eastbound flyer. The train had crossed the Detroit river and had proceeded a good way over into Canada before the conductor came through. He handed his ticket to the conductor. The conductor said, "Man, you are on the wrong train. Your ticket says 'Grand Rapids' and here you are going in the wrong direction over into Canada." The man got excited. He wouldn't believe the conductor. He wanted to argue about it. He felt so sure he was right. Finally he said to the conductor, "Well, what shall I do?"

The conductor said, "Get off at the first stop, take the next train back to Detroit, and get on the right train for Grand Rapids" The man had ridden forty miles thinking he was on the right train, when he was going in the wrong direction all the time. "There is a way that seemeth right to a man, but the end thereof is death." You will find this in Proverbs 16:25. The wisest man who ever lived said that.

If a man is on the wrong train, he will never reach the right destination, no matter how sincere he may be, unless he changes and gets on the right train. Don't forget that God's heaven-bound train runs on the Christ-track of the commandments. Put down Revelation 22:14. "Blessed are they that do His commandments, that they may have right to the tree of life, and may enter in through the gates into the city."

Friends, we ought to keep the seventh day, just as we keep the eighth commandment by being honest, and just as we keep the ninth commandment by being truthful, or as we keep the third commandment by being reverent in the use of God's name. I want to be true to Jesus Christ and I am sure you do.

> "Keep me true, Lord, keep me true;
> Keep me true, Lord, true to you.
> May all I say or strive to do,
> Prove dear Lord I am true to you."

A troubled father once came to Jesus regarding his afflicted son. He said, "Jesus, if you can do anything for him, have mercy on him, and heal him." The poor man put the "if" in the wrong place. See what he said, "If you can do anything for him." There isn't any "if" in regard to the ability or power of Jesus Christ to help troubled souls. All power in heaven and in earth is given unto Him.

Jesus replied, "If thou canst believe, all things are possible to him that believeth." The man put the "if" in the wrong place. He put the "if" on Christ's part. Christ showed him that the "if" was on his part He fell at the feet of Jesus and cried, "Lord, I do believe, help my unbelief." And the blessed, loving Jesus did for that father what he so much wanted done.

Friends, I think this describes our situation. We believe in Jesus Christ We want to follow Him all the way. We need more help to follow Him on the Sabbath question. Shall we not fall at His feet and cry, "Lord, I do believe. Give me more faith and more grace to follow Thee all the way!" I believe everyone in this auditorium wants to be remembered in prayer that the Lord will help you to be true to Jesus. How many want to be remembered in this closing prayer, "Lord, help me to follow Jesus all the way?" May I see your hands? Yes, it seems that nearly every hand is raised.

(Prayer)

Our blessed Jesus, we thank Thee for this incident that we have just talked about. Lord, like many of us, he put the "if" in the wrong place. He said, "If Thou canst do it." Lord, there is never any "if" as to what Thou canst do. The "if" is on our own part. Thou hast said, "If we can believe, all things are possible." O, God, give us more faith. Lord, we do believe, but we pray Thee to help our unbelief. Jesus, give us more grace, more love, that will help us to follow Thee closely step by step until we come to that great day, when Thou shalt come and we will see Thee face to face and be with Thee forever. We ask it in Thy precious name. Amen.

Unlocking Truth's Mightiest Secret
(Preached on the Fifth Saturday Afternoon of the Campaign)

A minister was talking one day to a little girl whose first name was Eve. He asked her, "Do you attend Sunday School regularly?"

"Oh, yes, sir," she said.

"And you know your Bible?"

"Oh, yes, sir."

"Could you tell me something that is in the Bible?"

"I could tell you everything that is in the Bible." "Indeed?" and the minister smiled. "Do tell me, then."

She said, "Sister's beau's photo is in it, and ma's recipe for' vanishing cream is in it, and a lock of my hair that was cut off when I was a baby is in it, and the ticket for Pa's watch is in it."

I am afraid that many people's knowledge of the Bible resembles the knowledge of little Eve: There is not anything more important for you and me to know than the real truth as set forth in the Bible. Why is this? Why is it more important to know the real truth of the Bible than everything else? The main reason is found in Isaiah 26 2. "Open ye the gates, that the righteous nation which keepeth the truth may enter in."

You will notice that it is those who keep the truth who will enter in through the gates to live forever in God's beautiful heavenly home. You cannot keep the truth, until you first know what is truth. On the basis of Isaiah 26:2 it is evident that our very salvation, our eternal happiness depend upon learning and following the truth of God's Word.

Unless we know the real truth of the Bible we are very liable to be deceived and led astray by false teachings. Put down Matt. 22 29. It is just as Jesus told the Sadducees, "Ye do err, not knowing the scriptures." If we do not know the real truth of the Bible, then we are liable to be overtaken with error and false ideas. The right meaning of scripture brings truth and salvation. The wrong meaning of the Bible brings error and destruction. Oh, how important it is that we obtain the right meaning of the Bible!

Any man who attempts to explain the Bible according to his own ideas will not find the true meaning of the scriptures. Put down 2 Peter 1:20. "Knowing this first, that no prophecy of the scripture is of any private interpretation." Unfortunately, most people who try to explain the Bible, explain the Bible according to their ideas. Mark this point well. It doesn't matter how wise a person may be; it doesn't matter how many letters he may have after his name, if he attempts to explain the Bible according to his own ideas he will not find the true meaning of the Bible. "No prophecy of the scripture is of any private interpretation."

When people interpret the Bible according to their own ideas, two things usually happen. First, they will try to explain away some of the plainest truths in the Bible, if those truths happen to be contrary to their ideas. Second, they will try to use the Bible to prove a certain doctrine when in reality the Bible teaches just the opposite.

The Bible declares that some people wrest the scriptures to their own destruction. Put down 2 Peter 3.15, 16. It is a serious thing to misinterpret the Bible. When you misinterpret the Bible, your actions will be wrong, because your actions will be in harmony with your misinterpretation.

If we follow a religious teacher in a wrong interpretation of scripture, it may result in our own destruction. I want to give you a striking illustration. This is taken from the temptation of Jesus in the wilderness as recorded in Matt. 4:5-7. You will recall how Satan attempted to defeat Jesus in the first temptation. Jesus had been fasting for forty days. He was very, very hungry. Satan appeared and said, "If you are the Son of God, make these stones into bread and you will have something to eat to satisfy your intense hunger." Jesus met the issue with the words of scripture. He said, "It is written, man doth not live by bread only, but by every word that proceedeth out of the mouth of the Lord." He quoted Deut 8:3.

The devil evidently said to himself, "I'll show you a thing or two. You have quoted scripture to me, I am going to quote scripture to you." He took Christ up on the highest pinnacle of the temple. He said, "Just throw yourself off from here. It won't hurt you. It is written, 'He shall give His angels charge over thee, to keep thee in all thy ways lest thou dash thy foot against a stone'." He quoted Psalm 91:11, 12. The devil tried to prove his point by scripture. I don't want you to miss this. He tried to prove his point by scripture, but he misinterpreted scripture.

Tell me, what would have happened if Jesus Christ had followed Satan's misinterpretation of Psalm 91:11, 12? What would have happened if Christ had cast Himself off the temple? He would have been destroyed. This shows how a scripture may be wrested to one's own destruction.

There is a proper place to use Psalm 91:11, 12. It is a very beautiful passage. Some time I should like to talk to you on "Who are the Angels?" If I were talking on angels, I would use Psalm 91:11, 12.

The Bible teaches us that every Christian has a guardian angel. One certain angel has been assigned to every child of God as his angel, his guardian angel. On this point you can use Psalm 91. "He shall give His angels charge over thee." But God didn't mean that we could go to the top of a ten-story building, and jump off and say, "Now the angel will bear me up in his hand, so this won't hurt me." That would be presumption. That would be a sin, and God would not take care of us under that kind of misinterpretation.

The fact that the right meaning of the Bible brings truth and salvation, and the wrong meaning of the Bible brings error and destruction shows how important it is that we follow the right system of interpretation. It is interesting to notice how different people have read the Bible.

"It is one thing to read the Bible through,
Another thing to read—to learn and do.
Some read it with design to learn to read,
But to the subject pay but little heed.
Some read it as their duty once a week,
But no instruction from the Bible seek.
While others read it with but little care,
With no regard to how they read nor where.
Some read it as a history, to know
How people lived three thousand years ago.
Some read to bring themselves into repute,
By showing others how they can dispute;
While others read because their neighbors do,
To see how long 'twill take to read it through.
Some read it for the wonders that are there,—
How David killed a lion and a bear;
While others read it with uncommon care,
Hoping to find some contradictions there!
Some read as though it did not speak to them,

But to the people at Jerusalem.
One reads it as a book of mysteries,
And won't believe the very thing he sees.
One reads with father's specs upon his head,
And sees the thing just as his father said.
Some read to prove a pre-adopted creed,—
Hence understand but little what they read;
For every passage in the book they bend,
To make it suit that all-important end!
Some people read, as I have often thought
To teach the book instead of being taught,
And some there are who read it out of spite—
I fear there are but few who read it right.
So many people in these latter days,
Have read the Bible in so many ways
That few can tell which system is the best,
For every party contradicts the rest!
But read it prayerfully, and you will see,
Although men contradict, God's words agree.
For what the early Bible prophets wrote,
We find that Christ and his apostles quote!
So trust no creed that trembles to recall
What has been penned by one and verified by all."

Now we come to the question, "How can I understand the Bible?" I want to give you three guiding principles and three rules of interpretation, not from my mind, not according to my way of thinking, but from the Bible itself, which, if followed, will enable you to understand your Bible.

It must be remembered that the Bible is different from any other book in the world. The Bible is a spiritual book. It takes spiritual conception and spiritual perception to understand the Bible.

You can take the books of men and master them by the sheer force of your mentality. But it takes more than brain power to master the Bible. We must have spiritual enlightenment from God in order to understand the Bible. Put down Luke 24:45. "Then opened He their understanding, that they might understand the scriptures."

Notice that Jesus opened their understanding, that they might understand the scriptures. So we must have spiritual enlightenment from God to understand the Bible. This is why Paul said in 1 Corinthians 2:14 that "The natural man receiveth not the things of the Spirit of God . . . neither can he know them, because they are spiritually discerned."

We need to pray like David in Psalm 119:18, "Open thou mine eyes, that I may behold wondrous things out of Thy law." Never should the Bible be opened without prayer. Before we open the Bible we should pray that God will open our minds to understand it, and that He will open our hearts to obey what we find. This will put you where God will be your teacher.

In Prov. 1:23 we read, "Turn you at my reproof: behold, I will pour out my spirit unto you, I will make known my words unto you." When God pours out His spirit on a person, He makes known the meaning of His words. In other words, **having the meaning of God's Words made known to us is the result of receiving the Holy Spirit.**

The Bible cannot be understood, the meaning of the Bible cannot be grasped wthout the aid of the Holy Spirit. Why? Because this Word was given by the Holy Spirit. Put down 2 Peter 1.21. "The Word of prophecy came not in old time by the will of men, but holy men of God spake as they were moved by the Holy Ghost." This is what makes this book different from any other book in the world. The Bible is the Holy Spirit expressing Himself in human language.

You must know the Chinese characters to understand the Chinese language. So you must have the Holy Spirit to understand the language of the Spirit in the Bible.

Jesus has made a very precious promise to us in John 16:13. He says, "When He, the Spirit of truth, is come, He will guide you into all truth."

We should not go to the Bible to prove our own theory or ideas. If a person goes to the Bible to find proof for his own theories, he will probably find what he is looking for. We should go to the Bible, not to prove our ideas, but to learn the will of God that we may do it.

Here are the three guiding principles for the understanding of the Bible: First pray God to open your understanding to understand His Word; second, look to God for the Holy Spirit to guide you into the truth; third, have your heart open to follow the truth. A person doesn't have to be a preacher or a Bible scholar in order to possess these three requisites. Every person may possess these three requisites if he so desires.

Suppose that here is a safe filled with money. The combination is, turn the dial left to 5, right to 7, and then left to 4. Whenever you do this, the door will come open. Could you open this safe? Certainly, if you know the combination.

There is a three-point combination for unlocking the Bible, and it comes from the Bible itself. It is not my idea at all. Put down 1 Cor. 2:13.

"Which things also we speak, not in the words which man's wisdom teacheth, but which the Holy Ghost teacheth; comparing spiritual things with spiritual."

We are to compare spiritual things with spiritual. The way to understand the Bible is to compare scripture with scripture, and let the Bible explain itself. Now we shall have a demonstration of the value of this principle. We shall have three texts read by three persons.

(Three men came to the front with their Bibles, and read respectively, Luke 21:5-7; Matt. 24:3; Mark 13:3, 4.)

These three texts deal with a certain question, which was asked of Jesus regarding the sign of His coming and the end of the world.

Let us listen to the reading of Luke 21:5-7. "As some spake of the temple, how it was adorned with goodly stones and gifts, He said, As for these things which ye behold, the days will come, in the which there shall not be left one stone upon another, that shall not be thrown down. And they asked Him, saying, Master, but when shall these things be? and what sign will there be when these things shall come to pass?"

Notice that it says, "they asked Him." But it doesn't tell you who "they" were. It doesn't say whether it was the disciples, the Sadducees, or the Pharisees, or the Romans, or the Greeks. It merely says, "they" asked Him. Now, to understand the Bible you must compare scripture with scripture. We shall compare Luke 21:5-7 with Matt. 24:3, to see who asked this question.

Listen to Matt 24:3. "As He sat upon the mount of Olives, the disciples came unto Him privately, saying, "Tell us, when shall these things be? and what shall be the sign of Thy coming, and of the end of the world?"

This says that the disciples asked this question. There were twelve especially chosen disciples. Did all twelve ask this question, or just who did ask it? Again we must compare scripture with scripture. We shall compare Matt. 24:3 with Mark 13:3, 4.

Listen now to Mark 13:3, 4. "As He sat upon the mount of Olives over against the temple, **Peter** and **James** and **John** and **Andrew** asked Him privately, Tell us, when shall these things be? and what shall be the sign when all these things shall be fulfilled?"

Tell me, who asked this question?

(Voices) (Peter, James, John and Andrew.)

Yes, you can be absolutely sure of this. Whose explanation is it? Is it Shuler's explanation? No! It is the divine explanation of scripture. The way to understand the Bible is to compare scripture with scripture. You can see by this how beautifully scripture interprets itself.

I shall give you a few additional illustrations, and you may put these down if you wish. For instance, put down Psalm 50:3. Speaking of the second-coming of Christ, it says, "God shall come, and shall not keep silence." To understand this, you must compare it with 1 Thess. 4:16. Speaking of the second-coming it says, "The Lord Himself shall descend from heaven with a shout." Now you can see how our God shall come and shall not keep silence. See how beautifully the Bible explains itself? Our God will come and not keep silence, because He comes with a mighty shout. Then if we wanted to go further, we could take another scripture and learn what is the purpose of this shout. We could find out what this shout will do. It is very fascinating to compare scripture with scripture.

Here is another one. Put down Isaiah 66:15. Speaking of the second coming of Christ, it declares, "The Lord will come with fire, and with his chariots like a whirlwind." What does it mean? We compare it with Psalm 68:17: "The chariots of God are twenty thousand, even thousands of angels." The chariots of God are the angels. Now put down Matt. 25:31. "The Son of man shall come in His glory, and all the holy angels with Him." The chariots of God are His angels, and when Christ comes all the angels come with Him.

There is a chain of three links—Isa. 66:13 tells us that the Lord will come with His chariots. Psalm 68:17 says that the chariots of God are the angels. Yet Matt. 25:31 tels us that when He comes all the angels will come with Him. This is how to let the Bible explain itself.

When you do this, whose explanation is it? Is it a Methodist explanation? a Baptist explanation? an Adventist explanation? No! It is God's explanation of God's word. So, the first point of the three-fold combination for unlocking the truth of the Bible is to COMPARE SCRIPTURE WITH SCRIPTURE.

You have had a demonstration of this method in this Bible Institute. You have not seen Mr. Shuler take a text, then close the Bible, and go on talking about other matters. Every time you have heard Mr. Shuler speak you have seen him open the Bible and link scripture with scripture, and let the Bible explain itself. You have seen this in every lecture, and you will see it in every lecture, as long as you keep on coming, for this is the right way to learn the truth.

Comparing scripture with scripture is not merely running the marginal references found in a reference Bible. These marginal references are not a part of the inspired Word of God. The original Scriptures did not have any marginal references. These references have been inserted by men, after the Bible was first penned. Comparing scripture with scripture is not simply running the marginal references in a reference Bible. You need to remember that those references were not in the original scripture that God gave by the Holy Spirit. In some cases these marginal references are helpful, but in some cases they refer you to references that are misleading, in respect to the true meaning of Scripture.

I will give you one example. In Revelation 1:10 he says, "I was in the spirit on the Lord's day." The marginal reference on Lord's day in my Bible is 1 Cor. 16.2, which says, "upon the first of the week let everyone of you lay by him in store." Now this is misleading. There is not a word in 1 Cor. 16:2 about the Lord's day.

The expression "Lord's day" is used only once in the entire Bible, and to find out what day is the Lord's day you will have to find out which day it is, of which Christ is Lord. Matt. 12:8 says, He is Lord of the Sabbath. This case of Rev. 1:10 shows how the marginal references may be misleading

The marginal references are the work of men. Being the work of men, you must evaluate them as the work of men, and follow only what is in harmony with the plain meaning of the Bible.

The second point of this three-fold combination for unlocking the truth is found in Isa. 28:9, 10. "Whom shall he teach knowledge, and whom shall he make to understand doctrine? . . . For precept must be upon precept, precept upon precept; line upon line, line upon line; here a little, and there a little."

To understand the truth, we must take everything the Bible says about a given subject and put it together. All the truth about any certain topic is not found in any one chapter. This is why Jesus said, "S-E-A-R-C-H the Scriptures." If all the truth about any given subject was in one chapter, it wouldn't take any searching. The truth about these great Biblical doctrines is scattered all through the Bible. To find the real truth, we must take everything the Bible says about a given subject, and put it together as line upon line, precept upon precept.

For example, take the subject of Baptism. Some night we will talk about it. There is some truth about baptism in the book of Matthew, but you can't stop there, because Matthew doesn't tell all the truth about baptism. There is some truth about baptism in Mark; there is some truth in the book of Acts, the book of Romans, etc. The only way to find the real truth about baptism is to take everything the Bible says about baptism, and put it together. You can't find the real truth about baptism by just taking one text like many preachers do or even by taking three or four texts. People who do this are liable to draw wrong conclusions, and adopt erroneous ideas.

If we follow God's method of arriving at truth, we must take everything the Bible says about baptism and put it together to find out what God wants us to do about baptism. Then whose doctrine is it? The Baptist doctrine? No! The Adventist doctrine? No! The Methodist doctrine? No! It is God's doctrine from God's own word. This is why I refuse to put a denominational tag on my Bible lectures.

The second point of this three-fold combination of the Bible-safe of truth on the matter of doctrine, is to **take everything the Bible says on a given topic and put it together.**

This is the way Jesus taught the Bible. Put down Luke 24:27. Beginning at Moses and all the prophets, he expounded unto them in all the scriptures the things concerning Himself. The Messianic prophecies are scattered all through the books of the Old Testament. Jesus went from book to book. He told them what Moses said about the Messiah; He told them what the Psalmist wrote about the Messiah; He told them what Isaiah wrote about the Messiah. He went from book to book, taking here a little, and there a little, and putting it all together to show them God's doctrine about the Messiah. There is no better way of teaching truth. **This is Christ's method.**

This is the method we have followed in this Bible Institute. This last Sunday night when we spoke on the Millennium, we took here a little, and there a little, and brought it all together, linking scripture with scripture and letting the Bible explain itself.

This is the way Paul taught the Bible. Put down Romans 3:10-18. Here we read:

"As it is written," (see, he is quoting from the Old Testament) "there is none righteous, no, not one: There is none that understandeth, there is none that seeketh after God. They are all gone out of the way, they are together become unprofitable; there is none that doeth good, no, not one. Their throat is an open sepulchre; with their tongues they have used deceit; the poison of asps is under their lips: Whose mouth is full of cursing and bitterness: Their feet are swift to shed blood: Destruction and misery are in their ways: And the way of peace have they not known: There is no fear of God before their eyes."

Paul is here making an argument to prove that everyone in the world, Gentiles and Jews, are all under sin. They are all sinners by nature. How does Paul prove it? He proves it by quoting the Scriptures. In these nine verses he quotes from eight different chapters, ten various verses, and from three different books of the Old Testament, taking here a little, and there a little, and bringing it together as line upon line.

He said, "There is none righteous, no, not one: there is none that understandeth, there is none that seeketh after God. They are all gone out of the way, they are together become unprofitable, there is none that doeth good, no, not one." Paul took this from Psalm 14:1-3, and Psalm 53:1-3.

He said, "Their throat is an open sepulchre; with their tongues they have used deceit." That is a direct quotation from Psalm 5 9. "The poison of asps is under their lips." He is quoting from Psalm 140.3. "Whose mouth is full of cursing." That is from Psalm 10 7. "Their feet are swift to shed blood, destruction and misery are in their ways." That was taken from Isaiah 59.7, 8. "There is no fear of God before their eyes." That is a direct quotation from Psalm 36:1.

In nine verses he quotes from eight different chapters, ten different verses, and three different books, taking here a little and there a little He put this togther into an incontrovertible argument to show that all are under sin.

In John 7.17 Jesus says, "If any man will do his will (that is, the Father's,) He shall know of the doctrine." The third point of this three-fold combination to unlock truth of the Bible, is to **be willing to obey the truth** as fast as it is made plain to you from the Bible.

Remember that Jesus doesn't show you at one time all that He wants you to do. Put down John 16 12. He says, "I have yet many things to say unto you, but ye cannot bear them now." He reveals truth as fast as we are able to bear it, as fast as He sees it is best David says in Psalm 119:105, "Thy word is a lamp to my feet, and a light unto my path."

If you are taking a journey on a dark night for one mile and you have a flashlight, do you expect the flashlight to show you the path for the whole mile when you take the first step? No! The flashlight shows you the path step by step. This is what God wants us to do with the Bible. The Bible is our flashlight, a lamp to our feet, and we are to walk step by step as the Bible shows the way.

If we are doing wrong ignorantly, God will give us light from the Bible to show us wherein we are doing wrong. To be a true Christian means to obey the truth and do right just as fast as we learn the truth from the Bible. "If any man will do His will he shall know the doctrine " Doing the will of God, the disposition to do the will of God, is what enables God to show you the truth. If a man isn't willing to obey truth, God will not show him the truth.

If a certain truth is brought to a man from the Bible, and he refuses to obey it, there can be no further progress in the discovery of truth for that man. Why should God show a man more truth if he will not walk in the truth He has already shown Him? If a man isn't willing to obey the truth, God will not show him the truth fully.

The ticket that admits one into the temple of God's truth has three coupons to it; namely, a humble spirit, willing to sit before the Bible and be taught; an open mind, willing to let life-long, deeply-rooted ideas go when the light coming in shows that they should go; and an obedient life, willing to change and shape the daily habits of life to whatever the Book may teach.

There is one question that we all do well to meditate upon. Am I willing to follow the truth, wherever it may lead? If you follow the truth all the way, you will go through the gates. Isaiah 26·2 says, "Open ye the gates, that the righteous nation which keepeth the truth may enter in."

How many are determined under God that by the help of God and by the grace of God you will follow the truth as fast as it is made plain to you from the Bible. Will you lift your hands? Thank you. It seems that every hand is raised.

(Prayer.)

Our dear heavenly Father, we thank Thee for the Bible as a light to our feet in this dark world. How glad we are to follow the way of truth. Help us, we pray, to walk step by step in Thy truth. We thank Thee that we have in our heart a determination to follow the truth as fast as Thou dost make it plain from the Bible. Bless these dear people. We thank Thee, Lord, for their honest hearts. We thank thee for the love they have for the Word of God. Lord, they want to know the truth and they want to follow the truth. So, dear Lord, just take us all and give us that grace divine and strength from above that we may walk in the light of God's Word step by step until we come to the end of the way, where we will meet Thee face to face, and be with Thee forever. We ask this in Jesus' name. Amen.

Who Changed the Sabbath?

(Presented Under the Form of a Jury Trial on the Sixth Sunday Night of the Campaign)

JUSTICE R. N. RAWSON: As this meeting is to take the form of a Jury Trial, our first business is to select a jury.

Men who are attending these Bible lectures placed their names on cards last Tuesday night, indicating their willingness to serve on the jury tonight, if their names were drawn. Cards containing names of these men are in this box. A drawing will now be made for these names, and the first 12 names of men who are present will constitute the jury. I am sure that the audience sees that this is a fair way to select the jury.

The bailiff will conduct the drawing of the jury. As soon as any man hears his name called will he please rise from his seat promptly and come forward and go into the dressing room here on my right where you will select your foreman and get ready to try this case.

The bailiff will now impanel the jury.

(The following jurymen were drawn, challenged, and impanelled:)

    (1) W. Thomas Barnett
    (2) Lyle Hatfield
    (3) Hugh Lyons
    (4) C. B. Frey
    (5) Robert W. Coffman
    (6) W. P. Wright
    (7) O. M. Strouson
    (8) Carl Von Brauchitsch
    (9) John A. Kepler
    (10) Ebert M. Munko
    (11) Frank H. Miller
    (12) George Derham

JUSTICE R. N. RAWSON: I will now examine the jury. **Gentlemen of the jury:** Has Mr Shuler talked to any of you about this case? If so, please raise the hand.

No hands were raised. This is evidence that Mr. Shuler has not talked to any of these men about this case.

Has anyone else talked to you to try to influence you to vote a certain way? If so, raise your hand.

No hands were raised.

Gentlemen of the jury:

Do you now promise to render a true verdict in keeping with the evidence that will be presented from the Word of God and authentic history? If so, raise the right hand. (Each juror raised his right hand.)

We shall now tell the religious affiliations of these gentlemen chosen for the jury.

JUSTICE R. N. RAWSON: Three are members of no church; three belong to the Church of Christ; two are Methodist, and two belong to the Christian church.

JUSTICE RAWSON: Will the audience kindly indicate by a show of hands if this jury is acceptable to them. (The audience responded with their hands.)

Thank you. The jury is now seated.

Mr. Shuler, on behalf of the prosecuton, may now make his opening statement.

EVANGELIST SHULER: Gentlemen of the special Jury, ladies and gentlemen of the general jury, the purpose of this trial is to discover who is responsible for attempting to change God's Sabbath from the seventh-day, commonly called Saturday, to the first day of the week, commonly known as Sunday. The Bible shows that in the very beginning, after Christ, the eternal Son of God, had made this world in six days, He rested on the seventh day. After He had rested on the seventh day, Genesis 2.3 says, "God blessed the seventh day, and sanctified it: because that in it He had rested from all His work which God created and made."

This word "sanctified" means set apart for a holy use. Therefore it is clear that Christ, as Creator, set apart the seventh day for man in the very beginning. In the Ten Commandments Christ commands man to keep the seventh day, which He set apart for man when He made the world.

In Exodus 20:8-11 the Lord declares that, "the seventh day is the Sabbath of the Lord . . . in it thou shalt not do any work; . . . for in six days the Lord made heaven and earth, . . . and rested the seventh day . . . wherefore the Lord blessed the Sabbath day, and hallowed it."

Today the majority of Christians are not keeping the seventh day, but are observing the first day of the week as the Lord's day, or as the Christian Sabbath. This brings up three big questions. Who changed the Sabbath from the seventh day to the first? How was it changed? When was it changed? I shall cite evidence in this trial to answer these three questions. Remember that a printed copy of this evidence will be sent to everyone who fills out a ballot card, so please be sure to fill in your ballot card and place your name on it.

(Special ballot cards had been placed in the hands of the jury and the audience before the trial began. Copy of this ballot card appears at the close of this lecture.)

Will everyone please take your ballot card in hand? You will notice that there are six propositions listed on the card. There will be six parts to this trial, corresponding to these six propositions. I shall take up these six propositions one by one and present evidence to this jury to establish each of these proposition. I ask you, gentlemen of the special jury, and every man and woman on this general jury, to follow me with your pencils in hand and check each item if the evidence plainly establishes it.

Look at the first proposition: God never changed the Sabbath from the seventh day to the first.

Is there positive proof that God never changed the Sabbath from the seventh day to the first day of the week? Yes, there is. The best way is to let God speak for Himself. The first witness in this trial will be the great God of heaven and earth, Jehovah, the Monarch of the universe.

In your courts in Des Moines you find it necessary to cross question the witnesses when they testify, to make sure if possible that they are telling the truth. But gentlemen, you will not need to cross question my first witness. Hebrews 6 18 says, "It was impossible for God to lie." Since it is impossible for God to lie, there is no need to cross question His testimony.

In Psalm 89 34 we have the record of God's testimony concerning the immutability of His Ten Commandments. I have placed this on muslin so that everyone of these twelve men, good and true, might see for himself just what God says. In this text God is the speaker. Now, gentlemen, I should like to have you twelve men read this text with me, and let us read it so the man on the back seat will hear it. All right, now altogether.

THE JURY: "My covenant will I not break, nor alter the thing that is gone out of my lips."

EVANGELIST SHULER: Now look at that word "alter." You know what that means. "Alter" means "change." God says, "I will not change the thing that is gone out of my lips."

There is only one document in this world, not two, but only one document that ever came direct from the lips of God to man. That is this great law of Ten Commandments The Lord God came down upon Mount Sinai and spoke the Ten Commandments with His own lips Then He wrote them on two tables of stone.

You will notice in the very heart of this decalogue, God says, "The seventh day is the Sabbath of the Lord" Now, Gentlemen, follow me closely. This came direct from the lips of God. You can see that since God will not alter or change the thing that has gone out of His lips, and from His lips came the words, "The seventh day is the Sabbath," it is forever settled that God has not changed the Sabbath from the seventh day to the first.

So, gentlemen of the special jury, and every man and woman on the general jury, I ask you to take your pen or pencil and put a check mark in the square opposite the first item as being clearly proven, not by my word but by God's own word.

If any man says, "No, I believe God has changed the Sabbath from the seventh day to the first," he is actually accusing God of doing the very thing that God said He wouldn't do. "I will not alter," or change, "the thing that has gone out of my lips." If we believe God, what else can we do but check the first proposition?

God has positively forbidden man to change the Ten Commandments. He is not to take anything away from them or to add to them. In Deut 4·2 I read, "Ye shall not add unto the word which I command you, neither shall ye diminish ought from it, that ye may keep the commandments of the Lord your God which I command you" God has positively forbidden men to change the Ten Commandments. If anybody has not checked the first statement, please, if you believe God, and I know you believe God, take your pencil and check the first proposition. According to God's word the seventh day is still the Sabbath.

Look at the second proposition: Jesus Christ did not change the Sabbath from the seventh day to the first

Many people think Christ changed the Sabbath from the seventh to the first day in honor of His resurrection. How do I know that Jesus Christ never changed the Sabbath? The best way, gentlemen, is to let Jesus Christ speak for Himself. My second witness will be the Lord Jesus Christ. He is the true witness. He never told a lie. You cannot doubt His testimony.

In Matthew 5·18 we have the testimony of Jesus Christ concerning the unchangeable character of the Ten Commandments. I have placed this text on cloth, so that everyone in this auditorium might see for himself what Jesus says about the unchangeable character of the law. I should like to have everyone read this with me.

GENERAL JURY. "Till heaven and earth pass, one jot or one tittle shall in no wise pass from the law."

What is a jot? It is the smallest character in the Hebrew alphabet. What is a tittle? A tittle is even smaller than the smallest character. It is the point of a letter. A tittle is like the dot on the "i" and the cross on the "t," which distinguishes one letter from another.

Jesus Christ declares that the Ten Commandments cannot be changed in the smallest item, not even so much as the smallest letter, or the point of a letter, so long as heaven and earth stand. Follow me closely, gentlemen. If Jesus Christ had changed the Sabbath from the seventh day to the first, He would have had to change these Commandments in far more than a jot or a tittle. But notice that He declared, "till heaven and earth pass, one jot or one tittle shall in no wise pass from the law." You can see that since Jesus Christ declares that the law cannot be changed in a jot or a tittle, so long as heaven and earth remain; it shows that Christ did not change the Sabbath from the seventh day to the first.

So gentlemen of the Special Jury, and every one in the General Jury, I ask you on the basis of Christ's own words, not upon my words, but according to His own words, to place a check mark in the square opposite the second item. If you believe Jesus Christ, and you do, what else can you do but agree with Christ? He says the law of God cannot be changed a jot or a tittle. So it must stand as it was given

Some one may say, "Mr. Shuler, did Jesus Christ ever mention the Sabbath in a way that we can know that He didn't change it?" Yes, He did. Put down Matthew 24 20. In a prophecy about the destruction of Jerusalem which was to take place in A. D. 70, He said to His disciples, "Pray ye that your flight be not in the winter, neither **on the Sabbath day.**" He shows that the same seventh day which was the Sabbath before His crucifixion would still be the Sabbath when Jerusalem would be destroyed in A. D. 70. This shows that Christ had no idea of changing the Sabbath from the seventh day to the first day at the time of, or following His resurrection.

I ask you on the basis of Christ's own unimpeachable testimony to place a check mark opposite the second proposition. Notice that in so far as the word of Jesus Christ is concerned, the law still stands and the seventh day is still the Sabbath.

Look at the third item: The apostles did not change the Sabbath of the fourth commandment, but the change was made after the apostles passed away, or after 100 A. D.

How do I know, gentlemen, that the apostles did not change the Sabbath? Here is how we know this. The fifth book in the New Testament is the Acts of the Apostles. In this fifth book of the New Testament it is made plain that the apostles recognized the seventh day, or Saturday, on which the Jews met in their synagogues for their weekly worship, as being the Sabbath day in the days of the apostles after the resurrection of Christ.

Here is one instance in Acts 13:14. In this case the Jews had assembled in their synagogue at Antioch on their regular meeting day, which was the seventh day. Paul went in and preached to them. The record says, "When they departed from Perga, they came to Antioch in Pisidia, and went into the synagogue on the Sabbath day, and sat down."

The Holy Spirit, in speaking through Luke, calls this day on which the Jews had met for their weekly worship the Sabbath day. Tell me, gentlemen, on what day did the Jews meet for the weekly worship in the time of Paul? There is only one answer that any man could ever give to that question. Everyone must agree on the answer. The Jews met on the seventh day of every week, the day we now call Saturday. This is when they met for their weekly worship. The Holy Spirit calls this Saturday meeting day of the Jews the Sabbath day in the days of the apostles.

Some will say, "Why yes! Paul went in there on Saturday so he could preach Christ to the people. This is granted. But that doesn't change the fact that the Holy Spirit calls this day on which the Jews met "the Sabbath day." He doesn't say it was the "old Sabbath" or the "abolished Sabbath," but **the Sabbath day.**"

If the apostles had changed the Sabbath to the first day of the week, as some people claim, the Acts of the Apostles could not call this seventh day on which the Jews met "the Sabbath day." This evidence is repeated eight times in the Acts of the Apostles.

I have these references to give to you. They are as follows: Acts 13:14;

Acts 13:27; Acts 13:42; Acts 13:44; Acts 15:21; Acts 16:13; Acts 17:1-3; and Acts 18:4. There you have eight texts in the Acts of the Apostles. These texts deal with events which took place fifteen or more years after the crucifixion and resurrection of Christ. Each of these texts refers to the seventh day on which the Jews met for their weekly worship, as "the Sabbath day." There you actually have eight proofs, not one, but eight proofs from the book of Acts of the Apostles, that the apostles did not change the Sabbath. If the apostles had changed the Sabbath, then the Acts of the Aposles eight times over could not refer to the seventh day on which the Jews were meeting in the days of the apostles as being, THE sabbath day at that time.

Gentlemen, I ask you on the basis of this evidence to please take your pencils and place a check mark opposite the third item on the ballot card. According to the Acts of the Apostles the seventh day is still the Sabbath day.

These gentlemen of the jury know that the apostles did not have any authority to change the Ten Commandments. The apostles followed Jesus Christ. He said, "Till heaven and earth pass, one jot or one tittle shall in no wise pass from the law." Everyone who has ever read the New Testament through knows there is not a line in these twenty-seven books of the New Testament about the Sabbath being changed from the seventh day to the first. Since the transfer from the seventh day to the first was not made in New Testament times, it must have been made by uninspired men after the New Testament was written. Then the change rests solely on the authority of man without the authority of scripture.

This brings me to the fourth proposition: The substitution of the first day, or Sunday, as a day of rest for Christians in the place of the seventh day, or Saturday, was a gradual change that took place during the third, fourth and fifth centuries.

If you ask, "Mr Shuler, when did this change take place from the seventh day, or Saturday, to the keeping of Sunday, the first day of the week?" I cannot give any exact date. No one can put his finger on a certain year and say, "This is the year when everybody stopped keeping Saturday and began keeping Sunday." It was a gradual change that took pace over a period of several hundred years, during the third, fourth and fifth centuries. Many of the professed Christian people worshipped on both Saturday and Sunday for a long time.

In fact a large portion of the professed Christian world worshipped for centuries on both Saturday and Sunday. All through the centuries since the apostles some people have kept the seventh day down through the ages.

If you ask, "How was it changed?" Here are two of the greatest steps in the transfer of the day of rest from Saturday to Sunday. On the seventh of March, 321 A. D., Constantine, the Emperor of Rome, signed the first law ever made requiring people to rest on Sunday. Forty-six years after this, or in 364 A. D., a church council at Laodicea decreed that Christians should henceforth cease to rest on the seventh day, but should rest on the first day of the week.

The Apostle Paul predicted that after the apostles died there would come a falling away from the truth. You will find this in your Bible in Acts 20:29, 30. This is exactly what happened. Rites and ceremonies of which Peter and Paul never heard, crept silently into use, and then claimed the rank of divine institutions. The keeping of Sunday was one of them.

Gentlemen, I could go to the library of Drake University, or any large library in this city, and bring in books by the armsful, to establish this fourth proposition. There is no question about it. I shall merely show you two testimonies on the screen to establish this item.

Neander is recognized as the greatest of all church historians. This first quotation is taken from page 186 of the translation by Henry John Rose, B. D., of Doctor Augustus Neander's book, "The History of the Christian Religion and Church."

"The festival of Sunday, like all other festivals, was only a HUMAN ORDINANCE, and it was far from the intention of the apostles . . . and the early apostolic church, to transfer the laws of the Sabbath to Sunday."

Notice first that Dr. Neander says that the keeping of Sunday was "only a human ordinance." It was not something that came from God. It was not based on divine authority. It was something that men agreed they would do. It was a "human ordinance."

He also declares that it was far from the intention of the apostles, or of the apostolic church to transfer the Sabbath to Sunday. This shows that the Sabbath was not changed in the days of the apostles.

Here is a clear testimony from a bishop named Eusebius. He was an eminent father in the early Catholic church, who was contemporary with Emperor Constantine, the man who made the first law requiring people to rest on the first day of the week Eusebius is often called the father of church history. Here is something from his Commentary on the Psalms, Column 1171 in Vol. 23 of Migne's Greek Fathers .

"All things whatsoever that it was duty to do on the Sabbath, those WE have transferred to the Lord's day (Sunday.)" (Emphasis mine.)

Notice that he doesn't say that Jesus changed the Sabbath. He doesn't say that the apostles changed it. He declares that the change was made in his day. When he says, "all things whatsoever that it was duty to do on the Sabbath, those we have transferred to Sunday," by "we" he refers to himself as a Catholic bishop, and to other Catholic bishops of that day. He shows that the change was made in his day, back there in the time of Constantine in the third century, nearly three hundred years after the resurrection of Christ.

Gentlemen, I have some things here that you might like to look at after the trial. I shall be pleased to have you examine them. Here is a photographic reproduction of the page of Dr. Neander's church history in the German language, containing his statement about Sunday being only a human ordinance. I also have a photostat of Dr. Rose's translation of this statement.

Here is a photostat of Eusebius' statement in the original Greek in which he wrote.

You have no doubt heard of Dr. H. G. Wells. He wrote a famous book "The Outline of History." I have the actual reproduction of a certain page from Dr. Wells' "Outline of History," where he makes it plain that the Sabbath was transferred from the seventh day to Sunday about the time of Constantine.

Gentlemen, I ask you on the basis of these statements from Paul, Neander, Eusebius, and H G. Wells to check this fourth proposition. It is clearly proven by authentic history In fact, if a man denies this fourth proposition, he must deny the open facts of history.

Look at the fifth proposition: The prophet Daniel prophesied that papal Rome would attempt to change the law of God in respect to the Sabbath day.

Where is the proof for this? We shall let Daniel testify. My next witness, gentlemen, is the prophet Daniel in Dan. 7.25. In the vision of the seventh chapter he saw four great beasts come up from the raging sea. A lion with eagle's wings. A bear with three ribs in his mouth. A leopard with four heads and four wings. And a terrible non-descript beast with ten horns on his head. A little horn arose among them that plucked up three of the first ten by the roots. Daniel 7 25 is talking about this little-horn power.

All of this seventh chapter of Daniel was explained on the third Tuesday and the third Friday nights of this Bible Institute. We found that there is no other power known in history which answers to the specifications of this little horn, as set forth in Daniel 7, except the papacy.

We have no enmity against Catholics There are just as fine, sincere, and godly people in the Catholic church as in any other church. I have friends and relatives who are Catholics. Nothing I say is aimed at any individual Catholic. All we are doing is investigating scripture and history, to see who is responsible for changing the Sabbath.

Notice this text in Daniel 7 25 "He shall speak great words against the most High, and shall wear out the saints of the most High, and **think to change times and laws.**" We have found the power who will try to change the Sabbath. The papal power shall "think to change times and laws."

Look the Ten Commandments over. Where do you find any **time** mentioned in these commandments? The fourth commandment, the Sabbath commandment, is the only commandment that talks about time. It talks about the seventh day; it talks about six days The fourth commandment is the only commandment where God ever told man how to count time. He asks man to work the first six days of the week and rest on the last day of the week. This is how God told men to count time.

When it says that the papal power will attempt to change the times and law of God, it is evident that this power will attempt to change the Sabbath commandment. So, Gentlemen, I ask you on the basis of Daniel 7·25 to check the fifth proposition. The prophet Daniel actually prophesied that papal Rome would attempt to make this change in the law of God.

Look at the sixth proposition· This ecclesiastical power acknowledges that she made the change: her friends say that she did, and her enemies agree with them.

Does the Catholic church claim that it made this change? Gentlemen of the jury, the DEFENDANT will now plead his own case. Remember this. It is not necessary for the Catholic authorities to appear on this platform in person. We have their printed testimony, which they have printed in their catechisms by the millions of copies Here are "The Convert's Catechism of Catholic Doctrine." "Doctrinal Catechism," "Catholic Christian Instructed," and "The Question Box" by Father Conway. These are only a few of many which could be used. This is their written testimony. Each of these books bears the imprimatur of a Catholic bishop. This makes the book a standard authority on Catholic doctrine.

Now the DEFENDANT will take the stand. (Quotations from various Catholic sources were flashed upon the screen)

The "Catholic Encyclopedia" in Vol. 4, p. 153 says,

"The Catholic Church . . after changing the day of rest from Saturday, the seventh day of the week, to Sunday, the first day, made the third commandment refer to Sunday as the day to be kept as the Lord's day."

Notice that they tell you plainly that they changed the day of rest from Saturday to Sunday.

"Doctrinal Catechism," page 174, says:

"Question: Have you any other way of proving that the church has power to institute festivals of precept?

Answer: Had she not such power, she could not have substituted the observance of Sunday, the first day of the week, for the observance of the Sabbath, the seventh day, a change for which there is no scripture authority." They even admit there is no Bible authority for changing the Sabbath from the seventh day to the first. They openly admit that they substituted the observance of Sunday, the first day of the week, for the observance of the seventh day of the week, or Saturday.

The "Convert's Catechism of Catholic Doctrine," says on page 50:

"Question: Why do we observe Sunday instead of Saturday?"

"Answer . . . Because the Catholic church, in the Council of Laodicea, transferred the solemnity from Saturday to Sunday." This edition received the blessing of the Pope on January 10, 1910.

Here is a statement from a paper called the CATHOLIC MIRROR of September 23, 1893.

"The Catholic Church for over one thousand years before the existence of a Protestant . . . CHANGED THE SABBATH FROM SATURDAY TO SUN-DAY."

I notice that two of these twelve jurymen belong to the Christian Church, while three others are from the Church of Christ. Here is a testimony which these men will especially value. It is from Dr. Nicholas Summerbell, who along with Alexander Campbell led out in founding the Disciples of Christ, or the Christian Church. We have a photostat of his statement. He wrote a book called the HISTORY OF THE CHRISTIAN CHURCH.

Dr. Nicholas Summerbell is not a Catholic, far from it He led out in certain reforms, which brought about the establishment of the Disciples of Christ Church. He was the first president of the Union Christian College. On pages 417 and 418, in speaking about the Catholic Church, he says: "It has reversed the fourth commandment, by doing away with the Sabbath of God's word, and instituting Sunday as a holy day."

My friends, this is a very weighty testimony. This isn't a Catholic talking. This is a great Protestant theologian speaking. He freely admits that the Catholic church attempted to change the fourth commandment, by doing away with the keeping of the seventh day, and instituting the observance of Sunday in its place.

Here is one from a Catholic priest, Father Brady. It is from a speech he made at Elizabeth, New Jersey. It was printed in the Elizabeth, New Jersey, "News" of March 18, 1903. He said:

"It is well to remind the Presbyterians, Baptists, Methodists, and all other Christians, that the Bible does not support them anywhere in their observance of Sunday. . . . Sunday is an institution of the Roman Catholic church, and those who observe the day observe a commandment of the Catholic church."

Gentlemen, if you would like to see the photostats of these testimonies, I should be very happy to show them to you.

The Pope of Rome claims to hold the place of Jesus Christ on earth. That is the foundation on which the papacy is built. They boast that because of this power invested in them, they established the keeping of the first day in the place of the keeping of the seventh day. I ask you, gentlemen, on the basis of these testimonies from standard Catholic works and on the basis of this testimony from Dr. Summerbell, to check the sixth proposition as being clearly proven.

Now, gentlemen, I will rest my case. I call you to witness as men, good and true, that I have presented Bible evidence and the testimony of authentic history to prove every one of these six points.

Your Honor, my plea to this jury is very brief. Suppose, gentlemen, a man charged with stealing an automobile is brought into court and tried. The witnesses prove he did it. Then, to cap the climax, he says, "Your honor, I have a statement to make." He stands before the jury and confesses he stole the automobile. Tell me, gentlemen, what would the jury say? What could the jury do? What could they possibly do, but find him guilty as charged?

Gentlemen, I have brought before you the evidence, and you have heard representatives of the Catholic power in their own official documents admit point blank, yes, even boast, that they made the change from Saturday to Sunday. Gentlemen, there is only one possible verdict. Not on the basis of your own personal opinion, but on the basis of this evidence, gentlemen, I ask you for a verdict that the defendant is guilty as charged. Your Honor, the case is now in the hands of the jury.

JUSTICE RAWSON: The jury may now retire to the jury room for deliberation on the evidence of the witnesses and the argument of the attorney. When you have arrived at a fair and impartial verdict, you may come into the courtroom with your decision.

(The jury retired to their room.)

* * *

EVANGELIST SHULER: I have a question on which I believe everyone will raise his hand in the affirmative. Tell me, how many of you believe that the evidence which we have cited, proves that the Catholic power made the change? Will you just raise your hands, please? (Nearly all hands went up.) I appreciate that you are with us on this question. Your vote is, "yes."

Everyone who raised his hand, please look on the back of your ballot card, and where it says, "According to the evidence cited from the Bible, and other authentic statements, I vote "YES" Will you kindly fill in your name, street number and city, in the spaces under, "YES." If you are a member of a church just check "yes" or "no," and if so, fill in what denomination.

If you do not believe that we have proved that the Catholic Church changed the Sabbath day, your vote would be "NO." Then where it says, "NEGATIVE," "I do not believe that the evidence establishes the proposition, because ...." please tell us why you vote, "NO."

Cast your vote on the card which you have. If you desire a copy of one of these cards as a souvenir, ask the ushers and they will give you one. But please go ahead and cast your vote on the one that you have.

There is one special favor which we ask of every person in the auditorium. Please do not leave until the benediction is pronounced. The service is not over when the jury reports, I have a little statement to make. Then we shall have prayer, and the ballots will be collected We thank you in advance, for staying until the benediction is pronounced.

Please fill in your ballot quickly. Fill in "yes," if you believe that the evidence is sufficient. If you think the point was not proved, fill in "no" and tell us why.

While the jury is deliberating I shall call your attention to the subjects for the week.

* * *

(The jury returns.)

JUSTICE RAWSON: Gentlemen of the jury, have you reached a verdict?

FOREMAN: We have.

JUSTICE RAWSON: Will you tell the court what it is?

FOREMAN: We find the defendant guilty, as charged, by a vote of 12 to 0.

JUSTICE RAWSON: Mr. Shuler, you may make your final statement.

EVANGELIST SHULER: There is one item that every person in this auditorium needs to settle for himself. Shall I obey God? Or shall I obey man?

Some will say, Mr. Shuler, you have the facts on your side, but I do not think it makes any difference what day we keep, just so we keep a day."

Listen! The issue before us tonight is not whether we shall rest on Saturday, or whether we shall rest on Sunday. It is a bigger issue than this. The real issue is, "Shall I obey the Lord Jesus Christ? Or shall I obey the dictates of the Anti-christ, the man who claims to be Christ on earth?

The Lord Jesus Christ spoke the Ten Commandments. He says, "The seventh day is the Sabbath." Jesus Christ commands us to keep the seventh day. The papal power, the Roman pontiff, who claims to hold the place of Jesus

Christ on earth, has tried to establish the keeping of the first day of the week in the place of the seventh day, which Jesus Christ sanctified for man. This papal power commands man to keep the first day of the week. Here is your test. Will you keep the seventh day as Jesus Christ commands? Or will you keep the first day of the week, or Sunday, as the Catholic power has ordained?

All Christians, both Protestants and Catholics, ought to repudiate this unauthorized change in the Ten Commandments. They ought to repudiate it and take their stand to keep the seventh day as God commands us.

I have a striking statement from a Catholic priest, and by the way it was made here in Des Moines. It was made by the late Father Enright when he was making a speech here. He says·

"It was the Catholic Church that changed the day of rest from Saturday, the seventh day, to Sunday, the first day. Which church does the whole civilized world obey? The Bible says, 'Remember that thou keep holy the Sabbath day,' but the Catholic Church says, 'No! Keep the first day of the week!' and all the civilized world bows down in reverent obedience to the mandates of the Catholic Church."

I do not know what your answer is to this, but I can tell you, that God helping me, here is one who will not bow to the mandates of the Catholic Church. Can you say "Amen," brother?

This Sabbath question presents a great test to every soul. Whom will ye obey? Will you keep the seventh day and obey the Lord Jesus Christ? Or will you keep the first day of the week in obedience to the mandates of the Catholic Church? I hope, friends, that your love for Jesus is so true, so strong, and so compelling, that you will say, "God helping me, I will henceforth keep the seventh day which Jesus, my Saviour, sanctified for me"

We need what Joshua had, when he got up before that large assembly and said, "As for me and my house we will serve the Lord." We need what Peter had, when the authorities ordered him to stop preaching Jesus Christ. He said, "We ought to obey God rather than man"

There is a Medical College in California which endeavors to train doctors to work as medical missionaries in lands over-seas. Every graduate from that college is given a blank on which he fills in his first choice, second choice, and third choice, as to the field to which he would like to go. There was one doctor who recently graduated there, whose heart was set on being a missionary to Africa. When his blank was returned to the president, it read, "First choice, Africa; second choice, Africa; third choice, Africa." He really wanted to go to Africa.

With a true Christian, there is really only one choice as to what he will do about the Sabbath. First choice, Jesus; Second choice, Jesus; Third choice, Jesus. O, I hope you will decide this Sabbath question in favor of the Lord Jesus Christ.

We all need help from God to make a right decision. How many want to be remembered in prayer that God will help you to be true to Jesus Christ? Will you lift your hand? Every man on this jury, and everyone here it appears, has raised his hand. Shall we bow our heads in prayer?

(Prayer.)

Blessed Lord Jesus, we love Thee. We have in our hearts a great desire to be true to Thee. Lord, we recognize that we are confronted with a great test. We have learned tonight what Thy Word says about Thy Sabbath. We acknowledge that Jesus is the Creator. He is One Who made the world in six days, and then rested on the seventh day, and then sanctified, or set the day apart for man. Men have tried to change Thy law. They can never change it in reality. They have changed the practice of many of the people, but Thy Sabbath still stands unchanged. We all need help and strength to follow Thee all the way, and to make the right decision.

Now, dear friends, keep your heads bowed. The prayer isn't over. I now ask everyone who is determined, by the help of God, to henceforth keep the seventh day as Jesus commands you, to take your pen or pencil and place the mark of the cross in that square at the bottom on the backside of your ballot card.

God will help you. Perhaps you can't do it right away; perhaps your business will have to be adjusted, but everyone who is determined to keep the Sabbath, which Jesus sanctified for man, please make the mark of the cross in the square. Remember, that you are doing this for Jesus. This is between Jesus and you. Now we shall continue our prayer.

(Prayer continued.)

Lord Jesus, we thank Thee for Thy cross and all that it means. Lord, we want to obey Thee. We want to keep Thy day that Thou hast sanctified. Thou hast done so much for us. Lord Jesus, we are glad to make the mark of the cross in the square to signify our determination to henceforth keep Thy holy day. Lord, bless these dear people. Many of them have problems which they will have to solve, but dear God help them. Many have made up their minds to do what Jesus wants them to do. We pray that Jesus will help them to solve their problems. So bless each one who has made this decision for Jesus Christ to follow Him all the way. Bless each one who has asked an interest in this prayer tonight. Bless also those who may have hesitated. May Thy Spirit continue to plead with their hearts on this great subject. We ask in His precious name. Amen.

ADDITIONAL NOTES ON THE CHANGE OF THE SABBATH

Some declare that the observance of the first day of the week (or Sunday) in the place of the seventh day (or Saturday) as commanded in the ten commandments, could not possibly have been brought about by the Catholic Church, because Sunday was being kept by Christians before the Roman Catholic Church came into existence It is true that Sunday was being honored to some extent as a religious festival by some Christians before the Catholic Church came into existence as an ecclesiastical organization. However, no Christian writer during the three generations following New Testament times claims any Scriptural behest for it. The facts of history abundantly attest that the practice of the keeping of the first day of the week, or Sunday, as a substitute for the keeping of the seventh day, as commanded in the ten commandments was brought about and established under the rule of the papacy.

Every person who knows history must admit that the papacy ruled supreme over Christendom for over one thousand years from the sixth to the sixteenth century. During this period of papal rule the keeping of Sunday was established in the place of the original seventh day Sabbath of the decalogue.

If you adopt an orphan boy, he becomes your boy He takes your name. You become responsible for him as a father. This is true whether the boy is one year old or fourteen years old when you adopt him.

So it is with the papacy and the Sunday institution. The papacy adopted the keeping of Sunday as the weekly holy day for Christians. They attempted to make the day of the S-U-N into the day of the S-O-N. The Sunday sabbath or alleged Lord's day is therefore a child of the papacy, and Rome is responsible for the establishment of the practice of the keeping of the first day of the week instead of the seventh, the day which Christ sanctified for man.

YOUR JURY BALLOT

Check
Here

☐ Please send me a free copy of the testimonies and the evidence presented at this trial.

We Shall Cite Evidence to Establish

☐ First: That God never changed the Sabbath from the seventh day to the first.
☐ Second: That Jesus Christ did not change it.
☐ Third: That the Apostles did not change the Sabbath of the fourth commandment, but that the change was made after the Apostles passed away, or after 100 A. D.
☐ Fourth: That the substitution of the first day, or Sunday, as a day of rest for Christians in the place of the seventh day, or Saturday, was a gradual change that took place during the third, fourth and fifth centuries.
☐ Fifth: That the prophet Daniel prophesied that papal Rome would attempt to change the law of God in respect to the Sabbath day.
☐ Sixth: That this ecclesiastical power acknowledges that she made the change: her friends say that she did it, and her enemies agree with them.

(See Other Side)

AFFIRMATIVE

According to the evidence cited from the Bible, and other authentic statements,

I vote "Yes"

Name..
Street Number. ...   .
City..
Are you a church member? ☐ Yes   ☐ No
If so, what denomination?. ....

NEGATIVE

I do not believe that the evidence establishes the proposition, because:

....
....
....
....
Name ....
Street Number.. ....
City..
Are you a church member? ☐ Yes   ☐ No
If so, what denomination?. ....

☐

Four Ways You Will Know Your Friends in Heaven

(Preached on the Sixth Tuesday of the Campaign)

The New York police discovered something peculiar on the body of a man, who was recently found dead in his hotel room on Thirteenth Street. When they searched the dead body to identify the man, they found the man had written on his identification wallet card, "Mr. Nobody," for his name, and "Heaven," as his address. "Mr. Nobody, Heaven." I hope this man was correct regarding his destination. But there is one thing that you can know right now, people who go to heaven, will not become Mr. or Mrs Nobody.

The Bible sets forth certain definite, specific ways by which people in heaven will be known and recognized. The purpose of this address is to discover from the Holy Scriptures four ways by which you will know your friends in heaven.

Everybody sooner or later loses a loved one by the hand of death. In that sad hour when our loved ones are swept from our side by the cruel hand of death, great questions arise in our hearts. Will I meet this dear one again on the other shore? Will I hear the same loving voice that is now stilled by death? Will I see "those angel faces that I have loved long since and lost awhile?" Will I know mother in the next world? Will I recognize father? Will I know my brothers and sisters?

God only knows what lies beyond death. Hence the only way we can ever know about life after death is to note what God has said about the other side of death in His holy Word. Before we can understand how we will know each other in heaven, we must first know what will be people's condition when they go to heaven. Will people go to heaven merely as disembodied, invisible spirits? Or will they go to heaven as real, tangible beings? On the authority of the Holy Scriptures we declare that people in heaven will be just as real as any people you have ever known in this world.

So I raise the question, What will people in heaven be like? Here is a direct, sure, positive answer in I John 3 2. I read, "Beloved, now are we the sons of God, and it doth not yet appear what we shall be; but we know that, when He shall appear, we shall be like Him; for we shall see Him as He is."

You will notice that this text declares that the saved in the future life will be just like Jesus. "We shall be like Him." Some people think that this means merely that people in heaven will be like Jesus Christ in character, like Jesus Christ spiritually. But it includes more than this. It includes having a real body like Christ's body after He came from the grave. Here it is in the Word of God in Philippians 3 20 and 21: "Our conversation is in heaven; from whence also we look for the Saviour, the Lord Jesus Christ: Who shall change our vile body, that it may be fashioned like unto His glorious body, according to the working whereby He is able even to subdue all things unto Himself."

Isn't that plain? It declares in so many words that the bodies of the saints will be changed to be like Christ's glorious body. When the saints go to heaven they will have bodies just like Christ's glorious body.

Did Jesus Christ have a real body after He had passed through death? Yes, most assuredly He did. When Jesus Christ met His disciples for the first time, after He had passed through the grave, He gave them three positive proofs that He had a real body. We find in Luke 24:36-43, that on the evening

159

of the day He arose from the dead, He appeared to His disciples as they were eating their evening meal. They were terrified. They thought they had seen an apparition or a ghost of some kind. But Jesus said, "Why are ye troubled? and why do thoughts arise in your hearts? Behold My hands and My feet that it is I myself: handle Me, and see; for a spirit hath not flesh and bones, as ye see Me have. And when He had thus spoken, He shewed them His hands and His feet." (Luke 24 38-40.)

Here is proof number one that He had a real body after He had passed through death. He showed them His hands and His feet. He could not have had hands and feet unless He had a real body. Then He said, "A spirit hath not flesh and bones, as ye see Me have." He was flesh and bones. And that is proof number two that He had a real body after He had passed through death Then He asked them, "Have you any food?" And they gave Him a piece of broiled fish and a piece of honey comb. He ate this food. Now there is proof number three. The fact that He could eat real food proved that He had a real body.

I thank God that we do not worship a dead Christ. "Not in the tomb where once He lay, but a living Christ, a risen Saviour." We are not trusting in a ghost Christ, but we have a real Christ of flesh and bones at the right hand of the Father.

The Word of God says, "We shall be like Him." He will change this vile body like unto His glorious body. This means that in heaven people will have bodies that will be real and tangible, as the body that Jesus Christ had after He passed through death. Paul helps us to understand this in I Cor. 15:44. He says, "There is a natural body, and there is a spiritual body." At the present time we have natural bodies. In the future home, in that home in the sweet by and by, we will have spiritual bodies. "There is a natural body, and there is a spiritual body."

Now the spiritual body will not be like this natural body. It is a higher order of body. Yet the spiritual body is just as real and just as tangible as the natural body. Jesus Christ taught that life in heaven will be so real that people in Heaven will eat real food. In Luke 22·29, 30 we read, "I appoint unto you a kingdom, as My Father hath appointed unto Me; that ye may eat and drink at my table in My kingdom, and sit on thrones judging the twelve tribes of Israel."

"We shall be like Him." Our bodies will be made like His glorious body. If we can discover how Jesus Christ was known and recognized by his disciples after He had passed through the grave, this will be a key that will unlock the other side of death, in regard to how people in heaven will know each other. The Scriptures tell of three different ways that Christ was recognized by His disciples after He had passed through death. When you know what these three ways are, you will see three ways by which people in Heaven will know their friends and loved ones.

When Mary Magdelene went to Christ's tomb on Sunday morning she found the tomb was empty. The Lord was gone. She began to cry. Turning about through tear-blinded eyes, she saw a man whom she took to be the gardener, or caretaker of the place But this man was Jesus Christ. She had not recognized Him. Then Jesus spoke her name, just as he used to speak it in His previous association with her. He said, "Mary." The moment He called her name, she recognized Him instantly. "Oh! this is Jesus."

Here is the Scripture record for that: "When she had thus said, she turned herself back, and saw Jesus standing, and knew not that it was Jesus. Jesus saith unto her, Woman, why weepest thou? Whom seekest thou? She, supposing Him to be the gardener, saith unto Him, Sir, if Thou have borne Him hence, tell me where thou hast laid Him, and I will take Him away. Jesus saith unto her, Mary. She turned herself, and saith unto him, Rabboni; which is to say, Master." (John 20:14-16.)

Mary recognized Jesus by His voice after He had passed through death. We shall be like Him. This means that we shall recognize our friends in heaven by their voices. Notice in the case of Jesus that in His resurrected body there was the same well-remembered cadence to the voice. The vocal cords had the same resonance as of old.

"We shall be like Him." So we shall know our friends on the other side by their familiar voices. Everybody realizes that we recognize our friends by their voices even when we cannot see them. A friend two thousand miles away may call you on long distance telephone. You cannot see him, but you recognize your friend.

I had a blind man in my congregation in a certain city where I preached for one year. He did not know what I looked like. He had never seen my face. Ten years after that in another city I saw him walking along main street one day. I placed my hand on his shoulder, and said, "Do you know me?" "Oh, it is Brother Shuler," he said, and clasped my hand in warm recognition.

There have been cases where children who could not recognize their own fathers and mothers by their appearance, did recognize them by their voices. In the early days of New England history a band of Indians captured some children who were only three or four years old. They kept them in captivity until they were thirteen of fourteen, when the white settlers delivered them out of the hands of the Indians. When these children were brought back to their mothers, they did not recognize their own mothers by their appearance. Then one mother began to sing a nursery rhyme, just as she had sung to her children when they were three or four years old. Before she was half way through that nursery rhyme, two of them ran up to her and cried, "Mama! Mama!" Notice that even though they did not recognize their own mother by her appearance, they did recognize her by that familiar voice in that familiar song.

In 1945 the Associated Press told about a three year old baby, who had never seen his father, yet recognized him by his voice. The boy came after the father had gone to war. The father sent back phonographic recordings of his voice. The mother played them to his son. When the father returned from the far east, the boy did not know him from any other soldier, but when he spoke, the little boy cried out, "That's my daddy! That's my daddy!"

Yes, we will recognize our friends in heaven by their voices. Isn't this truly comforting to you who have lost loved ones? Isn't God good to make it possible for you to recognize your loved one by that same familiar voice that has meant more to you than any other voice in the world?

> O, how sweet it will be in that beautiful land,
> So free from all sorrow and pain;
> With songs on our lips and with harps in our hands,
> To meet one another again!

Jesus Christ was also known and recognized by His disciples after He passed through death by his appearance and features. When Thomas saw the Lord Jesus after His resurrection he said, "My Lord and my God." He recognized Jesus Christ by His looks and by His familiar face after the Lord Jesus had passed through the grave. The glorified body of Jesus Christ retained its personal identity. The disciples recognized those same familiar features which they had looked upon so often during their three and one-half years of association with the Lord Jesus.

You understand how we recognize and distinguish our friends by the way they look. "We shall be like Him." As Jesus was recognized by His appearance and features, so we will know our friends in heaven by their appearance and features.

Every person differs from every other person. Each of us has his own peculiar mannerisms or make-up. Each one has his own way of walking, talking, laughing, etc. These are what make him a distinct personality. Jesus had a unique way of asking the blessing at the meal. It was different from what anybody else did.

In Luke 24:13-34 we read how two of Christ's disciples actually walked seven miles with Jesus on the day of His resurrection and did not recognize Him at first. After they had walked those seven miles with Jesus, these two disciples entered their abode. They invited the stranger to go in and eat with them. They invited the stranger to return thanks. They saw Him put out His hands, just as Jesus always put out His hands when He asked the blessing upon food. They recognized Him instantly. They said, "Oh, it is Jesus!" They reached out to take hold of Him, but He had vanished from their sight.

We shall be like Him. Just as Jesus was recognized by this peculiar way of breaking bread or of giving thanks, it means we will recognize our friends and loved ones by their dear, familiar ways of doing things, ways which were peculiar to themselves by which we knew them in this life. As Jesus Christ was recognized after He passed through death by His voice, by His features, by His personal ways, so we will know our friends in heaven by their voices, by their features, by their dear, remembered knack of doing things.

Going to heaven will not wipe out the identity of the individual. The identity of each person will be preserved in heaven. We notice this in Matt. 8:11. In speaking of that better land where the good will enjoy perfect happiness, Jesus Christ said that they will sit down with Abraham, Isaac and Jacob in the kingdom of God. Abraham, Isaac and Jacob are three old patriarchs who have been dead for thirty-five hundred years, but they have not lost their identity as individuals. They will not lose their identity as individuals in heaven. In heaven they will be known as Abraham, Isaac and Jacob. As surely as the identity of the individual will be preserved in heaven, just so sure are people to know each other. I am glad that the identity of the individual will not be lost sight of or wiped out in heaven. This means there will be recognition of fathers, mothers, brothers, sisters.

Do you know that in heaven, we shall recognize thousands of people we have never seen before, people who actually lived hundreds and thousands of years before we were born? This is made plain in Matt. 17:1-5. On the Mount of Transfiguration, Moses and Elijah came back to earth from heaven. Elijah was taken to heaven without tasting death. Moses was resurrected shortly after he died, and was taken to heaven. But notice that they did not lose their identity when they were taken to heaven. When they returned to visit Jesus on the Mount of Transfiguration, they were still known as Moses and Elijah. The three disciples who witnessed the transfiguration, Peter, James and John, had never seen Moses and Elijah. In fact, Moses and Elijah left the earth hundreds of years before Peter, James and John were born. Yet, on the Mount of Transfiguration, these three disciples recognized Moses and Elijah instantly. This indicates that in heaven we shall know thousands of people we have never seen. Yes, we shall know Moses, Elijah, Abraham, Paul, Peter, John and all the rest. O think how wonderful it will be to instantly recognize these millions of the saved!

God is the only one who truly knows any person in this present world. In Jeremiah 17:9, 10 we are told that the human heart is deceitful and desperately wicked. The question is asked, Who can know the human heart? The next verse gives the answer. "I the Lord." Yes, the Lord really knows our hearts. In the world to come or in the heavenly state we shall know each other just as truly and as fully as God knows each of us in this life.

We read about this in 1 Cor. 13:12. "Now we see through a glass darkly; but then face to face: now I know in part; but then shall I know even as also I am known."

In this life, at best, we have only partial knowledge. The apostle says, "we know in part." In heaven we shall have perfect knowledge. And perfect knowledge will mean perfect recognition. We shall know each other in heaven as fully and as truly as God knows each of us now.

> "We shall know, as we are known,
> Never more to walk alone;
> In the dawning of the morning,
> Of that bright and happy day,
> We shall know our dear ones better
> When the mists have rolled away."

We shall know each other in heaven not only by our voices, our features, our individual characteristics, but by the open manifestation of our characters.

Friends, think now of the glorious prospects God sets before you and me. When Christ shall appear those who have obeyed Him will be made like Him. He shall change this earthly body to be like the glorious heavenly body of Jesus Christ. Everyone who is thus changed will have a body that will never have an ache or a pain, that will never die. It will be a body in which you will enjoy perfect happiness without end.

Wouldn't you like to have a body like that? Certainly you would. If you had a billion dollars, you would give it all if you could have a body like that, if you could have your body changed into a body that would never have an ache or a pain, that would never get old, that would never be subject to sorrow or trouble of any kind, and never die   But all the money in the world can never buy such a body. Yet everyone may have such a body if he really wants it. Christ has opened the way for you and me to have it. "God so loved the world that He gave His only begotten Son that whosoever believeth in Him should not perish but have everlasting life." All it takes is to surrender yourself to Jesus Christ and become one of God's born-again, obedient children.

In Heb. 5:9 the apostle tells us how many people will be saved in heaven. He declares that Christ, being made perfect, became the Author of eternal salvation unto how many people? Unto all that join the church? No. Unto all that make a profession of Christianity? No. Unto all that are baptized? No. What does it say? He became the author of eternal salvation unto all that obey Him. If I should ask how many people want to be saved, everyone would raise his hand on that proposition. I have never met anyone who wanted to go to hell. Everyone can be saved if he will obey the Lord Jesus Christ. O friends of mine, I beg of you to decide to follow Jesus all the way!

(Copy of the Bible lesson outline, which was distributed to the people preceding the twenty-fourth lecture.)

Lesson IV - The Key to the Nature of Man

1. The idea is widespread that every person is born with an immortal, never-dying soul, and that the moment he dies, this soul leaves his body and goes immediately to heaven or hell, to live eternally in bliss or torment, according to whether the person was saved or lost.

2. The English Bible uses the word "soul" 533 times and never once speaks of the soul as being immortal, or never dying.

3. The Bible positively teaches that the soul of man is subject to death..........

4. In 11 different places the Bible speaks of the soul as dying or being subject to death: (Jas. 5:20; Matt. 26:38; Rev. 16:3; Eze. 13:19; 18:4; Job 7:15; 36:4 (margin); Jud. 16:16; Ps. 33:19; 78:50; Isa. 53:12.)

5. The word "immortal" is only used once in the entire Bible and is used to denote one of the distinguishing attributes of the Deity............................. ..

6. Scripture declares that God only has immortality. (I Tim. 6:15, 16.)

7. The only persons who will ever live forever are those who obey Jesus Christ (Jno. 3:36) and their souls will not be made immortal until the resurrection day at the second coming of Christ ....

8. The soul of man is not something which existed before his body was formed nor something which God puts into man after his body was formed ....,.. ....

9. The soul of man means his individual personal existence. (Gen. 2:7.)

10. Since the breath of life made man a living soul, when the breath of life is taken away at death, he must be a dead soul until the resurrection. (I Cor. 15:16, 18.)

11. The Bible does not speak of the soul as being capable of any conscious existence apart from the body. (Ps. 124:5.)

12. It is not the meaning that men have attached to certain religious terms that determines what is truth, but rather the way the Bible uses that term. (Jno. 8:31, 32.)

13. The word "soul" has three general meanings as used in the Bible.
    (a) A person, (Ex. 16:16 margin; I Pet. 3:20; Acts 27:37; 2:41; Gen. 2:7; Lev. 7:20; Prov. 25:25.)
    (b) Life or vitality, (Job 12:10; Luke 12:20; Gen. 35:18; Kings 17:21, 22, 17.)
    (c) The natural mind, thought, intellect and affections, (Ps. 139:14; Deut. 11:18; Ps. 103:1.)

14. All the trouble that has ever come to our world had its origin in the acceptance of a wrong idea regarding immortality. (Gen. 3:1-6.)

15. The only way we can live forever is to obey the Lord Jesus Christ. (Jno. 3:36; Heb. 5:9.)

References which were filled in as the study was presented, (3) Eze. 18:4; (5) I Tim. 1:17; (7) I Cor. 15.51-54; (8) Gen. 2:7.

The Mystic Ladder

(Preached on the Sixth Friday Night of the Campaign)

The Bible tells of a lonely and weary traveler, who lay down one night upon the ground beneath the broad canopy of heaven, with a stone for his pillow. As he slept that night he dreamed a wonderful dream. I suppose it was one of the sweetest dreams any mortal ever had. He saw a ladder, the base of which rested upon the earth at his feet. As his eyes swept up that ladder step by step, he saw that the ladder reached to the very throne of God in the highest heaven.

As he watched he saw the angels of God ascending upon this ladder from earth to heaven, while other angels were descending from heaven to earth upon it. **Here was the way to heaven!** Here was the first step at his very feet, and by climbing this ladder step by step, one could go to God's glorious home on high. The ladder that Jacob saw in his dream is a figure of the Lord Jesus Christ. Put down John 1:51.

The Lord Jesus in explaining to Nathanael about the way to heaven, made a very direct reference to Jacob's ladder as being a figure of Himself. He said, "Ye shall see heaven open, and the **angels of God ascending and descending upon the Son of man.**" This shows that the ladder which Jacob saw, upon which the angels of God were ascending and descending, is a figure of the Lord Jesus Christ, as the way to heaven.

Christ is **the** way to heaven. Put down John 14:6, "Jesus saith unto him, I am the way, the truth, and the life: no man cometh unto the Father, but by Me." Notice that Jesus did not say, "I am **a** way." He said, "I am **the** way." Yes, the **only** way, "no man cometh to the Father except by Me." **Jesus Christ is the way, the true way, the right way, and the only way.** If you want to go to heaven, and have eternal happiness in the city of God, you must follow Jesus Christ step by step, because He is the way. There is no other.

The bright, shining, Christ ladder will take you step by step to God's glorious happy home where you will enjoy eternal happiness. Tell me, friends, of what is a ladder composed? You say, "Mr. Shuler, it is composed of a series of steps." Right! A ladder is composed of a series of steps. So the Lord Jesus Christ has marked out a series of steps for you and me to take. The important thing is to know our Bibles, and to understand the steps to heaven.

In 1 Pet. 2:21, we read, "Hereunto were ye called: because Christ also suffered for us, leaving us an example, that ye should follow His steps." Christ has marked out steps for you and me to follow. He left us an example, that we should follow His steps.

Tell me, how do you climb a ladder? The way to climb a ladder is to take a step at a time. The way to heaven is to follow Christ's steps. We must walk with Christ step by step. He left us an example, that we should follow His steps. Going to heaven means taking a step at a time with Jesus as He leads the way. Going to heaven means obeying the truth step by step, as the Lord Jesus has marked it out for us in His holy word.

This Bible Institute has been in progress for six weeks. During these six weeks, as we have opened the blessed Bible, the Lord Jesus has pointed out the way step by step. I want you to notice tonight some of the steps in this shining ladder to heaven. Let us recall some of the steps that Jesus has made plain to us in His Word.

The first step in this ladder is inscribed, **"Jesus My Personal Saviour."**

There is no other way for a man to get started to heaven but by accepting the Son of God as his personal Saviour. Let us all repeat that supreme text of scripture, that one text which is a summary of the entire Bible, John 3:16: "God so loved the world, that He gave His only begotten Son, that whosoever believeth in Him should not perish, but have everlasting life "

Everything depends on what you do with Jesus Christ. In John 3 36 we are told, "He that believeth on the Son hath everlasting life: and he that believeth not the Son shall not see life; but the wrath of God abideth on him." Everything depends on what you do with Jesus Christ. So, as you think of this bright shining ladder reaching to heaven, I want you to see the first step inscribed, "Jesus, My Personal Saviour."

The second step in this ladder to heaven is labeled, "The Bible My Only Guide." The Bible is the guidebook to heaven. In Psalm 119:105 we read, "Thy word is a lamp unto my feet, and a light unto my path." Just as you take a lantern or a flashlight to guide your feet on a dark night, so God has given us this precious book to guide our feet step by step on the way to heaven.

Another step in the ladder, which we have learned from the Bible in these meetings, is labeled, "Salvation Only By Grace." In Ephesians 2 8, 9, we read, "By grace are ye saved through faith; and that not of yourselves: it is the gift of God not of works, lest any man should boast."

As we look at these steps, see how they come into view. Jesus My Personal Saviour; The Bible My Only Guide, Salvation Only by Grace. The next step is labeled "Conversion," or "The New Birth." No one can ever enter heaven without taking this step of being converted, being born again, being regenerated.

In Matt. 18 3 Jesus says, "Except ye be converted . . . ye shall not enter into the kingdom of heaven." In John 3 3 He says, "Except a man be born again, he cannot see the kingdom of God."

There is no other way to enter into life in this natural, or physical world, except by a physical birth. Aside from Adam and Eve, who were created in the beginning, there has never been a human being who has lived on this earth, who got here any other way than by being born. Even Jesus, the Son of God, entered this world through the womb of a virgin. There is no other way into this natural, or physical world, except by a natural, or physical birth. In the same manner, there is no other way into the Christian life except by experiencing a spiritual birth. "Ye must be born again."

Would you like to know how a person can be born again? This has been made plain many times during the six weeks of these Bible Lectures. Jesus Christ has marked out certain steps in the way of salvation. As a man takes those steps that Jesus has marked out, Divinity responds to that man's effort and does for him things that he can never do for himself.

Some of the steps on man's part are as follows: Yielding himself to the pleadings of the Holy Spirit; a sense of His need of the Saviour; the acceptance of Jesus Christ as his personal Saviour; a sense of sorrow for his past sins; making up his mind to turn from sin; confessing his sins and believing that God forgives all his sins; and believing that God cleanses his heart, and that Jesus Christ by the Holy Spirit enters his heart to dwell in him. These are some of the steps on man's part.

As man takes these steps, God takes certain steps in his behalf. Some of the steps on God's part are as follows: Drawing the man to Christ by the Holy Spirit; forgiving all his sins; imputing Christ's righteousness to cover all his past sins; imparting Christ's righteousness day by day so he can live right; creating in him a new heart; dwelling daily in his renewed heart by the Holy Spirit; giving him power to obey God's commandments and to overcome sin.

A further step in this shining ladder to heaven is, "Obedience to All the

Ten Commandments," through the indwelling of Jesus Christ in the heart. I should like to ask a very plain question. I think it needs to be asked.

When people hear that Mr Shuler has preached that the seventh day is the Sabbath, what will many say? Some will be quick to say, "Those Ten Commandments, that talk about the seventh day, have all been done away with. They were nailed to the cross, didn't you know that? You are not under the law, you're under grace A Christian isn't bound by those old Ten Commandments at all. A Christian doesn't have to keep them."

So I raise the question, "Did Jesus Christ teach that it is necessary to keep the Ten Commandments to be saved?" Put down Matt 19·16-17. "One came and said unto him, Good Master, what good thing shall I do, that I may have eternal life?" This is a tremendous question. In fact this is the most important question any man can ever ask. What did Jesus say? "He saith unto him, if thou wilt enter into life, **keep the commandments.**"

Now, what commandments was He talking about? Some may say, "Jesus didn't mean those Ten Commandments from the Old Testament, He was referring to some new commandments which He was about to give." I think we had better listen to what Jesus said. He knows.

This young man immediately asked Jesus what commandments he was referring to. And Jesus told him. "He saith unto Him, Which?" Jesus said, "Thou shalt do no murder, Thou shalt not commit adultery, Thou shalt not steal, Thou shalt not bear false witness" You know what commandments these are. Jesus cited certain commandments from the second table of the law. Christ did not quote any of the first four commandments He did quote certain commandments from the second table of the law, to help the young man to see that He was talking about no other commandments, but the Ten Commandments.

This is so plain that no one ever needs to make a mistake about it. Jesus Christ taught that it is necessary to keep the Ten Commandments. He said, "If thou wilt enter into life, keep the commandments," and it is clear that He was talking directly and specifically about the Ten Commandments.

In these words Jesus pronounced the great principle of restoration to the Kingdom of God. What Adam lost through disobedience can be regained only by obedience A disobedient mind is unfit for heaven.

We are saved from the stain of past sins by the gift of Jesus on the cross—both record and penalty may be cared for in the salvation He has offered. Thus we are reinstated here and now to a righteous standing with God. What we should do with our life from this point on is a matter of obedience to God's requirements. Each command is a test to us as was the tree of knowledge of good and evil to Adam. If we disobey again, we then despise His re-instating grace and call upon ourselves the displeasure of God as did Adam and Eve proving that we are not yet fit for either Eden or heaven One of the great purposes of grace is to make a person obedient to God's requirements. Thus in Romans 8.3, 4 we read, "What the law coud not do, in that it was weak through the flesh, God sending His own Son in the likeness of sinful flesh, condemned sin in the flesh: that the righteousness (margin, requirements) of the law might be fulfilled in us, who walk not after the flesh but after the Spirit."

Some people will tell you that Jesus Christ Himself did not keep the Sabbath. They say He broke the Sabbath. In fact there were two people here Sunday night, who voted "No" in the jury trial, because they said Christ Himself broke the Sabbath. I thank God, that Jesus Christ kept the Sabbath. Do you know why? If He had broken the Sabbath one time, He could not have been your Saviour. He would have been a sinner.

Here is where people become confused. Jesus Christ did break the man-made Jewish Sabbath laws. He brushed them aside. They said that He broke the Sabbath when He healed people, but God had given the Sabbath as a day to do good, and Christ went about doing good on the Sabbath. That isn't breaking the Sabbath. It was breaking the Sabbath according to the Jews' ideas, but not according to His Father's ideas. This is what He meant when He said, "My Father worked hitherto and I work."

1 John 3:4 tells us what sin is, "Whosoever committeth sin, transgresseth also the law: for sin is the transgression of the law." A part of the law is the keeping of the seventh-day It is the fourth commandment of the ten. If Christ had broken the Sabbath one time when He lived on this earth, He would have been a sinner and He could not have been your Saviour. You need to thank God that Christ kept the Sabbath. Where would we be tonight if He had broken the Sabbath? We would be without hope, if Christ had ever broken the Sabbath.

He violated man's ideas about keeping it, but He didn't break the seventh-day Sabbath as commanded in the Ten Commandments. He kept the commandments perfectly.

Do you know that if Christ had taught people to keep Sunday, the first day of the week, instead of keeping Sabbath the seventh day, or Saturday, He would have gone contrary to His own law? In such a case Jesus Christ would have been against Himself.

Jesus Christ, as the Creator, sanctified the seventh day, and set apart the keeping of the seventh day for man after He made the world in six days and rested on the seventh day. Then He came down upon Mount Sinai and spoke the Ten Commandments from heaven, in which He commands men to keep the seventh day, which He sanctified for man in the beginning. The Lord Jesus Christ never changes. Hebrews 13.8 says, "Jesus Christ the same yesterday, and today, and forever." He never goes contrary to His own word.

When Jesus Christ came here nineteen-hundred years ago, if He had taught people to keep the first day of the week, or Sunday, as the Sabbath in place of the seventh day which He sanctified in the beginning and commanded in the Ten Commandments, **Christ would have been going against Himself.** But He never does such a thing as this.

So another step in this bright shining ladder is, **"The Keeping of the Seventh Day as the True Lord's Day."** Can we be sure about this? We certainly can. Just think of these Biblical facts. Read your Bible for yourself. Read it through a hundred times, and what will you find? You will find that the seventh day of the week is the only day of weekly observance which the Lord Jesus Christ ever sanctified for man. Genesis 2:3 says, "God blessed the seventh day, and sanctified it." This is the only time in the Bible that it talks about God sanctifying a certain day for man to keep. The seventh day is the only day Jesus Christ ever sanctified or set apart for man or ever commanded man to keep. The Scriptures show that the seventh day is the Sabbath of the Lord Jesus Christ. They show that the seventh day is Christ's day, the true Lord's day.

The seventh-day Sabbath is Christ's own chosen sign that He is the Creator and the only Saviour. Put down two texts, Eze. 20:12 and Exodus 31:16, 17. I have paced a part of Eze. 20:12 on muslin so that you may see for yourself just what the scripture says. Notice that God says, "I gave them My sabbaths to be a **sign.**" **God gave the Sabbath to be a sign.** A sign of what? Look at Exodus 31:16, 17.

"Wherefore the children of Israel shall keep the Sabbath, to observe the sabbath throughout their generations, for a perpetual covenant. It is a sign between Me and the children of Israel forever." Why is the Sabbath a sign?

The very next clause tells us. **"For** in six days the Lord made heaven and earth, and on the seventh day He rested, and was refreshed."

The Sabbath is a sign that the Lord made this world in six days, and on the seventh day He rested. He appointed the seventh day to be the Sabbath, because He made this world in six days and on the seventh day He rested.

Evolution has tried to rule out God as man's Creator. Evolution claims that man and the world were evolved by a series of processes through millions of years. Listen to me. Here are two facts that completely explode the theory of evolution. All attempts (and there have been plenty of them) to find any transition from animal to man have ended in total failure The missing link **has never been found and never will be found.** The idea that original life sprang into existence spontaneously from non-living matter is a myth that has never been proven.

The seventh-day Sabbath is Christ's sign that the earth and man came into existence by Christ's direct creative power during a period of 144 hours, or six days of twenty-four hours each. If the Sabbath had always been kept by mankind, there wouldn't be an infidel, an idolater, a heathen, or an evolutionist on the face of the earth tonight. The true Sabbath has been lost sight of almost entirely by Christian people, and that is why evolution has practically captured all the churches. Think this through. If you knew tonight how many preachers believe in this erroneous theory of evolution you would be amazed. The seventh-day Sabbath is God's answer to evolution.

The Sabbath not only points to Christ as the Creator, but it points to Christ as the Saviour. In Ezekiel 20:12, we read: "Moreover also I gave them My sabbaths, to be a sign between Me and them, that they might know that I am the Lord that sanctify them." The Sabbath is a sign of the great power of Jesus Christ to save from sin and to sanctify the believer to His service.

The Sabbath not only points to Christ as the Creator, but to Christ as the re-Creator or the Saviour. The Sabbath is not only a sign of the mighty power of Jesus to make this world in six days, but it is a sign of His mighty power to regenerate our hearts and reconstruct our lives from sin to holiness.

Friends, I love the Sabbath. I love it, because it is a two-fold sign of Jesus my Saviour. It is a sign of His power as the Creator of this world. It is a sign of His power to recreate or make new creatures of those who receive Him. Keeping the Sabbath is a sign on my part, that not only do I honor Christ as the Maker of all things, but I honor Him as my Saviour. It is a sign that I have truly accepted Him as my Saviour, and that He is truly sanctifying me.

Just as surely as you believe that Christ is the Creator and the only Saviour, you ought to keep the seventh day, because the seventh-day Sabbath is His own appointed sign of Himself as Creator and Recreator, or the only Saviour.

Another question I want you to think through is, "What day did Jesus Christ keep when He lived here upon the earth?" There can be only one answer. It does not matter to whom you put that question, there can be but one answer. The only answer that can be given to this question, is that when Jesus Christ lived here on the earth, He kept Saturday as the Sabbath. He kept the seventh day according to the Ten Commandments.

Peter says, "He left us an example, that we should follow His steps." If you follow Jesus in the day that you keep, then what day will you observe? You will keep the seventh day as He did. Has Jesus changed? No! Hebrews 13:8 says, "Jesus Christ the same yesterday," (that is when He was here) "and today," (that is right now) "and forever," (takes in all the future.) Since Jesus kept the seventh day, or Saturday, when He was here, and He has not changed, isn't it plain that if He were here in 1946, He would keep this same seventh day?

Revelation 14 shows that the keeping of the seventh day is an important part of Christ's special message for the last days You will remember that on the second Thursday night of this Bible Institute, I gave a lecture on the prophecy of Revelation 14·6-14. We found that it contains Christ's message for our day. In this prophecy he saw three angels flying through mid-air, and the three of them together were preaching a great three-fold message.

One of the features of the first angel's message is, "Worship Him that made heaven and earth." You will find this in Revelation 14:7. The first angel calls upon men to worship God as the Creator. Tell me, how do you show that you worship Him that made heaven and earth?

Exodus 31:16, 17, which I just read, shows that the keeping of the seventh day is God's own appointed sign, that He is the One who made heaven and earth. Consequently, you can see that this prophecy of Revelation 14 indicates that the keeping of the seventh day will be restored under this threefold message, between 1844 and the coming of Christ on the cloud.

This explains why this Sabbath truth has not been found out before. God in His own Word appointed that under this last great message, the Sabbath truth would be brought to the forefront. The prophecy of Daniel showed that the papal power would attempt to substitute a man-made sabbath in the place of Christ's true Sabbath. Prophecy indicated that the true Sabbath would be lost sight of for hundreds of years, and then restored between 1844 and the second coming of Christ. You will find this brought out in such texts as Dan. 7 25, Dan. 8 12-14, and Revelation 14 6-14.

Mark this point: The keeping of the seventh day under the message that we are preaching in this Bible Institute has come in fulfillment of divine prophecy. The keeping of the seventh day is not a matter of denominationalism. It is a vital part of Christ's special message for these last days.

Now put all these facts together and see what you have: The seventh day is the only day Jesus Christ ever sanctified or set apart for men. The seventh day is the only day of weekly observance that Jesus Christ ever asked man to keep. The seventh day is Christ's chosen sign as Creator and Redeemer. Jesus Christ kept the seventh day when He was here as our example. If He were living here today, He would keep the same seventh day. The keeping of the seventh day is a vital part of Christ's special message for our day.

Dear friends, as you see how plainly and surely that the keeping of the seventh day is a step with Jesus Christ, I am sure that you are determined to take that step. As surely as you love Jesus, you will decide to keep the seventh day. He said in John 14:15, "If ye love Me, keep My commandments." If we really love Him, it is the joy of our hearts to do what He asks us to do.

Some people think, "Oh, what a terrible burden it will be to keep holy a different day from all the rest of the people." What does Jesus say? In Matt. 11.28-30 His word is, "Come unto me, all ye that labour and are heavy laden, and I will give you rest. Take My yoke upon you, and learn of Me; for I am meek and lowly in heart. and ye shall find rest unto your souls. For My yoke is easy, and My burden is light."

No burden can be heavy if it is borne in love. It is easy to step out and keep the seventh day, if you love Jesus Christ. I John 5:3 says, "This is the love of God, that we keep His commandments: and His commandments are not grievous."

Some people will say, "It will ruin my business, if I close on Saturday." Another man will declare, "I'll lose my job, if I don't work on Saturday." Another will assert, "I cannot afford to lose one day's wages." Some people think,

"Friends will ridicule me and scorn me, if I keep the seventh day." "My husband or my wife would be opposed to my keeping of the seventh day."

Let us think of some of the things on the other side. Think what Jesus went through to purchase your salvation. He gladly left His place at the Father's side in heaven. He gave up all the glories of heaven He came to this world to suffer for us. He sweat those terrible drops of blood in the garden of Gethsemane He had the cruel nails driven through His hands and His feet on Calvary. He gave His life for you.

In view of the great sacrifice He made for us, how could we hold back from keeping His day because of job, business, friends, loved ones, or difficulties? What would you think if Jesus should point to the scars in His hands, and say to you, "Do you think this was too hard? Do you think this was too much for me to do for you?" Friends, the least we can do is to surrender our all to Him. The least we can do is take the cross and follow Him.

> "I will take my cross and follow,
> My dear Saviour I will follow;
> Where He leads me I will follow;
> I'll go with Him all the way."

Are you ready to go with Him all the way on the Sabbath question? I believe that you are I appeal to you tonight to make your decision to henceforth keep the same day of the week on which Christ rested after He made the world, the same day of the week He kept when He lived here nineteen-hundred years ago. I can tell you frankly, I want to walk with Jesus regarding the Sabbath and every other item that He has marked out for me. The best thing you can ever do is to take this Sabbath step with Jesus, and every other step that He asks us to take in His holy word.

If we obey the truth step by step, as fast as we learn it from this blessed Bible, then we shall ascend this bright shining ladder, and some sweet day step off the last step over into God's happy home. Have you ever seen a father or a mother lead a little child by the hand? Yes, it is a very common sight; but listen, it preaches a striking sermon. Every time you see a father or mother leading a little child by the hand, it is a picture of how our heavenly Father wants to lead us to His heavenly home. Will you not let Him hold your hand in His? If so, He will lead you step by step, just as the father or mother leads their little child. He wants to take your hand. Will you reach up your hand just now and let Him lead you?

How many want to say; "Preacher, pray for me tonight that God will help me to follow Jesus all the way"? May I see your hands? Yes, it seems that every hand is raised.

(Prayer.)

Blessed Jesus, we thank Thee for Thy love. We thank Thee that Thou dost even want us to put our hand in Thine, that Thou mayest lead step by step all the way. Lord, we want to walk with Thee step by step, until we come to Thy wonderful home on high. May it be that each of us, in love to Jesus, will take every step with Him as He leads the way, until we come to be with Him forever in His wonderful kingdom. We ask in Jesus' name. Amen.

Does It Pay To Be Good?

(Preached on the Sixth Saturday Afternoon of the Campaign)

Were you to be offered one million dollars if you would walk fifteen miles without stopping, do you think you would consider the offer? Most likely you would, and you would do your level best to walk that distance without stopping. I have a far better proposition for you this afternoon than this. My proposition is from your Saviour, the Lord Jesus Christ. His offer pertains to something that is worth far more than a million dollars or even a billion dollars. In fact, it is worth more than all the gold, the silver, the diamonds, the stocks, the bonds, and title deeds in the entire world.

Christ's proposition has to do with the keeping of the Sabbath. As you have listened to these Bible lectures on the Sabbath question, you have learned two outstanding facts. First, there is no Bible authority for keeping the first day of the week, or Sunday. Second, the seventh day, or Saturday, is the only day of the week that the Lord Jesus Christ ever sanctified, or set apart for man, or ever asked man to observe.

These facts have brought home to your heart certain questions. Shall I make the effort to step out and keep the seventh day? Will it be worthwhile to change from the keeping of Sunday to observe the seventh day, or Satur-day?

We all know that the keeping of Saturday as the Sabbath is inconvenient. It is unpopular. It is often regarded as foolishness by the world, and it is generally opposed by nearly all churches.

In many cases the keeping of Saturday as the Sabbath means the loss of a day's wages each week. The acceptance of the Sabbath in the cases of some people may mean that you will hear the foreman say, "Sorry, we can not use you any more if you will not work on Saturday." In some cases it may mean changing our line of work to some other line of work where we can keep the Sabbath.

The keeping of the seventh day means going against the current of the world. It means one must have courage to be different from others. Don't forget, any dead fish can float down stream, but believe me, it takes a live one to swim up stream. In some cases keeping Saturday as the Sabbath means having to meet opposition and ridicule from one's own husband or wife, father or mother, brothers, sisters, friends or acquaintances.

Here is something I hope will sink deep into your heart. The Holy Scriptures show us scores of places that sacrifice, trials, persecution and opposition, being looked upon as peculiar, and even being regarded as foolish and crazy, will be the lot of people who obey the real truth. In 2 Timothy 3:2 Paul says, "All that will live godly in Christ Jesus shall suffer persecution." Did you get that? He does not say that possibly a few Christians will suffer persecution. He says, "All who live godly in Christ Jesus shall suffer persecution." He does not say, that they may be persecuted, but he says, "All that live godly in Christ Jesus SHALL suffer persecution."

In Mark 13:12 Jesus said, "Ye shall be hated of all men." This shows you what you may expect. Did Jesus Christ have an easy time in obeying the truth? No person ever lived on this earth who was opposed, despised, persecuted, and lied about more than Jesus Christ. And what did He say? "If they have persecuted Me, they will also persecute you." "If the world hate you, ye know it hated Me before it hated you."

Dear friends, you may wonder why I am saying these things. If you do not know now, you will likely know very soon. I am saying this to put you on your guard so that if any of you meet with ridicule, rebuff, persecution, sacrifices, and opposition from your own loved ones as you step out to keep the Sabbath, you will not be surprised, and above all will not become discouraged and back out.

I am sure that there are some people here who have already met with ridicule, sneers, reproach, and opposition regarding the keeping of the Sabbath. How many have met with ridicule, reproach, rebuff and opposition over the question of keeping the Sabbath? Yes, just look at the hands. This is exactly what scripture declares will be the case. So we need not be surprised.

Do you know what Jesus tells you to do in this kind of a situation? You may put down Luke 6.22, 23. He says, "Blessed are ye, when men shall hate you." You are surprised at this? Jesus says you are actually blessed when people hate you. You say, "I do not like people to hate me." If you are a true Christian, there are some people who will hate you.

Let us read on: "Blessed are ye, when men shall hate you, and when they shall separate you from their company, and shall reproach you, and cast out your name as evil, for the Son of man's sake." It is difficult for some people to see through this, but that is the word of Jesus Christ. He declares that you are actually blessed when people hate you and cast out your name as evil, when you are obeying the truth.

What shall we do when people persecute us because we obey the Lord's commandments? Jesus says, "Rejoice ye in that day, and leap for joy: for, behold, your reward is great in heaven: for in the like manner did their fathers unto the prophets."

The Lord Jesus tells us that we shall have trials, hardships, sacrifices, opposition, difficulties, and persecution in obeying the truth. However, He does not stop there. He also tells us of the great peace, and joy and fellowship we shall have with Him while obeying His word. He tells us about the eternal happy home in heaven that will come to the obedient. Over against the trials and difficulties and opposition in keeping the Sabbath, I want you to listen to what Christ promises you if you will be true and obedient.

Do you have your pencil and paper ready? Take down these four texts: John 15:14, John 14:23, Isa. 48.18, Rev. 22:14. In John 15:14 Jesus says, "Ye are My friends, if ye do whatsoever I command you." What a privilege to have Jesus Christ, King of Kings, as your personal friend! You would think you were highly honored if you were a personal friend of the President of the United States, or the Prime Minister of Great Britain. But here is something bigger than that. Jesus says, "You are my friends if you obey My commandments."

Then John 14:23 is a most lovely promise. He says, "If a man love Me, he will keep My word: and My Father will love him, and We," (that is, the Father and the Son,) "We will come unto him and make Our abode with him." O friends, let the world despise you, let the world hate you if it will. What need you care if people snub you, ridicule you, persecute you, when Jesus says, "If ye keep My words, the Father will love you, and the Father and Myself will come by the Holy Spirit and make our abode in your heart."

In Isaiah 48:18 the Lord says, "O that thou hadst hearkened to my commandments! then had thy peace been as a river." When we obey His commandments we will have peace like a river.

Then perhaps one of the most glorious promises is found in Revelation 22:14. "Blessed are they that do His commandments, that they may have right to the tree of life, and may enter in through the gates into the city."

Do you know that two of the greatest promises that God has ever made to any people, He has made to the people who will step out and keep the Sabbath in these last days?

The first of these is found in Isaiah 56:1-5. This prophecy applies to both the time of Christ's first advent and the time of His second advent. In verse one we read, "Thus saith the Lord, Keep ye judgment, and do justice: for My salvation is near to come."

Notice, he is talking about the time when God's salvation is near to come. God's salvation being near must refer first of all to the time when Jesus Christ died on Calvary and made salvation possible to every believing soul. Second, it refers to the time when Jesus Christ will come the second time to bring eternal salvation to those who have accepted of His sacrifice. In Hebrews 9:28 we read, "So Christ was once offered to bear the sins of many; and unto them that look for Him shall He appear the second time without sin unto salvation." God's salvation being near in reference to our day must mean that Jesus Christ is about to come, and bring eternal salvation to His people.

Now follow me closely. What item does God especially single out for His people to do in the last days? Notice the second verse of Isaiah 56, "Blessed is the man that doeth this, and the son of man that layeth hold on it, that keepeth the Sabbath from polluting it, and keepeth his hand from doing any evil."

Why does God especially single out the keeping of the Sabbath in the last days? Because He knew before hand it would be generally lost sight of during the centuries preceding the last days. In the Bible lecture which I gave on the sixth Sunday night of this Bible Institute, we found in Daniel 7:25 that God foretold how the papal power would attempt to change the Sabbath. "He shall think to change times and the laws." This substitute Sabbath was to be kept quite generally for hundreds of years.

In the Bible lecture on the sixth Friday night of these meetings we found in Daniel 8:12-14 and Revelation 14:6-14, that between 1844 and the second coming of Christ, God will send a special message to enlighten the people regarding the Sabbath question. One of the important items of this message is, "Worship Him that made heaven and earth." It will call people back to the creation Sabbath. It will lead people to keep the seventh-day Sabbath, which is God's own appointed sign, whereby we show that we worship Him that made the heaven and the earth.

In verses 4 and 5 in this 56th chapter of Isaiah, God tells what He will give to those who step out to obey the Sabbath and keep His commandments. "Thus saith the Lord unto the eunuchs that keep My sabbaths, and choose the things that please Me, and take hold of My covenant; Even unto them will I give in Mine house and within My walls a place and a name better than of sons and of daughters: I will give them an everlasting name that shall not be cut off."

Notice that God declares that He will give a place in His house, unto those who choose to keep the Sabbath and do the things that please Him. "In My Father's house are many mansions," (many places of abode) "I go to prepare a place for you. And if I go and prepare a place for you, I will come again; and receive you unto Myself; that where I am, there ye may be also."

A place in God's heavenly house means eternal happiness. In Psalm 16:11 we are told that in God's presence there is fullness of joy; and at His right hand there are pleasures for evermore. In Isaiah 35:10 we are told that the redeemed will come with everlasting songs of joy upon their heads and sorrow and sighing will flee away.

Friends, how much would you be willing to give, if you could have an eternal happy home in God's house this very minute? A million, if you had it? Yes. A billion? Yes. The entire world? Yes! A place in God's house is worth more than the entire world. God has pledged His word to give you a place in His house, if you will step out, and observe His Sabbath, and do what pleases Him.

In the light of what God declares He will give you if you lay hold on the Sabbath, just ask yourself, "Will it be worthwhile for me to endure the opposition, the trials, the ridicule, the sacrifices to keep the Sabbath?" When you think of that eternal happy home that God has for you in His heavenly house if you will obey Him, it will be worthwhile ten thousand times. Thirty minutes inside the New Jerusalem will repay you ten thousand times for all the trials, sacrifices, losses, and persecution that you ever had to suffer in keeping the seventh day for Jesus Christ. "What shall it profit a man, if he gain the whole world, and lose his own soul?" I want to tell you that there isn't anything you can do that will pay you better than to make up your mind to obey the Lord, "Blessed are they that do His commandments, that they may have right to the tree of life, and may enter in through the gates into the city."

The second of these great promises is found in Isaiah 58:13, 14. "If thou turn away thy foot from the Sabbath, from doing thy pleasure on my holy day; and call the Sabbath a delight, the holy of the Lord, honourable; and shalt honour Him, not doing thine own ways, nor finding thine own pleasure, nor speaking thine own words: then shalt thou delight thyself in the Lord; and I will cause thee to ride upon the high places of the earth, and feed thee with the heritage of Jacob thy father: for the mouth of the Lord hath spoken it."

Notice the first clause of this 13th verse. "If thou turn away thy foot from the Sabbath." God is calling people to take their foot off His Sabbath. In the fourth commandment of the Ten, God says, "Remember the Sabbath day to keep it holy. Six days shalt thou labour, and do all thy work: but the seventh day is the Sabbath of the Lord thy God: in it thou shalt not do any work."

God gives man the first six days of the week for his work, his business, his affairs. But God has reserved the seventh day as His holy day, and we are to render that day to Him. If we use the seventh day, which is God's day, for our regular business, then we are trampling under foot God's holy Sabbath. We have our foot on the Sabbath.

I have three charts to help you to visualize this matter.

(Three different charts were successively brought to view.) Notice this woman is ironing on Saturday. Do you see where her foot is? Her foot is on the fourth commandment. When we use Saturday for our work, we have our foot on God's Sabbath. The message of God is, "Take thy foot from the Sabbath."

Here is a lady who is at Younker's store today, buying material for a new dress. God says in the Bible that there is to be no buying or selling on the Sabbath. Notice where her foot is. Her foot is on the fourth commandment. She is trampling under foot God's holy day. It may be that she doesn't know it, but God will bring the light to her. When the light comes to her, let us hope that she will heed God's call to take her foot from the Sabbath.

Here is a carpenter doing carpenter work on Saturday. Notice where his foot is. His foot is on the fourth commandment. He is trampling under foot God's holy Sabbath.

I once had my foot on the Sabbath. I worked at my trade every Saturday. Then God's message came to me just as it has come to you in this Bible Institute. The call of God came to me to take my foot from the Sabbath. I obeyed His call. I stopped working on Saturday and began to keep it holy. I took my foot from the Sabbath. The wisest and best thing any soul can ever do, is to heed the call of the Lord.

When we really love Jesus we want to do what He says. He declares, "If ye love Me, keep My commandments." When Jesus says, "Take thy foot from the Sabbath," what else can we do but say, "All right, Jesus, I am glad you have shown me where I was wrong. Now I will keep Thy day."

Notice what God has promised to those who take their foot from the Sabbath. I turn again to the first portions of verse 13 and verse 14 of this 58th chapter of Isaiah. "If thou turn away thy foot from the Sabbath . . . Then shalt thou delight thy self in the Lord." God has promised that we will have a joy and peace surpassing anything we have ever had before. "O that thou hadst hearkened to my commandments! then had thy peace been as a river, and thy righteousness as the waves of the sea."

Have you ever noticed just how Genesis 2:3 reads? "God blessed the seventh day, and sanctified it." God blessed what? "The seventh day." Of course God blesses His children on every day of the week. But He has placed a definite blessing on the seventh day, and people cannot secure that particular blessing on any other day except the seventh. So, in keeping the seventh day you will receive a blessing that you never found in keeping the first day of the week.

I know this is true. I used to keep Sunday strictly and I was happy in my religion. But I found a special blessing when I turned to keep God's holy Sabbath. I still remember that first Sabbath I kept. It just seemed as though the trees were clapping their hands for joy. O, how I rejoice with those here today who are keeping their first Sabbath!

I am sure there are a number of people in this audience, who have kept the true Sabbath for years, and they will tell you that they have found a peace and joy and satisfaction of soul in keeping the seventh day, that they never found in keeping Sunday How many can testify that since you stepped out to keep the true Sabbath, you have found a joy, peace and rest of soul you never had before? May I see your hands? Yes, just look at those hands! "Ye are my witnesses, saith the Lord."

In Isaiah 58 God says, "Then shalt thou delight thyself in the Lord; and I will cause thee to ride upon the high places of the earth, and feed thee with the heritage of Jacob thy father for the mouth of the Lord hath spoken it." The Lord says that if we will take our foot from the Sabbath, He will bestow on us the heritage of Jacob. This word "heritage" means inheritance. The inheritage of Jacob is the inheritance of Isaac, because Jacob was Isaac's heir. The inheritance of Isaac is the inheritance of Abraham, because Isaac was Abraham's heir. The inheritance of Abraham is the New Earth as an everlasting possession. Think of that! This promise in Isa. 58:13, 14 really means that God will give you an eternal happy home in the new earth, if you will take your foot from the Sabbath and choose the things that please Him.

Is this enough? What do you say? What more could He promise? O, friends, there is no greater promise that God could make than the promise He has made in Isaiah 56 and 58 to those who will keep the Sabbath in these last days.

There are some present today who were keeping the Sabbath before these meetings began. I pray that God will keep you true to the end. My appeal is especially to you who have recently learned about the Sabbath in these Bible lectures. There is something in these texts to help you. In fact, I do not know of anything that should prove more helpful than these promises which God makes in Isaiah 56 and 58, to those who decide to keep His Sabbath in the last days.

Remember that this offer which I extend to you today from Isa. 56 and 58 is not Mr. Shuler's proposition. It is God's invitation. God declares in Isaiah 56, that if you will lay hold on His Sabbath and do the things that please Him, He will give you a place in His heavenly house. In Isaiah 58 He asserts that if you will take your foot from the Sabbath, He will give you an eternal happy

home in the new earth, and you will have a part in the inheritance of Abra_
ham, Isaac, and Jacob.

This is absolutely the best proposition that has ever been offered to
you in all your life. Are you ready to accept the Lord's invitation? I am sure
that you are. The best thing you could do would be to say, "Lord, I gladly
accept Thy proposition. I will lay hold on the Sabbath to henceforth keep it
holy. Lord, I will surrender my all, to do the things that please Thee."

I appeal to those of our friends who have been coming to these meetings,
and have here learned about the Sabbath. I want to have special prayer for
you. Will those of you, who are willing to accept God's proposition, and will
lay hold on His Sabbath, and enter into these great promises of God, please
stand for a moment? Everyone who has made up his mind to accept God's
proposition stand, please. Just remain standing for a moment. I believe there
are other people here who want to say, "Jesus, I'll take my stand." Yes,
thank the Lord here is another one. Are there not others who want to stand,
and thus signify, "Lord, I will accept this great proposition that Thou dost
offer to me."

In just a moment I want to invite all who are standing to form a prayer
circle here at the front. I want to extend this call to three other classes of
people. Is there a young person here today or an older person, who has never
given his heart to Jesus Christ? Decide just now that you will give yourself
to Jesus Christ. Come and take your stand with these dear ones here at the
front. Is there a person here who once followed this last-day message, but you
have wandered away, and today you will say, "God helping me, I decide to return to God?" Is there one here who was keeping the Sabbath before these
meetings began, and you haven't yet taken your stand with these Sabbath-seek-
ing people? All right, will you who are standing and those in the three classes
I have mentioned, who are willing to make this full surrender to the Lord,
please come forward and sit here in these vacant seats for a word of prayer?
(Choir sang "O, Lamb of God I Come," while people were coming forward. A
total of thirty-nine persons came forward.)

Is there another one? There surely must be another one, who will make
up his mind that henceforth you will keep Jesus' day. You know that the seventh day is the only right day to keep, and you know you ought to obey the
Lord. Remember that it is a dangerous thing to know this and not act on it.
James 4:17 says, "To him that knoweth to do good and doeth it not, to him it
is sin." The only wise course, the only safe way is to decide to obey the Lord.
O, I hope many others will yet come forward.

Some of you will say, "Brother Shuler, I must have more time to decide
this big question." I sympathize with your objective, but listen, do you know
how soon God expects you to begin to keep the Sabbath after you hear about
it? When you go home, read Psalm 18:44. In Psalm 18:44 God says, "As
soon as they hear of Me, they shall obey Me. This is what God wants us to do.
As soon as we hear about the Sabbath, God expects us to keep it.

O, I wish that Jesus would draw back the curtain and let you have a view
inside the New Jerusalem so that you might see what is in store for you! The
best thing to do is to accept God's proposition. The worst thing you could
ever do is to fail to accept His proposition.

O, friends, think how Jesus gave His all for us! Just think how He sweat
those terrible drops of blood to save us. Think how those nails were driven
through His hands and feet, for you and for me. How could you refuse to
come to such a wonderful Saviour?

Is there still another who will walk up here and say, "God helping me, I
take my stand." Is there one here, who once followed this message, and you
have wandered away? Make today the great day when you will decide to re-

turn to the Lord. Is there a boy or girl here, a man or a woman, who has never given his heart to Jesus Christ who will take his stand for Jesus?

Think of that great day when everyone will either be inside, "Saved," or ouside, "Lost." Where will you be? Remember you are going to be "inside" or "outside" according to the way you decide to obey the Lord. Coming forward in a meeting like this may make all the difference between being inside or outside. I do not want to see any soul left out of this prayer. I appeal to you who have not come forward. How many of you want us to pray, that God will give you the strength to obey Him? Will you lift your hands? Yes, thank the Lord for these hands.

This prayer will close the regular meeting, but immediately after the prayer I should like to meet all who have come forward. I have a tract to give you which will help you.

(Prayer.)

Our heavenly Father, we thank Thee for Thy love. We thank Thee for Jesus. We thank Thee for the great message for the last days. We thank Thee that this great message is going to every country under heaven, and wherever it goes it finds honest hearts. It finds those, Lord, who are willing to walk in the light.

We thank Thee that this message found us. We thank Thee for what the message has done for us. Now Lord bless these dear ones, who are making the full surrender today to Jesus Christ. Lord, they are accepting Thy proposition. Lord, may everyone of these who stand here at the front be conscious of the presence of Jesus Christ in his life as never before. Then in that great day when Jesus comes, may it be that we shall all have been true to our part of the proposition; we shall have kept His Sabbath, we shall have walked in His ways and chosen the things that please Him, and then He can say, "Here is a place in My house. Come and enjoy it with Me forever." We ask it in Jesus' precious name. Amen.

What About Hell?

(Preached on the Seventh Sunday Night of the Campaign)

The lecture tonight deals with the future punishment of the lost. The limitations of the available time for this one lecture will not permit me to cover all the texts in the Bible concerning the subject of "Hell." If any point in my lecture is not clear to you, or if some point seems to be out of harmony with certain other texts in the Bible, please place that item on a question card, and we will deal with it in the next few meetings.

The Bible never contradicts itself on any doctrine. Texts on any given point, which at first may seem to be contrary to other texts, will be found to harmonize perfectly by comparing scripture with scripture.

I was brought up to believe that hell is an ever-burning lake of fire down under the earth, into which the unsaved are cast at death, where they will be tormented throughout the ceaseless ages of eternity. There came a day when I determined to find out for myself what the Bible really teaches about the punishment of the lost. I want to tell what I found when I searched my Bible. I invite you to take a delightful tour of investigation with me regarding this subject.

I discovered that there is no place in the Bible where "hell" means an ever burning lake of fire into which the souls of the lost are cast as soon as they die. Some will say, "What about the rich man and Lazarus in Luke 16? Did not the rich man go into hell fire as soon as he died?" Later on in this Bible Institute I will give a special lecture on the story of Dives and Lazarus. There is nothing in this story about any disembodied soul leaving the rich man's body, and going into hell-fire immediately when he died. The account of the rich man and Lazarus in Luke 16.19-31 is a parable, and cannot rightfully be taken literally.

I have a letter from a certain citizen in Des Moines, R. J. Affolter. It was written on October 11, 1946. Here is a copy of the letter.

Reverend J. L. Shuler
1311 63rd Street
Des Moines, Iowa.
Dear Sir:
　　I offer you, or anyone else a new crisp $100 bill, if you will give me the chapter and verse of any text in the Bible that says that when a wicked man dies, his disembodied soul leaves his body and goes into hell-fire to be tormented as soon as he dies. If there is such a text in the Bible, I want it. In my reading of the Bible, I have found that the wicked will not be cast into hell-fire until the last great day of judgment.
Yours sincerely,

R. J. AFFOLTER

There is a brand new crisp $100 bill for anyone, who will take the Bible and find one text, which says that when an unsaved man dies some disembodied soul, without any form or parts, goes out of him into hell-fire to be tormented.

Jesus Christ is the Way. There is no other. If we will take what Jesus Christ taught about hell, then we can be sure that we have the exact truth. Millions of people have been taught that when an unsaved person dies, his disembodied soul leaves his body when he draws his last breath, and goes into hell-fire to be tortured throughout all eternity. Do you know that Jesus Christ taught just the opposite of this?

The tragedy of it all is, that Jesus Christ has been blamed for teaching something about hell which He never taught at all. I tell you frankly that I am here tonight to wipe this libel off the name of my Saviour. I am here to hold up my heavenly Father and Jesus my Saviour, as the God of love, and mercy, and justice.

I want you to put down some references. Here are four references that will show what Jesus Christ really taught about hell. They are as follows: Mark 9:43-48; Matthew 5:30; Matthew 13:38-42; Matt. 10:28. Here is what you will find in these texts.

In Mark 9:43-48 Jesus speaks about, "having **two hands** to be cast into hell," "having **two feet** to be cast into hell," "having **two eyes** to be cast into hell-fire." Listen to me. Jesus taught that when people go to hell they will go there with two hands, two feet, two eyes, in bodily form.

In Matt. 5:30 He says their whole body will be cast into hell. Jesus Christ never said one word about a disembodied soul leaving a man's body and going into hell-fire. Instead of the unsaved going into hell-fire at death, Jesus taught that the unsaved will not be cast into hell-fire until after the day of judgment at the end of the world. Listen to His words in Matt. 13:38-42.

"The field is the world; the good seed are the children of the kingdom; but the tares are the children of the wicked one; The enemy that sowed them is the devil; the harvest is the end of the world; and the reapers are the angels. As therefore the tares are gathered and burned in the fire; so shall it be in the end of this world. The Son of man shall send forth His angels, and they shall gather out of His kingdom all things that offend, and them which do iniquity; and shall cast them into a furnace of fire: there shall be wailing and gnashing of teeth."

Isn't that plain? Jesus declares that sinners will be cast into the furnace of fire at the end of the world. This is Christ's doctrine. And that is the doctrine I want. I do not want simply a church's doctrine, but Christ's doctrine. The doctrine of Jesus is that the wicked do not go to any place of punishment when they die, but they will be cast into the furnace of fire at the end of the world.

Jesus never taught that the unsaved would be tormented through the ceaseless ages of eternity He declares that the lost will be wiped out of existence soul and body in hell. Here it is in Matt. 10:28. "Fear Him which is able to destroy both soul and body in hell."

The Bible teaches, and nearly all churches are agreed, there will be a great day of judgment at the end of the world when all mankind will be judged. I want to ask you a question. Just think it through. Do you think a just God would send the unsaved people into hell-fire when they die, and after they have been burning in hell-fire for hundreds of years, take them out at the final day of judgment and judge them to see if they deserve to go to hell?

What would you think of a judge in Des Moines who would consign an accused man to the penitentiary for ten years and after he had served ten years in prison, give him a trial and judge his case? You say, "Mr. Shuler, we wouldn't stand for that in Des Moines. It would not be just. No state has any right to punish an accused man until his case has been judged in court." I agree, but listen. Shall not the Judge of all the earth do right? God is just. He will not punish sinners until after they have been judged at the day of judgment.

Notice how the apostles taught the same doctrine that Jesus taught. Put down 2 Peter 2:9. "The Lord knoweth how to deliver the godly out of temptations, and to reserve the unjust unto the day of judgment to be punished." Isn't that plain? There is no room here for a quibble. The apostle Peter says specifically that the unjust, the wicked, the unsaved, are reserved unto the day of judgment to be punished. Then they are not being punished in hell now.

It is altogether a mistaken idea to teach that the unsaved go to their punishment when they draw their last breath. Scripture says that they are reserved unto the day of judgment, to be punished.

Some will say, "Mr. Shuler, where are they reserved from the time that they die unto the day of judgment?" Here is the answer in John 5:28, 29.

Jesus says, "Marvel not at this: for the hour is coming in the which all that are in the graves shall hear His voice, and shall come forth: they that have done good, unto the resurrection of life; and they that have done evil, unto the resurrection of damnation."

Jesus taught that the unsaved people who have died are in their graves, and that they will be brought forth in the resurrection of damnation to receive their punishment. Mark this point well. He declares the unsaved will hear His voice from the grave. That is what He said. They will hear His voice from the grave at the last day and will come forth in the resurrection of damnation.

This is the teaching of Jesus Christ. Jesus taught that the unsaved people who die rest quietly in the grave until the day of judgment when they will be brought forth to receive their punishment. Do you know how many people are in hell-fire tonight? Not one. There is not a single person in hell-fire tonight. Scripture says that the unjust are reserved unto the day of judgment to be punished. Every unsaved person who has ever died is resting in the grave until the day of judgment when he will be brought forth in the resurrection of damnation to receive his punishment according to his sins.

When I searched the Holy Scriptures regarding the final fate of the unsaved, I found four great outstanding facts. I hope you will put these down. Here is the first fact: **The unsaved do not go to any place of punishment as soon as they die, but they are reserved in the grave until the day of judgment to be punished.** You will find this clearly set forth in Matt. 13:38-42 and 2 Peter 2:9.

Here is the second fact: **None of the unsaved will be cast into hell-fire until after the second coming of Jesus Christ at the end of the world.** Revelation 21:8 says, "The fearful, and unbelieving, and the abominable, and murderers, and whoremongers . . . and all liars, shall have their part in the lake which burneth with fire and brimstone: which is the second death."

Notice that the casting of the wicked into the lake of fire is the second death. This shows that the wicked will not be cast into hell-fire until after they get a second life, when they are raised in the second resurrection at the end of the one-thousand years of Revelation 20. Can a man get a second wife until he finds a second woman who will have him? The very fact that the casting of the disobedient into the lake of fire is the second death, shows that sinners will not be cast into hell-fire until after they get a second life, when they are raised in the second resurrection at the end of the one-thousand years of Revelation 20.

Does the Bible tell how the wicked will be cast into hell-fire? Yes, it does. Put down Revelation 20:7-9:

"When the thousand years are expired, Satan shall be loosed out of his prison, and shall go out to deceive the nations which are in the four quarters of the earth, Gog and Magog, to gather them together to battle: the number of whom is as the sand of the sea. And they went up on the breadth of the earth, and compassed the camp of the saints about, and the beloved city: and fire came down from God out of heaven, and devoured them."

The Scriptures show that the New Jerusalem, which is now in the third heaven, will descend from heaven to this earth at the end of the one-thousand years of Revelation 20. In connection with this, all the wicked will be raised from the dead in bodily form, with two eyes, two hands, and two feet just as Jesus talked about people going to hell. The devil will lead them to believe that they can capture this New Jerusalem which will be resting upon the earth. They organize the greatest military drive that has ever been known. They surround the New Jerusalem on every side. They think they are sure to capture it. But what happens? "Fire came down from God out of heaven and devoured them."

God will rain down coals of fire and brimstone upon them as they surround the New Jerusalem. What will the coals of fire do to them? Zechariah 14:12 shows that while they stand there in bodily form around this New Jerusalem, the fire will fall on their eyes and burn their eyes out of their sockets. The coals of fire will fall on their tongues and burn their tongues out of their mouths. These coals of fire will burn the flesh off of their bones while they stand upon their feet. Read Zechariah 14.12 and see what it says.

If a person is lost, he must be punished for every sin he ever committed. This is according to scripture. Hebrews 2.2 says, "every . . . disobedience received a just recompence of reward."

Take the man who has indulged in swearing, a terrible habit. He has disobeyed the third commandment by taking the Lord's name in vain. If that man doesn't repent and turn to Christ, God can at the day of judgment drop a coal of fire on his tongue for every curse word he ever uttered.

Take the thief who has broken the eighth commandment, "Thou shalt not steal." If he doesn't repent, God can at the day of judgment drop a coal of fire on his hand for every time that hand reached out to take the property of others. Yes! It is a fearful thing to fall into the hands of the living God. "Every disobedience received a just recompence of reward."

This fire that God rains down upon the wicked people will turn the entire earth into a lake of fire. This is set forth in 2 Peter 3 10. The apostle declares that at the last great day of judgment, "The elements shall melt with fervent heat and the earth also, and the works that are therein shall be burned up."

After the wicked people have been punished according to their deeds, they will be wiped out of existence in the lake of fire. Then this molten mass will be recreated into a beautiful new earth, as perfect as the earth was in the beginning, and the righteous only will live in this new earth. 2 Peter 3.13 says, "Nevertheless we, according to His promise, look for new heavens and a new earth, wherein dwelleth righteousness."

I promised to answer the following questions: What is hell? Where is hell? How long is hell? How wide is hell? Here is the Bible answer. Hell will be this earth turned into a lake of fire at the day of judgment. The Bible shows that the wicked will be punished for their sins in the lake of fire at the day of judgment, and that this lake of fire will be the entire earth melted by God's atomic power.

God knows a million times more about the atom than man will ever find out. He controls all atomic power. Don't forget that!

This earth will be melted by God's atomic power. You know what happened in New Mexico when they dropped that first atomic bomb. The sand was melted into a sea of glass. By God's atomic power this earth will be melted at the day of judgment, preparatory to the construction of this sinful world into a perfect, sinless earth where God's redeemed will live forever in perfect happiness. Hell will be as big as this earth. It will be 8,000 miles in diameter, and 25,000 miles in circumference.

Here is fact No. 3: **Hell as a place of punishment will be this earth turned** into a lake of fire at the day of judgment. You say, "Mr Shuler, how long will the wicked suffer in this lake of fire?" I do not know. What I do not know I do not try to tell. Nobody knows that but God. Each one will be punished according to the number and degree of his sins, and the length of time will vary according to the number and degree of his evil deeds. In the end they will all be wiped out of existence soul and body and be as though they never had been.

There is no scripture which when rightly compared with other scriptures indicates that the wicked will burn throughout all eternity. Here is one positive proof. Put down Revelation 20:15 and Revelation 21 1. Those references show that the lake of fire into which the wicked are cast at the day of judgment will in due time be turned into a new earth where the righteous will dwell. Therefore you can see there cannot be any such thing as an unsaved man being burned to all eternity.

The Bible shows that the soul of man is not naturally immortal. We had a Bible lesson on that here this last Thursday night. Since the soul of man is not naturally immortal, there is no such thing as eternal torment for the unsaved.

Some will say, "Mr. Shuler, doesn't the Bible say that this hell-fire into which the wicked are cast will never be quenched?" Yes. That is exactly what the Bible says. And it never will be quenched. The wicked cannot put it out, so it will never be quenched

Let me illustrate this point. Here is a frame house out in the country. They have no water or chemicals with which to put out a fire. The house catches on fire. It cannot be quenched. Will that house burn throughout all eternity? No. How long will it burn? It will burn just as long as there is anything there to burn. In the end the house will be reduced to smoke and ashes.

It will be the same way with the wicked. The fire that falls on these wicked people cannot be put out. It will not be quenched. In the end it will reduce the wicked to ashes. I will read this very item from the Bible in a few minutes. The Scriptures in speaking about a fire that never will be quenched do not mean a fire that will burn throughout all eternity. They mean a fire which cannot because it will not be put out. It means sure and complete destruction to the object that it starts to consume.

Some will say, "Mr. Shuler, doesn't Christ say that hell-fire is everlasting?" Yes, He does. He will say to the wicked, "Depart into everlasting fire prepared for the devil and his angels." What does the Bible mean by ever lasting fire?

The Bible must be allowed to explain its own terms. It is the meaning that the Bible attaches to a term that counts in the discovery of truth, and not the meaning that men have put on that term in their theology. Does the Bible say that everlasting fire is a fire that burns throughout all eternity? No. The Bible says just the opposite.

Here it is in Jude the 7th verse. "Even as Sodom and Gomorrah and the cities about them in like manner, giving themselves over to fornication, and going after strange flesh, are set forth for an example, suffering the vengeance of eternal fire."

The fire that fell on Sodom and Gomorrha back in Abraham's day was everlasting fire, eternal fire. Is that fire still burning over there in Sodom? No. The Dead Sea now rolls over the very spot where Sodom and Gomorrah once stood. This helps us to understand what the Bible means by everlasting fire. It wiped out those cities everlastingly. So the everlasting fire will wipe out the wicked everlastingly.

We learn in 2 Peter 2.6 that it overthrew those cities in a moment and reduced them to ashes, and this is an express example of what will finally overtake the impenitent. This is not Mr. Shuler's explanation of everlasting fire. It is God's explanation from His own Word.

Some will say, "Doesn't Christ say the righteous go into eternal life and the wicked go into everlasting punishment? Yes, He does. The punishment of the unsaved will be just as long as the eternal happiness of the saved. The righteous receive eternal life, and the disobedient receive just the opposite—everlasting death. In 2 Thessalonians 1:7-9, Paul declares the unsaved will be punished with everlasting destruction. Destruction is a punishment, hence everlasting destruction is everlasting punishment according to the Bible's own explanation of the term everlasting punishment.

The punishment of the wicked will be as long as the eternal life of the righteous. After the wicked are punished for their sins, God inflicts on them the second death. This second death will be just as long as the eternal life of the righteous. The righteous receive eternal life and the wicked receive just the opposite, which is everlasting death.

Notice what God says in Malachi 4:1, 3. "Behold the day cometh that shall burn as an oven; and all the proud, yea, and all that do wickedly, and shall be stubble: and the day that cometh shall burn them up, saith the Lord of hosts, that it shall leave them neither root nor branch. And ye shall tread down the wicked; for they shall be ashes under the soles of your feet in the day that I shall do this, saith the Lord of hosts."

God declares that the fire will burn them up. Some men have preached that the unsaved will burn for millions and billions of years, and never burn up. God declares that the fire will burn them up. Now whom shall I believe? There is nothing else I can do, or want to do, but believe God. What do you say? Do you say "Amen," brother?

Notice how complete the destruction of the wicked will be. "The day that cometh shall burn them up, saith the Lord of hosts, that it shall leave them neither root nor branch." Tell me, if you take a tree and put all the roots and branches into a big bonfire, how much is left of the tree? Nothing but ashes. So the wicked will be burnt up and reduced to ashes.

Here it is in the 3rd verse, "Ye shall tread down the wicked; for they shall be ashes under the soles of your feet." God takes the ashes of the wicked to fertilize the new earth. God doesn't say that "they shall be as ashes," He says, "they shall be ashes." Here is fact No. 4: **After the unsaved are punished according to their sins, they will be wiped out of existence soul and boly.**

Dear friends, God does not want to put any of us in hell-fire. "God so loved the world that He gave His only begotten Son that whosoever believeth in Him should not perish but have everlasting life." Jesus Christ died upon the cross for your sins. He paid the penalty in full for us. All you need to do is to accept Jesus Christ, obey Jesus Christ, and you will have an eternal happy home in heaven.

There are only two possible destinations for every person in the world. You, and I, and every other person in the world, are going to heaven or hell. There is no third place to which any soul can go. Every person must make his choice between two places, heaven, or hell.

If you do not choose to go to heaven, you will have to go to hell. God has provided eternal life and heaven through the sacrifice of His Son upon the cross. If a man does not choose eternal life in heaven, he will have to take everlasting fire in hell. God has left every person free to choose which he wants, eternal life in heaven, or everlasting fire in hell. Which do you want? Which do you take? It ought not to take any person in this house five minutes to decide in favor of Jesus Christ and eternal life.

Just as there are only two destinations for every soul so there are only two roads for travelers in the journey of life. There is the way of disobedience and sin that leads to hell. There is the way of righteousness and obedience that ends in heaven. There is no third road. Friend of mine, which road are you traveling tonight?

Are you truly on the way to heaven, or on the way to hell? I appeal to every soul who is walking in the ways of sin to accept the Lord Jesus Christ and let Him put you on the way to heaven tonight. I appeal to every soul here to make his decision to obey the commandments of God and follow in the way of obedience to the city of God.

There is only one thing that will ever cause any person to go to hell, and that is sin. What is sin? How can we tell what sin is? Put down 1 John 3:4, Romans 3:20, and Romans 7:7. I John 3:4 says, "Sin is the transgression of the law." The law means the Ten Commandments. In Romans 3 20 we read, "By the law is the knowledge of sin." In other words, we know what sin is by what the Ten Commandments require. Romans 7:7 shows that the law that reveals sin is the law of the Ten Commandments, which the Lord spoke with His own voice direct from heaven at Mt. Sinai and afterwards wrote on two tables of everlasting stone.

Listen! This is the law that tells you and me which day we ought to keep holy unto the Lord. Exodus 20:10 says, "The seventh day is the Sabbath of the Lord thy God: in it thou shalt not do any work." Obeying the Lord includes the keeping of the seventh day as marked out in the fourth commandment by the Son of God. This is why it is so important for you to make up your mind to follow Jesus in keeping the seventh day as He did. The Lord in mercy overlooks where you have kept the wrong day ignorantly, but when the light comes the only wise course is to turn and keep the seventh day as He commands us in His commandments.

O, how important it is that we permit the Lord Jesus to come and live in us a life of obedience! This is why the best decision any soul can ever make is to decide to keep the commandments of God and the faith of Jesus.

There is one fateful question which even the wisest man cannot answer. The wisest angel in heaven cannot answer this question. Even the all-wise God cannot answer it, and I speak that reverently too. The question is "How shall you escape if you neglect so great salvation?" There is no answer, because there is no escape.

If any of you go to hell, it will not be God's fault. You will go to hell in spite of all that God can do. You will go to hell over the love of God, over the pleadings of God, over the warnings of God, over the wooings of the Holy Spirit. You will go to hell over the cross of Calvary. God has done everything that is possible for a loving God to do to keep men out of hell. But if men will not repent of their sins, if they will not heed the call of God, there is nothing left for God to do, but to send them with their sins to hell.

O, friends, I hope every soul here will face this issue squarely. You and I have a choice to make. We can give up our sins to the Lord Jesus Christ and let Him forgive all of them and permit Him to live in us a life of obedience and make us ready for heaven. Or, if you are determined to do it, you may cling to your sins, go on transgressing God's commandments and go into hell-fire to suffer for your sins. Which do you choose?

Surely everyone in this auditorium wants God to help him to make a wise choice. How many want God to help you give up all your sins to Jesus Christ? and to follow Him all the way, so you may have a home in heaven? Will you lift the hand? Yes, it seems that every hand is raised.

(Prayer.)

Our blessed Jesus, we thank Thee for the real truth about hell. We are so happy to know that Thou art not the horrible monster that men have pictured Thee to be, ignorantly teaching that Thou wilt torment poor helpless creatures

for millions and billions of years without end. Lord, Thou hast said if we continue in Thy Word we will know the truth, and the truth shall make us free.
We thank Thee for the real truth. Help everyone of us to know that there are
only two destinations, that there are only two roads. O God, help every person
in this house tonight to give up his sins to the Lord Jesus Christ and to permit
Jesus to live in him a life of obedience that he may have an eternal happy home
with Thee in heaven. We ask it in Jesus' name. Amen.

The Mystery of Death

(Preached on the Seventh Tuesday Night of the Campaign)

About fifty years ago there lived in the little town of Cuttingsville, Ver-mont, a man named John Bowman. He firmly believed that he would live on after his death. In fact he declared he would return to his house after death. He believed it so firmly, that when he made his will he ordered his executors to provide a fund for the perpetual maintenance of his house in this little town.

For the past fifty years the furniture in this house has been dusted every day. Clean sheets have been placed upon the beds once every week. The pan-try has been stocked with fresh food, waiting for Mr. Bowman to return. No one has slept in those beds for fifty years. No one has sat down at that din-ing table to eat the food brought in once a week, because Mr. Bowman has not returned.

Science has tried in vain to discover what lies on the other side of death. Nobody knows what lies beyond death except God. If we desire to know the real truth about man's condition in death, we must turn to God's book, the Holy Scriptures, the Bible, the Word of God. I promised to tell tonight what it is that leaves a man when he dies, and where it goes, and when it will come back to him.

Here is some valuable information in Eccl. 12:7. "Then shall the dust re-turn to the earth as it was; and the spirit shall return unto God, Who gave it."

When a man dies his body goes back to dust in due time. The spirit re-turns to God who gave it. The question comes, what is that spirit which re-turns unto God at death?

There isn't a man on the face of the earth who of himself can tell you for a certainty what this spirit is that returns unto God. Only God Himself can reveal the nature of this spirit. God will tell us if we will let Him speak to us through His Word. I will give you two texts, one from the New Testament, and one from the Old Testament. In the mouth of two witnesses every word shall be established.

In James 2 26 we read: "As the body without the spirit is dead, so faith without works is dead also." The spirit is what keeps the body alive. "The body without the spirit is dead." The margin in some Bibles gives the word "breath" in the place of "spirit." The spirit that returns unto God who gave it, is the **breath of life.**

In Job 27.3 we read, "All the while my breath is in me, and the spirit of God is in my nostrils." This spirit that returns unto God at death is that which is in a man's nostrils. What did God put into man's nostrils when He made him?

Genesis 2:7 says, "The Lord God formed man of the dust of the ground, and breathed into his nostrils the breath of life; and man became a living soul." The spirit that is in a man's nostrils is the breath of life.

Remember, this is not Mr. Shuler's explanation. This is not the Methodist or Baptist or Adventist explanation. This is God's explanation of the nature of the spirit that returns unto Him when man dies. He shows us plainly in these two texts of scripture, James 2.26 and Job 27:3, that the spirit is the breath of life.

The breath of life that returns unto God when a man dies is not the air that you breathe. You know that there is just as much air left in this world after a person dies, as there ever was before he died. It is the animating touch of the great Creator by which we live. It is that divine spark of life from the great Source of life.

Listen again to how Eccl. 12:7 reads, because every word counts. The dust shall "return to the earth as it was; and the spirit shall return unto God, who gave it." That word "return" shows that this spirit is something that previously came from God to man.

If you say, Mr. Shuler, I have returned to the Hoyt Sherman Place to hear you deliver another Bible lecture" this shows me that you have been here before The very fact that you say, "I have returned," shows that you have been here previously. The Scripture says, "The spirit shall return to God." This shows that it is something that previously came from God to man.

Just ask yourself, "What was it that came from God to man in the beginning?" Genesis 2:7 tells you, "The Lord God formed man of the dust of the ground and breathed into his nostrils the breath of life." The "breath of life" is what came from God to make him a living soul. That is what returns to God when man dies.

In other words, death is the reverse of the beginning of life. In the beginning God took dust, or clay, and made a complete man and then breathed into that man the breath of life, or the spirit of life, and man became a living soul. At death God takes the spirit of life back to Himself and the man's body in due time goes back to dust.

Here is a question that we do well to think through. Since the breath of life made man a living soul, what will that man be when the breath of life is taken away at death? What do you say? He will be a dead soul. Yes, he is a dead soul until the resurrection puts the spirit back into him again. Since the breath of life makes man a conscious personality, he is bound to become an unconscious personality when the breath of life is taken from him at death.

Here is an object lesson that will help you to understand what we are talking about. Here is an electric lamp. Let this globe represent man's body. Let the illumination that the globe produces represent the consciousness of man. I press the switch and the light appears. What produced this illumination? It is produced by the flow of electric current into the filament of this globe. The illumination is the result of the union of the current and the globe

I press the switch again and the light is gone. Where has the light gone? Back to the dynamo? No. It has not gone anywhere. It is simply non-existent until the current is reunited with the globe. I press the switch again, and as soon as I restore the union of the electric current with the globe the light reappears.

Let your mind go back again to Genesis 2:7, as to how God made man. Remember this point: Globe plus electric current equals illumination. So body of man plus breath of life equals living soul or consciousness.

I press the switch and break the union of the globe and the electric current. Notice now that the electric globe minus electric current equals no illumination. So the body of man minus the breath of life at death equals no life, or no consciousness. Since the union of the electric current with the globe produces illumination, the separation of electric current from the globe takes away the illumination. So the separation of the breath of life from the body at death simply takes away consciousness until this union is restored again at the resurrection day.

This electric light is really a miracle. If you had told a man a hundred years ago, that I could just stand here and get a light just by pressing a little switch, he would have said there was nothing to it. This is a miracle. It is one of the modern miracles. How easy it is to press this switch and restore the union of the electric current and the globe so that the light shines again. So, friends, at the resurrection day the great God will restore the union of the breath of life with the body, and the dead will live again.

We have an illustration of this in Luke 8:52-55. A little girl had died. The breath of life had left her. Jesus came and restored her to life. The record says, "Her spirit came again and she arose." The breath of life had left her and gone back to God who gave it. Jesus is the life giver. He had power to put the breath of life back into that little girl. Her spirit came again and she lived.

The only way a person can know anything after he dies is to have the breath of life put back into his body by the Lord.

On the cross Jesus said, "Father, into Thy hands I commit My spirit." He committed His life back unto the Father for safe keeping. He knew His Father would give Him His life back again on the third day when He would be raised from the dead. In the same way Stephen, the first Christian martyr, as he was dying, said, "Lord Jesus receive my spirit."

When a Christian dies, his life passes into the hands of Jesus Christ for safe keeping, until Jesus shall return to receive His people unto Himself. In Colossians 3:3, 4 we read, "Ye are dead, and your life is hid with Christ in God. When Christ, who is our life, shall appear, then shall ye also appear with Him in glory."

Some will say, "Mr. Shuler, didn't Jesus tell the penitent thief on the cross that He would take him to paradise that very day?" Here is the text. We have placed the text upon the blackboard that everyone may see for himself, "Jesus said unto him, Verily I say unto thee today, shalt thou be with Me in Paradise."

Look at that text a moment. The meaning of Chrst's statement depends on where the comma is placed. If we placed the comma after "thee," we would make Christ say that this thief would be with Him in paradise that very day. If we put the comma after "today," then Christ is simply telling him that day that sometime in the future he would be with Him in paradise.

You are aware of the fact that the meaning of language often turns upon how it is punctuated. I shall give you a statement that tells two lies if it is punctuated wrong, or if it is punctuated correctly, it tells the truth. I will not change a word in either case.

"Every person in the land has 20 nails on each hand; five and 20 on hands and feet; this is true without deceit." No! It tells two lies the way it is now punctuated. No one in the land has 20 nails on each hand. No one has five and 20 on hands and feet.

Now listen, I'll not change a word. I shall simply change the punctuation. I shall remove the semicolon after "hand" and "feet" and place a semicolon after "nails;" and a comma after "five." Now it reads: Every person in the land has 20 nails; on each hand five, and 20 on hands and feet. This is true without deceit. It tells two lies, or it tells the truth according to how it is puncuated.

On the desk of Czar Alexander III, there lay a paper relating to the sentence of a political prisoner. On the margin of this request for pardon the Czar had written, "Pardon impossible; to be sent to Siberia." His wife happened to pick up the paper, and since she was a tender-hearted woman, she said, "I don't want to see that man sent to Siberia." She took an eraser and erased the semicolon after impossible, and placed the semicolon before the word impossible. Then it read: "Pardon; impossible to be sent to Siberia." It was allowed to stand. There was a man whose fate turned on just a semicolon.

Now it is the same way with Luke 23.43. If you put the comma after "thee" then you make Christ say that the thief would be with Him in paradise that very day. However, if you put the comma after "today" then Christ is simply telling him that day, that some time in the future he would be with Him in paradise.

There were no commas in the Scriptures when they were written by the holy men of God. In fact the comma was not invented until 1490. You see, the last book of the Bible was written A. D. 96. The comma was not invented until 1400 years after the last book in the Bible was written.

Where does the comma belong? Who has the right to say? The comma should be placed where the text will harmonize with the rest of the Scriptures. That is just good sense. Unfortunately the translators of the King James Version placed the comma after "thee." They thought it belonged there. But if you place the comma after "thee" you make the Bible contradict itself in two places. You say, "How can that be?" Put down two texts and you will see it. John 19:31-33 and John 20:17.

The thief to whom Jesus made this promise didn't die on the day Christ made the promise to him. We have Bible for this. The crucifixion of Jesus Christ took place on the day before the Sabbath.

Some one asked a question a few nights ago about whether the crucifixion of Christ took place on Wednesday or Friday. I know there are some people who argue that Christ was crucified on Wednesday. Mark 15:42 shows that He was crucified the day before the Sabbath. These people declare that this means the Passover Sabbath, but it was not the Passover Sabbath. Luke 23:56 speaks of this Sabbath as being **"the Sabbath according to the commandment."** Anybody knows that the commandment specified there, must be the fourth commandment of the Ten Commandments, which refers to the seventh-day weekly Sabbath.

He was crucified on the day before the Sabbath. The day closed at sunset. The Jews had a law that no criminal should be allowed to hang on the cross on the Sabbath day. So a little while before sunset on the day we now call Friday, the Jews came to Pilate and said, "We have a law that no criminal can hang on the cross on the Sabbath day. We want you to order the soldiers to take these three men off their crosses."

Pilate gave the order, and they took Jesus Christ off of His cross. When they saw that he was dead, the record says, "They brake not His legs." They knew He couldn't get away. They took the two thieves off from their crosses and broke their legs. Why? Because they were still alive and might get away.

We understand that Jesus was actually nailed to His cross. They counted Him such a terrible criminal that they nailed Him to the cross, through His hands and through His feet. But we understand that the two thieves were simply tied to their crosses and naturally that woudn't kill them in those few hours. Anyway we know that those thieves did not die that day. Here they were alive just a little while before sundown. Since the thief did not die that day, he couldn't go to paradise with Jesus that particular day.

In John 20:17 we find that Jesus Himself did not go to paradise until the third day after His crucifixion. In the Bible lecture on heaven we learned that paradise is located in the New Jerusalem. In Revelation 2:7 we are told that the tree of life is in the midst of the paradise of God. In Revelation 22:1, 2, we find that the tree of life grows on the banks of the river of life that proceeds from the throne of God. To go into paradise is to go into the very presence of God.

The Sunday morning He arose, (the third day after He told the thief about being in paradise with Him,) Jesus told Mary Magdalene that He had not yet been to the Father in heaven. When she wanted to worship Him He said, "Touch Me not for I have not yet ascended to My Father." This shows that even Jesus did not go to paradise until the third day after his crucifixion.

Hence the thief could not have gone to paradise with Jesus Christ on the day of the crucifixion, because Jesus Himself did not go.

So, if you place the comma after "thee" you make the Bible contradict itself in two places. If you place the comma after "today," then Luke 23.43 harmonizes with all the other scriptures. The Bible certainly must be interpreted in such a way that it harmonizes with itself.

Christ simply promised the thief that He would be with Him in the future. Think of this. Did the thief say, "Lord, remember me when I die?" No. He said, "Lord remember me when Thou comest in Thy kingdom." His mind went forward to the end of time, when Jesus would come into His kingdom. The Bible plainly teaches that Jesus will come in His kingdom at His second advent.

When Jesus comes the second time He will raise that penitent thief to immortality and take him to heaven along with all the redeemed, and the promise of Jesus Christ will be literally fulfilled. The thief will then be with Him in paradise.

Why did Christ use the word "today"? He used "today" for emphasis. We often do this in our conversation. If you lend fifty dollars to some friend who is not in the habit of paying what he borrows, your wife may say, "I tell you right now your money is gone." Did your wife ever tell you that? Did she mean that your money was actually lost that very day you made the loan? No. You did lend the money that day, but she is using the words, "right now," for emphasis. So Jesus used the word "today" for emphasis in His statement to the penitent thief.

If you will think of the circumstances under which Jesus made this promise, you will see why He used the word "today." Jesus was dying helplessly upon the cross. It looked as if He would never have a kingdom. His own disciples had lost faith in Him as the Messiah. But the thief had more faith that day than Peter, James or John. He believed that even though Jesus was dying helplessly upon the cross, rejected by His own people, forsaken by His own disciples, He would nevertheless have a glorious kingdom some day. Jesus said to him, "I tell you **today**, although it looks impossible for Me to be able to save anybody, **today**, when I am dying rejected by My own disciples, forsaken by My own people, **today**, I tell you that you will be with Me in paradise." "Today" was used for emphasis.

There is one question that towers above every other question. Will the Lord Jesus remember you when He comes in His kingdom? Will He remember me? The saddest thing that ever could happen would be for you or me not to be remembered on that great day, when Jesus makes up the number who will live with Him in eternal happiness "What will it profit a man if he gains the whole world, and lose his own soul?" If we lose a home in the kingdom of God, we lose everything. If I should ask how many here want the Lord Jesus Christ to remember them with an eternal happy home in His kingdom, I know every person here woud raise his hand, and rightly so.

I think we ought always to put up our hand on such a call. In fact, I would like to put up both hands. There is nothing I desire more than to have the Lord Jesus Christ remember me when He comes in His kingdom. Will the Lord remember me? Will the Lord remember you? That all depends on how you remember Him now. If we remember Him now, He will remember us then.

In Revelation 22:14 He has told us, "Blessed are they that do His commandments, that they may have right to the tree of life, and may enter in through the gates into the city."

All of the Lord's commandments are important. God never gives an unimportant command. They are all necessary for us, but do you know there is only one of God's commandments to which He attached the word "remember." Which one is it, friends?

It is the one most people have forgotten. That is why Jesus attached the word "remember" to it. He knew how it would be. There is only one of His Ten Commandments He has ever asked us especially to remember.

In Exodus 20.8-11 we read: "Remember the Sabbath day, to keep it holy. Six days shalt thou labour, and do all thy work: but the seventh day is the sabbath of the Lord thy God· in it thou shalt not do any work:"

Notice that the Lord has not asked us to remember to keep the first day of the week, or Sunday. But He does ask us to remember that He made the world in six days, and then rested upon the seventh, and then sanctified, or set apart the seventh day as a weekly holy day for man.

Mark this point. Instead of remembering the seventh day to keep it holy and doing no work upon this day the Lord commands, people today are using the seventh day for their own work, and their own business. This commandment for keeping the seventh day has been forgotten more perhaps than any other commandment that God has given. That is why Christ attached the word "remember" to it. "Remember the Sabbath day to keep it holy."

I am glad that so many of our friends here have made their decision to begin to remember the seventh day to keep it holy as the Lord has commanded. My prayer is that every soul will make this decision. Friends, if we remember Jesus now to do what He says, He will remember us when He comes in His Kingdom.

We talk about being a true Christian, but what is it? It simply means to obey the truth and do right as fast as you learn the truth from God's book. God is good. He freely forgave you when you worked on Saturday, without being aware that it is His holy day.

I used to work every Saturday at my trade. But God is good. I didn't know any better. He forgave me, and He forgives you where you have worked on Saturday and didn't know that it was the Lord's holy day. The Lord loves you. He wants to bring you into full harmony with His will. God has sent this message to you in these meetings to show you the right way to make you ready to meet Jesus.

I hope you will open your heart to this little thought. **The greatest blessings of all your life are just ahead for you if you will walk in this light.** The best is just ahead for you, if you will walk in the light. In 1 John 1:7 we read, "If we walk in the light as He is in the light, we have fellowship one with another, and the blood of Jesus Christ His Son cleanseth us from all sin. I count it the wisest and best decision I ever made when I promised God I would henceforth keep the seventh day as He did, and walk according to all His commandments.

Friends, we ought to be ready to respond to the call of Jesus, and say, "Yes, Lord, I will walk in the light. I will obey the truth as Thou dost send it to me from Thy blessed word." We need help to follow Jesus all the way. O, how important it is in these closing days when He is coming so soon, that we follow Him all the way and leave off nothing that He has asked us to do. How many tonight would like to send a silent prayer to Jesus, "Lord, help me to remember Thee now, to do Thy will, that Thou mayest remember me when Thou comest in Thy kingdom?" Will you lift the hand just now? Yes, it seems that everyone here wants to send up this kind of request.

(Prayer.)

Blessed Lord Jesus, we thank Thee for Thy great love. We thank Thee that Thou didst die upon the cross for our sins. We are so thankful that Thou couldst answer the request of the penitent thief, and give him the assurance that he would be with Thee in paradise. O, Lord, we have come a long way since Thou didst die upon the cross. We are coming now to that day when Thou wilt return upon the cloud to consummate this great plan of redemption.

(Copy of the Bible lesson outline, which was distributed to the people preceding the twenty-ninth lecture.)

Lesson V - Do the Dead Know What Happens After They Have Departed This Life?

1. The doctrine of Jesus concerning the state of the dead is that all the dead are resting in the graves until the resurrection of life or the resurrection of damnation ....

2. Jesus taught that life after death depends upon the resurrection (Jno. 6:39.) Without the resurrection the righteous dead are perished. (1 Cor 15:16-18.)

3. Every person goes to the grave when he dies. . .. .

4. There are ten places in the Bible that speak of the soul's going to the grave at death. (Job 33:18, 22, 28, 30; Ps. 16:10; 30:3; 49:15; 89;48; Isa. 38:17; Acts 2 31.)

5. After David had been dead for one thousand years, Peter declared that David was not in heaven. (Acts 2:34.) (Ps. 17:15.)

6. The righteous will go to heaven at the second coming of Christ. (Jno. 14.3; 1 Thess. 4:16, 17.)

7. People do not go to their reward at death, but according to the teaching of Christ they receive their reward at the second coming of Christ. (Matt. 16.27; Luke 14·14.)

8. The theory of people's going to hell or heaven at death is directly contrary to the Bible doctrine of the judgment, the second coming of Christ, the time of reward and the resurrection.

9A. There is no intelligent or understanding part of man that lives on after he dies ....,......... ... .

9B. Since man cannot think after he dies, the dead are bound to be unconscious. The soul cannot maintain a conscious existence apart from the body. (Ps. 146 3, 4.)

10. The inability of the dead to praise the Lord shows that the righteous do not go to heaven at death ....

11. The dead do not know what takes place after they depart this present life ....,............... ....

12A. Jesus taught that death is a sleep. (Jno. 11:11; Luke 8:52.)

12B. As a person in deep sleep is unconscious, so the dead are unconscious. Fifty-four times in the Bible death is referred to as a sleep.

13. The dead do not know anything . ...

14. A man who had been drowned, was asked, "How much did you know from the time you sank the last time till your rescuers restored breath to you?" He replied, "I knew nothing." "Then how much would you know now if you had never been restored to life?" The only answer he could give was, "I wouldn't know anything."

15. To the Christian it will seem but the next moment after he closes his eyes in death until he awakes to be with his blessed Saviour forever.

References which were filled in as the study was presented. (1) John 5: 28, 29; (3) Eccl. 3:20; (9A) Ps. 146.4; (10) Ps. 115.17; (11) Job 14:21; (13) Eccl. 9:5, 6.)

Protestantism's Two Unanswered Questions

(Preached on the Seventh Friday Night of the Campaign)

(Before the speaker began his sermon, four special tracts dealing with various phases of the Sabbath question were displayed and offered to the audience. Request cards for these four tracts were passed by bundles to the ends of the rows of seats, to be filled out by those who desired the tracts. The cards were collected after the lecture.)

Some few years ago, as one of the Czars of Russia was walking in his park one day, he came upon a sentry standing guard over a little patch of weeds. He said, "What are you doing here?" The sentry replied, "I don't know what I'm doing. All I know is that the captain of the guard ordered me to stand guard over this spot."

The Czar sent for the captain. He asked him, "Captain, what is this man guarding here?" The captain said, "All I know is that the regulations call for a sentry to be posted at this spot." The Czar ordered an investigation. But no man in the government of Russia could tell what the man was guarding at that spot.

Then they opened the archives. The mystery was solved The records showed that a hundred years ago, Catherine the Great had planted a rose bush on this plot of ground. She gave an order for a sentry to be posted there to keep people from trampling on the rose bush. The rose bush died. Nobody thought to cancel the order. And for a hundred years men were standing guard over a spot where a rose bush once had been and didn't know what they were guarding.

Every religionist will do well to open the archives of the Word of God, and check on the religious plantings that he follows. Many Christians have been and are following certain practices which they think are in the Bible when they are not in the Bible at all.

Truth alone will survive in the end. Truth endureth forever.

> "Truth, crushed to earth, shall rise again,
> The eternal years of God are here;
> But error, wounded, writhes in pain,
> And dies among his worshippers."

Every doctrine, every practice, and every religion that is not founded upon the Word of God will be destroyed ultimately. Listen to what Jesus Christ says in Matt. 15·13. "Every plant, which My Heavenly Father hath not planted, shall be rooted up." That means that every doctrine, every practice, and every religion that is not according to the Bible will be destroyed ultimately. "Every plant, which My Heavenly Father hath not planted, shall be rooted up."

Two different days of the week are being kept by Christian people as the Lord's day, or the Christian Sabbath. One class of people declares that Christians should keep the first day of the week, or Sunday, as the Lord's day, or Christian Sabbath. Another class of Christian people says that Christians should keep the seventh day, or Saturday, as the Lord's day.

Jesus says, "Every plant which My Heavenly Father hath not planted, shall be rooted up." The question ought to come to us, "Who planted the keeping of these two different days of the week that Christians are following? Who started the keeping of the seventh day?"

Listen, you will find the answer on the second page of your Bible. You don't have to seek very far. Anybody can find it who wants to. Genesis 2:1-3 tells us that after God had made the world in six days He rested on the seventh day, or the last day of the week.

God Himself kept the first Sabbath on the first seventh day of time. We have a series of charts for you to look at, which will serve to illustrate the days of creation. (At this juncture a series of seven charts was displayed one after another, which illustrated the days of the creation week.)

On the first day of the week, or Sunday, God made light. Then on the second day, or Monday, God created the air or the atmosphere. On the third day, or Tuesday, God made the dry land, and created the grass, the herbs and the trees. On the fourth day, or Wednesday, God caused the earth to take its place in relation to the moon, the sun and the other planets. On the fifth day, or Thursday, God made the fishes and the fowls. On the sixth day, or Friday, God made all the beasts. Then came the crowning work of creation, man in God's own image. Then on the seventh day, or Saturday, what did God do? He rested. After He had rested, He blessed and sanctified the seventh day for man to keep. That is the record which we find in the first and second chapters of Genesis.

It takes the New Testament to help a person understand Who made the world. When you read the book of Genesis, it tells you that "God created the heavens and the earth." When you read the New Testament you find that the God of Genesis 1 is Christ, the eternal Son of God In Genesis 2.3 we find that after the Son of God had rested on the seventh day, He "blessed the seventh day and sanctified it because in it He had rested from all His work which God created and made." Sanctified means to set apart for a holy use.

Christ, the Son of God, the great Author of Christianity, set apart the keeping of the seventh day for man at the beginning of the world. So we can drive down a stake, and say that the keeping of the seventh day was something that God planted. Remember, "Every plant that My Heavenly Father hath not planted, shall be rooted up." There is no one who can rightfully deny that God planted the keeping of the seventh day.

. Let us inquire, Who planted the keeping of Sunday? We take our Bible, which is our guide, and when we read the Bible from Genesis to Revelation, we find that there isn't any place where God ever told anybody to keep the first day of the week for any reason whatsoever. This means that we must look **outside the Bible** to find the origin of Sunday keeping. Where does Sunday keeping come from? Look at the word. Cut it in two. It becomes two words, Sun-day. That is where Sunday comes from. It was the day of the sun

The dictionary or any encyclopedia will tell you that the first day of the week is called Sunday, because it was the day of the week upon which the heathen people honored the sun in their heathen worship.

(At this juncture the speaker directed attention to three flower pots and a green shrub, which appeared on a table beside the pulpit)

This shrub and these three flower pots will serve to illustrate how Sunday keeping entered the Protestant churches. We are talking about plants, "Every plant, which My Heavenly Father hath not planted, shall be rooted up." This shrub represents the Sunday institution. These three flower pots represent the three great religions, Paganism, Catholicism, and Protestantism. Let us say that this red pot represents Paganism; the yellow, Catholicism; the green, Protestantism.

It is a well established fact that the keeping of Sunday started in sun worship. Historians tell us that Sunday was the wild solar holiday of all pagan times. The honoring of Sunday by the heathen people in their worship of the sun, can be traced back to the days of Abraham, centuries before Christ was born in Bethlehem. So I take this Sunday shrub and plant it in the pagan pot. There it flourished for centuries as the wild solar holiday of all pagan times.

Now what happened in reference to the keeping of Sunday by Christians during the 3rd, 4th, and 5th centuries after Christ? The Bible shows that the Lord Jesus Christ kept the seventh day when He was here on earth. The apostles kept the seventh day. The early Christians faithfully kept the seventh day as the Christian Sabbath. But during the fourth century, or about 300 years after the apostles passed away, the church decided to stop keeping the seventh day as the Sabbath, and to make Sunday the rest day for the church. They had no Bible authority for so doing. You say, "Why did they do it?" I shall read you the answer from a prominent Sunday-keeping minister. Here is a statement from the Reverend William Frederick in his book, "Three Prophetic Days, or Sunday and the Christian Sabbath," pp. 169, 170. Remember this statement is not from some seventh-day man. It is from a prominent minister who keeps Sunday himself and is arguing in favor of keeping Sunday.

"The Gentiles were an idolatrous people, who worshipped the sun, and Sunday was their most sacred day. Now, in order to reach the people in this new field, it seemed but natural, as well as necessary to make Sunday the rest day of the church . . . the church could naturally reach them better by keeping their day."

They tried to convert the Day of the S-U-N into the Day of the S-O-N. This matter of leading the Christians to change from keeping the seventh day, or Saturday, to keep the first day of the week, or Sunday, was a gradual change. At first some of the Christians held a meeting at sunrise on Sunday morning in honor of Christ's resurrection and then went to their work of raising crops, building houses, etc. They never thought of resting on the day. They rested the day before Sunday, which is the seventh day, commonly known as Saturday.

It wasn't very long until some began to argue that Sunday was the Lord's day and people should not work on this day. The matter grew until the bishops decreed at the council of Laodicea in 364 that Christians should no longer rest on the seventh day, but should rest on Sunday. Thus in due time the keeping of Sunday was substituted for the keeping of the seventh day which Jesus sanctified or set apart for man.

In my Bible lecture when we had the Jury Trial to discover who changed the Sabbath, we learned that God actually foretold that the Catholic power would attempt to change the Sabbath. In Dan. 7:25 we read, "He shall think to change times and laws." Catholics openly admit, yes, even boast, that their church made the change. In a Catholic paper called The Catholic Mirror in the issue of September 23, 1893, we have the following statement: "The Catholic church for 1,000 years before the existence of a Protestant . . . changed the Sabbath from Saturday to Sunday."

There is no misunderstanding this statement. They openly declare that one thousand years before there was a Protestant, the Catholic church changed the Sabbath from Saturday to Sunday.

So we must take a part of this Sunday shrub and plant it in the Catholic pot. Here it flourished during those centuries of the Dark Ages when Catholicism ruled Western Europe.

What happened with reference to the keeping of Sunday in the sixteenth, seventeenth, and eighteenth centuries when these great Protestant churches such as Methodist, Baptist, Presbyterian, and others were established? The answer is that the Protestant church leaders adopted the Sunday-Sabbath of Catholicism and made it the weekly holy day for Protestants. So I must take another part of this shrub and plant it in the Protestant pot.

Catholics are well aware that Protestants do not follow the Bible in keeping Sunday, but are following the church of Rome. Here is a striking statement from a Catholic paper called the "Pittsburg Catholic" from the issue of June 11, 1914. "Protestants deem it their duty to keep Sunday holy. Why? Because the Catholic church tells them to do so. They have no other reason." That is certainly plain, isn't it?

There is no text in the Bible that directs people to keep Sunday. Sunday-keeping rests on the same authority as the use of holy water, purgatory, confessing to a priest, the observance of Lent, Ash Wednesday, the worship of Mary, etc. There is no Bible authority for any of these. They rest solely on the authority of Catholic tradition.

Let me raise a question. Why does the present generation of Protestants keep Sunday? The present generation keeps Sunday because their fathers before them kept Sunday. Why did their fathers before them keep Sunday? Because their fathers before them kept Sunday, and on until you get back to that time when the Protestants came out of the Catholic church, and took Sunday keeping with them. The Catholic church in turn took it from the heathen people.

Do you know that a prominent Baptist minister admits all this? The Reverend E. T. Hiscox was a most prominent Baptist preacher. In fact he wrote the Baptist Church Manual. The Baptist ministers in New York State held a conference in Saratoga, New York on August 20, 1893, at which time Mr. Hiscox made the following statement to them: "Of course, I quite well know that Sunday did not come into use in early Christian history as a religious day . . . but what a pity that it comes branded with the name of the sun-god, then adopted and sanctified by the papal apostasy, and bequeathed as a sacred legacy to Protestantism."

Notice that he told those five hundred Baptist ministers, "What a pity it comes branded with the name of the sun-god." Yes, that is right! It started to grow in the pagan pot, branded with the name of the sun-god, Sunday. Then he said, "It was adopted and sanctified by the papal apostasy." There it is in the Catholic pot. Then he said, "Bequeathed as a sacred legacy to Protestantism." There it is in the Protestant pot.

What about that striking question with which Catholic priests have silenced Protestant ministers? Catholics constantly challenge Protestants regarding the Sabbath question. They ask Protestants, "Since you Protestants profess to take the Bible as your only guide, why do you keep Sunday when there is no Bible authority for it? If you are willing to accept Sunday-keeping on Catholic authority, how can you consistently refuse to accept the rest of the Catholic doctrines on the same authority?" This is Rome's challenge to Protestants.

How many Sunday-keeping ministers have been able to answer this question? Not one! This question has silenced all Sunday-keeping Protestant ministers. Can it be answered? Yes. You can answer it. You can answer it tonight if you want to. How? By being a true Protestant and following the Bible and the Bible only, and by keeping the seventh day as Jesus Christ kept it according to the Bible, and the question is answered. There is no other way to answer this challenge.

Listen to me. So long as any Protestant keeps Sunday, he is standing on Catholic ground whether he realizes it or not. He is standing on the Catholic ground of the Bible and tradition when he ought to stand on the Bible and the Bible only. He is standing on the ground of the Bible and the voice of the church, when he ought to stand on the ground of the Bible and the Bible only. Friends, I appeal to you to be true Protestants,. to follow the Bible and the Bible only.

The book of Revelation shows that in the closing days before the second coming of Jesus Christ, this matter of the keeping of the seventh day or the first day will line up the entire world into two classes. One class of people will be true Prostestants, and follow the Bible and the Bible only in keeping the seventh day according to the Bible. The other class will accept Sunday-keeping on the authority of the Catholic power and will be counted by heaven as followers of the papal power, which claims to hold the place of Christ on earth.

Every soul will make his decision on this question. This message will be brought to the forefront so that every soul will know about it, and will make his decision. I hope you will decide to take your stand on the side of Jesus Christ to keep the seventh day which He sanctified for man, and which He Himself kept when He lived among men.

Catholics recognize that the Sabbath issue is the key to being a true Protestant. Listen to a statement from the **Catholic Mirror** of September 23, 1893. "Reason and common sense demand the acceptance of one or the other of these alternatives, either Protestantism, and the keeping holy of Saturday, or Catholicism, and the keeping of Sunday. Compromise is impossible."

You can see the real issue in this matter of Sunday-keeping versus the observance of the seventh-day Sabbath of the Bible, Catholics say that it is just one of two things, either be a true Protestant and go strictly according to the Bible, and keep the seventh day which the Bible commands, or take Sunday on the authority of the Catholic church, and all other Catholic doctrines on the same authority.

The main question is, "What are you going to do about it?" I can tell you what I am going to do. I will not bow to the authority of the papal power. By the grace of God, I purpose to walk according to the commandment of the true and living God. Like Martin Luther I say, "Here I take my stand, God helping me, I can do no other." How about you, friends? Can you say "Amen" to that? Let all the people say, "Amen." (Many amens heard.)

I once kept Sunday, but when light came to me, I saw that according to the Bible the seventh day was the only day Jesus Christ ever blessed, hallowed, or sanctified. There was only one course I could take and be true to my Saviour. I turned from keeping Sunday to keep the seventh day, or Saturday. My heart cries,

> "Keep me true, Lord, keep me true;
> Keep me true, Lord, true to you;
> May all I say or strive to do,
> Prove, dear Lord, I'm true to you."

There are thousands of true Protestants who do not yet have this message for our day. But some day, somehow it will reach them. When they see that there is no Bible authority for keeping Sunday, and that the seventh day is the only day Jesus Christ ever sanctified or ever told man to keep, the true Protestant will make his decision to follow Jesus Christ all the way. He will begin to keep the seventh day. "Every plant which My Heavenly Father hath not planted, shall be rooted up." (As the speaker said this he plucked up the Sunday plant from the green pot of Protestantism.)

There are thousands and thousands of true Christians in the Catholic church. As God's message reaches them, they will see that the church had no authority to change the fourth commandment of God. They will recognize that the authority of the Bible is above the authority of the church and tradition, and they will turn from the man-made Lord's day and begin to keep the seventh day. "Every plant which My Heavenly Father hath not planted, shall be rooted up." (As the speaker said this, he plucked up the Sunday shrub from the Catholic pot.)

There are thousands of sincere pagans who are bowing down to gods of wood and stone. But as the message of God comes to them, they see that the sun isn't God They see that their idols are not God but that the true God is the Creator and that the seventh-day Sabbath is a sign of the true God as the Creator. As they see this, they are turning to keep the true Sabbath. "Every plant, which My Heaveny Father hath not planted, shall be rooted up." (As the speaker said this, he plucked up the Sunday plant from the pagan pot.)

God is sending this message to every country in the world to enlighten people about this great Sabbath issue. In every land as the message reaches sincere hearts, they are stepping out to keep the seventh day. Pagans, Catholics, and Protestants are responding at the rate of 35,000 a year now to keep the true Lord's day.

The wisest and best decision that you can ever make is to determine to keep the commandments of God and the faith of Jesus. Friends, just keep the facts before you. It will help you to make the right decision. We are concerned that God may help you to make the right decision. Just think it through carefully.

The keeping of the seventh day was instituted by the Son of God at the beginning of the world. The keeping of the first day, or Sunday, was instituted not by God, not by Christ, not by the apostles, but by men contrary to God's commandment. Jesus Christ blessed and sanctified the seventh day. Christ never blessed nor sanctified the first day of the week for people to keep. Christ commands the keeping of the seventh day in the Ten Commandments. He has never told people to keep the first day of the week for any reason whatsoever.

When Jesus Christ lived here on earth He kept the seventh day. He never kept the first day. When we hear the Word of God, Jesus wants us to do something about it. In Luke 11:28 He says, "Blessed are they that hear the Word of God, and keep it."

Christ warns us against hearing the Word of God and doing nothing about it. Listen! One of the most dangerous things any man or woman can ever do, is to hear the truth and do nothing about it. In James 4 17 God says, "To him that knoweth to do good, and doeth it not, to him it is sin."

Never forget that although you do nothing about the Word of God, the Word of God will do something about you, if you fail to obey it. In John 12:47 Jesus said, "If any man hear my words and believe not, I judge him not . . . but the word I have spoken, the same shall judge him in the last day."

The same sun that softens wax will harden clay. So the same Word of God to which men listen, will save one and condemn the other according to how they react to it.

In His sermon on the mount Jesus told about two men who built their houses side by side. One of these men was very careful how he built his house. He dug deep for the foundation so his house was founded upon a rock. After he had finished his house a great storm came. The wind blew a terrific gale. The rain fell in torrents. The valley was flooded. The waters surged against his house, but it stood, because it was founded upon a rock.

The other man wasn't careful how he built. He thought it didn't make any difference. He built his house upon the soft ground. It looked all right while the weather was fair But there came a day of testing. The same storm that tested the other man's house smote this man's house. The house fell and all who were in it perished.

Say, if you had been living in one of those houses, which house would you have preferred to have been in? You say, I should want to be in the house that was built on the rock. Yes, we shall all agree with this. No one wants his house to fall. You want your house of character to stand forever. Remember that Jesus said that the person who hears the truth and fails to obey it, is like a man who builds his house on the sand, while the person who hears the truth, and obeys it, is like the man who built his house on the rock.

Friend of mine, which one of these men are you going to be in regard to this great Sabbath truth? I appeal to you again, friends, to decide to obey the truth and build on the rock.

Many of you are standing at the fork of the road. After I learned about this great Sabbath truth, I stood at the fork of the road. That is where many of you are standing tonight. You are wondering which road you will take.

There is a signboard on one road that says, "The first day of the week is the Sabbath and Lord's Day by agreement of man." You look down that road and you see millions of people going that way. There is a signboard on this other road which says, "The seventh day is the Sabbath or Lord's Day by the sanctification and commandment of the Lord Jesus Christ" When you look down that road you see only a few people traveling that road.

On the side of Sunday I see the bishops and priests and popes of Rome; also thousands of Protestant ministers, the majority of whom have never searched the Bible regarding the Sabbath question. If they did search the Bible, more of them would step out and keep the seventh day, but they just take it for granted. On the side of Sunday I see the millions of good church members who just take it for granted that the keeping of Sunday is according to the Bible.

On the side of the seventh day I see Abraham, Moses, Elijah, Daniel, David, Isaiah, Jeremiah, Ezekiel, all the prophets, John the Baptist, Peter, James, John, Paul, all the apostles, and the apostolic church.

On which side shall I take my stand? I look again to the side of the seventh day and I see a figure towering above them all. He is the fairest among ten thousand, Jesus of Nazareth, Son of God, and Son of man. He raises His nail-pierced hands and beckons me to come. Friends, I can hesitate no longer. I cry out, "Jesus, I will take my stand with Thee in keeping the seventh day." Take the world, but give me Jesus.

Wouldn't you like to stand with me on the side of Jesus? Friends, if you are determined to keep the seventh day with Jesus, will you please take that little card that was given to you at the beginning of the sermon and make the mark of the cross? Place the mark of the cross on the card if you really mean to keep the seventh day with Jesus. If you didn't receive a card, just take a slip of paper and write your name and address on it and put the mark of the cross on that. Even if you placed the mark of the cross on the jury ballot card one week ago this last Sunday night, go ahead and put it on this card. Since Jesus bore the cross for you, don't you want to take the cross and go all the way with Him?

All right now, every one who is determined, as a solemn act of obedience to the Sabbath of Christ, just take your pencil, and place the mark of the cross on the card.

(Prayer.)

Blessed Jesus, precious Saviour, we thank Thee for Thy precious Word. Lord, Thou are sending a great message to the world to call men back to obedience to all Thy commandments, that they may be ready to meet Thee in Thy coming kingdom. Lord, we are happy that the message has reached us.

Speed the day when the world will be enlightened and every sincere heart will have an opportunity to take his stand on Thy side. Help us to make a true decision for Thee. We ask it in Jesus' name. Amen.

Does the Bible Contradict Itself?

(Preached on the Seventh Saturday Afternoon of the Campaign)

Infidels claim that Christianity is an unreasonable religion. They say it is actually impossible for anyone to be a Christian according to the teachings of Jesus Christ. Here is one of their examples.

In Ephesians 5:25 Paul says, "Husbands, love your wives, even as Christ also loved the church, and gave Himself for it." In Luke 14:26 Jesus says, "If any man come to me, and hate not his wife . . . he cannot be my disciple." Isn't Christianity a most unreasonable religion when a man must hate his own wife in order to be a Christian? Isn't this a case of a plain contradiction in the Bible? One text says he must love his wife, and the other text says he must hate his wife.

This apparent contradiction is easily dissolved. I turn to Luke 14, and read verses 25 to 27. "There went great multitudes with Him; and He turned unto them and said, If any man come to me, and hate not his father and mother and wife and children, and brethren and sisters, yea, and his own life also, he cannot be My disciple. And whosoever doth not bear his cross and come after Me, cannot be My disciple."

As the people listened to Christ's wonderful teaching they heard Him say over and over again, "Follow Me; Follow Me." Many thought that this meant just to walk along behind Jesus. They didn't understand that to follow Jesus meant to live as Jesus lived, a life of full surrender and obedience to God.

On this particular occasion a great crowd of people were walking along behind Jesus. They thought, "We are following Jesus." He turned around and looked at them, and said, "If any man will come to Me and hate not his father, and mother, and wife, and children, and brethren, and sisters, yea, and his own life also, he cannot be My disciple."

The word **hate** is not used here in the way in which we commonly use the word hate. We use the word hate in the sense of detest or abhor. In this case it is used in the sense of **love less**. In other words this text means that he must love Jesus Christ more than his father, mother, wife, brother, sister, and himself. He must put obedience to Jesus Christ above the cravings and desires of his flesh, above all the opposition of his loved ones.

The Lord Jesus knew what you would have to go through. Jesus knew that when people were about to step out and keep the Sabbath and surrender their all to God, oftentimes their own loved ones, husband, wife, father, mother, brothers, sisters, friends, would attempt to disuade them from going forward to obey Him. I am sure that many of you have already had people try to disuade you from accepting the Sabbath. That is why Jesus said, "If a man come to Me, and hate not his father, and mother, and wife, and children, and brethren and sisters, yea, and his own life also, he cannot be My disciple."

In other words, he must put obedience to Jesus Christ before everybody in the world. He meant that they would have to place obedience to Christ ahead of their own husband, or wife, or father, or mother, or brothers, or sisters. Many, many people will actually lose an eternal happy home in heaven because they listened to their husband, or wife, or father, or mother, or friends, who advised them not to keep the Sabbath. Many, many people will lose an eternal happy home in heaven, because they allowed some friend or loved one to hold them back from walking in the light sent to them.

God holds every person personally responsible to walk in the light as it comes to him. Notice what Eze. 18:20 says: "The soul that sinneth, it shall die. The son shall not bear the iniquity of the father, neither shall the father bear the iniquity of the son" God declares that the son shall not bear the father's sins, and the father shall not bear the son's sins. Every soul is responsible for himself. Every soul is personally responsible to walk in the light as God sends the light to him. Everyone of us shall give an account of himself to God.

Just think this through. It is as plain as can be since you are personally responsible to God for walking in the light, you cannot afford to allow even your dearest loved one to hold you back from responding to the call of Jesus for obedience.

In the judgment, when your case is decided for hell or heaven for eternity, God will not ask the wife, "What did your husband do about the keeping of the seventh day holy?" He will not inquire, "What did your father or mother do about it? Or what did your brothers or sisters think about it? Or what did your neighbors say about it? Or what did your pastor do about it?" No! No! There will be just one searching question. **What did you do about it? What did you do about my call to take your foot off from the Sabbath?**

You will stand or fall, be accepted or rejected, according to the way you lived up to the light that God sent to you. Friends, this means that I must go forward to obey God regardless of what anybody else says or does. Isn't that true? Yes. Listen, if nobody else in the world obeys a certain truth, and you know it is the truth, you ought to go ahead and obey it anyway; even if you are the only one in the world who follows this truth.

Instead of Christianity being unreasonable, it is the only reasonable thing for any man or woman to do. I turn to Romans 12:1. There is a word here for anyone who thinks that Christianity is an unreasonable religion. "I beseech you therefore, brethren, by the mercies of God, that ye present your bodies a living sacrifice, holy, acceptable unto God, **which is your reasonable service.**" When you surrender all to Jesus Christ, it is only a reasonable service.

One day a minister was walking around a beautiful cemetery. Over in one corner he saw a man decorating an old grave with the very choicest of flowers. The man was weeping profusely. Thinking he might offer some comfort, he ventured to speak to the man. He said, "You will pardon me for intruding, sir, but I dare say you have a very dear one buried here, perhaps a wife?"

The man shook his head. "Son maybe?" The man said, "No." "Then perhaps a brother?"

The man looked at him and said, "Here lies the man who died for me. When the war broke out between the States, I was a man of middle age. I had a family, a wife and four little children. They were entirely dependent upon me. My name was drawn in the draft for the army. You couldn't possibly understand what distress that brought to my home. My wife and my four little children clung to me. They couldn't bear to think of my going off to war, perhaps never to return. O, it brought terrible distress to our home!

"One night when we were in the deepest distress over the problem a knock came on the door We opened the door and there was a young man who lived on the next farm. He was the only son of his widowed mother. He came in and said, 'I came to tell you that I will volunteer to go as your substitute'." (This was allowed back in the days of the Civil War.)

The weeping man continued his story. "This young man made good his promise. When I received my notice to appear at the county seat, he went to report. When my name was called he stepped up and said, 'Here I am.' He answered to my name for induction into the army. He was killed in the very first battle in which he fought.

He died for me. His mother has lived with my family ever since that time.

It is a pleasure for me to care for her. I support her just as her own boy would have done had he lived. He died in my place. I live in his place."

Do you think this man did the right thing in taking care of the mother of the boy who died for him? Certainly! Wouldn't you have done the same thing? I can hear some of you men say, "Mr. Shuler, any man who wouldn't do that would be unfair, ungrateful, unreasonable." Listen, there is One who has done far more for you than this young man did for that drafted man.

You have sinned. All have sinned. "All we like sheep have gone astray, and have turned aside every one to his own way." God says, "The soul that sinneth; it shall die." The law of God condemns you to be punished for your sins. You are drafted for destruction in hell. Jesus, the Son of God, volunteered to die in your place. God took Him that knew no sin and made Him to be sin for us that we might be the righteousness of God in Him. On Calvary's cross He died in your place. He bore in His own body your sins upon the tree.

Now the question is, Have you surrendered yourself to the blessed Christ to live for the One who died for you? Are you living for the One who died for you? Or are you living to please yourself? Listen to me. No man has any right to live for himself. Did you know that? Put down 2 Cor. 5:14, 15. "The love of Christ constraineth us; because we thus judge, that if one died for all, then were all dead: And that He died for all, that they which live should not henceforth live unto themselves, but unto Him which died for them, and rose again."

We have no right to live for ourselves. We are to live for Him who died for us. It is only right. He died in your place. You must live in His place.

When I think how much Jesus has done for me, I am ready to say, "Jesus, you can have anything I have. Give me strength to obey on every point." Isn't that the way you feel? How many of you feel that way this afternoon, will you lift your hands? Yes, nearly every hand is raised. It is the only reasonable thing. It is the only right thing to simply surrender all and follow Him all the way.

A little while ago I read from Romans 12:1 the words: "I beseech you therefore brethren, by the mercies of God, that ye present your bodies a living sacrifice . . . which is your reasonable service." Did you get the force of that? "I beseech you by the mercies of God."

Here is an illustration. A man walking home from his place of business one night. As he nears home a fire truck suddenly dashes by. He wonders, could my house be on fire? As he turns on his street he sees his house in flames. He runs to the scene. He finds his wife and all his children safe except one. The smallest child is still in the burning building.

The next instant a fireman dashes into the burning building, fights his way through flame and smoke, lifts the little child in his arms, carries her out, and puts her in the father's arms safe.

Weeks go by, misfortunes overtake this fireman. He comes to this man and shows him his hands. He says, "Behold my love and mercy to you. I need help. I beseech you by my mercies to your child that you help me." Do you think that father would respond to the call of that fireman for help? There is nothing he has that he would not give him, up to half of his kingdom.

The blessed Lord Jesus comes to you and me, and holds out His nail-pierced hands and says, "My child, behold my mercy to you. I saved you from the guilt and penalty of sin. I brought you from death to life. I died in your place. I beseech you by my mercies, give your life to Me. Give Me your heart in full obedience to My commandments."

Friends, what can we do on such a call, but say, "Jesus, I come. Jesus, I come." How can anybody refuse to surrender all to such a wonderful Saviour?

God has done so much for us, and He asks us to do so little for Him, how can we refuse or fail to follow Him all the way?

There is a striking incident in 1 Samuel 15. There we read how God told King Saul to do a certain thing. Saul lost his soul because he failed to do all that God told him to do.

God told Saul to march against the Amalekites, a certain heathen nation, and to destroy every Amalekite and all their cattle. Saul went down against them, and God gave him the victory. He destroyed all the Amalekites except one.

I want you to see how near he came to doing what God told him to do. He destroyed all of them except one. God sent this message to him through Samuel: "Because thou hast rejected the Word of the Lord, the Lord has rejected thee." Isn't that a solemn warning to Christians who are keeping all of God's ten commandments except what? Except one? Except the one that says, "The seventh day is the Sabbath: in it thou shalt not do any work." Friends, for the sake of your own eternal interests, you should not fail to follow all of God's Ten Commandments.

Saul saved the best of the cattle And he thought he had a wonderful excuse for so doing. He said, "We killed all the cattle except a few choice ones. We intend to sacrifice them, as an offering to the Lord, and when we sacrifice them they will be destroyed anyway." The message came to him, "To obey is better than sacrifice, and to hearken than the fat of rams."

No excuse we can ever make, no matter how plausible or justifiable in our sight, will excuse us with God for our failure to keep His commandments exactly as He has given them. Some say, "I know that the seventh day is the right day to keep, and I intend to begin keeping it a little later. I must have more time to make my decision." Do you know what God's Word says about this? I want you to listen to Psalm 119.60, "I made haste, and delayed not to keep Thy commandments."

Instead of postponing your decision to keep the Sabbath, you ought to be in a hurry to do it. "I made haste, and delayed not in keeping Thy commandments." You ought to do it this minute. Not at 4:00 P. M. today, but do it this minute at 3.45 P. M.

2 Corinthians 6 2 says, "Now is the accepted time; behold, now is the day of salvation." Hebrews 4:7 says, "Today if ye will hear His voice, harden not your hearts." Listen. To delay to obey is sin. Maybe you hadn't thought about that. I say, to delay to obey is sin. James 4:17 says, "To him that knoweth to do good, and doeth it not, to him it is sin."

When God sends light, as He has sent to you on the Sabbath question, the only safe course, the only wise way, the only right thing to do, is to begin to keep it, immediately. Our love for Jesus should be so true, so strong, and so compelling that we would quickly answer His call and say, "I will take the cross and follow, all the way."

We need to love Jesus more. Every soul who is ever saved will be saved by love. Salvation is a three-fold cord of divine love. The love of the great Father in giving His only begotten Son; the love of the blessed Son in giving Himself; the love of the converted, born-again child of God, who in love gives himself in full surrender to God to obey His law.

I was made very happy last Sabbath to see so many come forward to surrender to Jesus to keep all of His commandments. I am sure that there are many additional souls here today, who have purposed to surrender themselves to the call of the Lord to keep all of His commandments. I want those who came forward last Sabbath afternoon to the call to obey all the commandments of God to lead the way when we extend the invitation today. Friends, just think of this! If Jesus Christ had known that only one soul among all of earth's unnumbered millions would have made the surrender to obey Him, He would still have left heaven for that one soul. He would still have left heaven and come down to this earth to sweat those terrible drops of blood in Gethsemane, and to be nailed to that cruel cross. O, the wonderful love of Jesus for you and me! I would detest myself if I refused to surrender my heart to obey such a wonderful Saviour.

I want to invite those who came forward last Sabbath to form a prayer circle here at the front. And in addition to those, I want to invite every soul, who has commenced to keep the Sabbath since these meetings have begun. I want to invite those who, just this minute, say, "By the help of God I will begin next Friday night to keep the Sabbath, that Jesus has sanctified for me." I want to invite forward every young person, or older person, who has never given his heart to Jesus Christ. The call of Jesus to you is, "My son, my daughter, give Me thine heart."

I invite forward those who once followed God's last-day message and have wandered away. Your only hope, brother, sister, is to return. I invite forward anyone who may have been keeping the Sabbath before these Bible Institute meetings began, but you have not yet taken your stand with God's Sabbath-keeping people.

Shall we stand and come down to the front for this prayer service? (Choir sang, "Lord, I'm Coming Home," and many came forward.)

I invite anyone here who has never given his heart to Jesus. There must be boys and girls here, who are not Christians. Will you not come and give your heart to Jesus? Some of you older people have never given your heart to Jesus. I urge you to come. Some of you once walked in this message, but you have wandered away into the world. Let today be the day when you take your stand for God anew.

Thank God they come. May that still small voice say what you ought to do, and when you hear that voice, I pray that you will yield to it. The Holy Spirit is here to draw us to Jesus The Holy Spirit is talking to you right now, and you know you ought to do it. Why not walk up here and say, "Jesus, with Your help I will do it."

(Prayer.)

Blessed Lord Jesus, we do respond to Thy call today. "By the mercies of God," Lord, how could we resist it, when we think of how much Jesus has done for us? Lord, Thou didst give Thy life for us. The least we can do, is to give our lives for Thee.

Lord, we are not here to please ourselves. We are not here to live for ourselves. We want to live for Thee. Thou didst die in our place, and we want to live in Thy place. Father, we pray thou wilt bless those who stand around the altar today. Lord Jesus, may Thy sweet Holy Spirit warm their hearts. May they hear the still, small voice of Jesus saying to them, "Be of good cheer, you are My son, you are My daughter, with whom I am well pleased."

O, Lord, we pray that Thou wilt bless those who did not come. Lord, they intend to do this. They want to do it. They do love Thee, and we pray that Thou wilt help them to love Thee more, until they yield themselves to obey Thee

Lord, there are some who have problems. We pray Thou wilt show Thyself strong to make a way through each problem. Bless those who may be giving their hearts to Jesus for the first time. O, we pray that each heart will be so fully yielded to Jesus, that He can come in and possess the heart fully. Recreate that heart in His own likeness. We ask all this in Jesus' precious name. Amen.

Three Generals Appointed for Armageddon

"I saw three unclean spirits like frogs come out of the mouth of the dragon, and out of the mouth of the beast, and out of the mouth of the false prophet. For they are the spirits of devils, working miracles, which go forth unto the kings of the earth and of the whole world to gather them to the battle of that great day of God Almighty And he gathered them together into a place called in the Hebrew tongue, Armageddon." This is the reading of the Word of God in Revelation 16 13, 14, 16

The word of God thus declares that in the final movements that usher in the return of our Lord Jesus Christ, the kings of the earth and of the entire world will be gathered to the battle of Armageddon, by three unclean spirits which go forth from the dragon, the beast, and the false prophet. This shows that these three, the dragon, the beast and the false prophet, are the three great generals on the side of Satan in the final battle between truth and error. These are the three powers through whom the devil will especially work in his endeavor to swing the whole world to his side in that final battle.

No person can understand the Battle of Waterloo in 1815 unless he knows who Napoleon Bonaparte was and who the Duke of Wellington was. Why? Because they were the two commanding generals on the two opposing sides on the field of Waterloo. So no one can understand the world-ending battle of Armageddon unless he knows who is the dragon, who is the beast, and who is the false prophet. Why? Because they are the three generals on the side of error in the last mighty conflict that will close the history of this world.

God has unveiled the identity of these three powers in Revelation 12 and 13. Take the first member of this false trinity, or triumvirate of error, the dragon. I turn to Revelation 12.3. "There appeared another wonder in heaven; and behold, a great red dragon, having seven heads and ten horns, and seven crowns upon his heads." (As the speaker read this text a chart depicting this red dragon was lowered into view.)

Now the question naturally arises, Who is this dragon? What power does it represent? Look at Rev. 12.9. "The great dragon was cast out, that old serpent, called the Devil and Satan." This dragon primarily represents the Devil. But the Devil works in this world through human agencies. In Revelation 12:4, 5 God unveils the identity of this dragon power in our world.

"His tail drew the third part of the stars of heaven, and did cast them to the earth: and the dragon stood before the woman which was ready to be delivered, to devour her child as soon as it was born. And she brought forth a man child, Who was to rule all nations with a rod of iron: and her child was caught up unto God, and to His throne."

This tells about a certain woman, who gave birth to a certain man child, who was to rule all nations, and how this dragon attempted to destroy the boy as soon as he was born. If we can learn who that man child was and what power attempted to destroy that man child as soon as He was born, you will know then who is this dragon.

Is it possible to know for a certainty who this man child was whom this woman brought forth? Most assuredly it is. Prophecy gives two points of identity regarding this man child. Notice verse 5. "She brought forth a man child, who was to rule all nations with a rod of iron: and her child was caught up unto God and to His throne." This man child was the One who has been appointed by the Lord to rule all nations, and He was caught up from this earth to sit on the throne of God in heaven.

There have been millions and millions of boys born into the world, but among these millions of boys there is **only one** (not two, not three, not four) only one boy that has ever been born into this world, who was divinely appointed to rule all nations. There has been only one boy born who was caught up from this world to sit on the throne of God. Tell me, who is He? Jesus Christ, the Son of man, and Son of God, born as a baby boy of the Virgin Mary.

Christ is the only man who ever trod this world, who could truthfully say, "All power in heaven and earth is given to me." Yes, He has power to rule all nations.

Enoch and Elijah were caught up from earth into heaven, but they did not become co-rulers with the Great Father upon His throne. But after Jesus paid the price for our sins upon the cross and rose again, He was caught up to sit on the right hand of the Father. We need not have a doubt as to who this man child was. We know for a certainty that the man child of Revelation 12 was the Lord Jesus Christ.

Follow me closely. Notice where the dragon enters the picture. I read again the last part of verse 4. "The dragon stood before the woman to devour her child as soon as it was born." Tell me, you Bible readers, who attempted to kill Jesus Christ as soon as He was born? (Voices, Herod.) Right! Who was Herod? He was a Roman king. He was the representative of that great pagan system of Rome that ruled the world when Jesus was born. So here is the answer to the first question, Who is the dragon? The dragon represents paganism.

In 1 Cor. 10:9, 20 Paul shows that idol worship is devil worship. The devil has made paganism the greatest of all religions in point of number. He has deceived untold millions by paganism. He has led countless millions to believe that when they worship their idols or images they are worshipping God, when in reality they are worshipping the devil himself, because idol worship is devil worship.

Notice how rapidly the world today is reverting to pagan ways of living. Talk about the world becoming Christianized! It has never followed pagan ways of living to the extent it follows them now. Men are worshipping gods of lust, gods of pleasure, gods of money, and gods of appetite. If you know your Bible, you should recognize this as a masterful plan of Satan to sweep millions upon millions into his net in the last struggle.

Let us turn to the second member of this false trinity, the beast. Who is the beast? I read Revelation 13.1, 2: "I stood upon the sand of the sea, and saw a beast rise up out of the sea, having seven heads and ten horns, and upon his horns ten crowns, and upon his heads the name of blasphemy. And the beast which I saw was like unto a leopard, and his feet were as the feet of a bear, and his mouth as the mouth of a lion: and the dragon gave him his power, and his seat, and great authority." (As this scripture was read, a chart depicting this beast was lowered into view.)

The question comes, What power does this beast represent? Did you notice that this beast has exactly the same number of heads, and the same number of horns as the dragon? More than this, the dragon gave this beast his power, his seat, his authority. This shows that the leopard beast is a continuation of the power of Rome in a different form.

In other words, God showed John how this beast would come up and take the place of the dragon. It is as plain as 2 and 2 make 4 that the beast is that religious system which followed pagan Rome in ruling over western Europe in the Middle Ages. Listen. Ask any Catholic priest this question: What religious power arose to supremacy over the nations of western Europe after the fall of the Roman Empire in the West? What will he say? What can he say? There is only one answer that can be given to that question. The facts of history show that papal Rome, or the Catholic hierarchy, is the only power that arose to supremacy over the nations of western Europe after the fall of the Roman Empire in the West.

The dragon gave the beast his seat. What is the seat of any government? It is the capitol of the government. The seat of this country is Washington, D. C. The seat of the government of France is Paris. The seat of the government of Russia is Moscow. The seat of the government of the Roman Empire was the city of Rome.

What happened to the city of Rome in 330 A. D.? Do you know your history? Constantine, the emperor of Rome, in 330 A. D. moved the capitol of the Roman Empire from Rome on the Tiber to Byzantium on the Bosporus, and changed the name of that city from Byzantium to Constantinope, or the city of Constantine. And what became of Rome? It became the seat of the bishops of Rome, who quickly built up an ecclesiastical Empire. To this day the city of Rome continues to be the seat of the pope's world-wide ecclesiastical Empire. Yes, the dragon gave the beast his seat. It is as plain as can be, isn't it?

Do you know that the Bible makes it plain that the beast power will have one certain man at its head, and even gives you his number? Here it is! Put down Rev. 13:18. "Here is wisdom. Let him that hath understanding count the number of the beast: for it is the number of a man; and his number is six hundred threescore and six."

That indicates that there will be one certain man at the head of this beast power and his number will be 666. Everybody knows that the man at the head of the Catholic system is the pope. Does this number 666 apply to the pope? Catholic officials deny this. They say no! But what are the facts?

All Catholic officials admit that the basis of the authority vested in the pope grows out of the claim that he is the vicar of Jesus Christ or the Vicar of the Son of God. The entire papal system is built on the assumption that the pope is the Vicarius Filii Dei. This is a Latin expression which means the Vicar of the Son of God.

When the pope is crowned, the cardinal who places the tiara on his head, pronounces him to be Vicarius Filii Dei. He is crowned as the vicar of the Son of God.

I have here (displaying a photostat) a photographic reproduction of a letter written from Cardinal Gibbons' office in Baltimore by one of his assistants on January 26, 1904, in which this assistant states that the cardinal, who puts the crown on the pope's head, uses these three Latin words, Vicarius Filii Dei.

Here is a photographic reproduction of a page from Ferrari's "Religious Encyclopedia, a standard Roman Catholic authority, in which he shows that all the power of the pope grows out of the claim that he is Vicarius Filii Dei. Here it is in the original Latin, and there you will see the three words, "Vicarius Filii Dei."

I have a photostat of a page from the canon law, which is the official law of the papal system. In this canon law the pope is referred to as Vicarius Filii Dei. There is no mistake about this. According to the Roman Catholic doctrine the pope is Vicarius Filii Dei. Of course you know that their official documents are in Latin. This is the Latin term that is used in reference to the power of the pope.

Scripture declares that we should count his number. Here are the three Latin words which, more than any others perhaps, express the alleged position of the pope—"Vicarius Filii Dei." This word "Vicarius" may also be spelled, "VICARIVS." In the old Latin usage "U" and "V" had the same value. You may see traces of this today. I have seen church buildings where the word "church" was carved in stone as "CHVRCH." I have seen public libraries where the word "Public" was carved "PVBLIC." I have seen "building" where it was spelled "BVILDING" in the place of "building" It is just the old Latin usage of "V" and "U" being used interchangeably.

Let us count the numerical value of this VICARIVS FILII DEI:

V— 5	F— 0	D—500
I— 1	I— 1	E— 0
C—100	L— 50	I— 1
A— 0	I— 1	
R— 0	I— 1	
I— 1		
V— 5		
S— 0		
___	___	___
112	53	501

112 in VICARIUS
53 in FILII
501 in DEI
___

Total 666

Brother, sister, you have his number tonight. It is 666 exactly as the prophecy declared it would be. It is interesting to notice that in the Greek the word for "Latin man" or "Latin church," equals 666. In the Hebrew the word "Roman kingdom" equals 666, and in the Latin, Vicarius Filii Dei equals 666. One writer says, "We challenge the world to find another name in the languages of Greek, Hebrew, and Latin that shall designate the same number 666."

The prophecy foretold how long this papal power would rule until he would receive a deadly wound. In Rev. 13:5 we read these words, "There was given unto him a mouth speaking great things; and power was given unto him to continue forty and two months" The supremacy of the papal power was to continue for forty-two months

In Bible times under the Jewish calendar they figured 30 days to the month. 42 x 30 equals 1260. The papal supremacy began in 538. He was to continue 42 months or 1260 days. In prophecy a day represents a year. You will find that in Eze. 4:6. God says, "I have appointed thee each day for a year." His supremacy was to continue for 1260 years. Add 1260 to 538 and you get 1798.

The prophecy indicated that this papal power would go into captivity at the end of forty-two months. The end of this forty-two months was 1798. Notice the last part of verse 5: "Power was given unto him to continue forty and two months." Verse 10 says, "He that leadeth into captivity shall go into captivity." Did this come true? It certainly did.

What happened on February 10, 1798, at the end of the forty-two months of Revelation 13.5? On February 10, 1798, a French army led by General Berthier, entered Rome, took the pope prisoner, carried him to France and placed him in prison. This power continued for forty-two months and went into captivity. The pope was put in prison in 1798.

In 1797 Napoleon was ordered by the French Directory to abolish the papacy. He disregarded the order and on his own responsibility made peace with the papacy. In 1798 the French Directory ordered Berthier to abolish the papacy, and he did it. The pope was just as helpless in 1797 as in 1798. Why did not Napoleon go ahead and take him prisoner in 1797? It was one year too early according to the prophecy. The appointed forty-two months had not expired. Scripture cannot be broken. "Heaven and earth shall pass away," says Jesus, "but My words shall not pass away."

The pope whom the French imprisoned in 1798 died while in prison in France the next year, or in 1799. The French refused to allow the Catholic cardinals to elect another pope. It looked as if the papacy was dead. For a time there was no pope. In 1800 Napoleon came into power in France, and he permitted the cardinals to elect a successor to the pope and they have had one ever since. Do you know that all of this was foreshadowed in the prophecy?

In Revelation 13:3 John, in talking about the papal power, said, "I saw one of his heads as it were wounded to death." It looked as if he had received a wound that would be the end of him. All Europe thought that the papacy was dead. But prophecy said, "His deady wound was healed" The papacy was destined to continue. The prophecy goes further than this. It indicates that in the closing days of this world's history, the pope's prestige will be increased again until almost the entire world will follow his direction. Here it is in Revelation 13·3. "His deadly wound was healed: and all the world wondered after the beast."

Have you noticed how the influence and prestige of the pope of Rome are steadily increasing during these recent years? Do you know what happened February 11, 1929? On that day the pope of Rome became king again. He became one of the earth's civil rulers, as the King of the Vatican City, as well as the spiritual ruler of hundreds of millions of Catholics all around the world. Do you know what happened March 13, 1939? A new pope was crowned at that time as the successor to Pope Pius XI, who died February 13, 1939. Joseph P. Kennedy, the United States ambassador to England, was sent from London to Rome to represent the United States government at the coronation of the new pope Forty different nations in the world had their official ambassadors present to honor the pope at his coronation.

Vatican City, over which the pope rules as a civil ruler is the world's smallest state. It consists of only 109 acres It isn't as large as a good Iowa farm. Tell me, why could a man, who was being crowned the head of 109 acres command the homage of the entire world? Here it is, "His deadly wound was healed; and all **the world wondered after the beast.**"

The prophet saw a third power, or the one that is called the false prophet, arising as this papal power went into captivity in 1798. We turn to Revelation 13:11. "I beheld another beast coming up out of the earth; and he had two horns like a lamb, and he spake as a dragon." (As the text was read, a chart depicting this beast was lowered into view)

He saw another beast come up out of the earth, and he had two horns like a lamb. This two-horned beast was an entirely separate beast from the leopard beast that received the deadly wound. This leopard beast, as we have already shown, had to do with the countries of the Old World in their relation to the papal power. Since the two-horned beast was entirely separate from the leopard beast, it must have to do with the territory of the New World, or the American continent.

He saw this third power coming up as the papacy went into captivity in 1798. Put those two specifications together and you can locate this third power: This third power pertains to some power that arose in North or South America in 1798. The only independent power that arose on the American Continent in 1798 was the United States of America. This two-horned beast must represent the United States of America.

This prophecy of Revelation 13:11-17 concerning the two-horned beast, makes it clear that the two-horned beast is not dealing with the United States merely as a civil power, but rather with Protestantism in the United States.

Prophecy indicates that the United States will compel people by the force of civil law to obey this papal power, even above obeying God. Here it is in Revelation 13 12. "He exerciseth all the power of the first beast before him, and causeth the earth and them that dwell therein to worship the first beast, whose deadly wound was healed."

The power symbolized by this two-horned beast will actually compel its citizens to obey this beast power, whose deadly wound was healed. This prophecy indicates that the Protestant churches will form a union, or federation, and that they will join hands with the Catholics in forcing all people to obey the papal power. Notice how this is set forth in Revelation 13:14. "And deceiveth them that dwell on the earth by the means of those miracles which he had power to do in the sight of the beast; saying to them that dwell on the earth, that they should make an image to the beast, which had the wound by the sword and did live."

The two-horned beast is to make an image to this beast, that had the wound by the sword, and did live. What is an image? An image is a likeness. You hear people say, "That boy is the very image of his father." The papacy was a union of church and state, enforcing obedience by the power of civil law. The image to the beast will be a union of Protestant churches with the United States government to enforce submission to the papal power by civil law.

Are things shaping up for this final conflict? See how the Protestant churches are combining? The order of today is church union. Denominations that we thought never could unite are uniting. The churches are seeking platforms of unity. See how Protestants and Catholics are drawing nearer and nearer together. See how the Protestant churches are trying to gain control of the government to enforce dogmas by law.

Look what happened on December 23, 1939. The president of the United States sent Myron Taylor as a special envoy to the pope without consent of congress and without consulting the American people. He sent this man to represent the United States government with the pope. Without the consent of congress, without the consent of the American people, this government was made to bow the knee to the papal power. See how Catholic influence in this government is constantly increasing.

Some will say, "Mr. Shuler, what connection does all this have with preaching the gospel of Jesus Christ?" I am glad to answer this. Revelation 14.6-14 shows that these prophetic items are some of the chief elements in the everlasting gospel of Jesus Christ for the last days. The gospel of Jesus Christ in the correct setting for our day is set forth under the symbolism of three angels flying in mid air, preaching a great three-fold message to every nation in the world. (At this juncture a chart of the three angels of Revelation 14:6-14 was lowered to view.)

In Revelation 14 6-14 the prophet saw three angels flying through mid air one behind the other. These three angels together were preaching a great three-fold gospel message to every people in the world The third angel was preaching the message that deals with these particular items. "The third angel followed them, saying with a loud voice, If any man worship the beast and his image, and receive his mark in his forehead or in his hand, the same shall drink of the wine of the wrath of God, which is poured out without mixture . . . and he shall be tormented with fire and brimstone in the presence of the holy angels and in the presence of the Lamb."

God's message solemnly warns people today against worshipping the beast, and against worshipping the image of the beast, and against receiving the mark of the beast in the forehead, or in the hand. This Bible institute is dedicated to the exposition of God's great inter-denominational message for these last days. These Bible lectures have now come to the very heart of this message. The lecture tonight has shown that the beast is the papal power: the image of the beast is a union of Protestant churches in this country enforcing submission to the papacy.

Next Sunday night we shall take up the sixteenth chapter of Revelation, and shall show that the seven last plagues are the wrath of God without mixture, of which those who receive the mark of the beast must drink. The most fearful punishment that God has ever pronounced upon any people is pronounced upon those who receive the mark of the beast. He says, "If any man," (it doesn't matter whether he is a Methodist, Baptist, Mormon, Christian Scientist, or a Seventh-day Adventist,) if he receives the mark of the beast he must drink the unmingled wrath of God.

On the other hand, the powers of earth will unite and decree that you cannot buy anything or sell anything, unless you have the mark of that beast. Put down Revelation 13:16, 17: "He causeth all, both small and great, rich and poor, free and bond, to receive a mark in their right hand, or in their foreheads that no man might buy or sell, save he that had the mark of the beast."

God says that if you take the mark of the beast on your right hand or forehead, He will torment you with fire and brimstone. The powers of earth will decree that if you do not take that mark, you can't buy or sell, and finally they will say you must be killed. It becomes a tremendous question, "What is the mark of the beast?"

Two weeks from tonight, behind closed doors, I will open the Bible on what is the mark of the beast, and how that mark is placed on people's foreheads, or in their hands. Admission will be by ticket only, but the tickets are free. The tickets will be distributed next Sunday night.

Notice that this Protestant power in the United States is the false prophet of this triumvirate, by which Satan will attempt to lead all mankind to obey him instead of God. In Revelation 19.20 the false prophet is identified as the power which deceives people into receiving the mark of the beast and into obeying the image of the beast. In Revelation 13:11-17 you will find that this power which deceives the people into receiving the mark of the beast and into obeying the image of the beast is the Protestant power in the United States. Hence apostate Protestantism in the United States is the false prophet of Revelation 16 13.

Friends, this world is now entering the final conflict between truth and error, between the commandments of God and the commandments of men. Every soul will be enlisted on one side or the other. The world's millions will be on the side of the beast and the Anti-christ. In comparison, there will be only a few on the side of Jesus Christ and His commandments. Put down Revelation 13.8. It declares that all the people in the world will obey this beast power except a few whose names will be in the Book of Life.

The all important question is, On which side will you stand? Whichever side you choose determines your fate for eternity. This is why it is so important for you to make your decision to keep the commandments of God and the faith of Jesus. This is why I have appealed to you over and over again, and will keep on appealing to you, to surrender your heart to Jesus Christ to keep all of His commandments. Not just nine of them, but to keep all of them. The wisest course you can ever follow is to make your decision to keep all the commandments of God and the faith of Jesus.

Every soul here needs help from God to do this. We cannot do it of ourselves. How many of you want us to pray that God will help you to keep all the commandments of God and the faith of Jesus? Let us see your hands. Yes, it seems that every hand is raised.

How You Can Postpone Your Own Funeral

(Preached on the Eighth Tuesday Night of the Campaign)

The way to postpone your own funeral as long as possible is to follow the counsel of the Lord in Exodus 15:26. "If thou wilt diligently hearken to the voice of the Lord thy God, and wilt do that which is right in his sight, and wilt give ear to his commandments, and keep all his statutes, I will put none of these diseases upon thee, which I have brought upon the Egyptians: for I am the Lord that healeth thee."

You may expect the best possible health for yourself by following the health instructions given in the Bible. One of the fixed laws of God is, "Whatsoever a man soweth, that shall he also reap." That holds good whether you sow good seed or bad seed. If you want to reap corn, you must plant corn. If you want to reap oats, you must sow oats. If you want to reap health, you must sow health, by obedience to the laws of health.

Why is there so much sickness? It is largely because people are disobedient to the laws of health, either ignorantly, or knowingly. God has ordained laws of health for this body just as He has ordained laws in the natural world. To illustrate: There is a law that when the temperature of water is reduced to thirty-two degrees Fahrenheit, it will freeze. That never varies. By working with this law, men are able to make artificial ice when the temperature is one hundred degrees in the shade on the outside.

In the same way God has ordained fixed laws of health for our bodies. By living in harmony with these laws, and by obeying them, we shall have health. And the reverse is true. If we disobey these laws we reap the inevitable result of ill health, sickness, disease, and finally, premature death.

It is true that "the disease and suffering that everywhere prevail are largely due to popular errors in regard to diet."—"Ministry of Healing," p. 295. Dr. Osler, that well-recognized authority in medicine, declared that ninety per cent of all pathological conditions, except contagious diseases, acute infections, and accidents, are due to wrong diet.

There is hardly one person in a hundred who lives as long as he ought to live, or as long as he might live. Think a little bit! How many people can you recall in the last ten years who have actually died of old age? Man kills himself by disobedience to nature's laws.

It is as you read in Hosea 4:6. "My people are destroyed for lack of knowledge." People are killing themselves for the lack of knowledge. If people knew beforehand the ultimate evil results of liquor drinking, cigarette smoking, and the use of such common things as tea and coffee, they would never take on those habits. "My people are destroyed for lack of knowledge."

Some people think that this matter of what a man eats or drinks has nothing to do with his religion. When someone attempts to outline what is best for people to eat, some will say, "I shall eat and drink what I please." I should like to raise a very plain question, and give it a plain answer from a supreme authority. That question is, Has a Christian a right to eat and drink as he pleases? Here is the answer in 1 Corinthians 10:31. "Whether therefore ye eat, or drink, or whatsoever ye do, do all to the glory of God."

This is a command of God through the apostle Paul. We are to eat and drink as will be pleasing to God. We belong to God. This body is the temple of God. God's command is that we eat and drink as is pleasing to Him. There is only one way anybody can eat and drink that will please God, and that is, to **eat and drink according to the principles laid down in God's Word**, which is the Guidebook for the Christian.

Has God told us what to eat? The Bible is a very practical Book. Many people think that the Bible is merely to be carried under the arm to church on Sunday, and after that it is to be left on the shelf until the next Sunday. But this is a Book for every day. It tells man how to eat, drink and dress. It tells him how to live each day.

Does the Bible tell us what to eat? Here it is in Isaiah 55:2. "Wherefore do ye spend money for that which is not bread? and your labour for that which satisfieth not? hearken diligently unto me, and eat ye that which is good."

How can you tell what is good to eat? Not merely by appetite, because appetite has been perverted through sin. You can't tell what is good to eat by taking what people think or say. In the Orient there are people who say that the most delicious food they know is young mice before their eyes are opened, dipped in honey, and swallowed alive while they are kicking. They can have my share, and I suppose they can have your share, too. I conclude from this that you can't settle this question of what is good to eat by what people say.

Has God told us what is good to eat? Here it is in Genesis 1:29, 31. As soon as God made man He told him what to eat. "And God said, Behold, I have given you every herb bearing seed, which is upon the face of all the earth, and every tree, in the which is the fruit of a tree yielding seed; to you it shall be for meat. And God saw every thing that he had made, and, behold, it was very good."

God ordained a diet of fruits, nuts and grains for man in the beginning. He pronounced this kind of a diet "very good." A little later on vegetables were added to that diet. I would like to have you do a little thinking with me. Does the God who made man know what is best for man? If I were to ask you to put up your hand if your answer is "yes," I believe every person would put up his hand. You know that an all-wise God who made man, knows what is best for man. This means that a diet of fruits, grains, vegetables, nuts and dairy products is the ideal diet for man. It means that if you will live on what God has ordained for man you are bound to be better off, and you will have better health. If you want the best health follow the diet prescribed by the Chief Physician.

Three of the greatest causes of premature debility and death are diseases of the heart, circulatory system, and kidneys. If you wish to keep your kidneys healthy, your blood vessels young, and your heart strong, it is well to follow four simple dietetic rules.

The first rule is: **Eat fruits and vegetables freely.** They contain the precious minerals and vitamins that we so much need and are so likely to be short on in this day of de-mineralized foods. It may not be best for some people to eat fruits and vegetables at the same meal. They may "fight each other" down below. It may be best for some people to eat fruits at one meal and vegetables at another. But the point that I am bringing to you is this, seventy-five per cent of the food that appears on your table ought to be fruits and vegetables.

The second rule is: **Eat cereals moderately.** By cereals we mean rice, corn, wheat, et cetera. Cereals are not something for a person to fill up on. You can fill up on fruits and vegetables, but cereals should not be eaten liberally.

The third rule is: **The heavy protein foods like eggs, cheese, beans and nuts should be eaten rather sparingly.**

The fourth rule is: **Use salt and sugar sparingly.**

A good practical workable rule is that **three out of four or four out of five** servings, or dishes, of food should be fruit, vegetables, and milk—while breads, cereals, and high protein foods may constitute the other one fourth or one fifth of the food. With 75 or 80 per cent of the food made up of fruit, vegetables, and milk, an alkaline ash of the food and body chemistry is maintained. This is also important to preserve the characteristics of youth well into old age. Of these foods Sherman specifies four servings of vegetables, five or six of fruit, and a quart of milk (four glasses) a day Breads and cereals should be whole grain or enriched.

God never gave man permission to eat the flesh of animals, or what we commonly call meat, until after the flood. In the beginning He ordained that man should live on a diet of **fruits, grains and nuts, vegetables and dairy products**, because that is best for man After the flood God gave men permission to slay animals and eat their flesh. But when God told man that he could eat flesh, He was very particular to point out that certain animals were unclean or unfit for food, and others were clean and could be safely eaten. Two whole chapters in the Bible are devoted to instruction as to what meats are good, and what meats are not good to eat These are Leviticus 11 and Deuteronomy 14.

God told man that every animal that "divides the hoof and chews the cud" like the cow and sheep are clean and may be eaten. Let me read that in Deuteronomy 14:6-8: "Every beast that parteth the hoof, and cleaveth the cleft into two claws, and cheweth the cud among the beasts, that ye shall eat. Nevertheless these ye shall not eat of them that chew the cud, or of them that divide the cloven hoof; as the camel, and the hare, and the coney: for they chew the cud, but divide not the hoof; therefore they are unclean unto you. And the swine, because it divideth the hoof, yet cheweth not the cud, it is unclean unto you: ye shall not eat of their flesh, nor touch their dead carcase."

Somebody will say, "Mr. Shuler, why did God make the swine if they are not to be eaten for food?" I will ask you a question, Why did God make a turkey-buzzard? Certainly not to be eaten! He made a turkey-buzzard as a scavenger. And that is what He made the swine for, and he serves his purpose admirably.

Do you know that a hog is constructed differently from any other animal? If you should examine the two front feet of a hog you will find two little holes on the inside of each leg just above his hoof. If you took hold of his legs and squeezed them, a mass of corruption and pus would ooze out. If the man who kills a hog will take a syringe filled with mercury and inject that fluid into these holes he will be able to trace little tubes or pipes throughout the hog's body that lead to these two holes. He is so full of corruption that he has to have an extra sewer system to drain off the poisons of his body. If these holes get stopped up, what happens? Ask a farmer what happens to a hog when these holes get stopped up. He will say, "If they don't get unstopped, Mr. Hog dies."

Everybody has heard the warning sent out by the government that people should be sure to cook pork until it is thoroughly done. Why? Do you want the facts? The advice is given to make sure that you kill certain microscopic worms that may be in the pork. These microscopic worms or parasites are called trichinae. If they get into your system alive you will suffer with trichinosis.

You say, "Doesn't the government inspect all meat today, and this eliminates the danger of trichina in pork?" The government has no inspection for trichina. All that they attempt to do on the matter of these worms in the pork is to send out the warning to cook pork until it is thoroughly done. The incidence of trichinous pork among hogs in the United States during the past fifty years has remained practically unchanged at a level of approximately 1.5 per cent.

When these trichinae get into a person's body they multiply by the millions in a short time. These worms pass through intestinal walls and penetrate the lymph glands and the muscle tissues. There is no cure once they get into the system, because there is no medicine that can kill them without killing the individual.

In the "Country Gentleman" of February, 1937, there appeared an article which shows that on the basis of the findings of Dr. Maurice Hall, Chief of the Zoological Division of the Public Health Service at Washington, one person in every seven in America has trichinosis from eating infested pork. This article says:

"Doctor Hall concludes that far more than ninety-nine per cent of acute trichinosis cases are missed by the diagnostician. The sickness is called variously typhoid fever, intestinal flu, malaria, rheumatism, heart disease, intercostal neuritis, and a host of other things. The list runs up to at least forty. Many of the patients die of pneumonia about the fifth week of a severe attack. In light infestations the patient is not bedridden, but it is easy to imagine the lowered vitality and the aches and pains that must come from thousands of little worms encysted here and there throughout the muscles of our bodies. In many of the post-mortem examinations serious damage has been done to the heart muscle."

Thousands of people are suffering from trichinosis who do not know what ails them. The public press frequently tells of an acute outbreak of trichinosis in certain localities, and of some people dying as a result. Think of the suffering people would save themselves in many cases, if they would obey the Lord's counsel to leave pork alone! His laws are always for our good. God knows that the use of pork is not good for man's body. Therefore in speaking of what meats may be eaten, He declares that the flesh of the hog is not to be used for food.

Some will say, "Mr Shuler, wasn't this prohibition against swine's flesh abolished when the Mosaic law passed away?" It is true that the Mosaic law of which Deuteronomy 14 is a part, was done away when Christ died on the cross. But this matter of a certain animal being unclean is not predicated by only the Mosaic law. Centuries before Moses was ever born we read in Genesis 7:2 how God told Noah to take the clean animals into the ark by sevens, and the unclean by twos. This shows that centuries before there was a Mosaic law, God recognized that certain animals were unclean and unfit for food. In Revelation 18:2 long after the Mosaic law was done away, God still recognizes that certain birds are unclean.

I read a little book one time called "Helps to Bible Study." It asked a number of questions on different subjects and listed certain Bible references which answered the questions.

There was one topic in this little book called "Health and Temperance." One night I looked up the references on this topic. One of the questions was, "What will happen to people who are found eating swine's flesh when the Lord comes?" For an answer it gave Isaiah 66:15-17, which I will read to you. "Behold the Lord will come with fire, and with his chariots like a whirlwind, to render His anger with fury, and His rebuke with flames of fire. For by fire and by His sword will the Lord plead with all flesh; and the slain of the Lord shall be many. They that sanctify themselves, and purify themselves in the gardens behind one tree in the midst, eating swine's flesh, and the abomination, and the mouse, shall be consumed together, saith the Lord."

This is talking about the second coming of Christ when the Lord will come with fire to slay the disobedient. It cannot refer to the first coming of Christ nineteen hundred years ago. He came then as a baby and lived as a man among men. Notice that those who are found eating swine's flesh at the end of time will be slain and consumed by the fire of Christ's glory. This shows that God's prohibition against the use of swine's flesh or pork by His people must necessarily be binding to the end of time.

I said to myself that night, "I am looking for the second coming of Jesus. I want to be ready when Jesus comes. If I am found eating pork, this text says I will be consumed. I don't want to be burned up when Jesus comes, so I am through with pork forever." I have never used it since. Even if I did not believe the Bible, I would not go back to eating pork, because I have so much better health since I have excluded it from my diet.

God loves us. Since He loves us He will not deprive us of anything that is for our own good. When He tells you to leave pork alone, He knows that it is not good for you. He knew the trichina was in it. He made the swine for a scavenger. He never made them for man to eat.

1 Corinthians 10 31 says, "Whether therefore ye eat, or drink, or whatsoever ye do, do all to the glory of God." This means that a Christian should not use any kind of food or drink which is out of keeping with the instruction of the Bible.

1 Corinthians 6 10 declares that no drunkard shall ever enter the kingdom of heaven. This means that if we drink to the glory of God, we will never use intoxicating liquors, such as beer, wine, gin or whiskey. The habitual use of any poisonous herbs cannot be to the glory of God. Do you know that there are three poisonous herbs in almost daily use by millions of people who profess to follow Jesus Christ? The first is tobacco in the form of smoking, chewing and snuff-rubbing.

Some will ask, "Do you think smoking is a sin?" I will give you six reasons why the use of tobacco is wrong. I think these six reasons will convince anybody. Tobacco contains nicotine, which is the most deadly poison known to science, except prussic acid. If you extract the nicotine from one cigarette, and place one drop of it in a sparrow's mouth, it will kill it in sixty seconds. One half a drop will kill a snake in twelve minutes. A half a drop will paralyze a mouse instantly.

Tobacco is craved because of the sedative effect produced by the absorption of small amounts of nicotine. If people were to absorb all the nicotine in the tobacco, they would not live to tell the story. If some man could produce tobacco that contained no nicotine, nobody would want it, because it would not have any sedative effect.

People say, "When I get all jittery a cigarette just calms me right down." If you took a tenth of a grain of morphine it would do the same thing. Tobacco is a sedative, and it is used for the sake of the **narcotic effect** which it produces. Hence it is wrong to use it.

Second, Tobacco injures the health. The smoking of one cigarette will often cause the blood pressure to rise from ten to fifteen points. Sooner or later every cigarette smoker gets "tobacco heart." In the draft it was discovered that about one third of our young men called for military service were unfit physically. The largest proportion of them were unfit because of heart ailments. And the greatest single cause of these heart ailments is cigarette smoking.

The Mutual Life Insurance Company checked on the mortality among tobacco users and abstainers. They found that among the tobacco abstainers there was but fifty-nine per cent of the expected mortality. The total abstainers lived nearly one third longer than the tobacco users. This is pretty good evidence on "How to Postpone Your Own Funeral."

Cigarette smoke contains nineteen active poisons, each one of which is capable of producing deadly effects. See what happens when you blow cigarette smoke through a white handkerchief. It deposits a dark brown stain on it. When men inhale the smoke, this poison is deposited on the tissues of the lungs and throat. That is the cause of smoker's cough.

One of the most lamentable conditions of our day is the increase of cigarette smoking among women and girls. Forty-nine out of every one hundred cigarettes smoked are used by women. Recently a certain cigarette firm paid a girl $10,000 to use her picture for a cigarette advertisement on a billboard poster, to get men to smoke more cigarettes. As soon as they had her signed up for the picture, they put another contract before her, in which they agreed to give her another $5,000 if she would never smoke cigarettes, so that her beauty might be preserved for other poster ads. It is a well known fact that cigarette smoking destroys feminine beauty.

Third, Tobacco defiles the body in violation of the commandment of God found in 1 Corinthians 6:19, 20 and 1 Corinthians 3:17. "Know ye not that your body is the temple of the Holy Ghost which is in you, which ye have of God, and ye are not your own? For ye are bought with a price: therefore glorify God in your body, and in your spirit, which are God's." "If any man defile the temple of God, him shall God destroy; for the temple of God is holy, which temple ye are." This is what makes the use of tobacco so serious. It defiles the temple of God, "which temple ye are." God says, "If any man defile the temple of God, him shall God destroy."

Fourth. It is a waste of money. If a man spends sixty cents a week on tobacco, that amounts to $31.20 a year. In forty years he has "puffed away" $1,248.00. He had far better put the $1,248.00 in the stove and burn it up. To be sure he would lose the money, but he would not have injured his body.

Fifth, Tobacco is a "fleshly lust" that wars against the soul. In 1 Peter 2:11 we are told to "abstain from fleshly lusts, which war against the soul."

Sixth, It is a violation of the command of God in 2 Corinthians 6:16, 17. God commands us to come out from the world and be separate, "and touch not the unclean thing."

The big question is, How shall we quit the use of tobacco? There are scores here who would like to quit. How shall we quit? Most people say, "Taper down on it until you are rid of it." Let us consider this matter of tapering in reference to the word habit. Smoking is just a bad habit. Suppose we plan to taper down. We take away the "h" and what do we have? "A bit." Let us go on tapering. Take away the "b" and what do you have? You still have "it!"

My friends, there is only one way to get rid of "it," and that is to lay the axe at the root of the tree. Don't begin to trim the leaves at the top. Put the axe at the root of the tree. When you take a tree up by the roots you are rid of it for good.

Some will ask, "Isn't there some cure that will help a man to quit?" Yes, there are medicines that will help. Spraying the tongue and throat with a half of one per cent solution of siver nitrate, or washing the mouth out after each meal with three fourths of one per cent solution of silver nitrate will help.

But the **real cure is Christ.** "I can do all things through Christ which strengtheneth me." "If the Son shall make you free, ye shall be free indeed." "If any man be in Christ, he is a new creature: old things are passed away; behold all things are became new."

I have good news for you. There is a living, all-powerful Saviour Who can break the chains that bind you to tobacco. There isn't any man or woman but can have victory over the tobacco habit, through the Lord Jesus Christ, if he wants it. "Thanks be to God, which giveth us the victory through our Lord Jesus Christ."

I have seen hundreds delivered. I have a picture here which was taken in connection with a Bible Institute held in 1940 in California, in which you will see eight men who had used tobacco for over fifty years They were delivered by Jesus Christ and secured the victory. Those men are holding up a banner above them, which says, "If the Son shall make you free, ye shall be free indeed." On the basis of my own observations, I have come to this conclusion, that there is no man, woman, boy or girl who, if they want the victory over tobacco, cannot have it by truly taking hold of Jesus Christ. He is able to save to the uttermost.

There are two other poisonous herbs in common use by the majority of professed Christians which ought not to be used. I refer to the use of tea and coffee. A cup of coffee or tea, or a glassful of a certain cola drink contains from one to two grains of a poisonous alkaloid known as caffeine. The presence of caffeine in these beverages makes them unwholesome stimulants and unfit for use. In large doses caffeine is a marked poison. The caffeine which many pople take into their bodies by using tea, coffee or cola drinks frequently causes nervousness, palpitation of the heart, insomnia, and indigestion, and is a contributing factor in producing high blood pressure and fatal diseases of the heart and blood vessels.

Tea, in addition to its content of caffeine, has another harmful constituent, tannic acid, which has a pronounced astringent effect upon the digestive organs. This action is detrimental to digestion as it retards the circulation in the area it touches.

The New York Life Extension Institute reveals that "out of 16,562 men examined by the institute, the excessive use of alcohol was considered to be responsible for seven per cent of the physical impairment, while coffee and tea were assigned as a cause of forty per cent of these ailments and impairments."

There are certain brands of coffee from which about ninety-seven per cent of the caffeine has been removed. These are naturally not as injurious as the coffee from which none of the caffeine has been removed.

The presence of caffeine in tea, coffee, and cola drinks tends to produce a habit in those who use them which is frequently difficult to overcome. While their use is not objectionable to the same degree as the use of tobacco or liquor, yet they do represent lesser degrees in the scale of artificial stimulants, whose use is a violation of Christian temperance

Everybody in the world would be better off spiritually, physically and financially if he never used tea, coffee, coca-cola, tobacco, pork or liquor. I have lived on both sides of this question so I know what I am talking about. I once partook of these. But nothing would induce me to go back to them, even if I were so foolish as to think there is no heaven nor hell. I am better off in this world without tobacco, tea, coffee, coca-cola or pork. I have better health and enjoy life more by having left them off many years ago. I am receiving benefits every day from having quit tobacco, tea, coffee, coca-cola and pork. It pays to be good to one's self.

Our common sense tells us that we should refrain from taking into our bodies injurious beverages or foods. If we leave religion out of this subject of healthful living, it is still only good sense to refrain from using liquor, tobacco, coffee, tea and coca-cola.

Notice how this teaching on healthful living is a part of the great three-fold message of Revelation 14 to which these Bible Institute meetings are dedicated. The purpose of this great three-fold message is to make ready a people for the second coming of Jesus Christ. The apostle John tells us in 1

John 3:2, 3 what effect a true belief in the soon-coming of Jesus Christ will have on a person's life.

"Beloved, now are we the sons of God, and it doth not yet appear what we shall be; but we know that, when He shall appear, we shall be like Him; for we shall see Him as He is. And every man that hath this hope in Him purifieth himself even as He is pure."

If we are looking for Jesus to come, and if we expect to be made like Him when He comes, notice what effect it will have on our life. "Every man that hath this hope in Him purifieth himself, even as He is pure." A person who believes that Jesus is coming will purify himself even as Jesus is pure.

Think of the physical implications of purifying one's self as Jesus is pure. If you purify yourself as Jesus is pure, it means that you will never use intoxicating liquors in any form. Jesus refused to defile His body with liquor. It means that you will not use pork. Jesus Christ never tasted a bite of pork in His life. He obeyed the laws of God.

It means too that you will not use cigarettes or tobacco in any form. Could you picture the Son of God walking down the street puffing a cigarette or a cigar, or spitting out tobacco juice? "Every man that hath this hope in Him, purifieth himself as He is pure." Tea and coffee were not known in that part of the world at that time, but if they had been offered to Him, He would have refused them, because they are harmful stimulants.

Jesus is the Way. There is no other. He is the mystic ladder that reaches from earth to heaven. One of the steps in that ladder, that you and I need to take, is the practice of Christian temperance. What is Christian temperance? I do not mean just ordinary temperance. A lot of people think that temperance means abstinence from the use of liquor. That is only a part of it. But what is Christian temperance? Christian temperance is the total ABSTINENCE from all that is harmful, and the moderate use of that which is good. I hope you are ready to take this step with Jesus. Christ will give the victory over all these habits.

There was a man in Chicago who was terribly addicted to liquor. He tried again and again to quit, but he went back to it every time. He couldn't go near a saloon without yielding to the temptation to take a drink. There came a day when that man was genuinely converted. He was born again. He received Christ into his heart. That gave him victory.

He went past saloons and didn't have the least desire to go inside. One of his former pals dragged him inside one day, and put a glass of liquor in his hand. He pushed it aside. He had the victory. The news spread around town that this confirmed drunkard was a transformed man.

A man stopped him one day on the street, and in a sort of taunting way said, "I hear that you have the mastery of the devil." The converted man said, "No, but I have the Master of the devil."

Brother, that is what you need and you will have the victory. "As many as received Him, to them He gave the power." "Thanks be unto God who giveth us the victory through our Lord Jesus Christ." I know Christ will give you the victory, because He has given me the victory. I once used tobacco, coffee, tea, coca-cola, and pork. I quit all five of them at one time. I have never wanted any of them since. There is victory for every soul through the Lord Jesus Christ.

The Lord doesn't always take away our desire for these things. In my case the desire was taken away. I have never wanted them since I quit. The Lord does at least give grace and strength to conquer these habits.

Friends, every soul here needs Jesus Christ in his heart. We need the full reception of the Lord Jesus Christ for victory. How many want to be remembered in the closing prayer. Yes, it seems every hand is raised.

Lesson VI - The Rich Man and Lazarus - Luke 16:19-31

(Copy of the Bible lesson outline which was distributed to the people preceding the delivery of the thirty-fourth lecture.)

1. Some claim that Christ was relating an actual literal experience of two real individuals at death. They use this Scripture to support the idea that the righteous go to heaven when they die, while the wicked go into hell-fire at their parting breath.

2. Others teach that the rich man and Lazarus is a parable, and cannot be taken literally. They hold that it has no reference to people going to hell or heaven at death. It is merely a story, told in the terms of the Pharisee's belief in a hereafter, for the purpose of administering a supreme rebuke to them for their rejection of the Son of God.

3. This Scripture cannot be taken literally because:
   (a) It would place heaven and hell within seeing and hearing distance of each other for eternity.
   (b) Abraham's bosom is not the place of future happiness for the righteous. (Jno. 14·2, 3; Heb. 11:10, 16.)
   (c) If taken literally it does not teach that any disembodied soul of the individual goes to hell or heaven at death.
   (d) If taken literally it would make the Lord Jesus contradict His own teachings ....

4. Since it cannot be taken literally it must be a parable.

5A. Parables have a figurative meaning, and cannot be taken literally For example, the parable of the prodigal son, the unjust steward, etc.

5B. It is a perversion of the Word of God to apply a parable literally.

6A. Sometimes parables are based on things which never happened and never could happen literally ....

6B. They may be merely a made-up story to illustrate a certain point.

7. Jesus often used figurative language in talking to the Pharisees (Matt. 23:24, 14.)

8. The Lazarus of this story in Luke 16:19-31 was not the Lazarus whom Jesus later raised from the dead. The name Lazarus was given to the beggar, to administer to the Pharisees under the veil of a parable, a supreme rebuke for their persistent rejection of the Son of God.

9. This Abraham's bosom, with a burning hell within hearing and seeing distance of it, was the kind of hereafter in which the Pharisees believed.

10. The Pharisees believed a rich man was sure of a place of happiness in the hereafter, while a poor man was doomed to hell.

11. Christ told this story of the rich man and Lazarus in the setting of their own ideas to rebuke their reliance on riches their condemnation of the poor and their unbelief in Him ....

12. Christ told this story according to the Pharisees' ideas of the hereafter, so they could not object to the form of the parable and so His point would go home to them the more forcefully.

The following Scripture references were filled in on the blank lines as the study proceeded: (3d) Matt. 13.38-42; 16.27; (6a) Judges 9:7-15; (11) Luke 16:14, 15.

The Woman in White

"There appeared a great wonder in heaven; a woman clothed with the sun, and the moon under her feet, and upon her head a crown of twelve stars." This is the reading of Revelation 12.1 The question naturally arises, Who is this woman? Of what is she a figure or symbol? The best way to ascertain this for a certainty is to compare scripture with scripture and let the Word of God tell us who this woman is.

Put down Jeremiah 6 2 and Isaiah 51:16. Read Jeremiah 6:2, and notice how the Bible explains itself. You don't have to guess who this woman is. God tells you who she is. In Jeremiah 6:2 I read, "I have likened the daughter of, Zion to a comely and delicate woman."

God declares that He has compared the daughter of Zion to a beautiful woman. This woman is the daughter of Zion Well, who is Zion? What does Zion stand for? In Isaiah 51:16 I read, "I have put My words in thy mouth, and I have covered thee in the shadow of Mine hand, that I may plant the heavens, and lay the foundations of the earth, and say unto Zion, Thou art My people." God says Zion is His people, His church, His followers.

Place the three texts together, and see how beautifully the Bible explains itself. In Revelation 12:1 God showed the prophet a beautiful woman with the sun over her head, the moon under her feet, and upon her head a crown of twelve stars. In Jeremiah 6:2 He makes it plain that this woman is the daughter of Zion. In Isaiah 51:16 He declares that Zion is His people, His church. It is as plain as can be that this woman is a figure or symbol of the true church of Jesus Christ.

In the Bible, the church of Jesus Christ is repeatedly spoken of under the figure of a woman. Put down 2 Cor. 11:2. In this verse the church of God at Corinth is referred to as a chaste virgin. The relation between the church and Jesus Christ is frequently compared to the marriage relation. Jesus Christ, the bridegroom, or the husband, and the church His bride, or wife. This is based on the figure of a woman being used to represent the church.

What is the meaning of the moon under her feet and the sun over her head? The moon represents the light of the Mosaic age of types and shadows. The sun represents the light of the Christian age.

The moon has no light in itself. The moon is a dead planet. We say, "See how the moon shines." But, technically speaking, the moon does not shine. It appears to shine, but it merely reflects at night the light of the sun which is shining on the other side of the earth. So the ordinances of the Mosaic dispensation shone with a borrowed light, pointing forward to the realities of the Christian Age. In other words the Mosaic age was the moonlight of the gospel. The Christian age is the sunlight of the gospel.

The offering of those lambs for sin pointed forward to the true sacrifice for sin on Calvary's cross. The moon being under her feet, and the sun over her head, represents that the Mosaic age was passing away, and the Christian age was being fully ushered in.

This twelfth chapter of Revelation, under the figure of a pure woman, presents three brief glimpses of the true church during the Christian era. In Revelation 12 2-5 the church is pictured as bringing forth that wonderful man-child, the child of promise, the Messiah, the Redeemer, the Lord Jesus Christ. In Revelation 12:6, 14 the church is pictured as being in hiding in the wilderness for 1260 days. That represents how the real truth would be obscured, and hidden-from view during that long reign of the papal power from 538 to 1798. Then the last verse in the chapter, Revelation 12:17, pictures how after 1798 the last part of the true church will appear before the world in the last days.

The most important item for you and me to discover is to know how to identify this true church of Jesus Christ in relation to our day. Dr. John Milner was correct when he said: "There is but one inquiry to make; namely, which is the true church . . . By solving this one question, 'Which is the true church?' you will at once solve every question of religious controversy that ever has been, or that ever can be agitated." That is found in his book, "The End of Religious Controversy," p. 95.

It is easy to open a safe if you know the right combination. So you can readily and with certainty find the real truth when you know which is the true church. In 1 Timothy 3:15 Paul tells us that the church of God is the "pillar and ground of the truth." The church of God is the bank or depository of the truth of God. It has the truth which Jesus wants Christians to follow. Hence when you have located or identified, the true church of Jesus Christ in relation to our day, you will have found the true doctrine of Jesus Christ and the true way of the Lord. More than that, you will have found the answer to the inmost question in the heart of every true Christian, "Lord, what will you have me to do?"

Every true follower of Christ desires to find the true church of Jesus Christ, and he wants to know beyond all doubt that he has found it. If you can discover which is the true church for 1946, if you can discover which church today is this true original church of Jesus Christ, the church which He started when He was here, you will have found something worth more than a million dollars. In fact you will have made one of the most valuable and practical religious discoveries that any person can ever make When you have located that true church of Jesus Christ in relation to our day, you will know which body of Christians Jesus Christ has chosen through whom to present His special message to the world for our day.

Some will say, "There are 212 different denominations. How in the world can I ever know for a certainty which is the true church of Jesus Christ for our day?" There are many different flags in use in the world. In fact there are as many different flags in the world today as there are different independent nations. If you saw all the different flags in the world hung up on a line, could you tell for a certainty which is your flag? Certainly!

There are several flags in the world that have stars on them, but there is only one that has forty-eight stars on it. There are a number of flags that have red stripes and some flags have blue stripes, but there is only one flag that has seven red stripes and six white stripes Just as you can easily locate your flag by certain specifications, so you can easily and with certainty locate which is the true church of Jesus Christ for our day by certain specifications.

God gives three specifications in the Book of Revelation by which every person may locate the true church in our day. This is such an important item, and so much depends upon it, that I make this earnest request. Will you not please take a piece of paper and make note of those three divine specifications or marks of the true church for our day. This is something that I want you to think through for yourself, and find the true church for yourself.

Put down Revelation 12:17 and Revelation 19:10. I have Revelation 12:17 printed on a chart and I want you to read it with me. "The dragon was wroth with the woman, and went to make war with the remnant of her seed, which keep the commandments of God, and have the testimony of Jesus Christ."

Did you notice how many times that little word "the" is used in this text? How many times? Five times. Correct! This verse talks about the dragon, the woman, the remnant, the commandments of God, and the testimony of Jesus Christ. To understand this verse we must know who is the dragon, who is the woman, what is the remnant, what are the commandments, and what is the testimony of Jesus Christ.

Take the first one. Look at Revelation 12.9. "The great dragon was cast out, that old serpent, called the Devil, and Satan." The dragon is the devil. Who is the woman? We have already cited Scripture to show that the woman is the true church.

What is the remnant? Here is where the ladies can qualify. Every lady here could quickly tell us what a remnant is. When you go to a department store and you see a table with an assortment of various pieces of cloth, and a sign, "Remnants," do you know what this means? Certainly! A remnant is the last part of a bolt of cloth.

Is the remnant of the same pattern as the first part of the bolt? Yes, it certainly is. The remnant of a bolt of cloth is a continuation of the same pattern as the first yard. So, this remnant church will be a continuation of the original church of Jesus Christ, which the Author of truth founded when He was here. It will be the last part of His church before He returns to the earth.

Take another question. At what time in the world's history will this remnant church be carrying on its work? The answer is, In the last days, in the closing age of the earth's history. You can see that the last part is bound to be here in the last days, in the last generation. We are living in the last days. The fulfillment of the signs which Jesus has given, attests that His coming is near, even at the door. So this is the day of the remnant. If you can discover which church is the remnant church, you will have located the true church of Jesus Christ for our day.

Now the question comes, How can you tell which church among all these different denominations and religious bodies is the remnant? God has not left you in doubt. He tells you how you can know it when you see it. Look at Revelation 12:17. "The dragon was wroth with the woman, and went to make war with the remnant . . . **which keep the commandments of God.**"

Isn't this plain? The remnant church will be distinguished by the keeping of the commandments of God. They will also have the testimony of Jesus Christ. Please notice that the keeping of the commandments of God is not at variance with the acceptance of Jesus Christ. The keeping of the commandments of God and the testimony of Jesus Christ go together. God has joined them together.

This remnant will keep the commandments of God, and they will have the testimony of Jesus Christ. What is meant by the commandments of God? If you read the sixty-six books of the Bible through a hundred times, you will find that the only commandments, which God ever spoke with His own voice to His people, or ever wrote with His own hand are the Ten Commandments. The Bible contains many commandments from God aside from the ten commandments. The commandments of God include all that God requires of man. But "the commandments of God," must mean pre-eminently the Ten Commandments.

Here are two questions for you. The remnant keep the commandments. Now, which day of the week do the Ten Commandments require man to keep? What is the answer? The seventh day. Yes. In the fourth commandment of God's commandments, He says, "Remember the Sabbath day to keep it holy. Six days shalt thou labour and do all thy work, but the seventh day is the Sabbath of the Lord thy God: in it thou shalt not do any work." You will find that in your Bible, Exodus 20:8-10.

The seventh day is the only day of weekly observance that God has ever commanded man to keep. Since Christ's remnant keep the commandments, what day then will they keep? The seventh day. Yes. If they do not keep the seventh day, they are not keeping the commandments. It is as plain as 2 and 2 make 4 that the remnant church, or Christ's true church for the last days, will be composed of a seventh-day, Sabbath-keeping people.

There is no command of God for the keeping of the first day of the week, or Sunday. Hence any church that keeps the first day of the week or Sunday, cannot be the remnant church of Revelation 12:17.

God has many true Christians in all the churches who are keeping Sunday. The Protestant churches have been greatly used of God in helping to restore certain truths of the gospel of Jesus Christ. But no Sunday-keeping church can be the remnant church, this last part of the original church of Jesus Christ for the last days, because God says, the remnant keep the commandments of God.

This remnant church has the testimony of Jesus Christ. What does this mean? Turn with me to Revelation 19:10. "He said unto me, I am thy fellow servant, and of thy brethren that have the testimony of Jesus: worship God: for **the testimony of Jesus is the Spirit of Prophecy.**

The testimony of Jesus is the Spirit of prophecy. The remnant church will be a people of prophecy. The remnant people of God will understand prophecy. They will teach prophecy. They will have among them the revelation of truth that God gives through the gift of prophecy.

Take your paper and write. Specification No. 1 of the true church for the last days. **They keep the commandments of God and have the spirit of prophecy.**

We turn now to Revelation 14:12. This text shows that the remnant of Revelation 12:17 will constitute the people who preach that great three-fold message of Revelation 14 to the entire world. In Revelation 14:6-14 we have God's special message for the last days set forth under the symbolism of three angels flying in mid-air, preaching a great three-fold message to every nation. In verse 12, God describes the people whom He will use to carry this three-fold message to the entire world. "Here is the patience of the saints: here are they that keep the commandments of God and the faith of Jesus."

Take note that the people who give this three-fold message will be those who keep the commandments of God. Hence, they must be the same people who compose the remnant church of Revelation 12:17, who are distinguished by the keeping of the commandments of God. In order then to find what people compose the remnant church, or true church of Jesus Christ for these last days, we must find a world-wide church, which is telling the people of every nation, that the hour of God's judgment has come; Babylon is fallen; not to worship the beast or his image, or to receive his mark in one's forehead, or in his hand; but to worship God as the Creator. In fact it is the preaching of this three-fold message that calls out this remnant church.

Put down the **second specification.** They give the special three-fold message to the world. The third specification is, they do their work between

1844 and the second coming of Jesus Christ. This is made plain in the 14th chapter of Revelation.

In these Bible lectures we have shown that this three-fold message applies to the closing period of earth's history between 1844 and the coming of Christ on the cloud at the last day. According to Daniel 8:14 the hour of God's judgment began in 1844. This has been established from the Scriptures in past lectures.

Revelation 14:14 shows that the second coming of Jesus Christ will take place when this three-fold message has been preached to every nation. Therefore it is as plain as can be, that this three-fold message belongs to the period between 1844 and the end. Hence, this remnant church will be composed of a people who will come on the stage in 1844, and will do their work between 1844 and the second coming of Jesus Christ.

This is made plain on this chart entitled, "The Prophetic History of the Church." (At this juncture a chart was lowered, and a series of items were revealed by removing pieces of paper) This first item marks out the birth of Christ in B. C. 4 when the woman brought forth that man child who was to rule all nations   Then it indicates the 1260 day-year period from 538 to 1798, during which the true church was to be in the wilderness. Next it points out how the closing period from 1844 to the second coming of Jesus Christ will be the time of the remnant church.

The remnant church comes in between the hour of God's judgment in 1844 and the second coming of Christ   This period between 1844 and the coming of Christ is the time when the dead are judged. It is the time when the work of God will be finished in the earth. It is the time when this three-fold message will be preached to every nation, kindred, tongue, and people.

Any church, then, that began its work before 1844 could not be the remnant church, because prophecy appointed 1844 as the time when it would appear. It is interesting to note in this connection the dates when the great Prostestant bodies were established. The Lutheran church was established in 1524. It is the oldest of all Prostestant churches so far as an outward organization is concerned. The Episcopal church dates back to 1534. The Congregational church was established in 1560. The Presbyterian church was established in 1560; the Baptist in 1617; the Quakers in 1647; the Methodist in 1784, and the Disciples of Christ in 1810. Notice that all of these churches began their work before the time came for the remnant church to come on the stage of action.

Now put the three specifications together. These are not my specifications. They are God's specifications or marks of the remnant church. How can you know the remnant church? They keep the commandments of God and have the spirit of prophecy. They will deliver to the world the great three-fold message of Revelation 14. They will do their work between 1844 and the coming of Christ.

Now you should take these three specifications, and find the church which fits them, and you will know for a certainty which is the remnant church, the true church of Jesus Christ for the last days. According to the Word of God it will be composed of a people who keep the commandments of God and have the spirit of prophecy, a people who are going to every nation with the special message of Revelation 14, and a people who arose in 1844, and are doing their work between 1844 and the second coming of Christ. Where can you find such a people today? Who are the people who fit these three specifications of the prophecy?

Observe how sure you may be which church is the true church for 1946. Your own Bible settles it. You need not take my word or any other man's word. There is no guesswork about it. All you need to do is to find the church, that fits these three specifications, and it will be the remnant church of Jesus Christ for our day.

Ask yourself the question: Among all the different churches and religions, how many are there, who keep all the commandments, including the fourth commandment, which requires the observance of the seventh day, and who are telling the world that the hour of God's judgment is come, not to worship the beast or his image; and not to receive the mark of the beast, but to worship God as the Creator; and who arose in 1844? How many are there who fit those three specifications? How many? There is only one. If there is only one, it must be the right one Regardless of how many denominations there are, there is only one that fits the three specifications, just as there is only one flag in the world, which has forty-eight stars and seven red stripes and six white stripes

This doesn't mean that there will be no one saved except those who belong to the remnant church. The Scriptures show that God has true children scattered in all denominations and in all religions. But the Bible plainly shows that God is sending this three-fold message, to gather them into the remnant church.

Do you know that the Catholics admit that the seventh-day keeping people are the only people who keep all the commandments? A Catholic journal, in dealing with the authority for Sunday observance, made the following statement. "If our authority for keeping Sunday be the fourth commandment . . the whole Christian world lies convicted of a serious breach of God's law. Stay! This is not true. There is a curious sect, called, I believe, Seventh-day Adventists, which literally obeys. They alone, then, of all Christians keep the whole of God's commandments."

Did you know that Abraham Lincoln actually looked for the remnant church? In 1913 a Mr. LeRoy T. Nicola made a sight-seeing trip to Washington D. C. In connection with this trip he had an experience which he describes as follows: "While downtown the other day, viewing Oldroyd Memorial Collection in the house in which Abraham Lincoln died, I heard a lady from the city make certain statements to friends who were with her, that attracted my attention. She said: 'Major Merwin was a near friend of Mr. Lincoln. The major is now advanced in years, and he seldom converses very long without some mention of his relations with that great man. He has related to me that Mr. Lincoln once told him that if he ever found a church that kept the ten commandments, he would join that church '"

It is a well-known fact that Abraham Lincoln did not belong to any church, but he was a man who prayed and read the Bible. His mind was saturated with the Bible. Abraham Lincoln made the statement that if he ever found a church that kept the Ten Commandments he would join it. "Then this lady added· "There is a church that keeps the Ten Commandments, all of them and they have a large encampment out north of the city." (That is, Takoma Park.) "They are the Seventh-day Adventists, and they are a very fine people!"

A curious thing happened in the Washington, D C. post office a few years ago. A letter came to the United States Post Office with nothing on it but, "Fourth Commandment Keepers, Washington, D C." To whom did the United States postal authorities deliver that letter? Do you know where they took that letter? Now there must have been some one in the post office that thought about the Methodists, and the Baptists, and the Catholics, but evidently he said, "No, they do not keep the **Fourth commandment**. You take that letter out to the Seventh-day Adventists. They keep the Commandments of God."

One day a railroad president, who had a private fortune of one hundred million dollars, ordered his magnificent private car to be attached to a certain train for a trip. He knew the engineer personally He was one of the best on the entire railway system, and the president always felt safe if this man's hand was on the throttle.

As the train was passing through the mountains of Montana, a boulder rolled down off the side of the mountain and lodged itself on the railroad track just fifty feet ahead of the flying locomotive. The engineer couldn't possibly stop the train in fifty feet. The engine struck the boulder. It turned the engine over on its side and pinned the engineer beneath his cab nearly crushing out his life.

The president rushed to the overturned engine. He saw the dying engineer's lips just barely moving He put his ear down close to the man's mouth, and this is what he heard him say, "I know in whom I have believed, and I am persuaded that He is able to keep that which I have committed to Him against that day."

Then putting his own mouth down close to the engineer"s ear he said, "Jim, I would give all my fortune to have a faith like that." Again he saw the engineer's lips move and bending low his ear he heard him say, "It will take just that."

It does take an entire surrender to the Lord Jesus Christ. "Whosoever he be of you that forsaketh not all that he hath, he cannot by My disciple." Everyone of us needs help from God to surrender his all to Jesus and to go all the way with Him. How many want to send up a silent prayer to Jesus just now, "Lord, give me strength to follow Thee all the way? May I see your hands? Yes, thank God we all want to pray that prayer.

(Prayer.)

Blessed Jesus, we thank Thee for Thy love We thank Thee for Thy truth. We thank Thee, Lord, that we have not been left in darkness. We have not been left to go by guess work. We have not been left to depend on what men tell us, but we have Thy precious Word to show us the way.

Jesus, we thank Thee for the great three-fold message, that thou hast placed in the Bible, to be preached at this time. We thank Thee for the people who are preaching it, who are giving their all to carry that message to the world.

We need special help to follow our dear Saviour all the way. Tonight Thou hast seen every hand that has been raised earnestly in silent prayer, "Lord, give me strength." May each one know that Jesus will give him the strength he needs to follow step by step, all the way, until that wonderful day, soon to come, when Jesus appears on the cloud, and we can go with Him to the wonderful mansions He has prepared. We ask it in His precious name. Amen.

Why So Many Denominations?

(Preached on the Eighth Saturday Afternoon of the Campaign)

A college president tells of a Chinese lad who came to his office to arrange to enter college. On the application blank there was a column marked "Reli gion," where each prospective student filled in the name of the religion which he followed. This Chinese lad, like millions of the Chinese, was a follower of Confucius. Unfortunately when he filled out on the application blank, he misspelled the word "Confucius," and in the column marked "Religion," he wrote, "My religion is confusion." He told the truth without being aware of it If people today would compare their religion with God's Guide Book, they would, in many cases, find that their religion is largely confusion.

Many people wonder why there is so much confusion in the religious world. Why is there so much confusion as to the right way in religion, when there is only one guide book for all people? Why are there so many different denominations teaching so many different ways, when they all profess to be guided by one and the same Bible? My answer is that if all the professed followers of Jesus Christ had been willing to walk in the light, Christendom would not be divided into numerous sects, but would be united as it was in the days of the apostles.

Time and again new denominations have arisen as some man of God discovered additional truth in the Bible, and the church to which he belonged refused to advance with the increasing light of God's truth. We must never forget that truth is progressive. In Proverbs 4 18 I read this beautiful statement: "The path of the just is as the shining light, that shineth more and more unto the perfect day."

This scripture shows that the precious light of God's truth is to shine more and more unto the perfect day. The perfect day will come when the Lord Jesus Christ returns at the end of this age. The light of truth is to shine more and more until the end of time

This is why no one should refuse to accept the seventh-day Sabbath, or other truths, because his father, or his mother, or his grandfather, or his grandmother didn't know about it. The light shines more and more unto the perfect day. The people who lived fifty or one hundred years ago could not see all the truth as God has ordained it for the present time.

Some have said, "Since this truth about the seventh-day Sabbath is so plain in the Bible, why do not the other churches see it and follow it?" Largely because they have been unwilling to walk in the light Each denomination has been content to advance no further than its own creed. But the light of God's truth has gone on and left them behind. You cannot tie God's truth down to a creed. The making of creeds and strict adherence to them has held the churches back in the discovery of additional truth.

I thank God that the remnant church has no creed. If a creed contains more than the Bible, it contains too much. If it contains less than the Bible, it does not contain enough. Why not, then, take the Bible and follow it carefully? What do you say? (Many "Amens.")

Pastor John Robinson told the Pilgrims as they were about to embark for America: "I charge you before God and his blessed angels, that you follow me no farther than you have seen me follow the Lord Jesus Christ The Lord has more truth yet to break forth out of His Holy Word. I cannot sufficiently bewail the condition of the reformed churches, who have come to a period in religion, and will go at present no farther than the instruments of their reformation. Luther and Calvin were great and shining lights in their times, yet they penetrated not into the whole counsel of God. I beseech you, remember it—'tis an article of your church covenant—that you be ready to receive whatever truth shall be made known to you from the written Word of God."—John Robinson, pastor at Leyden, Holland, in Farewell to Pilgrims sailing for New World, July, 1620; cited in "A History of the United States," George Bancroft, Vol. 1, chap. 8, pp. 306, 307. Boston: Little, Brown and Co.

One of the main reasons that Christians in general do not see these plain truths, that you have heard in these Bible Institute meetings, is that the churches have failed to advance with the increasing light, as it has come from the Word of God. It was the same way 1900 years ago when the Lord Jesus Christ brought new light to the Jewish people. I turn to Matt. 13:15. "This people's heart is waxed gross, and their ears are dull of hearing, and their eyes they have closed; lest at any time they should see with their eyes, and hear with their ears, and should understand with their heart, and should be converted."

Jesus told the Jews that they had closed their own eyes, lest they should see the truth, and be converted. It is the same way today. He told those Jewish leaders that it was a case of the blind leading the blind. When the blind lead the blind, tell me what happens? They both fall into the ditch. Today it is a case of the blind leading the blind, and the results will be disastrous.

When God reveals truth from the Bible to a person, and he refuses to obey it, he cannot make any further progress in learning truth until he is willing to obey the truth, which God has sent to him from His Word. Why should God reveal any additional truth to a person if he refuses to walk in the truth which God has already sent to him? Jesus says in John 12:35, "Walk while ye have the light, lest darkness come upon you: for he that walketh in darkness knoweth not whither he goeth."

Here is a question to think through. It may strike home to your own heart. Why are people today so willing and so eager to accept every new improvement in automobiles, for example, and yet the same people are so slow, and so unwilling, to accept advanced light as it comes from the Bible? Can you tell me?

I want to explain a little further the statement which I made about new denominations having come into existence, when some man discovered additional truth in the Bible, and the church to which he belonged refused to accept that truth, and he was led to form a new denomination, which would follow this truth.

Take Martin Luther. You might, in a certain sense, call him the first Protestant. It was a notable event when, on October 31, 1517, Martin Luther nailed those ninety-five theses against the selling of indulgence on the cathedral door in Wittenberg. Let me tell you, if Martin Luther was alive today, he would be preaching this special message of Revelation 14. He had the light for his day. He couldn't see the light of our day, which was four hundred years ahead from his day.

Martin Luther did not plan at first to establish a separate denomination. He was a good Roman Catholic. He sought to reform the Catholic Church. He saw the errors of Catholicism. When the Catholic church refused to accept the truths that he had found in the Bible, he was driven on to leave the Catholic church and establish a new denomination, known today as the Lutheran church.

Later on, Roger Williams discovered new truths in the Bible. He was a member of the Church of England. When the Church of England refused to follow the increased light, he came out of the Church of England, and established a new denomination known as the Baptist church.

John Wesley discovered new truths in the Bible. When the Church of England to which he belonged, refused to accept increased light, John Wesley came out of the Church of England and established what we now call the Methodist Church.

James White was an ordained minister of the Disciples of Christ, commonly called the Christian Church. When he found that there is no Bible authority for keeping the first day of the week, and that the seventh day is the only day of the week that Christ ever blessed or sanctified, or told man to keep, he decided to follow the increased light of God's Word, and became a seventh-day Sabbath keeper. Other men saw it, and in due time he and other men, who accepted the true Sabbath of the Bible, were led to establish what is now known as the Seventh-day Adventist Church.

This word "Adventist" is a very significant word. If you will look up the word "Adventist" in the Standard Dictionary, you will find that Adventist means one who lays special stress on the second-coming of Christ The Adventists are a people who believe Jesus is coming, and that He is coming soon. They lay special stress on this; hence, they are Adventists. Since the keeping of the seventh-day distinguished them from other Adventists who kept the first day of the week, they took the name **Seventh-day Adventist**.

In the Bible lecture last night we found from Revelation 14.6-12 and Daniel 8.14 that Christ's remnant church, which keeps the commandments of God, was to begin its work in 1844 when the hour of God's judgment began in heaven. History shows that in the very year 1844 a company of forty people at Washington, New Hampshire, who believed Jesus was soon coming, began to keep the seventh day, as specified in the fourth commandment. For a good many years these people did not have any official name. They thought at first that they wouldn't need to have any organization, but they found that they would have to have some kind of organization to hold property and to carry on the work of the Lord. In 1860, or about 16 years after they came into existence, they adopted the name Seventh-day Adventist. They have devoted themselves exclusively to proclaiming to every nation the great three-fold message that is found in Revelation 14·6-12.

Here is something I hope you will not miss. It will help you in taking your stand for the truth of God. Seventh-day Adventists are not merely another denomination. I want to repeat this, and then I will make plain what I mean by it. **Seventh-day Adventists are not merely another denomination.** What are they? They constitute a special, world-wide movement raised up by the Lord for the purpose of carrying out God's inter-religious and inter-denominational message to every nation.

Just as God called Noah to preach a special message regarding the impending flood, so God has called the Adventist people to preach the special message of Revelation 14 regarding the imminent return of our Lord. Just as God called John the Baptist to prepare the way for the first coming of Jesus, He has called these people to prepare the way for the second advent of our Lord. The Seventh-day Adventist people are not merely another denomination, any more than Noah, or John the Baptist, were leaders of another denomination in their day.

If the various denominations would accept God's interdenominational message as set forth in Revelation 14, it would bring them together just as Jesus prayed in John 17:20, 21. How do I know this? It is proven by the fact that this three-fold message today takes people from all religions. It takes them from atheism, infidelity, from paganism, from Mohammedanism, from Confucianism, from Buddhism, from Catholicism, and from every branch of Protestantism and binds their hearts together as one in this blessed hope.

If the Protestant churches had walked in the increasing light of God's Word, God would have used them to carry this special message of Revelation 14 to every nation, kindred, tongue, and people. But the established churches had their creeds. They refused to go beyond their creeds, and God couldn't use them to give the message, when it came due in 1844. When they refused to walk in the increasing light, God had to raise up a new people, a separate people through whom He could work to give this great three-fold message to the world. As God's message is being proclaimed all over the world, He is calling out those who are willing to walk in the light into this separate movement.

The other churches are in a certain sense responsible for the Adventists being here as a separate people. If they had given God's message to men, as God wanted them to, the Adventist people would never have come into existence. There wouldn't be any Seventh-day Adventist people, because there would be no reason for their existence. All other churches would have become in a certain sense just what the Adventists are now, or at least they would follow the same truths. If they had accepted God's message, it would have brought them together into one body, instead of this confusing array of conflicting beliefs that is seen today.

Some people say that there are so many different denominations, teaching so many different ideas in religion, that it is confusing to the average man who is seeking to find the one true way of Jesus Christ. Listen. No one need be confused in regard to which is the one true way of the Lord. The messages of those three angels of Revelation 14 constitute the true way of Jesus Christ for our day. All you need to do is to find the people who are teaching that message, and take your stand with them.

The Bible tells you how you can know the true people when you find them. Put down Revelation 14:12. "Here is the patience of the saints: here are they that keep the commandments of God, and the faith of Jesus." How can you tell who are the Lord's people? God says, "They . . . keep the commandments of God and the faith of Jesus." In order to find the true way, you must find the people who keep the commandments of God and the faith of Jesus.

There is a mission station in the high Andes mountains of Peru that is called the Broken Stone Mission. It has an interesting story back of its name. Years ago an Indian chief from that section came to an Adventist missionary nearby and begged him to send a teacher to his tribe. The missionary said, "I am sorry, but we have no teacher available to send at the present time."

This chief pressed his request. He said, "Our people are dying and they do not know the truth. We want some one to come and teach us the truth."

The missionary replied, "The best I can say, is that as soon as we have an available teacher, we will send him at the very first opportunity."

The chief said, "That will be all right. But the other churches are sending missionaries among our Indians, and we want the truth as you teach it. I am old, and a new chief may be in charge. How are my people going to tell when this teacher comes from you to teach the truth?"

The missionary picked up a piece of soft rock, and broke it in two pieces. He handed one to the chief and said, "Put that in your pocket and take it back home. I will give my teacher the other half of this rock, and when the teacher arrives, you check to see if the piece of rock you have fits the piece of rock the teacher has. If it does, you may know that he is the right one." This is why this mission is called the Broken Stone Mission.

Just as the old chief could tell which was the right teacher, you can tell, which church is the right church to which God wants you to belong. In the book of Revelation God gives you the rock of the true church with three notches in it. In the Bible lecture last night we found from Revelation 12 17 and Rev. 14:12 that there are three marks of the true church of Jesus Christ for our day. First, they keep the commandments of God and have the Spirit of Prophecy Second, they will proclaim this great three-fold message to all the world. Third, they will do their work between 1844 and the end of time

God has placed in your hands through His holy Word an identifying rock of His remnant church with three notches in it. He tells you to look for a people who fit into these specifications and then take your stand with them. Wouldn't it be well to check up on your church according to the three notches of the rock of truth which God has placed in your hands? God says, "Prove all things, hold fast that which is good."

Does my church keep the seventh day according to the commandments of God, and does it have the Spirit of Prophecy? Is it preaching that special message to every nation about not worshipping the beast or his image, and not receiving his mark in the forehead, or in the hand; and about the fall of Babylon and that the hour of God's judgment has come? Did this church arise in 1844, thus doing its work between 1844 and the end of time? If your church does not fit into these three notches in the rock of truth, then as a lover of truth you should find a people who fit these three divine specifications of the Book of Revelation.

I should like to ask you this question, have not these meetings brought to you a people who do agree exactly with the three notches in the rock of truth as specified in the book of Revelation?

Here is a piece of cardboard representing the rock of truth. It contains three notches. This is the part of the rock that God gives you. You can know the remnant church by the fact that they keep the commandments of God and have the Spirit of Prophecy. That is notch No. 1. The remnant are the people who are giving this three-fold message to every nation. That is notch No. 2. They arose in 1844 when the judgment-hour message was due. This is notch No. 3.

Now take this first piece and find the people who fit into these three notches. Then you will have the remnant church of Christ for our day. (At this juncture the speaker took another piece of cardboard, which fitted exactly into the piece of cardboard with the three notches in it.) This piece represents the preaching at the Hoyt Sherman Place, and just watch how it fits in this rock of truth that God gives you.

Ever since I found these specifications in the Book of Revelation, I have not had a shadow of a doubt as to what people I should affiliate with. When a sincere soul learns which is the true church of Jesus Christ for his day, he will let nothing hinder him from uniting with that church. Jesus declares that His sheep will respond to His call and come into His fold. In John 10:16 He says, "Other sheep I have." He has thousands and thousands of them scattered everywhere. He says, "Other sheep I have . . . them also I must bring, and they shall hear my voice; and there shall be one fold, and one shepherd."

Sometimes the question is raised, "Is it really necessary to unite with any church?" There are some folks who think it is not necessary to ever unite with a visible body here upon the earth. I turn to Acts 2:47. It just takes one text to answer that question. Acts 2:47. "Praising God, and having favour with all the people. **And the Lord added to the church daily such as should be saved.**" It is God's plan to add to the church those who are to be saved. If we want to be saved, it is God's plan for us to be added to the church.

I want to read to you a very important proposition. It is not my propo-

sition at all. It is a proposition from the Lord Himself. I read this in Isaiah
1:19, 20. I want you to think it through, because everyone here has to do
something with this proposition sooner or later. You cannot help but do something with it.

God says, "If ye be willing and obedient, ye shall eat the good of the land
But if ye refuse and rebel, ye shall be devoured with the sword for the mouth
of the Lord hath spoken it."

Every person who is ever born into this world has a choice to make, and
everything depends on how he chooses. The Lord says, If you are willing
and obedient, you will eat the good of the land forever in that glorious eternal home that he has prepared for His people. If you refuse to obey, and
rebel against His commandments, you will be punished with everlasting destruction. Which of these will you choose?

Each of us has a choice to make. I cannot tell you what you are going to
do. Your own heart before God must tell you that, but there is one thing I
can tell you. I can tell you what I am going to do about it. My decision is
made By His blessed grace I am purposed to be willing and obedient to the
call of Jesus Christ. Can you say "Amen" to that? Yes!

I was happy to see so many come forward on the last two Sabbath afternoons to show that they are purposed to be willing and obedient to the call
of Jesus Christ to keep His 'Sabbath and to follow His commandments. Today I invite forward to form a prayer circle all who have come forward the
two previous Sabbath afternoons, and with them I want to invite every other
soul who is willing to show his purpose to be willing and obedient to Jesus
Christ.

I want to invite forward every soul who has never given his heart to
God. There may be young people here, boys and girls, and older people,
who have never given their hearts to God. I want to invite you today to come
and stand here at the front in this prayer circle. We want to pray for you.

I want to invite forward those who may have known this blessed message,
but have wandered away from it. I want to invite you today to return to the
Lord and take your stand for this precious truth. I want also to invite every
one who will make his decision to keep the true Sabbath. The finest thing that
you could do would be this very minute to tell the Lord, "By Thy help I will
begin to keep the Sabbath even the remainder of this day, and next Friday
night I will begin to keep my first Sabbath."

We will stand and ask you to come forward. (Choir sang, "Just as I Am.")
We are forming the prayer circle. O, friends, everyone here needs special help
from Jesus to be true. I am inviting everyone who has made his decision to
keep the Sabbath since these meetings started. Or if you haven't made it before, tell Jesus right now that you will start next Sabbath.

This is the best time there will ever be to settle this great question. Let
us settle it now. It is the wisest decision, the best decision you can ever make.
Let's settle it now, while we sing.

Is there a boy or girl here today, or young person, or older person, who
has never given his heart to God? "Now is the accepted time " Why not
walk down here to signify, "Lord, here is my heart just as I am." If there is
one who once followed this message, but has wandered away, will you not
come and take your stand and say, "God helping me, I am going to live this
message."

I do not want to see a single soul left out of this prayer. How many who
have not come forward want to say, "Preacher, pray that God will give me the
strength to make my decision to obey His commandments?" Yes, I see a number of hands.

The Seven Last Plagues

If you were driving along the highway tonight, and came to seven red lanterns strung across the road, would you plunge through that line of red lanterns? Certainly not! No man in his right mind would do this. You know that a red lantern means danger. But it means more than that. It means safety if heeded.

In Revelation 16, God has hung seven red lanterns across the path of this generation Seven fearful and terrible plagues are soon to smite the world. God is sending the message of warning.

Listen as I read: "I saw another sign in heaven, great and marvelous, seven angels having the seven last plagues; for in them is filled up the wrath of God . . . And I heard a great voice out of the temple saying to the seven angels, Go your ways, and pour out the vials of the wrath of God upon the earth. And the first went, and poured out his vial upon the earth; and there fell a noisome and grievous sore upon the men which had the mark of the beast, . . .

"And the second angel poured out his vial upon the sea; and it became as the blood of a dead man: and every living soul died in the sea.

"And the third angel poured out his vial upon the rivers and fountains of waters; and they became blood.

"And the fourth angel poured out his vial upon the sun; and power was given unto him to scorch men with fire. And men were scorched with great heat, and blasphemed the name of God, which hath power over these plagues: . . .

"And the fifth angel poured out his vial upon the seat of the beast; and his kingdom was full of darkness; and they gnawed their tongues for pain . . .

"And the sixth angel poured out his vial upon the great river Euphrates; and the water thereof was dried up, that the way of the kings of the East might be prepared. And I saw three unclean spirits like frogs come out of the mouth of the dragon, and out of the mouth of the beast, and out of the mouth of the false prophet. For they are the spirits of devils, working miracles, which go forth unto the kings of the earth and of the whole world, to gather them to the battle of that great day of God Almighty . . .

"And the seventh angel poured out his vial into the air; and there came a great voice out of the temple of heaven, from the throne, saying, It is done. And there were voices, and thunders, and lightnings; and there was a great earthquake, such as was not since men were upon the earth, so mighty an earthquake and so great . . .

"And there fell upon men a great hail out of heaven, every stone about the weight of a talent. and men blasphemed God because of the plague of the hail; for the plague thereof was exceeding great."

This is the reading of the Word of God in Revelation 15:1 and the 16th chapter in part. These seven last plagues are so fearful, that I dare not stand before you to preach on such a subject, without a special anointing from God. Will you bow your heads with me in special prayer?

(Prayer.)

Father, we thank Thee that in mercy Thou dost warn us of what is coming. We know as surely as this is in Thy Word, just so surely it will come. Lord, make plain to every soul here the way of escape. Father, help us to be wise and accept Thy way of escape. May we not be foolish like the people in

Noah's day, who refused to heed Thy warning, and the flood came unexpectedly and took them all away. Grant that tonight we may heed the still small voice that shows us what to do. May not a man, or woman, or young person, leave this building without being right with God. We ask it in Jesus' name. Amen.

One of the main items that you would like to know about these seven last plagues is, when will these terrible judgments come? The seven last plagues are God's last judgments upon this sinful world. This shows that these plagues will come just before the end of time. Since they are God's last judgments, they will come just before the last day.

The Book of Revelation indicates that the first plague will begin about one year before the end of time. Here it is in Revelation 18·8. "Therefore shall her plagues come in one day." When the Word declares that these plagues will come in one day, that does not mean a day of twenty-four hours. Why not? Because Revelation 16 shows that the seven last plagues are not confined to a period of only twenty-four hours. When it says the plagues will come in one day, that one day must be a prophetic day. The Bible plainly shows that a day in prophecy represents a year. You will find that in Ezekiel 4.6. God says. "I have appointed thee each day for a year."

On this basis you can see that the seven last plagues will cover the space of about one year. I have a diagram here that will help you to understand this matter (At this juncture, a diagram was lowered into view, from which strips of paper were successively removed to reveal the period of time to which the plagues apply, and certain events connected with them.)

We shall remove the first paper, and there are the words, "Christ as Advocate!" At the present time Christ is our Advocate, our Mediator, our Intercessor, our Great High Priest. He sits at the Father's right hand, pleading pardon and eternal life for every soul who chooses to come under His blood. The day of salvation will continue just as long as Christ pleads His blood for sinners. But the time is drawing near when Christ will close His mediatorial work.

We now remove the second paper, and you will notice a line, which marks the end of Christ's work as our high Priest. This will bring the day when Jesus will no longer plead His blood for sinners. What will happen when Christ closes His intercessory work? The day of salvation will end and the great day of the wrath of God will begin. Then the Seven last plagues will be poured out upon the disobedient people of the world.

Next we remove the third paper and you will notice how the end of Christ's work as man's Intercessor will bring the end of the day of salvation and the beginning of the day of wrath, and the beginning of the seven last plagues.

What will happen when the seven last plagues have all been poured out? The book of Revelation shows that after the seven last plagues are poured out, the Lord Jesus Christ will appear before the world in visible form upon a cloud, to gather the righteous from the earth, and to slay the disobedient. So when we remove the fourth paper we notice the words. "The Second Coming of Jesus Christ."

This shows that the seven last plagues will come during the space of about one year between the end of Christ's work as High Priest, and the day when He will actually appear as King of Kings on the cloud at His second advent. The seven last plagues will bring the worst time of suffering; the worst time of trouble that has ever been or ever will be. Put down Daniel 12 1, "At that time shall Michael stand up . . . there shall be a time of trouble such as never was." The seven last plagues will bring upon the disobedient a time of trouble such as never was, or ever will be again.

In Revelation 15:1 and Revelation 14:9, 10 we learn that the seven last plagues are the wrath of God without any mercy, because Jesus does not plead for sinners during the time that those plagues are being poured out.

The book of Exodus shows that God sent ten plagues on Egypt just before He took His people out of Egypt. The book of Revelation shows that God will send seven plagues on the world just before He takes His people out of the world at the second coming of Christ The first plague on the Egyptians was the outbreak of painful boils on every Egyptian. The first of the seven plagues will be a painful, incurable sore, or canker, that will burst out in the flesh of the disobedient people.

Notice how many people are to have this incurable sore or canker. I read Rev. 16.2. "The first went, and poured out his vial upon the earth; and there fell a noisome and grievous sore upon the men which had the mark of the beast." Every person from the richest to the poorest, from the highest to the lowest, who has the mark of the beast, will have that incurable sore.

This is why you must not fail to be here next Sunday night to learn from your Bible how you can avoid receiving the mark of the beast. It is so important that you will do well to cancel every other engagement. Put a circle around November 10, a week from tonight. Admission will be by ticket only. The biggest preacher in Des Moines cannot walk through these inside doors next Sunday night without a ticket. But the tickets are free. If you failed to receive tickets as you entered the auditorium tonight, stop at the box office as you leave and get as many as you need.

According to Revelation 16.2, some day soon, entirely unexpectedly, while men are going about their ordinary pursuits, a terrible, incurable canker will break out in the flesh of millions of people in the same hour all over the world. In fact, everyone who has the mark of the beast will have that terrible sore burst out in his flesh.

Business will be completely paralyzed. Factory wheels will stop. The majority of the employees will have the mark of the beast, and they will be unable to work because of these terrible sores. Trains will stop. Airplanes will be grounded, because most of the men who operate them will have these terrible sores. Stores will stop selling goods There will be no clerks on duty. No customers at the counter. This will be the time when people will telephone for the doctor, but the doctor will not come, because the majority of the doctors will have the mark of the beast, and will have the sore.

A few days later comes the dreadful news that the sea has turned to blood. Every living creature in the sea will die Think what a stench will come up from their putrefying carcases.

Then a little later the third plague strikes The rivers, the lakes, the springs, the sources of man's drinking water, are turned to blood and those who have refused to obey God will have nothing but blood to drink. This is what scripture says. "For they have shed the blood of saints and prophets and Thou hast given them blood to drink, for they are worthy "

In the second book of your Bible, you will find that God turned the waters of Egypt to blood for seven days, and for seven days the Egyptians had no water.

Then a short time after this, the fourth plague will be poured out. The heat of the sun will be increased till it will sear the flesh where it strikes. Then will come the fifth plague and there will be a darkness that can be felt. Here is something I want you to notice These plagues do not kill people. Notice that the people, who have this terrible sore eating their flesh inch by inch, are still alive in their misery when the fifth plague comes.

Scripture says, "The fifth angel poured out his vial upon the seat of the beast, and his kingdom was full of darkness and they gnawed their tongues for pain, and blasphemed the God of heaven because of their pains and their **sores.**" Those who are afflicted with that terrible sore under the first plague are still alive gnawing their tongues for pain when the terrible darkness comes. They will long for death and not find it. They will desire to die and death will flee from them·

Each plague just adds to their misery and their suffering. The people who have refused to obey God will have this terrible sore eating their flesh like a slow fire. This in turn will produce a most burning thirst. They will struggle to the spigot with a glass, thinking they will get some cool water, but when they open the spigot, blood gushes into the glass. They will throw the glass to the floor in desperation. Then they think of some cool spring where they have quenched their thirst in days gone by, and they drag their sore-eaten bodies to the spring but lo, it bubbles forth blood and then, to crown all their suffering, the sun pours out as it were liquid fire. Their thirst is intensified all the more. Oh how they will long for a few drops of cool water.

This is the time when those who receive the mark of the beast will have no rest day nor night. How could they rest day or night with those sores eating their flesh like a slow fire, and nothing but blood to drink, with the sun scorching them and intensifying their thirst.

As surely as God lives, this is how the people who refuse to obey Him will be punished As I have said to you many times, the wisest thing, the best thing you can ever do, is to make your decision to keep the commandments of God and the faith of Jesus.

Under the sixth plague the nations are to be gathered for that last world-ending battle of Armageddon. Under the seventh plague will come the greatest earthquake that ever has been. This earthquake will lay every city in ruins. If you could see what Des Moines will look like when that great earthquake takes place, you would hardly believe your own eyes.

Revelation 16 19 declares that the cities of the nations fell. New York falls! London falls! Paris falls! Calcutta goes down. Shanghai is destroyed. Every city in the world will go down under that terrible earthquake. In fact, in Isaiah 24 20 we learn that this earthquake will be so severe that the entire world will reel to and fro like a drunken man

Then, in connection with this great earthquake, the largest hail stones that I suppose have ever been hurled down from heaven, will fall. Scripture says "Every stone about the weight of a talent." A talent is a Jewish standard of weight equivalent to fifty-seven pounds. Think of such hail! Hail stones as large as half bushel baskets!

On June 25, 1920, at Hillsdale, Wyoming, hail came down as large as apples. It made kindling wood out of the houses. Think of what destruction and death there will be when the hail comes down as large as half-bushel baskets.

After the hail, the heavens will open and Jesus Christ and all the holy angels will be seen coming to the earth, to catch away the righteous, and to slay the remainder of the wicked.

Some will say, "Mr. Shuler, what will happen to the people who obey God, when these terrible plagues smite the world?" Here it is in Daniel 12.1. "There shall be a time of trouble such as never was since there was a nation, and at that time Thy people shall be delivered, everyone found written in the book." If your name is written in God's book of Life, you will be protected from every plague. "Thy people shall be delivered, everyone found written in the book."

Have you ever read the 91st Psalm? This Psalm will likely mean more to you, than it has ever meant in all your life after you have heard this sermon. I turn to Psalm 91:7-10. "A thousand shall fall at thy side, and ten thousand at thy right hand; but it shall not come nigh thee. Only with thine eyes shalt thou behold and see the reward of the wicked. Because thou hast made the Lord, which is my refuge, even the most high, thy habitation; there shall no evil befall thee, neither shall any plague come nigh thy dwelling."

When those terrible plagues came upon the Egyptians, God protected His people. When the Egyptians were smitten with boils, the Israelites did not have a single boil. When the hail destroyed the crops and the cattle of the Egyptians, not a hail stone fell where the Israelites lived. When the oldest child in every Egyptian home died at mid-night on a certain fateful night, God told His people to put a mark of blood on their door. Every house that had that appointed mark was spared from death.

Paul tells us in 1 Corinthians 10:11, that all these things happened unto them for types, and they are written for our admonition upon whom the ends of the world are come. As God protected the Israelites from those plagues that came on Egypt, God will protect those who obey His commandments from these seven last plagues. The disobedient will have nothing but blood to drink but God will supply water to those who keep His commandments. When the sun scorches the disobedient, God will draw a shade over His people. When the hail falls, not a stone will fall on His children.

The Book of Revelation shows that when the seven last plagues come, every person in the world will either have the seal of God on his forehead, or he will have the mark of the beast in his forehead or in his right hand. Whichever of these two marks you receive settles your fate for eternity. Those who have the seal of God on their foreheads will be protected from the seven last plagues and will be taken to heaven when Jesus appears. Those who have the mark of the beast will have to drink the wrath of God in these seven last plagues.

The most important question of all is which of these two marks will you have? You are bound to have one or the other in that final crisis. This is why you need to be here Tuesday night without fail. The Bible lecture for that night will show what is the seal of the living God, and how you can have it placed on your forehead and be protected from the plagues. Then on next Sunday night, one week from tonight, you will learn what is the mark of the beast so you can avoid ever receiving it. It will be worth more than a billion dollars to have the seal of God on your forehead.

There is one question that every person needs to quietly ask himself to-night. "Am I ready for these terrible plagues to come?" You cannot avoid meeting these plagues. Some may say, "Mr. Shuler, there is nothing to what you preach." But the seven last plagues will come, nevertheless. Nobody can stop these plagues from coming. Just as surely as they are mentioned in this Bible, they will come. The word of God warns. It will not fail.

Listen to me. Since we cannot stop them, it is only good sense to get ready for them. Since God has told us that they are coming, we should be the most foolish people in the world if we did not prepare.

In Matt. 24:37 Christ compared the last days to the days of Noah. He says, "As the days of Noah were, so shall also the coming of the Son of man be." When the flood came, what happened to all the people who were unprepared? The flood took them all away. The reason only eight people were saved, is that only eight people were ready.

When the flood came, how many different ways were there by which people could be saved? Five ways? No! Four ways? No! Two ways? No! How many? There was only ONE way. That was God's way. "As the days of Noah were, so shall also the coming of the Son of man be."

Today we have religions, beliefs, and denominations by the hundreds, but there is only ONE WAY in which you, or I, or any other person can ever be saved from the seven last plagues. Here it is in Revelation 14 12. "Here is the patience of the saints: here are they that keep the commandments of God, and the faith of Jesus."

It takes the faith of Jesus to enable us to keep the commandments. Some people want to separate the ten commandments from the faith of Jesus. God joins them together. The only way you can ever keep the commandments of God is by the faith of Jesus. Those who keep the commandments of God and the faith of Jesus will be protected from the seven last plagues and will be prepared to meet Jesus when He appears on the cloud. I want to tell you, dear friends, in all the earnestness of my soul, that the most important matter demanding your attention, above everything else is to make your decision for the commandments of God and the faith of Jesus.

If you have been attending these Bible lectures regularly, you know by this time that the keeping of the commandments of God includes the keeping of the seventh day, the day we call Saturday This is the day Jesus kept. This is the day He commands us to keep. You will notice that His people are said to keep the commandments of God and the faith of Jesus. If I were to ask how many people want to be protected from the seven last plagues, everyone here would raise his hand, and rightly so. Nobody wants God to inflict these plagues on him. I do not want to suffer these seven last plagues. You do not want to suffer the seven last plagues. Why not, then, take God's way of escape? What do you say? God's way of escape is to keep the commandments of God and the faith of Jesus.

If you haven't stepped out to keep the commandments of God and the faith of Jesus, I hope you will make that wise decision this very night. When the flood came in the days of Noah, it was worth more than all the world to be safe in that ark. When the seven last plagues come, it will be worth more than all the wealth in the entire world to be found obedient to the commandments of God and the faith of Jesus.

Tell me, what will all the money in the world amount to if a man has to suffer the seven last plagues? What will the highest office, what will the most lucrative position, or the best paying business, amount to if a man must suffer these plagues? I hope every soul will do the wise thing, the safe thing, the right thing—make your decision for the commandments of God and the faith of Jesus

This message is set forth under the symbolism of three angels flying through mid-air, one after another, preaching a great three-fold message to every nation. The great purpose of this Bible Institute is to unfold this message step by step, and to locate sincere souls who are ready to accept God's message. The wisest and the best thing you can ever do is to be one of those who accept this great message for the last days.

Some man will say, "I believe, Mr. Shuler, that you are preaching the Bible. I believe that you preach the truth, but I shall wait until I see that sore break out on people. I shall wait until I see the rivers turn to blood I shall wait until I see the armies of the nations gather in the Holy Land for the last mighty battle, and then I shall begin to obey the commandments."

I tell you on the authority of the Word of God, that if you wait to prepare until you see these plagues come, you will never be able to prepare. Why not? Because the door of opportunity will be closed forever before the first plague starts. Here it is in Revelation 22.11, 12. "He that is unjust, let him be unjust still: and he which is filthy, let him be filthy still: and he that is righteous let him be righteous still· and he that is holy, let him be holy still. And behold, I come quickly; and my reward is with me, to give every man according as his work shall be."

This text has puzzled many Bible readers. Jesus declares that the man who is unjust must stay unjust; the man who is filthy must stay filthy. What about that? Does Jesus Christ want the man who is filthy in sin to stay filthy? No. What does it mean? He says in Isaiah 1:18, "Come now, and let us reason together, saith the Lord: though your sins be as scarlet, they shall be as white as snow."

However, Jesus can make our sins as white as snow, only so long as He pleads as our High Priest, as our Mediator, as our Intercessor. Remember, He will close His intercessory work before the first plague starts. In fact, the first plague cannot start until He lays down the golden censer and says, "Father, it is finished. The last one who is to accept of My blood has accepted. Now let him that is unjust, be unjust still; and let him that is filthy, be filthy still And behold I come quickly." This "quickly" is about one year, and during that period these terrible plagues will fall.

This shows, dear friends, that it will be forever too late to pray after the first plague begins. Why? Because the door of mercy will have been closed forever. Jesus will have terminated His intercession for sinners. The time is coming when a man may pray forty days and forty nights and it will not do him any good. It will be too late. The door of mercy will have closed.

This is why the Scripture says, "Seek ye the Lord while He may be found, call ye upon Him while He is near." "Now is the accepted time; now is the day of salvation" Some day soon, when people least expect it, the Lord Jesus will close His intercessory work as our High Priest, and He will pronounce this fateful decree of Revelation 22:11.

On the cross 1900 years ago, there came a moment when He said, "It is finished." The time is fast coming when He will come to the end of His work, as Priest and Mediator and He will say again, "Father, it is finished." Then the terrible plagues will begin.

When He says these awful words, the unjust man must remain unjust forever. He can never change. The man who is filthy in sin must stay filthy. He never can get clean, because the blood of Christ no longer avails for him.

As that moment finds you, living right or living wrong, obedient to God's commandments or disobedient to His commandments, so you will remain forever. You cannot make any changes after that. "He that is unjust let him be unjust still: and he which is filthy, let him be filthy still" Whatever you intend to do about obeying the commandments of God, you must do it before Jesus Christ closes His work of intercession, and before the first plague begins.

I wish that I didn't have to say what I am about to say. The Bible shows that millions of people will wait until it is too late. Millions of people will knock on a door that will never be opened to them. The door will have been closed forever. The door will never open to them. They will pray, but their prayer will be too late.

O, friends, we need to be ready now for this fearful time. O, unsaved man or woman, or unsaved young person, why not come to Jesus tonight while His blood still avails for you? I appeal to every Christian, who has not made his decision to keep the commandments of God and the faith of Jesus. Why not decide tonight?

Jesus wants to come into your life tonight, and make your life just what it ought to be. Will you let Him do it? He says, "Behold, I stand at the door and knock! If any man will hear My voice and open the door, I will come in to him and sup with him, and he with Me." Why not swing the door open just now by full surrender, and let Jesus Christ come into your life and live in you a life of obedience? I believe every soul here wants the Lord to help him.

How many want to say just now, "Preacher, pray for me that Christ may come into my life and make my life all that it ought to be?" Will you lift your hands? Yes, it seems that nearly every hand is raised for prayer.

The Seal of the Living God

(Preached on the Ninth Thursday Night of the Campaign)

Have you ever heard about the mystical mark, which, when placed on the door, kept death out of the house? You may read about that mark in Exodus 12 1-20 The last plague on the Egyptians just before God delivered His people from bondage was the death of the oldest child in every Egyptian home Before that plague came, God sent a message through His servant Moses and told the people what to do that they might be spared from this most fearful plague

He told them to take a lamb without blemish, because that lamb was to represent the perfect Son of God, who was to offer Himself without spot for the sins of humanity They were to slay the lamb and take some of the blood and smear it on the door post God said, "When I see the blood, I will pass over you "

When the angel of death flew over the land at midnight, and the fearful plague of the death of the first-born struck, every house that had this mark of blood on the door was spared from death But there was death in every house that night—even the death of the first-born—where there was no mark of blood upon the door The mark on the door kept death out of the house

This was a type of how the blood of Jesus Christ alone can save us from everlasting death "When I see the blood I will pass over you " This mark was also a type of a certain mark that God will place on His people in the last days to protect them from the seven last plagues Paul says in 1 Cor. 10 11, in speaking of the experiences which came to the Israelites· "All these things happened unto them for ensamples· and they are written for our ad--monition, upon whom the ends of the world are come "

The book of Revelation tells about this mark, which God will place upon the foreheads of His people in the very last days to protect them from those seven terrible plagues of Revelation. I read about this mark in Revelation 7 1-3

"After these things I saw four angels standing on the four corners of the earth, holding the four winds of the earth, that the wind should not blow on the earth, nor on the sea, nor on any tree And I saw another angel ascending from the east, having the seal of the living God, and he cried with a loud voice to the four angels to whom it was given to hurt the earth and the sea, saying, Hurt not the earth, neither the sea, nor the trees, till we have sealed the servants of our God in their foreheads "

The prophet tells of four winds which are about to overwhelm the world with universal destruction He notices that four angels are holding back, or restraining, these four winds from destroying civilization He looks to the east and sees an angel with the seal of the living God in His hands This seal is to be placed on the forehead of everyone of God's true people, that he may be protected from the impending destruction The angel with the seal cries for the four angels to hold back the threatening destruction until the seal has been placed on the forehead of God's people What does all this mean?

You will recall that in the Bible lecture which we gave on Daniel 7, we showed from the Scriptures that the four winds represent war, strife, uprising, revolution, and commotion. How fitting it is to compare war to a destructive cyclone. When you think of some of the pictures of the damage wrought by war in such cities as Berlin, Amsterdam, Warsaw, and Hamburg, it is as if you looked at a picture of a city which had been swept by some terrible hurricane, or cyclone. How fitting it is to compare war, with its fearful destruction, of life and property, to destructive wind.

These four winds, which are about to destroy the world, represent the ravages of war in the east, west, north, and south that are to wipe out civilization. Let me ask you, "Isn't that exactly what we have seen and do see?" You may look in any direction you wish tonight, you may look east, west, north, or south, and you see trouble, commotion, upheaval, and the threatened destruction of civilization. You see now, not next month, or next year, but you see now what the Bible said would prevail in the final movements of this world's history

When these four winds are loosed, then the great war of Armageddon will come We talked on this subject on the second Sunday night of this Bible Institute This conflict will not and cannot take place until these four angels loose their four winds In this Armageddon conflict all the people in the world will be slain, except those who have the seal on their foreheads

Thus it is that before this final destruction comes, God is sending a message over the world to put His seal on the foreheads of His people that they may be protected When those four winds are loosed, I should rather have the seal of God on my forehead than to have that gold which is now stored at Fort Knox, wouldn't you? What will all that gold at Fort Knox amount to when the seven last plagues come? When the third plague strikes, and all the drinking water is turned to blood, you couldn't take all those billions of gold and buy even one glass or water I tell you, we need to evaluate things in the light of the great day of the Lord

There are three items that you would like to know. What is the seal of the living God, which will protect His people from the seven last plagues? How is that seal placed on the forehead? Where is the special message that will place this seal of God on the foreheads of His servants?

Take the first question, What is the seal of the living God? Everybody understands that the seal of any nation is some design which that nation has chosen to represent its authority Put down 1 Kings 21 8 Jezebel wrote letters in Ahab's name, and sealed them with Ahab's seal Ahab's seal on those letters meant that the orders contained in those letters, had behind them the authority of the king of Israel

Every independent nation has its own seal Mexico has a seal, England, Spain, Brazil, Russia, each of these countries has its own seal Our government has its seal In Washington, D C, in the office of the Secretary of State is the great seal of the United States When that seal is placed on a document, it places behind that document the authority of the United States Government

In any case the seal of any government is some distinctive design that stands as a sign of the authority of that nation The seal of God must be some distinctive spiritual design that God has chosen as the sign of His authority as the only true God

The seal of God and the mark of the beast are not literal marks The seal of God on the forehead doesn't mean that some certain mark will actually be stamped upon a person's forehead The law of God written upon man's heart doesn't refer to any visible or literal writing being traced upon his person God is a Spirit The seal of God is some distinctive spiritual design that God has chosen to represent His authority as the only true God

Throughout the Bible God appeals to the fact that He as the Creator, is the supreme evidence that He is the only true God Here are two references, Psalm 96 5 and Jeremiah 10 10-12 In Psalm 96 5 the false gods of' the heathen nations are declared to be idols, while Jehovah, as the true God, is identified as the One Who made heaven and earth The Psalmist says, "All the gods of the nations are idols, but the Lord made the heavens" In Jeremiah 10 10-12 the false gods of the heathen people are singled out as the gods who did not make the heavens and the earth, while the true God is set forth as the One Who made heaven and earth by His mighty power.

The seal of God must be some distinctive spiritual design, that God has chosen as the sign of His power, as the only true God What has God chosen to be His distinctive sign, that He is the great Creator and the only true God? I turn to Exodus 31 16, 17.

"Wherefore the children of Israel shall keep the Sabbath, to observe the Sabbath throughout their generations for a perpetual covenant. It is a sign between Me and the children of Israel forever, for in six days the Lord made heaven and earth, and on the seventh day He rested, and was refreshed."

In these words God shows specifically that the Sabbath is His chosen sign as the Creator He declares in so many words that the Sabbath is a sign He is talking about His Sabbath, which comes upon the seventh day of the week This seventh-day sabbath is the sign that the Lord made the world in six days You can see that since God has chosen the seventh-day Sabbath as His distinctive spiritual sign, that He is the Creator and the only true God, the Sabbath must be the seal of the Living God

(At this juncture the speaker held up a notary's seal) What is this in my hand? Yes, it is a seal, a notary's seal We shall place a piece of paper in it and find out more about it (A piece of paper was placed in the seal, and imprinted with the seal) It reads, "William R Howder, Notary Public, Washington County, Tennessee " Notice that there are three items, William Howder was the name of the man who once owned this seal, Notary public was his distinguishing title, and Washington County, Tennessee was the territory in which he was authorized to act as a notary The seal contains a combination of three items. Name, distinguishing title and territory

When the President of the United States makes a proclamation, do you know how he begins the pronouncement? He imparts his authority to the proclamation by a combination of three items name, distinguishing title, and territory For instance a few weeks ago the President made a Thanksgiving Proclamation He began the pronouncement by saying "I, Harry S Truman, President of the United States " There you have the three essential items which constitute a seal Harry S Truman, his name, President, his distinguishing title, United States, his territory

Here is a photostat of the seal of the King of England The present king is George VI Here is a photograph of the seal of the King The inscription is in Latin, but when it is translated it reads, "George VI King of England, Etc " There you have three essential items of a seal George the VI, his name, King, distinguishing title; England, etc, territory It takes these three items to constitute a seal

So the Seal of God will contain these three items in reference to God When you find the seal of God, it will be something that reveals the name of God, the distinguishing title of God, and the territory over which He rules

Where can you find this? Do you know that there is only one institution mentioned in the sixty-six books of the Bible, that contains the three essential items of a seal? Let us look at the Ten Commandments

The first commandment says, "Thou shalt have no other gods before Me " This doesn't even mention the name of God The second commandment, the third commandment and the fifth commandment do mention the name of God They say, "Lord thy God," but they do not reveal the distinguishing title of God as the Creator, or His territory

Now look at the fourth commandment, the Sabbath institution "Remember the Sabbath day to keep it holy Six days shalt thou labor and do all thy work, but the seventh day is the Sabbath of the **Lord thy God.**" There is

His name—"Lord thy God" Then God tells us why we are to keep the seventh day "For in six days the Lord made heaven and earth" There is the distinguishing title of God. It reveals God as the Maker, the Creator. There too is the territory over which He rules He rules over the earth and everything in heaven, or the universe

This sabbath commandment constitutes the seal of the living God The Sabbath commandment is the only commandment and the only institution mentioned in the Bible, that gives the name of God, His distinguishing title, and the territory over which He rules Here is the seal of God—"Lord thy God," "Creator," "Heaven and Earth."

Notice how conclusive this evidence is. The seventh day Sabbath is the only institution, or commandment, that God has ever given in the Bible, that reveals the three essential items, which, when combined together, constitute a seal of authority. Hence, the Sabbath is found to be the seal of the living God.

The Sabbath is a double sign of God It is not only a sign that the Lord made the world in six days, but it is a sign that the Son of God is the only Saviour Put down Ezekiel 20 12. The Lord says, "Moreover also **I gave them My Sabbaths, to be a sign** between Me and them, that they might know that I am the Lord that sanctify them." Did you get that? God gave the Sabbath to be a sign That is His seal He made the Sabbath to be a sign He chose the Sabbath as His distinctive sign

The words "sign" and "seal" are sometimes used interchangeably in the Bible The word "seal" in Revelation 7 2 is rendered "sign" in John Wycliffe's translation of 1380 and in the Douay or Catholic version of the Bible in 1609 In the place of saying, "having the seal of the living God," it is rendered, "having the sign of the living God"

Four times over in the Holy Scriptures God calls the Sabbath His sign. Here are the texts Exodus 31.13, 16, 17, Ezekiel 20.12, 20. That is the same as saying four times over the sabbath is the seal of God.

Some people will tell you that the keeping of the seventh-day Sabbath is contrary to salvation by grace They say, "These people, who are trying to get you to keep the seventh day are trying to get you back under bondage These people are legalists' They are trying to save themselves by their works Salvation is only by grace. When a man is saved by grace, he has nothing to do with keeping the seventh day." God knows far more about this than any preacher God shows that the seventh-day Sabbath is actually a sign of salvation by grace Here it is in Ezekiel 20 12 "I gave them My sabbaths to be a sign between Me and them, that they might know that I am the Lord that sanctify them"

Sanctification is a work of grace. So the sabbath is actually a sign of salvation by grace This is a good thing to remember when people bring up the point about the keeping of the seventh day being contrary to grace

The Sabbath is, as it were, the flag of the Lord Jesus Christ as the Creator and the Re-creator, or Saviour. You know perfectly well that every sovereign nation has chosen some distinctive design for its flag as the sign or emblem of its power (At this juncture the speaker displayed the United States flag and the flag of England) Our own country has chosen the stars and stripes for its flag These forty-eight stars and seven red stripes and six white stripes are a distinctive design chosen by our federal government, as the sign of the mighty power of this republic England has chosen the "Union Jack" So we could go on and on Mexico has its own flag Russia has her flag, etc.

Listen The Bible shows that Christ has chosen the seventh-day Sabbath, as a flag, or sign of His power to create and to redeem from sin "Moreover also I gave them My Sabbaths to be a sign between Me and them that they might know I am the Lord that sanctify them "

Every true American loves the Stars and the Stripes. We say from our heart, "Long may it wave o'er the land of the free and the home of the brave." This flag is more than just a piece of cloth   There was a time when this flag in my hand was only a piece of cloth. I presume this was once just a piece of white muslin   Then there came a day when this design was stamped upon it.   Then it became the consecrated sign of our government, and must be reverenced and respected as such   Will a true American take this flag and wipe his shoes with it? No   Will a true American take this flag and walk on it? Never.

So, the Sabbath is more than just a day of rest   It is a portion of time, consecrated by the Lord Jesus Christ as His sign, as the Creator and the only Saviour. We must not trample on Christ's flag by using the seventh day, or Saturday, as an ordinary working day.

Here is something strange   There are millions and millions of Americans who would never think of walking upon the flag, but those same millions of Americans are trampling God's flag into the ground every week by working on God's holy day   This is why God sends a message in these last days about taking our foot off the Sabbath   In Isaiah 58 13, 14 we read, "If thou turn away thy foot from the Sabbath"   God asks us to take our foot off from the Sabbath. When a person keeps the Sabbath it is a sign that he accepts the Lord Jesus Christ as his Creator and Saviour.

Some people say that a day is a day and that it makes no difference which day of the week we keep, and that Sunday is just as good as any other day. That is a mistake   You might as well say that this flag is only a piece of cloth and it makes no difference which flag we recognize as our flag   Loyalty to the United States demands that we honor the stars and stripes   So loyalty to Jesus Christ demands that we keep the seventh day that He sanctified for us

Revelation 7 3 declares that the seal is placed on the foreheads of His servants   How is the seal placed on the forehead? The forehead represents the mind   Many times in this Bible the forehead is used to represent the mind. Tell me what is the first word of the fourth commandment? What is it? **Remember** the Sabbath day."

How do you remember? You remember with the mind (pointing to the forehead). When you remember the Sabbath, that puts the seal of God on your forehead   To receive the seal of God on the forehead means to surrender the heart, mind and soul to do the will of God. It means having the character and image of the Lord Jesus Christ stamped upon one's life

How can you have the seal of God placed on your forehead? God tells you what to do in Ezekiel 20 20. "Hallow My Sabaths; and they shall be a sign between Me and you that ye may know that I am the Lord your God "
Notice the first three words. "Hallow My Sabbaths " The word "hallow" means to keep holy   It is the same thought as is found in the first sentence of the fourth commandment, "Remember the Sabbath day to keep it holy." God declares that if you will remember the Sabbath day to keep it holy, it will become His sign or seal on you, that you are His obedient child, and that He is your God

This prophecy of the sealing message is being fulfilled today   The Sabbath truth is being preached to all nations   These truths which you have been hearing are being preached in over 800 languages and dialects all the world around. Wherever it is preached it is calling out a people, who are marked off from every other people in the world by the keeping of the true Sabbath

Do you know that there isn't anything a person can do, that will mark him off from other people as quickly or as distinctly, as just to keep the seventh day or Saturday as the Sabbath? I can remember when I first began to keep the Sabbath When I would walk down the street in our little town, the little boys would say, "There goes one of them There's one of those seventh-day fellows" Marked? Yes, a marked man, marked by God

A minister was visiting a large army camp in the South where there were thousands and thousands of soldiers Night had come He was tired and weary, but there was one more seventh-day keeping soldier on his list, whom he was determined to find He went to the sergeant in charge of the filing system He said, "I want you to help me find Mr Griffin"

The sergeant went to the files and there were dozens of Griffins He said, "Man, what are you asking for? This would be almost like hunting for a needle in a haystack for you to find the Griffin you want in this great big army camp" The minister said, "Hold on a minute! The man I am looking for is a Seventh-day Adventist and he goes to church on Saturday"

"Oh, yes!" the sergeant said "Sure! That Saturday man! Everybody in the camp knows that Saturday man!" In just a few minutes they brought the man, and he and the pastor had a fine visit.

It might have taken hours to find "Mr Griffin," but they found the "Saturday man" very easily Do you know why? "Hallow my sabbaths; and they shall be a sign between Me and You" Keeping the Sabbath marks a person off from other people If a man follows the ten commandments as God gave them it marks him off today in this modern world from everyone else Thank God for it

At that fateful midnight hour when death struck the oldest child in every Egyptian home, there was only one item that really counted That was the mark of blood on the door Regardless of how wise or rich, or how religious the family was, if the mark was not on the door there was death in that house.

Some people may have said, "How can some lamb's blood keep death away? What is there about lamb's blood to keep death away? What difference will it make whether you put the mark on the door or not?" The difference was life or death Life if they obeyed, death if they failed to obey

We are coming to another fateful hour when the only thing that will count will be to have the seal of God on our foreheads This sealing work is described in Ezekiel 9 The prophecy shows that every person rich or poor, high or low, old or young, learned or unlearned, will be destroyed unless he has God's mark on his forehead Put down Ezekiel 9 4, 5, 6

"The Lord said unto him, Go through the midst of the city, through the midst of Jerusalem, and set a mark upon the foreheads of the men that sigh and that cry for all the abominations that be done in the midst thereof" This tells how God will place His seal or mark upon the foreheads of those who will be true to His commandments

Notice what will happen in the final conflict "And to the others he said in mine hearing, Go ye after him through the city, and smite Let not your eye spare, neither have ye pity Slay utterly old and young, both maids, and little children, and women but **come not near any man upon whom is the mark.**" The only ones who will be spared are those who have the mark The all important question will be—Do I have the seal of God on my forehead?

It will be worth more than all the wealth of the world to have the seal of God on your forehead in that fateful day The only way you can have that seal on you then, is to fully surrender your will to do the will of Jesus Christ now and follow Him all the way Are you determined to fully yield your mind to the will of Jesus Christ, that He may place His seal on your forehead? I am sure that every soul here wants to send up a prayer to Jesus Christ, "Lord, help me to be true to Thy commandments, that I may receive the seal of God on my forehead" How many want to send up that kind of a prayer? Will you raise your hand? Yes, it seems that every hand is raised.

(Prayer.)

(Copy of the Bible lesson outline, which was distributed to the people preceding the thirty-ninth lecture)

Lesson VII - Can One Enter Heaven Who Has Not Been Baptized?

1 Four different methods of baptism are now being practiced—sprinkling, pouring, trine immersion and single immersion

2 As there is only one true God, and only one true Christ, there is only one true baptism (Eph 4 4-6).

3 The one true baptism ordained by Jesus Christ is the way that He was baptized as our example.

4 Jesus Christ was immersed in the river Jordan

5 John the Baptist baptized people only by immersion

6 True Christians follow in Jesus' steps (1 Pet 2 21)

7a If you follow Jesus in baptism, is it not plain that you will be immersed as He was?

7b If a person has only been sprinkled, has he really been baptized as Jesus was?

8 In true baptism both the minister and the believer must go down into the water   Then the minister baptizes him   Then they both come up out of the water

9 The Greek word used in the New Testament for baptism limits baptism to the one action of being dipped under the water

10 Believers are commanded to be buried with Christ in baptism

11a Baptism is a burial (Rom 6·4)

11b If a person has only been baptized by sprinkling or pouring, he should according to God's holy Word, be buried with Christ in baptism at the first opportunity, by going forward in the Christ-ordained ordinance of immersion

12 True baptism is a memorial of the burial and resurrection of Jesus (Col 2 12)
Single immersion with the face upward is the only form that rightly represents the burial and resurrection of Jesus

13 There will be people in heaven, who obeyed the truth according to the light they had, but were never immersed (Luke 23 40-43)

14. If the penitent thief had accepted Christ at a time when there was opportunity to be baptized, and had refused to comply with God's ordinance, he would not have been saved

15 Any person, who knows what he ought to do, and continues to fail to do it will be lost

16 In order to be saved, we must make Christ's death our death, or we must die with Christ to sin   Jesus Christ died for the transgression of all ten of the ten commandments (1 Jno 3 4)   In order for a person to be truly buried with Christ, he must die with Christ to the transgression of all the ten commandments

17 If you have been baptized or immersed in the past on only nine of the ten commandments, why not give God the honor of being baptized again on all ten commandments, when you accept His special message for the last days?

References which were filled in as the study was presented, (4) Mark 1:9-11; (5) John 3·23, (8) Acts 8 35-39; (10) Col 2 12, (15) Heb 10·26

The Woman in Scarlet

(Preached on the Ninth Friday Night of the Campaign)

"There came one of the seven angels which had the seven vials, and talked with me, saying unto me, Come hither, I will shew unto thee the judgment of the great whore that sitteth upon many waters . So he carried me away in the spirit into the wilderness and I saw a woman sit upon a scarlet colored beast, full of names of blasphemy, having seven heads and ten horns And the woman was arrayed in purple and scarlet color, and decked with gold and precious stones and pearls, having a golden cup in her hand full of abominations and filthiness of her fornication.

"And upon her forehead was a name written, MYSTERY, BABYLON THE GREAT, THE MOTHER OF HARLOTS AND ABOMINATIONS OF THE EARTH."

(As this was read a chart depicting this woman in scarlet was lowered into view)

This is the reading of Revelation 17.1, 3-5. The question naturally arises, who is this woman? Of what is she a figure? In Bible symbolism a woman represents a church The character of this symbolic woman, whether pure of impure, determines whether the Scripture is referring to a pure church or an impure church

A pure, virtuous woman is used to represent the true church of God An impure harlot woman is used to represent the apostate, corrupt, worldly church

In Revelation 12 we have the figure of a pure woman with the sun over her head, the moon under her feet, and upon her head a crown of twelve stars In the Bible lecture last Friday night we found from the Scriptures that this pure woman is a symbol of the true church of Jesus Christ

Revelation 17 presents just the opposite kind of woman from Revelation 12 In Revelation 12 we have a pure woman, in Revelation 17 an impure woman. You can see that the woman of Revelation 17 is bound to represent just the opposite from the woman of Revelation 12 Since the pure woman represents the true church, the impure woman of Revelation 17 and 18 must represent the false church system. Since the pure woman represents the Lord's true system of worship, the impure woman must represent Satan's counterfeit system.

Here is a point that I hope the Holy Spirit will sink so deep into your mind, that you will never forget it Every soul in this world will follow either God's commandments as recorded in the Bible, and be in the Lord's true system as prefigured by this woman, or he will follow God's commandments as changed by man, and be in the great, false system prefigured by this unchaste woman of Babylon Every soul will stand with one or the other of the two systems of worship prefigured by these two women

Whichever you choose, determines whether you will be saved or lost O, how important it is for you to understand this matter from the scriptures so that you may make the right choice My prayer is that God will make this so plain that you will see just what the Lord wants you to do, and that your heart will be so true to Jesus that you will obey His call this very night Will you bow your head with me in prayer?

(The speaker offered a brief prayer)

You will notice that the harlot woman has in her hand a beautiful golden cup You would naturally expect something very choice from a cup of pure gold But in this case the cup is filled with poisonous wine that has made untold millions drunk, in a spiritual sense   The wine in the golden cup represents the false doctrines of a universal, counterfeit religious system

Nearly all the people in the world have been affected by her false doctrines   That is what the prophecy declares in Revelation 17 2   "With whom the kings of the earth have committed fornication, and the inhabitants of the earth have been made drunk with the wine of her fornication"   The inhabitants of the world have been made drunk spiritually with the wine of her false doctrines   This is the woman who has made millions drunk

Countless millions have been deceived, and millions tonight are being deceived by her false doctrines   Just think of the tragedy of it!   Millions think that they are in the Lord's true system when in reality they are standing with a false, counterfeit system   O, how we need to have our eyes opened to the real truth that God has placed in His precious Book for our day!

Did you know that the Roman church has used a woman with a cup in her hand as an emblem of their church?   I have a photograph of a medal that was struck off in 1825 by Pope Leo XII   On one side it bore his own image or likeness   On the reverse side was a representation of the church of Rome, symbolized by a woman holding in her left hand a cross, and in her right hand a golden cup   Isn't this most striking in the light of this symbol?   In other words, this is as it were, an admission that the church of Rome is identical with the woman of Revelation 17

Did you notice the two colors which this woman chooses for her attire?   What are they?   "The woman was arrayed in purple and scarlet"   Here is a question for you   What are the two chief colors used in the official robes of the Catholic cardinals and bishops?   Purple and scarlet   God even foretold the two colors they would select   You know that when the pope makes a new cardinal, he gives him a red hat.   This is significant in the light of this prophecy

Did you notice the name which God gives to this false system?   You will find it in Revelation 17 5   "Upon her forehead was a name written, MYSTERY, BABYLON"   God gives this woman the name of "Babylon"   This of course, is a symbolical name

Every person must have a clear understanding of what the name "Babylon" means   Why?   Because you cannot understand God's message for our day unless you know what Babylon is   Second, because you cannot understand fully the call of the Lord to His people in these days, unless you know what Babylon is, and what implications are involved in this term in relation to Christian duty

I turn to Revelation 14 8   "There followed another angel saying, Babylon is fallen, is fallen, that great city, because she made all nations drink of the wine of the wrath of her fornication"   The second angel's message pertains to this religious system of Babylon   It is a solemn warning that Babylon is a fallen church, an apostate church system from which Christ's true fellowers must be separated

In this prophecy of Revelation 14 God's special message for our day is set forth under the symbolism of three angels flying in mid air, preaching a mighty three-fold warning to the people of every country   (At this juncture a chart depicting these three angels of Revelation 14 was lowered into view)   He saw three angels flying one behind the other   The three of them together were proclaiming a mighty message to every nation, kindred, tongue and people

Before we opened this Bible Institute, we placed in the advertisement that these meetings would be dedicated to the exposition of this great three-fold message for every people   As these meetings have proceeded from week to week, we have explained this message step by step from the Bible

We have pointed out from the Bible how the hour of God's judgment has come. We have shown from the Scriptures that we are to worship Him that made heaven and earth according to the first angel's message. We have explained from the Bible the significance of the beast. We explained the meaning of the image of the beast Last Sunday night when we talked on the seven last plagues, we explained the significance of the wrath of God without mixture We have shown from this blessed Book what it means to keep the commandments of God and the faith of Jesus. This Sunday night behind closed doors we shall show what constitutes the Mark of the beast, and how you can avoid receiving that mark either in your right hand, or in your forehead

In this meeting tonight, we shall let the Bible tell you the significance of the term "Babylon" This is one of the main items in God's message for our day. I turn to Revelation 18 2, 4 and read in part "He cried mightily with a strong voice, saying, Come out of her my people"

Please notice that the call to come out of Babylon is an important part of the call of the Lord Jesus Christ to His people in these days The call of Jesus to His followers is to come out of Babylon "Come out of her, my people" God's people cannot come out of Babylon, unless they first know what Babylon is No Christian can obey this call of Jesus Christ, unless he knows what Babylon is

Some may say, "What difference will it make if I don't know what Babylon is, just so I love Jesus?" If you love Jesus you will want to know what Jesus wants you to do, so you can do it One of the things Jesus wants you to do is to come out of Babylon, in case you have not already responded to His call in Revelation 18 4

When Saul was converted on the road to Damascus, his first question was, "Lord, what wilt thou have me to do?" He was ready to do what Jesus wanted him to do This is one of the outstanding signs or marks of a truly converted person Do you wonder whether or not you are really converted? Here is a decisive test A converted man is ready to do just what Jesus wants him to do without any reservations

He doesn't say, "Lord, it is too hard" "My folks didn't go this way." "I'll lose my job" No If God wants him to do it, he does it He takes his stand like Martin Luther, "Here I stand, God helping me, I can do no other"

Revelation 18 4 shows that a part of following the Lord Jesus Christ in this closing period of human history is to come out of Babylon Unless you know what Babylon is, you cannot obey that call We must find out what Babylon means, so we may know what Jesus wants us to do

Babylon is composed of three leading parts or divisions How do I know that? The Book of Revelation so declares We find this made plain in Revelation 17 18, Revelation 16 19, and Revelation 16 13

In Revelation 17 18 we read, "The woman," (referring to this woman of Revelation 17) "which thou sawest is that great city, which reigneth over the kings of the earth" The angel declares in so many words that this woman is a great spiritual city

Revelation 16 19 tells us that this great city has three parts Here it is "The great city was divided into three parts" Great Babylon, then, has three leading divisions

Revelation 16 13 shows that these three parts of Babylon are the three great powers in the triumvirate of error—the dragon, the beast, and the false prophet In the Bible lecture on the eighth Sunday night of this institute we found from the Book of Revelation, that these three are respectively Paganism, Catholicism, and apostate Protestantism These three divisions embrace the entire religious world outside the fold of God's special message

Many Protestants declare that the harlot woman, whom God calls Babylon, is the Catholic church But the book of Revelation shows that Babylon in-

cludes far more than the Catholic church   Listen as I read Revelation 17·5
"Upon her forehead was a name written, MYSTERY, BABYLON THE
GREAT, THE **MOTHER**."

This woman Babylon is a mother   She has a whole group of daughters
who follow her erroneous ways   We must never forget that those Protestant
churches, who follow the errors of Catholicism, are the daughters of Babylon
God's message is, "Babylon is fallen!"   That especially applies to the Protestant
churches which were once comparatively pure and spiritual, but which now
have become worldly and formal

I have some facts here which will startle you   In 1931 Professor George
Betts of the Chicago University addressed a letter to 500 Protestant ministers
of all different denominations and to 250 divinity students, regarding their
beliefs in certain fundamental truths of the Bible   Do you know what tremendous changes he discovered had taken place in the attitude of many
Protestant ministers toward the truths of the Bible?

Here are the facts   He asked these ministers if they believed Jesus
Christ would return to earth again as the Bible teaches   Six out of every ten
of the ministers who responded told him that they did not believe in the
second coming of Jesus Christ   Among the ministerial students nine out of
every ten denied that Christ would return   What does this mean?   Babylon
is fallen, is fallen!

He asked them if they believed in the virgin birth of Jesus Christ   One
out of every four of the preachers denied that Jesus was virgin born   Among
the ministerial students nine out of ten didn't believe that Jesus was virgin
born. He asked them if they believed in the existence of the devil   Four out
of every ten preachers denied that there is any such being as the devil Among
the ministerial students eight out of every ten said there was no such thing
as a devil

He asked the ministers if they believed in the day of judgment   Four out
of every ten denied that there would be a day of judgment   Among the ministerial students eight out of ten declared that there never would be a day
of judgment

Remember that these ministers and divinity students were from all the
leading Protestant bodies   What does this mean?   Babylon is fallen, is fallen!
She has fallen away from the Bible, fallen away from the truth   It means that
God is calling those who love the truth, and who want the truth, to come out
of those Protestant churches who have departed from such cardinal truths of
the Bible   You want to bear in mind that these shocking figures show the
attitude of the ministers in 1931   Modernism has greatly increased since 1931,
and the unbelief of ministers in these cardinal truths of the Bible is far worse
today

A pure woman is ever true to her one husband   If she turns aside to
unite with any other man, she becomes a fallen woman, an impure woman
So when the church turns aside from following Jesus Christ to follow the sinful ways of the world, she becomes a fallen church and is guilty of spiritual
adultery   That is the meaning of James 4 4, which says, "Ye adulterers and
adulteresses, know ye not that the friendship of the world is enmity with
God? Whosoever therefore will be a friend of the world is the enemy of God "

The true church of Jesus Christ will be separate from the world and will
not follow the sinful ways of the world such as dancing, card-playing, drinking,
theatre-going, etc   When you find the true church, you will find a people
who have come out from the world and do not partake of the unclean things
of the world   God's message is, "Babylon is fallen"   This means the
churches are guilty of spiritual adultery in following the sinful ways of the
world   Is this the case with the Protestant churches today?

I want to ask you a series of questions which every thinking man and

woman can answer very quickly   Is there any place today where the people
of the world go, such as dances, theaters, prize fights, card parties, cocktail
parties, but what many church members go to the very same places of amuse-
ment?   Is there anything that the people of the world drink in the way of
intoxicating liquors, but what many church members partake of the same?
Is there anything that the people of the world do, but what many church
members also do?   What difference is there today between the average pro-
fessing Christian and the non-church people of the world?   What does this
mean?   Babylon is fallen!   "Come out of her, My people"   By following these
worldly ways, Protestant churches are fallen   Hence, God must call His
true people out of these churches

I thank God that there are a faithful few in every denomination, who do
not partake of these worldly ways   They walk in the narrow way with Jesus
God's eye is upon these true Christians in Protestant churches   Notice what
God says in Revelation 18 2, 4   "He cried mightily with a strong voice,
saying Babylon the great is fallen, is fallen, .   and I heard another voice
from heaven, saying Come out of her"

Some may say, "Mr Shuler, doesn't this call to come out of Babylon
apply to the time of Martin Luther, when he called people out of the Catholic
church to form the first Protestant church?"   All you need to do is to read
the call and you will see for yourself   Notice again as I read it, "I heard
another voice from heaven saying, Come out of her, My people, that ye be
not partakers of her sins, and that ye receive not of her plagues"

What plagues does this refer to?   It cannot refer to anything else but
the seven last plagues of Revelation 16   In the Bible lecture last Sunday
night we showed that those plagues will come during the space of about
twelve months before the appearing of Jesus Christ on the cloud at the end
of time

Martin Luther lived 400 years ago   The seven last plagues did not pertain to his time   This call of Jesus Christ to come out of Babylon, lest ye
receive of the plagues, could not possibly have any reference to Martin
Luther's time   The call to come out of Babylon can apply only to Christian
people who are living just before the plagues are poured out   I think that
is so plain that every person here sees it   ·

How many of you see that this call of Jesus Christ to His people to
come out of Babylon, lest they receive of the seven plagues, must apply to
these last days in which we are living?   Will you raise your hands?   Thank
you   I was sure that you did see this because it so plain

The call to come out of Babylon did not pertain to people, who lived two
hundred years ago, or people who lived one hundred and fifty years ago   It
pertains to people who are living now   This is the call of Christ for our day
It means that Jesus is calling His true followers out of the Protestant churches,
out of the Catholic church, and out of the heathen religions   These are the
three divisions of Babylon, and Christ's followers are coming out of these
by the thousands

There are certain questions that naturally arise at this point   What plan
is Jesus using to call His followers out of Babylon?   Where are His people
to go when they come out?   Into what is Jesus Christ calling His people?
Put down two texts and you will see the answer to these questions   Revelation 14 12 and Revelation 12 17

The 14th chapter shows, that there will be a great three-fold message
preached to every nation in the last days to call out a people who will keep
the commandments of God and the faith of Jesus   I read in Revelation 14 12
"Here is the patience of the saints   here are they that keep the commandments of God, and the faith of Jesus"   God tells you how you may know

His people whom He will call out from other religions   He declares that His people are those who keep the commandments of God and the faith of Jesus

You who have been coming to these meetings know that the fourth commandment of the eternal ten says that the seventh day is the Sabbath and in it thou shalt not do any work   Since this special people whom the Lord is calling out in the last days will keep the commandments, just ask yourself, What day will they keep as the Sabbath?   Yes, they will be a seventh-day Sabbath keeping people

Revelation 12.17 shows that these seventh day Sabbath keeping people who give this three-fold message to the entire world will constitute the remnant church, the last part of the true church of Christ in the last days   I read in Revelation 12 17, "The dragon was wroth with the woman, and went to make war with the remnant of her seed, which keep the commandments of God, and have the testimony of Jesus Christ"

This verse mentions five different items, **the dragon, the woman, the remnant, the commandments,** and **the testimony of Jesus Christ.** In the Bible lecture last Friday night we found the meaning of those five terms   The dragon is the devil   The woman is the church   The remnant is the last part of the church in the last days   The commandments of God are pre-eminently the Ten Commandments   The testimony of Jesus is the Spirit of Prophecy.

Now read the verse according to the Biblical meaning of these terms. "The devil was angry with the true church and went to make war with the last part of the true church in the last days which keep the Ten Commandments and have the Spirit of Prophecy"   That certainly is plain, isn't it? It shows beyond any doubt that the seventh-day Sabbath keeping people, who preach this three-fold message, are Christ's remnant church, into which He is calling His true followers from all other religions and churches

These words of Revelation 18 4, "Come out of her my people," show that there are true followers of Jesus Christ in all different denominations   In fact, Christ's true disciples are scattered in all different churches and religions   Sometime, somehow, someway, God's special message will reach them and they will come out into His remnant church   If Christ's followers were not in Babylon, then Christ would never say, "Come out of Babylon My people"   .

Here is something I want you to notice   When we preach this call of Jesus Christ to His people, to come out of other churches into the remnant church to keep all the commandments, we are not preaching denominationalism and we are not proselyting   We are merely sounding the call of Jesus Christ for His people today

The night that followed the last day of the Battle of Gettysburg was a terrible night   There were 50,000 dead and wounded strewn over the battlefield. About 9 o'clock a little spot of light appeared over the field of battle   It was an old Quaker with his lantern, hunting for his boy, who was in the Union army

As he went along with his lantern looking into the faces of the dead and wounded, once in awhile he would stop and call, "John Hartman, thy father calleth thee"   Some poor boy nearby would say to himself, "Would to God that were my father!"   He goes a little further on and holds up the lantern and calls, "John Hartman, thy father calleth thee"   He hears men groan, and he hears men curse

Suddenly away over there he hears a voice, a very weak voice, but the ears of love are keen   He hears a voice saying, "Here, Father! here, Father! This way, Father"   At last he finds his son   He moves a great pile of dead soldiers to get down to his own boy   He pulls his son out covered with blood, and lifts him to his shoulders and carries him to home and healing

Your name may not be ·John Hartman, but whatever it is, thy heavenly

Father calleth thee. Have you accepted His call? He wants to carry you to His wonderful home on high Friends, I want to accept His call and go home with Him, don't you? I want to go home with Jesus when He comes. How many of you want to accept the call of Jesus to go home with him? (It seemed that every hand was raised) Yes, we all want to do it

(Prayer)

Our dear heavenly Father, we thank Thee for how plain Thou hast made the truth. We stand tonight amid eternal issues These two symbolic women present a supreme test to every soul The pure, virtuous woman represents Thine own true system of worship This fallen harlot woman represents the great counterfeit universal system O, God, every soul in this world will stand under one or the other of these two systems Help each one to make a wise choice Help us to keep Thy commandments as Thou , hast given them, and not to follow them as they have been changed by men May every soul hear the call of God and permit Jesus to take him as it were, gently upon His own shoulder and bear him step by step, day by day, until His great second advent, when we shall go to be with Him in His home on high We ask it in His precious name Amen

THE SECRET OF SECURITY
AND PROTECTION

(The after-meeting talk which was presented on the Ninth Friday Night at the close of
the lecture on "The Woman in Scarlet")

The secret of security and protection is revealed in Proverbs 18 10, "The name of the Lord is a strong tower the righteous runneth into it, and is safe "

In the days of Noah, the greatest storm that ever struck the world up to that time took place All the people on the earth perished in that storm except eight How did God protect those eight people from destruction? Seven days before the flood began He called those eight people out from all the rest of the people into the ark God had said "Come out from the rest of the people and enter the ark." They responded to the call of God, and were saved

In the days of Lot, God rained down fire and brimstone upon Sodom and completely destroyed that city All the people in Sodom were destroyed except four How did God protect those four from being consumed? Just before the fire and brimstone fell, God called them out of Sodom, out from the rest of the people

These illustrations are especially applicable to us in these last days The Scriptures declare that as it was in the days of Noah and Lot, so it will be in the last days A most fearful storm is about to break upon this world We learned last Sunday night how the seven terrible plagues of Revelation 16 are about to smite the world How will God protect His true children?

Here is the answer in Revelation 18 4 "I heard another voice from heaven saying, Come out of her, (Babylon) that ye be not partakers of her sins, and that ye receive not of her plagues " God will call His people out just as He called those eight out in the days of Noah, and just as He called the four out of Sodom God will call His people out, so that they may be protected

God's true people are scattered in all the different religions and denominations. But God's message is calling them out into His remnant church, to keep the commandments of God and the faith of Jesus

Some may say, "Mr. Shuler, does this call to come out of Babylon mean that a person must leave the churches where people keep Sunday, and come into the church where they keep the seventh day?" It is not for me to tell you what to do. My commission is to preach the Word The Word of God will show anyone here what to do if he really wants to know.

God answers this question in Revelation 18 4. "I heard another voice from heaven saying, Come out of her, my people, that ye be not partakers of her sins" Why is God calling His people out of Babylon? "That ye be not partakers of her sins" What is sin? I John 3.4 says, "Sin is the transgression of the law." The law there referred to is no other law than the Ten Commandments

The law of God, the transgression of which is sin says that "The seventh day is the Sabbath . . in it thou shalt not do any work." You can see that any church which does not follow the practice of keeping the seventh day according to the Ten Commandments is guilty of sin The call of Jesus Christ to come out of Babylon that ye be not partakers of her sin, must mean coming out of the churches which do not keep the seventh day, and coming into the remnant church, that keeps the seventh day and follows all the commandments

If a person is not a member of any church, the call of Jesus Christ to him is to come out from the world and take his stand with the remnant church in the keeping of the commandments of God and the faith of Jesus. If he is a member of some church, which is not keeping the seventh day according to God's commandments, and is not giving this three-fold message to the world, then the call of Christ to him is to come out of that church into the remnant church, which keeps the commandments, and which is giving this three-fold message to the world.

If it were not necessary for His people to leave the churches, Jesus Christ wouldn't say in Revelation 18 4, "Come out of Babylon, My people" This matter of coming into the remnant church is another step with Jesus that the Lord wants you to take "Thy word is a lamp unto my feet and a light unto my path." As the Word shows you the next step, I know that you want to take it When we love Jesus, how can we do otherwise than to take each step with Him as He shows us the way?

Many of you who have been coming to these meetings for nine weeks have accepted every point of the message as it has been brought to you from the Bible. I know that you will gladly respond to this call of the Lord to come out of Babylon into His remnant church. The Word of God has revealed to you tonight that accepting God's message means coming out and taking one's stand with His remnant church.

Friends, every man and woman here is facing the tremendous question, **what will you do with God's message?** There is only one thing that I could ever think of doing and that is to accept it Since this message is from God, what else can you do but accept it? The only wise course, the only safe way, the only right thing is to respond to the call of the Lord and come out and take your stand with Christ's remnant

When the light of God's threefold message for these last days came to me, I was a member of a certain church that keeps the first day of the week, or Sunday I loved that church When I joined that church, it was my intention to remain in that church for the rest of my life But when I saw that the call of the Lord Jesus to His followers is to come out of Babylon, what else could I do as a Christian, but say, "Yes Jesus, I will come out in answer to Thy call, and take my stand to keep all of Thy commandments"

Friends, I want to tell you that this was the best decision I have ever made in all my life. I have been thankful ten-thousand times that I took my stand with Christ's remnant. When a person has a true heart, he is ready to do all that Jesus wants him to do. This is just as when Saul of Tarsus met Jesus. The first thing he said was, "Lord, what wilt thou have me to do?" He was ready to do just what God wanted him to do.

Every one who loves Jesus should think most carefully and prayerfully about this call of Jesus to come into His remnant church. Remember, the call is not from Mr Shuler If it were only a call from Mr. Shuler, you could go to bed and forget it.

Did you notice where this call is from? I want you to get this point because it is very important Listen again, to Revelation 18:4, "I heard another voice from heaven saying, Come out of her my people."

This is a call from the Lord. It is not something which I have made up. My purpose is to bring you only what God says in His book. The call is from heaven. It is the call of the Lord to your soul. When Jesus calls, we shouldn't allow anything or anybody to keep us from obeying the call.

I am closing this meeting with prayer, and I especially want to remember in this prayer, everyone who is determined under God to respond to the call, that the Lord has brought to him I invite you to form a prayer circle here at the front. We are facing tremendous issues. We need the help of God. I invite everyone here, who is determined to obey the call of God and come out and take his stand with God's remnant people. I invite you to come and stand here at the front for prayer.

Many of you have come forward before in these meetings, but this call goes further than any call we have ever given. This call is for the full acceptance of God's threefold message. It is a call to come out and take your stand with Christ's remnant. So, even if you have been forward before, this means that every soul who is purposed to accept God's message should come forward for this closing prayer.

As we stand I invite everyone, who is determined to respond to the call of the Lord, and to come out and take his stand with Christ's remnant to fill in here at the front. (As the choir sang, "I Surrender All," a large number came forward)

This is just what it takes "All to Jesus I surrender." Jesus went all the way for you Aren't you ready to go all the way for Him?"

I want to do the will of God. I want to obey my Saviour. When He says, "Come out," there isn't anything I can consider, but to "come out." He is my general. He is my captain It is not for me to say, "Lord, it is too hard. I don't see how I can do it. It isn't the way that I was raised." No! If Jesus says, "Do it," all I know is to do it.

I don't want to see a soul left out of this prayer. I am so happy to pray for these who have come forward to take their stand. But there are many who have not come forward who will take this step a little later. You want to do it You know it is right, and you want God to help you to do it. I want to pray for you, because if you want God to help you, He will help you. God can do everything for the man who wants His help. How many are there, who haven't come forward, who would like to signify by lifting your hand, "Brother Shuler, pray for me that God will help me do it?" Yes, there are many hands going up.

(Prayer)

"Lord, What Wilt Thou Have Me Do?"

(Preached on the ninth Saturday afternoon of the Campaign)

"Thus saith the Lord God; behold, I, even I, will both search My sheep, and seek them out As a shepherd seeketh out his flock in the day that he is among his sheep that are scattered; so will I seek out My sheep, and will deliver them out of all the places where they have been scattered in the cloudy and dark day" This is the reading of the Word of God in Ezekiel 34 11,12

You will notice that God is talking about searching out and gathering His sheep Every Bible reader knows that when God speaks about His sheep, He refers to His true followers upon the earth In this prophecy God declares that His sheep have been scattered But God is purposed to gather them from all the places where they have been scattered

The prophecy of Ezekiel 34 11,12 should be studied in connection with the prophecies of Revelation 18 2,4 and Revelation 14·6-12, which were explained in the Bible lecture last night Revelation 18 2,4 tells how Babylon has fallen from the truth, and that in view of this, God will call His people out of Babylon The fourth verse sounds the call, "Come out of her, My people, that ye be not partakers of her sins, and that ye receive not of her plagues" The text indicates that God's people have been scattered in that great false religious system known as Babylon.

God is calling His people out of Babylon If His people were not in Babylon, God could not, and would not, call upon them to come out of Babylon This shows that His true people are scattered in all these religions and denominations that comprise this great, universal system known as Babylon the great

In Revelation 14 6-12 we find that God will send a special three-fold message to every nation in the world, for the express purpose of calling His true followers out of Babylon into His remnant church, to keep the commandments of God and the faith of Jesus I thank God that He has made the truth so plain Isn't the truth sufficiently plain, so that every sincere soul may know for a certainty what the Lord wants him to do?

Here are three decisive points from the book of Revelation which show what God wants people to do at this time I draw the first point from Revelation 18 4 This verse shows that God's true people have been scattered in all the different denominations

I draw the second point from Revelation 12 17 This text shows that in the last days just prior to the return of Christ, God will have a remnant church upon the earth who will keep the commandments of God

The third decisive point is found in Revelation 14 6-12 and Revelation 18 4 These scriptures show that God will send a special message to every country, which will call His true followers from these religions and churches where they have been scattered, and bring them together into His remnant church

These three points from the Word of God make the truth very plain They show that the Lord wants every soul, who has not come out and taken his stand with His remnant church, to respond promptly to the call to come into His remnant church, to keep the commandments of God and the faith of Jesus This is the call of the Lord to His people today. This is what the Lord wants His people to do at this time

Every sincere Christian longs to know what the Lord wants him to do,

so that he can do it   His inquiry is, "Lord, what wilt Thou have me to do?
Lord, show me what to do, and I will gladly do it"

The Lord has answered this heart inquiry of every sincere soul   "I heard
another voice from heaven saying, come out of her, My people, that ye be not
partakers of her sins, and that ye receive not of her plagues"

Mark this point well   Everyone of Christ's true followers will in due time
respond to His call, and will come into His remnant fold   How do I know
that?   Here it is in John 10 27   Jesus speaks of His church as His fold, and of
His true disciples as His sheep   He says, "My sheep hear My voice, and I
know them, and they follow Me"

What will His sheep do?   His sheep will heed His voice   They will follow
Him   His sheep obey His voice   When Jesus calls upon them to come out
of Babylon, they will come out and take their stand with His remnant   Just as
surely as you are one of Christ's sheep you will come out and take your stand
with His remnant to keep His commandments   "My sheep hear My voice,
and they follow Me"

Jesus came unto His own, and, sad to say, His own received Him not
Have you ever wondered why it was that the great majority of the Jewish
people rejected the Son of God?   Why did only a few of the great mass of
Jewish people believe on the Lord Jesus?   When Jesus was here among them,
He told them why they didn't believe on Him

Jesus didn't hesitate to tell the truth   He was a plain preacher   He didn't
preach smooth things to please the people

In John 10 26 He told the Jews, "Ye believe not, because ye are not of My
sheep´   . My sheep hear my voice,   and they follow me"   This was the
same as saying, "If you were My sheep, you would accept Me as your Saviour
You would accept the truth that I have brought to you, but you believe not,
you reject the truth, because you are not of My sheep!"

This explains why only a comparative few of professed Christians, in these
days will obey the call of Jesus Christ to come out of Babylon into His remnant church   But please let every soul bear in mind, that if you are one of
Christ's true sheep, you will both hear and respond to His call, to come out of
Babylon into His remnant to keep the commandments of God and the faith
of Jesus.

A church can be the true church of God at one time, and later on it will
be necessary to even come out of that church, and unite with another church,
in order for one to continue to be in the true church of God   The Jewish
church was the true church of God in the days of Moses and David   But in
the days of Jesus Christ, when the Jewish people refused to accept the truth,
it became necessary for the Lord Jesus Christ to call His true followers out of
the Jewish church, to form a new church, even the Christian church

Consecrated honest people in all these various churches will accept God's
message as truth as the message reaches them   There is no hope of a complete
or collective restoration to the real truth for any Protestant church as a body
Hence, the only way that God's truth can march forward is for Christ to call
from these churches those true Christians who are willing to obey all His
commandments

You have an exact parallel of this in the days of Jesus and the apostles
The Jewish church was once the true church of God, His peculiar people, His
special treasure   But when the Jewish church, as a body, rejected the message
of God that Christ brought to them, what did God do?   He called His true
ones out of the Jewish church to form the Christian church.

Never forget that James and John and Peter and all the twelve apostles had
to come out of the Jewish church, to become the disciples of Jesus Christ   Of
course there came a time when the Gentiles began to accept Christianity and
entered the Christian church, but the first people to enter the Christian church

in the days of Christ came from the Jewish church. Every one of those 3000 people who united with the church of Christ on the day of Pentecost had to come out of the church where they were, in order to be in the church where God wanted them to be

It is the same today. When the Protestant churches rejected God's special message for these last days, God proceeded to call His true people out of these churches to form His remnant church Some people think it is sacrilege to leave their church to join another church Other people say, "I don't see how I could leave my present church in order to unite with the Sabbath-keeping church" The Lord Jesus has really settled this matter for us He says, "Come out of her, My people," and our only thought should be to obey His commandments

A good soldier needs only to know the orders of his captain Let us be good soldiers of Jesus Christ and follow His orders on coming out of Babylon We must never forget that the Christian church in the days of Jesus Christ began with a few faithful souls, who came out of the Jewish church in which they had been born and raised Think of this! What if they had refused to leave their church? All Christian people greatly honor Peter, James, John, and Paul. But listen to me You would never have heard of Peter, James, John, or Paul, and they would never have become Christ's apostles, if they had not left the church in which they had been born and raised, to unite with Christ's new church for their day.

If Martin Luther had remained in the Roman church and followed its creed, there would never have been a Lutheran Church If Martin Luther had taken the position that most Lutheran people take, about staying in their church, there never would have been a Lutheran Church He would have remained in the Catholic Church.

If John Wesley had remained in the Church of England and been satisfied with its teachings, there never would have been a Methodist Church

If John Knox had remained in the Catholic Church, there never would have been a Presbyterian Church in the United States

If Roger Williams had remained in the Church of England, he never would have been the founder of the Baptist Church in the United States

If Alexander Campbell had remained in the Church of England, he never would have been the founder of the Disciples of Christ Church

If James White had remained with the Disciples of Christ, he never would have been used of God along with other men to inaugurate the remnant church

God expects us to move forward with the advancing light Some people say, "I don't see how I can go into a different church from the one to which my husband belongs, or a different church from that to which my mother and father belong, or a different church from the one which my brothers and sisters attend " We must ever bear in mind that if the situation demands it, we must be prepared to place obedience to the call of Jesus above love of father, love of mother, love of wife, love of husband, love of brothers and sisters, and all earthly friends

In Matthew 10:37 He says, "He that loveth father or mother more than Me is not worthy of Me " In Luke 14.25-27 He says, "If any man come to Me, and hate not his father, and mother, and wife, and children, and brethren, and sisters, yea, and his own life also, he cannot be my disciple And whosoever doth not bear his cross, and come after Me, cannot be my disciple "

Do you know that the man whom God called to be the father of the faithful had to leave his own kinfolks, and go into a land of which he knew nothing, in order to respond to the call of the Lord? We should ponder carefully the call of Abraham If we are of the children of Abraham, we shall do the works of Abraham. We shall have the spirit of Abraham It takes the spirit of Abraham to go through to the kingdom of God.

I turn and read Genesis 12 1, 5 "Now the Lord had said unto Abram, Get thee out of thy country, and from thy kindred, and from thy father's house, unto a land that I will shew thee" God called upon him to leave his own kinfolks, and go into a country which he had never seen

Did Abraham hold back and say, "O, Lord, I don't see how I can leave my kinfolks I can't go so far away, that I may never see them again I don't see how I can go into a new country of which I know nothing How will I make a living? Maybe I will starve to death over there" Abraham didn't talk that way What did he do? Look at verse 5

"Abram took Sarah his wife, and Lot his brother's son, and all their substance that they had gathered, and they went forth to go into the land of Canaan; and into the land of Canaan they came" They started out to Canaan, and they kept on until they got there It takes that kind of a spirit to go to heaven We read in Hebrews 11 8 that by faith Abraham went out to a land not knowing whither he went. Friends, we need the same faith and surrender to the will of God that Abraham had

Some people say, "It is so hard to leave my church where I have been all these years All my friends are in that church I've been in that church for years, and it is hard for me to even think about separating myself from that church" I will grant that all this is true But what does Jesus say? In 2 Corinthians 12 9 he says, "My grace is sufficient for thee" In Luke 14 27 He says, "Whosoever doth not bear his cross and come after Me, cannot be My disciple" For your encouragement He says in Isaiah 41 10, "Fear thou not, for I am with thee, be not dismayed, for I am thy God. I will strengthen thee, yea, I will help thee; yea, I will uphold thee with the right hand of My righteousness"

We should not hold back when the Lord wants us to go forward Even though you think it is going to be hard, His grace is sufficient The blessings that He has for you in the future, if you will be true to Him will far outweigh the sacrifices of the present When Jesus calls, we mustn't let anything or anybody hold us back from responding Notice how important it is to heed the call of Jesus In Luke 9:59-62 I read:

"He said unto another, Follow Me But He said, Lord, suffer me first to go and bury my father" This looked as if it were quite a reasonable request, didn't it? The Lord said, "Follow Me" The man said, if you will wait a little while, Lord I will do it, but let me go and bury my father first Notice what Jesus said to the man "And Jesus said unto him, Let the dead bury their dead. but go thou and preach the kingdom of God"

He shows us the supreme importance of responding to His call You can't put the love of father above responding to the call of Jesus Christ He must be first, last and always He must be our supreme Lord

"Another also said, Lord, I will follow thee; but let me first go bid them farewell, which are at home at my house" Just let me go and say good-bye to my folks at home This looked like a very reasonable request It wouldn't take long to go and say good-bye Jesus said unto him, "No man, having put his hand to the plough, and looking back, is fit for the kingdom of God"

The poet has well said,

> "Who answers Christ's insistent call
> Must give himself, his life, his all,
> Without one backward look
> Who sets his hand unto the plow
> And glances back with anxious brow,
> His calling hath mistook
> Christ claims him wholly for His own;
> He must be Christ's—and Christ's alone"

We have a striking lesson in Matthew 4 18-22 on how we should respond to the call of Jesus, as soon as His call comes to us "And Jesus, walking by the Sea of Galilee, saw two brethren, Simon called Peter, and Andrew his brother, casting a net into the sea; for they were fishers And He saith unto them, Follow Me, and I will make you fishers of men " Notice now how quickly they responded "And they straightway left their nets, and followed Him "

"And going on from thence, He saw other two brethren, James the son of Zebedee, and John his brother, in a ship with Zebedee their father, mending their nets, and He called them " Notice what happened? "And they immediately " They didn't say, O, Lord, we have our fishing nets to take care of Just wait until we put our nets away, and tomorrow we will come " No! "They immediately left the ship and their father and followed Him "

Matthew had a lucrative position He was a tax collector This was a good-paying job Jesus passed by his desk where he was taking in the money and said, "Matthew, follow Me" Matthew turned to one of his assistants, and said, "Here, you take care of this tax money, I am leaving to follow this man Jesus " This is why he became one of Christ's chosen apostles, and his name has come down to us as one of those great Christian leaders

Friends, it takes that kind of spirit if we are one hundred per cent for the Lord Some people think, "O, if I could have been back there and had heard Jesus speak to me, as He spoke to Peter, and James and John and Matthew, Yes, I would have left everything too, and responded without any delay " You can check up on yourself How are you responding to the call of Jesus in Revelation 18 4 to come out of Babylon into His remnant church? Take note of this, and then you will see how you would have responded if you had been among those who first heard Jesus

May it be said of you and me—

> He saw God's truth, but did not stay
> To ask if others saw the way
> Content was he in heart to know
> That Jesus walked there here below
> And evermore He walks with men,
> That men may walk His paths again
> And He is more than all besides,
> For others fail, but He abides

The wisest thing, and the best thing, and the only safe course is to obey the call of the Lord The most fatal mistake that any man can ever make is to fail to respond to the call of Jesus Christ To reject the call of Jesus Christ means to suffer eternal loss To obey the call of Jesus Christ will bring you an eternal happy home in that heavenly city which He has prepared for His own

One evening, about dark, a farmer in Minnesota started to cross a lake in a small sail boat The wind changed suddenly, as it can on those lakes, and a gust of wind overturned his boat in the middle of the lake He was a good swimmer, so he started to swim to the part of the shore where he thought his house stood

It was in the winter time and the water was covered with masses of floating ice It was dark and he became confused and went in the wrong direction His strength began to give out As he was sinking in the freezing water, he heard a voice It was the voice of his little girl on the back porch of their home calling, "Father, father "

Her voice put fresh life into him He thought, "If she would only call once more, I could tell then which way home is by the sound of her voice But, I am afraid she will go in the house and close the door, because she has heard no reply to her call "

Just as he was about to go under, another call came, "Father " He turned and struck out in the opposite direction, because he had been going away from home all the time He had gotten turned around in the darkness, and was going in the wrong direction He fought his way through the ice, and reached the shore and home at last

Friends, there is a voice calling you today, which, if you will heed, will bring you home to God In Isaiah 30 21 we read, "Thine ears shall hear a word behind thee, saying, This is the way, walk ye in it " That still small voice has been speaking to you during the nine weeks of this Bible Institute As you have heard the Word of God, this still small voice has said to your heart, "This is what you ought to do This is the right way This is the truth This is the way, walk ye in it " O, I hope that none here will fail to heed this still small voice It will guide you home if only you will heed it

In the case of this farmer, his very life depended on heeding that call, and turning in the opposite direction, so he could follow the call So it is life or death according to how we respond to the call of Jesus It may mean going in the opposite direction from the way you have been going, but following His voice leads home

The highest privilege that can ever come to a human being in these last days is the privilege of responding to the call of Jesus Christ "Come out of her, My people, that ye be not partakers of her sins, and that ye receive not of her plagues "

We were happy to see so many people respond to the call of the Lord last night I am sure that there are others here today, who have made their decision since last night There are likely some present who were not here last night, whose minds are prepared to respond to the call of the Lord

I invite you to form a prayer circle here at the front I want those who came forward last night to come forward again I want you to lead the way today, because there are others who will follow you in responding to the call of the Lord We shall stand and sing as you come forward for prayer

(After the people came forward, the speaker asked them to take seats at the front and remain for a little further instruction The rest of the audience was dismissed)

(Prayer)

Heavenly Father, we thank Thee for these dear ones who are responding to the call of Jesus today Jesus has shown them what to do They have heard His call The voice from heaven is saying, "Come out of her My people Come out from among them, and be ye separate Come out and obey My commandments "

Dear Lord, we thank Thee that they have a heart to respond to this call We pray, O, Jesus, that Thou wilt fill every one of them with great joy for having made this good decision May Thy peace that passeth understanding fill their hearts Jesus has said, "O, that thou hadst harkened to My commandments! then had thy peace been as a river "

Dear Lord, bless others here There are many, Lord, who have heard the message Some must lead the way There will be many others Lord, who will walk this path ere these meetings shall close We thank Thee for them We thank Thee that there are scores of other sincere hearts who will respond to the call of Thy Son When Jesus comes may it be that each of us will be ready and will be able to see Him face to face We ask it in His precious name Amen

Mark of the Beast

I have an important radiogram tonight from the New Jerusalem to Mr. and Mrs Everybody. It reads: "If any man worship the beast and his image and receive his mark in his forehead, or in his hand, the same shall drink of the wine of the wrath of God, which is poured out without mixture into the cup of his indignation, and he shall be tormented with fire and brimstone in the presence of the holy angels, and in the presence of the lamb; and the smoke of their torment ascendeth up for ever and ever. and they have no rest day nor night, who worship the beast and his image, and whosoever receiveth the mark of his name" You will find that in your Bible in Revelation 14.9-11

This is the most solemn warning that has ever fallen upon mortal ears I. will not attempt to preach on such a solemn warning from God without asking God for special help Will you join me in a word of prayer (Prayer followed).

Regardless of what the mark of the beast is, there can be no doubt about the fearful consequences of receiving this mark God says, "If any man" It matters not whether he is a Methodist, or a Baptist, a Catholic, or a Christian Scientist, a Jew, or an infidel If any man receives the mark of this beast, he must drink the unmingled wrath of God and be tormented with fire and brimstone by the Lord In view of this we ought to make up our minds tonight, that if it takes our life, we will never receive the mark of the beast

In view of this fearful warning, you would naturally think that no one would ever choose to receive the mark of the beast, but on the contrary the Bible shows that in the final crisis nearly everyone in the world will have the mark of the beast in his forehead, or in his right hand You will find this in Revelation 13 16, 17 "He causeth all, both small and great, rich and poor, free and bond, to receive a mark in their right hand, or in their foreheads. and that no man might buy or sell save he that had the mark, or the name of the beast, or the number of his name"

The mark of the beast will be offered by the power of civil law The powers of earth will decree that no person may secure employment, that he cannot get a job, that he cannot buy or sell anything unless he has the mark. Think of this fearful issue just ahead The powers of earth will decree that you cannot buy or sell, unless you have the mark; and then later on they will pass a law that if you will not receive the mark of the beast you will be sentenced to death On the other hand, Almighty God declares that if you take the mark of the beast, He will punish you with fire and brimstone Just think of what we are coming to! If any people ever needed the help of God to show how to take their stand on the right side, it is you and I today

Prophecy says, "He causeth all, both small and great, rich and poor, to receive a mark in their right hand, or in their forehead." In Revelation 13 8 we find that all the people in the world will obey this beast power, even above God, except a faithful few who will cling to God's commandments at all costs The prophecy shows in Revelation 14 9-14 that when the warning against the mark of the beast has been preached to the people of every nation, the Lord Jesus Christ will return from heaven to gather the righteous and to slay the disobedient That makes it clear that the warning against the mark of the beast is God's last call to humanity

Think of the solemnity of this! God's last call to men If a man rejects

God's last call, what hope is there for him? What hope could there be for him? The warning against the mark of the beast is God's last call to men Read the chapter for yourself In Revelation 14 9-12 you find the warning, and then when you read on, you will note that the next event is the coming of Christ on the cloud.

The third angel's message about the mark of the beast is the third and final part of the three-fold message that God has appointed for these last days This three-fold message is pictured in Revelation 14 under the symbolism of three angels flying in mid-air, preaching a mighty three-fold message to the people of every country. It is the third angel who sounds the warning against the mark of the beast

This series of meetings has been dedicated to the exposition of this great three-fold message As these meetings have been conducted from week to week for ten weeks, each successive feature of this great three-fold message has been explained from the Holy Scriptures Tonight we come to the last item—the mark of the beast O, friends, if you have never made a move in these meetings, I pray that tonight God's last call will move you into action

No one can understand what the mark of the beast is, until he first knows what the beast is This beast of Revelation 13 and 14 against which God gives such a solemn warning, is not a literal animal It is not an animal like a lion or a bear The beast is symbolic of a certain power on the earth In just the same way, a lion is used today to represent England, a bear to represent Russia, or the Buffalo the United States The beast power is described in Revelation 13 1-10, and the image of the beast is explained in Revelation 13·11-15

Many of you have been coming to these meetings for nine weeks, and we are happy that this is so You will recall that we explained the identity of the beast and the image of the beast on the eighth Sunday night, or two weeks ago tonight I recognize that there are people here tonight, who are attending this Bible Institute for the first time Will all who are here at this institute for the first time please raise your hands? (About fifty raised their hands) We are glad that you are here There are others present who have heard only a very few lectures You who just raised your hands, and others who have only heard a few lectures, you will have to bear in mind, that the limits of time in one lecture will not permit me to go back and repeat the Biblical explanations that I have been making here for nine weeks In this lecture I must necessarily build on Biblical conclusions which have been clearly established in former lectures

We have shown by the Scriptures that the beast referred to in Revelation 13 is a symbol of the papacy or the Roman Catholic hierarchy The image of the beast is a federation of Protestant churches in the United States, which will eventually gain control of our government and enforce certain religious practices by the power of civil law The wrath of God without mixture refers to the seven last plagues on which I talked last Sunday night

The mark of the beast is not a literal mark that will be stamped on people's foreheads or on their hand Why not? Just think a little bit The beast is symbolic hence, the mark of the beast must be symbolic Prophecy would not couple a literal mark with a symbolic beast The mark of the beast is something you can resist God charges you to resist it If the mark of the beast were a literal mark that could be stamped on a man's forehead or stamped in his hand and he couldn't resist it, they could tie a man down and place the mark on him whether he wanted it or not But God charges you to resist it, and the fact that you can resist it shows that it is not a literal mark, because you could not resist receiving a literal mark They could overpower you physically and make you take it.

The mark of the beast has to do with the rejection of the authority of God

This is why God prounounces such a fearful warning It is the accepting of something else in the place of the authority of God You know perfectly well that marks are used for the purpose of identification The laundry puts a mark on my collars and on my shirts to distinguish them from other men's collars and shirts A rancher puts a mark on his cattle to distinguish them from other ranchmen's cattle So the mark of the beast is symbolic of some spiritual observance, which distinguishes those who accept it as obeying the authority of the Catholic power on this particular point

Those who resist the mark of the beast will be distinguished as being obedient to God in that particular issue This is exactly what you find in the Bible Put down Revelation 14 12

In verses 9-11 in Revelation 14 we find the warning against the mark of the beast, and in the very next verse God tells you what to do to escape the mark of the beast It reads· "Here is the patience of the saints here are they that keep the commandments of God, and the faith of Jesus "

This shows that those who refuse to receive the mark of the beast will be those, who keep the commandments of God and the faith of Jesus The mark of the beast must be some disobedience to one of God's commandments It also shows that the only way a person can ever avoid receiving the mark of the beast in the final crisis is to make his decision to keep the commandments of God and the faith of Jesus This is why, night after night, we have appealed to you to make your decision to keep the commandments of God and the faith of Jesus I repeat, The only way that you will ever avoid receiving the mark of the beast is to make your decision to obey the commandments

Revelation 14 7 shows that the mark of the beast is in direct opposition to the commandment of God that reveals Him as the Creator Look at the Ten Commandments Here on this chart are the Ten Commandments as they are recorded in the Bible in Exodus 20 1-17 It is an undeniable fact that the fourth commandment, the Sabbath precept, which requires the keeping of the seventh day, or Saturday, is the only commandment of the ten that reveals God as the Creator

Now follow me closely Jesus Christ bids men keep the seventh-day Sabbath He is the Creator of the world As the eternal Son of God He made the world in six days On the seventh He rested Then He sanctified, or set that day apart for men to keep Jesus Christ bids men keep the seventh day as a sign that He is the Creator and the only Saviour The Catholic Church bids men keep the first day of the week, or Sunday, as the sign that they have the power to change God's commandments So **the mark of the beast is the attempted change that the Catholic power has made in reference to the weekly Sabbath.**

Do you know that Catholics admit that the instituting of the first day of the week, or Sunday as the day for Christians to keep is a mark of their power? On October 28, 1895 a certain gentleman wrote to Cardinal Gibbons, who at that time was the only Catholic cardinal in America He asked Cardinal Gibbons if the change of the Sabbath from the seventh day to the first was a mark of the authority of the Catholic Church The answer from the Cardinal's office was as follows "Of course the Catholic Church claims that the change of the Sabbath was her act   And **the act is a mark of her ecclesiastical power and authority in religious matters."** Just as Jesus holds up the Sabbath as a sign of His power, the Catholic power holds up Sunday as a sign of their power

Here is a statement from a Catholic catechism called the "Abridgment of Christian Doctrine" written by Rev Henry Tuberville On page 58 we find this Question How prove you that the church has power to command feasts and holy days? Answer· By the very act of changing the Sabbath into Sunday" The Catholics openly admit that the change of the Sabbath from the seventh day to the first by their church is a mark of their power to make laws binding on the consciences of men

Catholics openly boast that the keeping of Sunday by Protestants without any Bible evidence is an act of worship to the authority of the Catholic church. Listen to this statement from a book written by Father Segur, which bears the title, "Plain Talk to Protestants" On page 213 he says, "The observance of Sunday by the Protestants is an homage they pay, in spite of themselves to the authority of the Catholic church"

Some will say, "Mr Shuler, I don't think it makes any difference what day a man keeps just so he keeps a day" But bear in mind that the Sabbath question is not merely a matter of days It is not a question merely of whether you will rest on Saturday or Sunday If that is all there is to it, I would not take one minute of my time, or of your time to ever talk about it This is a question of whether we will obey Jesus Christ as our supreme Lord by keeping the seventh day, which He sanctified for man, or whether we will put the papacy above Jesus Christ by keeping Sunday, which they have attempted to substitute for the keeping of the seventh day This is the most tremendous of all questions, Whom will we acknowledge as the supreme authority in religious matters? Choosing Sunday in the place of the Bible Sabbath is actually placing the authority of the Catholic church above the authority of God This is a very serious matter

Jesus Christ says in Matthew 15 9, "In vain they do worship Me, teaching for doctrines the commandments of men" That is the way it was when He was here, and it is just the same today They are in many cases teaching for doctrines the commandments of men If we substitute the commandment of man in the place of the commandment of God, then our worship is in vain Jesus plainly says, "In vain they do worship Me, teaching for doctrines the commandments of men"

The keeping of the seventh day is a commandment of Jesus Christ The keeping of the first day, or Sunday, is a commandment of man The keeping of the first day in the place of the seventh is putting a commandment of man above a commandment of Jesus Christ

When this light was brought to me, there was only one way I could go and be a true follower of Jesus Christ, and that was to make my decision to obey Jesus Christ as my supreme Lord in keeping His seventh day Jesus has done so much for me He left the glories of heaven and came and died on the cross in my place to save me How could I think of being untrue to Him? How could I obey any earthly power above Jesus Christ? O, I think of that little song:

> "Keep me true, Lord, keep me true
> Keep me true, Lord, true to you
> May all I say or strive to do
> Prove, dear Lord, I'm true to you"

The book of Revelation shows that God has ordained that the Sabbath question shall be the final test on which men and women will decide for or against Jesus Christ in these closing days In Revelation 7 1-3, on which I preached Tuesday night, we find that God will send a message in the last days to place the seal of the living God on the foreheads of His servants In Revelation 13 16, 17 we find that the powers of the earth will attempt to cause all people to receive the mark of the beast on their forehead, or in their right hand

Every soul will have to choose between receiving the seal of God on his forehead, or the mark of the beast on his forehead, or in his right hand If a man doesn't choose to receive the seal of God by surrendering his heart and mind to obey God, he will have to take the mark of the beast on his forehead, or in his hand   This shows that the mark of the beast is just the opposite of the seal of God.

In my Bible lecture on Tuesday night I read four texts from the Bible where God declares four times over that the seventh-day Sabbath is His sign or seal   Now you can see, that since the mark of the beast is just the opposite from the seal of God and the seal of God is the Sabbath which Christ has appointed, then the mark of the beast must be the Sunday institution, which the Catholic power has attempted to establish in the place of the seventh day that the Lord sanctified for man   This is another proof that the mark of the beast consists in the attempted change of the Sabbath by the Catholic power

There is a principle in Romans 6 16 that I wish you to notice   I shall ask you two questions and let you answer them, and you will see for yourself what is the mark of the beast   Romans 6 16 says. "Know ye not, that to whom ye yield yourselves servants to obey, his servants ye are to whom ye obey." There are eight words in that verse that I should like to have you keep in mind **"To whom ye obey, his servants ye are."**

I want to ask you two questions   First, when a person keeps the seventh day as the Sabbath, whom does he obey? Yes, he obeys God   That question admits of only one answer.

The seventh day of the week is the only day that the Lord has ever sanctified for His people to keep   The seventh day of the week is the only day of weekly observance that God ever commanded men to hallow   So when a man keeps that seventh day holy, he shows that he obeys God   Scripture says, "To whom ye obey, his servants ye are"   So when a man keeps the seventh day, he shows that he is a servant of God

Here is the second question   When a person keeps Sunday as the Sabbath, or Lord's day, whom is he obeying? Many Christians honestly think that in keeping Sunday they are obeying Jesus Christ. But God is sending a message to enlighten the people concerning the Sabbath truth   The fact is that the person who keeps Sunday as the Lord's day does not obey Jesus in reference to the day that he keeps.

He may obey Christ in everything else, but if he keeps the first day of the week, he is not obeying Jesus Christ in the matter of the day that he keeps Why not? Bcause there is no place where Jesus Christ, or God, has ever told anybody to keep the first day of the week for any reason whatsoever   There is no command in the entire Bible to keep the first day of the week

Now let us go a little further   If there is no command in the Bible to keep the first day of the week, and a man selects Sunday as a holy day, whom then is he obeying? There can be only one answer to that question   The answer is, that he is obeying the authority of the Catholic church   Remember that "To whom ye obey, his servants ye are"   So in keeping the first day of the week he shows that he is a follower of Rome in that respect   Again you see how the attempted change of the Sabbath constitutes the mark of identification between those who obey God as the supreme authority regarding the Sabbath, and those who obey the authority of the papacy as supreme in regard to Sunday

This brings every soul face to face with the most important issue of all his life   Will you receive the seal of God? Or will you receive the mark of the beast? You ought to say like the psalmist in Psalm 119 60, "I made haste and delayed not to keep thy commandments"   Without a moment's hesitation we ought to choose Christ's way.

During World War II people had to choose between two different flags (At this juncture the speaker held up the Stars and Stripes in one hand, and the flag of Japan in the other). People had to choose whether or not they would follow the flag of the rising sun, or the glorious Stars and Stripes. If you had to choose between these two flags, it wouldn't take you a split second

to make up your mind what you would do, would it? Why not then, without
delaying another hour choose the seventh day, which is Christ's flag, or sign,
in the place of the first day, or Sunday, which is a sign of the Catholic power?

Some will say, "I would be glad to keep Saturday, but it interferes with
my work, my job, or my business" If your job or business is holding you
back, think of Christ's great question, "What shall it profit a man if he shall
gain the whole world and lose his own soul?" It would be better to starve to
death keeping the true Sabbath than to gain the whole world and die in disobedience to God's commandments But you will not starve to death. Jesus
Christ has promised that if you obey Him, He will provide for you In
Matthew 6:33 He says, "Seek ye first the kingdom of God and His righteousness, and all these things shall be added unto you"

If you want to escape the mark of the beast, you will have to put obedience
to God above all money matters, because the time will come when you cannot
buy or sell, or get a job unless you have that mark. You will have to put
obedience to God above all money matters, above all church ties; and if need
be even above family ties.

Some say, "It is too hard to keep the seventh day when you have to go
against your own relatives and your friends." If you feel that way, I wish
you could see Jesus tonight, as He hung upon the cross for you. See the
blood falling from His hands and feet into which they drove the cruel nails to
free you from sins Look at His back torn to shreds where they had beaten
Him Hear the crowd jeering at Him and ridiculing Him Can you look upon
the suffering Jesus and say, "Jesus, it is too hard to keep your day, the seventh
day?" No! He says to you, "Whosoever doth not bear his cross, and come
after Me, cannot be My disciple."

If we escape the mark of the beast, we must have the courage and back-
bone to stand alone for God. In Revelation 13 8 it says, "All that dwell upon
the earth shall worship him, (this beast) except those whose names are written
in the book of life" I do not know what trials and tribulations may await
you in keeping the seventh day, but this I know, those who stand true to
God's commandments will gain the victory and will stand triumphant upon the
sea of glass in front of God's throne

In a certain battle the Duke of Wellington called for volunteers to capture
a certain hill This hill held the key to victory. He knew they would never
win the battle unless they captured this certain hill. It was very heavily fortified and he knew it would mean a great loss of life. But the only way to win
the battle was to capture the hill

So he addressed his army, which was common in those days He said,
"Men we shall never win this battle unless we capture that hill. It is a dangerous undertaking Many a man who goes out to take that hill will never
come back But it must be done. I have the power as your commander-in-
chief to select certain regiments and simply say, 'Regiments 55, 56, 57, charge
and take the hill,' and you would go. But today I shall not do it that way.
I shall call for volunteers. I do not want you to be influenced by looking at
me. I shall turn my back, and every man will make his own decision I want
every man in this army, who is willing to volunteer to take the hill to advance
two paces in front of the rest of the army"

He turned his back a little while. Soon his aide saluted him and said,
"General, you may turn around and look! The entire line has advanced" O,
friends, can't we do the same for the Captain of our salvation? What do you
say? Those men were willing to take their life in their hands to win the favor
of the king Our great General, the Lord Jesus Christ, is calling for an advance
step He wants us to step two paces in front of other people by following
His commands as He gave them.

Wouldn't it be fine if we could just send up the signal to our heavenly

General and say, "Jesus the entire line here in this auditorium, November 10, 1946 has stepped forward to obey Thee"? O, how my heart yearns to see this! Can we not send this word up to Jesus tonight? How good it would be if every soul would make his decision to receive the seal of God and surrender his heart, his soul, and his mind, to do what Jesus Christ says and to keep His commandments How many want to send the signal up to Jesus by your up-lifted hand, that by His grace and power you will keep the seventh day, as Jesus sanctified it for you? How many hands do I see on this? (Many, many hands were raised) O, I wish we could see every hand!

(Prayer)

Our dear heavenly Father, we thank Thee that Thou hast sent this great three-fold message to enlighten people concerning the issues that lie just ahead Lord, we see that everyone must make his choice between Thy seal on his forehead, or the mark of the beast on his forehead, or in his right hand

Help us to choose Thy seal Help us, Lord, to surrender our hearts and minds to Jesus Christ He gave His all for us. Help us to give our all for Him

Bless those who have raised their hands Give them strength from heaven to obey Thee Bless others who believe and want to do what is right.

Help every soul to accept this message that Thou hast sent May it be that when Jesus comes we shall have Thy seal on our foreheads and be able to greet Jesus with joy at His appearing and go with Him to be with Him forever We ask it in His precious name Amen

One Hundred Thieves Caught in One Church

(Preached on the Tenth Tuesday Night of the Campaign)

There is only one right plan of church finance, and that is the plan set forth in God's Word I invite you to consider three questions First, Should the minister of the gospel be paid for preaching? The answer is found in Luke 10 7 The Lord Jesus, in speaking about those whom He sent out to preach, said, "The labourer is worthy of his hire "

My second question is, How much shall the minister of the gospel be paid? According to the principles set forth in the Bible, he should be paid a sufficient wage to support himself and his family The practice in certain city churches of paying ministers large salaries of four, five, seven, ten, and sometimes twenty-thousand dollars a year, is contrary to Christ The paying of these large salaries makes money a factor in the minister's call and is out of keeping with the spirit of true ministry.

To illustrate A minister at a certain church in Baltimore is receiving $4,000 a year A church in Chicago hears about this man, and they want him to preach at their church So they send word to this minister, "If you will come to Chicago and preach at our church, we will pay you $5,000 a year" Next Sunday the minister in Baltimore gets up before his congregation, and says "Brethren, the Lord has called me to Chicago" Did He? No It was that extra thousand a year which called him to Chicago It was not the call of the Almighty, but it was the call of the "almighty dollar "

Is it any wonder that people of the world who see such things, and hear such things, have lost confidence in religion, and think that religion is just another racket? As long as these city churches vie with one another as they do in paying men large salaries, this unfortunate situation will continue to exist

The practice of paying large salaries to ministers puts the ministry on a commercial basis, which is something entirely foreign to the true spirit of the gospel ministry It is proper and right that the doctor, the lawyer, and the dentist should make as much money as they can, provided they make it honestly But being a minister of Jesus Christ cannot and must not be placed on a money-making basis This practice of one church offering a minister $500 or $1,000 more a year than he is getting from another church is leading some ministers to preach for money and not for souls They preach to please the people, and will not tell the people the plain truth for fear the salary would not be forthcoming

No man can be a true preacher unless he is called of God One of the evidences that a minister is called of God is that he will not be greedy for money If a minister is greedy for money, he cannot be a true minister of God The Bible condemns in scathing language ministers who preach for money You never need expect to learn the truth from a man who preaches for money.

My third question is, How shall the money be secured with which to pay the minister? Shall the board of deacons assess each member a certain amount? If there is a shortage, shall the sisters give a "Bean Supper," or a "Rag Doll Party" or a "Fair," or a "Bazaar" to earn money for the church?

Here are two theater tickets (displaying) which have a story back of them I was preaching in a certain city in Illinois when a certain church in that city was facing a shortage on the pastor's salary What do you suppose

271

they did? They rented the city opera house, and took certain people from the congregation, whom they organized into a theatrical company. Then they put on a regular drama or play at the city opera house to raise money to meet the shortage on the pastor's salary. Strange to say, the preacher whose salary was in arrears, acted a leading part in the play. In fact, he played the part of the devil in the drama.

They gave all the preachers in that city complimentary tickets. They sent me two tickets, one for my wife and one for myself. We did not attend. I resolved that wherever I preached the Word of God, I would exhibit these tickets to the audience in condemnation of such unholy practices on the part of any professed Christian church I will not give the name of that denomination for it would be embarrassing to some of our friends who belong to that denomination. But here (displaying) are the actual unused tickets to that church show at the city opera house.

I have some interesting things to show you tonight Here (displaying) is a facsimile of a lottery ticket A certain church wanted to raise money to build a church building. They raffled off three automobiles Tickets were sold for one dollar apiece Friends, I would rather preach in a barn than in a church paid for in a lottery. (Amens) What is a lottery of raffling? It is gambling.

Christians may well hang their heads for shame when the governor of a certain state sometime ago had to ask the legislature, to pass a law to stop the gambling that was being carried on at church fairs and church bazaars.

Dr. Gallup, in one of his sample "polls," found that five persons out of every ten are indulging in some kind of gambling Here are the figures· Nine per cent of the people who were interviewed admitted that they gambled on the numbers game. Ten per cent admitted that they were betting on horse races. Thirteen per cent of the people had gambled on sweepstake tickets. Nineteen per cent were betting on elections Twenty-nine per cent were playing cards for money. Twenty-three per cent on slot machines Twenty-six per cent on punch boards. Twenty-nine per cent gambled in church lotteries Think of it! Nearly three times as many people are gambling at church lotteries as at horse races This is based on an actual cross-section poll of America. It indicates that the church or parish house is the most popular gambling house in America. What an indictment of modern Christianity!

One church used little socks like this (displaying a doll's sock) to raise money for the church. Attached to the sock was a card which contained this little poem:

"This little sock we give to you is not for you to wear,

  Please multiply your size by two and place inside with care,

In silver or in cents, twice the number that you wear

        (we hope it is immense).

  So if you wear a No. 10, you owe us twenty; see,

Which dropped in this little sock will fill our hearts with glee

  So don't forget the place and date, we'll answer when you knock,

And welcome you with open arms, but don't forget your sock."

I will not give the name of the church that used this method to raise money Suppose I wanted to give my mother a present Would I pass little socks among my friends to secure the money to purchase a present for her? No I would not insult my mother that way. How much worse it is to insult Almighty God by trying to raise money for His cause by such methods!

Another church needed money, and they sent out little panties like this (displaying doll's underthing) with this piece of poetry:

"These little panties are sent to you,
And this is what we want you to do.
Measure your waist line inch by inch,
And see that the tape line does not pinch
For each small inch you measure around,
Place a penny in your pocket sound,
And when returned, the pocket we'll search,
And with the money we'll pay for our church"

Friends, I would rather preach in a barn than in a church that is paid for by such methods

When Jesus Christ came here 1900 years ago, and found the Jews carrying on commercial business in the temple, what did He do? He drove them out He said, "Make not My Father's house an house of merchandise" If Christ were to enter these churches today where money is being raised for His cause by such unholy methods, He would drive them out like He did in old Jerusalem

Is there some plan that God has ordained for the support of His ministers? Yes God has ordained the tithing plan for the support of His workers Notice in Leviticus 27 30 how all the tithe is the Lord's. "And all the tithe of the land, whether of the seed of the land, or of the fruit of the tree, is the Lord's It is holy unto the Lord."

What is the tithe? It is one-tenth of our net income Please note that "all the tithe," or one-tenth, "is the Lord's" Not fifty per cent of that one-tenth, but **all** the tithe is the Lord's It is the Lord's whether you ever pay it or not. You cannot give the tithe to Him, it is the Lord's

Just as the seventh day of every week belongs to God, so the one-tenth of our net income belongs to God The seventh day is the Lord's holy day, even though most people are using it for their own business and their own work It is still the Lord's even if men appropriate it to their own use, and fail to keep it holy So the tithe is the Lord's whether a man pays that one-tenth or not If a man is an infidel, and does not believe in God, one-tenth of every dollar that he makes belongs to God

Everybody understands the principle that if you live in a house that belongs to another person, you are due to pay rent for the use of that property Everything in this world belongs to God In Psalm 24 1 David says, "The earth is the Lord's, and the fulness thereof, the world, and they that dwell therein" This world and everything in it belongs to God

In Haggai 2 8 He declares, "The silver is mine, and the gold is mine, saith the Lord of hosts" In Psalm 50 10 He says, "For every beast of the forest is mine, and the cattle upon a thousand hills" In Deuteronomy 8 17, 18 we learn that it is the Lord that gives us power to get wealth God is the one that keeps your heart beating Every breath you take is from God One-tenth is due the Lord for the use of His property, just as rent is due the landlord for the house you rent

If a landlord owns a farm, and furnishes everything such as stock, implements, fertilizer, seed, he is entitled to one-half of everything that grows on that land See how much better the Lord is with His tenants! He furnishes everything He keeps your heart beating He keeps you alive He gives you health in addition to temporal wealth, and all He asks is one-tenth—not a half!

You say, "Mr Shuler, isn't this tithe a part of the old Mosaic law that was done away with when Christ came?" The law of the tithe antedates the Mosaic law You will find that Abraham paid tithe at the Lord's direction He lived hundreds of years before Moses was ever born Jacob paid tithe The law of tithing is not dependent on the Mosaic law for its binding obligation It was in force long before Moses was born, and the law of tithe remains after the Mosaic law was abolished

Jesus endorsed tithe paying   I read in Matthew 23 23· "Woe unto you, scribes and Pharisees, hypocrites! for ye pay tithe of mint and anise and cummin, and have omitted the weightier matters of the law, judgment, mercy, and faith· these ought ye to have done, and not to leave the other undone "

This word "ought" is stronger than the word "should " To illustrate We **should** be polite, but we **ought** to tell the truth   You see how "ought" is a stronger word than "should " The use of "ought" in connection with telling the truth signifies a moral obligation, but there is no moral obligation to be polite

Jesus uses the word "ought" in connection with tithe paying Tithe paying is a moral obligation, just like being honest   If a man does not turn over that one-tenth to God, he is really violating the eighth commandment, which says, "Thou shalt not steal "

The Mosaic church was financed by the tithe   I read in Numbers 18 21, "And behold, I have given the children of Levi all the tenth in Israel for an inheritance, for their service which they serve, even the service of the tabernacle of the congregation "

God's plan for the support of the church in the days of Moses was the tithing system   God's ministers, who carried on the work of the church, received their living out of the tithe that was contributed by the rest of the Israelites

God has ordained the same plan for the support of the gospel ministry   I read in I Corinthians 9 13, 14· "Do ye not know that they which minister about holy things live of the things of the temple? and they which wait at the altar are partakers with the altar?" In this 13th verse Paul was speaking about the plan that was followed for the support of the work of God in the days of Moses   Then he goes on to say, "Even so hath the Lord ordained that they which preach the gospel should live of the gospel "

In precisely the same manner that God ordained the tithing system for the support of His ministers under the Mosaic law, He has ordained the same plan for the support of the gospel ministry   The gospel minister is to live from the tithes of those who accept the gospel   This is how to pay the preacher without using your own money

What about those hundred thieves that were caught in one church? Let us look at Malachi 3 8   "Will a man rob God? Yet ye have robbed Me   But ye say, Wherein have we robbed Thee? In tithes and offerings " If a man doesn't turn over that one-tenth to God, he is a robber and a thief   I think you will agree with me that there are many churches where there are far more than a hundred people who do not pay tithe   There you have one-hundred thieves in one church.

"Will a man rob God?" This is a striking question   If He said, Will a man rob his fellow man, you would not be surprised, because that is going on all the time   But, "Will a man rob God?" Will a man rob the One who gives him everything?   "Yet," He says, "ye have robbed Me " And when they raise the question, "Wherein have we robbed Thee?" the answer comes back, "In tithes and offerings " If a man does not pay tithe, he is a thief   I Corinthians 6:10 declares that no thief will ever enter the kingdom of heaven

Do you know that our government recognizes God's claim on a man's money is first? "In the beginning God " In paying income tax the government allows a man a 15% deduction for charitable purposes   In other words, a man can pay the tithe to God, that is 10 per cent, and he can give 5 per cent in freewill offerings. Then when he comes to figure up his income tax, he is permitted to deduct the 15% and his income tax is figured on the remaining 85%   So even the government recognizes that God's claim on a man's money is first

Someone says, "I think all this is correct, but I could not afford to pay one-tenth of my salary   I do not make very much money   It takes all I make to pay the bills   If I took out one-tenth from my salary, we would not have enough to live on.   I just cannot afford to do it "   Brother, you just have that wrong   You **cannot afford not** to pay tithe

Let me read to you **why** in verse 10 of Malachi 3.   "Bring ye all the tithes into the storehouse, that there may be meat in Mine house, and prove Me now herewith, saith the Lord of hosts, if I will not open you the windows of heaven, and pour you out a blessing, that there shall not be room enough to receive it "

Notice who is talking here   The One who says this is the One Who never fails to do what He says   If this were the promise of man, you might have cause to question it, but you never need question the promise of God.   "Bring ye all the tithes   . and prove Me," He says, "if I will not open you the windows of heaven, and pour you out a blessing, that there shall not be room enough to receive it "

Nine-tenths **with** God's blessing, actually goes further than ten-tenths **without** His blessing   Nine-tenths **plus** God, is better than ten-tenths **minus** God   I have talked with hundreds of people in regard to this matter, and I have never met any one who really tithed, but that he found Malachi 3.10 to be true   (Amens)

This shows that God is a true God   His promises never fail   I never met anyone that really tithed, but who would tell you that he has found by experience that nine-tenths with the blessing of God actually goes further than ten-tenths without His blessing

I can testify to the glory of God's name, after paying tithe many years, that I have found that nine-tenths goes further.   I have come to the place where, if it were not an obligation, I would want to do it because nine-tenths with God's blessing goes further than ten-tenths without it

I will test this out right here   I find that today there are people in every denomination who are tithers   There is an increasing number of people who are paying tithe to the Lord   How many here who have actually tithed will stand to testify that you have found that the nine-tenths goes further with God's blessing, than the ten-tenths without it?   Let us see?   "Ye are my witnesses"   Thank you   (A large number of those present stood)

I will repeat it again   I have never found anybody who has actually carried out God's instructions, but what has found that His promises are true. So you see, dear friends, you cannot afford not to pay tithes.   You cannot afford to lose this blessing   "Bring ye all the tithes into the storehouse, . . . and I will .   open you the windows of heaven, and pour you out a blessing that there shall not be room enough to receive it."   Above all you cannot afford not to do it from the standpoint of losing heaven by robbing God.

I have another question on which I hope everybody will stand   It will at least give everybody a chance to act on the Lord's instruction.   How many here believe that the tithing system is right, and you are willing to stand to say that by the help of the Lord you will accept His proposition to bring all the tithe into the storehouse, and let Him give you the blessing?   (Nearly the entire audience stood)

FULFILLING ALL RIGHTEOUSNESS

(Preached after the Forty-third Lecture. Outlining the importance of coming into the Remnant Church by re-baptism)

(Some thoughts on the question of whether the people, who have been immersed before they accepted the true Sabbath, should be re-immersed when they accept God's message for these last days)

"Jesus answering, said unto him, Suffer it to be so now, for thus it becometh us to fulfill all righteousness " This is the reading of the word of God in Matt 3.15.

When the Lord Jesus Christ came to John the Baptist to be baptized of him in Jordan, John the Baptist at first refused to baptize Jesus John told Jesus, "You do not need to be baptized by me, but I need to be baptized by You " This was true How easily Jesus might have said, "You are right I am not a sinner I have not committed a single sin There is really no need for me to be baptized " But no, Jesus said, "Suffer it to be so now, for thus it becometh us to fulfill all righteousness "

Jesus Christ was determined not to leave off any right thing So He was immersed beneath the waters of Jordan In the light of His example, when a person who has not been baptized by immersion accepts Christ's message for our day, he will plan to be immersed as Jesus was The individual who has been immersed before he accepted Christ's special message for these last days should consider carefully whether or not he will be re-immersed under this special message

Some may ask, "I was immersed once to show my faith in Christ. If I should be re-immersed wouldn't that be a denial of my faith in the Lord Jesus?" The answer is, "No " Being re-immersed under this message of the commandments of God and the faith of Jesus would be showing your faith in Jesus Christ more than when you were immersed the first time I refer you to Col 2 12, which says

"Buried with Him in baptism, wherein also ye are risen with Him through the faith of the operation of God, who hath raised Him from the dead."

One purpose of baptism is to show the Christian's faith in the death, burial and resurrection of the Lord Jesus Christ Immersion is the true memorial of Christ's resurrection The keeping of Sunday in honor of Christ's resurrection is a man-made memorial of His resurrection, which men contrary to the Word of God have instituted in the place of Christ's appointed seventh-day Sabbath

When I was immersed the first time, I was keeping Sunday as an alleged memorial of the Lord's resurrection Since I was keeping Sunday as a false memorial of Christ's resurrection, this first immersion could not take its divinely appointed place in my life as the true memorial of Christ's resurrection. When Christ's special message for our day came to me, and I learned that Sunday is a false memorial of Christ's resurrection, and that immersion is the true memorial of Christ's resurrection, I decided that I should be re-immersed, that this second baptism might stand in my life as the God-ordained memorial of the Lord's resurrection How could immersion be to me the true memorial of Christ's resurrection until the false memorial of Sunday keeping was dislodged from my life, by the light of God upon the Sabbath truth? This is a point I wish you would think through carefully, if you were immersed while you were keeping Sunday

The question may be raised, "Do we know whether God approves of people being immersed more than once?" We have a record in the New Testament where God led people to be immersed at two different times in their lives You will find this in Acts 19 1-5 It reads as follows

"It came to pass, that while Apollos was at Corinth, Paul having passed through the upper coasts came to Ephesus; and finding certain disciples, he said unto them, Have ye received the Holy Ghost since ye believed? And they said unto him, We have not so much as heard whether there be any Holy Ghost. And he said unto them, Unto what then were ye baptized? And they said, Unto John's baptism. Then said Paul, John verily baptized with the baptism of repentance, saying unto the people, that they should believe on Him which should come after him, that is, on Christ Jesus When they heard this, they were baptized in the name of the Lord Jesus "

These believers were immersed two times They were immersed the first time when they accepted certain truths under the ministry of Apollos Then when Paul brought them the additional light for their day they were re-immersed Immersion is the right form of baptism In fact, baptism is immersion These disciples at Ephesus had been baptized in the right way before they had ever heard Paul preach, but notice, having been baptized in the right way did not make it unnecessary for them to be re-immersed

Some may say, "These people had to be re-immersed to show their faith in the Lord Jesus Christ as their Saviour So their re-immersion would not be any point in favor of Christians being re-immersed today " When we grant this to be the case, there is still a strong point here for re-immersion on the part of those, who have been immersed before they accepted God's message for the last days Their cases are parallel to the cases of these disciples in Acts 19 1-5 in several decisive particulars Like these disciples of Apollos they were immersed the first time when they heard only a part of God's gospel Later on when the full gospel is brought to them in God's special message for this last hour, it is right and proper that they be re-immersed as those disciples at Ephesus were, when Paul brought to them the additional light of God for their day

The instruction of Jesus regarding baptism needs to be carefully studied Let us notice His words in Matthew 28, verses 19 and 20 Jesus says

"Go ye therefore, and teach all nations, baptizing them, in the name of the Father, and of the Son and of the Holy Ghost "

Notice that teaching precedes baptism What does this teaching include? Jesus tells us in verse 20

"Teaching them to observe all things whatsoever I have commanded you, and, lo, I am with you alway, even unto the end of the world."

A person should be taught to observe all the commandments of Jesus Christ before he is baptized I wish that you, who were immersed before you heard God's special message for these last days, would ask yourselves the question, "Was I taught all the commandments of Jesus before I was immersed?" I think your answer will have to be in the negative

There are six different commandments pertaining to the Christian life that I was not taught when I was immersed the first time. Here they are

The commandment to keep holy the seventh day of the week (Ex 20 8-11)

The commandment to eat and drink to the glory of God, which involves the laying aside of tobacco, pork, tea, and coffee (1 Cor 10 31)

The commandment to render unto God one-tenth of one's income (Lev 27 30)

The commandment to refrain from following the sinful ways of the world, like dancing, card-playing, theatre-going, etc (2 Cor 6 17)

The commandment to dress modestly, and to not adorn one's self with ornaments such as earrings, necklaces, bracelets, etc (1 Tim 2 9, 10)

The commandment to wash each other's feet before we partake of the Lord's supper. (Jno 13 12-15)

This makes six commandments of the Lord that I was not taught before I was immersed the first time When God's message came to me, it taught me these six commandments, which I had not been taught before my first baptism. The instruction of Jesus concerning baptism is, that a person is to be taught to observe all the commandments before he is baptized Isn't it plain that according to the instruction of Jesus re-immersion was necessary in my case, when God's message came and taught me all His commandments?

Generally speaking, those who have been immersed before accepting God's last day message have been immersed into the various religious organizations administering that rite But God's message calls for further steps into truth and deeper consecration to that truth It is to be expected then, that God would call His people out of the confused religious concepts of the world today.

Much good has come from the reformation The various reformed churches have each made their contribution to Christianity But, I think that the reader can see, that the day of disunion is passing The emphasis in religious circles today is oneness It is all an answer to Jesus' prayer in John seventeen However, let that oneness be built upon God's last message for this hour God's call is, "Come out of her, My people" To come out of the confusion in the world today is it not fitting, is it not necessary and most gratifying to be re-immersed into Christ's remnant church that is proclaiming the judgment hour message throughout the world? Then each child of God will find his place at the conclusion of the prophetic picture, "Here they are that keep the commandments of God, and the faith of Jesus"

This special message for the last days sustains the same relation to Christ's second advent as the message of John the Baptist did to the first advent of our Lord There was a special baptism connected with John the Baptist's message, called "John's baptism" So there is a special baptism connected with this counterpart message for these last days

The Scriptures tell us that in order to have a true baptism, one must die with Jesus Christ to sin In Rom. 6 3 we read "Know ye not, that so many of us as were baptized into Jesus Christ were baptized into his death?"

I wish to ask a few questions What is sin? I John 3.4 says:

"Sin is the transgression of the law"

The law in this case means the ten commandments Did Jesus Christ die for the transgression of just nine of the ten commandments? Or did He die for all ten of the ten commandments? He died for the transgression of all ten of the ten commandments Since a person must die with Christ to sin in order to have a true baptism, and Jesus died for all ten of the ten commandments, on how many of the ten commandments must a person be immersed in order to have a true baptism? If you were immersed on only nine of the ten commandments, before you accepted the true Sabbath, isn't it necessary to be immersed again on all of the ten commandments, in order to die with Christ to sin, and to have a true baptism?

A person who has been immersed before he accepted the Sabbath may become a member of the remnant church on profession of faith without being re-immersed But these scriptural considerations show that it is better to be re-immersed when we accept this message My second immersion brought me the greatest spiritual blessings of all my life I believe that you, who have been immersed before you learned this special message for these last days, as you think over these scriptural considerations will say of being re-immersed, like the Saviour said on the banks of Jordan, "Suffer it to be so now, for thus it becometh us to fulfill all righteousness"

(Copy of the Bible lesson outline, which was distributed to the people preceding the Forty-fourth lecture)

Lesson VIII - The Real Truth About the Jew

1   The name "Israel" was used first in (Gen 32 28)   It came to Jacob, not by inheritance, as our surnames come to us, but was given direct from heaven to denote the born-again experience that came to Jacob through prayer and surrender   From Jacob the term "Children of Israel" was applied to his 12 sons and their descendants   These constituted the 12 tribes of literal or fleshly Israel of the old covenant

2   There are two different kinds of Jews, or two different Israels, under the old and new covenants.. .. ..

3   These are — (a) "Israel after the flesh," (1 Cor 10 18), composed of the literal descendants of Abraham   They were the Israel of the old covenant, which expired at the crucifixion   (b) Israel after the Spirit, or "the Israel of God" (Gal 6 16), composed of both Gentiles and Jews, who accept Christ as their Saviour .   .   ..

These are the Israel of the new covenant from the cross to the second coming of Christ

4   Paul's illustration of the olive tree makes plain the real truth about Israel   .. ..

5a   The olive tree represents Israel (Jer 11 16)

5b   The natural branches were the Jewish people, or the literal descendants of Abraham The breaking off of these natural branches was the rejection of the Jewish nation because of their national rejection of Christ (Rom 11 20, Matt 21 37-43)

5c   The wild olive branches, which are grafted in to take their place, are the Gentiles and Jews, who accept Jesus, and become God's Israel, in the place of the literal descendants of Abraham (Rom 11 17, 9 25-26, Eph 2 11-22)

6   The only way the literal Jews can now have any part in the promises and plans of God is by accepting Jesus Christ . ..   .

7   The literal Jews as a nation will not be restored as a divine kingdom in Palestine   ... .

8   The promises made to Israel in the Old Testament now apply in general to God's true Israel   These promises of the restoration and gathering of Israel to the holy land were partially fulfilled in the return of the Jewish exiles from Babylonian captivity   These promises and prophecies will be fulfilled to the highest degree in the establishment of God's Israel in the new earth, or heavenly Canaan

9   This true concept of Israel reveals—

(a) How all the saved will be Israelites (Rev 21 12)   .

(b) How the seventh-day Sabbath is binding today, as God's perpetual and everlasting sign between Him and Israel (Ex 31 16-17; Isa 66 23-23)

(c) How only a small number of literal Israel will be saved (Rom 9 27), but all spiritual Israel will be saved (Rom 11 26)

(d) How there is no such thing as any lost tribes in God's plan   (Jas 1 1, 5 7)

References which were filled in as the study was presented (2) Rom 2 28, 29, 9 6-8, (3b) Gal 3 29, 7, 6 15, 16, (4) Rom 11 13, 17-20, (6) Rom 11 23, (7) Jer 19 10, 11, Eze 21 25-27)

Preparing the Way for Christ to Come

(Preached on the Tenth Friday Night of the Campaign)

Thousands of people in the city of Des Moines today read the MORNING REGISTER and the EVENING TRIBUNE to get the news but do you know that the biggest piece of news, the best news of all, was not in the newspaper? It wasn't even announced over any radio station. What is it? The biggest piece of news, and the best news of all is that the world movement which is actually preparing the way for the end of the war, the end of all sorrow, the end of all trouble, is soon to reach its grand and glorious objective

The Bible shows that the second coming of Jesus Christ will bring to an end all sickness, sorrow, and trouble for the righteous In Revelation 14 6-15 we learn that in the closing age of this world's history just prior to the second coming of Jesus Christ, God will bring into existence an international religious movement that will actually prepare the way for the return of His Son from heaven

Let us notice how the apostle John describes the second coming of Christ in Revelation 14 14, 15 "I looked, and behold a white cloud, and upon the cloud One sat like unto the Son of man, having on His head a golden crown, and in His hand a sharp sickle And another angel came out of the temple, crying with a loud voice to Him that sat on the cloud, Thrust in Thy sickle and reap for the time is come for Thee to reap, for the harvest of the earth is ripe"

The prophet saw the Lord Jesus Christ coming on a cloud with a sickle in His hand, to reap the harvest of the gospel Jesus Christ Himself declared that the reaping of the harvest will come at the end of time Put down Matthew 13 39 He said, "The harvest is the end of the world" So this description of Jesus coming on a cloud with a sickle to reap the harvest must refer to the second coming of Christ If you will read the eight verses of scripture which precede this description of Jesus coming on the cloud, you will find that in the last days God will raise up a certain world movement that will prepare the way for Christ to come and reap the harvest

This movement is symbolized by three angels flying through mid-air preaching a striking three-fold message to the people of every country You will find this in Revelation 14 6-12 "I saw another angel fly in the midst of heaven, having the everlasting gospel to preach unto them that dwell on the earth, and to every nation, and kindred, and tongue, and people, saying with a loud voice, Fear God and give glory to Him, for the hour of His judgment is come. and worship Him that made heaven and earth, and the sea, and the fountains of waters

"And there followed another angel," (a second one) "saying Babylon is fallen, is fallen " And in Revelation 18 2, 4 we read that coupled with this warning that Babylon is fallen will come the divine call to God's people to come out of Babylon

"And a third angel followed them saying with a loud voice, If any man worship the beast and his image, and receive his mark in his forehead, or in his hand, the same shall drink of the wine of the wrath of God, which is poured out without mixture into the cup His indignation· and he shall be tormented with fire and brimstone in the presence of the holy angels, and in the presence of the Lamb."

Then we notice in verse 14 that just as soon as the third angel delivered his message, the prophet saw Christ come on the cloud to reap the harvest.

What does all this mean? Does this mean that three angels will actually appear in visible form in the air over every country and preach to the people? No! Why not? Because the preaching of the everlasting gospel has not been committed to angels. It has been committed to men. These three angels must represent a body of people whom the Lord will raise up in the last days to preach this great three-fold message to every nation.

The teaching of this message will bring forth an inter-national world movement that will prepare the way for the second advent of our Lord, as John the Baptist prepared the way for the first advent of our Lord. This present world movement with the three-fold message will actually bring to an end all war.

Some folks think that the UNO will bring the end of all war. I hope so. However we do know that the preaching of this three-fold message to every nation will actually bring the end of all war, because it will bring the return of Christ. This in turn will mark the end of all war under this present world order. It will bring the end of sorrow, the end of trouble, by ushering in that great day of days when Christ will appear to consummate the plan of redemption.

There cannot be any mistake about this. Why not? Because this prophecy of Revelation 14 shows definitely and specifically that Jesus will appear on the cloud just as soon as this three-fold message has been preached to every nation. The Word of Jesus Christ will never fail. He says, "Heaven and earth shall pass away, but My word shall not pass away."

Jesus Himself has declared unequivocally that the end will come when this last message has been preached to every nation. Did you know that there is only one place in the Bible that tells exactly when the end will come? In Matthew 24.14 Jesus says, "This gospel of the kingdom shall be preached in all the world for a witness unto all nations, and then shall the end come."

He declares positively that when the gospel of the kingdom has been preached to every nation, **then at that very time, the end will come.** When this message has been sufficiently made known to all men everywhere, Christ will appear on the cloud to gather those who are ready to the heavenly mansions. Jesus declared in John 14.3, "I go to prepare a place for you, and if I go and prepare a place for you, I will come again, and receive you unto Myself; that where I am, there ye may be also."

Think what a privilege it is to be a herald of this three-fold message! I thank God tonight for this message. In preaching it I am helping to bring Christ back again. I hope that from this Bible Institute there will be other men and women who will unite their efforts with ours in teaching the three-fold message of God for today.

It is the preaching of this message that will bring Christ out of heaven. If the message that you have heard in these meetings had been sufficiently made known to men, Christ would not stay in heaven tonight. He would be on His way, and we could say good-bye to all our troubles and sorrows and sicknesses, and go to a world where there will be no sorrow, nor sickness, nor pain.

The nearer we come to the point where this message is sufficiently made known to people of every country, the nearer we are to that great day of days when Jesus will appear. Before Christ can come to reap the harvest, the way must be prepared by giving men a chance to get ready to meet Christ, and by preparing a people to meet Him.

When the hour hand and the minute hand of the clock come together at twelve, you know the clock will strike twelve. If the clock is in working order, it will not strike twelve until the two hands come into line at the top of the dial So Jesus will not come, Jesus Christ cannot come **until these two condition of the prepared way and the prepared people come into line with each other.** When they come into line, God's great clock will strike and the end of human history, and the return of Christ will be here

All this brings us to three big questions Where is this world movement that God has appointed to prepare the way for the return of Christ? Who is preaching this three-fold preparatory message of Revelation 14? How are they succeeding in the task of making the three-fold message of Revelation 14 known to every country?

Please notice that there are five special truths contained in this three-fold message of Revelation 14. They are as follows 1) The date when the hour of God's judgment began in heaven 2) The appropriate recognition of God as the Creator 3) The warning against Babylon and the call to God's people to come out of her 4) A warning against obeying the beast or his image, or receiving the mark of the beast in the forehead or in the hand. 5) The keeping of the commandments of God and the faith of Jesus

Let us take this first question What people are proclaiming the special truths of this three-fold message to the world today? I can call you to witness that these five special truths are the very truths you have heard in these Bible Institute meetings I make bold to say that this series of meetings has been planned and conducted for the one purpose of making known this great three-fold message to the people of Des Moines We have advertised from the very first meeting that these Bible lectures are dedicated to the exposition of God's universal message

If you should investigate the work of all different churches and religious bodies in the world, you would find that there is only one people (not two or three) but only one people in the world who are actually proclaiming this three-fold message to every nation They are the people which this series of meetings represents

Can you be sure about this? Yes There is no guess work about it. Aside from the Seventh-day Adventist people there is no other church that even claims to preach this message Some of you folks have gone to church all your life, but how many sermons have you ever heard about the beast? Or the image of the beast? Or the mark of the beast? Or about Babylon? Or about the hour of God's judgment beginning in 1844 at the end of the 2300 days? How many sermons have you ever heard on these subjects? No, you never heard these matters explained until you came in contact with the Adventist people.

Let us consider the next question How are the Adventist people succeeding in proclaiming this message to every nation? It is a tremendous undertaking to preach any message to the people of every country in the world How are they succeeding?

If you should start from Des Moines tonight and go around the world either east or west, you would find adherents of this message all around the circle of the earth The message has already gone as far north as men live, and as far south as men live, and all the way between Do you know what is the northern most city in the world? It is Hammerfest, Norway And the message has gone there If you were to visit Hammerfest, you would find a company of forty people who have been called out by this message to keep the commandments of God, and who are waiting for the return of Christ from heaven

What is the southern most city in the world? It is a city called Punta Arenas on the very tip of the South American continent The message has gone there You would find a company of sixty people in that city keeping the commandments, and looking for the return of the Lord Jesus Christ. The message has gone as far north as men live, and as far south as men live, and it is all the way between

The prophecy of Revelation 14 6 foretold that the message would be preached in every tongue   The Adventist people are now preaching this message in over 800 languages or tongues   The fact that this message is being preached in over 800 languages shows how nearly it is being preached in every tongue

Listen! During most of the time since 1929, Adventist preachers have been adding a new language on the average of every nine days   Think of that! Almost every week that goes by this message is being given in some additional language, dialect, or tongue   At that rate it will not be long until it is preached in every tongue, then Christ will come   Adventists are today preaching, and teaching, and printing gospel literature in more languages and tongues than any other Protestant denomination, yet they are very small in number compared to other great denominations

The message is being given today in over 400 countries and island groups Over 9,000 churches in all parts of the world have been established in this movement   The total number of adherents to this message now exceeds half a million   In the eight years from 1929 to 1937 the growth in membership equalled that of the first seventy-three years of its development   More people are accepting this message every year than the total membership list reached in 1888 after the first forty-four years of the proclamation of the message   The Adventists have doubled their numbers every ten years since 1845, and have increased their missionary activities nearly 500% with every succeeding decade

This movement started in 1844 with a group of forty people who accepted the Sabbath in an obscure mountain hamlet at Washington, New Hampshire From that small beginning in 1844, it has grown into a world movement that is operating in over 400 countries and over 800 languages

(At this juncture three successive maps of the world were thrown on the screen which showed how the message has spread around the world)

Here is a point I want you to mark well   The Seventh-day Adventists owe their existence to the prophecy of the three-angels' messages of Revelation 14   Notice how the prophet describes the people who will be called out or raised up by the preaching of this three-fold message   Put down Revelation 14 12   "Here is the patience of the saints· here are they that keep the commandments of God, and the faith of Jesus "   Remember that this verse is a part of the third-angel's message

The preaching of this three-fold message will raise up a people who will be distinguished from other people by the keeping of the commandments of God and the faith of Jesus   This prophecy of the three-fold message indicated that when the hour of God's judgment came in 1844, a people would be raised up to keep the commandments of God and the faith of Jesus   In that very year the first group of Adventists began to keep all the commandments

Prophecy called for a certain people to do a certain work at a certain time at a certain climactic period in the world's history   The Seventh-day Adventist movement was brought into existence by the Lord to do this appointed work   They owe their very existence to this prophecy of Revelation 14 6-12 The great God of heaven ordained over 1800 years ago in the Book of Revelation, that this three-fold message would be preached during a certain period, and He appointed that as the result of the preaching of this message, a great world-wide movement should be raised up   Scripture cannot be broken   The Word of God is always fulfilled in its season   When the great judgment hour struck in 1844 at the end of the 2300 days of Daniel 8 14, the movement began by which this three-fold message is being given to all the world

Mark this well   Seventh-day Adventists are not merely another denomination   **They constitute the appointed, last-day, world movement for the preaching of this three-fold message to prepare the way, and to make ready** a people to meet the Lord. **This is a God-ordained movement for the consummation of the work of the gospel.** God is working in marvelous ways to bring this three-fold message to every nation.

In the heart of Africa, in Nyasaland, an Adventist missionary asked the chief in charge of that country if they might have permission to preach the message to his people The chief refused to grant them a permit to preach One night a little later this chief had a remarkable dream This dream troubled him greatly No one could tell him what it meant

About that time the missionary came before the chief again to renew his request for permission to preach to the people of his country. The chief said, "I have had a dream, and if you can interpret it, I will grant your request"

He said, "In my dream I saw an angel fly through the air and he had a scroll in his hand that had certain writing on it. As he flew along he kept waving the scroll up and down Finally the angel came and sat on stump near where I was I asked him, 'What is that in your hand?' He said, 'This is the everlasting gospel'."

How easy it was for the missionary to interpret the chief's dream He simply took his Bible and began to read, "I saw another angel fly in the midst of heaven, having the everlasting gospel to preach unto them that dwell on the earth "

The chief stopped him He said, "Listen, you are reading my dream from that book " The missionary said, "Yes, this everlasting gospel is what we want to preach to your people, but you have been unwilling to grant us permission to do it " The chief said, "No longer do I refuse " He sent out runners to every part of the country, and they brought the people in by the hundreds to hear the message A new Book of Acts is being written today of the wonder-working power of God in connection with this message.

When I was in San Francisco in 1941 I met a chief from the Solomon Islands, a man who has been marvelously used of God in preaching the message to those Islands Thousands of his people have accepted the message This chief, Kata Ragoso, helped save the lives of scores of American fliers who had to "bail out" of their planes over the Solomon Islands during the war with Japan.

Of course this angered the Japanese Kata Ragoso was flogged, imprisoned, and then when he would not yield, the Japanese threatened to kill him He told them, "You can kill me, but I will never disobey God "

I thank God that He can take a black man of the Solomon Islands and change his heart to be true to Jesus I have heard this man tell how his father used to eat human flesh He showed us the club with which they killed people before they feasted upon their flesh How marvelously God has worked to transform these hearts! "I am not ashamed of the gospel of Christ, for it is the power of God unto salvation "

The Japanese told him that if he did not give in to the Japanese government they would kill him A Japanese army officer called for a squad of soldiers and said, "Now, I am going to count one, two, three, and when I say 'three,' you shoot " They led Ragoso out to the place of execution and tied him up The soldiers aimed their guns The officer started to count "one—two—," but he could not say "three " He tried again, "one—two—" then there was silence again He could not say "three " Once more he tried with the same result; so he walked away For a day and a half this Japanese officer could not speak a word Tell me that there is not a God in heaven, Who can take care of His own! How marvelously God worked to save that man!

When this three-fold message is brought to you, as it has been in these meetings, you can be sure that you have found the true way of Jesus Christ for these last days, and the wisest and best thing that you can ever do is to decide to accept the message that God has sent   This message that you have heard from Revelation 14 is God's last message, because the second-coming of Christ and the reaping of the harvest are the next items on God's program after this three-fold message has been sufficiently preached to the world.

Just think it through   If a person rejects God's last call, what hope is there for him?   If he rejects God's last call, there is no hope for him   Among all the millions of people who will be lost, there will not be one soul cast into the lake of fire because God couldn't save him   The people who will be cast into the lake of fire will go to that most fearful fate because they would not let God save them   God tells us that He has no pleasure in the destruction of the wicked   His appeal is, "Wherefore turn yourselves, and live ye" "Cast away all your transgressions   make a new heart   . . for why will ye die?"

Why will so many people be lost eternally?   Christ tells us in John 5·40 He says, "Ye will not come to Me that ye might have life"   This is why so many people will be lost   They will not come and take their stand for Jesus Christ   "Ye will not come to Me that ye might have life"   Neglect, indecision, and procrastination will cause more people to go to hell than perhaps any other sin of which humanity is guilty   "How shall we escape if we neglect so great salvation?"

Some will say, "Brother Shuler, I know that what you have preached here is the real truth from the Bible, and I intend to accept it a little later." O, friends of mine, do not make the mistake of thinking you can accept this message whenever you get ready.

One day the carcass of a calf was floating down the Niagara River on a cake of ice   A great eagle soaring in the air, spotted this carcass on the piece of ice   He flew down and dropped upon it   Leisurely he sat devouring his easy prey, while the swift current was all the time bearing him down toward the falls.

He wasn't uneasy   Couldn't he leap off the cake of ice into mid-air in just a moment, even when the ice got to the very brink of that awful cataract? Hadn't he done this a thousand times before in his bird experience?   So he floated on, just as you go on not accepting the message

By and by he neared the brink where the waters take that fearful leap to the rocks below   It was time to leave!   He stretched his great pinions, but he could not rise   Unnoticed by him, his talons had sunk in the ice and frozen hard and fast   His fate was sealed   He flapped his great wings; he struggled with all his might, but all in vain!   In a few moments he was swept over into the abyss to his death   He had delayed too long, thinking he could get away any time he so desired

In like manner, many a person will perish in the fiery abyss of hell, because he delayed to begin to obey God's commandments, thinking he could make a start whenever he desired   He kept promising himself that a little later on he would do it   Why do people delay their decision on this supreme issue which is more important to them than all else put together?

People are in a hurry to make money   People are in a hurry to get a seat at the theater   People are in a hurry to rush the season and get into spring clothes or winter clothes   They certainly rush the season on clothes these days   Life is just one hurry, hurry in every direction!   But there is just one thing that is worth hurrying for, and that is the eternal welfare of your soul Yes, people are hurrying today after every will-o'-the wisp that the devil dangles before their eyes   But when it comes to stepping forward to obey God and to secure life's grandest prize, they move at a snail's pace, if they go at all

May God open your eyes to see the true values of life!   Do you know what the Word of God declares we should be in a hurry to do?   There are some things we should be in a hurry to do   Here it is in Psalm 119 60 "I made haste, and delayed not to keep Thy commandments " That is the thing you ought to be in a hurry to do If you have not made your decision to keep all the commandments of God, I hope you will do it this very night I hope you will take this to heart, and be able to say when you go out of this place, "I made haste, and delayed not to keep Thy commandments "

Friends, we have no time to lose Jesus says, "Therefore be ye also ready for in such an hour as ye think not the Son of man cometh " The preparatory message has nearly finished its work, the journey is almost over, a few more steps will suffice to bring us home It is really true that "In a little while we are going home."

Jesus is coming to take those who are ready to His heavenly home He said, "I go to prepare a place for you, and if I go and prepare a place for you, I will come again, and receive you unto myself " The all important question is, Will you be ready to go with Jesus when He comes? He has sent this message to make you ready. It will make you ready if you will accept it and adhere to it to the end.

If you have stepped out to obey this message, I pray that you will determine in your heart to be true to the end Then you will go to be with Jesus forever If you have not stepped out to accept the three-fold message you have heard in these meetings, why not take your stand for it this very night? Last night a large group of people came to the front in the after-meeting to signify that they would go all the way with Jesus and accept the message they had heard.

There must be many more who are determined to accept the message God has brought to them How many who did not come forward Friday night are determined to go all the way with Jesus Christ? May I see your hands? Yes, I see several hands. How many tonight want to send up a silent prayer that the Lord will help you to be true to His message in order that you may be ready when Jesus comes? Will you raise your hands? Yes, nearly every hand is raised

(Prayer)

Blessed Jesus, we thank Thee for this great message for the last days Lord, how plain this 14th chapter of Revelation is! Here are the three angels who deliver the message, and then the next thing is the coming of the Son of man upon the cloud It is so plain, that this three-fold message is the message to be preached just before Jesus comes to make ready a people to meet Him

Lord, bless those who have taken a stand for this message Keep them true Bless those here who are determined to accept it Bless those who just raised their hands to signify that they want Jesus to help them to be ready We pray that not one will make the serious mistake of postponing his acceptance until it is too late

Keep us true, and when Thou dost come, may everyone here be ready to go with Thee to that wonderful home Thou hast prepared. We ask it in Jesus' name Amen

The Master Key to Your Ideal Life

(Preached on the Tenth Saturday Afternoon of the Campaign)

In the office of the superintendent of the Internal Revenue building at Washington, D C, there is a magic key, which confers great power into the hands of him who holds the key   There are 1800 rooms in the Internal Revenue building   Everyone of those rooms has its own respective doorlock and its own different key   But the master key in the superintendent's office will do all that the 1800 different keys will do   It will open every one of those 1800 rooms even though every one of those locks is different from the others

Today I want to tell you about the great master key of life   This key will open the way to an ideal life of happiness for every soul who will accept it This master key of life is Jesus   In John 10 10 He says, "I am come that they might have life, and that they might have it more abundantly"

Jesus Christ is the true light that lighteth every man that cometh into the world   All that can satisfy the needs and longings of the human heart for this world and for the world to come is found in Jesus   I want to repeat that It is so meaningful that I hope every word will register in your heart   **All that can satisfy the needs and longings of the human heart for this world and for the world to come is found in Jesus.**

Paul tells us in Ephesians 1 3 that "God hath blessed us with all spiritual blessings in heavenly places in Christ"   Christ is ALL and in ALL

Do you need peace?   Yes! everybody needs peace   Every normal person longs for that inner peace of heart and of soul   The answer to that need for peace is Jesus   He is our peace   In Romans 5.1 Paul says, "Being justified by faith, we have peace with God, through our Lord Jesus Christ"

Do you need victory?   Yes, every soul needs victory over sin   The answer to that need for victory is Jesus   He is the victory   1 Corinthians 15 57 says, "Thanks be unto God, which giveth us the victory through our Lord Jesus Christ"

Do you need salvation?   Yes! every soul needs salvation   If he does not gain salvation, he will perish forever   The answer to this need for salvation is Jesus   On that memorable night when Mary brought forth her first born and laid him in the manger, the angel Gabriel said, "Thou shalt call His name Jesus, for He shall save His people from their sins"   In Isaiah 53 6, 5 we read, "All we like sheep have gone astray, we have turned everyone to his own way; and the Lord hath laid on Him the iniquity of us all   He was wounded for our transgressions, He was bruised for our iniquities· the chastisement of our peace was upon Him, and with His stripes we are healed"

Do you need happiness?   Yes! every person in this world longs to be happy   It is strange the different ways people try to find happiness   Some men think they can find happiness in a whiskey bottle   Some people think they can find happiness by gorging themselves with food until they get sick Then they find that they are not so happy   Some people think they can find happiness by going into a smoke-filled dance hall and dance until two or three o'clock in the morning   Then the next day they find that they have a splitting headache, and they do not feel very happy

The true answer to man's need for happiness is Jesus   Jesus is the joy of heaven let down to earth   In John 15 11 Jesus said, "These things have I spoken unto you, that My joy might remain in you, and that your joy might be full"

When you swing the whole circle of human needs, Jesus is the only One Who answers to the circumference of every necessity. Everything you need, everything you should have, everything you ought to be, Christ is, and can make possible. Paul tells us in Phil 4.19, "My God shall supply all your needs according to His riches in glory by Christ Jesus." Yes,

> I've found a friend in Jesus,
>   He's everything to me,
> He's the fairest of ten thousand to my soul.
>   He's the lily of the valley, in Him alone I see,
> All I need to cleanse and make me fully whole

Jesus is the Master Key to an ideal life   Now the question comes, "How can you have Jesus as the Master Key to make your life what it ought to be? There are a lot of people in this world who only exist. They do not live; they just exist. What we need, friends, is that more abundant life.

There was a certain political party who took as their slogan, The more abundant life for the American people   They declared that if they could manage the country, there would soon be two chickens in every pot, and two cars in every garage. Is that the abundant life?   No! That is not the abundant life which God wants us to have   "A man's life consisteth not in the abundance of the things which he possesseth"

Often times those who have the most of this world's goods are the most unhappy people in the world.   Only a few years ago there were fifty-seven millionaires who killed themselves in one year   Were they happy? No! Didn't they have plenty?   Yes, they had millions   But it is literally true as Jesus said, "A man's life consisteth not in the abundance of the things which he possesseth."

God wants you and me to have the truly abundant life   One of the striking answers as to how we can have this abundant life is found in the last book in the Bible.   In Revelation 3 20 it says, "Behold, I stand at the door, and knock. if any man hear My voice, and open the door, I will come in to him, and will sup with him, and he with Me."

Jesus says, "Behold, I stand at the door."   Christ is at the door today in two particular ways.   He is at the door in respect to His speedy return to the earth to consummate the plan of redemption.

In the Scriptures Jesus has pointed out certain signs which will appear when He is about to return   In Matthew 24 33 He said, "Likewise ye, when ye shall see all these things, know that it (margin, He) is near, even at the doors"   The striking fulfillment of these signs today shows unmistakably that Jesus is at the door.   His coming is very near.   O friends, you have no time to lose in getting ready!   You have no time to lose in coming into line with the great message that He is sending to the world in these last days.

Jesus is also at the door of your heart in point of opportunity for making your life all that it ought to be   In Revelation 3.20 He says, "Behold I stand at the door and knock."   Everybody knows the significance of a knock at the door.   It means that the one who is at the door wants to come in.   Jesus says, "I stand at the door and knock"

Do you know how Jesus knocks at the door of your heart?   You will find that explained in John 16 8   Speaking of the Holy Spirit, or Holy Ghost, which is His special representative, Jesus says, "When He is come He will convince the world of sin and of righteousness and of judgment"

The Holy Spirit speaks to your heart through that still small voice, that inner voice, which when you are about to do something wrong says, "Now that is wrong   Do not do it."   Or when you are thinking about what you ought to do, He says, "This is the right way. This is what you ought to do"   Every desire for purity, every longing for holiness, every yearning for a better life, is Christ knocking at the door of your heart.

As you have attended these Bible Institute meetings, you have experienced desires for greater purity You have had longings for a better life, haven't you? I want to ask right now, How many of you, as you have attended these meetings, have experienced in your heart a longing for a better life? Yes, these many uplifted hands testify that the words of Jesus are true "Behold I stand at the door and knock" Jesus is knocking at the door of your hearts.

Those longings that you have had for a better life are proof that by the blessed Holy Spirit Jesus has been knocking at the door of your heart This is positive assurance that He will come into your life and make it what it ought to be, if you will open the door Jesus wants to come into your life in a fuller, deeper, closer way The fact that He has been knocking at the door of your heart is proof of this   ‸

Now the entire question of whether He will do it depends on how you respond to His knocking He says, "Behold I stand at the door and knock If any man hear My **voice, and open the door, I will come in to him."** The entire question of whether Christ does come into your life and make your life what it ought to be depends on whether you open the door "If any man open the door," He says, "I will come in "

You say, "Brother Shuler, please make it plain what it means to 'open the door ' How do I open the door to let Christ in?" You open the door when you fully surrender your will to do His will You open the door when you yield to the pleading of the Holy Spirit You open the door by making your decision to keep all the commandments of Jesus. You open the door by making up your mind to go all the way with Jesus in accepting this special message for the last days

I appeal now to you who have not yet stepped out to unite with Christ's remnant in keeping all the commandments of God and the faith of Jesus I want you to think how supremely important, how urgent it is, that you make this good decision, and make it **now.** Why should you hold back any longer? Your decision is the connecting link between what Jesus is doing in knocking at the door of your heart, and the greater things He will do for you, if you let Him in by making your decision now

No one can keep you from being saved except yourself. Whether you will be saved or lost depends on whether or not you will open the door Remember, Jesus will never force the door of your heart to open to Him

He loves you He died to save you He wants to come into your heart and make your life all that it ought to be He is knocking at the door **But He cannot do any more for you until you open the door.** When you get this thoroughly in your mind, I am sure you will make your decision to obey His call, and thus open the door

Why should you stop where you are? Christ cannot do any more He is knocking at the door of your heart, but that is as far as He can go. He says, "Behold, I stand at the door and knock. if any man hear My voice, and open the door, I will come in " He cannot go any further until you make your decision to surrender all to keep His commandments Are you ready to open the door this afternoon by surrendering yourself to go all the way with Jesus in accepting His special message for these last days?

Some will say, "Brother Shuler, I believe that what you have preached in these meetings is the truth; I know it is according to the Bible, and I intend to take my stand a little later But I feel that I must wait until I am more impressed to do it " Listen If you wait until some compelling power comes on you to make you do it, you will never make a decision This is where so many people will be lost They are waiting for some certain feeling They want something to take hold of them, and make them do it But God does not work that way.

You should take yourself in hand Christ is knocking now You should act on His knocking and open the door   If you are ever saved, you must choose to obey Jesus Christ   You must decide to follow Him all the way

Many people will be lost, while hoping and desiring to accept God's message for our day. They want to do it. They plan to do it   They promise themselves that they are going to do it   But they drift on and on, and fail to come to the point of yielding their will to God   They do not choose to follow Jesus all the way

There was a great artist, who once worked long and hard to illustrate this text on which I am preaching today—Christ knocking at the door   He painted a picture of a beautiful entrance doorway to a cottage, with a lovely vine arched over it   Just outside the door stood Jesus, Saviour of men, knocking for admittance

His painting was a masterpiece   He sought to express in the face of Jesus His great yearning for admittance through the closed door   As one looked at the painting, he might almost be seized with an impulse to walk up and push the door open so Jesus could enter

One day he placed this painting on exhibition so his friends could come and view it, and give him their constructive criticism   The people came   One of his friends, after looking at the picture carefully, said, "Mr Hunt, your painting of the face of Jesus is a masterpiece   I have never seen anything that expresses the yearning of a person for admittance at this does   But," he said, "Mr Hunt, you have forgotten one item "

"What is that?" asked Mr Hunt

This friend said, "Just look at that picture   There is no latch outside the door with which to pull the door open "

The great artist looked at him quietly and said with great feeling, "There is no mistake on this point   The door through which Jesus enters into human hearts **opens only from the inside.**"

The door which lets Jesus into your heart, so that your life may be what it ought to be, opens only from the inside. If He ever comes in, **you** must open the door   Everything depends on the right action of the will   You cannot save yourself   You cannot change your heart   But you can choose to obey His commandments   You can give Jesus your will   You can make your decision to accept His message, and then He will work in you to will and to do of His good pleasure

Jesus is ready to do His part right now, not next week, not next month, not next year, but he is ready to do His part now   Are you ready to do your part now? Are you ready to open the door?

There is nothing we need more than to have Jesus abiding in our hearts

When Jesus comes, the tempter's pow'r is broken,
When Jesus comes, the tears are wiped away
He takes the gloom and fills the life with glory,
For all is changed when Jesus comes to stay.

You can have Jesus in your heart to stay, if you just surrender your heart to keep His commandments   Listen to His most wonderful promise. It is a promise that I greatly love   In John 14 23 Jesus says, "If a man love Me, he will keep My words   and My Father will love him, and We will come unto him and make Our abode with him "

Isn't that wonderful! Just think, these hearts of ours, that have been so sinful can be transformed and become the living temple of the great heavenly Father and the Son of God by the Holy Spirit! As a matter of fact, you may have God and Christ and the Holy Spirit in you

"If a man love Me " Oh, we need to love Jesus more! If we love more, we will obey more   "If a man love Me, he will keep My words and My Father will love him, and We will come unto him, and make Our abode with him "

I appeal today to every soul in this auditorium who has not yet responded to the call of the Lord to come out and take his stand for the commandments of God   I am not referring merely to a decision to keep the Sabbath   That is a good decision

Scores of you have already filled out a decision card to keep the Sabbath That is fine, but that is only a good start toward accepting God's message   I am talking about a decision to go **all the way,** to throw the door of your heart wide open, to go all the way with Jesus in accepting His message, and to come out and take your stand with Christ's remnant

We shall now have a little song about opening the door

> You must open the door,
>   You must open the door
> When Jesus comes in,
>   He will save you from sin,
>   But you must open the door

Now I want everyone, who is determined to go all the way with Jesus, to sing this song together, and sing it this way,

> "I will open the door,
>   I will open the door
> As Jesus comes in,
>   He will save me from sin
>   For I do open the door "

Having told Jesus that you will open the door, I am sure you are ready to express your surrender to Him, so we can remember you in prayer ˙ How many who have not come forward to take your stand with God's remnant are determined under God to accept the message you have heard, and to go all the way in taking your stand with God's remnant?   Will you rise?   (Several began to rise)

Thank God here they come   One by one they are responding to the call of God   There must be others   Just remain standing   Is there another who wants to throw the door wide open to Jesus?

The Lord is speaking to hearts   Are there others?   Tell Jesus by standing, "Jesus, you may have anything I have   I love you with all my heart You have done so much for me, and I want to go all the way with You " Is there another who will stand and say, "God helping me, I will go all the way with Jesus "

You know it is right   You know you ought to do it   There will never be a better time to settle this great question than right now

Will you who are standing please come to the front and form a prayer circle as the choir sings, "Just As I Am?"   As you come, I believe others will follow you   You are leading the way today

In invite forward every young person, who has never given his heart to Jesus   Will you open the door and let Him come in?   I now invite those who may have once followed this message, but you have wandered away   You need to return   It is the only hope you have

Jesus is able to save to the uttermost all who come unto Him   If you will do the coming, He will do the saving   Will you do it today?   Come forward just now and say, "Jesus, I will open the door "

He has been knocking at the door of your heart   You know that   He cannot go any further until you open the door   Do it today?

If I should ask those who have not made a decision, "Do you have a desire to obey the Lord?" You would say, "Yes "   I know you have this desire You would not be here today, if you did not have it   Listen!   It is fine to have this desire, but if you stop there, you will never be saved   You must act

It is good to wish to do well, but if you do not go further than that, you will remain lost   Thousands will be lost who wanted to obey the truth, and keep the Sabbath and take their stand   Why?   Because they failed to act on the desire they had   They never made a start   They held back from making their decision   O, friend of mine, you have the urge in your heart   Act upon it!   Will you say, "God helping me, I act on that desire   I will go forward and take my stand with Christ's remnant "

The next stanza will close the call   It may be the last opportunity for some one who has not made a move today   Your last chance   I do not know   There is something about those words that wring my heart, "the last chance, the last invitation "   O, brother, act on it today!   This is your chance

It is the best chance you will ever have   You will not have a better chance Sunday night   Your best chance is now   This is the best chance you will ever have   The longer you put it off, the less chance there is that you will ever do it   As we sing the last stanza closing the invitation, will you come?

I do not want to see anyone left out of this prayer   I know that there are others who ought to respond   I want to pray for you, as well as for those who have responded   You need a little more help to make the decision   How many want us to pray that God will help you to take your stand?   Will you raise your hands?   Thank you, I see many hands

(Prayer)

Our dear heavenly Father, we thank Thee for the working of Thy blessed Spirit here today   We thank Thee for these dear ones, who have heard the still small voice saying, "This is the truth, this is God's message, this is the way "   They have said, "Yes, Lord, I will follow Thee all the way "

As they swing the door of their heart open, Jesus does come in with new happiness, new peace, new victory for them   Then, Lord, bless these dear ones, who need extra help   Lord Jesus, do send them that extra help   It is so important that we take our stand   It is just as important as it was for the people of Noah's day to come into the ark   Help us all to do this, and to be ready in that great day when Jesus shall appear   We ask it in His precious name   Amen

Four Mysterious Horses

(Preached on the Eleventh Sunday Night of the Campaign)

"I saw when the Lamb opened one of the seals, and I heard, as it were, the noise of thunder, one of the four beasts saying, Come and see And I saw, and behold a **white** horse and he that sat on him had a bow, and a crown was given unto him and he went forth conquering, and to conquer

"And when he had opened the second seal, I heard the second beast say, Come and see And there went out another horse that was **red**: and power was given to him that sat thereon to take peace from the earth, and that they should kill one another

"And when he had opened the third seal, I heard the third beast say, Come and see And I beheld, and lo, a **black** horse, and he that sat on him had a pair of balances in his hand .

"And when he had opened the fourth seal, I heard the voice of the fourth beast say, Come and see And I looked, and, behold, a **pale** horse And his name that sat on him was Death, and Hell followed with him And power was given unto them over the fourth part of the earth, to kill with sword, and with hunger, and with death, and with the beasts of the earth " (The reading of Rev. 6 1-5, 7-9).

Four mysterious horses riding through the world A white horse, whose rider goes forth conquering and to conquer A red horse, whose rider is given power to take peace from the earth, that men should kill one another A black horse, under whose rule it takes a day's wages to buy enough food for one meal A pale horse, through whom one-fourth of all the people in the world are killed What does all this mean?

Under the first seal, a white horse appears whose rider goes forth conquering and to conquer In Bible symbolism, white denotes purity Put down Psalm 51·7. When David desired a pure heart, he prayed, "Wash me, and I shall be whiter than snow " So this white horse represents the purity of the gospel faith in the days of the apostles Notice how strikingly the white color depicts the pure gospel which the apostles preached They received it directly from Jesus Christ, who Himself is the Way, the Truth, and the Life There was no admixture of tradition and error in the gospel that Jesus gave them It was pure

Notice how this rider going forth conquering and to conquer, depicts so wonderfully the triumphs of the pure gospel in the days of the apostles On the day of Pentecost according to Acts 2, one sermon conquered 3,000 hearts The apostles went out and preached the truth with mighty power Wherever they went preaching, believers were established and churches were raised up The gospel went with such rapidity that in just a few decades it had been taken to the known world The apostle Paul, in writing to the Colossians in Col 1·23, could tell them that the gospel had been preached to every creature under heaven

As the white horse disappears, a red horse appears This white horse covers what we commonly call the Apostolic Age, from about A D 31, when the apostles began to preach after Jesus had gone back to heaven, until about A D 100, when the last of the apostles passed away You can see that since the color white in the first horse denotes the purity of the gospel in the days of the apostles, the color red in the second horse would indicate, that after the apostles passed away, the pure gospel would be corrupted with error This is exactly what happened

Just as soon as the apostles died, and the church no longer had inspired men to guide her, she began to wander from the path which the Lord Jesus had marked out for her Rites and ceremonies of which Peter or Paul never heard, or even dreamed of, crept silently into use, and then claimed the rank of divine institutions

Never forget that the keeping of Sunday in honor of the Lord's resurrection was one of those rites and ceremonies of which Peter and Paul never heard It crept into use after the apostles died The keeping of Sunday is post-apostolic It is beyond the lids of the Bible, and no man can prove that Sunday keeping is in the Word of God

This second seal covered the second stage of the Christian dispensation, reaching from about A D 100, when the last of the apostles died, to the alleged conversion of Constantine about 323 A D The so-called conversion of Constantine in 323 introduced a new era in the external history of the church

The red horse disappears and, lo, a black horse! Black is just the opposite of white Since the color white in the first horse denoted that pure gospel which Jesus gave to His apostles, the black in the third horse would indicate, that during this third period the pure gospel would be utterly corrupted That is exactly what happened

During the third period, as the papacy was arising to power, the pure gospel of Christ was utterly corrupted with human traditions They left off many items which Jesus had told people to do, and they added on many things which Jesus never intended people should do The third seal covers the third period in the external history of the church from about 323 A D to about 538, when the papacy became supreme in Christendom

The black horse disappears and, lo, a pale horse Pale means death You know, we have a saying, "He is as pale as death " This pale horse represented the slaughter of the saints during the Dark Ages after the papacy gained her long-wanted supremacy

This slaughter of the saints is especially noted in the prophecies of Daniel and Revelation In Daniel 7 21 and Daniel 7 25 it talks about that little horn, which is a symbol of the papal power God said that this horn would make war with the saints and prevail against them "He shall wear out the saints of the Most High " In Revelation 13 this same papal power is set forth under the symbol of the leopard beast rising out of the sea with seven heads, and ten horns In speaking of that power in Revelation 13 7 John says, "It was given to him to make war with the saints, and to overcome them "

This was the time of which Isaac Watts sang,

"Must I be carried to the skies on flowery beds of ease,

While others fought to win the prize and sailed through bloody seas?"

During this age of persecution, millions sealed their testimony with their blood They were slain for the Word of God and the testimony of Jesus which they bore

The fourth seal covered the fourth period in the external history of the church from about 538, when the papacy was established, until about 1517 when the Protestant Reformation under Martin Luther broke the rule of the papacy

Consider the color of these horses There is something very significant about it The color of each horse is a key which unlocks the identity of the period to which it applies The white is a symbol of the purity of the gospel in the days of the apostles The red is a symbol of the errors of pagan philosophy entering the church during the second and third centuries The black is the papal apostasy rising to supremacy during the 4th, 5th, and 6th centuries The pale is the slaughter of the saints by the millions during the rule of the papacy in the middle ages

The fifth seal extends to the time of the reformation This is pictured in the sixth chapter, as the blood of the martyrs crying for vengeance and white robes being given to them   It represents the vindication of the truth in the Protestant Reformation   We should never forget what happened October 31, 1517   Do you know?   I hope you do   On October 31, 1517 that noble soul, that great man of God, Martin Luther, walked up to the door of the Catholic Cathedral in Wittenburg and nailed on the door ninety-five theses against the Catholic doctrine of indulgences, and the Protestant Reformation was inaugurated

We owe Martin Luther a debt of gratitude for the liberties we enjoy, and for the open Bible that we prize, or should prize so highly.   There never would have been a Declaration of Independence on July 4, 1776, if it had not been for the stand Martin Luther took on October 31, 1517.

Unfortunately, the reformation was not carried through for the full restoration of the gospel as God had designed   The reformed churches formed creeds and ceased to move forward with the advancing light of God   One of the purposes of this great three-fold message to which this Bible Institute has been dedicated is to finish the arrested reformation. And it will   Put down Revelation 14 12   God says, "Here are they that keep the commandments of God and the **faith of Jesus."**

Those who accept this three-fold message will have the faith of Jesus   This three-fold message will complete the reformation from error to the full restoration of God's blessed truth   O, I thank God for the three-fold message, don't you?   Before these meetings close, I am hoping there will be hundreds in Des Moines who will be thanking God for the three-fold message.

The fifth seal covers the fifth period from about 1517, when the reformation broke the rule of the papacy, until 1755, when the first event of the sixth seal occurred   The sixth seal is described in Revelation 6.12-17.   Verses 12 and 13 of this 6th chapter of Revelation introduce certain signs which mark the rise of God's last message   Verse 14 tells how the heavens will be rolled back as a scroll, and through the opening in the heavens Christ will come at His second advent   Then verses 15-17 tell so graphically how those who are unprepared to meet Jesus will pray for the rocks to cover them.   This shows that the sixth seal extends to the very end of time, to the coming of the Lord.

Let us read Revelation 6.12, 13.   "I beheld when he had opened the sixth seal, and, lo, there was a great earthquake; and the sun became black as sackcloth of hair, and the moon became as blood, and the stars of heaven fell unto the earth, even as a fig tree casteth her untimely figs, when she is shaken of a mighty wind "

Here are four events—a mighty earthquake, the sun mysteriously darkened, the moon appearing in color as blood, and the stars falling to the earth   Have these come to pass?   Yes.   On November 1, 1755, the great earthquake prophesied for the opening of the sixth seal occurred.   It is known in history as the Lisbon earthquake, because on that day 90,000 people perished in the city of Lisbon   That earthquake shook four million square miles of this earth's surface   It was the greatest convulsion of nature since the deluge

Twenty-five years after that great Lisbon earthquake, on May 19, 1780, the sun was darkened   May 19, 1780, has gone down in history as the Dark Day   The sun came up bright and clear that morning   It looked as if it would be a beautiful bright day   About 8 o'clock people noticed an uncommon appearance in the sun   It began to get dark   By 10 o'clock they could not read common print in the open air   Birds sang their evening songs, and disappeared in their leafy retreats   Fowls went to roost, cattle came to the barnyard just as they do at sundown   People lighted candles in their houses, because they could not see without them   The darkness lasted all the rest of that day

Some will say, "O, that was just an eclipse   People back there were not as wise as we are   It was just an eclipse "   Was it?   No!

Look at this (At this juncture two charts were lowered in view of the audience One revealed the relative positions of the sun, moon, and earth, which are necessary for an eclipse of the sun; while the other depicted the relative positions of the sun, and earth on May 19, 1780)

Here are the positions necessary to make an eclipse You see the sun, moon, and earth must come into a straight line The moon then eclipses, or shuts off, the light of the sun for a brief period The darkness from an eclipse lasts for only about five to ten minutes But this darkness lasted from 10 o'clock through the rest of the day.

Notice, here are the positions of the sun, earth, and the moon on May 19, 1780 The relative positions of the moon and the earth in relation to the sun were not right to make an eclipse The earth, moon, and sun must be in a straight line

It was not an eclipse, for history says the moon was full the night before The American Encyclopedic Dictionary says, "An eclipse of the sun can appear only at new moon The sun, the moon, and the earth must be in a straight line, the moon being in the center"

It was not an eclipse To this day the wisest scientist has not been able to explain that dark day. They have written pages and pages about it, but when they get all done, their statements may be reduced to this,—it was dark, because there was a great darkness

Webster's Dictionary declares that the cause for this remarkable phenomenon is unknown Nobody could explain it Why not? Because it was the hand of Almighty God, hanging out in the heavens before all men, the first great sign of the approaching end and the coming of His Son from heaven.

Notice what happened the same night The night following this Dark Day of May 19, 1780, was probably the darkest night that ever has been since God said, "Let there be light." A sheet of white paper held before the eyes was just as invisible as the darkest velvet There was such a darkness as has not been known

The moon was in the full It should have been a bright moon-light night Why was it dark? Jesus had said, "The moon shall not give her light" After midnight the moon did appear Those who sat up that night, said that when they saw the moon after midnight, it had the appearance of blood, just as the prophecy said

Fifty-three years after this mysterious dark day, or on November 13, 1833, the greatest shower of shooting stars occurred that has ever taken place, so far as we know, since creation You can go out almost any night and see a few shooting meteors But on November 13, 1833, the stars were shooting in the heavens as thick as snow flakes in an Iowa blizzard in December or January. The whole heavens appeared to be on fire People who saw it never forgot it to their dying day

In the year 1937 I baptized an old gentleman in North Carolina who was 111 years old He was seven years old when the stars fell in 1833 He told us how his father got up that morning of November 13, 1833 at 4 30 to cut some wood, and ran back into the house and said, "Oh, Mom, the world is on fire"

The old man told how he went out and stood between his father and his mother, holding to his mother's skirts with one hand, and to his father's trousers with the other, and watched the shooting stars He said, "When they fell they didn't fall straight down like an apple falls when it gets ripe, but they shot in every direction"

Listen That is the way God said they would fall Notice Revelation 6 13 "And the stars of heaven fell unto the earth, even as a fig tree casteth her untimely figs, (not ripe ones, but green ones) when she is shaken of a mighty wind"

I am sure that there are people here who have heard their father or mother or at least their grandfather or grandmother, tell about that great shower of shooting stars   How many here have heard your mother or father, or grandmother or grandfather talk about that great shower of shooting stars?   May I see your hands?   (A number of hands went up)   Just look at these hands!   There is your proof for the falling of the stars on November 13, 1833

Verse 13 tells about the falling of the stars   What is the next event marked out in the prophecy?   Verse 14 tells, "The heaven departed as a scroll when it is rolled together, and every mountain and island were moved out of their places"   This has not happened yet, and it will not happen until the day when Jesus appears   It will take place in direct connection with the coming of Jesus   The heavens will be rolled back, and through the opening in the heavens Jesus will come

We are living tonight between the 13th and 14th verses of the 6th chapter of Revelation   The stars fell in 1833, and so far as this prophecy is concerned, the next event on God's program will be heaven split wide open, and the coming of the Son of Man

Revelation 14 helps to fill in this gap in Revelation 6, between the falling of the stars in 1833 and the appearing of Christ at the last day   Shortly after the falling of the stars, or in the year 1844, at the end of the 2300 days of Daniel 8 14, God's last message was to arise in the earth, and between 1844 and the end of time it was to be preached to every nation, to prepare the way for the coming of Jesus

The fifth seal was the age of the reformation from about 1517 to about 1755   Then comes the sixth seal   The Lisbon earthquake on November 1, 1755   The moon and sun darkened on May 19, 1780   The stars fell November 13, 1833   Then between 1833 and the end comes the closing work of the gospel   This will be the period during which God's great three-fold message will be carried to every nation   If you read Revelation 7 1-8, you will find that under this last message, the seal of God will be placed on the foreheads of His servants, so they will be protected from the seven last plagues, and be ready to meet Jesus at His appearing

Then under the seventh seal, time will be no longer   The sixth seal reaches to the parting asunder of the heavens and the appearing of Christ on the cloud   The seventh seal then covers the period of the second coming of Christ   In Revelation 8 1 we are told that under the seventh seal there will be silence in heaven about the space of a half an hour   What will make that silence?

In prophetic, or symbolic time, a day is reckoned for a year   On the year-day Biblical basis, a half hour would be the 48th part of 360, which would be about seven and one-half days   Everything in heaven will stop for seven days   Why?   Because Christ will leave heaven at the end of the sixth seal to come to the earth, to gather all the pure, and all the holy of all ages, and of all lands, to the heavenly mansions   When Christ leaves heaven to return to the earth, the Heavenly Father comes with Him, and all the angels leave heaven to come with Him   There is a pause in heaven for seven days   It is spoken of here prophetically as half an hour

The main lesson of this prophecy is that **we are living in the very last days.** Friends, the only wise course, the only safe way, the only right thing to think about, is to accept God's message, so that the seal of God will be placed on your forehead, and you be ready to meet Jesus

I am happy that so many of our friends have made this good decision to accept the message of God, which has been preached here from the Bible during these ten weeks   Many more will make this good decision in the next few weeks   Do you know what those who accept this great message, and are true to the end, will do when Jesus appears?   Put down Isaiah 25 9   "It shall be said in that day, Lo, this is our God, we have waited for Him, and He will save us this is the Lord; we have waited for Him, we will be glad and rejoice in His salvation "

The people who accept God's message will be ready to meet Jesus When they see Him coming, they will shout for joy and say, "There is Jesus! We love Him We have kept His commandments He told us He was coming We have waited for Him and He will save us "

That is one side of the picture I wish I could stop there I dare not I must declare the whole counsel of God What will people do, who have failed to accept God's message, when they see Jesus come? I read Rev 6 15-17

"The kings of the earth, and the great men, and the chief captains, and the mighty men, and every bondman, and every free man, hid themselves in the dens and in the rocks of the mountains, and said to the mountains and rocks, Fall on us, and hide us from the face of Him that sitteth on the throne, and from the wrath of the Lamb for the great day of His wrath is come, and who shall be able to stand?"

Those who have neglected to accept God's message will hold the greatest prayer meeting that has ever been held in the history of mankind But there will be two things wrong with that prayer meeting What are they? They will pray, but their prayers will be too late They will pray the wrong kind of a prayer "O, rocks cover us and hide us from the face of this Jesus "

There will be only two classes at that great day One class will be composed of millions and millions of people who will be caught unprepared They will not be living according to God's commandments When they see Jesus coming, they will be filled with terror They know they are not ready They know they cannot bear to look on the face of that holy God, and they pray the most horrible prayer a human being ever will pray "O, rocks fall on me, and hide me Cover me lest I see this Jesus who is coming" O, what wailing and gnashing of teeth, when they realize they are unprepared and lost, and they know it is their own fault, because they could have accepted the message when they heard it, but they failed to do so

There will be another class, comparatively few in number who will have obeyed God's message every day They will be ready Just think of the tremendous contrast Just think of it! While one class is praying for the rocks to cover them, another class is shouting for joy The great question is, In which class, friend of mine, will you be?

Think it through You cannot avoid being in one class or the other There is no third class when Jesus comes You and I and every other person who is alive will be in one class or the other If you live to see Jesus come, you cannot help being in one class or the other The fact that you are alive will cause you to be in one class or the other You cannot help being in one class or the other, if you live to that day There is one thing you can help You can help to determine which class you are in, by what you do with the message of God What you do with the message you have heard in this Bible Institute, determines in which class you will be

During the past ten weeks the message of God has been set before you step by step You are facing the most important question you ever faced, What will I do with the message God has sent to me? You must do something with it In fact you **are** doing something with it You are either accepting it, or rejecting it If we obey God's message and take our stand to keep His commandments and the faith of Jesus and be steadfast to the end, we will be ready. When He comes, we will say, "Lo, this is our God We have waited for Him, and He will save us " If you reject God's message and fail to heed His Word, you will be among those who will flee to the rocks and pray that awful prayer for the rocks to cover them O, friends, what will you do with God's message?

The decision I am talking about tonight is not merely a decision to keep the Sabbath   That is a good decision   Many have done this   Scores and scores of you have affixed your names to a decision card, to signify that by the help of God you will keep the Sabbath   Tonight I appeal for a decision to accept the whole message, to go all the way with Jesus and take your stand with God's remnant people, to keep the commandments of God and the faith of Jesus   I appeal to everyone here who has heard the message, and hasn't stepped out as yet, to make this good decision   Remember that to know this message and even to admit that it is true, but to go on without heeding it, is just as bad as rejecting it outright   "To him that knoweth to do good, and doeth it not, to him it is sin "

Many people who had intended to step out and take their stand for God's message will be lost at last   Why?   Because they put off their decision until it was too late   They just kept putting it off, and putting it off, until the last opportunity was past   Like Felix, they said, "When I have a convenient season I will call for thee "   But, alas! that time never came   They will pray when it is too late, because they failed to act on the conviction they once had   Do you know that the longer you wait to come out and take your stand, the less chance there is that you will ever do it?

An evangelist was preaching one night to an audience of 4000 people   He asked all to stand   They did   He said, "Now all you who accepted Christ before you were twenty years old, take your seats "   Hundreds and hundreds sat down   He said, "All of you who took your stand for God before you were forty, sit down "   Scores sat down   Only five were left standing out of 4,000   Then he said, "All who took your stand before you were fifty, sit down "   Only two out of 4,000 people were left.   The longer you wait, the less chance there is that you will ever do it.

Some one who has done some careful figuring declares that if a person is not a Christian by the time he is twenty-one, the chances are 5,000 to 1 he will never become a Christian.   If he doesn't take his stand for God by the time he is 30 years old, the chances are 15,000 to 1 that he will never do it   If he doesn't take his stand by the time he is 40, the chances are 50,007 to 1 he will be lost   If he isn't saved by the time he is 50 years old, the chances are 150,000 to 1 he will be lost forever   Yet all the time he is intending to take his stand.

This is why God says, "Now is the accepted time, now is the day of Salvation   Tonight if you will hear My voice, and harden not your heart "   Everything depends on what you do with God's message   I appeal to you to make the right decision now.   The still small voice has been saying to you, "This is the way, walk in it "   Why not say, "Lord, with Thy help I will take my stand?"   How many, who have decided to keep the Sabbath, or it may be that you haven't started as yet, but tonight you are purposed under God, that you will go all the way with Jesus Christ in accepting the message?   Will you lift your hand just now?   Yes, I can see quite a number of hands.

(Prayer)

Our dear heavenly Father, we are facing solemn realities tonight   Lord, help everyone here to know that the things of which we have been reading will soon transpire before our eyes   Help every one of us to realize that we cannot help being in one class or the other   Either we shall shout and sing for joy and be caught up to meet the blessed Christ and go to be with Him forever, or we shall flee and pray for the rocks to cover us and be struck dead as we flee   O, God, help every man, and woman, and young person here to put themselves on the side of Jesus Christ, and to do it now

Bless these dear ones who tonight are making up their minds to go all the way with Jesus   Some have problems, but Christ can solve the problems   He can take care of the business, the job, the opposition, or whatever it is   Help us to have faith in Thee   We ask it in His precious name. Amen.

(Copy of the Bible lesson outline, which was distributed to the people preceding the forty-eighth lecture)

Lesson IX - Examination of Five Reasons Why Ministers Reject the Keeping of the Seventh Day

1   It is claimed that the keeping of the seventh day was intended only for the Jews, because the Sabbath was never given until after the Jews left Egypt and was given only to them, and is declared in Ex 31.12-17, to be a special sign between God and the children of Israel forever
    (a) The keeping of the seventh day was set apart for man at creation, 2500 years before the Jews left Egypt (Gen 2.1-3; Ex 20.11, Mark 2 27)
    (b) The Sabbath is for the Gentiles (Isa 56.1-7)
    (c) God's Israel under the new covenant is composed of all Christians among the Gentiles and Jews (Gal 3 29, Jas 1·1; 5 8), and the Sabbath continues for Christian Israel forever
2   It is claimed that the laws regarding the keeping of the seventh day, show that God intended it only for the Jews when they lived in Palestine (Ex 35 3, 16 29)
    (a) These were only temporary rules binding during their sojourn in the wilderness
    (b) The abolition of these rules did not in any way lessen the binding obligation of the fourth commandment
3   It is claimed that the Sabbath was a part of the Mosaic law, which was done away in Christ (Col 2 14-17)
    (a) The handwriting of ordinances does not apply to the ten commandments, but to the ceremonial law.
    (b) The sabbath days of Col 2 16, 17, refer to the seven yearly sabbaths of the ceremonial law (see Lev 23)
    (c) The Acts of the Apostles mentions the seventh-day Sabbath eight times and thus proves eight times over that the seventh-day Sabbath was not done away with in Christ on the cross (Acts 13·14, 27, 42, 44, 15 21, 16 13, 17 1-3, 18 4)
4   It is claimed that Christians are under no obligation to keep the seventh day, because they are not under the law, but under grace (Rom 6 14)
    (a) Being under grace does not release us from the obligation to obey the decalogue (Rom 6 14, 15, 3 31; 1 Cor 9 21)
5   It is claimed that every one of the ten commandments is repeated in the New Testament with the exception of the Sabbath commandment, which shows that God never designed for Christians to observe the seventh day
    (a) Only three of the ten commandments are repeated verbatim in the New Testament (Rom 13 9)
    (b) The ten commandments have never been repealed, hence there was no need to repeat them in the New Testament
    (c) The New Testament recognizes the validity of every one of the ten commandments, including the Sabbath—Luke 23.33, 52, 55, 56; Acts 13 14)
    (d) Some reasons why some ministers do not see the truth about the Sabbath—(Matt 11 25, 13 15, Eze 22 26)
    (e) Our only safety is to do exactly what God commands us (Jas 4 17).

Why Do Ministers Reject the Bible Sabbath?

(Preached on the Eleventh Tuesday Night of the Campaign)

Many people have wondered why Protestant ministers who claim to follow the Bible, do not keep the seventh day as taught in the Bible In one city where I conducted a Bible Institute a group of people went to the most learned minister in the city, to inquire about this matter That gentleman was recognized as the outstanding authority on the Sabbath question in the city of Washington, D C They said to him, "Why don't you preachers follow the Bible in the keeping of the seventh day?"

He told them that the ministers had five reasons for rejecting the keeping of the seventh day A little later this clergyman delivered a lecture in a tabernacle in Northwest Washington in which he set forth those five reasons why preachers reject the keeping of the seventh day We had his sermon taken down by a stenographer, and thus we secured a copy of his five reasons for rejecting the keeping of the seventh day Mr Becker will now present these one by one and we will answer them by the Scriptures

"We ministers have five reasons from the Bible why we reject the keeping of the seventh day Here they are First The keeping of the seventh day, or Saturday, was intended only for the Jews God never told the Gentiles to keep the seventh day Since we are Gentiles and not Jews, the keeping of the seventh day does not pertain to us at all

"And here is our Bible proof for this The Sabbath was never given until after the Jews left Egypt and it was given only to them Exodus 31 12-17 declares that the Sabbath was a sign between God and the children of Israel forever This shows that God never intended the keeping of the seventh day Sabbath for Christians "

The apostle Paul tells us to prove all things and then to hold fast to that which is good Let us ask the question, Is it true that the Sabbath was never given until the Jews came out of Egypt?

"What says the Bible, the blessed Bible
This should my only question be
Teachings of men so often misled us,
What says the Book of God to me?"

I turn to Genesis 2 1-3 "Thus the heavens and the earth were finished, and all the host of them And on the seventh day God ended His work He had made, and He rested on the seventh day from all His work which He had made And God blessed the seventh day, and sanctified it because that in it He had rested from all His work which God created and made "

What did God do the seventh day after He had rested upon it? "God blessed the seventh day and sanctified it, because in it He **had** rested from all His work which God created and made " God sanctified the seventh day after He had rested upon the seventh day of the first week of time What does sanctified mean? Sanctified means to set apart for a holy or religious use

For whom did God set apart the keeping of the seventh day? You know and everyone ought to know that almighty God does not need any day set apart for Himself Then it is evident that God set the seventh day apart for the first man and the first woman That was 2500 years before the Jews ever left Egypt

We find in Exodus 20 11 that God Himself refers to the seventh day as having been the Sabbath when He blessed and hallowed it at the close of the first week of time He declares that the seventh day was the Sabbath day when He blessed and hallowed it   The Sabbath is just as old as the marriage institution   You know that marriage goes back to the first man and the first woman, Adam and Eve in the garden of Eden   Just as God ordained marriage at the beginning for the entire race of man, so the same God sanctified, or set apart, the keeping of the seventh day for the entire race of man

This is exactly what Jesus taught   Put down Mark 2.27   "The Sabbath was made for man"   And in this case the word "man" means, or takes in, the entire race of man   There is only one way a man can excuse himself from keeping the Sabbath, and that is to prove that he does not belong to the race of man, or that he is not a man   If anyone wants to do this, let him go!

Let us look at the Ten Commandments   Here is the fourth commandment which requires the keeping of the seventh day.   Notice that right next to the fourth commandment is the third commandment which says, "Thou shalt not take the name of the Lord thy God in vain"   Tell me, do you think that this was intended only for the Jews?   Is that binding only on the Jews? I hear you say, "Most assuredly not!   It applies to every person"

Then here is the eighth commandment "Thou shalt not steal"   Do you think that this was intended only for the Jews?   Was it binding only on the Jews? Most assuredly not!   So we might go on with all the rest of the Ten Commandments.   These Ten Commandments deal with great, eternal, principles of right, which are binding upon **all people** in **all ages.**

The keeping of the seventh day in the fourth commandment was no more intended only for the Jews than were the other nine commandments intended only for the Jews   God placed the keeping of the seventh day in with the other nine commandments, and that is where it belongs.   The fact that God placed the keeping of the seventh day in with the other nine commandments, shows that He intended the fourth commandment to be binding on all people just like the commandment not to steal, not to lie, or swear, or commit adultery, etc.

In Isaiah 56.1-7 God expressly declares that the keeping of the Sabbath is for the Gentiles, who are referred to in this Scripture as the "sons of the stranger"

It is true in Exodus 31 16, 17 that God says the Sabbath is a sign between Him and the children of Israel forever   But instead of this being something against Christians keeping the seventh day, it is one of the strongest proofs that Christians should keep the seventh day.   Please notice these facts from Scripture

The Bible speaks of two Jerusalems, the old Jerusalem in the land of Palestine, and the New Jerusalem in the heaven of heavens   The Bible speaks of two covenants, the Old Covenant and the New Covenant   It speaks of two sanctuaries, the earthly sanctuary and the heavenly sanctuary.

So the Scriptures speak of two Israels, a literal seed and a spiritual seed   Literal Israel is composed of the literal descendants of Abraham, or the people whom we commonly call the Jews   The spiritual seed is composed of all, both Jews and Gentiles, who accept Jesus Christ as their Saviour. Listen to the apostle Paul in Galatians 3 29.   "If ye be Christ's" (remember he was not talking to Jews, Galatians was written to the Gentiles)   "If ye be **Christ's, then are ye Abraham's seed."**   You are Israelites   You are the real children of Israel

Words could not be plainer   "If ye be Christ's, then are ye Abraham's seed "   This means that Christians are the true Israel of God

The apostle James in his epistle addresses all Christian people everywhere as the twelve tribes of Israel   You will find this in James 1 1.   These twelve tribes of Israel are referred to in James 5 8, as those who are looking for the return of Christ   "Be patient therefore, brethren, for the coming of the Lord draweth nigh"

Just as the New Covenant has superseded the Old Covenant, and the heavenly sanctuary has taken the place of the earthly sanctuary, and the new Jerusalem has superseded the old Jerusalem, so the Christian commonwealth of Israel has superseded literal Israel as God's true Israel   Hence, the keeping of the seventh day continues for Christian Israel, as a sign between God and Israel forever   In the place of Ex 31 16, 17 being against the keeping of the seventh day by Christians, you can see that it is one of the strongest proofs for the keeping of the seventh day

Now, we will hear the second reason

"Second: The very laws, which God made regarding the keeping of the Sabbath, show that He intended it only for the Jews when they lived in Palestine, and not for any other people in any other country.

"In Exodus 35 3 God plainly says, Ye shall kindle no fire throughout your habitations upon the Sabbath day   Since people are ordered to make no fires in their houses on the Sabbath day, how could people in cold countries ever keep the Sabbath?   Even the Adventists who profess to keep the Sabbath, break the Sabbath, by making fires in their houses on Saturday   In Exodus 16 29 God says, Let no man go out of his place on the seventh day   If you go outside your house on Saturday, you are breaking the Sabbath "

These texts are easily explained   The rule about people not going outside their houses on the seventh day was a rule given in connection with the falling of the manna in the wilderness   God told them that there would be no manna to gather on the seventh day, or the Sabbath day, and that they were to gather a double portion on the sixth day, the day we call Friday   When some of the people went out to gather manna on the seventh day, Moses made this rule that they were not to go out of their houses on the Sabbath

This was only a temporary rule while they were being fed by manna in the wilderness   When they crossed over Jordan and established themselves in Canaan, and built their synagogues, they all went out of their houses on the Sabbath day to the synagogues with God's approval, because that temporary rule had expired by limitation

The same thing was true about not building fires on the Sabbath day   When that rule was given they were in a warm country   They needed no fires because of cold, and their food was cooked on Friday   This rule against making fires on the Sabbath was enforced only while they were on their way to Canaan   The expiration of these temporary rules did not in any way affect the binding obligation to keep holy the seventh day, as set forth in God's great law of the Ten Commandments

Those rules about not going out of your house on the seventh day and not building fires were just like the rules we had for rationing gas and sugar   They were temporary rules during an emergency and that is the way it was about their rules

We do not keep the Sabbath according to the rules of Moses   No   If we kept the Sabbath according to the rules of Moses, we would have to kill two lambs every Saturday   God does not expect us to keep the Sabbath according to the rules of Moses   We should keep the Sabbath according to the fourth commandment of the Ten Commandments, as interpreted in the life and example of Jesus   Jesus kept the seventh day, and showed us how to keep it   We should keep the Sabbath, not according to the rules of Moses, but according to the example of Jesus.

Now we shall hear the third reason

"Third   The Sabbath was a part of the Mosaic law, which was done away in Christ   Paul specified in Col 2 14-17 that the Sabbath day was done away in Christ   The keeping of the seventh day, along with the rest of the Jewish law, was abolished at the cross and hence is not binding on Christians "

We shall examine this text in Col 2 14-17 and see what Paul says "Blotting out the handwriting of ordinances that was against us, which was contrary to us, and took it out of the way, nailing it to His cross" This refers to the ceremonial law that was nailed to the cross It has no reference whatever to the Ten Commandments

In the ceremonial law in Leveticus 23 the Jews were given yearly sabbaths, in addition to the weekly Sabbath of the Ten Commandments Those yearly sabbaths were nailed to the cross and done away with, but the seventh-day Sabbath continued binding after the cross, just as the other nine commandments continued binding

Paul is careful to specify that the sabbath days, which were done away in Christ, were the sabbath days of the ceremonial law, which were connected with the new moons and the feast days of the Jews I read in verses 16 and 17, "Let no man therefore judge you in meat, or in drink, or in respect of an holy day," (the Greek is feast day) "or of the new moon, or of the sabbath days **Which are a shadow of things to come,** but the body is of Christ"

The fifth book of the New Testament is the book of Acts It covers a period of about thirty years following the crucifixion and resurrection of our Lord In eight different places the Acts of the Apostles mentions the Sabbath during the days of the Apostles, after the Lord's resurrection Mark this well Every time without a single exception that the Acts of the Apostles mentions the Sabbath, it identifies the Sabbath as being the seventh day, or Saturday, when the Jews held their regular weekly meeting in the synagogues

These eight references to the Sabbath in the Acts of the Apostles are as follows Acts 13 14 Acts 13 27, Acts 13 42, Acts 13 44, Acts 15 21, Acts 16 13, Acts 17 1-3, and Acts 18 4 Here are the eight unimpeachable proofs that the seventh-day Sabbath did not expire at the cross Remember that the Acts of the Apostles is dealing with events after the resurrection of Christ and eight times in that book the Sabbath is identified with the Saturday-meeting-day of the Jews This shows that the seventh day continued to be the Sabbath in the New dispensation under the new covenant

Some will say that these texts in the Book of Acts about Paul preaching in the Jewish synagogues on the Sabbath day are no evidence in favor of the seventh day being the right day for Christians to keep They declare that he went to the synagogue on Saturday, because it gave him an opportunity to preach Christ to the unbelieving Jews This may be granted to be the case But the fact remains, that the Holy Spirit in speaking through Luke in the book of Acts, calls this seventh day, or Saturday, on which the Jews met for worship THE Sabbath day This shows that the seventh day, or Saturday, was the Sabbath in the days of the apostles

Please follow me further The Acts of the Apostles shows that the **only** Sabbath there was in the days of the apostles was the seventh day, or Saturday, the day on which the Jews held their regular weekly meetings at the synagogues Put down Acts 13 42, 44 You will find in this scripture that Paul preached on two successive Sabbath days in the city of Antioch At the close of his first sermon the Gentiles begged Paul to preach the same truths again the next Sabbath When did the next Sabbath come? In this case the Jews had assembled on Saturday as was their custom for their weekly worship, and certain Gentile believers in God were also in the meeting The Gentiles begged Paul to preach to them again the next Sabbath What was the next Sabbath? The record shows that it was the next seventh day, when the Jews again came together as per their custom This indicates that the **only Sabbath there was in the days of the apostles fell on the seventh day, the day we call Saturday.**

We can go a step further Since the only Sabbath there was in the days of the apostles came on the seventh day, or Saturday, then the seventh day, or Saturday, must be the only day there is for Christians to keep today

Now we shall hear the fourth reason

"Fourth Paul says in Romans 6 14 that Christians are not under law, but under grace Hence the keeping of the seventh day is not binding on Christians In fact the keeping of the seventh day typifies salvation by works If a Christian tries to keep the seventh day holy, he is fallen from grace "

Romans 6 14 does show that Christians are not under the law, but under grace What does it mean? "Under the law" sometimes means under the condemnation of the law, or under sin Sometimes "Under the law"- means subject to the requirements of the law Jesus Christ forgives all the believers' sins, so that Christians are not under the condemnation of the Ten Commandments, but under the unmerited favor of God However, Christians are still subject to the requirements of God Being a Christian does not put a man above the requirements of God Being under grace does not release a man from the obligation to keep the Ten Commandments

Paul was the man who wrote Romans 6 14 He must be allowed to speak for himself In 1 Corinthians 9 21 Paul says that Christians are under the law, as it is in Christ

Take the eighth commandment, "Thou shalt not steal " Ask yourself a question Does the fact that Christians are not under the law, but under grace, give them the right to steal? What do you say? No So in the same way being under grace, and not under the law, does not give Christians the right to work on Saturday in violation of the fourth commandment which says, "The seventh day is the Sabbath, in it thou shalt not do any work "

Why do not these people who talk about the Ten Commandments not being binding under grace, read the next verse after Romans 6 14? If they would read the next verse they would never have a question about it Put down Romans 6 14, 15 Paul evidently knew that people would misconstrue the meaning of his words, and he said something to help people to be on their guard

I read Romans 6 14, 15 "Sin shall not have dominion over you for ye are not under the law, but under grace " A lot of folks want to stop right there, but Paul did not stop there "What then? Shall we sin, because we are not under the law?" He then used the strongest negative he could muster, "God forbid "

What is sin? "Sin is the transgression of the law " See 1 John 3 4 Now put the Bible definition of sin into Romans 6 15 "What then? Shall we transgress the law, because we are not under the law, but under grace? God forbid " Paul makes it plain that being under grace does not release a man from the obligation to obey God, and to keep His commandments

The keeping of the seventh day is not opposed to grace On the contrary it is one of God's own appointed signs of the work of grace in the believer's heart Put down Ezekiel 20 12, "Moreover also I gave them My Sabbaths to be a sign between Me and them, that they might know that I am the Lord that sanctify them " The keeping of the Sabbath is a sign of the work of sanctification in a person's life That is a work of grace

Now we shall hear your last reason

"Fifth Seventh-day preachers repeatedly challenge Sunday keepers to produce one text in the New Testament which says that Christians should keep the first day of the week But we challenge them to produce one text in the New Testament which says that anybody ought to keep the seventh day The fact that every one of the Ten Commandments is repeated in the New Testament with the exception of the Sabbath commandment, shows that God never designed for Christians to observe the seventh day

"Ask them to explain why every one of the Ten Commandments is repeated in the New Testament (some of them many times), with the exception of the Sabbath commandment   In the entire New Testament there is not a single command to observe the Sabbath"

Take this statement that every one of the Ten Commandments is repeated in the New Testament with the exception of the Sabbath commandment   Check up on that and what do you find?   You will find that it is not true   Only three of the Ten Commandments are repeated verbatim in the New Testament, as they are given in the Old Testament   Those are the sixth, seventh, and eighth commandments in Romans 13 9

The fact that the first, second, third, fourth, fifth, ninth, and tenth of the Ten Commandments are not repeated word for word in the New Testament, as they are recorded in the Old Testament, does not mean that those commandments are not binding on Christians

Jesus Christ and His apostles treated the Ten Commandments as a divine law, which was binding in its entirety, hence, there was no need to repeat the Ten Commandments word for word in the New Testament in order to make them binding on Christians

When a law is once enacted, it remains binding until it is repealed by the law-making power, or until it naturally expires by limitation   To illustrate If the United States Congress enacts a law without any limitation expressed as to its duration, that law remains binding in the United States until it is repealed by the United States Congress   When a new Congress meets, they do not have to repeat all the previous laws that Congress ever passed to make them binding on the people   Unless a law was designed to expire by limitation, it naturally continues binding, until it is repealed by the same power which enacted it

The New Testament plainly shows that the ceremonial law was repealed at the cross   In fact, the ceremonial law expired by limitation   It was designed to be binding only until the death of Christ, but the New Testament never says anything about the Ten Commandments being repealed   On the contrary they are treated as being a binding code

There is no limitation of time expressed or implied in any of the Ten Commandments   Notice the eighth commandment, "Thou shalt not steal" Does it say, "Thou shalt not steal until Christ dies on the cross?" Is that the way it reads? "Thou shalt not steal until the New Covenant comes in?" No God simply says, "Thou shalt not steal" That is eternally binding   It is the same way with the Sabbath   It was not necessary to repeat any of the commandments in the New Testament in order to make them binding

The New Testament does, however, recognize the validity of every one of the Ten Commandments   The apostle James in his general epistle addressed to all Christians, refers to the Ten Commandments as a law that is binding in its entirety   You will find that in James 2 8-12

God knew that this question would come up and He so ordered the Scriptures, that the Sabbath commandment is the only commandment specifically spoken of as being binding after Christ died on the cross   In Luke 23 52, 55, 56 we read   "This man went unto Pilate and begged the body of Jesus"   This is talking about the sixth day of the week, that memorable Friday when Jesus was crucified   "And the women also which came with Him from Galilee, followed after, and beheld the sepulchre, and how His body was laid"   "And they returned and prepared spices and ointments, and rested **the Sabbath day according to the commandment."**

Christ had already died, but the commandment was still binding   "They rested the Sabbath day **according to the commandment."**

The Acts of the Apostles recognizes the validity of the Sabbath commandment eight times over by referring to the seventh day as the Sabbath day eight times in the book of Acts   The New Testament throws great light upon the Old Testament The New Testament shows that Christ is the One Who spoke these ten Commandments at Mt Sinai Hence, the fourth commandment is a commandment of Jesus Christ for the keeping of the seventh day When it says, "the seventh day is the Sabbath of the Lord thy God," that is equivalent to saying, "the seventh day is the Sabbath of the Lord Jesus Christ."

The New Testament shows that the One Who made the world in six days and rested upon the seventh day and sanctified, or set apart, the seventh day for man is the eternal Son of God, Jesus Christ Then the seventh day is Christ's sanctified day for Christians to keep The example of Jesus Christ enforces the keeping of the seventh day in the New Testament

If men should preach a hundred sermons against the keeping of the seventh day, if they write a hundred books, or a thousand books, against the Sabbath, when they are done there are two outstanding facts which can never be overthrown, and these two eternal facts settle forever, which day Christians should keep **The seventh day is the only day of weekly observance that Christ ever sanctified, or set apart, for man to keep. The seventh day is the only day of weekly observance that Christ ever asked people to keep.** Friends, aren't those facts sufficient to help you to make your decision to follow Christ in keeping the seventh day?

Some will say, "This Sabbath truth is so plain, I just cannot understand why the learned preachers do not see it and follow it " One of the main reasons is that most of the preachers have never searched their Bibles to find the truth about it. They just take it for granted.

A certain gentleman wrote to a prominent Methodist minister in Des Moines asking him why he observed the first day of the week, or Sunday, in place of the seventh day as spoken of in the Ten Commandments What do you suppose he wrote back? Under date of April 3, 1933, Reverend Dilman Smith, who was Chaplain of the Iowa Methodist Hospital in the city of Des Moines, said.

"I have never made a study of 'why I should observe the first day of the week as Sabbath rather than the seventh ' This is a mooted question, and is no nearer settlement than it was decades ago My ancestors have all kept the first day of the week and I have accepted their traditions and am very happy about it."

In other words, one man is a Democrat because his father was a Democrat Another man is a Republican because his father was a Republican So this says, as it were, "I keep Sunday because Dad kept Sunday."

In Matthew 11 25 Jesus says, "I thank thee, O, Father, Lord of heaven and earth, because Thou hast hid these things from the wise and prudent, and hast revealed them unto babes " Jesus actually declares that the truth is hid from these, who think they are so wise, and it is revealed to those who, in simple faith, take God at His word.

God makes a charge against some ministers It is a serious charge. Put down Ezekiel 22 26 Do you know that God declares that many of the ministers will hide their eyes from the Sabbath? Listen to what God says.

"Her priests (that is an Old Testament term that refers to the ministry) have violated My law, and have profaned Mine holy things: they have put no difference between the holy and profane   and have hid their eyes from My Sabbaths."

Why do they not see it? If a man hides his eyes from the Sabbath, he will never see it The higher religious authorities in Christ's day refused to admit that Jesus was the Son of God It was a case of the blind leading the blind Jesus told them that they had closed their eyes, lest they should see the truth and be converted

The religious authorities of His day fought against Jesus Christ just as the church authorities today fight against the seventh-day Sabbath   The religious authorities fought against the truth that the apostles preached, just as the religious authorities fight against this Sabbath truth

It is possible for a preacher to be perfectly honest, but terribly mistaken It is possible for him to be entirely honest and give other people wrong directions   Proverbs 16 25 says, "There is a way that seemeth right unto a man, but the end thereof are the ways of death"

Some will ask, "If a person is given wrong directions by a preacher, will God punish the preacher and let the person go free?"   God will judge each person according to the light given him, and according to the opportunity he had to learn the truth   God cannot excuse anyone who goes directly contrary to one of His plain, positive commands

We have a case in the Bible where one preacher told a deliberate lie to another preacher   He knew he was telling a lie when he told it   This lie led the other preacher to disobey a plain command of God   Did the Lord let the preacher go free who was deceived by the lie of a fellow preacher?   No, He did not   You will find all the details in 1 Kings 13

God told this preacher to go into a certain city, and to do a certain work God told him not to eat or drink while he was in that city   The preacher went to the city   He did the work God asked him to do   The king invited him to go home for dinner   The preacher said, "No   I would like to go, but God has told me not to eat bread or drink water in this city"   He stood firm

Then a little later when he was on his way out of town another preacher contacted this first preacher, and said, "Brother, I am a preacher just as you are   Come and go home with me"

The man said, "No, I cannot do it   God has told me not to eat anything in this town"

Then the other preacher told him a lie   He said, "An angel just came to me and told me to come out here and get you to come to my house to eat dinner"   He knew he was lying when he said this   The first preacher was deceived   He believed the lie   He went back to town   He sat down to eat at the dinner table in the second preacher's house in direct disobedience to what God had told him

When he left town a lion came out of the woods and killed him   Here is a case where one preacher lost his soul, because he listened to another preacher, who advised him contrary to the plain command that God had given

One of the most dangerous things you can do is to accept the word of man in place of the Word of God   God commands you to keep the seventh day   Your only safety is to obey God and keep it holy   "To him that knoweth to do good and doeth it not, to him it is sin"   You dare not run the risk of losing eternal life by listening to any person, preacher, friend or loved one, who advises you contrary to the plain command to keep the seventh day holy Thousands of people will miss heaven, because they allowed somebody, preacher, neighbor, husband, wife, brother, sister, father, or mother to turn them aside from keeping the seventh day, when they knew in their heart that they ought to do it

Some years ago two fast passenger trains collided head-on   Twenty-eight people were killed, and scores were injured   The air was filled with cries and shrieks of the wounded and dying   The engineer of one of those wrecked trains was lying pinned under his engine   A man saw him faintly waving a piece of yellow paper   It was the orders he had received from the dispatcher He was moving the piece of paper, and the man bent over to catch his dying words   He said, "Someone gave me the wrong orders"

God alone knows how many thousands will be wrecked for eternity, because they listened to the wrong orders on the Sabbath question   Our only safety is to heed God's orders   I should like to know tonight, how many are determined to heed God's orders about the Sabbath and henceforth keep the seventh day holy?   Let us put our hands up high   Thank God!   This is the best expression we have had here   (Nearly every hand was raised)

I wonder if there is someone here to whom the truth has been made a little plainer   The truth has been made so plain to some of you who have been holding back that you are ready to say, "God helping me, I will listen to God's orders henceforth and keep His day "   Is there someone, who has not previously made up his mind, but tonight you will make your decision?   Do I see a hand?   Yes, there is one   Is there another?   God says they shall be gathered one by one   Thank God somebody tonight is making up his mind

Prayer followed

How To Die and Live Again

There are three special days which ordinarily come to people in their natural lives in this world These are the day of their birth, the day of their marriage, and the day of their death. Do you know that baptism is comparable in a spiritual sense to these great days in a person's life? Baptism means a spiritual death to sin, a spiritual birth into the kingdom of God, and a spiritual marriage to Jesus Christ for time and eternity.

Baptism is a spiritual death, a spiritual resurrection, a spiritual birth, and a spiritual marriage As we conduct this baptismal service, we will have a spiritual funeral, a spiritual birthday, and a spiritual wedding, all combined in one No wonder this is the highlight of eleven weeks of preaching the Word of God.

Jesus Christ definitely connected baptism with the new-birth experience. In John 3.5 He said, "Except a man be born of water and of the Spirit, he cannot enter into the kingdom of God." Baptism marks the time when we were born of the water. When a person is baptized by immersion, he emerges from the waters as from the womb He is born of the water, and if his heart has been truly surrendered to the Lord Jesus Christ, he is not only born of water, but he also is born of the Holy Spirit.

Notice how important it is for you and me to enter into this experience Remember the solemn words of Jesus He says, "Except a man be born of the water and of the Spirit, he cannot enter into the kingdom of God "

One of the most important elements in being baptized is to receive the Holy Spirit You cannot live right after you are baptized unless you receive the Holy Spirit when you are baptized. There is only one way that you can ever live a Christian life, and that is to have the Lord Jesus Christ come and live His life in you, by the indwelling of the Holy Spirit The apostle Paul expresses this truth so graphically and so directly in Galatians 2 20. He says, "I am crucified with Christ: nevertheless I live yet not I, but Christ liveth in me " (That is the Christian life, Christ living in you) And he continues, "The life that I now live in the flesh I live by the faith of the Son of God Who loved me, and gave Himself for me."

The only way that Christ can ever live in you is by the Holy Spirit The Holy Spirit, is, as it were, the personal presence of Jesus Christ The Holy Spirit is His direct personal representative Christ in your heart, and the Holy Spirit in your heart are the identical and same experience

Let me say to these dear ones who are being baptized tonight, that God has promised to give you the Holy Spirit when you are baptized I turn to Acts 2 38, a verse taken from that sermon preached on the Day of Pentecost when 3000 were converted "Then Peter said unto them, repent, and be baptized everyone of you in the name of Jesus Christ for the remission of sins, and ye shall receive the gift of the Holy Ghost "

I say to these dear friends of ours who are being baptized tonight,—claim, by faith, the gift of the Holy Ghost God has promised to give Him to you when you are baptized, and now it is for you, by faith, to claim this highest of all gifts of the Father

The baptism of Jesus wonderfully illustrates this As you know, when Jesus was baptized the heavens were opened and the Holy Spirit in the bodily form of a dove came down upon Him. He received a special anointing of the

Holy Spirit when He was baptized   Jesus was standing there in your place
In fact He was baptized for you, and He was baptized for me   He didn't
have any sins to wash away such as you and I have   He never committed any
sin   He did not need to be baptized, but he said, "Suffer it to be so now
for thus it becometh us to fulfill all righteousness"   The gift of the Holy Ghost
to Jesus at His baptism, is God's assurance that He will give the Holy Spirit
to everyone who truly surrenders himself in baptism

The New Testament teaches that baptism marks the beginning of a new life
in Christ   I turn to Romans 6 4   "Therefore we are buried with Him by
baptism into death, that like as Christ was raised up from the dead by the
glory of the Father, even so we also should walk in newness of life"   After a
person is baptized there is to be a new life   He is raised up from the watery
grave to walk in newness of life   The day of his baptism is the day of
spiritual birth

The New Testament teaches that a Christian is to be united so closely to
his Saviour that he is actually married to Jesus Christ   He becomes one with
Jesus   When a man and woman are truly married, they become one in every
sense of the word   When the marriage takes place there is a ceremony at
which they exchange their vows   Baptism is the marriage ceremony where the
believer publicly becomes one with Christ   He takes Christ's name to henceforth live for Christ   Paul brings this thought out so beautifully in Galatians
3 27   "As many of you as have been baptized into Christ have put on Christ"
Baptism is the seal of your union with Christ for time and eternity

Baptism means to die with Jesus Christ to sin   We find this expressed
emphatically in Romans 6 3   "Know ye not, that so many of us as were
baptized into Jesus Christ were baptized into His death?" In other words if
you are really baptized into Christ, you are baptized into His death   The day
of your baptism should be your funeral to the sinful ways of the world and
to the sinful habits of the flesh

Think how much this service means to these dear friends of ours who are
about to be baptized   A spiritual death, a spiritual resurrection, a spiritual
birth, and a spiritual marriage all together in one service tonight

Some people think that since immersion is the true form of baptism, all
that there is to being baptized is to be dipped under the water   Do you know
that a person might be dipped under the water a dozen times, or even fifty
times, and not have a true baptism? What do I mean by that? A true baptism means following Christ into His death, burial, and resurrection

It takes three steps of spiritual experience in order for a person to have a
true baptism   He must die with Christ to sin, he must bury the old life of
sin, he must rise with Christ to walk in newness of life   If a person does not
take these three steps of spiritual experience, his will not be a true baptism,
even though he goes through the form of being dipped under the water fifty
times

I want you to notice how important these three steps are for every soul
The blessed Bible shows us that salvation centers, or revolves, around three
great acts of the Lord Jesus Christ   He died for our sins; He was buried
for us, He rose again to minister His life to us   In order for you and me to
actually experience salvation we must go with Jesus into His death, burial,
and resurrection

Salvation becomes yours personally when you follow Christ into His
death, into His burial, and into His resurrection. His death must become
your death to sin   His burial must be your burial of the old life of sin   His
resurrection must become your resurrection to a new life of holiness   Baptism
is God's own appointed sign of these three steps of spiritual experience

How many parts are there in the act of baptism? There are three   Everyone of these people whom I shall baptize tonight will enact these three parts

There will be a laying back in the water, a going under the water, and a coming up from the water   All this has a most beautiful meaning

Notice how beautifully the three parts of the act of baptism prefigure the three steps of spiritual experience that make salvation yours by following Jesus into His death, burial, and resurrection   As the believer is laid back in the water, it shows that he is dying with Jesus Christ to sin.   As he goes under the water, it shows that he is burying the old life of sin with Christ. As he is raised from the water, it shows that he is rising with Christ to walk in newness of life   O, how meaningful is true baptism   Beautiful, isn't it? Even the three parts that constitute immersion beautifully picture the three steps of spiritual experience by which salvation becomes ours

Some people, when they think about having a few drops of water sprinkled on their head, or a cup of water poured over their head, or actually being dipped under water, conclude that immersion is the best way, because there is more water employed   Immersion is not better than these other forms merely because more water is employed, but rather because single immersion alone sets forth the essential following of Jesus into His death, burial, and resurrection on the part of the believer   Any of you who have only been sprinkled will do well to ask yourselves, "Have I been buried with Jesus Christ in baptism?   Have I set forth in my baptism the three great steps of dying with Jesus, of being buried with Jesus and of rising with Jesus?" No Not unless you have gone through immersion

These dear ones who are being baptized tonight are making salvation their very own by following Jesus into His death, burial and resurrection   The all-essential consideration in being ready for baptism is to die with Jesus Christ to sin   Baptism is a burial with Jesus Christ

Any of you folks who are not just sure about immersion being the right way for you to be baptized really need only to read five words in the Bible Here they are in Colossians 2 12   "Buried with Him in baptism" Those five words are enough for me   You know and I know that sprinkling a few drops of water on somebody's head is not burying him with Christ in baptism If there was nothing else in the Bible, these five words are sufficient to show that we ought to be immersed and thus be buried with Christ in baptism in harmony with the command given in Colossians 2 12

You cannot be truly buried with Christ, unless you first die with Christ to sin   The question naturally comes, what does it mean to die with Christ to sin? It means this   If a man is addicted to swearing and he dies with Christ to sin, he simply stops swearing   He loves the name of God and Christ so dearly, that he will never think of misusing those holy names   If a man is addicted to the use of liquor or tobacco, and he dies with Christ to sin, he stops using liquor and tobacco

The way to have sure victory over liquor and tobacco is to be dead to sin Let me ask you a question   Can a corpse smoke a cigarette? No If you are dead to sin, you have the victory   Can a corpse drink a glass of beer? No Jesus Christ can give you the victory until a cigarette, or a glass of beer, will have no more power over you than if it were offered to a corpse

I can testify to the glory of God that He gives the victory   I once used cigarettes and liquor, but God gave me complete victory   I have never wanted them from the night I laid them down   "Thanks be unto God, who giveth us the victory through our Lord Jesus Christ"

Some months ago I was riding across Canada in a Pullman car   There was a naval officer on the car who became very friendly   After he had talked to me a little while he said to me, "I have here in my grip some of the choicest champagne that it is possible to get in France   Wouldn't you like a drink of this fine champagne?" I said "No, thank you, I wouldn't care for it" Soon he pulled out a package of cigarettes   He said, "Mr, wouldn't you like to have a cigarette?" I said, "No, I wouldn't care for any, thanks"

Although I at one time used both of those items, when he offered them to me, it aroused no more appeal in my body than if he had offered them to a corpse   Dead to sin   Yes   That is what God wants us to be   The sure way to have victory over sin is to die with Christ to sin

I am sure that there are scores of people here, who once used these items and have complete victory over those habits   I believe it is good to testify to the glory of God   How many wish to bear your testimony by the uplifted hand that God has given you victory over these habits?   Look at those hands (A number of hands were raised)   Think of the divine power back of those hands which have been raised   Back of every hand there is a living Christ who gives the victory

What happens to the leaves on a tree when the tree dies?   You say, "When the tree dies the leaves fall off"   Yes   Do they ever come back?   No, not if the tree is dead   That is how it is with the truly converted man and the sinful ways of the world   When you really die with Christ, those sinful ways of the world drop off, never to come back

2 Corinthians 5.17 says, "If any man be in Christ, he is a new creature old things are passed away, behold, all things are become new"   The way to have sure and lasting victory over liquor and tobacco and every other bad habit of life, is to die to sin with Jesus Christ

If a person has not been keeping the seventh day, or Saturday, and He dies to sin, he begins to keep the seventh day holy   If a man has been robbing God by not rendering to God His tithe and he dies to sin, he will begin to bring into God's storehouse, the one-tenth of his net income   If a person has been attending dances, the Hollywood movies, gambling, and playing cards, and he dies to sin, he will turn away from those sinful ways of the world   Romans 12 2 says, "Be not conformed to this world, but be ye transformed by the renewing of your mind"

If a person has been wearing ornaments forbidden by the Word of God, and he dies to sin, the ornaments will come off, never to return   Dying with Christ to sin means turning away from every habit and practice that is contrary to the teachings of Jesus Christ   It is not until then that a person is ready for baptism

No person can live a new life in Christ until he buries the old life   No person can bury the old life until he dies to sin with Christ   Does the undertaker have any right to bury a person in the cemetery unless he is dead?   No That would be a terrible thing   So, no minister has any right to bury a person in baptism, until that person gives evidence of being dead to sin

This is why Adventist ministers cannot baptize people who are not keeping the seventh day   If they do not keep the seventh day, they are still transgressing the law of God   "The seventh day is the Sabbath of the Lord thy God   in it thou shalt not do any work"   This is why we cannot baptize any person who is using liquor or tobacco because he isn't dead to sin   We cannot baptize a person, who is attending dances or playing cards, because he is not dead to sin yet   It is really impossible for a person to have a true baptism until he has left off these things

After a person is baptized he will live a new life   He will live the life of Christ   The apostle John expresses this in 1 John 2 6   "He that saith he abideth in Him ought himself also so to walk, even as He walked"   Some will say, "Aren't some people baptized and yet live no differently afterward than before?"   Yes, we have all seen such cases   In fact we have seen them too frequently, but why?   The reason is that those persons did not take the three steps of spiritual experience which are absolutely essential to having a true baptism   They failed to die with Christ to sin   Having failed to die to sin, they could not rise with Christ to live a new life

Some will say, "What shall I do if I sin after I am baptized?"   God tells us what to do in 1 John 2 1   God does not want us to sin   He has made full provision to save us from sin   So we read in 1 John 2 1, "My little children, these things write I unto you, that ye sin not   And if any man sin, we have an Advocate with the Father, Jesus Christ the Righteous"

Jesus will forgive us again if we fall back into sin   He will forgive us again as He did when we were converted, but Christ wants to keep us from falling   He is able to keep us from falling, and He will keep us from falling if we will permit Him

Do you know how we are to permit the Lord Jesus to keep us from falling? You will find this in Romans 13 14   Paul says, "Put ye on the Lord Jesus Christ, and make no provision for the flesh, to fulfil the lusts thereof"   We must enthrone Christ in our hearts, and make no provision to fulfil the lusts of the flesh

If a person has been addicted to smoking, he shouldn't even take a cigarette between his fingers   If he takes it between his fingers, he may put it in his mouth   We should make no provision to fulfil the lusts of the flesh   If he never puts it between his fingers, he will never put it in his mouth

If a man has been addicted to drinking and he quits drinking, then he should not stand outside the tavern looking at the liquor bottles in the window If a man has been accustomed to attending Hollywood movies, he should avoid looking at the posters of the movies   He ought to avoid everything that will keep alive the interests in the wrong things he once did   When he applies for a job, he should make provision for having the Sabbath in the clear   If you will stand firm, and refuse to make any provision for going back on God's commandment, God will see that you will win out completely

Baptism is a grave between the old life and the new   We bury the sinful past   We rise to walk in newness of life

Think what a privilege it is to put the sinful past where it will not rise up to plague you again.   It is a wonderful privilege that these people have tonight, to put the sinful past where it will not rise up to dominate them again

I appeal to you who are about to be buried in the watery grave   Make this baptismal fount a real grave where all the sinful ways of the world, the old habits, the haunts, the attachments, or friendships, that are contrary to Jesus Christ are buried forever   Remember Lot's wife   She lost her soul hankering after what she had left behind in Sodom   So it is liable to be with any of you who are baptized tonight, if you look back

Jesus says in Luke 9.52, "No man, having put his hand to the plough, and looking back, is fit for the kingdom of God"   If we are really raised up with Christ in baptism, we will set our affection upon things above as Paul says in Colossians 3 1-3.   "If ye then be risen with Christ   set your affection on things above, not on things on the earth"

A baptized person does more than leave off bad habits   The religion of Jesus Christ is not a negative religion   It isn't just "don't do this, don't do that"   No!   A baptized person does more than leave off bad habits   He takes on good habits in the place of the bad   Such as a daily reading of the Bible, daily prayer to God, attending church, keeping the Sabbath, coming to Prayer meeting, paying his tithe, eating and drinking to the glory of God, talking, dressing, and acting in accordance with the revealed will of God

You who are being baptized, should not conclude that the devil will leave you alone after you are baptized   Jesus Christ had the most wonderful baptism any person could ever have, but what happened immediately afterward? Have you read Mark 1 10-13?   The 10th and 11th verses tell how the heavens were opened, and the Holy Spirit descended on Jesus, and the Father's voice said, "This is My beloved Son," when Jesus was baptized The next verse says, "Immediately the Spirit driveth Him into the wilderness and He was there in the wilderness forty days, tempted of Satan " Immediately after the baptism of Jesus, came His great test of forty days of temptation

I heard one of the greatest evangelists in America declare, "I did not know what temptation was until after I became a Christian " But remember, Jesus Christ will never fail you He will see you through He declares in Jude 24 that "He is able to keep you from falling, and to present you faultless before the presence of His glory with exceeding joy " In 1 Corinthians 10 13 He says, "There hath no temptation taken you but such as is common to man, but God is faithful and will with the temptation also make a way to escape " In Isaiah 41 10 He says, "Fear thou not, for I am with thee be not dismayed, for I am thy God " I will strengthen thee, yea, I will help thee; yea, I will uphold thee with the right hand of My righteousness "

When God says all this to you, you have everything to go forward for Then in Philippians 1 6 we learn that "He which hath begun a good work in you will perform it until the day of Jesus Christ "

I appeal to you who are being baptized tonight to keep your eye on the surpassing prize at the end of the way The great prize comes not to him who begins, but to him who finishes the race I beg you to keep your eye on the surpassing prize that Christ has for you, if you will be faithful to the end Baptism puts your feet on the first round of the Christian ladder Now, add to your Faith, Virtue; to Virtue, Knowledge, to Knowledge, Temperance; to Temperance, Patience, to Patience, Godliness, to Godliness, Brotherly Kindness, to Brotherly Kindness, Love, (2 Peter 1 5-7) and then step off the last round over into the City of Gold

As the choir sings, "All to Jesus I Surrender," I invite those who are to be baptized tonight to come to the front for a prayer of consecration

This is a fine time for you who are planning on taking your stand in the near future, to come and stand wtih these who are coming forward tonight I ask that the entire congregation please stand, and I appeal to everyone who has a purpose in his heart to accept the great message that you have heard to come forward This is a fine time to come and say, "God helping me, I want to surrender all to Jesus "

(Prayer)

O, Lord Jesus, Precious Saviour, we present to Thee tonight in the arms of our faith, this company of men and women who have heard the great message of God during these weeks Lord, they are making their response tonight to the call of God They have come here to stand and say, "I surrender all "

Lord, we thank Thee for their sincere hearts We thank Thee for the love they have for Jesus He says, "If you love Me, keep My commandments "

O, God, we pray that to these who go forward tonight, this baptism will mean all that the Word of God says it should mean Make their baptism a real grave, where all the old habits of sin are buried forever May every one of them come up to walk in newness of life

We pray for these friends of ours who have come forward tonight to make their decision for Thy message We thank Thee for their honest hearts and for what they are purposed to do O, God, work in their lives and grant that in the next baptism we may see as large a number as we see here tonight We thank Thee for this, in the name of Jesus our Saviour Amen

Baby Buggy Religion

If I should give each of you a slip of paper and ask you to write on it the reason why you belong to your church, what would you write? I am sure there would be a large variety of answers

Some people belong to a certain church, because it happens to be the nearest church to where they live They reason, why should I go four miles, or six miles, to attend a church, while I can worship just a few blocks away, even if this nearby church does not teach just what the one does across town? Anyone who reasons along that line ought to remember that a faith that is not worth sacrificing for is not worth having

One of the first principles of Christianity is self-denial Jesus said, "If any man come after Me, let him, (what is the first thing?) deny himself" Yet this is the last thing that most people want to do When we talk to them about giving up tobacco, and refraining from the sinful ways of the world, such as dancing and theatre-going, and laying aside ornaments forbidden by the Word of God, some people begin to draw back They fail to realize that one of the first principles of Christianity is "self-denial" "If a man will come after Me," says Jesus, "let him deny himself and take up his cross and follow Me"

Some people join a certain church, because it has the finest edifice, the best pipe organ, the most talented choir. It seems that churches today are vying with each other to have the finest edifice and the most talented choirs and the finest pipe organs Of course, it is desirable to have the proper kind of place in which to worship God But when it comes to deciding which church you will join, you cannot settle that on the basis of the kind of a building they have, but rather on whether they have the truth

I think it is true as a rule, that the more elaborate the church edifice, the less religion you will find there Isn't that likely to be the case? If you put this to a test in any city, you will likely find that the more elaborate the church edifice, the less real religion you will find You will find a great deal of pomp and fashion and show and style, but where is the real christianity of the Bible?

Some people unite with a certain church, because the most influential people in town belong to it Perhaps the mayor is a member, or the Congressman or the United States Senator belongs to the church People like that need to remember that the way of truth will never be popular

Jesus said in Matthew 7 13,14, "Enter ye in at the strait gate, for wide is the gate, and **broad** is the way that leadeth to destruction, and **many** there be which go in thereat Because strait is the gate, and **narrow** is the way, which leadeth unto life, and **few** there be that find it"

A lot of people do not like that word "narrow" Of course, I do not believe in being narrow-minded But I accept the words of Jesus **"Narrow is the way, which leadeth unto life, and few there be that find it."** The gate is narrow The way is narrow It is so narrow, that you cannot walk in it with your arms bulging out with a lot of things of the world which most people want to take with them

The true church will always be ridiculed If any of you should unite with the Seventh-day Adventist church, thinking you will be in a church that is not ridiculed, you are mistaken before you take your first step The true church will be ridiculed and persecuted That is the way it was when Jesus was here That is the way it was in the days of the apostles In John 15 19 Jesus says, "If ye were of the world, the world would love his own" You see, if you will

316

go the way the world wants you to go, they will pat you on the back and tell you that you are doing fine So Jesus says, "If ye were of the world, the world would love his own but because   I have chosen you out of the world, **therefore the world hateth you."**

In Acts 28 22 we read that the Jews of Rome, in speaking about the Christian people in the days of Paul said "Concerning this sect, we know that everywhere it is spoken against " The people looked upon the followers of Jesus as a sect They declared that this sect was spoken against everywhere All that they ever heard about it was against it

In John 10 20 we find that Jesus Christ Himself was accused of being mentally deranged and of having a devil Just think of that! According to John 10 20 some said, "He hath a devil, and is mad, why hear ye Him?" If they accused the Son of God of being mentally deranged and of having a devil, what can you expect they may say about you and me? The fact is that the real truth never has been popular and it never will be popular

Some people join a certain church, because the pastor is such a wonderful man with a pleasing personality, charming manners, and eloquent tongue Such people should bear in mind that you should not take any man for a pattern There is only one pattern, even Jesus In 1 Peter 2 21 we read that "He left us an example, that we should follow His steps "

Some people unite with a certain church because their friends belong to it We should never decide our duty in religion by what our friends do If Paul had clung to his friends in the Jewish church, he never would have become a Christian This is something you need to think over seriously In Galatians 1 10 he said, "Do I now persuade men, or God? or do I seek to please men? for **if I yet pleased men, I should not be the servant of Christ."**

If he had listened to his friends, he never would have become a Christian He was one of the highest officers in the Jewish church He was a member of a special council of seventy, which corresponded to our supreme court, the Jewish Sanhedrin His friends were among the Sanhedrin If he had listened to his friends, he never would have become a Christian

The same situation prevails today in almost every case with people when they hear God's message for this hour If they follow the advice of their friends, they likely will never begin to keep the Sabbath There were people baptized last night, who will tell you frankly, that if they had listened to husband, or preacher, or if they had followed the advice of friends, they likely would not have begun to keep the Sabbath

It is a terrible thing to think how many people who hear God's message, and who know what they ought to do, allow their friends to dissuade them from accepting it One of the most terrible mistakes a person can ever make, is to allow his friends or even his father or his mother, his wife, husband, his brothers, or his sisters to sway him to decide against the commandments of God

Remember that any person who advises you contrary to the commandments of God is not your friend He may have been your friend in the past, but if he advises you against obeying God, he is unconsciously the enemy of your soul If you should lose some friends because you take your stand for the commandments of God, the Lord will give you many better friends in their place, among those who keep His commandments We must never forget that every soul is individually responsible to God This means that when we see what is right, we ought to go ahead and do it, irrespective of what anybody else says or does

Some people belong to a certain church, because their father or mother belonged to it A certain famous evangelist was once asked why he was a Presbyterian This man really knew the Bible quite well, but what did he say? "I am a Presbyterian, because pa and ma were Presbyterians If pa and ma had been Catholics, I guess I would have been a Catholic too "

The faith in which a person is brought up may be the truth, but there is only one way you can be sure, and that is, not to take it as the truth merely because your father and mother belonged to it, but take your Bible; prove all things, and hold fast to that which is good We must bear in mind that the light of God's truth is to increase with each passing generation Proverbs 4 18 says, "The path of the just is as the shining light, that shineth more and more unto the perfect day" We cannot be guided entirely by the religion of our fathers and mothers, because the light shines more and more, and the nearer we come to the end, the more light and more truth there will be The religion of your father may have been good enough for him, but it may not save you

Jesus Christ called Peter, James, and John and others, out of the Jewish church to start a new church, the church of Jesus Christ What if Peter, or James, or John had said, "The religion of the Jewish synagogue was good enough for my father, isn't that good enough for me?" If they had followed this reasoning, they never would have become followers of Jesus Christ Peter's father may have been saved in the Jewish synagogue, but Peter became responsible for the new light that Jesus brought to him So it may be in the case of your father and mother They may have been saved in the Methodist Church, the Baptist Church, the Disciples of Christ, The Presbyterian, or the Episcopal Church, but you are responsible for new light and increased truth, which God has sent you in this three-fold message of Revelation 14

If Luther had followed this reasoning that his father's religion was good enough for him, he would have remained a Catholic He would never have been used of God, to inaugurate the great Protestant Reformation

Some people like to sing about "The Old Time Religion" Do you know that song? It was sung frequently in Billy Sunday's meetings

> "It is the old time religion,
> It was good for Paul and Silas,
> And it is good enough for me
> It was good for my father and mother,
> And it is good enough for me"

I can endorse this sentiment one hundred per cent, if you mean real, genuine Christianity, Christ in the heart, and living a pure, clean, consecrated life But if you mean this in the sense of standing by some creed which is out of harmony with the Bible, then it isn't good enough for you

Suppose your father and mother had been Mohammedans, would that be good enough for you? Many people want to settle down on their father's creed They say, "My father's and mother's religion was good enough for them, and it is good enough for me"

The horse and buggy and the old tallow candle may have been good enough for your great-grandfather, because they were about all he had, in the way of transportation and illumination, but would they be good enough for you? Come now, the horse and buggy and old tallow candle were good enough for your great-grandfather, but are they good enough for you? I do not see you using them I go to your home and you are not using the old tallow candle I see you take a trip, and you do not use the horse and buggy

Listen Is it not more important to make advancement in the field of religion than in modes of travel or in illumination? Henry Ward Beecher said an amusing thing He said he would just as soon go a-courting with his father's love letters, as to join a church just because his father belonged to it His father's love letters were effective in winning his mother, but it wouldn't do for the son to take his father's letters to win his bride His letters must fit his girl

Some people say, "I was christened and confirmed in my church, and I feel I must stay there for the rest of my life" Didn't you once ride in a baby buggy? Yes Does this mean that you should ride in a baby buggy for the rest of your life? No! You took an advanced step when the time came for it The time came to leave the baby buggy   So God expects us to be ready to take advanced steps in religion, as the Word points the way   We need more than baby-buggy religion

Much might be said about the many considerations that lead people to join the churches with which they are affiliated, but in the light of eternity, in the light of your eternal welfare, in the light of the Bible, there is only one consideration that should influence a person in deciding what church he should join, and that is to join the church that has the truth   Can you say "Amen", brother? Yes, I would say "Amen" twice

We are told in 1 Timothy 3 15 that the church of the living God is the pillar and ground of the truth   Truth alone will count in the end, when it comes to getting through the gates of heaven   All these other considerations will fall short   When it comes to getting through those gates of pearl, to go inside the city of gold, the truth is the only thing that will count   Isaiah 26 2 says, "Open ye the gates, that the righteous nation which keepeth the truth may enter in "

No person ever needs to hesitate, or be in doubt, as to what church has the truth   There are three scriptural facts that make this as plain and true as 2 and 2 make 4   Here is the first one   In Revelation 12 17 the Word of God shows that in the last days, Jesus Christ will have a remnant church which will keep all the commandments of God, and will preach the three-fold message of Revelation 14 to all the world

Here is the second fact   In Revelation 18 4 the Word of God shows that God has true children scattered in a large group of churches, to which He gives the symbolical name of Babylon

Here is the third fact   In Revelation 18 4 the Word of God shows, that the call of Christ in our day is for the true Christians to come out of those churches into the remnant church to keep the commandments

When you put those three facts together you can see how plain it is, that Christ wants you to come out and take your stand with His remnant church if you have not already done so

Some people say, "I intend to always keep the Sabbath, but I must remain in my present church   I do not see my way clear to come out and join this Sabbath-keeping church "   I have yet to see the first person who ever made good on this proposition   One of two things happens   After a time they will cease to keep the Sabbath, in spite of all they have said about keeping it   They will give up the keeping of the Sabbath and forget God's message, and they will go on in the church where they are   Or they will go all the way with Jesus Christ and obey His call to come out of Babylon   We hope it will be the latter with each of you who have heard God's message

A person who attempts to keep the Sabbath and stay in another church is going directly contrary to the counsel of the Lord   God's call is, "Come out of her, My people, that ye be not partakers of her sins, and that ye receive not of her plagues "

If a person could keep all the commandments and remain in the other churches, Christ would not say, "Come out "   Christ does not ask us to do anything which is unnecessary   Jesus knows what you ought to do   You may safely trust your case in His hands   If it were possible to keep the Sabbath, and still stay in the other churches, then He would not say "Come out "   If a person is willing to do what Jesus Christ wants him to do, there is really nothing else he can do, but come out and take his stand with His remnant

In John 12 42, 43 we learn that many of the leaders among the Jews believed on Jesus. but they failed to take their stand because they would lose their place in the church   This is significant because we see how history repeats itself today   The record says, "Nevertheless, among the chief rulers also many believed on Him, but because of the Pharisees they did not confess Him, lest they should be put out of the synagogue, for they loved the praise of men more than the praise of God"

They believed on Jesus, but they would not come out and take their stand because it meant giving up their church They lost their souls, because "they loved the praise of men more than the praise of God"

A person who is truly sincere and honest will obey the truth, regardless of what it may cost him or what he may have to undergo In John 18 37 Jesus says, "Everyone that is of the truth heareth My voice" This matter of what we do with truth draws a testing line Jesus states in John 8 47, "He that is of God heareth God's words ye therefore hear them not, because ye are not of God" If we obey the truth, we are of God If we refuse or neglect to obey the truth, we are not of God

In John 10 26, 27 Jesus says, "Ye believe not, because ye are not of My sheep My sheep hear My voice and I know them, and they follow Me"

It is easy for people today to recognize or to believe that Jesus Christ is the Saviour It has actually become popular now to believe in Jesus Christ But back in the days when Jesus was here, it was a real test Even Nicodemus was ashamed to come during the day He came to see Jesus at night

I have already read from the gospel of John how the religious leaders believed in Jesus, but would not come out and take their stand It was a real test It was just as much a test then for the people to believe on Jesus as it is a test now to unite with the Sabbath-keeping church To unite with the Sabbath-keeping church today is just as unpopular, as it was to believe on Jesus Christ when He was here

God has sent you the message, and the all-important question is, what have you done with it? What are you doing with it? Every soul must do something with it There is no such thing as a man or woman being neutral In Matthew 12 30 Jesus says, "He that is not with Me is against Me, and He that gathereth not with Me scattereth abroad" The only wise course, the only safe way, the only right thing is to accept the message We are always safe in obeying the call of our heavenly Father

Some tourists were gathering flowers in the Highlands of Scotland They saw some very rare flowers growing on a ledge of a dangerous gorge They were afraid to go down there and get the flowers themselves So they approached a shepherd boy and offered him a large sum of money if he would let them tie a rope around his body and lower him over the wall to pick the flowers

The boy looked at the money It looked good to him It was a lot of money for a shepherd boy Then he looked at the wall which went straight down Finally he smiled and said, "Gentlemen, I will go down into the gorge and get the flowers, if you will let me go home and get my father to hold the rope"

Friends, your heavenly Father is holding the rope today Since He holds the rope, why not step out, even if it is just like going down a dangerous gorge God will safely hold the rope of His care about your life He tells us in 1 Peter 5 7, "Casting all your care upon him, for He careth for you"

He says in Isaiah 4 10, "Fear thou not, for I am with thee, be not dismayed, for I am thy God I will strengthen thee, yea, I will help thee, yea, I will uphold thee with the right hand of my righteousness" This is one text that I wish everyone of you would memorize Learn it Get it in your heart Believe it, and it will hold you fast It is one of the most precious texts in the Bible You should be able to repeat this text without even looking at a Bible When trouble comes, and you are facing trials, you ought to be able to quote this verse to yourself When you believe this promise of God, you will move forward

Every soul must make a choice between God's remnant and Babylon

There is no third place. There is no halfway station between the remnant church and Babylon. All the people in this world will be aligned under the pure woman of Revelation 12 or the harlot woman of Revelation 17. You and I will either stand with the faithful few, who keep the commandments of God in the remnant church of Revelation 12 17 or we will stand on the side of disobedience with the millions of church members, who make up great Babylon of Revelation 17. There is no neutral ground If we are not with Him, we are against Him. If we do not come out and take our stand for Christ and His great remnant, we are really against Him The great question is which do you choose, the remnant? Or Babylon?

This message brings people to a dramatic turning point in their life, something like what the Spanish soldiers of Pizarro faced when he was about to embark upon his conquest of Peru. His soldiers had endured indescribable suffering They were about to desert him Just at that critical moment when they were about to desert him, ships came into the harbor which would take them safely back to Spain.

Pizarro told his men that they could board the ships, and go back home if they wanted to. "But wait," he said, and he took his sword and traced a line from east to west upon the sand Then turning south he said, "Men, before you lies toil, hunger, drenching storms, disease, and possibly death, but there is victory and great wealth and glory Behind you there is ease and pleasure and safety. On that side lies Peru with its perils and riches. On this side is Spain with its comforts, but eternal disgrace. Now choose which side you will stand on As for me, I go south," and he stepped across the line.

He waited a moment and his faithful lieutenant said, "I, too, Sir." He too, stepped across the line and joined his commander Another stepped forward, and another, and another, until the entire band of brave soldiers had stepped over the line and Pizarro took those men and swept to a conquest that has been one of the marvels of succeeding generations.

Our great commander, the Lord Jesus Christ, has drawn a line. On one side is popularity and ease and fame in Babylon On the other side are trials, reproach, persecution with Christ's remnant. But at the end is victory on the sea of glass and an eternal happy home in heaven. Jesus says, "Choose now on which side you will stand." As for me, friends, I go with Christ's remnant. What do you say? Let everyone say "Amen" to that. That is the way I feel about it.

I am glad that so many have made their decision to go with the remnant. I wish it might be that each would step over the line until every soul who has been coming to these meetings will have made his choice for the truth of God. We do know that "one by one," each of God's true people will be gathered into His remnant fold In Isaiah 27 12 God says, "Ye shall be gathered one by one." Surely there must be some of those here today, who have not made their decision before, but are ready now to declare their decision.

I want to ask now, if there are those who have not previously made their decision to go all the way, who are ready to say, "By the grace of God I will be one of those whom the Lord is gathering!" Will you lift your hand? Yes, thank God here is one There must be others "Ye shall be gathered one by one " Isn't there another one this afternoon, who by putting up his hand will signify, "God helping me I will be one of those ones?"

Friends, it is the greatest privilege under heaven to be one of those "ones" whom the Lord is gathering I want to ask, How many who were not baptized last night have in their hearts the noble purpose to accept God's message? Will you raise your hands? I am glad to see so many hands. This looks fine.

We shall ask the workers to pass decision cards to any of you who have not filled out one before. This card is not merely for the keeping of the Sabbath. This is a decision card to go all the way in becoming one of God's Sabbath-keeping people   If you aie not sure about having filled out one of these cards, take one and fill it out because it doesn't hurt anything to fill out a card like this two or three times

"Ye shall be gathered one by one"   This is the way it is   One by one they make up their minds to obey the Lord and keep His commandments, and to come out and take their stand with His remnant   The day is coming soon, when it will be worth more than all the world to be on God's side fully

The Lord says, "If ye be willing and obedient, ye shall eat the good of the land, but if ye refuse and rebel, ye shall be devoured with the sword"

(Prayer).

Our loving Heavenly Father, we thank Thee for Thy presence with us in this Sabbath afternoon meeting   We thank Thee that Thou art gathering out a special people to keep thy commandments and the faith of Jesus

Lord, Thou hast said, "Ye shall be gathered one by one"   And they are coming one by one   We thank Thee for the group who took their stand last night   We thank Thee for those who will go forward this coming Sabbath   We thank Thee for these today who have held up their hand

Then, Father, here are all these requests   There are so many of us who have loved ones who are out of the ark of safety   They are far away from Christ   Jesus is able to save to the uttermost all who come   So, Lord, we would bring these cases to Thee   Dear Lord, wherever these people are, we pray that just now Thy Spirit will plead with their hearts   May the cords of love draw them to Thee   Show them the right way, and then give them the courage to take their stand   We ask it in Jesus' name   Amen

What Is the Unpardonable Sin?

(Preached on the Twelfth Sunday Night of the Campaign)

The worst thing that can ever overtake any person in this world is to come to the place where his sins can never be forgiven, no matter how much he may pray   Many people have wondered, what is this unpardonable sin? Some people say it consists in taking one's own life   Others say it consists in killing an unborn child   Some say it is uttering certain terrible words of cursing or blasphemy   Some people think it is some terrible crime which is so hateful in the sight of Almighty God that He cannot pardon it

I can definitely tell you that the unpardonable sin is not murder nor adultery.   David committed murder and adultery, and he was forgiven   The unpardonable sin is not some terrible words of cursing   Peter cursed Jesus Christ bitterly on the night of His betrayal, and Peter was forgiven and became a mighty man of God

Is it possible to know what is the unpardonable sin?   Yes, Jesus Christ makes it plain that the unpardonable sin is a sin against the Holy Ghost, or Holy Spirit   I read His words as recorded in Matthew 12 31, 32, "Wherefore I say unto you, all manner of sin and blasphemy shall be forgiven unto men: but the blasphemy against the Holy Ghost shall not be forgiven unto men   Whosoever speaketh against the Holy Ghost, it shall not be forgiven him, neither in this world, neither in the world to come "

Jesus makes it plain that the unpardonable sin consists in doing something against the Holy Ghost   What is it that people do against the Holy Ghost, or the Holy Spirit which puts them where God cannot forgive their sins?   The Scriptures show that the most common manifestation of the sin against the Holy Ghost consists in the persistent refusal to turn and obey God

The unpardonable sin may be explained in just three sentences   No person can ever receive forgiveness without repentance   He cannot receive repentance without the convicting power of the Holy Spirit   Thus, he who grieves away the Holy Spirit sins the unpardonable sin, since he cannot meet the conditions on which God grants pardon

I am happy to tell you tonight that God is ready to forgive every penitent sinner   In Psalm 86 5 we read, "For thou, Lord, art good, and **ready to forgive; and** plenteous in mercy unto all them that call upon Thee "   God is ready to forgive every kind of sin when a sinner repents of it, and believes on the Lord Jesus Christ as his personal Saviour

No man can ever receive forgiveness without the Holy Spirit   Why not? Because the Holy Spirit is the only agency by which he may come to repentance   He is the only agency by which one can meet the conditions on which God can grant pardon and forgiveness

Here is something to think through   It is impossible for any man to repent of himself   Man has a part to do in repentance, but the Holy Spirit also has a part, so that it is impossible for anyone to repent of himself   He can repent only under the convicting power of the Holy Spirit.

We read about this in John 16 8   Speaking about the work of the Holy Ghost, or the Holy Spirit, Jesus said, "When He is come, He will reprove the world of sin and of righteousness, and of judgment "   The Holy Spirit convicts men of sin and of righteousness   He points out wrong habits and evil practices which we should turn from   He then shows us right ways and right duties which we should do   "When He is come, He will reprove the world of sin, and of righteousness "

Have you ever been conscious of a still small voice, saying within your heart when you were about to do something wrong, "You had better not do that, it is wrong?" Or have you heard a still small voice saying, "This is the right way for you to go?" How many of you during these meetings have been conscious of a still small voice saying within your heart, "This is the right way This is what you ought to do?" Or it may be that this still small voice has shown you certain wrong things in your life from which you should turn

I wonder how many have been aware of such a still small voice speaking to you during these meetings? May I see your hands? (Many hands were raised) Yes, I think everyone here would put up his hand on that This still small voice is the convicting power of the Holy Ghost Your uplifted hand testifies that John 16 8 is true "When He is come, He will reprove the world of sin, and of righteousness "

The Holy Spirit has been doing His part in these meetings You have heard that still small voice speaking to your hearts The most important question of all is, What have you done about it? What are you going to do about it tonight? I hope you will never forget that your eternal welfare depends on how you respond to that still small voice of the Holy Spirit If you yield to the pleading of the Holy Spirit, you will be saved. If you reject the pleading of the Holy Spirit, you will be lost

We are just as dependent upon the Holy Spirit for conviction unto repentance, as we are upon the blood of Jesus Christ to cancel our sins Repentance is a gift from God A lot of people do not understand that Repentance is a gift from God by the Holy Spirit just as much as forgiveness is a gift of God by the blood of Jesus Christ.

I refer you to Acts 5 31 There you will read that God has exalted Jesus to be a Saviour to give repentance unto Israel, and the forgiveness of sin. Notice that repentance and forgiveness are joined together as being gifts of God through His son

If you want to be forgiven, you must take repentance when the Holy Spirit convicts you Some people think that they can wait, and turn to God when they get ready This may prove to be the most fatal mistake they have ever made No man can obey God, or come to Christ unless the Holy Spirit draws him You will find this thought in John 6 44 "No man can come to Me, except the Father which hath sent Me draw him " The Father draws him by the Holy Spirit I say again, that if you want forgiveness, you must take repentance while the Holy Spirit is convicting you There is danger in delay.

The Scriptures show that there is danger, possibly tragic For, if a person persistently refuses to yield to the pleading of the Holy Spirit, the Holy Spirit may leave him never to return Then his sins will be unpardonable.

Take your notebook and record some important references The first one is found in Genesis 6·3 God says, "My Spirit shall not always strive with man "

This shows that the Holy Spirit strives with a person for a certain period If he persistently refuses to yield and obey, the Holy Spirit may leave him In such a case, his sins would be unpardonable Why? Because they are so horrible that God could not pardon them? No! God says, "Though your sins be red as scarlet, they shall be as white as snow " But God cannot forgive, unless man repents, and man cannot repent if he grieves away the Holy Spirit Now you begin to see what is the unpardonable sin, don't you? This is a solemn warning to every soul not to go in disobedience against the pleading of the Holy Spirit "My Spirit shall not always strive with man "

The Bible speaks definitely about the Holy Spirit being taken from people Put down Psalm 51 11 David had sinned a most horrible sin. In fact a terrible double sin of murder and adultery He had gone directly against two of the ten commandments He feared that the Holy Spirit would be taken from him He knew perfectly well that if the Holy Spirit was taken from him, he was a lost man forever, whether he lived on for twenty years or forty years

So he pleaded with God, "Cast me not away from Thy presence, and take not Thy Holy Spirit from me" This shows that the Holy Spirit can be, and sometimes is, taken from people It shows that the Holy Spirit will be taken from those, who continue to go against the commandments of God

Next I refer to 1 Samuel 16 14 This is another significant statement It says, "The Spirit of the Lord departed from Saul" The Holy Spirit left him

Why did the Holy Spirit depart from Saul? Because he persisted in persuing a course that was contrary to the commandments of God I wish you would read 1 Samuel 15 when you go home, and see what led to his eternal ruin.

God told Saul to march against the Amalekites, and to slay every one of them and all their cattle Saul marched against them, and killed every one of them—except one He spared Agag the king He killed all the cattle—except a few choice specimens.

See how near he came to obeying the Lord's commandment He killed them all except one and all the cattle except a few choice ones He intended to sacrifice those few choice specimens on the altar, and then they would be destroyed He argued that he was doing the right thing People become so self-deceived, that they argue that they are doing the right thing, when they are doing the wrong thing

Samuel said to him, "Since thou hast rejected the word of God, God has rejected thee" Then he persisted in a wrong course until in the next chapter we have that tragic statement, "The Spirit of the Lord departed from Saul" Let me tell you that he was just as lost from that moment, as if he were already in hell He had sinned the unpardonable sin

We need to study this experience, because this has been placed in the Bible for a lesson to us Doesn't Saul's experience preach a powerful sermon to you and me on the question of keeping the seventh day as commanded in the fourth commandment? Saul lacked on only one point of obedience He killed all, except one

Many Christians obey all the Ten Commandments—except one The one that says, "The seventh day is the Sabbath; in it thou shalt not do any work" Of course, many Christian people are doing this ignorantly God graciously forgives their sins of ignorance, but God is sending light in these meetings to show people what to do about the Sabbath

Many have made a wise decision to walk in the light of God's word I hope every one of you will make that good decision while the Holy Spirit still pleads with you Remember "My Spirit shall not always strive with man" There is a danger, that if a person delays too long, if he refuses to turn and obey God, the Holy Spirit may leave him never to return

This is the worst thing that could ever happen to any man or woman You may talk about a man losing his legs and arms, having his eyes put out, or being crippled for all his days It is tragic, yes But none of these is as bad as the Holy Spirit leaving a man That is the worst thing which can ever happen to a man or woman while he lives on the face of the earth

The attitude that each soul takes toward the Holy Spirit seals his fate for everlasting joy or everlasting destruction The attitude that you and I take toward the Holy Spirit seals our destiny for everlasting joy or everlasting destruction Here are three texts

In Ephesians 4 30 Paul exhorts Christians to "grieve not the Holy Spirit, whereby ye are sealed unto the day of redemption"

In Acts 7:51 we read about people resisting the Holy Spirit In Hebrews 10 29 we read about those who have done despite unto the Spirit of grace

This is what leads people to commit the unpardonable sin, grieving the Holy Spirit, resisting the Holy Spirit, doing despite unto the Holy Spirit If a person persists in grieving and resisting the Holy Spirit he will finally sin the unpardonable sin

Some will ask, "How do people grieve the Holy Spirit? How do people resist the Holy Spirit?" When a man knows what he ought to do, and refuses to do it, or fails to do it, that is grieving the Holy Spirit Every time a man fails to turn and obey God as the Holy Spirit pleads with him, or impresses him, he is resisting the Holy Spirit Every time a call is given for a person to surrender to the Lord Jesus, and he resists that call, he is resisting the Holy Spirit When the Word of God shows a person the right way, and he refuses to walk in it, that is resisting the Holy Spirit Some of you have been doing this week after week in these meetings O, brother, sister, I hope tonight you will resist the Holy Spirit no longer, but yield to His pleading in full surrender to the Lord Jesus

I beg of you to listen to the call of the Spirit, because God cannot reach you except through Him If a man grieves the Holy Spirit away, his case is absolutely and completely hopeless, eternally hopeless The most terrible sin is the sin against the Holy Ghost, because He is the only One Who can ever bring you to Christ

God is merciful and kind He is longsuffering with sinners, but when people persist in disobedience, God finally gives them up Let me tell you that the saddest thing in this world is when God gives a person up It is bad enough when a husband gives up his wife The world is filled with divorces and broken homes It is sad to see a mother give up her children We sometimes see that, but listen, the saddest thing is when God gives a person up

Do you know why God gives people up? Hosea 4 17 says, "Ephraim is joined to idols· let him alone" God sends the Holy Spirit to lead people to give up their sins, and to draw them to Christ When a person persistently refuses to give up a certain sin in response to the pleading of the Holy Spirit, the time will come, when God will say, "He is joined to his idols· let him alone" Then the Holy Spirit will leave him, never to return "My Spirit," says God, "shall not always strive with man."

God sends us light from the Bible to show us the right way He gives us a desire to turn and obey He impresses us and pleads with our hearts to surrender all to Jesus Christ and to keep His commandments; but if a person persistently says, "No," to the call of the Holy Spirit, the Spirit will leave him and God gives him up This is the saddest thing that can ever happen to a human soul "Ephraim is joined to idols· let him alone" If the Holy Spirit leaves him, he cannot repent; and where there is no repentance there is no forgiveness, and where there is no forgiveness, there is no salvation

Judas Iscariot committed the unpardonable sin when he sold his Lord for thirty pieces of silver He was a man of good intentions, but he was covetous He was greedy for money The Holy Spirit pleaded with him to turn from his covetousness, but he allowed that covetous spirit to grow larger and larger He persisted in disobeying the tenth commandment which says, "Thou shalt not covet" Finally a persistent transgression of the tenth commandment led him to commit the unpardonable sin in selling his Lord to secure thirty pieces of silver.

It was unbelief that led the Pharisees to commit the unpardonable sin Put down Mark 3 28-30 There you will find that the unpardonable sin in their cases consisted in attributing the miracles wrought by the Holy Spirit through Christ, to the power of the devil. But it was their determination not to accept Jesus Christ of Nazareth as the Son of God, that led them to assert that He cast out devils by the power of the devil.

Any known sin that a person persists in against the conviction of the Holy Spirit may lead him to commit the unpardonable sin If a person has certain wrong things in his life, the only safe thing to do is to give them up, no matter how dear or how necessary those things may seem to him

Have you ever wondered what Jesus meant when He declared that if your hand offend you, cut it off? Let us read His words as given in Mark 9.43-48

"If thy hand offend thee, cut it off. it is better for thee to enter into life maimed, than having two hands to go into hell, into the fire that never shall be quenched where their worm dieth not, and the fire is not quenched And if thy foot offend thee, cut it off it is better for thee to enter halt into life, than having two feet to be cast into hell, into the fire that never shall be quenched where their worm dieth not, and the fire is not quenched. And if thine eye offend thee, pluck it out it is better for thee to enter into the kingdom of God with one eye, than having two eyes to be cast into hell fire where their worm dieth not, and the fire is not quenched "

Jesus did not mean for people to disfigure their bodies He was speaking figuratively Some people have sinful habits that seem as dear and necessary to them as their eyes, or hands, or feet There are people whose feet are addicted to dancing They had far better give up that dancing, than to dance their way to hell There are people who have evil habits, which are as much a part of their life as their own right hand.

Some people are in love with the sinful ways of the world These sinful things of the world are as precious to them as their own right eye. Some men have formed unlawful attachments for other men's wives or other women. Those attachments are as dear to them as their own right hand There are women, who have formed attachments for other women's husbands or for other men But these unlawful attachments will take people to hell if they cling to them.

These people had far better listen to that still small voice that says to turn from this unlawful way, than to cling to it and go into hell fire This is what Christ meant about cutting off your right hand or plucking out your right eye, or cutting off the right foot It is those unholy and sinful habits which are dragging people down to hell They had far better give them up than let those things drag them down to hell

Some people attempt to smother the conviction of the Holy Spirit with the thought that they can go on committing sin, and then break off whenever they so desire But the man who persists in sin against the conviction of the Holy Spirit may find himself bound or holden with the cords of his own sins

There was a snake charmer who had a boa constrictor that he had raised from birth It was his delight to step out in front of the footlights In a wing of the theatre was a cage in which he kept his boa constrictor, now fully grown He had caught that snake when it was a little tiny thing, and had raised it on a bottle

He trained it to mind every signal that he gave At a certain signal that snake would crawl from the cage and come out on the stage At another signal it would wrap itself around its master At another signal the snake would uncoil and go back to its cage

Day after day this man carried on his thrilling performance When the audience thought the man would be crushed to death; he would give the signal and the snake would uncoil and go back to his cage The man thought he had complete control, because he had had that snake from the time it was a little tiny thing

One day he signaled the snake It crawled out to him He gave another signal and the snake crawled around him He gave another signal, at which it was supposed to uncoil, but the snake did not obey He tightened his coil around the man Bones crushed and the poor man fell in a lifeless heap

So habits of sin grow and some day the sin you think you can control will master you The sinner will be holden with the cords of his own sin The only safe way is to yield to the pleadings of the Holy Spirit and let Jesus set you free

The unpardonable sin is a sin against much light I refer you to Matthew 11 20-22

"Then began he to upbraid the cities wherein most of his mighty works were done, because they repented not Woe unto thee, Chorazin! woe unto thee, Bethsaida! for if the mighty works, which were done in you, had been done in Tyre and Sidon, they would have repented long ago in sackcloth and ashes But I say unto you, It shall be more tolerable for Tyre and Sidon at the day of judgment than for you"

Jesus told these people that they had sinned against great light. The transgression of any of the commandments, if persisted in against the light of the Word of God, may lead to the unpardonable sin I turn to Hebrews 10 26 "For if we sin willfully after that we have received the knowledge of the truth, there remaineth no more sacrifice for sins"

If a person deliberately persists in disobeying God's commandments when he knows better, he will come to the place where there is no sacrifice for sin If there is no sacrifice, there is no forgiveness "If we sin willfully after that we have received the knowledge of the truth, there remaineth no more sacrifice for sins"

This is the text that led me to begin keeping the seventh day I once kept Sunday strictly There isn't any one in the city of Des Moines who believes any more sincerely that Sunday is the right day than Mr Shuler did at one time I thought it was the right day for Christians to keep But when I searched the Bible I found that the only day of the week that Jesus has ever sanctified, or set apart, for man is the seventh day The seventh day of the week is the only day He ever asked people to keep

When I found this out, I knew that I ought to keep the seventh day But like a lot of people I was slow to obey the light I didn't want to step out and keep a different day from other people. So I put off making a start to keep the Sabbath Then a man directed my attention to Hebrews 10.26. "If we sin willfully after that we have received the knowledge of the truth, there remaineth no more sacrifice for sins"

I want to tell you that that text put me in a corner where I had to do something I saw that if I continued to refuse to keep the Sabbath, I would come to the place where there was no sacrifice for my sins. I knew that if I got to that place, I would be a lost man So I made my decision; sink or swim, live or die, survive or perish, I would keep the Lord's Sabbath.

I could not afford to come to the place where there was no more sacrifice for my sins. Can you?

> "There is a line that is drawn by rejecting our Lord,
> Where the call of His Spirit is lost,
> And you hurry along with the pleasure-mad throng
> Have you counted, have you counted the cost?"

I appeal to you who have been attending these Bible lectures from week to week and have not yet begun to keep the true Sabbath You have heard the Word of God, and God tells you what day of the week you ought to keep He says, "The seventh day is the Sabbath, in it thou shalt not do any work"

This is the only commandment which God ever has given about the keeping of a weekly day unto the Lord Now you know what you ought to do The Word of God says, "If we sin willfully after that we have received the knowledge of the truth, there remaineth no more sacrifice for sins"

Friends, the worst thing that could happen to a person is to come to the place where there is no more sacrifice for his sins. I do not see how you can go another week without beginning to keep the seventh day holy as the Lord commanded.

Now the question comes, how can we tell when a person has committed the unpardonable sin? The unpardonable sin condition may manifest itself in any one of three different ways. The first way is in being indifferent to one's own spiritual condition. In Ephesians 4:19 it talks about people who are past feeling. The most tremendous appeal has no effect whatever upon them. If one has no desire whatever to turn and obey the call of God, that may be the unpardonable sin condition.

A second way it may manifest itself is in being calloused in disobedience. "There is a way that seemeth right unto a man, but the end thereof are the ways of death." Men can persist in disobedience until they think they are right even when they are disobeying God. If you can transgress any of the Ten Commandments and your conscience doesn't hurt you, you may well be alarmed.

The third way that the unpardonable sin may manifest itself is in open hostility to God, Jesus Christ, and the Bible.

A young man was taken very ill one night. His mother called the doctor, and the doctor told the mother, "Your boy will not be alive more than twenty-four hours." She knew the young man was not a Christian. After she had gained her composure, she went in and told the boy. She said, "Son, the doctor says you cannot live more than twenty-four hours. I have just telephoned my pastor to come and talk with you."

The boy looked at his mother and said, "Mother, I do not want to see your preacher. I will not even let him talk with me. Two years ago in a revival meeting I was powerfully impressed one night to go forward and give my heart to Jesus Christ, but I resisted that impression. I grabbed my hat and left the church. Outside the church I prayed, 'Holy Spirit leave me alone.' I determined I would blot the desire out of my heart to be a Christian. I have never had a desire to be a Christian since then. I am lost and I don't care."

Yes, "My spirit shall not always strive with man." You say, "How can I tell that I have not committed this fearful, unpardonable sin?" If you have a desire to obey God, then the Holy Spirit is still pleading with you. If you once lived a Christian life and you have wandered off into the sinful ways of the world, and you have a desire to return, that is the Holy Spirit still pleading with you. If you have never given your heart to the Lord Jesus Christ, and you have a conviction that you ought to be a Christian, that is the Holy Spirit still pleading with you. If you have heard these Bible lectures about the Sabbath and you know the seventh day is right, that is the Holy Spirit pleading with you. The important thing is to yield yourself to the sweet, tender, pleading, drawing power of the Holy Spirit. Thank God for the conviction the Holy Spirit gives you, and act on that conviction before it fades away and is gone.

If a person does not act on the conviction he has, it will likely get weaker until he will not even think about it. This is why God solemnly warns us to decide today. "Today, if you will hear My voice, harden not your hearts."

The unpardonable sin is that which hardens the heart. If the Holy Spirit impresses us to obey God, and we fail to respond, the heart will be a little bit harder. If a person goes on and on refusing, he will become so hardened that he will be past yielding, and the Holy Spirit will leave him.

There are some people who get to the place where an alarm clock will not awaken them. Why? Just because morning after morning they refuse to get up when the alarm sounds.

Some people attend meetings like this and hear lectures about the true

Sabbath   At first they are powerfully moved to begin to keep the Sabbath but they put it off and say, "I will do it a little later"   Then the conviction begins to fade   There are people tonight who are not half as much impressed to begin keeping the Sabbath, as they were two weeks or three weeks ago   This is a dangerous thing   Soon the conviction may be entirely gone and they will never even think of doing it

> "There is a line by us unseen,
>   That crosses every path,
> The hidden boundary between
>   God's patience and His wrath
>
> "Oh! where is this mysterious bourne
>   By which our path is crossed,
> Beyond which God Himself hath sworn,
>   That he who goes is lost?
>
> "How far may we go on in sin?
>   How long will God forbear?
> Where does hope end? and where begin
>   The confines of despair?
>
> "An answer from the skies is sent·
>   Ye that from God depart!
> While it is called today, repent
>   And harden not your heart"

O, friends, if we persistently refuse the call of the Holy Spirit, He may leave   By delaying, holding back, and putting off taking our stand we may grieve away the Holy Spirit forever   I beg you tonight for the sake of your own eternal welfare, not to trifle with God's Holy Spirit any longer, but yield to His pleading now

I want to remember in prayer those who have not made their decision to obey God   I wonder how many there are, who have not made their decision to obey the Lord, who would like to have us pray that God will give you strength to yield to the pleading of the Holy Spirit?   How many are there, who have not made your decision, and you want us to pray that God will give you strength and grace to yield to the pleading of the Holy Spirit?   Will you lift your hand please?   Yes, I see a number of hands

Friends, we do need help from God to do this, because we cannot do it of ourselves   The Holy Spirit has been pleading with you, but you must have help to obey God   How many want the help of God that you may fully yield yourselves?   Will you lift your hands?

(PRAYER)

(Copy of the Bible lesson outline, which was distributed to the people preceding the fifty-second lecture)

Lesson X - How God Leads Into the Truth

1. There are three special parts to the call of the Lord to the people in these last days.

2A The primary step of decision, which the Lord asks man to take, is to believe on His Son Jesus Christ (Jno 3 16)

2B By truly believing on Jesus a person receives remission of sin ..   ....
            .   and a change of heart, or the new birth   _

3   Your first step in responding to the call of the Lord is to give your heart to Jesus, so He can cleanse you from all sin and give you a new heart

4   The Lord gives the believer a new heart so he may keep His commandments _ ....

5. After a person takes the first step of receiving Jesus for justification and regeneration, then he can take the second step, which is obedience to the will of God, and walking in the commandments of the Lord (Ps 119. 146 margin).

6A. God Himself has appointed the keeping of the seventh day as the sign of man's obedience to God   _ _ _   _ _ _ _—_

6B The keeping of the Sabbath is the only item which God has ever appointed as the sign of the true God and the only Saviour.

7. Your second step in responding to the call of the Lord is obedience to God's commandments, with the keeping of the seventh day as the sign of your obedience and loyalty to God.

8. God is calling all those who keep His commandments into His remnant church ....   _   .... . _—.... _ _   _

9. Your third step in responding to the call of the Lord is to become a member of His remnant church

10A The call of the Lord to people today is a threefold call—"Give Me thine heart" (Prov 23 26), take thy foot off of the Sabbath (Isa 58.13) and come out of the world or Babylon into the remnant church (Rev 18 4)

10B The call of God is for conversion to Christ, the keeping of the Sabbath of Christ, uniting with the remnant church of Christ, and then being true to the commandments of Christ to the end (Mark 13 13, Rev 2 10)

11   Those who are truly born of God and have the right experience are victorious over sin (1 Jno 5 4, 18) and will not backslide from the truth (Jer 32 40, Ps 80 17,18)

12   We should respond to the call of the Lord just as soon as it comes to us   . _   ..   _   .... _ _ .... _

13   The devil's greatest weapon is—"Do it tomorrow" or "wait a little while" in direct contrast to God's do it "now" (2 Cor 6 2) and "today" (Heb 4 7).

14   It is of eternal impoitance that we respond to the call of God promptly.

15   If a person persistently delays and puts off responding to the call of the Lord, the time will come when he will call on God, but God will not answer him ..   ..   .   _

References which were filled in as the study was presented, (2B) Acts 10 43, John 1 12, 13, (4) Eze 11 19,20, (6A) Eze 20 12, (8) Rev 12 17, (12) Ps 119 60 (15) Prov 1 24-30

Five Million for One Pearl

Have you ever heard of that famous pearl that is worth more than five million dollars? The Lord Jesus tells about that pearl in Matthew 13·45,46 "The kingdom of heaven is like unto a merchant man, seeking goodly pearls· who when he had found one pearl of great price, went and sold all that he had, and bought it "

Jesus declares that the kingdom of heaven is like a merchant man who was seeking goodly pearls One day he saw the finest pearl he had ever seen The moment he saw it, there came into his heart a great desire to be the possessor of that one, choicest, most lovely pearl

He asked the man who had it how much he wanted for it. The man told him the price The merchant then began to do some figuring. He found that it would take everything he had in order to buy this one choice pearl.

But mark this point the man's desire for the pearl was so supreme, so all-absorbing, so compelling, that he went immediately and sold everything he had in the world in order to secure that one pearl He didn't say that the price was too high He didn't suggest that the pearl wasn't worth what the man asked He didn't indicate that he couldn't afford to buy it He didn't suggest that maybe he had better wait until he was in a little bit better shape to buy it No He gladly, eagerly, and immediately went and sold all that he had to buy the pearl

This is a parable This is what going to heaven is like This one choice pearl, this pearl of great price, represents Jesus Christ and eternal life It represents the eternal happy home in heaven which God has for those who choose to obey His will Heaven, just as it took everything this man had to secure that pearl of great price, so it will take an entire surrender, a full consecration, a full obedience to the will of God on your part and mine, in order to secure an eternal, happy home in God's heavenly city

Some people will say, "Doesn't the Bible show that all a person has to do in order to be saved is to believe on Jesus Christ?" Yes In Acts 16 31 the scripture says, "Believe on the Lord Jesus Christ and thou shalt be saved" But do you know what true faith in Christ will lead a person to do?

Look at the blackboard Do you see that word on the blackboard? What does it say? 'F-A-I-T-H' Faith in the Lord Jesus Christ Let us look at this word and see what faith in Christ will lead a man to do

F stands for Forsaking
A stands for All
I stands for I
T stands for Take
H stands for Him

Faith means "Forsaking all, I take Him " "Believe on the Lord Jesus Christ and thou shalt be saved " If you have genuine faith, you will say, "Forsaking all, I take Him " If your faith doesn't lead you to forsake all to obey Jesus, then your faith falls short

I hope that those of you who have been struggling with the matter of accepting God's message will have faith to go all the way I hope your faith will not fall short I think of what Jesus said to Peter He told Peter how Satan desired to have him, but He declared that He had prayed for him, that his faith would not fail

I pray for you, who are struggling about taking your stand, that your

faith will not fail to stand the test If you really want to gain an eternal happy
home in heaven, you must have the faith that forsakes all to obey the Lord
The kingdom of heaven is like a man who sold everything he had to secure
the one choicest pearl

If we allow anything, or anybody to hold us back from obeying Christ's
call to come out and take our stand, to keep all His commandments, then
our faith does not stand the test The saddest thing that could ever happen
to you would be for your faith to fall short, or for you to fail to stand the
test of giving up all for Christ, or to fail to go all the way for Christ, or to
fail to go all the way with Jesus

Some will say, "Do you mean that a person cannot be saved unless he is
willing to give up everything for Christ's sake?" It is not for me to say
what it takes for a person to be saved This has not been left in my hands
But I do refer you to the One in Whose hands it has been left Listen to what
Jesus Christ says, for He is the One, Who decides what it takes in order for
a person to be saved "So likewise, whosoever he be of you **that forsaketh
not all that he hath, he cannot be My disciple.**"

How much must you forsake in order to be His true disciple? You must
forsake all Suppose a person is willing to follow Jesus Christ in everything
except one item, which he feels he cannot give up, or one item he cannot
agree to do There are people, who when we talk with them about being baptized, say, "Now I agree with every point except one This person needs to
hear Jesus say, "Whosoever he be of you that forsaketh not all that he hath,
he cannot be My disciple"

If you have a hundred things that you ought to yield to Jesus Christ, and
you yield only ninety-nine of them, you have not fully accepted Him as your
sovereign Lord Unless we make Christ Lord of all, He isn't our Lord at all
Some Christians are willing to obey all the Ten Commandments except one
Except the one that says, "The seventh day is the Sabbath, in it thou shalt
not do any work" People like this need to hear the Word of God in James
2 10 "For whosoever shall keep the whole law, and yet offend in one point,
he is guilty of all"

Some people believe that the seventh day is the right day to keep They
are fully convinced that they ought to keep the seventh day, or Saturday
"But," they say; "I will lose my job if I take Saturdays off It will ruin my
business if I close on Saturday" If any of you are thinking along that line,
I pray that you will think of Christ's question "What shall it profit a man
if he shall gain the whole world, and lose his own soul?" What will that
job amount to in such a case? It may be a good-paying job, but what will that
job amount to and what will that business amount to, brother, if you disobey
God and are lost? If a man persists in disobeying God, he will be lost

Then some people say, "I believe the message is true I know that this
is the right way, but I cannot take my stand for this message because my
husband objects to it, my wife is opposed, or my folks are against it, my father
and mother do not want me to do it" If there are those here, who are being
held back by any such considerations, I hope that you will hear the voice of
Jesus saying unto you, "Whosoever loveth father or mother more than Me,
is not worthy of Me" I know this is a close test But God will give you grace
to stand

The Lord Jesus tells us in Luke 14 25-27, "If any man come to Me, and
hate not his father, and mother, and wife, and children, and brethren, and
sister, yea, and his own life also, he cannot be My disciple" In other words,
unless we are willing to obey Christ above husband, above wife, above our
father or mother, above our brothers or sisters, above a job, above business,
we cannot be a true follower of Jesus Christ Friends, it seems to me that if

people would just think this through, they wouldn't let the job, or the business, or some loved one hold them back from coming out and taking their stand for God's message

Other people say, "I agree with all of Jesus' message, except one item I cannot agree to keep the seventh day. I cannot agree to give up dancing, or card parties, or going to the theatre, or I cannot lay off this article of jewelry, or I cannot leave my own church and take my stand with the remnant church Friends, if any of those things are in the way, I pray the Lord that the still small voice may say to you, "Whosoever doth not forsake all, he cannot by My disciple."

One of the saddest stories in the Bible is the story of a man who lacked only one thing, and yet was lost. You perhaps know to whom I refer. You will find the story in Matthew 19.16-22.

There was a rich young man who came to Jesus one day with this question· "What shall I do to have eternal life?" I want you to notice some things He asked the right question. He came to the right person with the right question He came in the right spirit You read the account in Mark and you will find that he came running He was so eager to know the way, to know the truth, that he ran to get in contact with Jesus, and when he got to Jesus he kneeled He came as humbly as a man could come. He asked the right question, he came to the right person, he came in the right spirit, he got the right answer, but, he wasn't willing to accept the answer.

He said to Jesus, "What shall I do to have eternal life?" Jesus looked at him and declared, "If thou wouldst enter into life, keep the commandments" The young man said, "What commandments?" Then Jesus began to quote from the second table of the law. He did not quote any commandment from the first table of the law He began to quote, "Thou shalt not kill, Thou shalt not steal, Thou shalt not commit adultery, Honor thy father and thy mother"

The young man immediately perceived that Jesus was talking about the Ten Commandments Then he said, "Lord, I have kept all these things from the time I was a boy" This fellow had been raised in a good home. He had been brought up in a godly, Jewish home He had been taught the Ten Commandments He knew them by heart, but he didn't have them in his heart He thought he had kept them

Jesus did not contradict the young man's statement about having kept all of the Ten Commandments from the days of his youth But Jesus showed him that he had not kept them Jesus placed a test on him, which revealed that the young man had not kept even the first commandment Jesus told him, "One thing thou lackest If you want to be perfect, go and sell everything you have, and give it to the poor and then come and follow me" What did the young man do? The record says, "He went away sorrowful, because he had great possessions"

He lacked only one thing, but he was lost He loved his money more than he loved Jesus He thought he was keeping the Ten Commandments, but he hadn't even gotten as far as obeying the first one What is the first commandment? "Thou shalt have no other gods before Me" He had allowed his money to come in between him and Christ His money was his god He had another god before the Lord He wasn't even keeping the first commandment

What a solemn warning this is, in regard to allowing anything whatever to hold you back from going all the way in accepting God's message which has come to you in these meetings When we hold back from obeying the call of Jesus, He can actually put His finger on the very obstacle which we allow to come in and hinder us from taking our stand If you haven't taken your stand, and you are allowing something to hold you back, Jesus Christ places His finger on that one item tonight and says, **"One thing thou lackest."** It may be your job, your business, the opposition of friends or loved ones.

It may be tobacco, it may be theater-going, it may be dancing Whatever it may be that is holding you back, Christ, with eternal love for your soul, places His finger on it, and says to you, "One thing thou lackest Dost thou love Me more than this?"

I hope that none of you will make the sad mistake which the rich young ruler made He failed to stand the test that the Lord placed on him If you lack one thing, then be quick to remedy this lack, as the still small voice says, "This is the way, walk ye in it "

The man who goes on lacking one thing, will finally lack everything and lose everything I want to repeat that The man, or woman, who continues to allow any one thing, I don't care what it is, job, business, the opposition of loved ones, worldly pleasures, the giving up of some item, if he allows any one item to come between him and going all the way with Jesus, he will soon lack everything and lose everything

Do you know wherein a great many church members will fall short of reaching heaven? The majority of professed Christians have a cheap religion They want to live as they please, eat and drink and dress like the world, do like the world, and yet claim to be a follower of Jesus, hoping that somehow they will get to heaven at last

Mark this well There is no such thing as being a cheap Christian The world is full of cheap religion But there is no such thing as being a cheap Christian Jesus never taught a cheap religion One of the first principles of following Jesus is self-denial Put down Matthew 16 24 "If any man will come after Me, let him deny himself, and take up his cross, and follow Me " Jesus Christ never taught a cheap religion

You know that I have not preached a cheap religion If I wanted popularity, then I would preach a cheap religion I cannot be true to Jesus Christ and preach a cheap religion I must preach as Christ taught There is no such thing as being a cheap Christian You can be a cheap church member You can be a cheap professed Christian You can have a cheap religion But there is not such thing in being a cheap Christian

It costs something to be a Christian It cost Jesus something None of us can understand how much it cost Jesus to make it possible for you to be a Christian We may have some idea when we read 2 Corinthians 8 9 "Ye know the grace of our Lord Jesus Christ, that though He was rich,   He became poor, that ye through His poverty might be rich "

Jesus had to give up all the glories of heaven He had to leave His place at His Father's side, and come down here and be born as a baby He grew up as a man to be ridiculed, sneered at, spit upon and beaten He sweat blood, was treated like a criminal being nailed to a cross Yes, it cost Jesus something! Don't ever think you can follow Jesus without it costing you something

Since He gave His all for you, how could you hold back from giving your all to Him? He went all the way for you I hope that you will not refuse or fail to go all the way for Him

It is easy, friends, to accept this message if you make a full surrender It is impossible to accept it, if you do not make a full surrender

A gentleman was walking along the street one day with a bag of candy in his hand He met a little boy He held out the bag of candy to the boy, and said, "Son, wouldn't you like to have some candy?" The boy said, "Sure, I would like some candy " The man pulled the sack wide open and said to the boy, "Just put your hand down in there and take all the candy you want " The boy put his hand in the sack and pulled it out, but did not have any candy in it.

The man said, "Son, don't you like candy?" Then the man looked in the boy's hand and saw that his hand was full of marbles He was so eager to hang on to those marbles, that when he put has hand into the bag, he couldn't take any candy

You smile at this, and say, "Well, I would have had better sense than that I would have placed those marbles on the sidewalk, and then I could have taken a whole handfull of candy" Yes, you smile at that boy, but are you doing any better in regard to what God offers you?

Let me have a word with you who are holding back from coming into His remnant church, to keep all His commandments God offers you the pearl of great price Why don't you take this great prize? The facts are that some have their hands so full of worldly things, that they cannot take hold of God's pearl So long as people are holding on to their Saturday work or business, tobacco, the Hollywood movies, dancing, card playing, and other sinful ways of the world, they cannot lay hold on God's pearl

Why not lay aside these cheap, transitory, fading things of the world, so that you can take the pearl of endless joy and pleasure forever more? Jesus Christ was right when He said, "What shall it profit a man, if he shall gain the whole world and lose his own soul?" I think you recognize that eternal life in the kingdom of God is worth more than all this world

How many of you believe that eternal life in the kingdom of God is worth more than all the gold, silver, diamonds, mansions, bonds, stocks, and pleasures of the world all put together? Let me see your hands Yes, we are all agreed on this, and we ought to be It is right It is the truth Eternal life in the kingdom of God is worth more than everything in this world put together

Now let us go a step further I will not ask you to put your hands up on this You can tell the Lord about it Since it is true that eternal life is worth more than all the world, then why should you hesitate one minute, to give up a few paltry things of the world to secure eternal life? O, friends, we need to have more of the love of Jesus in our hearts! When you have the love of Christ dwelling in your heart, it is easy to make the full surrender.

I want to tell you tonight about a Japanese girl In Tokyo, Japan, there lived a Japanese girl who was the heir to a large fortune through her god-father He gave her a wonderful education She attended the University of Tokyo for ten years

Then she came in contact with this great three-fold message, for it is being preached in Japan just as it is here in America One day she went to the Adventist missionary When she heard the message, something told her that this was the truth As she attended meeting after meeting, she finally made up her mind that she would become a Christian and keep the Sabbath

When her people heard it, they felt disgraced that their fine daughter would even think of becoming an Adventist Her god-father determined to stop her from accepting the message He forbade her to attend any more meetings, but she went anyway Then he said, "If you don't stop going to those meetings, you must pack your clothes, and leave this home, never to return You may take your choice now between this fine home and the Adventist religion"

Think of what a choice that girl had to make! She had been reared in the lap of luxury She had had everything her heart could wish for She had servants to wait on her, as we say, hand and foot Now she must choose between taking Jesus Christ and being expelled from home and go out in the world alone, to make her own living the best she could, or rejecting Jesus Christ and remaining in this home of ease, wealth, and luxury Which would she choose? "Whosoever loveth father or mother more than Me is not worthy of Me"

At first she was greatly perplexed She said, "Where will I go if I am driven from home? What can I do to support myself?" But she was determined to follow Jesus all the way. She had seen the pearl of great price She was ready to sell everything to secure it She went to her room and got out her little trunk She began to pack her clothes, and as she packed the clothes, she sang,

> "Jesus I my cross have taken,
> All to leave and follow Thee
> All things else I have forsaken,
> Thou from hence my all shalt be
> Perish every fond ambition,
> All I've sought, or hoped, or known,
> Yet, how rich is my condition,
> God in heaven still my own"

In the university where she had received her education, she had learned three languages, English, German, and French, in addition, of course, to her own Japanese tongue So she decided that she would rent a bungalow and put up a sign that she would teach people either German, French, or English She was thus able to make a nice living for herself by teaching those three languages

Quite a long time afterwards her god-father came to her for a reconciliation He said, "I want you to come back home. We love you, and we cannot live without you The day I drove you away, happiness died in our home I want you to come back You can have your religion You can be an Adventist All I ask is, that you will promise that when I die, you will offer incense and pray to my spirit"

The girl said, "Father, I want to come home I will be good to you and mother as long as you live, but I cannot promise to worship you when you die I can worship only God and Jesus"

He flew into a rage. He drove her out into the street like a man who was beside himself He said, "I'll disinherit you forever I will adopt another daughter in your place and give her all my money" And he did that very thing

When that man died he left a fortune in Japanese yen that would equal in American money one million dollars, and he didn't give one penny to this girl, whom he had disinherited It cost that girl one million dollars to be a Seventh-day Adventist Did it pay? One proof of that would be to ask that girl She would tell you that Jesus is more precious to her than all the world She has the pearl of great price When the saints gather around the throne, I believe Jesus will point to her and say, "There is one who was willing to give up so much for Me" I believe that people like her will shine the brightest around the Father's throne

I hope you will make the same wise choice that this young lady did A home in heaven is of such surpassing value that you cannot afford to allow anything or anybody to hold you back from responding to the call of the Lord to come out and take your stand with His remnant church

We talk about hell, and not wanting to go there, but I want to tell you that the worst punishment of hell will not be the fire that burns people The worst part of hell for many people will be to realize what they have lost by their failure to step out and obey God O, what a fearful awakening it will be when the disobedient stand around the New Jerusalem in the final day and see inside the city the glories, the beauties, the joys, they have missed simply because they refused to take their stand for God, and allowed some little thing to hold them back.

When this message came to me I had a great struggle I'll not go into details, but I doubt if anyone here is having any greater struggle than I had when this light came to me. Finally I settled three items once for all

The first one was that the great prize that awaits me in heaven if I will be true to Jesus is of such surpassing value that I can't allow anything, or anybody to hold me back from being obedient to the call of God

Second, that I ought to be willing to give up all to comply with all of God's commandments to secure this great prize, the prize of prizes which He has for the obedient

The third item was that having once started to obey God, I must never even think of turning back I hope that you likewise will settle those three points once for all

During a certain battle in the Civil War there was a battery on a hill that was the key to the victory The opposing side charged up that hill again and again only to be forced back with great losses On another hill the general was sitting on his horse watching the battle through his field glasses. He saw his men being repeatedly defeated in their effort to charge up that slope and capture the battery

Finally he sent for one of his captains who was in charge of the battle The captain respectfully saluted his general and awaited his orders

"Will you take that battery?" asked the general

"I'll try, sir," and saluting his general, he turned to go

The old experienced general was not satisfied He signaled for the captain to return The young captain did so, and saluting as before, awaited once more his commander's orders

This time the general asked him with great emphasis, "**Will** you take that battery?"

The captain seeing how earnest his commander was, replied with a similar emphasis, "I'll **try**, Sir " The captain turned away to go and make the attempt

The battle-scarred general was not satisfied For the third time he called the captain back, and looking into the captain's eye, striking one gloved fist into the other, hand, he cried, "**Captain, will you take that battery?**"

The young captain, sensing the urgency of the situation unhesitatingly saluted and said, "**I'll do it or die, Sir.**" The battery was taken, and the battle won

Our heavenly general, the Lord Jesus Christ, is asking you and me, "Will you surrender all to do the will of God? Will you take your stand against the world if need be to follow all of My commandments?" If you have the determination that by His grace you will do it or die, you will have the victory

The Lord Jesus is holding out the grandest prize that He ever offered to a human being He is holding out the great pearl Why not just reach out tonight and take the pearl of great price? I am glad there are a group of people here, who are ready to take this pearl They have accepted the Lord and are going all the way with Him

As we listen to the song, "Is your all on the Altar of Sacrifice?", I would like for you who plan to be baptized tomorrow morning to come forward for a prayer of consecration, as your response to the question of the song Along with you, I invite all others to come who are ready to surrender all to Jesus to secure this pearl of great price

God can do everything for the person who wants His help, but God cannot do anything for the person who doesn't really appreciate his need of help or want God's help

How many who have not come forward would like to lift the hand and say, "Brother Shuler, pray for me tonight that God will help me to take my stand, and to go all the way in accepting His message? Yes, Thank the Lord I see a number of hands!

(PRAYER)

Half-Baked Christians

I am speaking today on the subject of "Half-Baked Christians." I suppose some of you have wondered where we find anything in the Bible about this You may say, "This subject seems quite strange Surely you cannot find anything about this in the Bible." Here it is in Hosea 7 8, the last part of the verse, "Ephraim is a cake not turned"

When a pancake is cooked on one side, the cook usually turns it over so it will bake on the other side I do not suppose anyone likes a half-baked pancake So God does not like half-baked Christians One of His charges against Ephraim was, that "Ephraim is a cake not turned." He has not been turned over and baked on the other side He is only half-baked That is the same as saying he is only half converted.

If he does not go further than this, he will never get to heaven He isn't ready for heaven Why is it that we see some people, who are only half baked spiritually? One of the tragedies in evangelism is to see some people, who are only half baked spiritually, just half way into the message Why do people go only half way? What is lacking in their experience? No one will ever have a true experience of God, until he first makes a full surrender to do the will of God

The key to this whole question of whether or not we are half baked is found in Luke 14 33 The words of Jesus are, "So likewise, whosoever he be of you that forsaketh not all that he hath, he cannot be My disciple" There is no mistaking the meaning of these words of Jesus

You do not hear very many sermons preached on this text Most preachers today place great emphasis on believing on Christ, and scarcely say anything about the necessity of a full surrender to Christ. Jesus declares that whosoever does not forsake all that he has, not nine-tenths, or ninety-nine hundredths, but all that he has, cannot be His disciple

God demands a hundred per cent surrender to His service In Romans 12 1 we have the call of God "I beseech you therefore, brethren, by the mercies of God, that ye present your bodies a living sacrifice, holy, acceptable unto God, which is your reasonable service" Even when you make a hundred per cent surrender you have only done the reasonable thing You have just done the right thing It isn't even extra measure, it is just your reasonable service

Why is it that so many people, who are apparently sincere, come to the Lord, but fail to get power to overcome certain things in their lives and are left only half-baked? I think of these meetings here, and I speak this with sorrow in my heart I think of men who are allowing only one thing to keep them from going all the way with Jesus The only thing that is holding them back from taking their stand is a worthless weed It is just a miserable weed called tobacco

The only thing which is holding some back, is that they are not willing to give up the Hollywood movies There are other people, who are willing to accept all the message, but they are unwilling to lay aside their ornaments for Jesus' sake

Why is it that some people come to the Lord, with a desire in their heart to do what is right, but fail to get the power to overcome? I want to read you one answer to this question In a book called **Acts of the Apostles** on page 299 there is a statement which I think will help us "The surrender must be

complete Every weak, doubting, struggling soul who yields fully to the Lord
is placed in direct touch with agencies that enable him to overcome"

"Every weak, doubting, struggling soul." O, we have so many of them
here There are many weak, doubting, struggling souls Jesus speaks about
not quenching the smoking flax I thank God for the spark of desire which
they do have I would to God I knew some way that I could fan that spark
into a blaze that would consume them on the altar of full consecration to God

Notice that "every weak, doubting, struggling, soul who yields fully to
the Lord is placed in direct touch with agencies that enable him to overcome"
If he does not overcome the wrong things in his life, it is not God's fault
God's power is available You know that If a man does not get the victory
over these wrong things, it is because he does not make the full surrender
It takes the full surrender to bring the power of God into a man's life and give
him victory Remember that you can assure the power you need in your life
for right living, only as you yield yourself fully to the Lord Jesus Christ

The reason that some people are only half-baked spiritually, or half-con-
verted is that they fail to make a full and complete surrender If you are 25%
surrendered, you are twenty-five per cent converted If you are fifty per cent
surrendered, you are fifty per cent converted Brother, fifty per cent is not
enough Seventy-five per cent is not enough It takes a hundred per cent
conversion What did Jesus say? "Whosoever he be of you that does not forsake
all that he hath, he cannot be My disciple." It takes a hundred per cent
surrender to make a man a hundred per cent converted

In **Testimonies**, Volume 6, page 92 we read this. "When the soul fails
to make this surrender, sin is not forsaken; the appetites and passions are
striving for the mastery, temptations confuse the conscience, so that true
conversion does not take place."

This reveals an important basic principle of Christian living. It is not
just for people who have not yet joined the church This may apply to those
who have been in the church for years Everyone of us needs to heed it Here
is the key to having a true conversion If you want true conversion, you must
make a full, complete surrender with no reservations

When the soul fails to make this full surrender, true conversion does not
take place A person who fails to make the full surrender is left half baked
This is the reason why people are only half-way into the message They did
not make the full surrender, and they are left, as it were, only half baked,
only half converted, only half-way into the message

True conversion cannot take place in the experience of those who fail
to make the full surrender If you want to be truly converted, you must make
the full surrender

Here is a question I would like to have you think through It is a very
pertinent question How much did the Son of God have to give up in order
to make salvation possible for you and me? Jesus Christ, God's eternal Son,
was up in heaven with the Father, even before the world was In fact the
Father made all the worlds by His Son, Christ Christ was the co-ruler of
the universe with His Father All heaven was Christ's The angels loved to
bow before Jesus and worship Him

How much did Christ have to give up in order to save you and me? He
had to give up ALL He had to give up everything that He had in heaven
and come to this world He came here and didn't even have a place to lay His
head He says, "The foxes have holes, and the birds of the air have nests, but
the Son of Man hath not where to lay His head"

In place of being worshipped by the angels, He came here to be ridiculed
and spit upon by men He had to give up everything He had in heaven and
come to this world, as poorest among the poor, and suffer the indescribable
agony of Gethsemane and Calvary Paul says in 2 Corinthians 8 9, "For ye

know the grace of our Lord Jesus Christ, that though He was rich, yet for your sakes He became poor, that ye through His poverty might be rich"

I do not think any of us will ever fathom the meaning of that text "He was rich" You never will realize how rich Christ was before He came to this world as a baby It is impossible. You will never know how poor He became either

He was rich, He had all heaven; He came here and became the poorest of the poor Why? He did not have to do it. If He had not come to earth, it would not have been a sin He did not have to come here at all He would not have been doing anything wrong, if He had stayed up in heaven But what would have happened to you? You would have been eternally lost

It was nothing but love that brought Jesus Christ out of heaven God so loved the world, that He gave His own dear Son Christ so loved the world, that He gave His all Since Christ had to give His all to save us, how much will you and I have to give up in order to enter into a true experience of salvation with Him? We will have to give our all "Whosoever he be of you that forsaketh not all that he hath, he cannot be My disciple"

> "I gave my life for thee,
> My precious blood I shed,
> That thou might'st ransomed be,
> And quickened from the dead
> I gave, I gave My life for thee,
> What hast thou giv'n for Me?"

I wonder, if the Lord Jesus Christ were sitting in that seat next to you, and He quietly said, "Son, daughter, how much have you given for Me? I gave My life for thee, what hast thou giv'n for Me?" What would you tell Him? What could you say?

There are thousands of professed Christian people who could not tell of one item which they ever gave up for the sake of Jesus Christ A minister once preached a sermon on how Christians should be willing to sacrifice everything for Jesus. He told how many people who claim to love and follow Christ have never denied themselves even one thing for Christ He told how many Christians were partaking of the sinful pleasures of the world, which are directly contrary to the teachings of Jesus He mentioned how many Christians were freely using tobacco, tea, and coffee and other items, which are out of keeping with the spirit and example of Jesus

There was one family among others, which was deeply impressed by the minister's earnest appeal When they returned home, they began to consider the appeal in relation to their lives They asked themselves, "What shall we do about it?" The father said, "I believe the preacher is right I cannot think of one item I have ever denied myself for the sake of Christ I have made up my mind to give up cigars for the sake of Christ"

The mother said, "I dearly love my cup of tea, but I have made up my mind to give up the use of tea for the sake of Christ" Alice, the daughter, said, "I don't see how I can get along without my cup of coffee in the morning You know I have a terrible headache if I leave off coffee I do not see how I can get along without my cup of coffee, but I have decided never to use it again"

Tom, the son was yet to be heard from After the father, the mother, and the daughter had spoken, Tom said, "I have decided that I will give up eating salt mackerel, I never did like the stuff anyway"

This illustrates the attitude of many professed Christians They are not willing to give up anything that they really like or desire, for the sake of the One Who gave His all for them Many people are willing to follow Christ up to a certain point, or up to a certain limit They are willing to obey Christ as long as it does not interfere with their own pleasure, their own appetites, plans and business

They should remember that the acceptance of Jesus Christ is not subject to any reservation "Whosoever he be of you that forsaketh not all that he hath, cannot be My disciple" Unless you make Jesus Christ Lord of all your life, He is not your Lord at all

Many Christians think that it is a matter of little consequence whether or not they give up the use of cigarettes They will argue by the hour about what a little thing it is to use cigarettes There are others who contend that it makes no difference whether or not they refrain from attending the Holly-wood movies Some will say, "What difference does it make whether or not I comply with such a little thing as taking off some ornament, or abstaining from reading novels?"

We need to look beyond what we think are little things to the real issue I would to God today that any of you, who are struggling on these points, might have your eyes fully opened to the real issue involved in these items There are only two controlling principles for every person's life You will find these set forth in Romans 8 5,6 "For they that are after the flesh do mind the things of the flesh, but they that are after the Spirit do mind the things of the Spirit For to be carnally minded is death, but to be spiritually minded is life and peace "

These are the two controlling principles There is the minding of the Spirit, or obeying the Spirit There is the minding of the flesh, or obeying the flesh Whichever of these two controls your life, settles your destiny for heaven or hell If you mind the Spirit, you will be saved If you mind the flesh, you will be lost and go to hell

The real issue is not merely what harm there is in smoking two or three cigarettes The real issue is not merely what harm there is in going to a Hollywood movie once in awhile The real issue is not merely what harm there is in an occasional game with a regular deck of playing cards The real issue is not merely what harm is in the wearing of some ornament No, the real issue, is living for the flesh, or for the Spirit

The entire question of the supremacy of God in a person's life may turn on a little point Remember that the question of the supremacy of God in your life decides whether you will be saved or lost The great question may revolve around what you do, on what appears on the face of it, to be a minor item It may revolve around whether or not you will give up going to the Hollywood movies, or the use of cigarettes or lay aside some ornament

Some one has well said, "It is not the greatness of the act of disobedience, that constitutes sin, but the fact of variance from God's expressed will in the least particular, for this shows that there is yet communion between the soul and sin The heart is divided in its service There is virtual denial of God, a rebellion against the law of His government "

Some will say, "Brother Shuler, you have been talking about the need of a full surrender Will you please tell us what you mean by making a full surrender? How can I proceed to make a full surrender?"

Reduced to its simplest terms, it consists of two steps

First, the complete abandonment, the immediate giving up of all evil desires, bad habits, wrong practices and unholy attachments, which are contrary to the will of Jesus Christ and which Christ cannot use in your life

Second, it is the dedication, or the turning over to the Lord of all good desires, talents, abilities and powers that the Lord can use It means giving to Jesus Christ **what we are,** our person, our wills, our bodies, and all their members It means giving **what we have,** to Christ, our time, our talents, our faculties, our capabilities It means giving **what we do** to Christ, our plans, our aims, our purposes.

There are millions of Americans, who are willing to go through every kind of hardship, suffering, and danger for the sake of the star-spangled banner Think of World War II and of what our boys went through in order to capture certain islands from the Japanese They were willing to give their all for their country's flag And this is true of the people of other countries

In a certain battle in China, before World War II really broke out, the Japanese tanks were plunging relentlessly through the Chinese lines The Chinese had no tanks or artillery with which to stop the Nipponese tanks It was impossible for the Chinese forces to hold their ground against the onslaughts of these mighty steel monsters of Japan It looked as if the entire Chinese army would be cut to pieces

In the midst of the battle the Chinese general asked a certain regiment to assemble at the rear where he could talk to them They gathered about him He said, "Men of China, there is no way for us to save China unless we can stop these tanks We have no artillery or tanks of our own There is only one way, that I know of to stop these Japanese tanks which are cutting our lines to pieces This is for some of you men to tie charges of dynamite to your bodies, and when you see a tank coming, lie directly in its path Then pull the fuse when the tank is just about to run over your body Every man who does this will be blown to pieces But the tanks will be stopped It means that every man who does this is giving his all to save China Do I have any who love China enough to volunteer for this?"

Do you think it was hard to get volunteers? Did he have to plead and beg his men to do it, as we have to stand here and coax and beg people to come and say, "I will do what I ought to do for Jesus Christ?" No! When he said, "Do I have any who love China enough to do this?" Hundreds of men stepped forward Hundreds more than were needed They said, "Here I am Bring the dynamite and put it around me "

O, friends, this should put us to shame If men are willing to give their all for their country, how much more should you and I not hold back for one split second, in giving our all to Jesus Christ for an eternal home in heaven Why should men be so quick to go forward in the face of death for their country, yet, when it comes to moving out for Jesus Christ, you cannot get people to make a move Friends, let us change the program today What do you say? When the call is given today, let us come up and say, we will go forward for Jesus Christ!

Why should we not be more willing and quick to follow the One Who has gone all the way for us? Why should we not be willing and brave to die for Jesus Christ if necessary, as men are to die for their country?

Some of you men think it will kill you if you quit using tobacco It will not kill you It will kill self "I am crucified with Christ " The cure you need, brother, is to die to self Then you will have victory over tobacco Why should we hold back? Brother if you will make this kind of surrender, you will have victory from this day You will not tamper with it again

Why shouldn't we be willing to even die for Christ? The time will come when the law will say that those who will not worship the beast will be put to death on a certain day But no one is asked to face death for Christ today He does ask us to quit tobacco and leave it alone He asks us to lay aside the sinful ways of the world. If He asked us to actually give up our physical lives, we should even be willing to do that If men are willing to die for their country, why shouldn't we be willing to die for Jesus Christ?

Let us go a little further Eternal life in heaven is worth more than everything in this world put together "What will it profit a man if he gain the whole world and lose his own soul?" Think how much eternal life exceeds in value this present life, which after all is so transitory! This means that you have as much more inducement to give your life to Jesus Christ now, as eternal life exceeds in value this present transitory life Yes, heaven is cheap enough at any price

How small these things are that we give up! What Christ asks you to give up is nothing compared to what He gave up for you When He asks us to give up worldly things, it is just like asking us to trade pennies for hundred-dollar gold pieces People who are not willing to give up worldly distractions are as unwise as a man holding on to pennies, when some one is waiting to pour twenty-dollar gold pieces into his hand How small these items are, like tobacco, jewelry, worldly pleasure, worldly friends, when compared to the everlasting joys and pleasures of heaven!

We are told that the Mohammedan conquerors always destroyed the idols in the temples of the territory which they conquered When Mahmud, the Mohammedan conqueror of India, came to a certain village in his conquest of India, his soldiers went to the temple to destroy the idols When they entered one temple to destroy the idols the priests gathered around a very small idol They begged most earnestly that they would not destroy this little idol

They said, "You see how little it is It is one that we cherish so highly Destroy the rest of them, but please, please don't destroy this little idol"

The idol seemed of little value and the soldiers were inclined to preserve it Some of them went and told Mahmud, and he went to the temple The priests gathered around him and pleaded that he would not destroy this small idol They offered him a large sum of money if he would just spare this one idol The offering was tempting

This little idol didn't look as if it were worth fifteen cents They offered a large amount of money if he would just spare this one He was just about to say, "Yes, I will do it" Then he lifted his battle-ax and with one blow he broke that little idol to pieces and from inside the idol there fell at his feet handsful of diamonds, sapphires, rubies and many other precious gems These jewels far exceeded in value the amount of money they offered him to spare this small idol

So the devil is trying to drive a sharp bargain with some of you folks He makes tempting offers to people today if they will just spare one of his chosen small idols "I will give you so much if you will just spare that one" He knows if you do, you will lose the jewels of eternal happiness

The Word of God is sharper than any two-edged sword Brother, sister, if there is even one item that you have not given up, which is keeping you from taking your stand with God's remnant people, why not take the Word of God at this minute and cut it loose? Do not let anything, friends, loved ones, wife, husband, father, mother, brothers, sisters, dancing, card-playing, theatre-going, jewelry, tobacco, or anything else cause you to lose the never-ending pleasures of a home in heaven! Are you ready to smite your idol today with the sword of the Spirit?

We ought to be just as definite about this matter of a full surrender to God as we are when we buy a piece of land, or when we buy a book, or any article There are many people who know they ought to do it They intend to do it, and they tell themselves, "Someday I will take my stand" But they never come to the definite point of actually doing it Hence they will lose eternal life.

I may intend to give a new Bible to one of my friends, but until I actually go to him and put the Bible in his hands, or send it to him, I have not given it to him It still remains in my possession

A North American Indian once heard a missionary tell of the great peace that God gives to those who come to Him with all their hearts The Indian went into the deep woods alone He said to himself, "I will secure that great peace that the missionary man has told about"

The best thing he knew was to build an altar He knelt at the altar and prayed But when he got up he didn't feel any better

Then he said to himself, "I will secure this great peace, if I give an offering to the Lord. I must give the Lord something" So he laid his blanket on the altar You know that a blanket is valuable to an Indian He laid his blanket on the altar. He got down and prayed. When he got up, he felt no better.

Then he laid his gun on the altar A gun is about all an Indian has with which to get something to eat He got down and prayed, but felt just the same

Next he laid his pony on the altar He tied the pony's four legs and laid it on the altar Again he knelt and prayed, but still felt no better Then he said, "Indian give himself" So he laid himself on the altar, yielding unreservedly Then that great peace which God gives to those who surrender all, entered his heart He had made a definite surrender, he received a definite blessing

So it will be with every soul who makes this matter of a full surrender a definite transaction in his life Your heavenly Father has proved His love for you in giving for you the best gift of heaven The blessed Son has proven His love for you in giving His all Now may it be that each of us will prove our love for Jesus and the Father by giving our all to them

Will you prove that today, by making a full surrender? I have never been able to understand how anyone can refuse to give his all to Jesus, Who has done so much for him Can you look at Jesus, suffering on the cross, and say, "I can accept all Thy message, which I have heard in these meetings, all except one certain item?" Could you tell Jesus that? No You should say

"Love so amazing, so divine,
    Demands my heart, my soul, my all"

When Abel laid his sacrifice on the altar, the fire of God fell and consumed it. So, when a person surrenders himself spirit, soul, and body, fully to God, when he lies like an offering on the altar of God, then the fire of God falls, to burn up the evil in that man, and to make the offering clean After an experience such as that, he will be a different person than before

"Laid on Thine altar, O my God divine,
    Accept my gift this day for Jesus' sake
I have not jewels to adorn Thy shrine,   ·
    Nor any world-famed sacrifice to make.
But here I bring, within my trembling hand,
    This will of mine,—a thing which seemeth small
Yet, Thou alone, O Lord, can understand
    How when I yield Thee this, I yield Mine all "

Shall we yield our all to God just now? During the last two Sabbaths we have had the pleasure of seeing two fine companies of people take their stand for this message A week ago Friday night we saw a fine company of people baptized, and the next day we had the privilege of receiving them into this great message This morning we saw another company of people baptized, and had the pleasure of receiving them into the great brotherhood of the message of God There are many more of you who intend to take your stand Today we should like to pray for you You need the help of God

I shall ask that the choir sing softly for us, "I surrender All" As the choir sings, I ask you, who intend to accept this message, to come forward You need the help of God to take this step My appeal is to everyone beyond the two groups whom we have already received Give your all to Jesus While the choir sings, will you please come and form a prayer circle here in front? (People began to come forward)

Yes, thank God, they are coming If men are willing to give their all for their country, brother, how can you sit back there? How much more you should give your all to Jesus Christ! Thank the Lord He is speaking to hearts today

Friends, how can we refuse to do it? How can we refuse to give our all to Him? Remember that I am appealing to everyone in this audience who intends to accept the message of God. Surely there are others. Men are willing to give up all for their country. Let us show that we are willing to give up all for the sake of Jesus Christ

As we stand I want to invite still others. Will you come and stand with these here at the front? We want to pray for you today. You need the help of God to do it. Thank the Lord here is another one!

The still small voice says, "This is the way." The Holy Spirit is urging you to come. Come now and take your stand. Thank God here is another one! The Lord bless you, brother, it is the best thing any man can do

"Ye shall be gathered one by one." God is gathering His people one by one

I want to tell an experience, which I think will help some of you. There was a man who had an incurable disease, leprosy. He was told that in order to be cured he must go and dip himself seven times in the River Jordan. He went to this river and dipped himself one time. But he looked just as he did before. He dipped the second time. Still there was no change. The third time, no change. And for the sixth time, and no change. What would have happened to that man if he had stopped after the sixth time? That is where some have stopped. Have you gone just so far in accepting the message? Then you stopped

This man went on and dipped himself the seventh time. A shout of joy went up because the leprosy was gone. Joy came when he went all the way. Will still others say, "God helping me I am going all the way?"

As we sing one more stanza we shall close the invitation. I dislike to say the word "close," because it may be the last time for some. I hope not. Some time the door will be forever shut, and, O, the tragedy of millions of people knocking on a door that will never be opened! Let us come today and take our stand. Let us go all the way today. Is there another that wants to come forward and stand for prayer today?

(Prayer.)

Our dear heavenly Father, we thank Thee for Thy great love. We shall never be able to fully understand how God gave the best gift He had for us. O, blessed Jesus, we shall never be able to fully understand how Thou hast given Thine all for us

Bless these who have come forward. Do for them what they cannot do for themselves. Set them free. Give them victory. Give them peace and strength. Bless others here who know that they ought to take this step. They intend to do it. We pray that Thou wilt remember them

Bless the people who have heard the truth, and know the truth. O, God, give them a heart to obey the truth

Guide us, keeps us, and may it be that everyone of us will have gone all the way with Jesus, that when He comes He can welcome us to an eternal happy home in that wonderful place He has prepared for His own. We will give Thee all the praise in Jesus' name. Amen

Jesus Is the Way

This afternoon I took the Des Moines telephone directory and looked up the churches in the classified portion of the directory I discovered that there are over fifty different denominations represented by the various church buildings and religious meeting places in the city of Des Moines Wouldn't it be interesting to know which one of these fifty different beliefs the Lord Jesus would follow if He lived in Des Moines today? You say, "Is it possible to know which church Jesus would join?" Yes, it is

All you need to do is to ascertain which of these churches is walking in the way that Jesus marked out for man The way of Jesus will endure until the end of time This means that there must be some church today which corresponds to the one which Jesus established when He came here 1900 years ago If you were sure which church Jesus Christ would belong to if He lived here, wouldn't you belong to it? I think everyone here will raise his hand on that If you were sure which church Jesus would belong to if He lived here today, how many would choose to belong to that church? Will you raise your hands? Thank you I am glad that all of us are agreed on this

On the last night that Jesus was with His disciples before He was crucified, He told them about that wonderful heavenly home that He would prepare for His own He said, "In My Father's house are many mansions if it were not so, I would have told you I go to prepare a place for you And if I go and prepare a place for you, I will come again, and receive you unto myself; that where I am there ye may be also "

Then Thomas asked the Lord a question which expresses the longing of every sincere heart He said, "Lord,   how can we know the way?" Jesus had been talking about this wonderful heavenly home This led Thomas to inquire, "Lord, how can we know the way to that wonderful home on high? How can we be sure, which is the right way that will take us to the heavenly home?"

Here is the answer, the true, sure answer Notice what Jesus said to him "Jesus saith unto him, I am the Way, the Truth, and the Life no man cometh unto the Father, but by Me " Jesus is the Way There is no other "I am THE way "

Jesus Christ is the answer to every question as to what a person ought to believe and do in religion If you want the real truth, all you need to do is to follow Him He is THE truth In John 1 14 we are told that Jesus Christ is full of grace and truth If you want grace and truth, you must get them from Jesus We cannot find grace or truth apart from Him

People who want truth will do what Jesus says In John 18 37 Jesus says, "Everyone that is of the truth heareth My voice " If you want the truth, you will follow what Jesus said

Everyone agrees that Christ lived a life of perfection, a life without sin We can go a step further If we pattern our lives after Jesus, our lives will be right I am sure you will agree with me in this How many of you agree, that if we follow exactly what Jesus said and did, we are sure to be right? May I see your hands? That is fine I am glad we all agree on this We are told in 1 Peter 2 21 that Jesus left us an example, that we should follow in His steps

The example and teaching of the Lord Jesus Christ is the authoritative and infallable standard of Christian doctrine, truth and duty. We do not have six different patterns, or three different patterns, not even two, but only one pattern.

Some people think that the various denominations are just so many different ways to heaven They say heaven is just like a great union depot The Methodist will ride over the John Wesley line The Presbyterians will ride in over the John Knox way The Baptists will come in over the Roger Williams way The Disciples of Christ over the Alexander Campbell way.

It is true that there will be people in heaven who were identified with each of the various creeds, but there is no such thing as a Methodist way to heaven, or a Baptist way to heaven, or a Presbyterian way to heaven or an Adventist way to heaven There is only one way to heaven and that is the Jesus way **"I am the Way"** There is no other. There is only one right way in religion and that is the way Jesus marked out when He was here as man's example

Some will say, "There are so many different denominations teaching so many discordant ideas and yet each one claims to be right It just seems a hopeless task for an average man like me to examine all of them and find out which is the right way"

I have a question for you How many counterfeit ten-dollar bills should you study, in order to recognize a genuine ten-dollar government note? The answer is that you need not study one counterfeit The government experts who can detect the most clever counterfeit bills, make themselves so familiar with the genuine that the moment they see a counterfeit they recognize where it falls short It is the same way in religion You do not need to take days and weeks and months and years, or a lifetime to study the beliefs of all the different denominations You do need to study the true way of Jesus When you know the true way of Jesus, you will know the way that you ought to go And when you know it well, you will recognize at once where all man-made ways fall short

Take another question How can you tell if a house that a contractor builds for you is built according to the right plan? The answer is that you check the building acording to the blue-print that you gave him Tonight we will look at the blue-print of the true way in religion as Jesus marked it out

There is great confusion in the religious world Hundreds of different denominations are teaching their discordant theories But no one needs to be perplexed or bewildered, as to which is the true way for him to go It is comparatively easy to find the true way amid all these denominational ways, and doctrinal puzzles if you will follow the Christ pattern

A little seven-year-old girl one Sunday morning was asking her father a great many questions Father wanted time to read the Sunday paper The little girl just kept pestering him with questions So he took a page of the paper that had a map of the world on one side Little girls don't know very much about a map of the world and how these various countries fit into the picture So he took the scissors and cut the map into all kinds of odd pieces, and then mixed them all up

He led the little girl into another room and said, "Now just take these pieces and fit them together in the right form to make the map of the world" He went back into his den to enjoy his Sunday paper In less than five minutes, the little girl came running in and said, "Daddy, come and see! It is all put together"

The father said, "Surely you couldn't get that all together so soon, could you?"

"Yes, I did Come and see," replied the little girl

So he went with her, and sure enough there was that whole sheet put together, right, into a complete map of the world He said, "How did you get all those odd pieces together so quickly?"

She said, "That was easy There was a big man on the other side, and all I had to do was to put the man together and the map of the world was right"

So if men would take the teachings of the pattern man and put them together, they would solve the puzzle of finding the right way in religion It doesn't take years to do it. You can do it here tonight If you have never heard me preach any other sermon, if this is your first sermon, you can get enough in this one talk to discover for yourself the one true way for people today

The Son of God came from heaven to this world to mark out the way that leads to heaven I invite you to look at some of the distinctive points which He marked out for man The limitation of time requires a brief presentation of these points, so in some cases we will merely list the scriptural references without quoting them

Jesus marked out that the Holy Scriptures, what we call the Bible, is the final arbiter of what a man should believe and do in religion Jesus taught that what the Scripture says is final, and must be believed, and that whatever the Scriptures command is final, and must be obeyed Jesus Christ endorsed the Old Testament as a guide for doctrine Here it is in John 5·39, 46, 47

"Search the scriptures; for in them ye think ye have eternal life· and they are they which testify of Me " This is what Jesus said to the Jews back in His day What Scriptures did they have? The only Scriptures they had were the Old Testament Not a line of the New Testament was written until many years after Jesus left this world

Please note that Jesus endorsed the Old Testament as a guide to doctrine He was even more emphatic when He said, "Had ye believed Moses, ye would have believed Me for he wrote of Me But if ye believe not his writings, how shall ye believe My words?"

There are many churches today which discard the Old Testament Any church that discards the Old Testament is not the true way of Jesus Jesus endorsed the Old Testament as a guide to doctrine

Jesus marked out the necessity of the new birth In John 3 3 He says, "Except a man be born again, he cannot see the kingdom of God "

Jesus marked out the necessity of His indwelling presence in a man's daily life for right living In John 15·4 He says, "Abide in Me, and I in you As a branch cannot bear fruit of itself, except it abide in the vine, no more can ye, except ye abide in Me "

Jesus marked out the necessity of obedience to every one of the Ten Commandments You will find this in Matthew 19 16-22 When the rich young ruler asked Him, "What shall I do to have eternal life?", Jesus directed him to keep the Ten Commandments In His sermon on the mount Jesus said, "Till heaven and earth shall pass, one jot or one tittle shall in no wise pass from the law, till all be fulfilled

If you and I follow the way that Jesus marked out for man, how many of the Ten Commandments will we keep? Nine of them? No All of them Just as you read in Psalm 119 6, "Then shall I not be ashamed, when I have respect unto all Thy commandments " In the New Testament Jesus Christ reveals Himself as the One Who made the world Put down John 1 10, 1-3, 14 Speaking of Christ John 1 10 says, "He was in the world, and the world was made by Him " See how plain that is! Speaking further, "the world was made by Him, and the world knew Him not "

In John 1·1-3 Christ is revealed as the Word by Whom all things were made This means that Christ is the Lord Who made the world in six days Christ is the Lord Who rested upon the seventh day after He had made the world in six days Christ is the Lord Who sanctified or set apart the seventh day after He had rested upon the first seventh day in the history of the world It is literally true according to the New Testament that Jesus marked out the keeping holy of the seventh day. He sanctified the seventh day for man

There is not a line or a word in the New Testament, or the Old Testament that shows that Christ ever sanctified, or set apart, the first day of the week commonly called Sunday for any man to ever keep Then mark this point well: It is an eternal fact that the seventh day, the day now called Saturday, is the only day of weekly observance that Jesus ever sanctified, or set apart, for man to keep

Jesus Christ is the One Who spoke the Ten Commandments In Nehemiah 9 12, 13 we find that the same God Who led the Israelites by the pillar of cloud by day, and the pillar of fire by night, is the One Who spoke the Ten Commandments

In 1 Corinthians 10 4 Paul shows that the One Who led the Israelites was Christ He says, "And did all drink the same spiritual drink· for they drank of that Spiritual Rock that followed them and that Rock was Christ " Then it is literally true that Christ commands the keeping of the seventh day as set forth in the Ten Commandments

The fourth commandment is a command of Jesus He spoke those words, "The seventh day is the Sabbath of the Lord thy God· in it thou shalt not do any work " There is not a line, nor a word written in the New Testament, to show that Jesus ever asked any man to keep the first day of the week, or Sunday, for any reason whatsoever.

Then, it is literally true, according to the New Testament, that the seventh day or Saturday is the only day that Jesus ever asked people to keep If you walk exactly in the way that Jesus has marked out for man, then what day will you keep? Yes, you will keep the seventh day This one decisive point should be sufficient to settle the Sabbath question for every person

If you walk in the true way of Jesus Christ, there is nothing else that you can do, but keep the seventh day which He set apart for man When he lived here on the earth He kept it Has He changed? No Hebrews 13 8 says "Jesus Christ the same yesterday, (That is 1900 years ago when He was here) today, (December 8, 1946) and forever, (that is all the days of the future to come) "Jesus the same yesterday, today, and forever "

Think it through Since Jesus kept the seventh day when He lived here nineteen centuries ago, and He hasn't changed, isn't it settled that if He lived here today He would keep the same seventh day? Jesus attended church every Saturday Put down Luke 4 16 It says, "As His custom was, He went into the synagogue on the Sabbath day " If He lived here now, where would He go every Saturday? He would go to the house of God If we walk in the way He marked out, then we will go to the house of God every Saturday

Jesus made it clear that when people die they fall asleep He also taught that the wicked do not go into hellfire as soon as they draw their last breath, but will be cast into the lake of fire at the day of judgment at the end of the world He taught that the righteous do not go to heaven immediately when they die, but that they go to heaven at the second coming of Christ Here are the references John 11 11, John 5 28, 29, Matthew 13: 38-42; John 14.3, Luke 14 14

Jesus clearly implied that the ministry is to be supported by God's method of tithing, and not by methods that man devises In Matthew 23 23 we find that Jesus endorsed tithe paying He told the Pharisees that they ought to pay tithe, but not leave undone mercy, judgment, and faith, which were the weightier matters of the law If you and I walk in the way Jesus marked out for man, what will we do with the one-tenth of our net income? We will do as God says "Bring ye all the tithes into the store house "

o

Jesus said that Christians should be separate from the world, and should not follow the sinful ways of the world   Put down John 17 14-16   He said, "I have given them Thy word and the world hath hated them, because they are not of the world, even as I am not of the world   I pray not that thou shouldest take them out of the world, but that thou shouldest keep them from the evil   They are not of the world, even as I am not of the world "

If we walk the way Jesus marked out we will shun card playing, dancing, theatre-going, and all other sinful ways of the world

Jesus taught that Christians should practice true temperance   Christ never used alcoholic liquors   He never tasted pork   If tobacco had been in use at that time in Palestine, He would not have used it   If we would walk in the way Jesus marked out, we will eat and drink according to the principles set forth in the Word of God   We will refrain from the use of alcoholic liquors, tobacco in all its forms, the habitual use of all narcotics, pork, and other unclean meats which His word condemns

Jesus marked out that Christians should dress simply, neatly, modestly He was noted for the simplicity of His attire   He wore no ear rings, necklaces or bracelets   If we walk in the way that Jesus marked out, we will rightly represent Him in our dress and personal adornment

Jesus marked out that Christians should practice the washing of each other's feet before they partake of the Lord's supper   Put down John 13 12-15 We find that before He gave them the wine and the bread as the emblems of His spilled blood and broken body He went around and washed their feet After He had washed their feet, He put on His outer garments again, and sat down to the Passover supper table.

Then He asked them, "Know ye what I have done to you?   Ye call me Master and Lord, and ye say well, for so I am   If I then, your Lord and Master, have washed your feet; ye also **ought** to wash one another's feet " This is something that Jesus says we ought to do   "I have given you an example," he says, "That ye should do as I have to you "   "If ye know these things, happy are ye if ye do them "

After He said these things, then He gave them the bread and the wine If we walk in the way that Jesus marked out, we will wash each other's feet before we eat of the bread and the wine at the Lord's Supper

Jesus marked out immersion as the way by which every believer should be baptized   You will find this in Mark 1.9-11   He set the example by being immersed in the river Jordan Himself

Sprinkling and pouring as alleged forms of baptism were established by the Catholic church   And I want to tell you that all other churches which use sprinkling for baptism are simply following the Catholic Church in this respect They are not following the Word of God, or the way of Jesus in this matter of baptism   Any church which does not hold exclusively to single immersion for baptism cannot be the true way that Jesus marked out for man   .

Take the question, If Jesus lived in Des Moines, what church would He join?   This is not a fanciful question to which no definite answer can be given If Jesus lived in Des Moines, He would attend and join the church which teaches exactly the way He prescribed for man

Christ cannot deny Himself   He would not belong to any church which does not follow the way that He ordained   Think it through   Where can you find a church that follows all these items that Christ marked out, like the keeping of the seventh day, tithing, separation from the world, the non-wearing of jewelry, the ordinance of feet washing preceeding the Lord's Supper, eating and drinking according to the principles of the Bible, and baptism only by single immersion?

There is only one church which follows all of these, and that is Christ's remnant church   These meetings have brought this kind of a church to you

Since you know now what church Jesus would attend and join if He lived here, surely you are ready to take your stand with this church, aren't you? Are you willing to turn aside from every other way to walk in the Jesus way?

Christ is the way There is no other. If we want to reach that wonderful home He has prepared, we must follow the way that He has marked out. One of the greatest privileges that can ever come to a human being is to know that he is walking in that true way of Jesus, the way that Jesus marked out. The message we have preached in these meetings has set before you the only true way of Jesus

One of the objectives of this great three-fold message is to restore the true way of Jesus Here it is. Put down Revelation 14 12 God describes the people who will accept that message, **the people who will be called out by that message.** "Here is the patience of the saints. here are they that keep the commandments of God and the faith of Jesus "

There is the true way of Jesus. They keep the commandments of God and the faith of Jesus This three-fold message will call His people back to the original faith of Jesus the true way He marked out for man. The call of the hour is to get away from man-made creeds and human ordinances to the simple, pure true way of Jesus.

Some of you, who have not yet taken your stand with Christ's remnant church will say, "I want to be sure I am right before I go ahead." Yes, every person needs to be sure he is right, then to go ahead But think how plain the true way of Jesus has been made in this one sermon If you never heard another sermon this lesson tonight has made the true way of Jesus stand out as plain, as highway number six from Des Moines to Davenport Isn't that right? You can see the true way of Jesus among all these discordant beliefs and theories, as plain as a twenty-four foot concrete highway between two cities .

If you want to be sure that you are right, take the Jesus way To take the Jesus way, means to take the entire Bible as your guide, not just the New Testament It means to be born again, to let Jesus live His life in you daily; to keep all the Ten Commandments by His grace, to keep the seventh day or Saturday as His holy day, to give God the one-tenth; to live separately from the world, to refrain from using liquor, tobacco, and pork, to lay aside ornaments, to practice feet washing before the Lord's Supper, and to be immersed.

To me this true way of Jesus is just as plain, as if there was snow five feet deep and a neighbor went out and shoveled a path five feet wide from his house to your house If you were going to your neighbor's house, you wouldn't wade through five feet of snow when there was a path five feet wide, which he had already cleared through the snow. Take the path which Jesus has cleared for you, from your house to His heavenly house.

Notice this. I have not asked you to take my word as to which church is the true way of Jesus. I have set before you from the Word of God, some of the distinctive features of the true way of Jesus, and you know for yourself which church teaches according to these items of Jesus.

Some people hinder their own progress by being too slow to act, too conservative to move forward There was a man who was in a hurry to get across a river in the winter time where there was no bridge. The river was frozen over, but he was afraid the ice wouldn't hold him up. So he lay down on the ice and crawled along slowly, to distribute his weight as much as possible so the ice wouldn't break.

Finally he heard a great noise behind him. Has the ice broken loose? No, he looked around and saw a colored man galloping a team of horses with a wagon across the river, singing "Glory Hallelujah" as he went The wagon passed him and went across the river. Then in the place of crawling he got up and walked.

Brother, it is time to stop crawling along with your own ideas. Let us get up and walk in the Jesus way, what do you say? Some of you folks, have been so slow to act Let us stop crawling and walk in the Jesus way. If you haven't stepped out, it is time to get up and walk in the true way of Jesus.

Friends, if you will study the words of Christ, you will find that to walk in the way of Christ, is more important than riches. It is more important than making a living It is more important than burying your own father. Jesus taught that obedience to his call must come ahead of all family ties and church ties, and above all money matters. If you love Jesus, you cannot do otherwise than take His way. No other way will do for me except the Jesus way I want the Jesus way. Can you say, "Amen?"

Will you choose this way tonight? It has been made so plain! You must not hesitate longer. We have had the blessed privilege of seeing three groups of people take the way of Jesus I want to appeal tonight to everyone here beyond these three groups.

My appeal is to all others who are purposed to follow Jesus How many here are determined to take the way of Jesus? Would you mind rising and remain standing? Everyone who intends to take the Jesus way, please stand (A number stood)

Are there still others who will stand to signify, "God helping me, I will take the way of Jesus?" Is there another? This is a good time to put yourself on the right side One more who will stand and say, "God helping me, I will take the way of Jesus?"

Jesus declares that if you confess Him before men, He will confess you before the Father. If you deny Him before men, He will deny you before the Father. Stand up for Jesus. Thank the Lord here is another. The Lord is speaking to hearts.

I crave the privilege of shaking the hands of those of you who are standing You need not remain at the front, but I would like to shake your hand, and the hands of others who will choose this way of Jesus. As the choir sings, "All to Jesus I Surrender,"I invite you to come forward to signify that you will take the way of Jesus.

Here is my hand, how about yours? Friends, how plain this is! How sure it is! God bless you for wanting to take the way of Jesus. O, friends, there is nothing else for me but the way of Jesus

I appeal to you who have not come forward. Would you signify by lifting your hands, "Pray for me, Brother Shuler, that God will help me to take the way of Jesus, to be like Jesus, and to walk in His ways?" (Many hands were raised)

(Prayer.)

O, blessed Christ, precious Saviour, Son of God and Redeemer of the world! We do thank Thee that Thou didst come from heaven to mark out the way that leads to heaven. O, Lord, help us to be willing to take the way of Jesus Help us to get away from man-made creeds, and man-made doctrines and man-made arrangements and take the pure, simple way of Jesus and walk in it.

Help us to have a heart, that loves Jesus enough to take His way. May we not love anyone else more than we love Jesus. Help us to love Thee with all our hearts It is easy to take the way of Jesus, when we truly love Him

Lord, we pray for those who have raised their hands, and those who didn't raise their hands. Lord, we pray that their heart will be so true, that they will not think of anything else, not make any other decision, but the decision to take the way of Jesus

Give them the strength to be in harmony with the teachings of Jesus. May it be that everyone here will have chosen the way of Jesus that when He comes we may all go with Him to that wonderful home He has prepared. We ask it in His precious name. Amen.

(Copy of the Bible Lesson outline, which was distributed to the people preceding the fifty-sixth lecture)

Lesson XI - The Key to Certainty in Religion

1. It is of the utmost importance in this uncertain world, that we be absolutely sure from the Bible that we are following the right religious faith (Luke 1.4, 1 Thess 5 21)
2. It is possible by a study of the last-day prophecies of the Bible, to know for a certainty which religious faith directly represents the truth of God and the work of God in our day
3. Isaiah prophesied that the time would come, when the hand of God would be put forth the second time, to gather from all nations a remnant for Himself   ___ __   __ __ __ _
4. The Exodus Movement in the days of Moses, by which God gathered the Israelites out of Egypt and led them through the wilderness into the land of Canaan, was the putting forth of God's hand the first time (Acts 13 16, 17).
5. This second Exodus Movement, as predicted in Isa 11 11, refers to a gathering out of God's people in the last day___   _ _ _   _ _
from every country in the world
6. The remnant whom God will gather in the last days will be distinguished by the keeping of the commandments of God, and by having the spirit of prophecy.... ... ., and by the giving of the three angel's messages of Rev 14 6-14 to every nation   _ _ _ _   _ _ _ _
7. Among all the religious faiths in the world, there is only one faith and one people, who fit these three specifications of God's remnant for these last days and that is   __ _ _ _ _ .   people
8. The Advent Movement has been raised up by the Lord, to give the threefold message of Rev. 14 to all the world for the purpose of gathering God's remnant from every country   (Rev 18 2, 4)
9. In the light of Isa 11 11 and Rev 14 6-14, this Advent Movement must be God's hand put forth the second time to recover the remnant of His people   We can therefore be just as sure that the Adventist faith is true and right and will be victorious, as we are that the hand of God is true and right and always victorious
10. Just as surely as God took the Israelites to the earthly Canaan and the old Jerusalem, He will take His remnant today to the heavenly Canaan and the new Jerusalem   __   _ _ __ _ _____ __ __ _____.
11. There is sure victory ahead for every one who will be true to the Adventist faith.
12. Since the Advent Movement is the hand of God put forth the second time (Isa 11 11), those who respond to God's call to unite with this movement, may be assured of God's everlasting arm to carry them through to victory (Deut 33 27)
13. In the first Exodus Movement God gathered His people all at one time in one body from one country—Egypt
14. In this last-day, second Exodus Movement God will gather His remnant one by one from every land, as His message comes to them and they accept of it (Isa 27 12).

References which were filled in as the study was presented   (3) Isa 11 11, (5) Isa 2 2, 11 12, (6) Rev 12 17, 19 10, 14 12, (7) Student will fill in the name which belongs here; (10) Rev 15 2, 3.

Is St. Peter in Charge of the Gates of Heaven?

(Preached on the fifteenth Sunday night of the Campaign)

Saint Peter has no more to do with opening the gates of heaven to you than John Doe, Will Smith, or Jim Williams Do you know who is actually in charge of the gates of heaven? Here it is in Revelation 21 2, 12 "And I John, saw the holy city, the new Jerusalem,   and had a wall great and high, and had twelve gates, and at the gates twelve angels " There are twelve gates to God's heavenly home   God has chosen twelve certain angels as the gate keepers to His heavenly home

The Bible does tell how many people these twelve angels will admit through these gates into heaven   Let us turn to Hebrews 5 9   Speaking of Christ it says, "Being made perfect, He became the author of eternal salvation unto"   (how many people?) Unto all who profess to follow Christ? No Unto all who are baptized? No Unto all who join the church? No   What does it say? "He became the author of eternal salvation unto all them that obey Him."

Some people tell us that since people are saved only by grace, the Ten Commandments are no longer binding on those who believe in Christ   But notice that Hebrews 5 9 shows that **obedience is necessary to salvation.** Christ gives eternal salvation unto all them that obey Him

We are saved only by grace, but grace does not do away with obedience In fact grace makes it possible to obey the Lord   There will be just as many people saved eternally in heaven, as there will have been persons in this world who will have obeyed the Lord Jesus Christ as far as they have had a knowledge of His will.

There will be thousands of people saved in heaven who did not know that Jesus Christ died for their sins   Zechariah 13 6 seems to indicate that there will be people in heaven who when they meet Jesus and see the nail prints in His hands, will ask, "Lord, what are these wounds in Thine hands?" You and I will never ask such a question as that   We know what made those nail prints   We have heard the story of the cross   We know Jesus died for our sins   But some sincere soul from a heathen land, who never heard the story of Calvary, yet has lived up to all the light that he had, will be saved   And when he sees those nail prints in the hands of Jesus, he will ask, "Lord, what are those wounds in Thine hands?"

There will be many people in heaven who have never been baptized in the right way   They did not have the light on true baptism   They did not have the opportunity to be baptized according to the Bible

There will be many people in heaven who did not keep the true Sabbath They didn't have the opportunity to learn that the seventh day, or Saturday, is the only true Sabbath according to God's Word   They honestly believed that Sunday was the day that Jesus wanted them to keep   They obeyed Jesus just as far as they had a knowledge of His will, as far as they had opportunity to learn the truth.

There isn't anything that I desire more than to have a home in the city of gold   "Lord, I want to be among that number when the saints go marching in " The most important question of all is, "Will you be among that blessed number who will be admitted through those gates of pearl to have an eternal, happy home in heaven?" It all depends on one item, and what is that? It depends on how you choose to obey Jesus Christ   Remember Hebrews 5 9, "He became the author of eternal salvation unto all them that obey Him" **It all depends on how you obey Christ.**

Every soul in this auditorium is settling the supreme issue of his life, as to whether or not he will have an eternal happy home in heaven, by the way he decides to obey the Lord Jesus Christ   This is why I have appealed to you again and again during these fourteen weeks of meetings, to make your decision to obey the commandments of God and the faith of Jesus   I have reminded you again and again that the wisest thing and the best thing that you can ever do is to surrender your heart to obey the Lord.

I want to ask two plain questions tonight in the light of God's special message which has been proclaimed from the Word of God in these meetings. We have just read from the Bible that Christ is the Author of eternal salvation unto all them that obey Him   Does this matter of obeying Christ include the keeping holy of the seventh day or Saturday?   The Bible settles this question so plainly that no one need have any doubts

The New Testament reveals Christ as the Creator of the world   Genesis 2 3 plainly shows that after the Creator had made this world in six days, He rested on the seventh day   He sanctified, or set apart, each succeeding seventh day for man to keep   The record says, "God blessed the seventh day and sanctified it. because that in it He **had rested** from all His work which God created and made"

Notice that the One Who sanctified the seventh day is the One Who made the world   Since the Son of God, or Christ, is the Creator, Christ is the One Who sanctified the seventh day for man at the beginning

In the Ten Commandments, which were spoken by the Son of God at Sinai, He commands the keeping of the seventh day, on which He rested, and which He sanctified or set apart for man

Mark this point well   The evidence for the seventh day is clear, specific and positive   There is no guess-work about it   We are not left to build up a list of far-fetched or uncertain inferences in regard to Christ having sanctified the seventh day, and having commanded its observance

Now look at the other part of the picture regarding the keeping of the first day of the week, now known as Sunday   Where can you find a line anywhere in the Bible which indicates that Christ ever sanctified the first day of the week?   Where is there a line to show that Christ ever commanded the keeping of the first day of the week?   It just isn't there   There is not even the semblance of any declaration of holy scripture in behalf of the sanctification of the first day of the week, or any requirement for its observance   All that any man ever has done, or ever could show from the New Testament in behalf of the keeping of the first day of the week are a few far-fetched, uncertain, unreliable inferences   These are like sinking sand, so far as constituting any solid foundation for such a vital matter as to which day each week, man should render unto the Lord

When you contrast the Biblical standing of the seventh day over against the first day in respect to which one is Christ's sanctified and ordained day, it really settles once and for all which day we should keep   The very fact that the seventh day of the week is the only day of weekly observance which the Son of God ever sanctified or ever asked man to keep, settles the question forever   What further evidence is needed?   Isn't this enough?   No matter how much may be said, or how much may be written, or argued or debated, when it is all done, it will still be a fact that according to the scriptural record, the seventh day of the week is the only day of weekly observance which the Son of God ever sanctified for man or ever asked man to keep

I am willing to do what Jesus wants me to do   What else can I do, but keep the only day of the week that He ever sanctified, the only day of the week He ever asked man to keep? So obeying Jesus Christ in the light of God's special message for these last days must include the keeping holy of the seventh day, now known as Saturday.

Here is my second question Does the matter of obeying Christ include coming out and taking our stand with His remnant church to keep all of His commandments? Yes The Bible settles this so plainly, that no one need have any doubt

In Revelation 12 17 we find that in the last days Jesus Christ will have a remnant church, which will keep the commandments of God and the faith of Jesus

In Revelation 14 12 and Revelation 18 4 we find that Jesus Christ will send a special message to the world in the last days to call His true followers out of every other religion and denomination into His remnant church The call of Jesus Christ Concerning Babylon is "Come out of her, My people, that ye be not partakers of her sins, and that ye receive not of her plagues "

So it is literally true in the light of God's message, that obeying Jesus Christ includes coming out and taking one's stand with His remnant church to keep the commandments of God and the faith of Jesus

We thank God that during the fourteen weeks of these meetings so many have come into line with Jesus on both of these matters Some have come into line on the matter of keeping the Lord's holy Sabbath, but have not as yet gone all the way with Christ in the matter of coming into His remnant church Some have not yet come into line with Jesus in keeping the seventh day which He sanctified for you Friends, if you only realized how supremely important it is for you to obey Jesus, you wouldn't hesitate nor delay in coming into line with Jesus on both of these matters

Some people will say, "Mr Shuler, do you mean to say that God will condemn a person to be lost who is good in every way, except he doesn't keep the seventh day?" What I say doesn't amount to anything In fact, it is not my business to ever say who will be saved or lost God is judge He decides every case for heaven or hell What He says is the last word There is no appeal from His sentence But we do well to heed those principles according to which God decides the cases of men

In James 4 17 you will read, "To him that knoweth to do good, and doeth it not, to him it is sin " God cannot have any person who isn't willing to do what he knows is right When a person knows what is right and fails to do it, or neglects to do it, God holds that against that man as sin And if God holds sin against a man, that man will never get to heaven, because no sin can be taken into heaven "To him that knoweth to do good, and doeth it not, to him it is sin "

Then in James 2 10 we read, "Whosoever shall keep the whole law, and yet offend in one point, he is guilty of all " Some will ask, "Does this mean that a person who breaks one of the Ten Commandments is as bad as the person who transgresses everyone of the Ten Commandments?" No God takes into account the number and degree of a man's transgressions The man who persistently and knowingly breaks two of the Ten Commandments will be punished more than the man who persistently and knowingly violates only one

Here is a lamp that is chained to the ceiling with a chain of ten links Tell me, how many links must I cut for the lamp to fall? Five? Three? Two? How many? Just one! If you cut one link that lamp will fall and be broken just as certainly as if you cut all ten at one time So the Ten Commandments are a chain of righteousness composed of ten golden links

If a man breaks any one of those ten willfully and persistently, he will lose heaven just the same as if he had broken all ten Some people plan to go on disobeying God That is a terrible thing Some people intend to go on disobeying God's fourth commandment, even though God has sent them the light This is a very serious mistake

Please mark well how God regards this In Hebrews 10 26 we have a striking text One that some people here ought to think through very seriously "For if we sin wilfully after that we have received the knowledge of the truth, there remaineth no more sacrifice for sins "

"If we sin wilfully . . there remaineth no more sacrifice for sins " Now what is willful sin? The person who knows what God commands, and will not do it, that is willful sin The person who knows that God commands the keeping of the seventh day, and yet goes on defying God by working on the day on which God says no work is to be done, is committing willful sin This is very serious.

O, that God would somehow awaken us to our peril! If we sin willfully after we have received the knowledge of the truth, there remaineth no more sacrifice for sins. Can you afford to come to the place where there is no more sacrifice for sin? No No one can afford to lose eternal happiness by coming to the place where there is no more sacrifice for sin This is so serious that if you have not commenced to keep the Sabbath, you ought not to leave this meeting without making your decision that you will begin to keep God's Sabbath How can you go another week without keeping God's Sabbath in the light of Hebrews 10 26?

Some person will say, "It really doesn't make any difference what day I keep just so I keep one day in the week And if I keep Sunday in honor of Christ's resurrection, I think the Lord will accept that " Anyone who thinks this, needs to consider Proverbs 16 25 and Matthew 15 9 "There is a way that seemeth right unto man, (you think it is all right) but the end thereof are the ways of death " "In vain they do worship Me," says Jesus "teaching for doctrines the commandments of men "

In Leviticus 10 12, 2 you will read about two young priests who went into the sanctuary to burn incense one day God had commanded the priests that whenever they burned incense on the altar, they were to take holy fire from the altar of burnt offering with which to burn the incense These two young men knew what God had commanded But they said to themselves, "Fire is fire What difference will it make whether we take some ordinary fire that we can kindle, or whether we take fire from the altar? The incense will be burned whichever kind we use " They reasoned like those who say, "A day is a day, and it makes no difference what day we keep."

These young men took common fire to burn the incense What happened? A bolt of lightning came down from heaven and struck them dead

Does it make any difference whether we do exactly what God says, or something that we think is equivalent to His requirements **The difference is life or death.** Life if you obey Jesus; death if you disobey

The difference between willing obedience, and willful disobedience will be the infinite difference between enjoying the glories of heaven, or being cast into the fires of hell The day is coming when people will regret with weeping and wailing and gnashing of teeth their own slackness in obeying the Lord

Do you know that there will be many people who will have even preached great sermons for Christ, even healed the sick in the name of Christ who will find themselves barred from heaven because they failed to keep one of the Lord's commandments? You will find this set forth in Matthew 7:21-23.

"Not every one that saith unto Me, Lord, Lord, shall enter into the kingdom of heaven; but he that doeth the will of My Father which is in heaven Many will say to Me in that day, Lord, Lord, have we not prophesied in Thy name? (They have preached great sermons in the name of Christ) and in Thy name have cast out devils? and in Thy name done many wonderful works?"

Jesus is not talking about ordinary sinners   These people are professed Christian people   They have taken the name of Christ   They have preached in Christ's name   They have healed the sick in Christ's name   They have done many wonderful works in the name of Christ   But Jesus says, "Then will I profess unto them, I never knew you   depart from Me, ye that work iniquity"   Iniquity is lawlessness, disregard of the law of God

The man who knows what Jesus Christ commands, and will not heed it, even his prayers become abomination to God   Notice this in Proverbs 28 9, "He that turneth away his ear from hearing the law, even his prayer shall be abomination"   It is a fearful thing for a person to come to the place where even his prayer is abomination   This is exactly what happens if people continue to refuse to obey the Lord

A transport plane loaded with thirty-six people crashed into a high mountain and everyone of those thirty-six people was killed   What was the trouble?   There was nothing wrong with the plane mechanically   The engines were functioning perfectly   What was the trouble?   The plane was off the beam

An aviator can fly through the darkest night and arrive safely at his destination if he keeps his plane on the radio beam   As long as the pilot keeps his plane on the beam, a steady signal keeps coming through   If he swings to the right or the left of the beam, the signal stops   He must find that beam again or face possible destruction in the darkness

God has given us a directed beam of guidance, in the life of His Son upon the earth, in the teachings of the Bible, and in the Ten Commandments   So long as we keep on the beam, we are safe   If we go to the left or the right in the way that is different from what Jesus has marked out, we are in danger   My advice to you is, keep your plane on the directed beam and you will arrive safely at the heavenly port   "Blessed are they that do His commandments that they may have right to the tree of life, and may enter in through the gates into the city" (Revelation 22 14)

There is only one safe way in religion and that is to do exactly what the Bible says and to do it as soon as we hear it   Is God particular how we obey Him in small items?   I refer you to a three-word sermon of Jesus   "Remember Lot's wife "

When she left Sodom the angel told her not to look back   Mrs Lot thought just as a lot of people think, "Well, that's a little thing   What difference will it make to God whether we just take a little glance back or not?"   She acted on her reasoning as people so often do, and what happened?   She lost her life and she lost her soul for eternity   "Remember Lot's wife "

If we persist in going contrary to God's commandments, we will certainly be lost   A person's standing before God is determined by the way he obeys the commandments of God   Let us read 1 John 2 4   "He that saith, I know Him and keepeth not His commandments is a liar and the truth is not in him." I didn't say that, but I read it to you from the Bible

Should you spend your time trying to find the truth from people who do not keep all the commandments?   Think it through   God declares that the one who does not keep His commandments is a liar, and the truth is not in Him   You will not find the real truth where the commandments are not kept   The truth and keeping the commandments are linked together in the Word of God

If people only knew how serious it is to disobey the Lord, they would make their decision for His commandments   Some say, "I know that what I have heard in these meetings is the truth and I intend to accept it a little later "   O, friend, God urges you to accept it now   "Now is the accepted time "

God never suggests tomorrow   He never says next week or next year   God never suggests some other time   He even warns you and me not to put off making our decision, because He says we do not know what tomorrow will bring "Boast not thy self against tomorrow for thou knowest not what a day may bring forth"

Many people have put off making their decision to obey the Lord, and they face eternity unprepared, lost, and doomed forever   Tomorrow never comes   What we do, we do today   I can tell you now that you will not make your decision tomorrow   When tomorrow comes, it will be today   That is why God says, "Today, if ye will hear His voice, harden not your hearts"

There was a farmer who needed feed from a grain mill, but he was out of money   So he decided he would drive to a mill and see if he couldn't secure some feed on credit   He took his boy with him in the wagon   When they got to the mill they saw a sign posted that said, "Today we sell cheap for cash, tomorrow we sell on credit"   He turned to his boy and said, "That is just fine   We're out of money, so we'll come back tomorrow and we can buy on credit"

The next morning they hitched up and drove to the mill   They got there and the sign read, "Today we sell cheap for cash, tomorrow we sell on credit   If he had gone back there a hundred days in succession, it would have read just the same   Tomorrow never comes   When tomorrow comes, it will not be tomorrow   It will be today   "Today if ye will hear His voice, harden not your hearts"

You ask, "How soon does God expect a man to step out and keep the Sabbath?"   In Psalm 18 44 He says, "As soon as they hear of Me, they shall obey Me"   God expects us to act on His word

If I should ask how many people in this audience want to have an eternal happy home in heaven everyone would raise his hand and rightly so   I have never met anyone who wanted to go to hell   Since we want a home in heaven, the only thing to do is to decide to obey the Lord Jesus Christ

God has left every person in this world free, free to obey, free to disobey   In the judgment, every one will have to give an account as to how he has exercised the power of choice   Your case, my case, every man's case will be decided on how we have used the power of choice   The important thing to keep in mind is that God will never force any man to obey   **If we are ever saved, we must decide to obey.**

If you haven't decided to keep the Sabbath, brother, sister, I appeal to you to exercise that high power of choice, by telling the Lord tonight, "I surrender myself to the Lord Jesus Christ to henceforth keep His day"   If you are keeping the Sabbath, but haven't obeyed the call to come into the remnant church, I appeal to you to exercise that high power of choice by taking the next step and saying to Jesus, "I'll go all the way with Thee and take my stand"

There was a man in Chicago who attended Moody's meetings in Farnell Hall   He came under deep conviction   Moody went to him and pleaded with him to accept Christ   But he said, "I want time to think it over, Mr Moody"

The man became dangerously ill.   Moody went to his room on the North side of Chicago   Again he plead with the man to decide for Christ   The man said, "Yes, Mr Moody, I am going to do it   But I can't do it now, because people will say I have been scared into religion."

The man got well   Mr Moody went to see him again.   He said, "Yes, Mr Moody, I am going to do it, but I am too busy now   I am planting a new peach orchard over at Benton Harbor, Michigan and when I get the orchard started I'll do it"

Soon the news came that the man had a relapse and was very ill.   Mr Moody took the next boat across Lake Michigan   He arrived at the man's house at midnight   He saw a light in the house and doctors and nurses bending over the man   Mr Moody went in and stood over the man and prayed

The man shook his head   "It is too late now"   Moody told him about the dying thief and tried to encourage him   The man said, "No, Mr Moody, I have rejected chance after chance   It is too late"   Moody prayed and prayed as no man could pray, but all in vain   Before he breathed his last they saw his lips move, and bending low heard him whisper, "The harvest is past, the summer is ended, and I am not saved"

A man can swim in the Niagara River above the Niagara Falls if he doesn't go too near the rapids   There is a place where the water begins to boil in those rapids where no human power can save a man from going over the falls to his death   On the bank of the river where the rapids begin to swirl so desperately for their final plunge, is a signboard that bears the startling words, "Beyond Redemption Point"   The man who passes that point, whether he is swimming, or whether he is in a boat, can never retrace his steps

So, if a man persists in refusing to yield to the pleadings of the Holy Spirit, he will go "Beyond Redemption Point," where he cannot be saved   "My Spirit," says God, shall not always strive with man"

The only safe way, brother, sister, is to act on the conviction which you have tonight   If in your heart you know you ought to begin to keep the Sabbath, decide tonight that you will start to keep it this week   If you are keeping the Sabbath, and know you should take your stand with God's remnant people, make up your mind to do it now

The same sun that softens wax will harden clay   The attitude that people assume toward the Word of God and the Spirit of God determines whether the heart will be softened for obedience unto eternal life, or hardened for eternal destruction   There is a softening and a hardening process going on in every life   I appeal to you who have not made your decision, to yield to the pleading of the Holy Spirit and be saved

There was a preacher named George Pentecost who climbed Pike's Peak alone one day   He became lost in a blizzard   He sought shelter under some overhanging rocks   Night was coming on   He would freeze to death, unless he had a fire

He gathered some twigs and firewood   He felt in his pockets, but found only one match   His life depended on one match   Unless he kindled a fire, he would be frozen stiff by morning   Would the match burn?   He felt that the most critical moment of his life had arrived

He took his coat and his hat to shield the match from the whirling gusts of wind   He struck the match   It burned   The twigs caught fire, and he was saved   But there was only one match between him and death

There are some people who have only one more 'No' between them and hell   If they say 'no' on the next call, it may be their last chance   Friends, don't say 'no' to Christ again, but make it 'Yes'   Saying 'Yes' to Jesus means eternal life   How many who have not previously said 'Yes' to Jesus, about keeping the seventh day are ready to say "Jesus, I will begin to keep the Sabbath?"   Do I see a hand?   Thank the Lord here are some!   Are there others, who haven't commenced to keep the Sabbath, determine to make it 'Yes' for Jesus?   The uplifted hand means 'Yes' for Jesus

Is there one who has commenced to keep the Sabbath or hasn't taken his stand with God's remnant people, who will make it 'Yes' to Jesus that you will do it now?   Will you raise the hand?

There is nothing I desire so much as for God to help me to obey that I may have eternal salvation   How many with me want to raise your hands as a prayer to Jesus, "Jesus, give me help to be obedient that I may have eternal salvation?"   May I see your hands?   Yes, every hand is raised

(PRAYER)

(Copy of the Bible Lesson outline, which was distributed to the people preceding the fifty-eighth lesson)

Lesson XII - What Faith Corresponds to the Divine Pattern?

1 It is only those who know the surety of the Adventist faith, who will be able to stand steadfast to the end (Mark 13 13)   -

2 In making a certain item, if you have a pattern to go by, and the pattern is right, you know when you make it like the pattern, that it is bound to be right

3 The Exodus Movement in the days of Moses, which took the Israelites from Egypt to Canaan, was a type or pattern of God's true movement for the last days   -   -   margin

4 This last-day movement will be God's hand put forth the second time (Isa 11 11), as the Exodus Movement was the putting forth of God's the first time (Acts 13 16, 17)

5 In order to be sure that the Advent Movement is God's appointed movement for the last days, we must see if it corresponds to the divine pattern given in the Exodus Movement

6 Both movements are founded on the same divine objective Israel was called out of Egypt as a separate people, to keep the ten commandments (Ps 105 43, 45)

    God is now calling His Israel out of Babylon as a separate people, to keep the same ten commandments (Rev 18 4; 1 Jno 3 4, Rev 14 12)

7 In connection with the call out of Egypt the people were tested on the keeping of the true Sabbath (Ex 16 4, 28, 29) In connection with God's last-day call, the people are being tested on the keeping of the true Sabbath (Rev 7 1-3, 14 9-12)

8 The Exodus Movement was not an accidental occurrence, because God had foretold that it would come at the end of a certain appointed period (Gen 15 13, 16, Ex 12 40, 41)

    In the same way God appointed 1844, at the end of the 2,300 day-years, as the time when His true message for the last days would arise (Dan 8 10-14, Rev 14 6, 7)

9 God has placed in the Advent Movement the same six special lines of truth, which He placed in the Exodus Movement
   (a) The sanctuary truth (Ex 25 8; Dan 8 14).
   (b) The tithing system for the support of God's workers (Num 18 21, 1 Cor 9 13, 14)
   (c) A dietetic reform (Lev 11) (1 Cor 10 31)
   (d) Dress reform (Ex 33 5, 6, 1 Tim 2 9).
   (e) A four-fold plan of organization (Ex 18 21)
   (f) The spirit of prophecy for guidance (Hos 12.13; Rev 12 17, 19 10)

10 The Exodus Movement could not fail, because God had marked it through Canaan in His prophetic word (Gen 15 16)

    The Advent movement cannot fail, because God has marked it through to the sea of glass before His throne   _ . _   _ _

11 CONCLUSION—The Advent movement is just like the divine pattern We can be as sure that it is of God, and will go through to victory, in the heavenly Canaan, as the Exodus movement was of God for the time of Moses, and did go through to victory in earthly Canaan

    References which were filled in as the study was presented (1) John 6 66-69, (3) 1 Cor 10·11, (10) Rev 14 12, 14, 15 2, 3

When God Makes His Last Call

(Scheduled for the fourteenth Friday night of the Campaign)

I have before me a striking question, "Is there any way of knowing when God makes His last call to a person?" There is one point on which we are all agreed If people only knew when God's last call was being extended to them, many who do hold back from responding to His call, and put off accepting His message, would not hesitate or delay to act on the call of God to their soul What a tremendous difference it would make as to how people would respond to God's call, if they only knew when it was their last chance

Before the flood came, God sent His last call to the people through His servant Noah Noah told the people, "A flood is coming" God is going to wipe man off the face of the earth with a great flood of waters I appeal to you to turn from your wicked ways and obey God's commandment Get ready to enter the ark so you will be saved"

People ridiculed Noah They refused to believe his message How differently they would have treated God's message if they had only realized that in a short time the waters would pour down upon them and wipe every living thing off the face of the earth, except those who entered the ark Mark this point If they had believed God's message, they would have known that the preaching of Noah was God's last call to their soul.

There is another striking illustration of God's last call in Genesis 19.12-14. "And the men said unto Lot, Hast thou here any besides? son-in-law, and thy sons, and thy daughters, and whatsoever thou hast in the city, bring them out of this place For we will destroy this place, because the cry of them is waxen great before the face of the Lord, and the Lord hath sent us to destroy it And Lot went out, and spake unto his sons-in-law, which married his daughters, and said, Up, get you out of this place; for the Lord will destroy this city But he seemed as one that mocked unto his sons-in-law."

It is the last night in Sodom The city is given over to dancing, drinking, immorality and revelry They are having their last fling, and do not know it Before the sun shall rise upon another day, fire and brimstone from God will wipe out every vestige of the city and its inhabitants A super-atomic bomb will explode on Sodom this night, and wicked Sodom will be no more forever

The two angels came to Lot's house in Sodom on this fateful night They told him to go quickly and tell his daughters and their husbands to flee from the city at once, because God would destroy the entire city that very night How did they regard the message? How did they regard God's last call to their soul? The record is, "He seemed as one that mocked " Think of it! They mocked God's last call to their soul And they paid the penalty for their mocking in being destroyed that very night

They went on with their fun They continued with their revelry, drinking, and dancing that night Just as they reached the height of their pleasure, the fire of God fell on the city and completely destroyed every building, and person in the entire city

How different the reaction of these sons-in-law of Lot might have been, if they had only realized that Lot's message was God's last call to their souls But mark this point well If they had believed that message, they would have known that it was God's last call to their soul **So those who believe God's message for our day as outlined in Revelation 14, know that it is God's last call to the people of this generation.**

God's message for all the various peoples of earth in these closing days of human history, is set forth in Revelation 14 6-12 under the symbolism of three angels flying through mid-air, preaching a mighty threefold warning to all people God revealed this to the apostle John in symbolic vision He made it especially plain that this threefold message of Revelation 14·6-12 would be His last call to the people, who would live in the last days

In this vision John was shown that the second coming of Christ and the end of the world would take place immediately after the threefold message was preached to every nation You will find this in Revelation 14·14, 15.

"I looked, and behold a white cloud, and upon the cloud **One** sat like unto the Son of man, having on His head a golden crown, and in His hand a sharp sickle And another angel came out of the temple, crying with a loud voice to Him that sat on the cloud, Thrust in Thy sickle, and reap: for the time is come for Thee to reap, for the harvest of the earth is ripe"

These verses show that the return of Jesus to this world is the **next item on God's program** after this threefold message of Revelation 14 has been sufficiently made known to the people of every country **This shows as conclusively as two and two make four that this threefold message is God's last call to men.**

This series of meetings has been devoted to presenting that threefold message In a very special sense you may know, that the message which you have heard in these meetings is God's last call to you

This is why it is of supreme and eternal importance for every truth-loving soul to make his decision to accept the message which he has heard in these meetings The most fatal mistake any person can ever make is to reject God's last call If a person rejects God's last call, what hope could there be for him?

This means that as you consider what you will do with the truths you have heard in these meetings, you should make sure above all else, that you do respond to the message of God for our day by coming out and taking your stand with His remnant who keep the commandments of God and the faith of Jesus Since this is God's last call to men, what else can you do, in the fear of God, and for your own eternal interests, but take your stand for this three-fold message?

Let us consider some additional clear, direct, sure evidences that this message you have heard is God's last call to people today Jesus Christ compares the last days just prior to His return to the days of Noah before the flood came Notice how He set this forth in Matt 24 37

"But as the days of Noe were, so shall also the coming of the Son of Man be"

Jesus also compares the closing days of history before His second advent to the days of Lot in Sodom prior to its utter destruction by fire from heaven Notice how He sets this forth in Luke 17 28-30

"Likewise also as it was in the days of Lot, they did eat, they drank, they bought, they sold, they planted, they builded, But the same day that Lot went out of Sodom it rained fire and brimstone from heaven, and destroyed them all Even thus shall it be in the day when the Son of man is revealed"

Just as the message of Noah which called upon the people to prepare for the flood, was God's last call to their souls, so this threefold message, which calls upon the people to prepare to meet their soon-coming Lord is God's last call to men today Just as the message of Lot was God's last call to his sons-in-law, so this threefold message, which you have heard in these meetings, is God's last call to you

One of the important features of this threefold message is the call of Christ for His people to come out of Babylon, lest they receive of those terrible seven last plagues which will smite great Babylon in the final days of this age See how plainly this is set forth in Revelation 18 4

"And I heard another voice from heaven, saying, Come out of her, My people, that ye be not partakers of her sins, and that ye receive not of her plagues"

Since this call to come out of Babylon into God's remnant is directly connected with the pouring out of the seven last plagues which will come just prior to the end of time, this call to come out of Babylon is bound to be God's last call to His people

The seven last plagues are spoken of in the book of Revelation as the wrath of God without mixture   The warning against the mark of the beast in the third angel's message is directly connected with the falling of these plagues as the unmixed wrath of God   Notice how plainly this is presented in Revelation 14 9, 10

"And the third angel followed them, saying with a loud voice, If any man worship the beast and his image, and receive his mark in his forehead, or in his hand, The same shall drink of the wine of the wrath of God, which is poured out without mixture into the cup of his indignation   "

This shows that the third angel's message with its warning against the mark of the beast must be God's last call to men

Think what this means to you who have heard this message in these meetings, and have not responded to God's call to come out and take your stand with Christ's remnant church   It means that you are trifling with God's last call to your soul   Since the message you have heard is God's last call, the only safe course, the only right decision, the only wise thing to do is to respond to this call   If a person fails to accept God's last call, what hope could he ever have for eternity?

Some of you are on the very verge of taking your stand   You are almost persuaded to step out and take your stand with God's remnant people   This is good as far as it goes, but it is also one of the most dangerous positions in which any person can ever be   If you go through and take your stand, it will be fine   But if you keep on lingering and hesitating and putting it off, and fail to respond to God's call, it will be the worst mistake you have ever made

The Bible tells of certain persons who were almost persuaded and yet died without hope so far as the record goes   When Paul pled with King Agrippa to make his decision for Christ, the king was profoundly moved   The king said, "Almost thou persuadest me to be a Christian"   But almost-persuaded, if we go no further than that, means that we will still be lost   If you, or I, or any other person, is ever saved, we must be so fully persuaded that we will move forward to act on the call of the Lord

It didn't matter how near a man was to entering the ark in the days of Noah   If he did not go all the way in accepting God's message, by going inside the ark at the call of the Lord, he was lost   The man who half-way believed that Noah was right, and lingered near the ark, but failed to go inside before the door was shut, perished, just the same as the most hardened unbeliever, who never went near the ark   The man who had his foot on the threshhold when the door closed was lost, just as much as the people who were a hundred miles away from the ark   To you who are on the verge of making your decision to enter God's remnant church, I would say, "Linger not around the door of the ark   Let us go on the inside   What do you say?

There comes a time in some people's lives when everything depends on what they do in the next five minutes   Such a time came to Felix when Paul preached the Word of God to him   In Acts 24 25 we read, "And as he reasoned of righteousness, temperance, and judgment to come   Felix trembled, and answered, Go thy way for this time, when I have a convenient season, I will call for thee"

As Paul talks to Felix about his duty to Christ, a strange fear begins to creep about the heart of Felix   Everything depends now on what happens in the next five minutes   Will he yield to the pleading of the Holy Spirit? Or will he resist the pleading of the Holy Spirit and say 'No' to the call of God? The tongue of the balance trembles and hesitates for a moment, and then slowly the wrong scale goes down He said, "Go thy way for this time; when I have a convenient season, I will call for thee" But, alas! that convenient season never came

Is it safe for you to wait for a more convenient season? No Death may overtake you and seal your fate forever on the side of disobedience against God The Holy Spirit may leave you and the conviction you have about taking your stand will fade entirely away A person may go on in disobedience until he loses the power to turn and obey God.

The Bible shows that those who persist in rejecting the call of the Lord will come to the place where God will give them up, and then their cases are absolutely hopeless Notice how this is set forth in 2 Chronicles 36 15,16

"And the Lord God of their fathers sent to them by His messengers, rising up betimes and sending, because he had compassion on his people, and on his dwelling place But they mocked the messengers of God, and despised His words, and misused His prophets, until the wrath of the Lord arose against His people, **till there was no remedy."**

There is a certain period in the year when men in the corn belt can plant corn and expect to reap corn But if a man waits too long to plant, if he waits until the planting season is over, he will not reap any ears of matured corn So if a man wants salvation, he must take it while God offers it to him

Lot almost lost his life because he was so slow to come out of Sodom The record says, "He lingered" Many a person will lose eternal life, because he is so slow to come out of Babylon.

I appeal to you who have been lingering about responding to the call to come out and take your stand with Christ's remnant church Isn't this matter about which you linger entirely too important for you to continue such lingering? Isn't the matter of your soul's welfare a matter too important for you to keep on hesitating, postponing, and putting it off? I hope you will say with the Psalmist, "I made haste, and delayed not to keep Thy commandments"

When men see that the last call has come to them in respect to their physical life, they act quickly and cast aside everything they have in order to save their life A miner was returning from the Klondyke gold fields He had made a fortune He had a belt around his body in which there was $200,000 worth of gold

The ship was wrecked a half mile off the coast He was a good swimmer, but he knew he could never swim to land with that load of gold around his body He dropped the belt of gold to the deck

No one picked it up Their last call had come All the money in the world was of no account at such a moment

By putting forth every possible effort, this man made the shore His last call had come to him in a physical way, but he acted wisely and was saved

I hope you will be as wise in letting go of the things of the world in order to make sure of everlasting life The message of God's last call has come to you in these meetings Why not cast aside everything that hinders you from acting rightly on His last call?

Every evangelist has seen tragic cases of souls who had their last chance and failed to accept In one city where I preached the message, a man and his wife attended every meeting week after week His wife began to keep the Sabbath and was ready to be baptized The husband believed the message, but he delayed to make his decision

One night I called at his home I urged him not to put off accepting God's message, but to begin to keep the Sabbath the very next Saturday He said, "In a few weeks I will start to keep the Sabbath"

Two days later he and his wife were walking to the hall to attend my Sunday night meeting.   An automobile struck them, and the man was killed instantly If he had only known two nights before this, when I urged him to surrender to Jesus Christ that night, that it was God's last call to his soul, do you think he would have put off accepting the message?   No, indeed, but his last chance came and he failed to accept the message

In a tabernacle campaign which I conducted in Washington, D C , a certain taxi driver attended the meetings   He sat very close to the front   He listened intently to the sermons   He was convinced of his duty to obey the message He intended to take his stand for the truth of God

One night the preacher spoke on the subject "Standing at the Parting of the Ways "   How significant that subject was to the taxi driver!   The very next morning, as this man was walking into his bathroom he slumped to the floor and his life was gone   If he had only known the night before, that the preacher's call that night was God's last call to his soul, how different would have been his response!

I hope that no one in this campaign will have his last chance and fail to accept God's last message   There is only one sure way to avoid such a terrible fate, and that is to accept the message, as soon as it is explained to you from the Bible

One night Evangelist D L Moody noticed that a certain man remained seated in the auditorium after all the others had left   He sat down beside the man, and found that the man was under deep conviction   The man had determined not to leave the building until he had the Lord Jesus Christ in his heart

Mr Moody prayed with him, and the man made a full surrender of his heart to the Lord Jesus Christ   He was born again and became a new creature in Christ   The next day he went to work in the coal mine   There was a terrific explosion that morning in the part of the mine where he worked He was carried out more nearly dead than alive

The people saw his lips move, and a friend bending low heard him whisper over and over again, "It is a good thing I settled it last night "   Yes, it was a good thing that he settled it last night   His last call came to him and he responded to it

Delays are dangerous   Procrastination is the thief of souls

> "The clock of life is wound but once,
>   And no man has the power
> To tell just when the hands will stop—
>   At late or early hour;
> Now is the only time you own,
>   Live, love, toil with a will,
> Place no faith in tomorrow,
>   For the clock may then be still "

Soon the last chance will come to every man   Soon Christ will close His mediatorial work and say, "He that is unjust, let him be unjust still, and he which is filthy, let him be filthy still and he that is righteous, let him be righteous still, and he that is holy, let him be holy still "   Then every man will have had his last chance

Many, many souls will put off accepting God's message until it is too late   They will join in that bitter wail, the most disappointing of all disappointments, "The harvest is past, the summer is ended, and I am not saved "   If people could only realize what will happen when the seven last plagues fall and Jesus Christ appears on the cloud, they would not allow anything to hold them back from making an immediate decision

When the flood came, it was worth more than all the world to be inside the ark of safety.   When the fire fell on Sodom, it was worth more than all the business and the pleasures in the entire city to have responded to the call of God in coming out of Sodom When the seven last plagues fall, and Jesus Christ comes, it will be worth more than all the property, the business, the positions, the stocks, the bonds, in this world just to be safe on the side of the commandments of God and the faith of Jesus

In that day the millionaire will be glad to give all his millions for one more chance to accept God's message, but there will not be another chance for him or for any other person who has not made his decision by that time Many will say, "O, if I only had accepted God's message when the preacher explained it to me from the Bible I would give all I have for one more chance to accept it" But they have waited too long   .

Now is the time to make the full surrender Now is the time to respond to God's call. God says, "Now is the accepted time, now is the day of salvation" "Today if ye will hear my voice, harden not your hearts"

In the great Lakes region years ago, an Indian and his son-in-law carried the mail from the distant shore of a certain bay to a fishing village on the opposite shore. One day in mid-winter, they set out from the south shore for the long trip across the great lake

All day they traveled on the ice, skirting the frozen shore of the bay. As night came, they pitched their tent and went ashore to look for firewood After gathering what they needed they started back to camp

Just as they stepped upon the ice, it broke loose from the shore and began to drift out into the lake The boy, alert and quick-witted, dropped his bundle of firewood and leaped ashore across the crevice in the ice The father-in-law hesitated for a moment and in that moment the gap widened too much for him to overleap it in one leap

The boy shouted to the old man to leap in and swim to shore If the man had made his decision to leap into the water immediately, he could have easily reached the shore in safety, but he hesitated He was undecided what to do.

The lad began to cry out more earnestly, "Leap into the water now. Leap into the water now before the ice drifts further from the shore It is your only chance"

Still the older man stood undecided as the wind drove the great ice-floe out into the lake Soon he began to call out farewell messages for his wife and children across the ever widening watery waste The last the boy saw of him he was standing with outstretched hands drifting to his death in the bitter cold and darkness of that night

He perished, a victim of deadly indecision If he had only made his decision at the right time, he would have been saved, but he hesitated So, many a soul will be lost eternally, because he failed to make his decision for God at the right time

The person who hears this message is brought face-to-face with the supreme question of all his life—**what will you do with God's last call?** What have you done with God's last call, as set forth from His Word in these Bible lectures?

Thank God many can say, "I have responded to His call I have come out and taken my stand with His remnant I have gone all the way with Jesus in accepting the message. This is fine. Now, the all-important item for you is to be true to the message to the end, whether it be the end of life or the end of time.

I appeal to you who have heard God's message, but have not decided to take your stand for the keeping of the commandments of God and the faith of Jesus What will you do with God's last call? Can you afford to neglect His last call to your soul? No Why not, then, step over the line at this very hour, and say, "By the grace of God, I will respond to the call of Jesus, by coming out and taking my stand with His remnant"

God wants you to do it. **He** appeals to you to do it. You know that you ought to do it. You have a desire to do it The Holy Spirit is impressing you to do it. Why not act on the impression and step out today?

Your chances for accepting God's message are passing every day. The first chance God gives a person to accept His message is the best chance He will ever have The last chance God gives us is our poorest chance

You have had many chances during these weeks of meetings If you have had chances before to accept God's message and have not done so, then you have the poorest chance tonight But listen, **it is the best chance you may ever have again.**

O, I hope you will make the best use of it Is there one who has not made his decision to take his stand with God's remnant church who is willing to say, "God helping me, I will make the best use of the chance I have tonight and make a full surrender tonight?" Will you lift the hand? I am glad to see a number of hands.

Will those of you who raised your hand come and give me your hand as we sing? God says, "My Spirit shall not always strive with man " May God help us to yield while the Holy Spirit pleads with our hearts

The Bible says that Jesus "is able to save them to the uttermost that come unto God by Him, seeing He ever liveth to make intercession for them." If you will do the coming, Jesus will do the saving

The Word of God says, "If there be first a willing mind, it is accepted according to that a man hath, and not according to that he hath not " May God help us to make our decision on His last message before it is too late

(Prayer closed the meeting)

(Copy of the Bible Lesson outline, which was distributed to the people preceding the sixtieth lecture)

Lesson XIII - The Practice of the Presence of God

1 Those who learn and apply the secret of the continual presence of God in their lives will enjoy rest of soul, peace of mind, happiness of spirit, guidance in the right path, freedom from worry and fear, and will develop a Christ-like character   Gospel Workers page 128

2 Your sense of the companionship of the Father and the Son with you every hour is what determines the reality, the depth, and the strength of your own Christian experience

3 Satan endeavors to get Christians to doubt the presence of God   Ps 42 10, 6, 7, 9

4 WHERE IS THY GOD? God's answers to cheer His children:

   (a) Ps 125 2 God is   me to   _ __   _ _ _ _ me

   (b) Deut 4·39, God is   me to   over me

   (c) Deut 33 27 God is   me to   _   _ _ __me

   (d) Ex 13·21 God goes   _   me to   __ __   _ _   me

   (e) Isa 52 12 God is   _   me to   _ __ _   _   __ me

   (f) Isa 41 10 God is   me to   _   me

   (g) Ps 56 9 God is   me to __   _   me

   (h) Isa 41·13 God _   _ _ ____   ___ _   __ __ to

          .   _ me

   (i) Ps 67 1   is shining upon me to make me   __ in Him

   (j) Ps 33 18 His   is upon me to   _ _   me

   (k) Ps 34 15 His   _   are open to   me

   (l) Ps 145 18 God is   .   to me to   me

   (m) Isa 57 15 God _ _   _ _ in me by His Holy Spirit,
      to make my life   in Him (Col 1 27, 28).

5 WHAT IS THE SECRET OF HAVING HIS CONTINUAL PRESENCE IN MY LIFE?

   Practice five simple every-day rules

   (a) Keep the morning watch with Jesus (Rev 3 20).

   (b) Be obedient to everything that Jesus Christ and God have asked you to do (John 14·22, 23) (1 John 3·24)

   (c) As you go about your work keep repeating Christ's precious promises over and over to yourself (Such as Heb 13.5; Matt 28 20; Matt 11 28-30, Isa 41·10)

   (d) Talk to Jesus within your heart as you go about your work

   (e) Be ever ready to respond to His still small voice (Isa 30 21). Remember, "As a shield from temptation and an inspiration to purity and truth, no other influence can equal the sense of God's presence " Education page 255

Words which were filled in by the people under the fourth proposition as the study was presented·

   (a) around, protect

   (b) above, watch

   (c) beneath, uphold

   (d) before, lead

   (e) behind, defend

   (f) with, help

   (g) for, sustain

   (h) holds my right hand, encourage

   (i) God's face, happy

   (j) eye, guide

   (k) ears, hear

   (l) near, comfort

   (m) dwells, perfect

Why I Am What I Am

The Lord expects you and me to give sound Biblical reasons why we are what we are religiously   I turn to I Peter 3 15   "Sanctify the Lord God in your hearts   and be ready always to give an answer to every man that asketh you a reason of the hope that is in you with meekness and fear."   The Word of God directs me to be ready always to give an answer to every man that asks me a reason for the hope that is in me

There are millions of professed Christians today who could not give any Biblical reason why they belong to their church   There are countless thousands of church members who have never stopped to examine their religious position. A certain man was asked, "What do you believe?   To what doctrine do you hold?"   The man said, "I believe what my church believes "   Then they asked him, "What does your church believe?"   He said, "My church believes what I believe "

Then they inquired, "Please tell us what do you and your church believe?" He said, "We believe alike "   This man was lost in a circle and did not know it   There are millions of church members who do not know where they are going religiously   They are going around in a circle and getting no where so far as ever learning the real truth is concerned

If you were to select six average church members from six of the largest denominations in Des Moines, and ask them the plain, pointed question, "Why do you belong to your church?"   I doubt if any of them could give you a Biblical reason   **No man can be really honest in his religion and not know what he is trying to be in faith and practice.**   The command of God is, "Be ready always to give an answer "

Why do I choose to be an Adventist?   I want you first to consider the significance of the word "Adventist "   This word "Adventist" comes from the word "advent," which means a coming   We talk about the advent of spring We mean the coming of spring   We talk about the advent of Jesus Christ to this world   We mean the coming of Jesus Christ to this world

The Standard Dictionary defines the word "adventist" as one who lays special stress on the second coming of Jesus Christ   Please hold this definition in your mind, for I shall refer to it again and again   An adventist is one who stresses that Christ is coming again   The word "adventist" may be used and is used in two different ways, in a general sense, and in a technical sense

In a general sense the word "adventist" includes every person in every country, in every age of the world's history, who laid, or does lay, stress on the fact that Christ will return   In other words if we spell the word "adventist" with a small "a," then it applies to every person everywhere, who has stressed the doctrine of the second-coming of Jesus Christ.

In a technical sense the word "Adventist" would include only those who are members of that particular religious organization   If we spell the word "Adventist" with a capital "A," then, of course, it would be limited in its application to the members of that particular religious body   I am using the word tonight with a small "a "

I raise the question, Where did this adventist doctrine come from?   Who was the first adventist preacher?   Do you know that the first adventist preacher is over 5,000 years old and he is still living?   You say, "Shuler, you are beside yourself   There is no one 5,000 years old "   But believe it or not, it is true, and it is all in your Bible   Do you have your notebook ready?   Put down Jude 14 and Hebrews 11 5

Six hundred and twenty-two years after the creation of the world a boy was born to whom they gave the name Enoch   That boy when he grew to be a man became the first prophet of God, who ever walked on this earth   Scripture declares that he walked with God   God revealed great truths to that man   In his prophecies Enoch, the seventh from Adam, laid special stress on the second coming of Jesus Christ   In Jude 14, we read, "Enoch also, the seventh from Adam, prophesied of these, saying, behold, the Lord cometh with ten thousands of His saints, to execute judgment upon all "

We do not know how many times Enoch preached   We do not know how many prophecies he uttered, but this we 'do know, out of all the items that this first prophet ever preached, or ever prophesied, the Holy Spirit saw fit to record only one and that was where he stressed the second-coming of Jesus Christ   The only statement we have in all the Bible from all that Enoch ever said, is, "Behold, the Lord cometh "

Keep in mind that an adventist is one who lays special stress on the second coming of Jesus Christ   Enoch stressed the second coming of Christ   That means that Enoch, the first prophet, who ever lived was an adventist

What happened to Enoch?   In Hebrews 11 5 we read that, "By faith Enoch was translated that he should not see death "   In other words, God picked that man up, changed him in the twinkling of an eye from mortality to immortality, and took him to heaven when he was 365 years old   He has never died, so the first adventist preacher is over 5,000 years old, believe it or not

Mark this   God so loved this man who first taught the adventist doctrine that he sent angels to pick him up and take him to heaven   The adventist doctrine, then, is a heaven-going doctrine   I tell you frankly, that if it is a heaven-going religion, if it will take me to heaven, brother, I want it   What do you say?   Can you say, "Amen"?

Do you know that every prophet who ever lived was an adventist?   Here it is in Acts 3 20,21   Peter here is talking about the second-coming of Christ   He directs attention to that day of days when the heavenly Father, Who sent His Son to the earth 1900 years ago as a baby, will say to that Son, "Go to the earth the second time and gather the saints "

In Acts 3 20,21 we read   "And He shall send Jesus Christ, which before was preached unto you, whom the heaven must receive until the times of restitution of all things, **which God hath spoken by the mouth of all His holy prophets since the world began."**

Enoch, the first prophet who ever lived, said, "Behold, the Lord cometh with ten thousand of His saints "   Every other prophet has picked up the strain and said, "The Lord will come," "Behold, He cometh "   Every prophet has stressed the second coming of Jesus Christ

Since an adventist means "one who stresses the second coming of Christ" and every prophet has stressed the second coming of Christ, every prophet was an adventist   I choose to be an adventist, because Enoch, Job, Moses, Isaiah, Jeremiah, David, Ezekiel, Daniel, and Zechariah were adventists   It is really good to be an adventist, isn't it?   When you become an adventist it means you have every prophet of God on your side

Who is the head adventist?   Put down these three texts   John 14 1-3, Matthew 26 64, Revelation 22 20   Just before Jesus left this world, He told His disciples about His return   He was about to leave them   He had been on the earth about thirty-three and one-half years from the time He had been born of the Virgin Mary   Now the time had come when He was about to go back to the great Father

The disciples were made very sorrowful, when Jesus said, "I am going to leave you "   Think how they had learned to love Him during the three and one-half years of their association with Him Their hearts were troubled because Jesus was about to leave them Then it was that Jesus spoke those sweet, comforting words of John 14 1-3

"Let not your heart be troubled ye believe in God, believe also in Me In My Father's house are many mansions if it were not so, I would have told you I go to prepare a place for you And if I go and prepare a place for you, I will come again, and receive you unto Myself, that where I am there ye may be also "

He stressed the fact that He would return He said, "If I go back to heaven, I will come back to earth I will come again."

Jesus stressed His second coming under the most unusual circumstances I refer to the time when He was on trial for His life, and was about to be condemned to death by the Jewish Sanhedrin It looked as if he never would have any kingdom He stood before them apparently powerless But He said to them, "Nevertheless I say unto you, Hereafter shall ye see the Son of man sitting on the right hand of power, and coming in the clouds of. Heaven "

Do you know what the last words are that Jesus ever gave us? How we treasure the last words of our loved ones! There are people here tonight who may have lost their mother or father twenty-five years ago, yet they can tell you what their last words were Do you know what the last words are that Jesus gave us? Here it is in Revelation 22 20

The last chapter in the Bible is Revelation 22 The last verse in the Bible is Revelation 22 21 This verse is a benediction pronounced by the apostle John "The grace of our Lord Jesus Christ be with you all Amen!"

Now look at the verse just before that They are the last words of Jesus "He (Christ) which testifieth these things saith, Surely I come quickly " In the last words which Jesus Christ ever gave us in this Bible, He stressed the fact that He is coming and coming soon "Surely I come quickly " John with the heart of a true Christian, speaking for the church of God responded with those words, "Even so, come, Lord Jesus "

Christ Himself stressed the great doctrine of His coming again So Christ Himself is an adventist Yes, He is the Head adventist, the Chief adventist The fact that Jesus is an adventist settles it for me, that I must be an adventist Does it settle it for you?

Do you know that the Apostles were adventists? Every apostle whose writings in part are found in the New Testament canon, stressed the second coming of Jesus Christ Where does Paul stand on the doctrine of the second coming of Jesus Christ? Put down I Thess 4 16,17 He said, "The Lord Himself shall descend from heaven with a shout, with the voice of the archangel, and with the trump of God and the dead in Christ shall rise first " Paul was a great adventist preacher In his epistles over and over again, he stresses the second coming of Jesus Christ

Where did Peter stand on this doctrine of the advent? In 1 Peter 5 4, in speaking about how preachers should be faithful in their tasks, he said, "When the chief Shepherd shall appear, ye shall receive a crown of glory that fadeth not away " Peter stressed the doctrine of the second coming of Christ Peter was an adventist

Where did John stand on this doctrine of the advent? Put down Revelation 1 7 He gives this keynote "Behold, He cometh with clouds, and every eye shall see Him " John stressed the coming of the Lord He was an adventist

Where did James stand on this doctrine? Put down James 5 7,8 Speaking to all Christians of all ages he says, "Be patient therefore brethren, unto the coming of the Lord stablish your hearts for the coming of the Lord draweth nigh " James stressed the second coming of Christ

Remember that the word "adventist" means one who stresses the second coming of Christ. That means that James, Peter, John, and Paul were adventists   Martin Luther, John Calvin, John Wesley, Richard Baxter, D. L. Moody, Spurgeon, Torrey, Billy Sunday, Wilbur Chapman, and on down the line stressed the second coming of Jesus Christ.

The true church in all ages has been, and is, an adventist church   Paul shows that every true Christian will love this doctrine. In 2 Timothy 4 6-8 He says, "Henceforth there is laid up for me a crown of righteousness, which the Lord, the righteous Judge, shall give me at that day, and not to me only, but unto all them also that love His appearing"   Did you get that? .Paul shows that **every true Christian will be a lover of Christ's second coming.** He will love His appearing. He will want Christ to come, that he may enjoy being with Christ forever

Paul shows that the second coming of Jesus Christ is the hope of the church in all ages   In Titus 2 13 he said, "Looking for that blessed hope, and the glorious appearing of the great God and Saviour Jesus Christ"   The true church has been and is now an adventist church

Do you know what the motto of the early Christians was? Here is something quite significant in 1 Cor 16 22, marginal reading   "If any man love not the Lord Jesus Christ, let him be Anathema"   Then Paul adds a very peculiar word   It is a word that has never been translated   It is the word "Maranatha" If you will look in the margin, you will find that this word means, "Our Lord cometh, or the Lord is coming" "Maranatha" means, "the Lord is coming"

This word was used just as we use the word "Hello," or "How are you?", or "Good Morning," or "Good evening"   Think how they stressed the second advent of Jesus Christ! When these early Christians met one another, in the place of saying "Hello," or "How are you?", they said "Maranatha," "the Lord is coming"   That was the word of greeting when they met one another   Since the second coming of Jesus Christ formed the basis of their greeting, it must have been the dominant theme of those early Christians

Dr. C E Jefferson makes this striking statement about the word "Maranatha."   "When one Christian met another Christian he greeted him with 'Maranatha' He lit up the day by the declaration that the Lord was coming When a Christian wrote a letter to his friends, he often wrote at the end of the last page, 'Maranatha'   That was a benediction   He wanted his friends to know that he was still rejoicing in the expectation that the Lord was coming 'Maranatha' was the slogan which the soldiers of Jesus Christ repeated to one another as they went forth   'Maranatha' was the password which Christians in the early times used when they went into their meetings   When they met before day in sequestered places, that was the watchword which gained them immediate admittance   'Maranatha'"   This is taken from "The Known Bible and Its Defense," Vol 1, pp 361, 362

You can see from this how these early Christians stressed the second coming of Jesus Christ   I chose to be an adventist, because Jesus Christ was an adventist, the apostles were adventists, the early Christians were adventists, and Christ's church in all ages had been and is an adventist church

Do you know that there are countless millions of adventists? You say, "I am afraid you are beside yourself tonight"   Here it is in the Bible   Put down Acts 1 9-11 and Revelation 5 11

In Acts 1 9-11 you will find that when Jesus ascended at the end of forty days after His resurrection, the two angels appeared to the disciples and they **stressed** that "This same Jesus, which is taken up from you into heaven, shall so come in like manner as ye have seen Him go"   The angels are adventists They laid special stress on the second coming of Jesus Christ

How many angels are there?   John says, "I heard the voice of many angels round about the throne   . and the number of them was ten thousand times ten thousand, (that is one-hundred million to start with) and thousands of thousands" So there are literally millions of adventists among the angelic throng

Do you know that everyone who prays the Lord's Prayer intelligently is an adventist? I do not know how many people have prayed the Lord's Prayer, but I do know that everyone who prays that prayer intelligently is an adventist

We pray, "Our Father which art in heaven, hallowed be Thy name Thy kingdom come, Thy will be done in earth as it is in heaven" Tell me, when will the kingdom come? The kingdom will come when Jesus comes the second time Put down 2 Timothy 4 1 There he speaks about God, the Lord Jesus Christ judging the quick and the dead at His appearing and His kingdom Notice the phrase, 'at His appearing and His kingdom' The second coming of Jesus Christ and the coming of the kingdom are identical in point of time

Matthew 16 28 says, "Till they see the Son of man coming in His kingdom" The kingdom will come when the King comes When you pray, "Thy kingdom come," what are you praying for? You are praying for Whom to come? You are praying for Jesus Christ to come Whenever you pray for Christ to come, aren't you putting much stress on the second coming of Jesus Christ? Then you are an adventist An adventist is one who lays stress on the second coming of Jesus Christ Everyone who prays the Lord's Prayer intelligently is an adventist

The Lord's Supper is an adventist ordinance Put down 1 Cor 11 26 "As often as ye eat this bread, and drink this cup, ye do shew the Lord's death till He come" Everyone who eats the Lord's Supper, according to its true implication, is an advenist

I will go a step further The New Testament is emphatically an adventist book There are 260 chapters in the New Testament The twenty-seven books of the New Testament mention the second coming of Jesus Christ 318 times The New Testament mentions the second coming of Christ fifty-eight times more than there are chapters in the book That is laying great stress on the second coming of Jesus Christ The New Testament is an adventist book

Those who say they have no use for an adventist book will have to dispose of the New Testament They claim that the New Testament is the only Bible that they want They do not want the Old Testament, now they will have to give up the New Testament

Have you ever stopped to consider that the "Battle Hymn of the Republic" is a real adventist hymn? It was not without purpose that Mr Rutherford chose the Battle Hymn of the Republic for the theme song of the American Bible Institute radio program over KSO

"Mine eyes have seen the glory of the coming of the Lord
He is sifting out the hearts of men before His judgment seat"
You see, this song mentions the great Adventist doctrine of the investigative judgment, as well as the doctrine of the coming of the Lord God is even now sifting out the hearts of men before His judgment seat

Why do I choose to be a Seventh-day Adventist? Who started the keeping of the seventh day? One of the outstanding truths of the New Testament is that Christ, as the eternal Son of God, is the Maker, or the Creator, of the world There are seven places in the New Testament that show that Christ is the Creator of this world

Since Christ is the Creator according to the New Testament, Christ is the One, Who made this world in six days, and rested upon the first seventh day in the history of the world According to Genesis 2 3, after He had rested on the first seventh day in the history of the world, the Son of God sanctified, or set apart, each succeeding seventh day for man to keep holy According to God's holy Word the seventh day, which we now call Saturday,

is the only day in the week that the Son of God, or Jesus Christ, ever set
apart for man to keep

There is not a line, not even a word in either the New Testament or the
Old Testament, that shows that the Son of God or Jesus Christ ever sanctified
the first day of the week, the day called Sunday, for any reason whatsoever

Friends, just think it through   You do not have to read a big book
Just take your Bible and do a little thinking   Since the seventh day of the
week, the day now called Saturday is the only day in the week that Christ,
the Son of God, the Creator, ever sanctified, or set apart, for man, then what
else can I do, since I want to obey Christ, than to keep the seventh day
which He sanctified and set apart for man?

I choose to be a Seventh-day Adventist because the seventh day of the
week is the only day of the week that Christ ever set apart   I choose to
keep the seventh day because the same Lord who commands me not to lie,
not to swear, not to worship idols in the same identical law commands me
to keep the seventh day holy, in Exodus 20 8-11

"Remember the Sabbath day, to keep it holy   Six days shalt thou labour,
and do all thy work but the seventh day is the Sabbath of the Lord thy God
in it thou shalt not do any work   For in six days the Lord made heaven
and earth, the sea, and all that in them is, and rested the seventh day wherefore the Lord blessed the Sabbath day and hallowed it"

If you will compare Nehemiah 9 12, 13 with 1 Corinthians 10 4, you will
find that Christ, the Son of God, is the Lord who came down upon Mt Sinai
and spoke the Ten Commandments   This means that the fourth commandment, of the Ten Commandments, is a command of the Lord Jesus Christ for
all people   The Lord Jesus Christ never asked people to keep the first day
of the week, or Sunday, for any reason whatsoever

Even though men may write a hundred books, or have a hundred debates,
when the Last Word has been said, it will still be an eternal fact that the only
day Jesus Christ ever asked anybody to keep is the seventh day

Friends, if we want to obey Jesus Christ, and I do and you do, what
else can we do but keep the seventh day? Can you say "Amen?"

I have three questions for you   What day did the Old Testament
prophets keep? You say they kept the seventh day   Everybody, even those
who oppose us, admit that the Old Testament prophets kept the seventh day
We have already found that every prophet stressed the second coming of
Jesus Christ   Hence, they were adventists.   Now tell me, since the prophets
kept the seventh day, what kind of adventists were they?

I have another question   What day did Jesus Christ keep when He was
here? The seventh day   And even those who oppose this seventh day
preaching admit this   They could not help but admit this   Jesus kept the
seventh day   We have already noticed how Jesus stressed the doctrine of
the second advent   Hence, He was an adventist   Since Jesus was an adventist, and a keeper of the seventh day, what kind of an adventist is Jesus
Christ? Doesn't this settle what you are going to be, Brother?

A third question   What day did the Apostles and early Christians keep?
In eight different places in the Acts of the Apostles, the seventh day, the day
on which the Jews met for their regular weekly worship, is called the Sabbath
day in the days of the Apostles   We have already noticed how the apostles
stressed the second coming of Jesus Christ   Hence, they were adventists
Now, tell me, since the apostles kept the seventh day, what kind of adventists
were they?

I choose to be an adventist and keep the seventh day, because Jesus
Christ, the Prophets, and the apostles were adventists and kept the seventh
day   See who is on the side of the seventh day and the doctrine of the
advent   all the prophets, Enoch, Moses, Isaiah, Jeremiah, Ezekiel, Daniel;

all the apostles, Peter, James, Paul, the early Christians, and towering above them all the blessed Man of Calvary, the Lord Jesus   This settles it for me where I will stand   I want to be on Christ's side, don't you?

Notice that the best people who have ever lived on this earth have been on the side of the seventh day and the doctrine of the advent   It is really good to be an Adventist isn't it?   When you become an Adventist you are standing on the side of the Lord Jesus Christ, the prophets, and the apostles

I choose to be an adventist, because Bible prophecy shows that the last part of Christ's true church in the last days will be a seventh-day-Sabbath-keeping church   You will find that in Revelation 12 17 and Revelation 14.12 It talks about the remnant church that will keep the commandments of God Revelation 14 12 says that the saints are those who keep the commandments of God and the faith of Jesus   Since they keep the commandments, they will keep the day specified in the commandments, which is the seventh day.

Now I have just one more question, and I am through   Do you think I did right in choosing to be a Seventh-day Adventist?   I haven't always been a Seventh-day Adventist   I used to be a Methodist   I was converted in Billy Sunday's meetings and joined the Methodist Church   There came a day when the call of God's message reached me and I left the Methodist Church.

The Methodist church is a good church.   I do not condemn them   You haven't heard me talk against the Methodist church, or the Baptist church, or any church   If the Bible says something, then we have read it

Do you think I did right in choosing to be an Adventist?   I have been talking to you folks now for over twelve weeks   Some of you have heard me practically every time   Will everyone here who believes that I did right in choosing to be an Adventist, raise your hand and raise it high?   Thank God, it looks as if you are all with me!   That is fine

There is only one thing that is going to be found worthwhile in the end, and that will be, to be found obedient to the commandments of the Lord   The last chapter of the last book in this Bible in Revelation 22 14 says, "Blessed are they that do His commandments, that they may have right to the tree of life, and may enter in through the gates into the city"   Isaiah 26 2 says the gates will be opened to those who keep the truth

A certain lady once attended a series of Bible lectures like the one you have been attending at these meetings   She became thoroughly convinced that she should observe the seventh day as the Sabbath   Her husband was very much opposed to her keeping the seventh day   He finally made her a proposition that if she would forget the Bible lectures she had heard, give up the idea of keeping the seventh day, he would buy her a new automobile, new furniture, all the new clothes she wanted   At first she said, "No, I am not interested."

Finally he prevailed on her to accept his offer, and he bought the things for her that he had promised   She stopped attending the Bible lectures She tried to forget the commandments of God

One morning a friend of theirs called at their apartment and knocked on the door   Nobody came   He thought maybe they weren't home   So he went out and looked in the garage to see whether or not the car was there The car was in the garage

Then he noticed that the newspaper was on the steps, and the milk bottle was still there   He felt sure they must be at home.   So he went back and hammered on the door, thinking they were asleep.   He hammered again. Then he thought, "There is something wrong"   He went to the corner and found a policeman and said, "Come down here   I think there is something wrong in this house   The people are in there, but something has happened"

The policeman forced the door open and immediately they smelled gas.

They rushed into the bedroom, and there they found the husband and wife lying dead upon their beds, killed by their own hand by turning on the gas "What shall it profit a man if he gain the whole world and lose his own soul"

What did that new automobile amount to as that lady lay there dead, a suicide, lost, doomed to hell! What did those new pieces of furniture amount to? the new dresses in the wardrobe? the diamonds sparkling on her fingers as she lay there dead, when she was eternally lost?

How different might have been that lady's fate if she had followed her conviction, when the Holy Spirit told her that the seventh day is the right day! I hope no one in Des Moines will repeat the history of this woman There are women here tonight, whose husbands do not want them to keep the Sabbath Perhaps they will offer you a new dress, or a new automobile, or something else I hope you will not sell the truth for anything. Remember, Judas sold out for thirty pieces of silver

The best thing, the wisest course, the safest way is to make your decision to obey the commandments of God and the faith of Jesus

I have stood here before you for many weeks in these Bible lectures I have done my best to present the Bible and not my own opinions I would like to take in this hand of mine tonight the hands of those of you who intend to take your stand for these truths of God's message Thank the Lord here they come The Lord bless you

Here comes another couple The Lord bless you O, friends, there will never be a better time This is God's time He says, **"Now** is the accepted time" If anything should happen to you between now and next Sunday night, you would be mighty thankful that you did this

We do not know what is going to happen That is why God says, "Now, now, today, tonight" The devil says, "Put it off" God says, "Do it now" The Devil says, "Tomorrow," but tomorrow never comes.

Whatever you do, you do today When tomorrow comes, it is today There will be many people lost, because they listened to the devil when he whispered "Wait awhile Do it tomorrow" O, friends, let us yield tonight to the Holy Spirit Is there another?

I don't want to leave anyone out of this prayer tonight I would like to ask how many of you who have not come forward would like to lift the hand to God and ask that He will help you, that you might take your stand for this great message? Will you lift your hand where you are? Yes, I see many hands going up God sees them, and He will help you take your stand. When you want to do it, remember, that then, you and God are agreed, and it will be done

(Prayer)

The Truth About the Law

(Sermons against the keeping of the seventh day were preached by many ministers in the city. In nearly every case they endeavored to show that the Ten Commandments are not binding on Christians This lecture was designed to meet this issue concerning the law.)

The keeping holy of the seventh day of the week is commanded in the fourth precept of the Ten Commandments If the Ten Commandments are binding upon Christians as a rule of life and duty, then the keeping holy of the seventh day, commonly called Saturday, is obligatory upon Christians What does the New Testament teach on this question of whether or not, the Ten Commandments are binding upon Christians as a rule of life?

In this discussion we are not dealing with the issue as to whether the keeping of the Ten 'Commandments should be regarded as a means of salvation, or as a way of obtaining righteousness, or justification Salvation is only by grace No man can save himself by keeping the Ten Commandments God has decreed in Romans 3 20 that, "By the deeds of the law there shall no flesh be justified in his sight."

There is only one way that any person can ever be saved, and that is by faith in the Lord Jesus Christ There is only one way any person can be righteous, and that is by the righteousness of the Son of God, obtained free by faith in Him

So the issue before us is not the keeping of the Ten Commandments as a means of salvation, or of justification, or of securing righteousness No! Here is the issue Is a Christian to live according to the Ten Commandments after he receives Jesus Christ as his Saviour? What did the apostles teach?

First we will call the apostle Paul to the witness stand "Paul, what did you teach about the Ten Commandments? Many people say that you taught that the Ten Commandments were nailed to the cross What did you really teach concerning the relation of Christians to the decalogue of the Old Testament?

Paul wrote the book of Romans about A D 60, or about twenty-nine years after the new dispensation had been ushered in by the death and resurrection of the Lord Jesus

Paul refers us to Romans 13 8-10 "Owe no man anything, but to love one another; for he that loveth another hath fulfilled the law "

What law is Paul talking about? Let Paul tell us in the next verse "For this, Thou shalt not commit adultery, Thou shalt not kill, Thou shalt not steal, Thou shalt not bear false witness, Thou shalt not covet " Mark this well Paul cites the sixth, the seventh, the eighth, the ninth, and the tenth of the Ten Commandments So it is definitely settled that he is talking about the decalogue

Please notice that Paul cites the Ten Commandments as a binding rule of life on Christians in A D 60 In other words, twenty-nine years after the crucifixion and resurrection of Jesus Christ, Paul pointed out in his epistle to the Romans that the Ten Commandments are a rule of life and conduct for Christians under the new covenant

If Paul believed that the Ten Commandments had been abolished at the cross twenty-nine years before he wrote the book of Romans, then he would not have cited the Ten Commandments as a binding rule of life and conduct in A D 60

In Romans 7·12 Paul says, "Wherefore the law is holy, and the commandment holy, and just, and good " There was some law that Paul regarded as being holy and good for Christians in A D. 60, twenty-nine years after the cross of Christ Well, what law was it? Look at verse 7 "What shall we say then? Is the law sin? God forbid Nay, I had not known sin, but by the law· for I had not known lust, except the law had said, Thou shalt not covet "

He is talking about the law that says, "Thou shalt not covet " What is the only law that ever said, "Thou shalt not covet?" It is the Ten Commandments? This is the law which Paul regarded as being holy and just and good for Christians in A D 60, twenty-nine years after Christ's crucifixion and resurrection

Also he points out in Romans 7 7 that the Ten Commandments are necessary for pointing out sin Did you notice his statement? I will read it again **"I had not known sin, but by the law."** He taught that the Ten Commandments must stand forever to convince men of sin

Let us turn to Romans 3 31 "Do we then make void the law through faith?" If you will read the preceeding verses, you will see that he is talking about the law of Ten Commandments by which is the knowledge of sin He raises the question, "Do we then make void the law through faith?"

This is the issue at stake in this discussion of which day Christians ought to keep Are Christians to live according to the Ten Commandments after they believe on Jesus Christ? "Do we then make void the law through faith?" Those who oppose the keeping of the seventh day say, "Yes " What does God's Word say? It says, "No " Paul used the strongest negative he could summon He says, "Do we then make void the law through faith? **God forbid: yea, we establish the law."**

Instead of faith in Jesus Christ as your Savior doing away with the keeping of the Ten Commandments, it actually establishes the keeping of the commandments in your life, by bringing Jesus Christ into your heart to live in you a life of obedience to the Ten Commandments

Now let us ask James where he stands on this question He presided at the first Christian council James says, "I wrote a general epistle about A D 60, addressed to all the Christians everywhere I advise you to read James 2 10, 11 "

Look at James 2 11 "He that said, (the margin in some Bibles says, 'That law which said') Do not commit adultery, said also, Do not kill Now if thou commit no adultery, yet if thou kill, thou art become a transgressor of the law "

He is talking about the law that said, "Do not commit adultery, and, Do not kill " Now you tell me what law is it that said, "Do not kill and do not commit adultery " It is the Ten Commandment law There can be no question about that He is talking specifically and directly about the Ten Commandments

We ask James how much of these Ten Commandments are binding on Christians as a rule of life and duty? He refers us to verse 10 "Whosoever shall keep the whole law, and yet offend in **one** point, he is guilty of· all " James taught that **all** of the Ten Commandments are binding on Christians in A D 60

Remember that this is twenty-nine years after the old covenant had passed away at the cross Twenty-nine years into the new dispensation he holds up the Ten Commandments as a rule of life for Christians, and bids all Christians to live according to the Ten Commandments Since all the ten are binding according to James 2 10, 11, the keeping of the seventh day, as the fourth one of the ten, is bound to be binding

Next let us talk to the apostle John, the beloved apostle, the one who wrote so much about love "John, what do you say about the Ten Commandments? What is your idea about the Christian's relation to the decalogue?"

He refers us to 1 John 3 4 "Whosoever committeth sin, transgresseth also the law: for **sin is the transgression** of the law"

When you place this along with Romans 7.7, it is plain, that the law of which transgression is sin, is no other law than the Ten Commandments

John was the last writer in the New Testament In fact he wrote near the close of the first century He wrote this epistle about A D 96 This was sixty-five years after the cross of Christ, sixty-five years after the new dispensation had been ushered in Yet, he teaches that the Ten Commandments are binding on Christians as a rule of life "Sin is the transgression of the law" Christians are not to practice sin

Here then is plain, direct, positive, New Testament, apostolic truth, which we can tie to as secure and steadfast Christians are to live according to the Ten Commandments as God's eternal standard of truth, right, and duty While the law of the decalogue is **not to be regarded** as a way of salvation, or a means of justification, yet **it is to be honored** and followed as a rule of life and conduct by Christians of today Since the keeping of the seventh day is commanded by the fourth precept of the ten, this means that Christians are under obligation to keep the seventh day

Scripture never contradicts itself when properly interpreted This means that any other text in Paul's epistles where he speaks about certain laws being abolished, cannot refer to the ten commandments, because Paul, and James, and John, are all agreed in teaching the Ten Commandments as a rule of life for Christians

There are in particular two texts in Paul's epistles where he speaks about certain laws being abolished at the cross These are Ephesians 2 15, and Colossians 2·14-17.

In Ephesians 2.15 he declares that Christ, "abolished in His flesh the enmity, even the law of commandments contained in ordinances" In Col 2·14 he refers to certain laws being abolished as, "The handwriting of ordinances that was against us," and which Christ took out of the way by nailing it to His cross

Mark this· In these two texts where Paul speaks about certain laws having been abolished at the cross, he specifies that those abolished laws were the laws regarding ordinances In Ephesians 2 15, it is the law of commandments contained in ordinances In Colossians 2 14, it is the blotting out of the handwriting of ordinances

What is an ordinance? The dictionary says an ordinance is a religious rite or ceremony This shows plainly that it was the ceremonial laws, those laws about the ordinances of the Levitical priesthood which were nailed to the cross and abolished Hence, Ephesians 2 15 and Colossians 2 14-17 have no reference whatsoever to the law of Ten Commandments

In Galatians Paul makes it plain that he is talking primarily about the ritual laws of the Jews, and not the moral law of Ten Commandments He declares that every man who is circumcised is debtor to do the whole law The issue was not whether or not Christians should live according to the Ten Commandments, but whether the Gentile Christians must be circumcised and keep the ceremonial laws of Moses So in Galatians Paul is talking primarily about the ritual law

He declares that this law was added because of transgression God's law which points out transgression was already in existence before the Mosaic law was added The ritual law was added as a temporary remedy for transgression until Christ should come and die for sin The ritual laws was a schoolmaster, teaching them of the Saviour Who was to die for the sins of the world When they believed in Christ, they were no longer under that schoolmaster of the ritual law

Those who oppose the keeping of the seventh day declare that the laws which God gave in the Old Testament constitute one integral system of law, and that it passed away at the cross in its entirety. They claim that the Ten Commandments cannot be regarded as being separate from the other laws which God gave in the Old Testament

Remember that Scripture never contradicts itself when properly interpreted If, as they claim, there is only one system of law, then Scripture would contradict itself In Romans 3 31 Paul declares that the law is established by faith in Jesus Christ. In Ephesians 2.15 he declares that the law of commandments contained in ordinances was abolished at the cross Think it through for yourself **How could the same law be abolished and still be established?** This would make the Bible contradict itself.

The fact is that Paul recognized a two-fold division of the laws. He recognized the moral laws as being a standard of life and established by faith in Jesus Christ, while the ceremonial laws of ordinances which prefigured the sacrifice of Christ were abolished at the cross, because the sacrifice which they prefigured was met You can see that the man who argues that all the laws of the Old Testament constitute only one law is making the Bible contradict itself, hence his teaching must be wrong

Our teaching that the Ten Commandments are a separate law from the other laws, which God gave the Jews, is not based on the terminology of calling the Ten Commandments the law of God and the ceremonial laws, the law of Moses In Luke 2·22-24 the ceremonial law is called the law of the Lord, and the law of Moses

This distinction between the laws of the Old Testament is not based on the idea that all the laws of Moses passed away at the cross and that the Ten Commandments only continued binding For example· The Mosaic law said in Exodus 23 2, "Thou shalt not follow a multitude to do evil." This is just as binding tonight as when Moses spoke it It is just as wrong to follow a crowd today in committing sin, as it was in the days of Moses

Again the Mosaic law declared that men should love God with all their hearts, and their neighbors as themselves This is just as binding tonight as when Moses spoke it So it isn't true that even all the Mosaic laws have passed away The only laws of Moses that passed away at the cross were the laws regarding the offering of animal sacrifices, circumcision, the ordinances of the earthly temple, the feast days, the yearly sabbath days, and judgments that were intended only for the Jews

The distinction in the law as to the moral laws, which continued binding after the ceremonial laws were nailed to the cross, is settled by the very nature of the laws in question The ceremonial laws of Moses consisted of rites and ordinances, which were designed to be binding only until Christ should die on the cross The moral laws, like the Ten Commandments, and those other moral laws which Moses spoke to the people, pertain to duties of morality applicable to all people, in all lands, in all ages

If the Scriptures recognize the Ten Commandments as a separate law from the laws that Moses gave, then you can see that the abolition of certain laws of Moses at the cross would not repeal the binding obligation of the Ten Commandments Do the Scriptures recognize the Ten Commandments as a separate law from the laws that Moses gave? Put down Deut 33 2-4

"And he said, The Lord came from Sinai, and rose up from Seir unto them, He came with ten thousands of saints from His right hand went a fiery law for them" In verse 4 it says, "Moses commanded us a law" Anyone can see that this shows that the Ten Commandments are a separate law from the laws which Moses gave The first tells how the Lord came down upon Sinai and from His right hand went a fiery law That was the Ten Commandments Then after that, Moses commanded them certain laws

God Himself made a clear distinction between the Ten Commandments and the laws of Moses The only commandments that God ever spoke with His own voice to Israel were the Ten Commandments The only commandments of God ever wrote with His own finger on tables of stone were the Ten Commandments All the other laws were spoken by Moses and written by his hand with pen and ink in a book

Thus you can see how God marked off the Ten Commandments as a separate law by speaking them with His own voice, and writing them with His own finger on everlasting stone Then God told the Israelites to place the two tables of stone inside the ark of the covenant, but the books containing the laws of Moses were placed in a pocket on the outside of the ark

Let us examine the strongest argument of our opponents They ask this question, "Didn't the old covenant pass away at the cross? Our answer is, "Yes" The Bible plainly shows that the old covenant passed away at the cross and that Christians are living under the new covenant Then our opponents try to prove that the old covenant is the law of Ten Commandments, and were abolished at the cross

So we raise a pertinent question Are the Ten Commandments binding as a rule of life on Christians under the new covenant? Put down Hebrews 8 8-10 This is talking directly about the new covenant Notice what it says "For finding fault with them, he saith, Behold the days come, saith the Lord, when I will make a new covenant with the house of Israel and and with the house of Judah. . . . For this (talking about what the new covenant is) is the covenant that I will make with the house of Israel after those days, saith the Lord. I will put My laws into their mind, and write them in their hearts."

Under the old covenant the Jews had the Ten Commandments written on two tables of stone Listen, brother, you might have two tables of stone in your house with all the Ten Commandments written on them, but if that is as close as the Ten Commandments ever get to you, they will not keep you from doing anything wrong When a man has the Ten Commandments on his heart, and the Holy Spirit stamps honesty on his heart, he will not steal. "Thou shalt not steal "

This becomes a promise of God, instead of being merely a legal requirement Jesus says to this man, "Having received Me, and since I have given you an honest heart, you will not steal " And the power of God will keep that man from stealing. This is the new covenant Under the old covenant, the Jews had these Ten Commandments on two tables of stone, and did not keep them because the commandments were merely on stone, outside of the man's life Under the new covenant, God declares, "By the Holy Spirit I will write this law on their hearts and they will keep it "

Therefore the same Ten Commandments which God wrote on stone under the old covenant, and which were not obeyed, are written on the Christian's heart by the Holy Spirit under the new covenant, so that they will obey them Remember, Scripture never contradicts itself This shows that 2 Corinthians 3 about the ministration of death written and engraven in stones being superseded by the ministration of the Spirit, cannot mean that the Ten Commandments have been done away with in Christ Any interpretation about the Ten Commandments being abolished with the old covenant is not rightly dividing the Word of truth.

The Ten Commandments are called God's covenant, but they are never called the old covenant Those who oppose the keeping of the seventh day fail to distinguish between the decalogue as God's eternal covenant with man, and the old covenant made concerning these commandments

The truth is that the Ten Commandments are not the old covenant, but they are by themselves, with nothing added to them or taken away, God's covenant made concerning these commandments

The Ten Commandments are by themselves, with nothing added to them or taken away, God's covenant of truth, and right, and duty for man. It is exactly true that the words on the two tables are the words of the covenant, and the covenant there referred to is God's covenant of truth and right and duty, which stands binding forever and ever.

The discussion of this law question as recorded in Galatians, Romans, and Acts, does not relate in any wise to whether or not Christians should live according to the Ten Commandments. The issue was not whether a Christian should live in harmony with the decalogue. No one ever argued about that in the days of the apostles. That was never brought up until some people sought to find a way around the keeping of the seventh day.

In Galatians, Romans, and Acts, there are implications of a controversy as to whether or not the ceremonial observances of Moses should be imposed upon Gentile Christians. There was also a controversy as to whether or not the keeping of the Ten Commandments should be a means of securing righteousness and justification. But there was never any question among Christians in the days of the apostles whether a Christian should live according to the Ten Commandments. All of them agreed that the Ten Commandments are a rule of life and duty for believers.

The real truth about the law question is summed up in three propositions

1. The ceremonial observances of the Mosaic law were abolished with the old covenant at the cross and are not binding on any Christian

2. The keeping of the Ten Commandments must never be regarded as a means of securing salvation or justification

3. The Ten Commandments are God's eternal standard of righteousness and are binding on Christians as a rule of life and duty and conduct.

Do you know that the Ten Commandments can never come to an end as long as God is God and man is man? The Ten Commandments regulate man's duty to God and to his fellow-man. The first four regulate in a general way man's duty to his Creator. The last six regulate man's duty to his fellow-man. Since they regulate man's duty to his Creator and his fellow-man, they will continue binding as long as God is God and man is man.

The Ten Commandments are summed up in two great precepts, love God with all your heart, and your neighbor as yourself. Therefore they will continue binding as long as men should love God, and as long as men need to love their neighbors as themselves.

The Ten Commandments deal with duties which are of perpetual obligation. Go back as far as you can think. Was there ever a time when it was right to steal, swear, hate, covet, worship idols, etc. No. Now let your mind go forward into the future as far as you can imagine. Will there ever be a time when it will be right to lie, swear, hate, covet, worship idols, etc? No! Therefore the ten commandments are a perpetual obligation.

The Ten Commandments are a transcript of the character of God. Man may as well talk about doing away with God as to talk about doing away with His Ten Commandments

Since the Ten Commandments will never come to an end, the seventh day Sabbath as the fourth commandment of the ten, will never come to an end. So Isaiah 66 22, 23 shows that the seventh-day Sabbath will be hallowed and kept throughout eternity by the redeemed of all ages in the earth made new.

CPSIA information can be obtained
at www.ICGtesting.com
Printed in the USA
LVHW080828070721
691891LV00047B/2458